# MASTERPIECES OF CHINESE PAINTING 700–1900

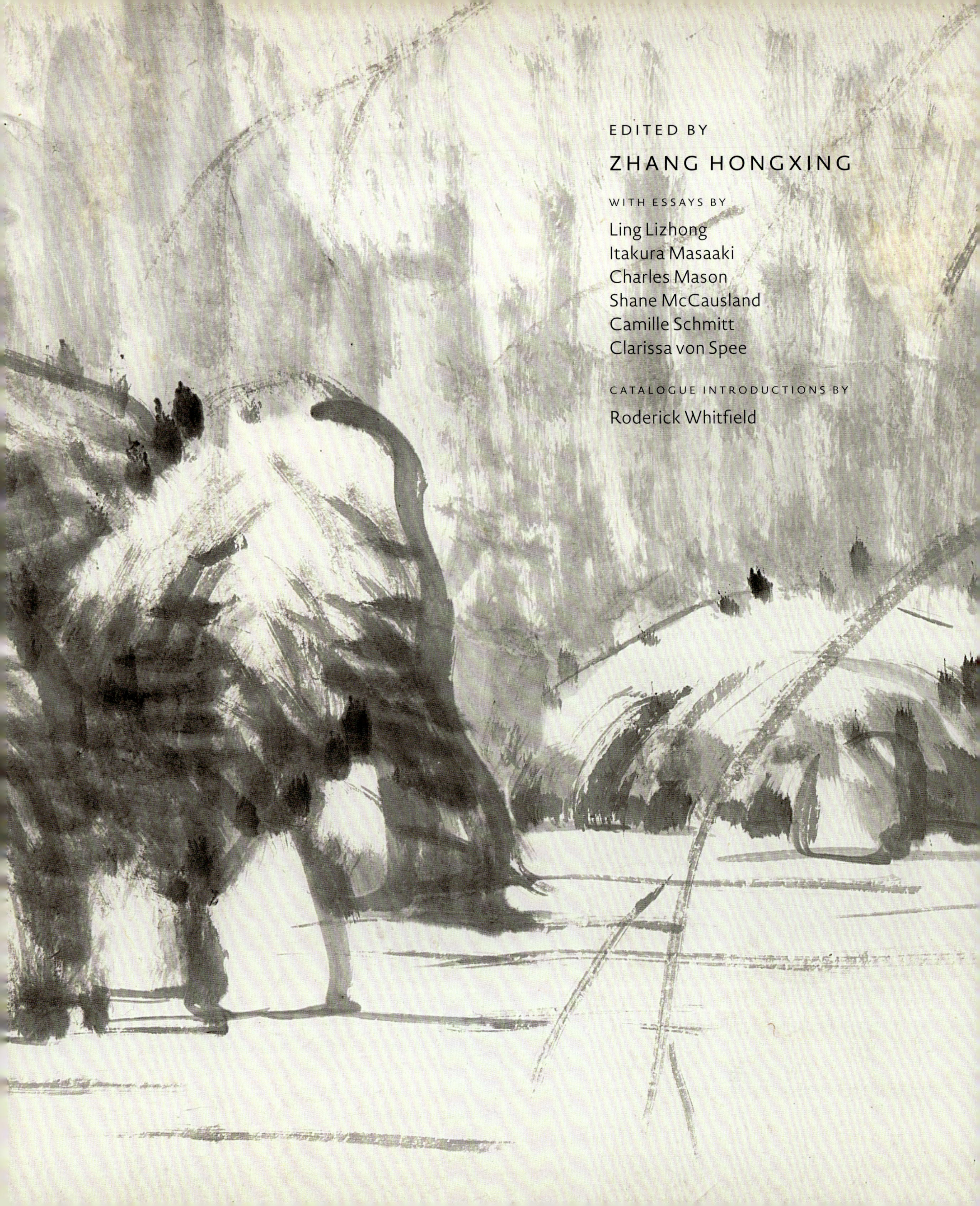

EDITED BY

ZHANG HONGXING

WITH ESSAYS BY

Ling Lizhong
Itakura Masaaki
Charles Mason
Shane McCausland
Camille Schmitt
Clarissa von Spee

CATALOGUE INTRODUCTIONS BY

Roderick Whitfield

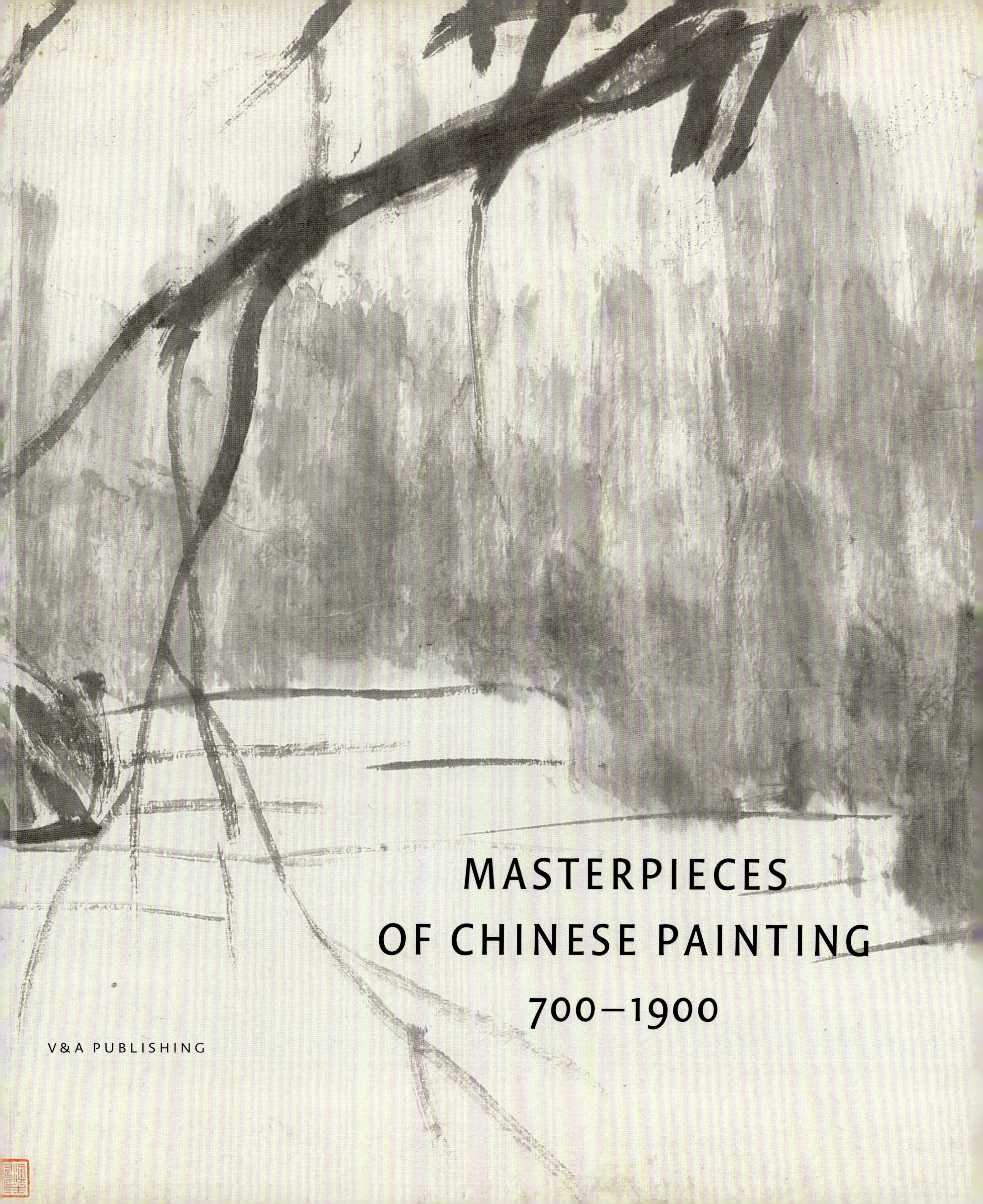

# MASTERPIECES OF CHINESE PAINTING 700–1900

V&A PUBLISHING

EXHIBITION SUPPORTED BY
The Friends of the V&A

RESTAURANT PARTNER
Ping Pong

TRAVEL PARTNER
Viking River Cruises

First published by V&A Publishing, 2013
Victoria and Albert Museum
South Kensington
London SW7 2RL
www.vandapublishing.com

Distributed in North America by
Harry N. Abrams Inc., New York


Hardback edition
ISBN 978 1 85177 756 3

Library of Congress Control Number 2013935666

10 9 8 7 6 5 4 3 2 1
2017 2016 2015 2014 2013

A catalogue record for this book is available
from the British Library.



Front jacket illustration: cat. no. 16 (detail)
Back jacket illustration: cat. no. 33
Pages 2–3: cat. no. 74 (detail)
Page 4: cat. no. 49 (detail)
Pages 114–15: cat. no. 61 (detail)
Pages 118–19: cat. no. 12 (detail)
Pages 148–9: cat. no. 38 (detail)
Pages 202–3: cat. no. 48 (detail)
Pages 230–1: cat. no. 55 (detail)
Pages 266–7: cat. no. 76 (detail)

DESIGNER Phillip Lewis
COPY-EDITOR Frances McDonald
INDEX Claire Hodgson

Printed in Italy

MIX
Paper from
responsible sources
FSC® C015829

**V&A Publishing**

Supporting the world's leading
museum of art and design,
the Victoria and Albert
Museum, London

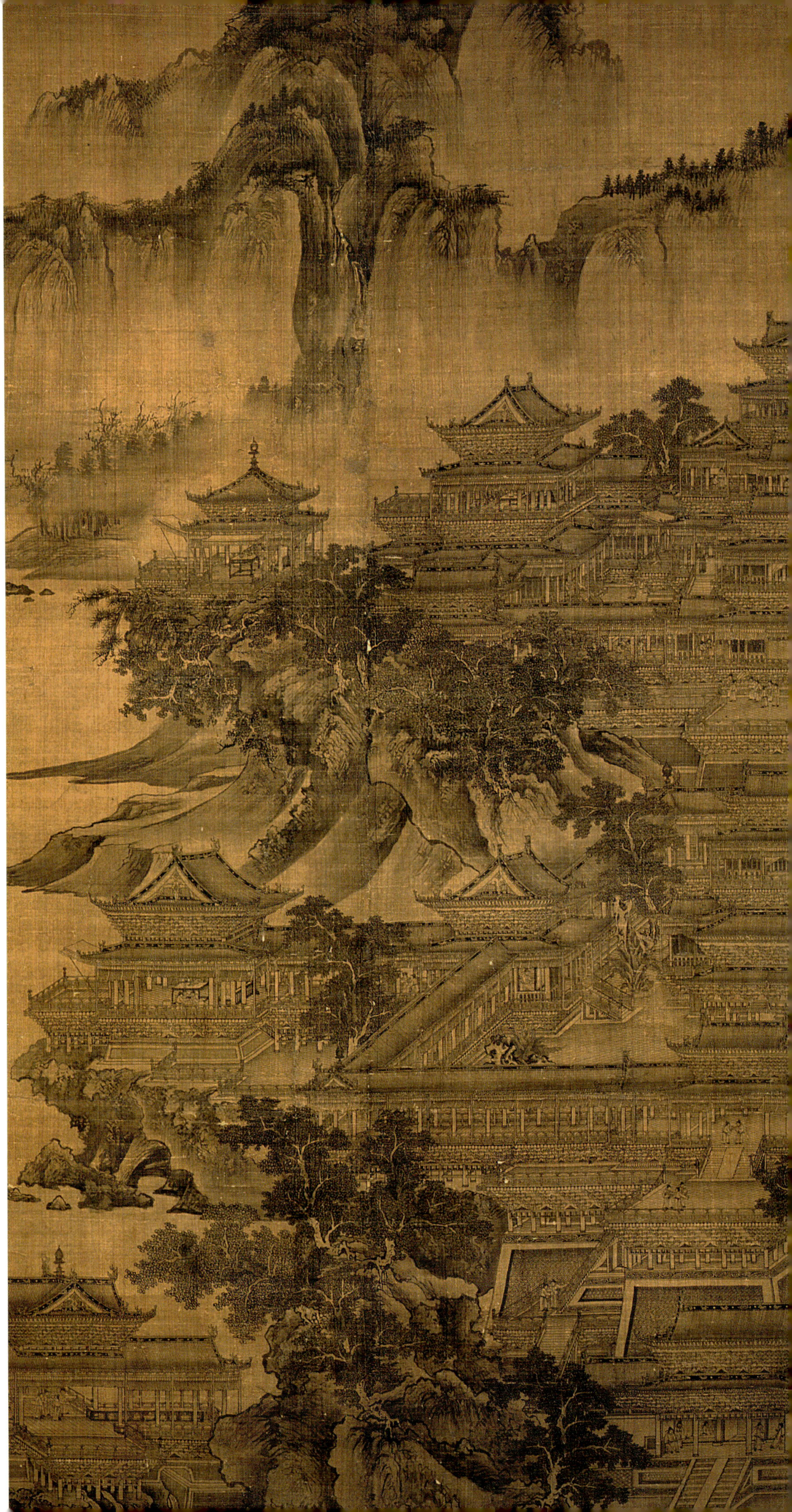

# CONTENTS

# DIRECTOR'S FOREWORD

THERE ARE COUNTLESS pleasures to be found in the masterpieces of Chinese painting – so many spectacular views, and innumerable poignant details. An exhibition presenting over a millennium of the very highest artistic achievements would naturally be expected to feature a bewildering variety of consummate techniques and styles; but here there are also many moments purely of delight, as we take to the air above the city of Suzhou, examine the tiniest grasshopper or share a private walk inside the inner walls of the imperial palace.

Considering that these paintings, executed on fragile silk or paper, were never intended for permanent display (even in East Asia today museums and galleries must rotate the paintings on view, so that visiting a famous collection does not guarantee seeing a particular work), their captured instants are even more startlingly thrilling. But how can we compare the naturalistic paintings we find here to the scenes of cavorting dragons, or to the eighth-century depictions of the Buddha in majesty? Do we look at these works through the lens of what we know of Western European art? Do we think of them as part-way between painting, drawing and calligraphy, as a kind of correspondence from the artists who created them? Can we imagine taking a brush and forming a tree from a single movement ourselves? These questions are addressed, explicitly or implicitly, in this exhibition and the accompanying catalogue, which is intended to provide an updated and authoritative guide to these great works of art.

The ambitious aims of this undertaking could not have been realized without the support of institutions and individuals beyond the Victoria and Albert Museum. I am grateful to all the lenders who have made their treasures available and to all the contributors to the catalogue, many of whom represent the museums and collections that serve as a custodian to the works in the exhibition. I am particularly grateful to Art Exhibitions China, which has coordinated the loans from museums across China.

MARTIN ROTH
*Director*, Victoria and Albert Museum

# CURATOR'S PREFACE

THIS CATALOGUE IS intended to be a guide to the history of Chinese painting from the period 700 to 1900. The lives of great artists, the development of schools and the evolution of styles are discussed – but this book is foremost a history of paintings.

The book confines its scope to portable paintings on silk or paper. Although stone engravings and murals are important for understanding Chinese pictorial art, those works can only be properly studied in the tombs and temples for which they were made, and therefore are excluded from the main focus of discussion. The chronological spread stems from the fact that few paintings dating before the eighth century have survived, and that fundamental changes to the nature of classical Chinese painting took place during the early twentieth century, including the abandonment of the right-to-left viewing tradition.

The book is divided into two parts. The first consists of eight essays outlining a variety of topics: the main types of paintings, their original functions and any subsequent alterations, the artist's profession and practice, technique and medium, genres of painting, inscriptions and seal marks, presentation and preservation, and finally the histories of collecting in Europe, America, Japan and China. The second focuses on individual paintings, and is arranged in five sections corresponding to the chronological display of these works in the exhibition. Each section opens with a brief text introducing the historical background, major artists and artistic trends of the period.

Although each entry is self-contained, it is hoped that the selection of works and their chronological arrangement, the variety of topics covered in the essays and catalogue entries, and the abundant cross-references will make it possible to use the catalogue as an introduction to the history of Chinese painting. Readers interested in exploring the meanings and provenance of the paintings may wish to consult the appendix, which provides a full transcription and translation of artists' inscriptions, as well as a brief description of collectors' inscriptions and seal marks.

ZHANG HONGXING
*Senior Curator*, Victoria and Albert Museum

# LENDERS

The British Library, London
The British Museum, London
Cincinnati Art Museum
The Cleveland Museum of Art
Dunhuang Academy
Hong Kong Museum of Art
Kyoto National Museum
Liaoning Provincial Museum, Shenyang
The Metropolitan Museum of Art, New York
Musée Guimet, Paris
Museum of Asian Art, Berlin
Museum of Far Eastern Antiquities, Stockholm
Museum of Fine Arts, Boston
The Nelson-Atkins Museum of Art, Kansas
Osaka City Museum of Fine Arts
The Palace Museum, Beijing
Princeton University Art Museum
Private collection, Kyoto
Shanghai Museum
Tianjin Museum
Tokyo National Museum

# MODERN CHINA

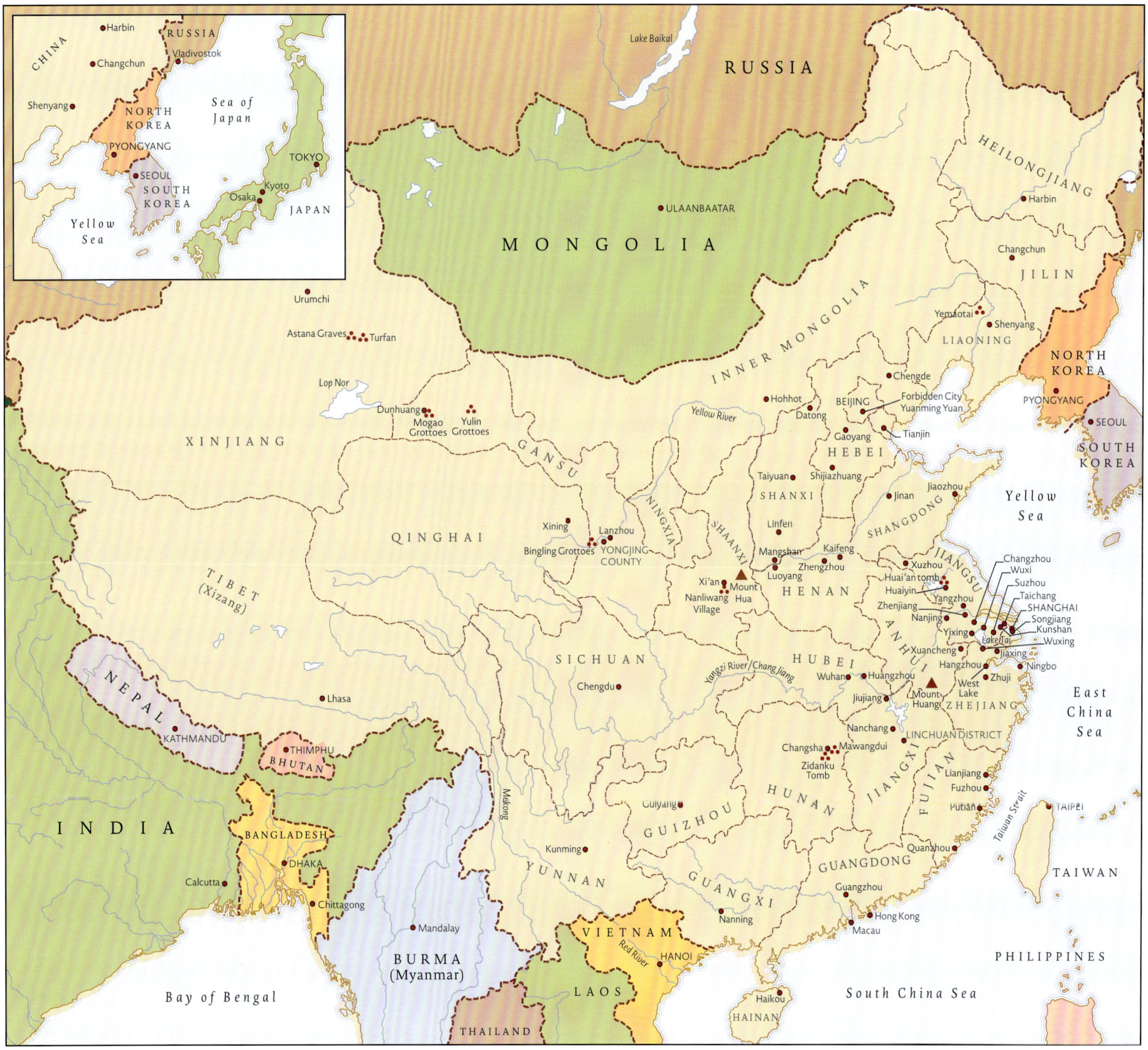

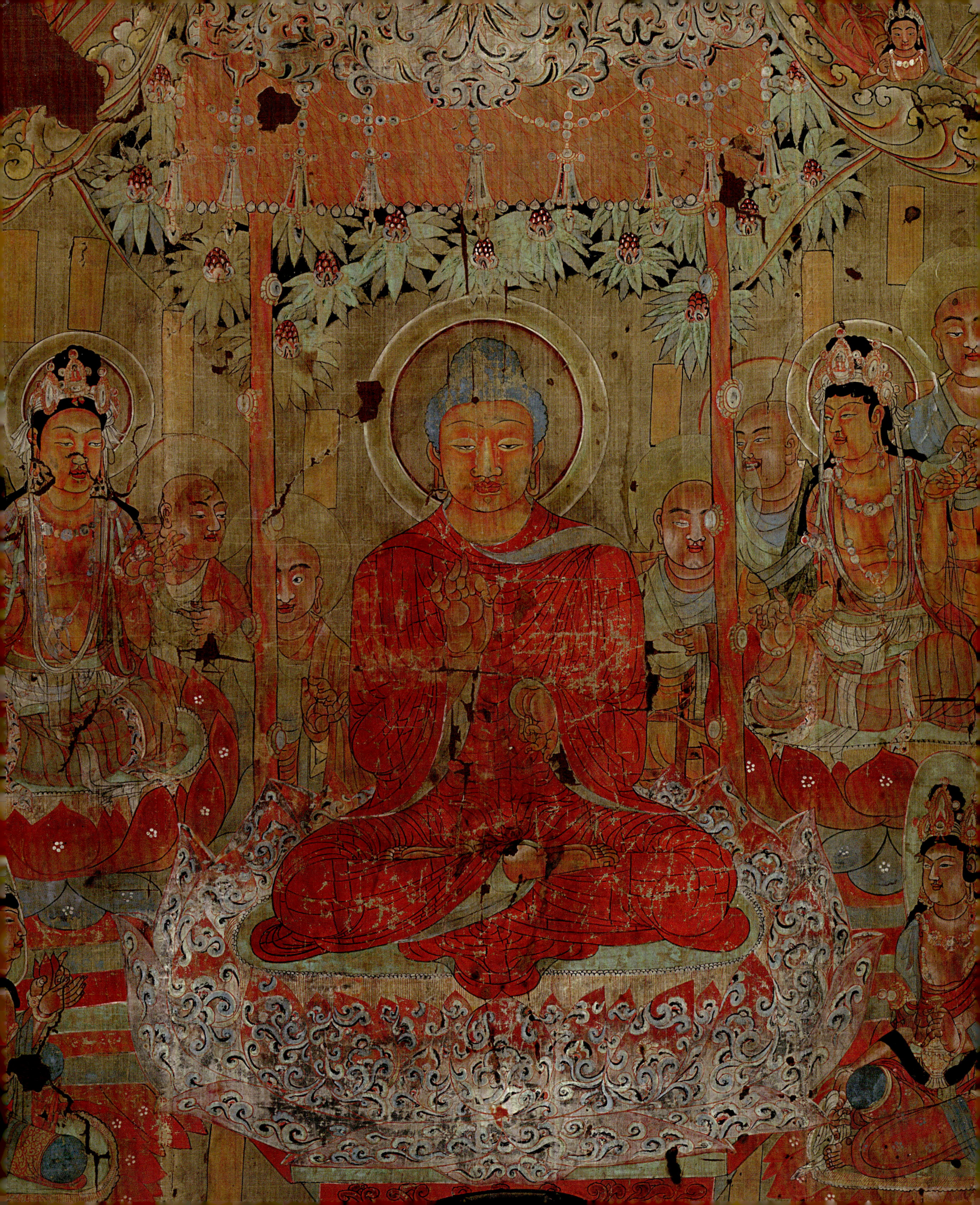

# INTRODUCTION

Zhang Hongxing

Today, one of the key aims of a museum is to situate the works on display within their original context. As such, elements of the design that might otherwise have been disregarded can be shown to have been dictated by the original function of an object, or by the intention of the artist or patron. This approach underlines two crucial aspects in understanding the portable Chinese paintings in this book: firstly, none of the paintings produced in the period covered by the exhibition were ever conceived to be seen in a gallery. In China, the first museum opened in the city of Nantong, Jiangsu Province, in 1905, and the first public institution dedicated to displaying works from the former imperial collections, including paintings, the Institute of Exhibiting Antiques (Guwu chenlie suo), was established inside the Forbidden City, Beijing, in 1914.[1] Secondly, Chinese paintings – from early Buddhist banners to scrolls made much later – were intended to be viewed on a temporary basis, for a period ranging from a few hours to several weeks. Most of the time, a Chinese scroll painting is stored in its box, rolled up.

Prior to the twentieth century, Chinese paintings were produced in diverse forms for many different purposes and comprised works of varied status – from the everyday to the highly prized. They were used in tombs, temples, palaces, domestic houses and private gardens. These variations in form and function have all too often been obscured by the subsequent fate of the works; for example, *Buddha Preaching the Law* (cat. no. 1), now displayed as a picture attached to a wooden board, can no longer easily be conceived as a banner that was once repeatedly folded and unfolded, to be suspended freely in a procession or inside a temple. When a painting was made, its form was related to its function, be it a banner, screen, hand-held fan, scroll or album – and a consideration of its function is important in understanding a work. Further, a study must also take into account the fact that, throughout history, the form a painting might take was subject to changes in fashion. One extreme consequence of this volatility was that paintings on banners, screens and hand-held fans declined and after the fourteenth century, scrolls and albums became the most typical forms.

## Form and Function

### PAINTINGS ON BANNERS

A painted banner was either commissioned by an individual or several donors, or purchased at a religious site. As a group, banners were one of the major types of early portable Chinese paintings, and often consisted of a painted image of Buddhist deities on silk or hemp, or occasionally on paper.

It was believed that offering an image of a Buddha or bodhisattva was a means of accumulating 'merit' (*gongde*), which could subsequently be dedicated for the benefit of ancestors and family members, or towards the success of the donor's current spiritual or worldly interests. Such painted devotional and votive banners were primarily used for temporary public display, typically during ceremonial rituals, where they were either hoisted on long poles in the open air, or hung on a wall or pillar or suspended from the ceiling inside a temple. Since images on cloth are light and can be rolled or folded easily, travellers could also carry them, as they might a portable altar, on a long and hazardous journey.

We know very little about when the use of Buddhist painted banners began, but some literary sources suggest as early as the fourth century. By the eighth, ninth and tenth centuries, they had become common across the Tang (618–907) empire; several classical art-historical treatises of the time record banner paintings made by well-known

cat. no. 1 (detail)

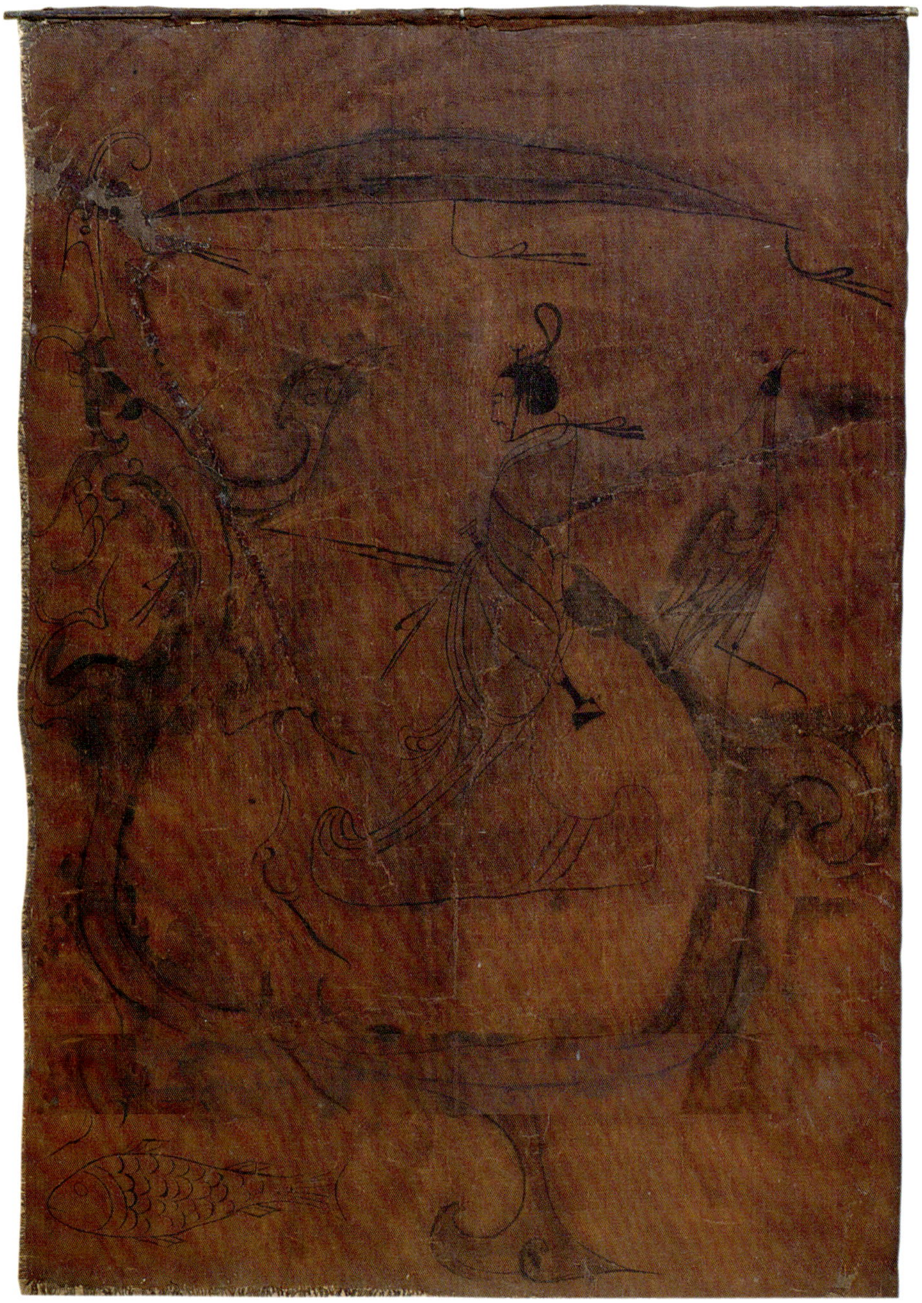

FIG. 1
*Man Riding on a Dragon* funerary banner, c.3rd century BCE. Ink and colour on silk, excavated from Zidanku, Changsha. Hunan Provincial Museum

artists, and single out votive painting as an established genre. Zhu Jingxuan (*c.*785–*c.*848), a scholar-official living in the capital, Chang'an (present Xi'an), in his *Celebrated Painters of the Tang Dynasty* of about 840, lists five painters who specialized in votive paintings.[2] According to Zhu, Lu Tingyao (act. before 840) was regarded by his contemporaries as the painter par excellence in the form. While Zhu does not make it explicit, these artists' works were presumably on cloth, and he records 12 painted elongated banners (*huafan*) illustrating the Buddha's life executed by Chen Hong (act. 1st half 8th century), one of the favourite court painters during Xuanzong's reign (712–55).[3] Zhang Yanyuan (815–76), another scholar-official in the capital, in his *Record of Famous Painters of Successive Dynasties* of 847–60, documents several painted icons on silk seen in the Zisheng and Baosha Temples in the capital; he identifies them as works by several leading painters of the time, including the great master Wu Daozi (*c.*685–758).[4] Elsewhere in his record, Zhang writes that a certain Zhang Liba (act. early 8th century?) produced 13 *huafan* for the teaching hall of the Eastern Dhyāna Cloister at Qing'ai Temple in Luoyang, the eastern capital.[5]

In 842, Emperor Wuzong (r. 841–6) began a great persecution of Buddhism, and iconoclasm spread across the empire. As a consequence, the physical evidence of early Buddhist banner paintings is much diminished. Those that survive are the banners found early last century in the so-called 'library cave' in the Mogao Grottoes at Dunhuang in north-west China, an oasis in the Gobi desert remote from the capital Chang'an and independent of Tang dynastic control during the period of the Buddhist persecution. These amount to more than 1,000 works of various sizes, and form the single largest body of paintings that have survived from the period between 700 and 1000.

The majority of the banner paintings from Dunhuang are the work of local artists whose names are unknown to us, but they are most likely the same painters who created the murals in the cave temples there. The size of the banners varies according to the subject and the means of the local donors, and ranges between 25 and 180 centimetres in width. They can generally be divided into two broad types in terms of format: rectangular or square (cat. no. 1), and an elongated form uncannily similar to the shape of the human figure (cat. no. 6). While the former, known as *zheng* in the Tang period, is often large, and usually shows a Buddha and assembly within a complex composition, the latter, called *fan*, without exception depicts a single divinity such as a bodhisattva or a Guardian King. The overall construction of the elongated banners is more elaborate than that of the rectangular or square ones: typically, the rectangular or square banner has a silk border sewn onto the edges, with several loops for hanging along the upper edge, to which, in the case of larger pieces, a silk-covered stave is added. In an elongated banner, the top consists of

FIG. 2
Fragment of a relief, 2nd or 1st century BCE. Terracotta, Mathura, India. Museum of Fine Arts, Boston

a triangular headpiece of bordered silk with a hanging loop at the apex. Along the base of the triangle runs a bamboo splint or stiffener wrapped in silk, and below this is the main part of the banner in the form of a long rectangle of silk. A second bamboo stiffener is sewn into the lower edge of the painting, from which hang silk streamers fixed into a weighting board; two long streamers are also attached to the upper stiffener at the base of the triangular headpiece.[6]

The use of banners for ritual purposes was in fact well developed in China before the arrival of Buddhism in the first century, and silk banners dating to the third and fourth centuries BCE have been excavated from several tombs in Hunan Province in central China (these were for funerary processions, as can be seen from the bamboo stiffener sewn into the upper edge of the painting, with a suspension loop in the centre) (fig. 1). Given that the artistic milieu in the Tang dynasty was cosmopolitan and that Dunhuang was strategically located on the Silk Route, however, the banner-painting form inevitably evolved under the influence of regions other than China, namely Central Asia, and above all, India. Although no early Buddhist banners from India survive, their existence can be established from pictorial evidence, of which the earliest is probably the medallion section of a red stone railing crossbar from Mathura in northern India (dating to the 2nd or 1st century BCE), where several large rectangular banners can be seen suspended from long posts on a stupa (fig. 2).[7]

In Dunhuang, banner paintings were generally displayed during special family ceremonies or annual Buddhist festivals.[8] These included several public lamp-lighting ceremonies, the city parade of Buddhist icons on the eighth day of the second lunar month, the Ghost Festival on the fifteenth day of the seventh month, funerals, rituals for the sick, and the sending off of loved ones. The inscriptions found on some of the rectangular votive banners suggest that their donors came from a wide variety of social backgrounds, ranging from local officials, clerks, military personnel, monks and nuns, to artisans and villagers.[9] The dedicatory inscriptions on these paintings provide rare insights into the donors' motivations and the circumstances in which the banners were made. Generally, such texts fall into three broad categories in terms of purpose: for the benefit of the deceased, for the living, or both (cat. nos 4, 8, 12).

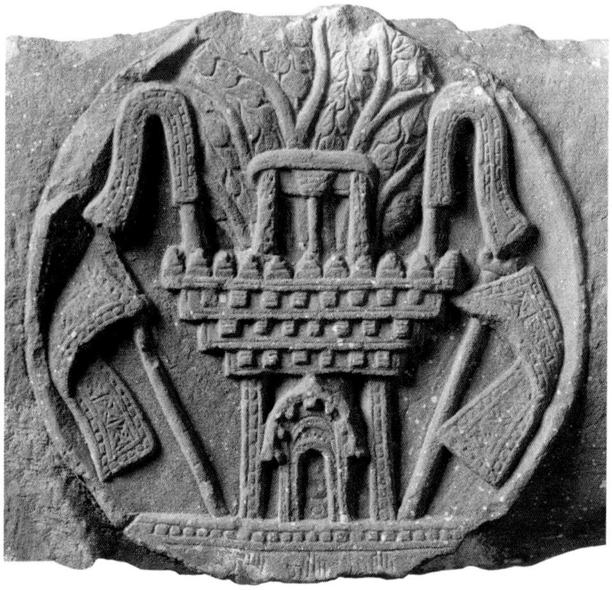

## PAINTINGS ON INTERIOR SCREENS

The typical dwelling house in imperial China was a timber-frame structure in which walls played only a secondary role. Prior to the development of solid partition walls, there were no rigid distinctions between private spaces and those open to all; rather, there were degrees of privacy and openness according to rank, role and the nature of the activity. When it was necessary to partition a space, typically a portable screen of one kind or another was employed. On formal occasions, a single-panel screen was usually placed behind the host or guest of honour as a sign of his or her high status. At night, a multi-panel screen would be used to enclose a canopy bed so as to create a completely private space; during the day, this screen might be opened or removed altogether, and the bed would become a seating area for several people.[10]

FIG. 3
*Dancing Beauty* from a six-panel folding screen, 7th–8th century. Ink and colour on silk, excavated from the Astana graves, Turpan. Xinjiang Uyghur Autonomous Region Museum

FIG. 4
Traditionally attributed to Gu Hongzhong (act. 960). *The Night Revels of Han Xizai* handscroll (detail), mid-12th century. Ink and colour on silk. The Palace Museum, Beijing

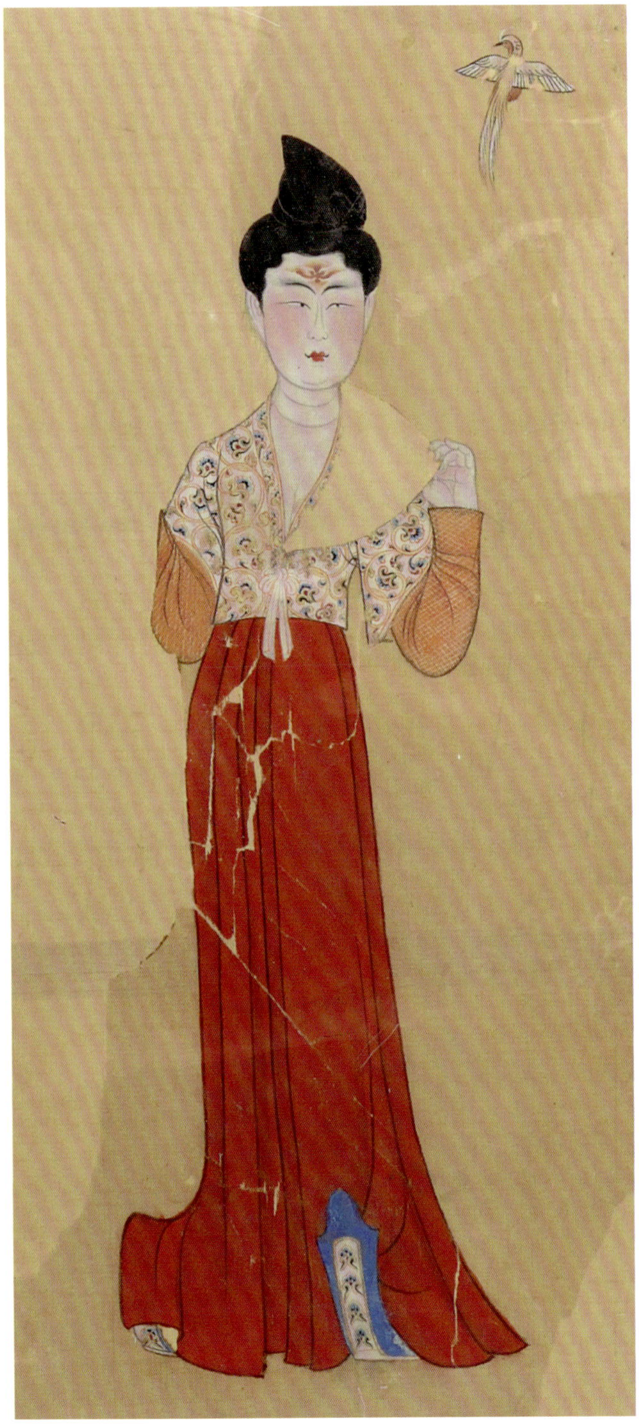

These movable interior screens were frequently adorned with painted decoration. The oldest decorated screen in existence is a small-size burial model dating to the second century BCE, which was excavated from one of the tombs at Mawangdui near Changsha in Hunan Province and is now in the Hunan Provincial Museum; it features a flying dragon on the front and geometric patterns on the back. Other rare early examples of screens include five panels found in the tomb of Sima Jinlong, a general and member of the Northern Wei dynasty (386–534) imperial family, which are painted with stories of Confucian paragons from the *Biographies of Exemplary Women* (see fig. 28). Both screens are made of wooden panels, and painted in lacquer.

It is not known exactly how and when painted silk or paper screens began to be used – R.H. van Gulik has speculated that it might well have been the court painter Fan Changshou (act. 1st half 7th century) who started the trend,[11] and physical evidence suggests that this type of screen had become popular by the first quarter of the eighth century, if not earlier. A six-panel folding silk-screen model featuring six female dancers and musicians, one on each panel, was excavated in 1972 from the tomb of Zhang Lichen, a member of the local nobility in Astana, Xinjiang, who was buried sometime between 703 and 721 (fig. 3).

Despite the rarity of surviving early painted screens, contemporary documents reveal that many painted silk or paper screens were produced in the eighth and succeeding centuries. These texts show not only that the screen was one of the primary painting formats for the majority of great artists until the thirteenth century, but also demonstrate that landscape, animals and plants gradually overtook human figures as the preferred subjects. Early evidence of this shift – towards the natural world – can be found in the *Celebrated Painters of the Tang Dynasty* by Zhu Jingxuan. In this book, he describes a single-panel screen by Wang Zai (act. late 8th century) which depicts two trees above a river, 'one a pine, the other a cedar. An old wisteria vine twisted around them, winding up towards the sky and reaching downwards to the water.'[12] Zhu also notes that at the Xingshan Temple in Chang'an there was another screen by Wang: a landscape over four folding panels that depicted the four seasons.[13]

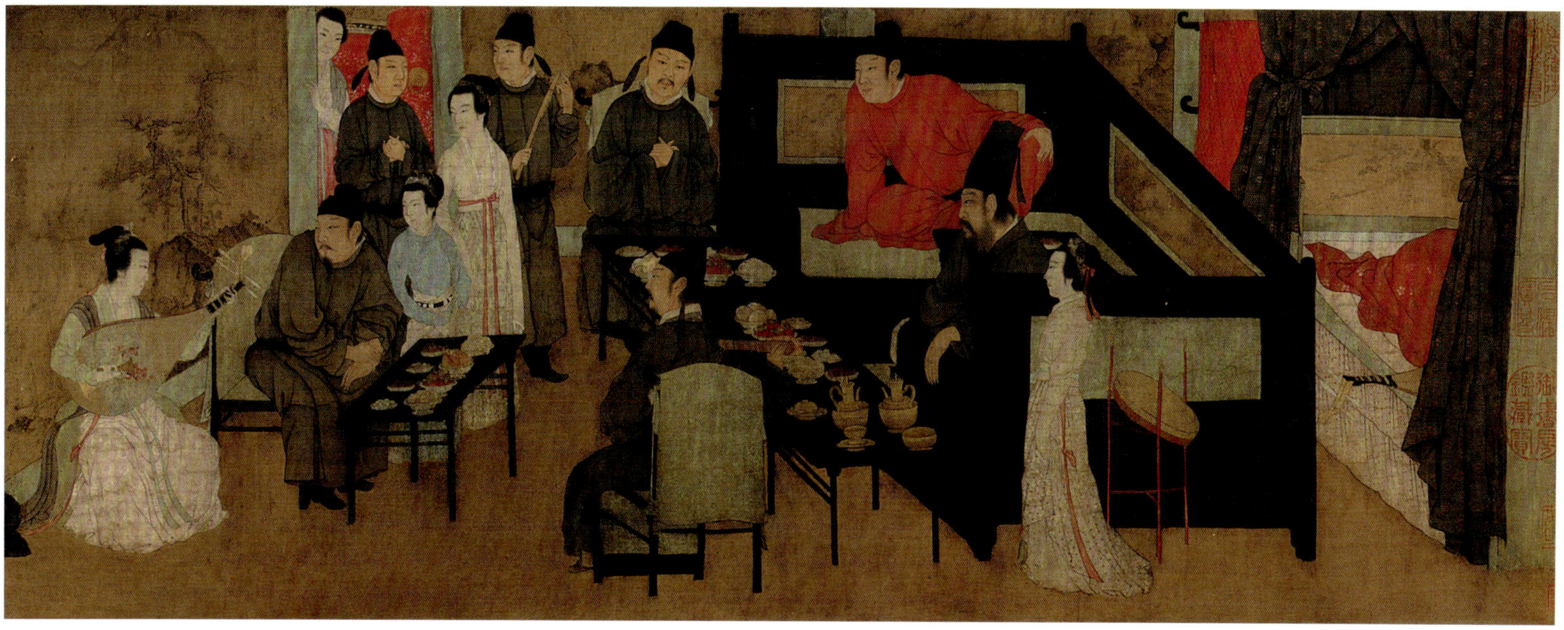

During the eighth and ninth centuries, screens were placed either on top of platforms and beds, or around groups of people seated on the floor – and were therefore quite small. From the tenth century, when it became customary to sit on high seats and use high tables, large floor screens developed, which in turn provided artists with much larger surfaces for painting and more prestigious commissions. Guo Ruoxu (*c.*1041–*c.*1098), a scholar-official and art lover living in the capital during the second half of the eleventh century, in his *Experiences in Painting* gives a vivid sense of the high status that screen painting enjoyed. The largest and most important commissions came from the imperial court, and usually involved painting for the large screen behind the throne. Typically, such a screen measured 3 metres high and 6 metres long.[14] Under the Xiangfu reign (1008–17) of the Northern Song dynasty (960–1127) emperor Zhenzong (r. 998–1022), Tao Yi (act. early 11th century), a specialist painter of flowers, bamboo and birds, was commissioned to paint several screens for the imperial throne, and so pleased the Emperor that he was subsequently promoted to be painter-in-attendance in the Hanlin Academy, the imperial institution confined to an elite group of scholars performing secretarial and academic tasks at court.[15] Yi Yuanji (act. mid-11th century), a court painter during the reign of Emperor Yingzong (r. 1064–7), painted a large three-panel screen for one of the palaces: 'On the centre panel he depicted rocks from Taihu Lake, and sketched in the well-known pigeons of the capital and the celebrated flowers of Luoyang, while on the two wings he represented peacocks ... In all of these his imagination reached its ultimate height.' As a result of this commission, he received an imperial summons. Apart from these grand screens behind thrones in palaces, court painters were also commissioned to paint large screens for the audience halls in other official buildings; examples given by Guo Ruoxu include those in the Court of Sacrificial Worship and the General Supervisorate in Hangzhou. Famous artists were at times requested to paint screens for the houses of high officials in the capital as well. For example, Yan Wengui (967–1030) was commissioned to paint a large screen for the audience hall of Lu Yijian (979–1044), as was Qu Ding (act. mid-11th century) for Pang Ji (988–1063).[16] Among the court painters, Guo Xi (*c.*1000–*c.*1090) was the most popular during his lifetime for his large-scale screens. Ye Mengde (1077–1148), a court official from a younger generation, wrote that in the Yuanfeng era (1078–85) of Emperor Shenzong (r. 1068–85) 'the screens for the audience hall of all the government buildings in the Forbidden City, including the Chancery, were decorated with landscapes by Guo Xi.'[17] The most spectacular painting Guo Xi created was arguably a landscape screen behind the throne in the Jade Hall in the Hanlin Academy; it measured 3 metres high and 16 metres long.[18]

Few paintings of this kind have survived, and those that have are now remounted as scrolls. However, they can occasionally be seen in pictures of interiors. One of these is the mid-twelfth century *The Night Revels of Han Xizai*, which

FIG. 5
*Ladies Adorning their Hair with Flowers*
(detail of fig. 6)

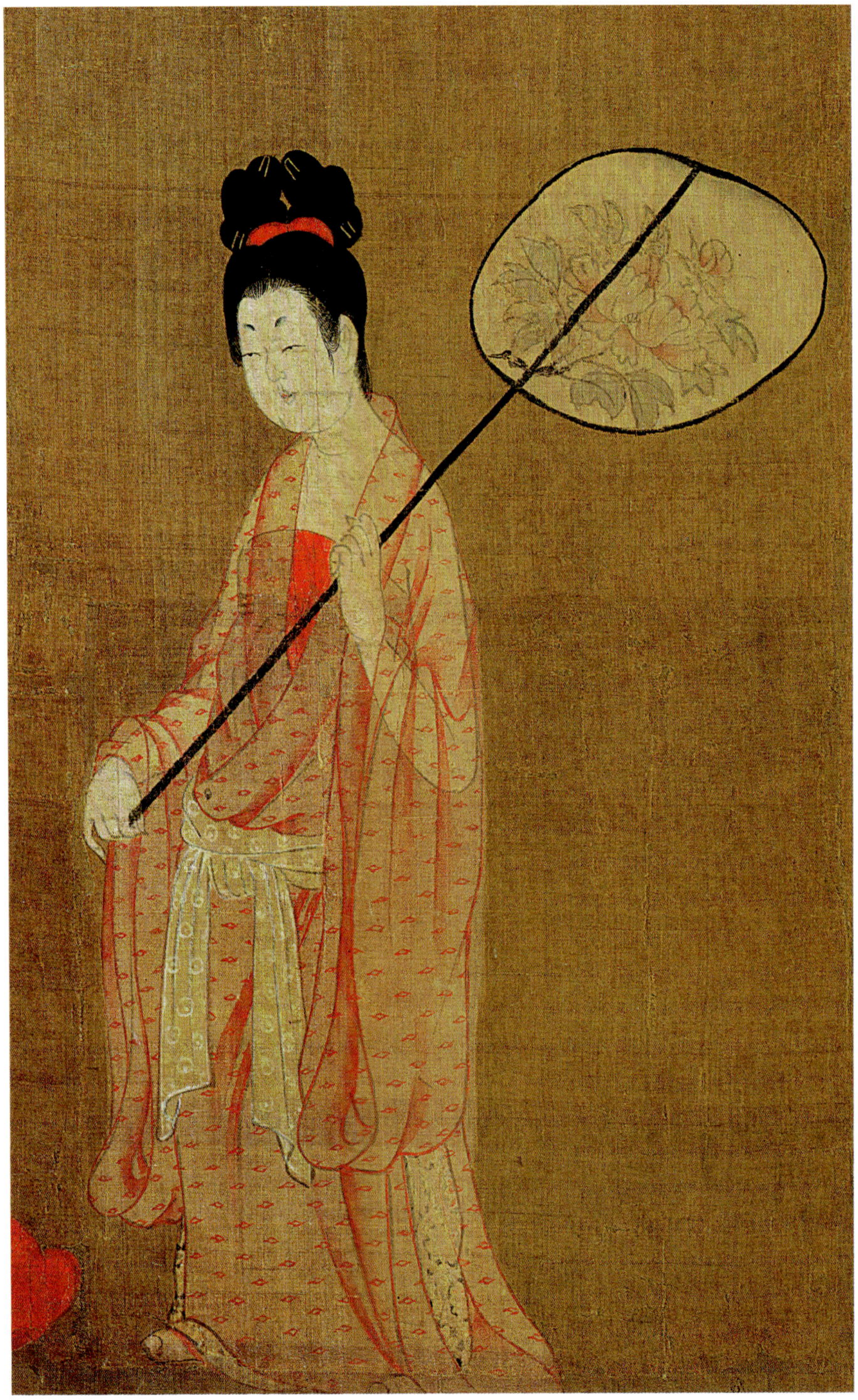

depicts an evening party hosted by a minister named Han Xizai (902–70), who served the Southern Tang dynasty (937–75) in Nanjing (fig. 4). In this five-section narrative scroll painting, seven painted landscape screens of four different types are shown.

Painted screens continued to be a conspicuous feature of the Chinese interior after the twelfth century, although the development of solid partition walls now deprived them of their role as a space divider, and for many great painters, they ceased gradually to be a vehicle for major works. Increasingly, artists looked upon painting as something personal, as a private means of communication between members of the gentry. As such, nothing could have been less suitable than the publicly exposed surface of a screen.

## PAINTINGS ON HAND-HELD FANS

Paintings on bed or couch screens, as seen in *The Night Revels of Han Xizai* (see fig. 4), could be fairly intimate, but the smallest paintings were executed on hand-held fans.[19] Fans in China were of two main types: stiff and round, or a butterfly-shaped folding fan. There is written evidence of the stiff, round fan being used at the imperial court in the first century BCE: the 'Song of a Round Fan' attributed to Ban Jieyu (48 BCE–2 CE), the concubine of Emperor Chengdi (r. 32–7 BCE) of the Han dynasty (206 BCE–220 CE), in which she describes a stiff fan as having a silk face as round as a full moon and being small enough to tuck into a sleeve.[20] The folding fan was introduced into China from Japan in the eleventh century, if not earlier. While folding fans were not painted until the fifteenth century, the round, stiff fans, in their basic form of two silk faces stretched over a bamboo or wooden frame with a central rib that extended as the handle, had been a common working surface for painters since at least the early eighth century. Physical traces of painted round fans earlier than the Song dynasty (960–1279) are rare, but evidence has been found; among the objects excavated from an early eighth-century tomb in Astana, Xinjiang is a long-handled silk fan decorated with painted patterns of birds and flowers.[21] Aside from the objects themselves, painted round fans can be seen in several paintings made by court artists. A small figure just off centre in *Ladies Adorning Their Hair with Flowers*, a work attributed to Zhou Fang (act. 2nd half 8th century), is shown holding a long-handled fan painted with a peony (fig. 5). A young woman of similar age also appears in *Court Ladies Preparing Newly Woven Silk* (cat. no. 16), an early twelfth-century remake of a mid-eighth century work; she is fanning the furnace with a short-handled fan painted with a snowy river scene.

Written evidence suggests that paintings made on small round fans continued to be highly popular both at court and in general society until the thirteenth century. In his *Evaluations of Song Dynasty Painters of Renown* of 1086–94, Liu Daochun (1032–98) relates that during the Duangong era (988–9) of the reign of Emperor Taizong (976–97) of the Northern Song, all court painters were ordered to present painted silk fans, and the Emperor was particularly impressed with Yan Wengui's submission.[22] In the *Painting Continued* of 1168–73, Deng Chun (*c*.1109–79/83) notes that during the Zhenghe era (1111–17) of the reign of Emperor Huizong (1101–25), fan paintings by the Emperor were so popular with the imperial family that every time he painted a fan with a new design, there would soon be hundreds of copies commissioned by the empresses and the princes.[23] A certain Liu Zongdao (act. early 12th century), who painted fans for the market in Kaifeng, tried to gain the upper hand against those who replicated his work by having copies made in his studio ready for sale before releasing a new design.[24] We know from miscellaneous thirteenth-century writings that small fan paintings were still popular a century later in Hangzhou; there was a Mr Chen who ran a famous fan shop in the city, according to Wu Zimu's (act. late 13th–early 14th century) *Record of the Millet Dream*,[25] while another contemporary writer, Zhou Mi (1232–98), notes that when the local people went on a spring or summer outing to the West Lake they took painted fans with them, and that during special flower shows in the imperial palace, painted fans were also laid out for display.[26]

## PRESERVING, COLLECTING AND REMOUNTING EARLY PAINTINGS

Despite the fact that banners, screens and hand-held fans were the main types of painting up until the thirteenth century, very few have survived. All of the banners shown in this exhibition, indeed almost all extant examples, come from a single region, Dunhuang, and we cannot be sure how representative they are of the form more broadly across China. By comparison, many hand-held fans survive, yet even so they must represent only a small fraction of the actual output.

This scarcity has been caused by a number of factors. With regard to religious paintings, apart from the catastrophic Buddhist persecution by Emperor Wuzong in the mid-ninth century, which destroyed much of the Buddhist art that had survived up to that time, there was a belief among Buddhists and Daoists that devotional or votive images were made solely to be used; it was considered improper to collect them in case they were treated irreverently. When the authorities decided that they would not, or could not, be used again, burial or burning was regarded as the proper means of disposal. For early paintings of secular subjects on screens or hand-held fans, the loss is largely associated with the ephemeral nature of the support. In his *Experiences in Painting*, Guo Ruoxu relates the fate of a large eight-panel screen painting called *Yuan An Lying in the Snow*: the painting was a gift from Emperor Zhenzong to his favourite court official Ding Wei (926–1033) on the occasion of the latter's departure for Nanjing as governor. 'When you reach Jinling [present Nanjing],' the Emperor said to him, 'be so good as to choose some spot with a superlative prospect and display the picture there.' In Nanjing, Ding had a pavilion erected in the north-west corner of the city, and placed in it a great screen, over which he had the painting stretched. While we are told that the view was indeed superlative, as the months lengthened into years the silk fabric came to show signs of wear and tear, with the result that from time to time people would cut pieces out of the screen and carry them off, until there was almost nothing left.[27] In some cases, changes in a patron's taste led to the loss of certain styles of work. As mentioned above, during Emperor Shenzong's reign, Guo Xi was so popular that most of the palaces and government buildings were decorated with his paintings.

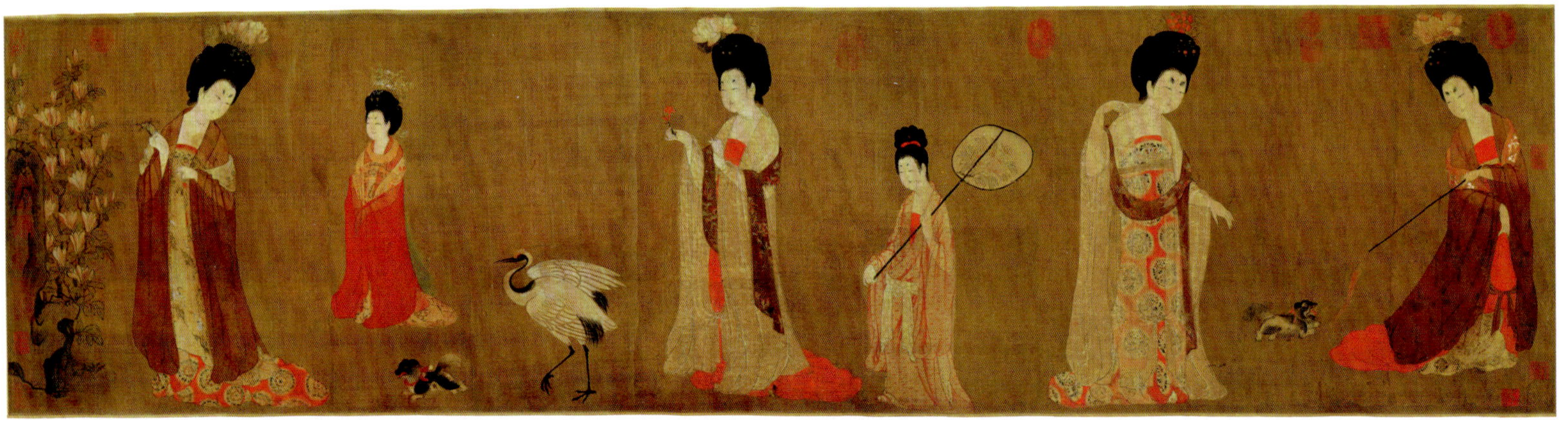

FIG. 6
Zhou Fang (act. 2nd half 8th century). *Ladies Adorning their Hair with Flowers* handscroll, c.8th century (or possibly later). Ink and colour on silk. Liaoning Provincial Museum

FIG. 7
Li Cheng (919–67)
*Luxuriant Forest and Distant Peaks* handscroll (detail of the colophon by Xiang Shui), c.960–1127. Ink and colour on silk. Liaoning Provincial Museum

After Emperor Huizong ascended the throne in 1101, however, Guo Xi's style lost popularity, and it was not long before his paintings were taken down and replaced. According to Deng Chun, who was the son of a high official at the imperial court under Huizong, his father one day discovered with a shock that the piece of cloth a mounter at the imperial mounting studio was using to clean the table was in fact one of Guo Xi's landscapes.[28]

Despite the losses, the very fact that any early paintings on banners, screens or fans survive at all is significant, as it demonstrates an important development for Chinese painting; the advent of connoisseurs and scholars. From the early ninth century, originally functional paintings started to become collectable objects and, in some cases, even highly saleable commodities. As recorded by Zhang Yanyuan in his *Record of Famous Painters of Successive Dynasties*, screen paintings by great masters could command very high prices: a single panel by the most celebrated painters, such as Yan Liben (d.673) and Wu Daozi, could fetch as much as 20,000 ounces of gold, while slightly inferior ones might sell for 15,000 each.[29] Zhang Yanyuan also records a story of how his contemporary, a collector in the capital, rushed to save two fragments of a large screen depicting a pair of cypresses and a single rock by Zhang Zao (act. late 8th century), succeeding only by the skin of his teeth as the wife of the deceased owner of the painting was just about to use them to mend the lining of a set of clothes.[30] Guo Ruoxu, in his 1070s account of the

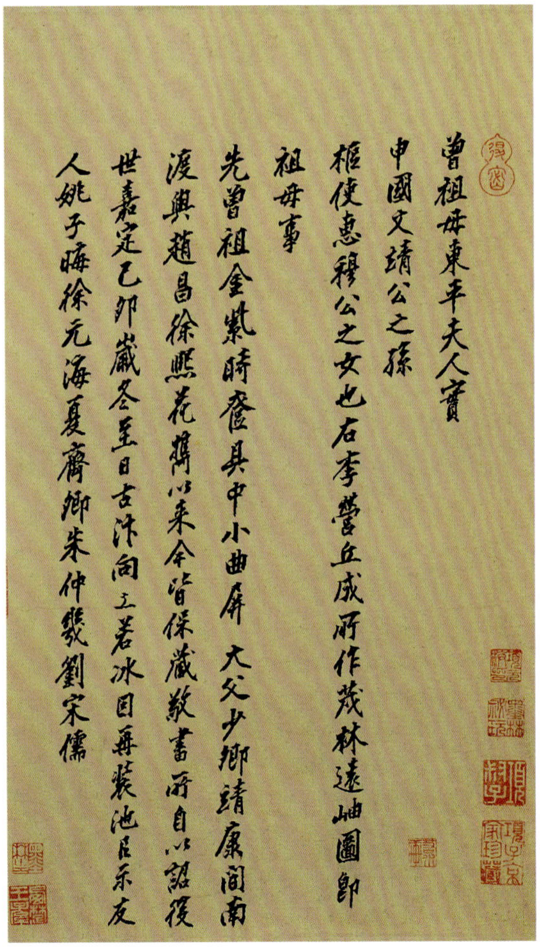
曾祖母東平夫人實
中國文靖公之孫
樞使惠穆公之女也右李營丘成所作茂林遠岫圖即
祖母事
先曾祖金紫時登具中小曲屏 大父少卿靖康間南
渡與趙昌徐熙花禽以來今皆保藏敘書所自以詒後
世嘉定乙卯歲冬至日古汴向水若冰因再裝池呂禾友
人姚子晦徐元海夏齋卿朱仲發劉宋儒

early Song dynasty collector Zhang Quhua (938–1006), mentions that Zhang was able to make his acquisitions of paintings of birds and flowers by the tenth-century master Huang Quan (d.965) and his school because he had an opportunity to supervise a refurbishment project for government buildings in Chengdu, in which old paintings were being replaced with new ones.[31] During the eleventh century, the scope of collecting seemed to include both secular and religious subjects. In the section 'On Collecting Icons' in his book, Guo Ruoxu writes that there should be no taboo on collecting icons:

> The theory is sometimes pronounced that it is not proper to collect Buddhist or Daoist icons; this in the fear that it would be difficult to unroll and enjoy them from time to time without treating them irreverently, or exposing them to the forbidden and unclean. My own opinion is quite the reverse. It is a general rule that when scholars and gentlemen meet for the pleasure of seeing and discussing calligraphy or paintings, the place must be quiet and clean; and where there is only appreciation for skill and respect for the images preserved from the past, how could any irreverence of heart exist?[32]

After collectors acquired paintings on banners, screens or fans, typically they would remount them as scrolls or albums, transforming them from functional objects into works to be valued aesthetically. A wealth of written evidence suggests that this type of remounting was common. There are also a number of extant early scroll paintings which, judging from their physical features or the documentary sources associated with them, would clearly have started their lives as screen paintings. *Luxuriant Forest and Distant Peaks* attributed to Li Cheng (919–67) (fig. 7), for instance, bears three colophons, the first of which was written in 1219 by Xiang Shui (act. early 13th century), who mentions that the painting was originally on a small folding screen and was part of the dowry of his great-grandmother, the granddaughter of Lu Yijian.[33] *Ladies Adorning their Hair with Flowers* is another example; while remounting it the museum's curator discovered that the long horizontal composition actually consisted of three separate short sections. These sections, each bearing two images of women, must have been removed from the three panels of a couch or bed screen (fig. 6).[34]

## HANDSCROLL PAINTINGS

While the formats of handscroll, hanging scroll and album were used by collectors to preserve functional paintings, between the eighth and thirteenth centuries they increasingly became the form preferred by artists. Indeed, by the fourteenth century these three formats had replaced the banner, screen and fan to become the paradigm for the portable painting, a status quo that remained unchallenged until the early 1900s, when the European tradition of easel painting began to provide an alternative.

Among the three forms, the handscroll was the first to be developed and employed for painting. The origins of handscroll painting were concurrent with the development of the scroll as a format for text.[35] The silk manuscripts found in the third tomb in Mawangdui, near Changsha, which date from the second century BCE, are an example of the earliest form of what came to be known as the scroll: following the precedent of the bamboo- or wooden-strip book, the text is written vertically in columns from top to bottom, with the columns arranged from right to left and at the end of the text a bamboo or wooden strip affixed to the silk to enable the book to be easily rolled up. In the first-century official bibliography *Treatise on Bibliography, Standard History of the Former Han Dynasty*, a substantial number of books are recorded as being *juan* or 'scrolls', indicating that the silk scroll, as well as the book made of bamboo or wooden strips, was a standard format of the time. By the fifth and sixth centuries, thanks to the widespread use of paper, the scroll had completely replaced strips for books, as suggested by the *Treatise on Bibliography, Standard History of the Sui Dynasty*, a bibliographical catalogue of the mid-seventh century.

Both these books list various pictures (*tu*), ranging from diagrams, charts and maps to illustrations of classic books made between the first and mid-seventh centuries. Records of the same types of pictures were also made in

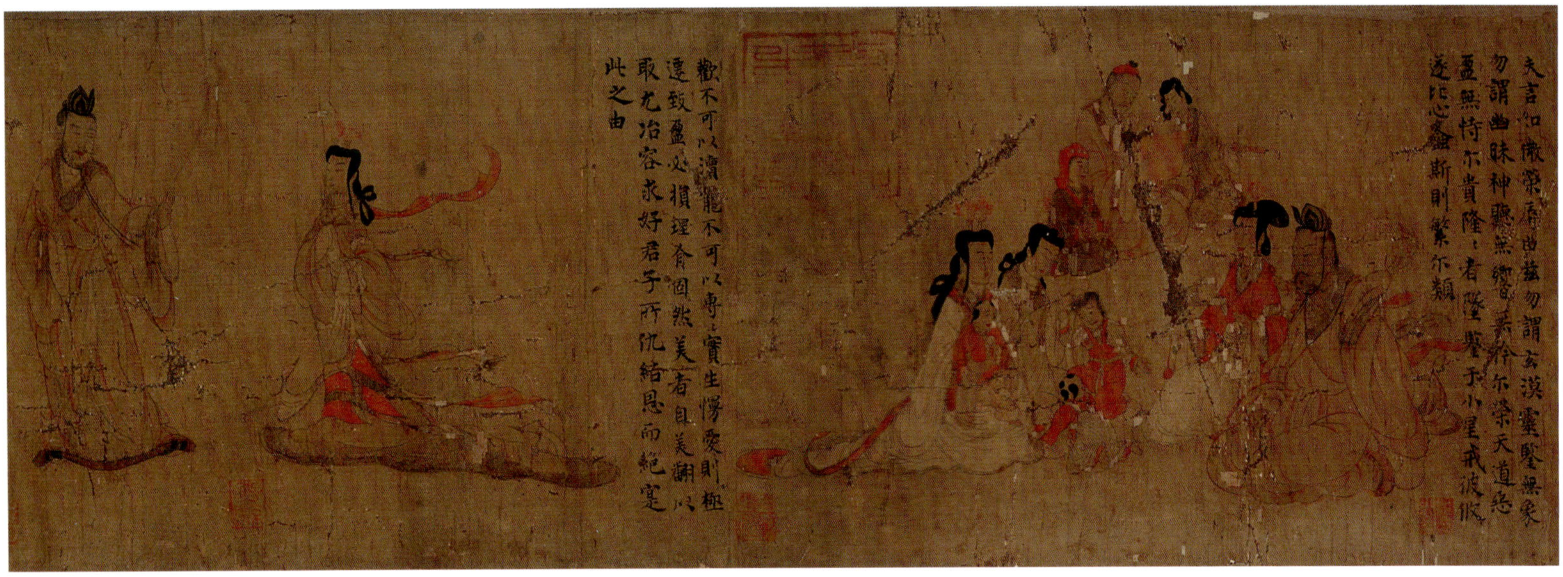

the ninth-century *Record of Famous Painters of Successive Dynasties*, where Zhang Yanyuan clearly considers them to be the earliest handscroll paintings.[36] The compositions of these paintings typically alternate text with illustration, as seen in *Admonitions of the Court Instructress to the Palace Ladies*, a sixth- to eighth-century copy of the lost original attributed to the famous painter Gu Kaizhi (c.344–c.406) (fig. 8). This early mode of text-and-picture continued to be adopted by artists in the following centuries, forming a special category of handscroll painting, in this exhibition

FIG. 8
After Gu Kaizhi (c.344–c.406). Copy of the *Admonitions of the Court Instructress to the Palace Ladies* handscroll (detail), 6th–8th century. Ink and colour on silk. The British Museum, London (1903,0408,0.1)

FIG. 9
After Gu Kaizhi (c.344–c.406). Copy of the *Goddess of the Luo River Ode* handscroll, c.960–1279. Ink and colour on silk. The British Museum, London (1930,1015,0.2)

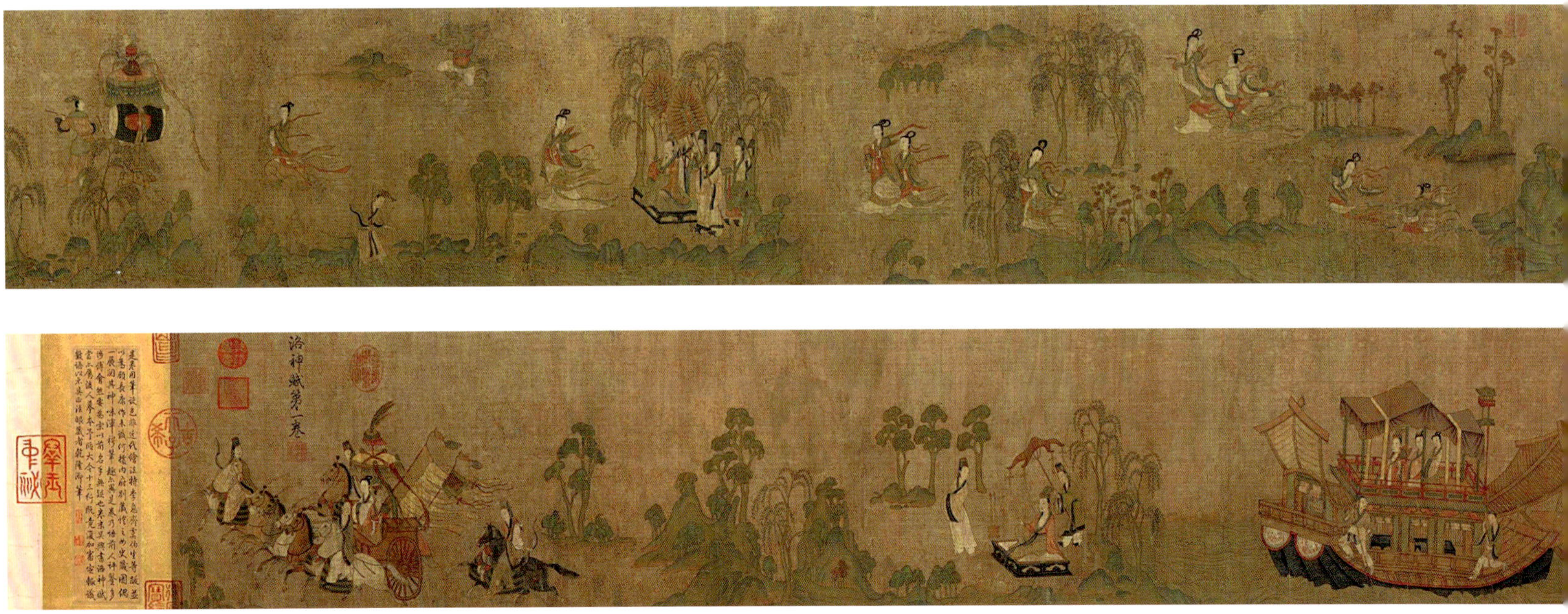

exemplified by *The Five Planets and Twenty-eight Constellations* (cat. no. 13), traditionally attributed to Zhang Sengyou (act. 490–540) but probably painted in the Northern Song or earlier.

Even as the text-and-picture tradition was being established and developed, some painters began to free themselves from the restrictions of the mode, and took advantage of the potential of a scroll's horizontal format to experiment with subjects that embodied temporal and spatial progression – above all, to create a new type of composition in which scenes were presented in a continuous sequence. This experimentation resulted in a new kind of narrative illustration relating to the great classical themes of the period, as seen in *The Goddess of the Luo River Ode* attributed to Gu Kaizhi. In a late Northern Song copy of this masterly scroll (fig. 9), the episodes of the story of the poet's ill-fated romance with the river goddess unfold through a continuous landscape, and the images of the two lovers and their attendants appear again and again.

It is unclear whether Chinese painters developed this technique of continuous and linear pictorial narration of classical subjects over the fourth, fifth and sixth centuries independently of the narrative tradition in Indian Buddhist art, which was being introduced into China during this period, or whether they adapted important elements from the illustrated Buddhist texts originating in India to develop their techniques for illustrating classical Chinese subjects.[37] It is also possible that the pre-Buddhist practice of decorating walls with depictions of processions and hunting scenes in long strips prepared Chinese artists to recognize the potential of the handscroll for sequential illustration. In any case, from the eleventh century on, painters worked to explore temporal and spatial progression in the horizontal format not just with classical poetry and Buddhist or Confucian tales, but also with landscape and genre scenes. For many artists, a continuous pictorial progression was important because they felt that the underlying purpose in painting such subjects was to

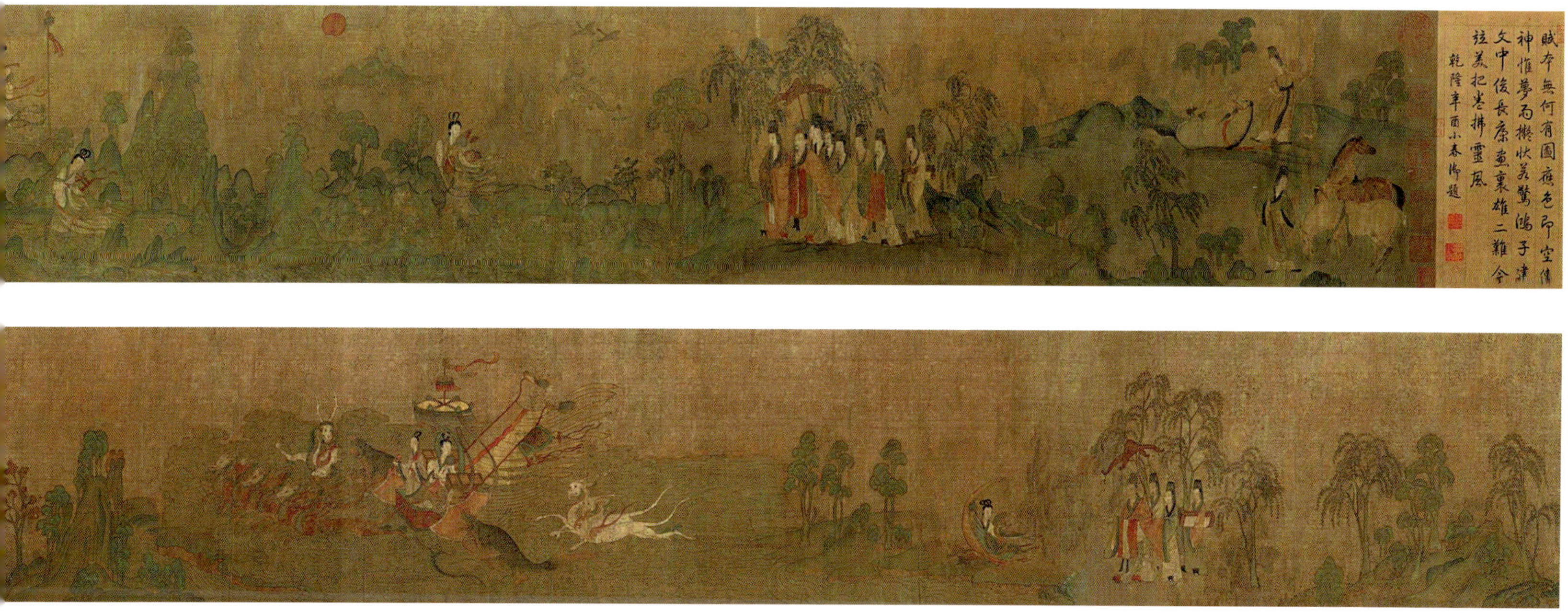

FIG.10
Wei Xian (act. 937–78). *The Lofty Scholar Liang Boluan* hanging scroll, c.907–960. Ink and colour on silk. The Palace Museum, Beijing

provide the viewer with an imaginary travelling experience. The painter Guo Xi writes in his landscape text *The Lofty Message of Forest and Streams*:

> There are those [landscapes] through which you may travel, those in which you may wander, and those in which you may live. Any paintings attaining these effects are to be considered excellent, but those for travelling and sightseeing are not as successful in achievement as those suitable for wandering and living.[38]

With a few exceptions, it is generally difficult to establish which of the surviving landscape paintings in handscroll format made between 1000 and 1300 were actually designed to be handscrolls, and which were initially destined for bed or couch screens. In 1082, the great writer, poet and calligrapher Su Shi (1037–1101) posted a horizontal scroll of a landscape by the contemporary painter Li Ming (act. late 11th century) to his close friend Wu Fugu (1004–1100) in Guangdong. In the covering letter, Su wrote: 'The scroll is long so that it would be suitable for the screen around your bed.'[39] By the fourteenth century, however, bed and couch screens had generally disappeared, and most horizontal scroll paintings were intended as handscrolls. It may be no coincidence that the word for handscroll, *shoujuan*, was coined in this period;[40] previously there were various words referring to a scroll: *juan* ('scroll'), *hengjuan* ('horizontal scroll') and *juanzhou* ('scroll with roller'). Viewing a painting in scroll format was an experience akin to reading a book, with the 'reader' controlling the pace at which they proceeded. Sometimes the viewer might stop to contemplate a particular scene, sometimes even retracing his steps and travelling back a few inches. One might even say that viewing a handscroll was less restrictive than watching a film today, as spectators in a cinema cannot focus or dwell on a scene of particular interest at leisure, nor can they go back a little to watch something again; all that is done for them on the screen. With a handscroll, however, the viewer was free to wander or dwell at will.

## HANGING SCROLL PAINTINGS

There are almost twice as many hanging scrolls in this catalogue as handscrolls, and although it is impossible to provide conclusive data, a survey of several authoritative lists of scroll paintings by the Chinese connoisseur Xu Bangda (1911–2012) suggests that this ratio of hanging scrolls to handscrolls probably reflects the true situation of painting production over the 12 centuries to 1900.[41] Looking through Xu Bangda's lists, it is evident that

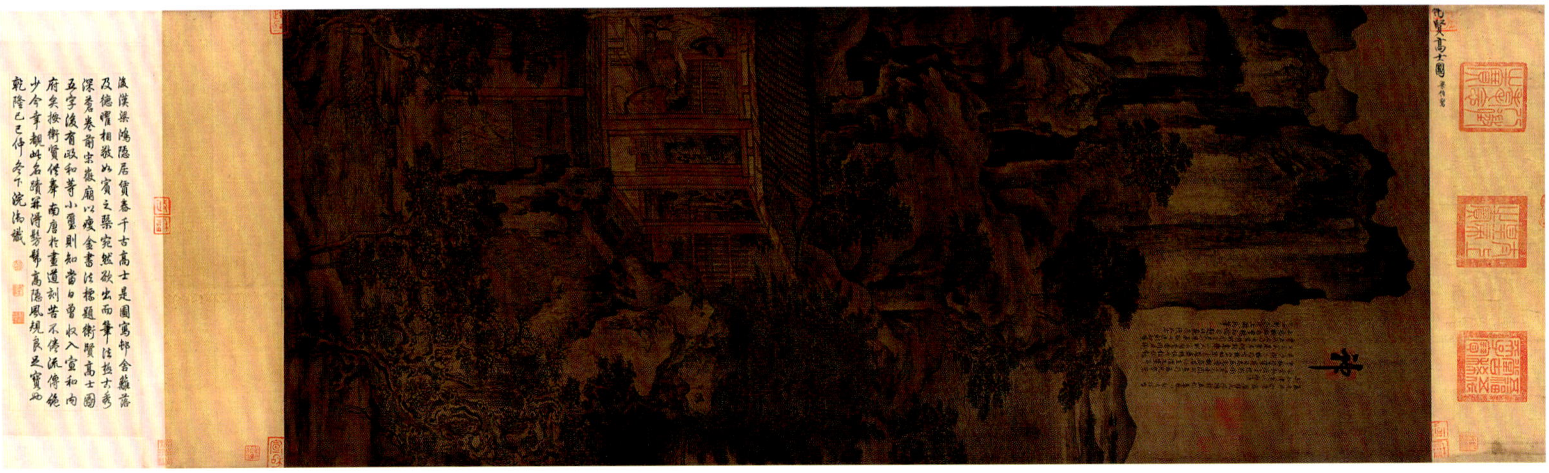

FIG. 11
Wooden 'house' excavated from the Yemaotai Tomb, Faku County. Liaoning Provincial Museum

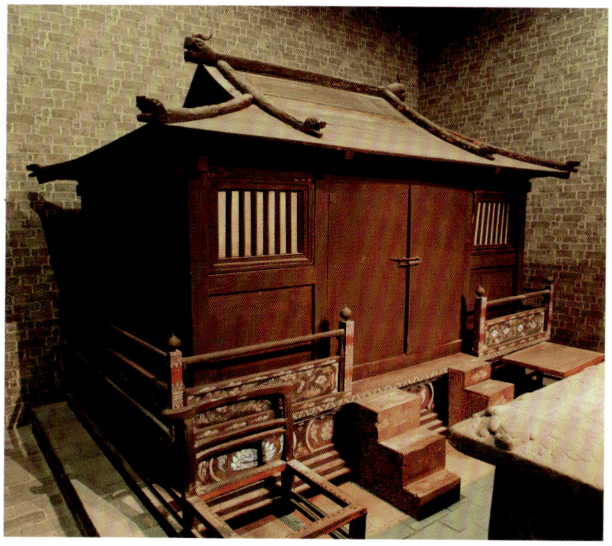

individual artists, and in some cases different local schools, preferred one or another of the two formats. Among the great literati-painters of the Yuan dynasty (1271–1368), Zhao Mengfu (1254–1322) (cat. no. 46) and Qian Xuan (*c.*1235–before 1307) (cat. no. 45) preferred to work on a handscroll, while Wang Meng (*c.*1308–85) and Ni Zan (1306–74) (cat. no. 51) evidently favoured the vertical format; indeed, Ni Zan does not seem to have painted a single handscroll. Many of the works produced by Zhe school painters during the fifteenth and sixteenth centuries were in hanging scroll format as well. There are also general trends across certain periods: for example, while the two-to-one ratio seems to remain constant until 1700, a greater number of hanging scrolls are listed for the eighteenth and nineteenth centuries, and by the end of the nineteenth century, handscrolls produced by contemporary painters become extremely rare. This seems surprising, given that the hanging scroll only emerged many centuries after the handscroll had matured as a form.

In spite of its relatively late development, the origin of the hanging scroll can be traced back to early funerary banners. One of the oldest surviving examples of such banners, found in Zidanku tomb no. 1 near Changsha, dates to the third or fourth centuries BCE, and depicts a man in profile riding a dragon. The banner has a loop for suspension attached to a stiffener at the top in a similar manner to a hanging scroll (fig. 1). Other precursors include Buddhist banners produced and used in the eighth, ninth and tenth centuries, as seen from the surviving examples from Dunhuang, especially the large rectangular pieces with a silk-covered stiffener attached to the upper edge of the mount (see cat. no. 5). The major formal difference between these early banners and a hanging scroll, however, is that the latter has a roller at the bottom of the painting as well as a stiffener at the top. The stave-and-roller design of the hanging scroll could have originated from more than one source: the elongated banners, which include a stiffener near the top and a weighting board at the bottom, and – perhaps a stronger and more direct influence – the mounting practice of handscrolls, as seen in the rare examples of early hanging scrolls in which traces of the mounting style of handscrolls still remain. For example, in the tenth-century hanging scroll painting *The Lofty Scholar Liang Boluan* by Wei Xian (act. 937–78) (fig. 10), a silk strip has been attached to both the upper and lower edges of the painting, but not to the left and right edges (which became prevalent in later hanging scrolls). Most unusually, the title of the painting, written later by Emperor Huizong, is placed horizontally at the upper edge of the picture. If one turns the painting clockwise by 90 degrees, it becomes clear that this vertical picture is mounted in the same style as a horizontal handscroll. The question of exactly when hanging scrolls came into being has yet to be answered conclusively.[42] It is possible that they existed as early as the ninth century, as suggested by William R.B. Acker's English translation of Zhang Yanyuan's *Record of Famous Painters of Successive Dynasties*, in which the word *huazhang* (literally 'painted fabric curtain or hanging') is rendered as 'hanging scroll',[43] although the text does not justify the preference for 'hanging scroll' over the more obvious 'hanging'. Further problems arise from the ambiguous meanings of the key word *zhang*.[44] Otherwise, the two silk hanging scrolls taken from a Liao dynasty (907–1125) tomb of the late tenth century at Yemaotai near Shenyang in Liaoning Province – the earliest surviving hanging scrolls with their original mounting intact – provide the terminus post quem.[45]

The discovery of the Yemaotai paintings (fig. 52) also gives a rare glimpse of how hanging scrolls were displayed in a domestic setting during the late tenth century. According to the excavation reports, the two paintings were found hung on the east and west walls of a wooden 'house' inside the tomb, within which was the stone sarcophagus containing the tomb occupant's body (fig. 11).[46] This method of pairing is also found in the murals in an early twelfth-century tomb at Mangshan in the north of

FIG. 12
Diagram showing the layout of the early 12th century tomb no. 12, Mangshan Tombs, north of Luoyang

Luoyang: here, two bird-and-flower hanging scrolls are depicted on the east wall, mirrored by another two on the west (fig. 12).[47] Indeed, this method of display remained fashionable in later periods, as reflected in the popularity of sets of paintings such as *The Four Pleasures: Music, Chess, Calligraphy and Painting*, traditionally attributed to Ren Renfa (1255–1327) but probably by an early fifteenth-century artist (cat. no. 53).

The owners of hanging scrolls typically displayed them on a temporary basis, in some cases due partly to concerns over their fragility. The Southern Song connoisseur Zhao Xigu (act. 1195–c.1242), in his *Record of Pure Happiness from Hermit's Cave*, gives a detailed description of how a hanging scroll should be displayed:

> Having selected some paintings by famous artists you should not suspend more than three or four in one room. After having enjoyed these to the full, every three or four days you should change them for other good pictures. In such a way you will (in course of time) see all your scrolls, and they will not suffer damage from overexposure to draughts or sunrays. If they are displayed in turns they will not get soiled. Besides, by continually changing the works of one or two masters you will never tire of them. For viewing your scrolls, you should have a careful person to handle the unrolling. When a painting is unrolled, you should lightly dust its surface with a whisk made from a horse tail or silk; you should never use a coir-hair brush. In the room there should never be burnt sandal wood, laka wood, camphor, or any other types of incense that contain oil and thus produce thick smoke. The only type of incense you may use there is *penglai*, *jia* or *qian*. The windows of the room should be covered by oil paper and the sunblind of the door should be kept lowered. Underneath each scroll there should be a low table to protect it. On this table there should be no objects that interfere with the scroll, there could be only such things as an incense burner, a lute or an ink stone. During the very hot days of summer, when it is warm and moist, no paintings should be left on the walls. During the severe cold winter a slow fire should be kept burning in the room to have a temperature like that of early spring. Then you can have the scrolls on the wall, provided that they are taken down for the night and put in their boxes to prevent them from being damaged and from getting frozen.[48]

In other cases, the owners changed their displays according to the season, so as to indicate the time of year and the various calendar festivals. During the seventeenth century, the heyday of connoisseurship, some collectors even tried to develop a formula to codify the centuries of

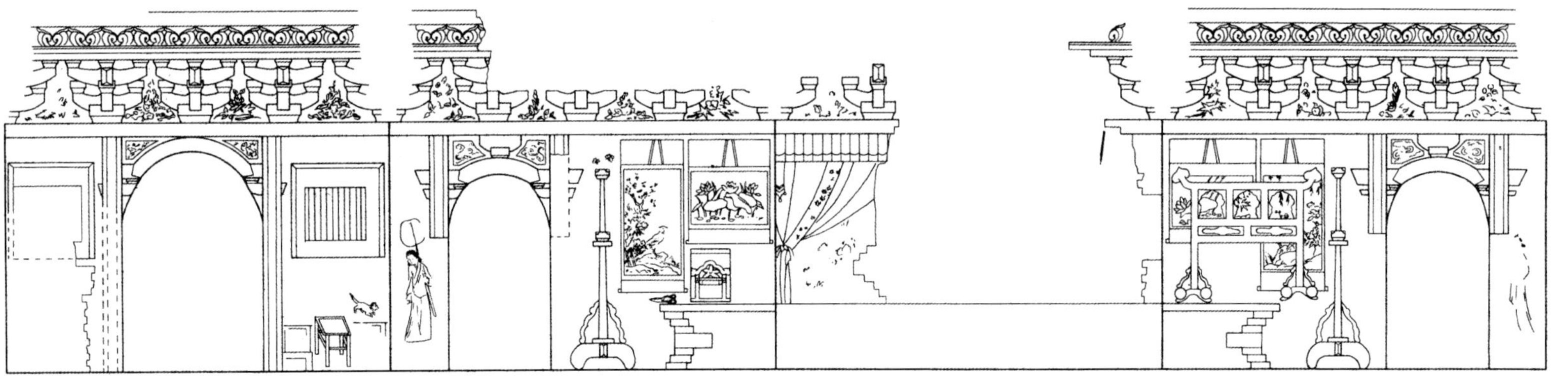

display practice. A typical example is the 'Calendar for the Displaying of Scrolls' by Wen Zhenheng (1585–1645), the great-grandson of Wen Zhengming (1470–1559).[49]

Chinese paintings that made their way to Japan prior to the modern era, via Japanese envoys, monks and traders, were for the most part hanging scrolls. In the case of hand-scrolls, hand-held fans and album leaves, most would have been remounted as hanging scrolls (cat. nos 26, 39, 41) to suit their new setting. During the Muromachi period (1336–1573), Chinese hanging scrolls were featured, as an example of 'Chinese things' (*karamono*), in a type of *kazari* – a formal display of art and decorative objects in the residences of the military elite set out for special occasions, such as visits from vassals, high-ranking court officials, Buddhist clergy, or even the emperor and his entourage (cat. no. 43). Typically, the scrolls were hung in the display alcoves of a 'guest hall' (*kaisho*), which were usually set slightly higher than the floor. In front of the scrolls, the host would also arrange flower vases and incense burners. The modes of *kazari* developed in this period had a profound influence on the display of Chinese scrolls throughout the early modern periods in Japan.[50]

## ALBUMS

The album was the last major painting format to develop. Like the handscroll, the origin of the album is related to the evolution of the book; the first leaf-books came into existence through the rise of reference materials such as rhyming dictionaries and encyclopaedias, as was observed by the great scholar Ouyang Xiu (1007–12) in his book *Jottings after Returning to the Fields*:

> The men of the Tang dynasty had all the books mounted in scroll form for their libraries. It was only later that the leaf-book, in a form close to today's album, came into being. It would have been difficult to consult texts for specific information frequently if they were written on a scroll as it would have had to be unrolled. That is why the leaf-book was invented.[51]

The first albums were probably made with the concertina format of binding (*jingzhe zhuang*), examples of which can be seen among the ninth-century Buddhist texts from Dunhuang. The second album format, the so-called 'butterfly binding' (*hudie zhuang*), was developed later, and consisted of multiple leaves folded inwards and bound together at the folds, leaf by leaf, with paste. Although it is difficult to establish the details of the early history of using albums for paintings,[52] it seems likely that the album was first chosen as a practical way to preserve small paintings such as those on hand-held fans, and subsequently adopted by artists as a new format for original work. Despite the scarcity of early albums in their original mounts, it has been suggested that some extant early scrolls were originally made as albums. The early twelfth-century work *Auspicious Cranes*, attributed to Emperor Huizong (cat. no. 17), which is now mounted as a handscroll, was probably once a leaf in the extensive series of painting albums *The Xuanhe Reign Album of Sagacious Viewing*, commissioned to depict auspicious signs and events under Huizong.[53] Other early examples include two thirteenth-century works, *The Preaching Śākyamuni Buddha* by Zhang Shengwen (act. mid-13th century, National Palace Museum, Taipei) and *Twelve Views of Water* by Ma Yuan (act. late 12th–early 13th century, The Palace Museum, Beijing) – the former was originally in a concertina binding, the latter in a butterfly binding.

Albums as a painting format achieved their popularity after 1350, and were employed for a wide variety of purposes. For artists whose favourite subjects were the country's well-known scenery or local gardens, the album was typically used to present multiple views in a sequential manner, as seen in *Twelve Views of Tiger Hill* by Shen Zhou (1427–1509) (cat. no. 57) and *Garden of the Inept Adminstrator* by Wen Zhengming (cat. no. 62). These works serve as pictorial guides to specific sites. In cases where albums display a wide and diverse range of subjects, styles and artistic quality, they were probably used for experimentation or to store ideas, and therefore would not originally have been intended for anyone but the artist himself. Albums of pictures with pedagogical intent were evidently created by a master as a tool for teaching his students (see fig. 15).

## Profession and Practice

Contrary to received wisdom,[54] both material and documentary evidence indicates that there was no distinction between painting and other arts, or indeed between any arts and crafts, in the early periods of Chinese history; until the emergence of academies in the tenth and eleventh centuries, painting was regarded as just another lowly profession for an artisan.

### THE ARTISAN-PAINTER AND WORKSHOP

According to the structure of traditional Chinese society, artisans ranked lower than scholars or farmers but above merchants and traders. A desire for social continuity meant that an artisan's profession was hereditary, and handed down from father to son. Although a painter's sons were not necessarily painters themselves, they generally practised trades related to the artisan professions, such as carpentry, goldsmithing or pottery. For example, while Dai Jin's (1388–1462) father was a painter, Dai Jin himself was a failed goldsmith before turning to painting,[55] and Qiu Ying (1494/5–1552) began his career as a lacquer artist.[56] In the Song period, Gao Wenjin's (act. 2nd half 10th century) family produced four generations of painters, and Ma Yuan's family, seven.[57]

Information about very early artisan-painters is extremely limited, but it is possible to examine the working life of artisan-painters in the eighth, ninth and tenth centuries in some detail based on contemporary official and private writings, and especially the surviving archives from Dunhuang.[58] These sources indicate that during this period artisan-painters most probably worked as members of a team rather than as individual artists. Their work was anonymous, and unsigned. Artisan-painters did not confine themselves to walls, banners, screens and fans; they also painted buildings, sculptures in wood, stone and terracotta, lacquerware and silk garments. As well, they provided the drawings in crafts where there was a division between conception and execution, such as embroidery and metalwork. This type of collaboration is illustrated by a banner fragment portraying the bodhisattva Dizang (S. Kṣitigarbha) (cat. no. 10), in which painting and embroidery techniques are combined. It should be noted that collaboration between a painter and embroiderer is a significant ancient tradition that can be traced back to the Zhou period (1045–256 BCE). The *Record of the Scrutiny of Crafts*, a fourth-century BCE text that purports to be a description of the products and working processes of different artisans attached to the ruling house of the Qi Kingdom (in today's Shandong Province), describes painting on silk as part of 'colouring' (*shese*) activities; others included embroidery, dyeing, printing and silk preparation. Here the role of the painter in the workshop could have been, in addition to making drawings, working in collaboration with the embroiderer and other textile artisans to apply colour to the silk fabrics.[59] The earliest surviving examples of this type of cooperative activity are a group of tenth-century BCE silk fragments attached to the remains of clay and wood, found in tomb no. 1 at Rujiazhuang in Baoji, Shaanxi Province (fig. 13). The contour lines of the patterns on these early fragments are embroidered in yellow thread, whereas the different colours for the areas within are painted with a brush.[60] There is good reason to suppose that painting on silk was a cheaper substitute for expensive and time-consuming embroidery work. This might help to explain why up to the Tang period, the word 'hui' (績 or 繪) could mean either 'to embroider' or 'to paint'. It is also interesting to note that at some point during the Tang the former character disappeared, and with it the meaning 'to embroider'; the second character then only possessed the meaning 'to paint', while 'to embroider' was allocated to another ancient word, 'xiu' (繡).

An artisan-painter was a member of a workshop. In Dunhuang, during the second half of the ninth and the tenth centuries, a workshop was typically attached to the local painters' guild. Members of the guild included masters (*boshi* or *shi*), assistants (*jiang*) and apprentices (*sheng*).[61] When painters were away from their home base, perhaps working on murals, a temporary workshop was usually arranged on site. As has been discovered at Dunhuang, when a donor decided to commission a new cave mural in the Mogao Grottoes, painters would use a smaller cave nearby as a storehouse for their materials and equipment.[62] In the Tang period, a painter's workshop would simply be a working space in their house in the residential area of the city. It was only in the second half of the tenth century, when the new rulers of the Song dynasty abolished the traditional imposition of a residential and market divide in urban administration, that it became possible for the painter's workshop to move to the busy marketplace and to comprise a shop that opened on to the street and a studio at the back. Two paintings by Zhou Jichang (act. 2nd half 12th century) from the late twelfth century (cat. nos 23, 24) were made in a workshop of this type in a commercial street in Ningbo.[63] By the seventeenth and eighteenth centuries, as a result of high land prices in the busiest commercial districts, the painters' workshop would have been a two-storey structure, with the studio on the upper floor and the shop downstairs (see fig. 23).[64]

## THE ARTISAN-PAINTER AT COURT

Many painters made their living by supplying work to the local marketplace – and there may have been many more than is sometimes supposed today – but not all artisan-painters worked in local workshops. From the earliest times, it was an established practice for the imperial court to recruit the most talented artisan-painters in society to work in the palace workshop on a temporary or permanent basis, and there was also a system in the early courts to reward them with official titles and privileges for good service; however, from the early eighth century, the most highly esteemed artisan-painters in the palace workshop were not only paid salaries, but were also elevated to the prestigious position of academician (a station traditionally reserved for scholar-officials).[65] At the court of Emperor Xuanzong, as well as being given such a post in the Hanlin Academy, Wu Daozi was appointed tutor in the school for palace ladies and companion to the prince, while both

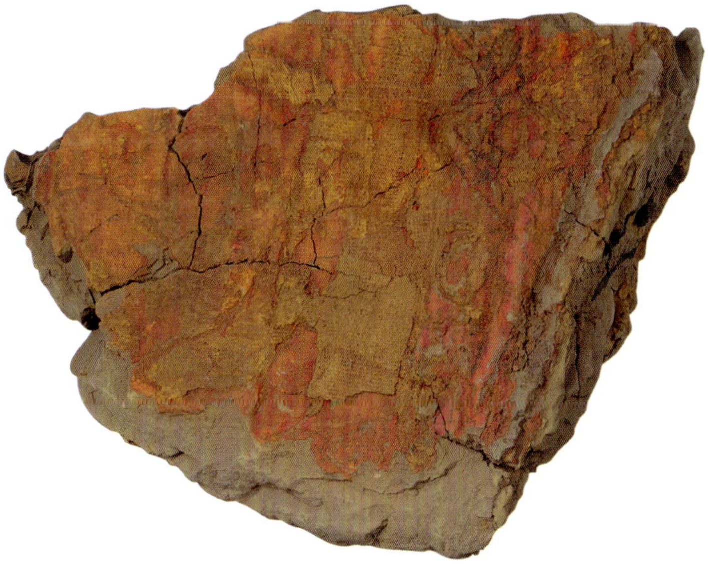

FIG. 13
Clay and wood remains showing the impression of silk fragments, 10th century BCE. Excavated from tomb no. 1, Rujiazhuang Tombs, Baoji. Shaanxi History Museum

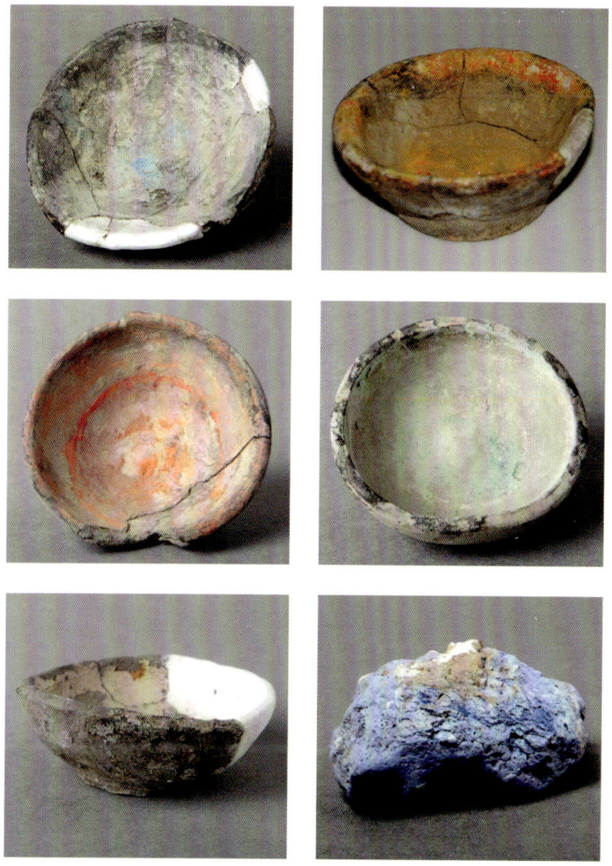

FIG. 14
Artists' colour pans, 861–1279, and ultramarine blue pigment, 960–1279. Excavated from the Mogao Caves, Dunhuang. Dunhuang Academy

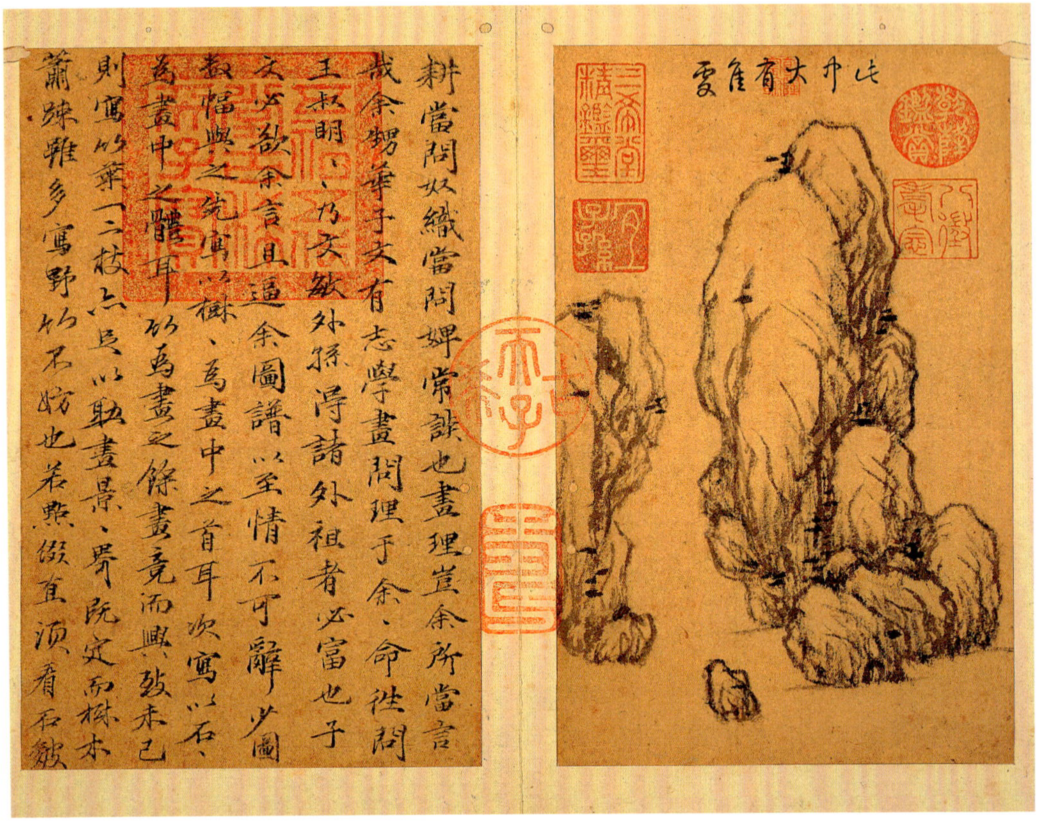

FIG. 15
Ni Zan (1306–74). *Two Rocks* from a painting manual, 1350. Two leaves from an album of 10, ink on paper. National Palace Museum, Taipei

Chen Hong and Zhang Xuan were given the title 'academician' in the Jixian Academy (Academy of Scholarly Worthies). In the following centuries, the elevated social status of the court artisan-painter was also matched by a new intellectual status attached to painting by writers. For example, in the ninth century, Zhang Yanyuan, extolling the powers of image-making and expounding a link between writing and painting, declared painters to be the equals of philosophers, historians, poets and calligraphers.[66] In the tenth century, following the destruction of the Tang empire, the status of court artisan-painters continued to rise in the regional courts, and in Chengdu, situated in the Later Shu Kingdom, and in Jinling, in the area controlled by the Southern Tang dynasty, artisan-painters were singled out from other craftsmen in the palace workshops to form the Hanlin Painting Academy, a branch academy of the Hanlin.

Artisan-painters were naturally attracted to these prestigious new positions at court and the accompanying generous monthly salary. Service at court also provided an escape from the pressure and competition of the market-place. However, in reality the bestowal of grand titles probably had little to do with the creation of great works of art, but rather had the merit – in the eyes of the emperor – of keeping the painters in permanent and close proximity, thus guaranteeing regular contact between artist and ruler. Hence, despite the grand title of 'academician', court painters remained artisans, with the subjects of their paintings still being chosen for them. They were artists of limited humanistic learning and of limited artistic ambition.

While the situation remained unchanged at court in the first 150 years of the Song dynasty, in the early twelfth century there was agitation for change. Emperor Huizong, himself a painting enthusiast and great collector, decided to break with the tradition of the workshop apprenticeship by founding a national School of Painting according to the principles of humanistic learning.[67] In 1104, the school opened with 30 selected students and a curriculum that combined technical training in studios and general studies. Studio training was organized around six genres: Buddhist and Daoist subjects, figure painting, landscapes, birds and beasts, flowers and bamboo, and architecture and trees. The general studies classes consisted of lectures on ancient dictionaries, which included the earliest lexicographical work,[68] and one of the *Five Classics*.[69] More- over, the Emperor made his collection of old masters available for students to study. Students' progress was also assessed regularly by means of examination. The principal criteria in the assessment were realism, originality and poetic evocation.

Although Huizong's School of Painting lasted only six years, it nevertheless signalled the end of the era when painters were perceived only as manual workers. However, perhaps more important than the school was the fact that a number of painters now came from backgrounds that might be described as 'scholarly', in that as children they had been schooled in the classics, poetry and calligraphy up to a relatively advanced age. This was certainly the case for Wen Tong (1018–79), Li Gonglin (*c.*1049–1106), Mi Fu (1051–1107) and his son Mi Youren (1074–1151/1086–1165). In the centuries that followed, people from the 'scholar' class continued working in the profession, and by the end of the seventeenth century they dominated the art world. Scholar-painters had two typical career paths: they either painted in their spare time while serving as a government official, or if they did not enter (or failed) the national examination for civil service, they became a 'professional' scholar-painter. In both cases, either through interest or necessity, they also produced calligraphy, poetry and other types of writing as well as paintings. A standard fee, set by six professional scholar-artists living in Zhejiang in 1660, listed the wide range of services they provided, including seal carving, painting, calligraphy, poetry and prose-writing.[70] Gong Xian (*c.*1619–89), who worked in Nanjing in the same period, also ran a teaching studio to subsidize his work.

The consequences of literati-painters entering the profession were extensive: for the first time, calligraphy and poetry as well as painting were treated as integral parts of the painter's practice, and scholarship became part of the artist's training. In the first half of the seventeenth century, Dong Qichang (1555–1636) summarized this preparatory work with the time-honoured motto: 'reading 10,000 books; travelling 10,000 miles'. In the studio, technical skills were acquired principally through two types of practice: calligraphy and the study of pictorial forms. In calligraphy, proficiency in different scripts (seal, clerical, regular, running and cursive) and styles formed the basic training for painters, and in the study of pictorial forms, analysis and categorization into almost calligraphic expressions was emphasized, which can be traced back to the *Manual of Plum Blossom Likeness* by Song Boren (act. mid-13th century). Master-pupil tutorials that employ this method are evident in several fourteenth-century works; for example, in 1350 Ni Zan produced an album of 10 leaves for his nephew Hua Ziwen, aiming to teach him basic forms in landscape (fig. 15). The seventeenth century further saw the publication of the *Mustard Seed Garden Manual of Painting*, a work that has been one of the most popular technical manuals of pictorial forms used in studio training ever since.

In later periods, the diverse range of artistic activities embraced in the literati-painter's studio – composing poetry and prose, calligraphy and painting – led to a fanciful view of the literati-artist as a high-minded individual no longer bound to institutional patrons (particularly the imperial court) and the commercial marketplace. This view, by and large, was created by the literati themselves by such means as the romanticization of their studios. In the treatise *Superfluous Things* of 1637, the literati-painter Wen Zhenheng in Suzhou advised his peers as follows:

> To live far out in the country is best; next best is to live in rural areas; next comes the suburbs. Even if we are unable to dwell among cliffs and valleys and to follow the path of the hermits of old, and we have to settle in city houses, we must ensure that the doors, courtyards, buildings and rooms are clean and smart, that the pavilions suggest the outlook of a man without worldly cares, and that the studios exude the aura of a refined recluse. There should be fine trees and interesting plants, and a display of antiques and books, so that those who live there can forget about age, the guest forget to leave, and the visitor to the grounds forget about fatigue.[71]

To reinforce this ideal, importantly, a literati-artist would attach a poetic name to his studio, which would be added to his signature in his works. For instance, Zhao Mengfu gave his studio the name *Songxue Zhai* ('Studio of Pines in Snow'), Dong Qichang had the *Huachan Shi* ('Room for Meditation on Painting') and Zheng Xie (1693–1765) the *Banqiao Shuwu* ('Study of the Wooden Bridge').

## STUDIO EQUIPMENT

Despite changes in studio practice, and the divergence of the literati-artist's studio and the artisan-painter's workshop, the standard tools and equipment of the artist in many ways remained unchanged for centuries and can be reconstructed from documentary and pictorial sources. Depictions of artists at work from various periods show that a typical painter's studio was furnished with stools, benches and tables. On the tables paintings could be laid flat, the ink was prepared in stone slabs and the colours in ceramic mortars and saucers. While later the saucers were made of porcelain, in the early period they were earthenware, a substantial number of which have been excavated by Chinese archaeologists in Dunhuang, many still containing traces of pigment (fig. 14).[72] For the ink, painters used stone or ceramic slabs, both to grind the ink cakes and to hold the liquid ink once it had been produced.

Brushes were typically made of rabbit or goat hair, which was bunched together and inserted into a bamboo tube.[73] The brush was not uniform, but structured in three layers: the core was composed of long, stiff hairs, with the intermediate layer consisting of shorter hairs disposed to form a mantle around the core, and the outer layer extending from base to tip and covering both the core and mantle, thus creating a 'reservoir' that would hold a quantity of ink or pigment. While we know a great deal about how the brush was made, our knowledge of how it was held is less complete. The standard account is that the usual method of holding the brush in China today has always been in use; the brush is held vertically and gripped between the thumb and the index and middle fingers, while the ring and little fingers are tucked beneath the shaft. However, it is arguable that this method was only gradually adopted in the ninth and tenth centuries, when raised furniture made its appearance in domestic houses and it was used for calligraphy, being suited to a horizontal surface placed in front of the writer. Previously, a calligrapher would have written on a scroll held in the hand at an angle, and would have held the brush more naturally between the thumb and index finger, very much as a pen is held today (fig. 16).[74]

There is good reason to suppose that painters would have held the brush in the same manner when they painted on a support positioned at an angle. In several depictions of artisan-painters at work, including one by a little-known illustrator, Wang Yi (act. Southern Song period [1127–1279]), on the frontispiece of a woodblock edition of the *Lotus Sutra* (fig. 17), in which the artist is shown painting a relatively large Buddha image, the painting support appears simply to have been propped against a single-panel free-standing screen. This illustration suggests that large paintings – such as *The Summer Palace of Emperor Minghuang*, traditionally attributed to Guo Zhongshu (d.977) (cat. no. 49), or other monumental landscape compositions made from the eleventh century onwards – might have been executed in a similar manner, with the brush held between the thumb and index finger rather than in the way it is used today.

The *Lotus Sūtra* depiction also shows that the painting support was stretched over a frame. Several artists' treatises, such as the 1318–19 *Manual of Bamboo Painting* by Li Kan (1245–1320) and 1758 *Painting Manual of Xiaoshan* by Zou Yigui (1688–1772), suggest that this type of frame was an essential tool in a studio if silk fabric was used as the painting support.[75] The frame seems to have been called a *zheng* until the fourteenth century, but by the eighteenth century the name had somehow been changed to *bengjia*.[76] Frames varied in size, but in every case the structure was the same, and was – significantly – very similar to that of the frame used for embroidery, consisting of two long wooden bars and two short crosspieces. The pair of long bars was joined at the ends by the crosspieces, which were slipped through horizontal holes in the bars and held in place with wedges. The silk was then laid on the frame, pulled taut, and carefully attached with flour paste to three sides of the frame: top, left and right. After the paste had dried and the silk was firmly attached, a bamboo splint was sewn onto the bottom edge of the silk, and then – with strong thread – laced together with the bottom long bar. The string could be pulled tight to stretch the silk (fig. 18). Other depictions suggest that it would not be uncommon for a painter to lace more than one side of the frame.

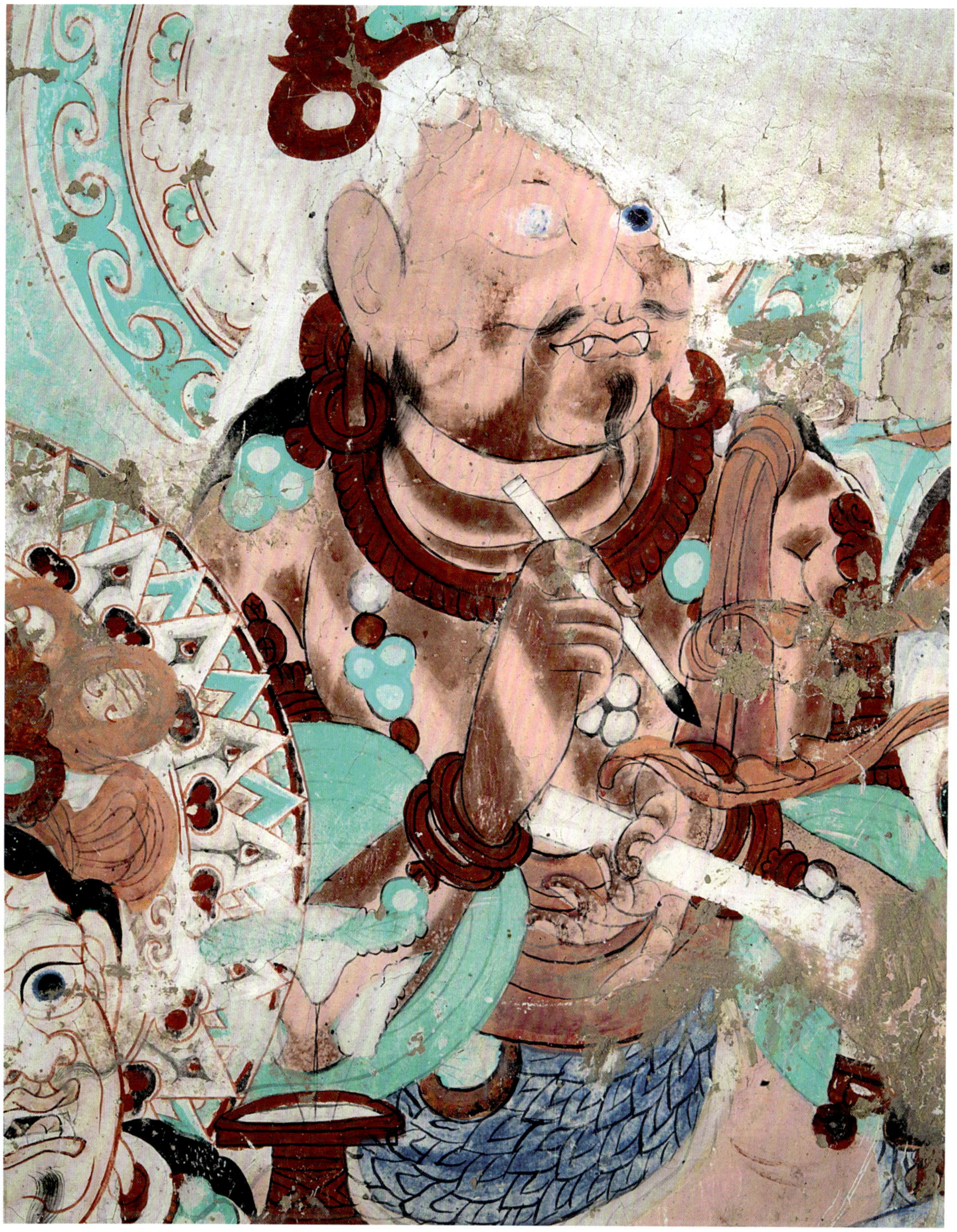

FIG. 16
A Dragon King holding brush and paper, c.907–60. Mural from Cave 36, Mogao Caves, Dunhuang

FIG. 17
First frontispiece from the *Lotus Sūtra* showing a painter at his stretcher, 1127–1279. Woodblock print on paper. National Palace Museum, Taipei

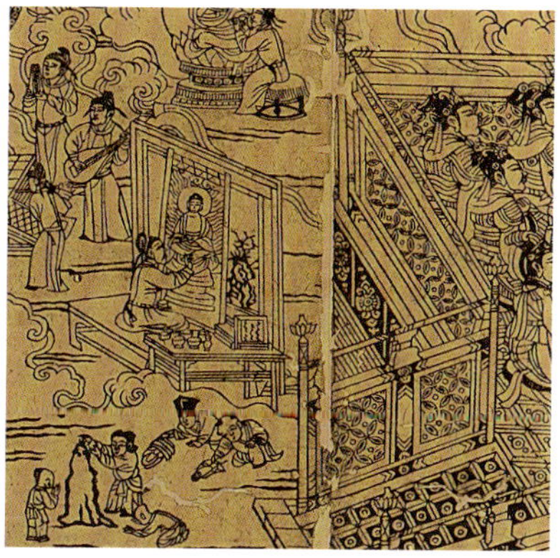

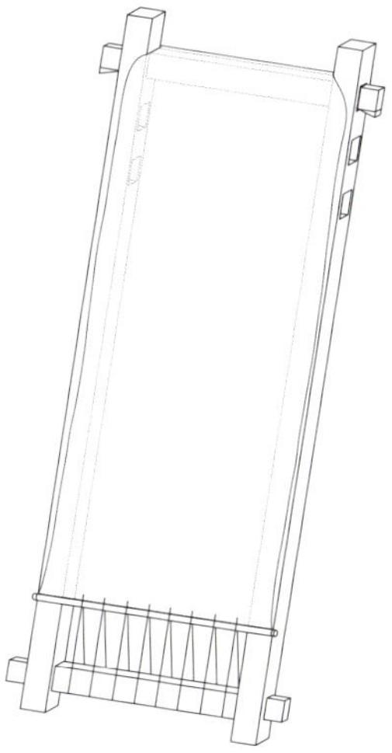

FIG. 18
Diagram of an artists' stretcher

# Materials and Techniques

## THE SUPPORT

Almost any material can support a painting, but in China the most common choices were silk and paper. Silk was available and in use earlier, and was the primary material for painting until around 1300; after that paper progressively became predominant – at least as far as we can tell from surviving works.

## SILK

Silk production was established in China much earlier than anywhere else in the world; there is evidence of a well-developed Chinese silk technology in 3500 BCE. The earliest surviving silk fragments were used to wrap the dead before burial, as well as the bronze or jade objects to be interred with them. Thus silk was apparently believed to be a medium, or agent, that enabled communication with the divine – which may partially explain why it was chosen for early paintings. The first significant group of paintings on silk are the Zidanku funerary banners dating from the third century BCE (see fig. 1). Although paper became the dominant support after the fourteenth century, artists continued to paint on silk until the end of the nineteenth, particularly if they were emulating the technical virtuosity of earlier masters. For example, the Yangzhou painter Yuan Jiang (act. *c.*1680–1730) used silk supports to emulate the Song masters, as seen in his spectacular *Pavilion of Nine Perfections* (cat. no. 72).

In the majority of cases, artists chose *juan*, or silk of a plain or tabby weave, made up of a simple alternation of warp over weft mostly using untwisted threads, although there are examples where fabric with a more intricate weave is used – the artist Huang Gongwang (1269–1354) once used *ling* or damask for a landscape (fig. 19). Some historical sources have suggested that a variety of plain-weave silks were available for painting from early times, and in the ninth century Zhang Yanyuan mentions several types used in his time: 'light closely woven prepared silks *wan* of Qi [in today's Shandong Province], heavy prepared silks *lian* of Wu [Jiangsu Province], icy raw silks *su*, and misty thin silks *xiao*'.[77] The seventeenth-century *Mustard Seed Garden Manual of Painting* comments that Tang silk had a coarse weave, while the Song silk used by court painters had a superbly 'clear, fine texture'.[78] Guo Wenlin, one of the copyists of early classical Chinese paintings in the Palace Museum, Beijing, states that after the thirteenth century the texture of the silk gradually became coarser, thicker and looser.[79] Further research needs to be conducted on the classification of painting silks according to their geographical and historical variations, and on the factors influencing an artist's decision to use a particular fabric.

The plain weave silk was an expensive commodity, and until the tenth century it was also used as a main currency together with the bronze 'cash' coins.[80] It is reckoned that in tenth-century Dunhuang, a standard unit of plain weave silk would have cost the equivalent of an agricultural labourer's wages for four years.[81] According to Tang regulation, the measurement of a standard unit of silk was one *chi* and eight *cun* in width, and four *zhang* in length (approximately 56 × 1200 cm).[82] The central strip of *Buddha Preaching the Law* (see cat. no. 1) at 53.7 centimetres, is not far off.

Typically, in this period larger paintings were achieved by adding extra pieces of silk to the first. In the case of *Buddha Preaching the Law*, to avoid having a join line across the seated figure of the Buddha in the centre of the composition, the first single width of silk was placed at the centre of the painting, and the second, cut lengthways into two equal halves, attached to it selvedge to selvedge. This method of constructing larger supports from several widths of silk was a standard practice in artists' workshops throughout Chinese history.[83] The larger formats of paintings in the mid-twelfth century – one and a half widths, two widths, three widths and four widths – are known from a record of mounting styles based on the imperial painting collection in Hangzhou during the Shaoxing era (1131–62) of the Southern Song dynasty emperor Gaozong (r. 1127–62), in the *Rustic Ramblings of Eastern Qi*, a book of miscellaneous historical notes written by Zhou Mi.[84] Physical evidence provided by surviving paintings suggests that from the eleventh century, the width of painting silk departed from the Tang standard measurement, becoming more varied – and in some cases, considerably larger. This development might have resulted from silk being no longer in use as a currency, further

FIG. 19
Huang Gongwang (1269–1354).
*Nine Pearl-like Verdant Peaks*
hanging scroll, c.1300.
Ink and colour on damask.
National Palace Museum, Taipei

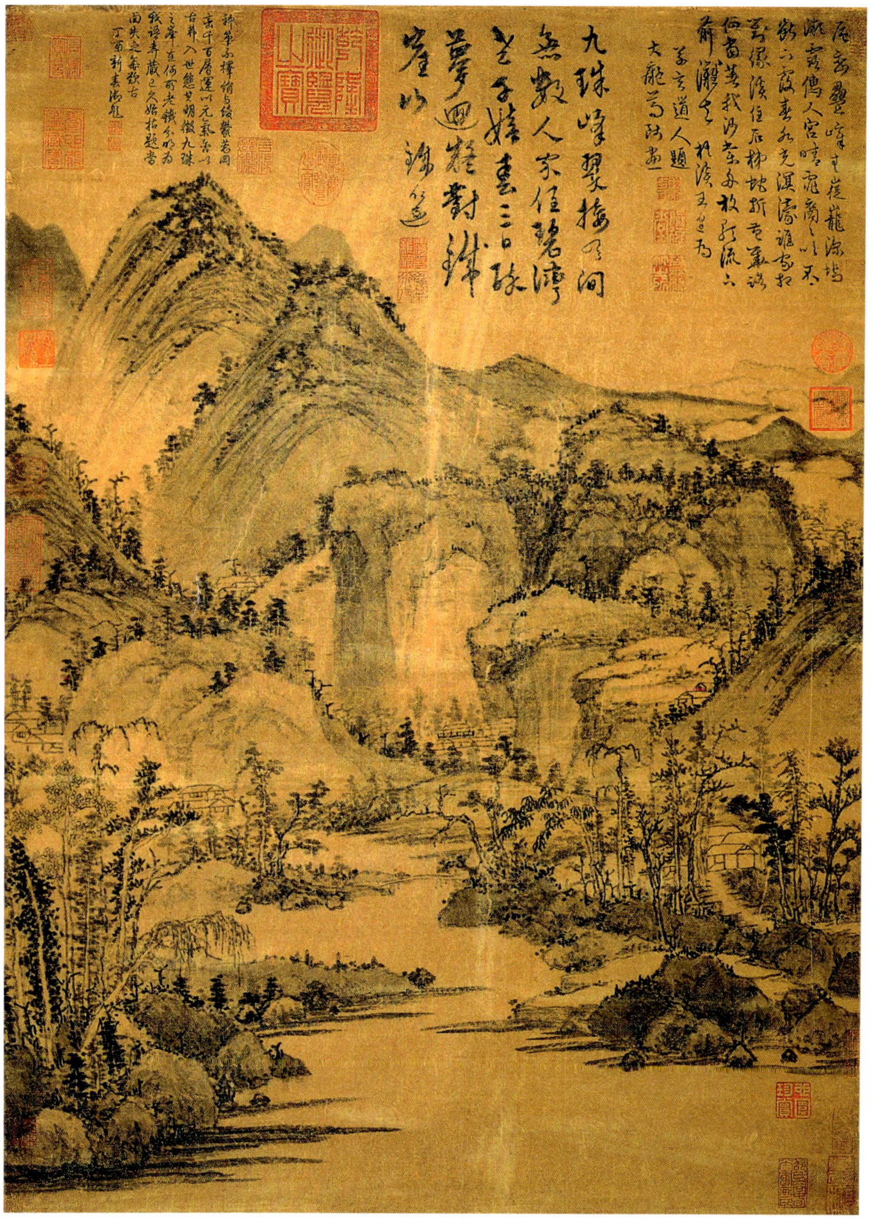

advancements in weaving technology, or both. In any event, it made it possible to complete a large painting on a single width of silk, as in *Magpies and Hare* by Cui Bai (act. 2nd half 11th century), dated 1061 (fig. 20).

## PAPER

Surviving paintings suggest that paper came into regular use as a support in about 1000 CE. Before this, it was typically used either for drawings or as an occasional substitute for the silk support. The advantage of paper over silk lay in its lower price, ready availability and greater durability. It was favoured by scholar-artists as a support earlier than by craftsman artists, perhaps because of its traditional association with scholarly education and calligraphy.

The fibre the paper was made from varied greatly, depending on the raw materials available and developments in manufacturing. Many surviving drawings, and occasionally paintings, from the fourth to the tenth century are on hemp or ramie. Hemp and ramie were rarely used for historical documents or loose sheets of paper after the tenth century, and from the eleventh century, various tree barks, bamboo and straw made from rice or wheat were used to make paper instead. Broadly speaking, paper made of mulberry (*sang pi*) or paper mulberry (*chu pi*) bark was rated highly for its smooth surface and off-white colour, and was preferred by both painters and calligraphers. Bamboo paper was typically used for printing books, while straw from rice or wheat was the principal raw material for low-quality paper, such as that used for wrapping.

Documentary evidence suggests that from the late sixteenth century, *xuan* paper became the favourite type for painters and calligraphers on account of its extremely soft, fine texture and white colour, surpassing paper made from mulberry. *Xuan* paper was made especially for artists, and its name refers to the Xuanzhou (present Xuancheng) region in southern Anhui Province, where the paper originated. Its principle was obtained from the inner bark of the *qingtan* or blue sandalwood plant (*Pteroceltis*

FIG. 20
Cui Bai (act. 2nd half 11th century). *Magpies and Hare* (or *Double Happiness*) hanging scroll, 1061. Ink and colour on silk. National Palace Museum, Taipei

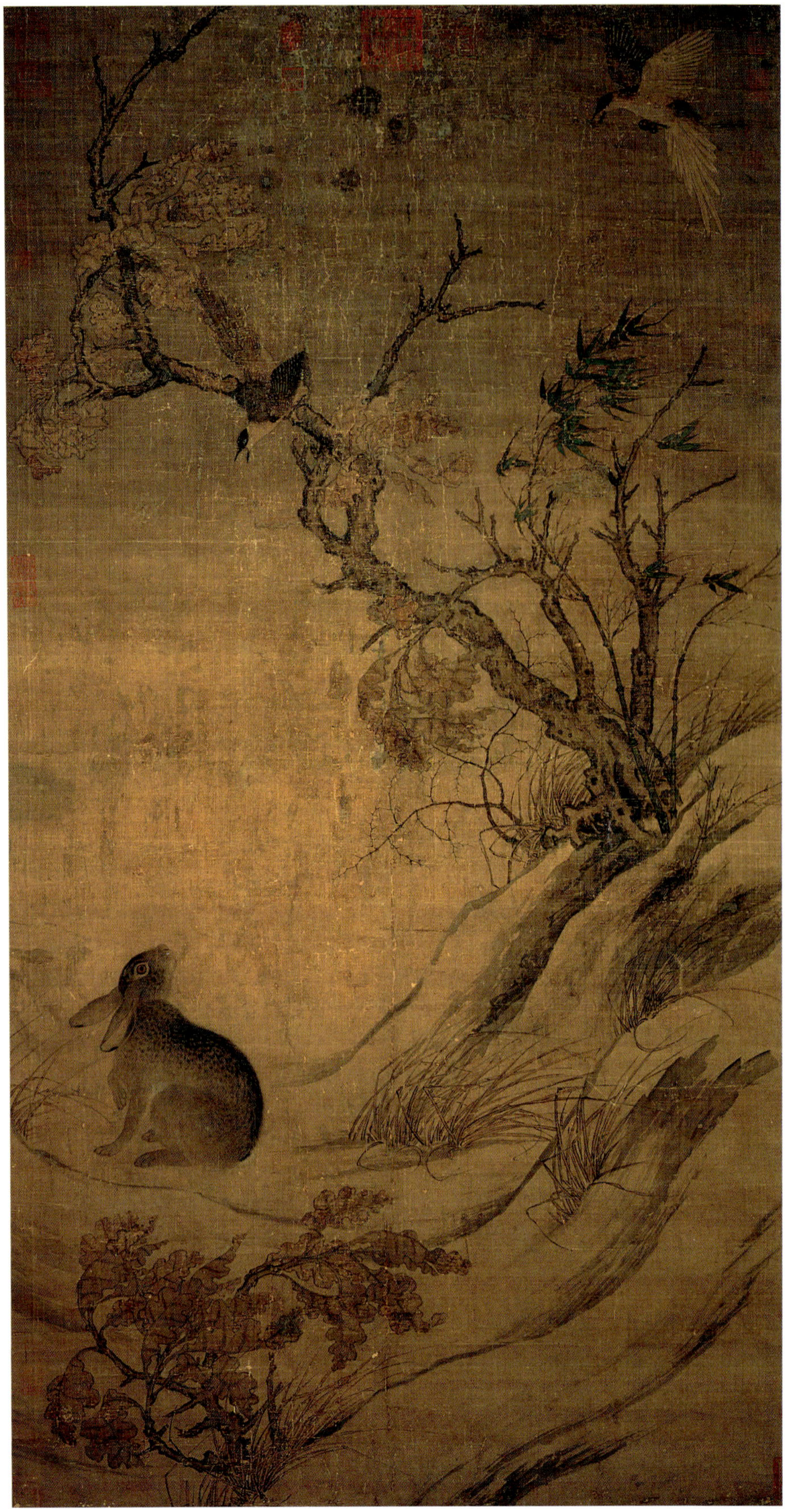

*tatarinowii*). In the late eighteenth century, the sandalwood fibres were mixed with local grass fibre such as rice straw, with the result that artists were offered papers of different grades depending on the mixture.[85] Unfortunately, at present analytical evidence taken from samples is not always available to support the historical documentation.

The size of the sheet was determined by the paper-making mould, measuring standards, the format of the final work, fashion and artistic decision. Paintings that survive today have sometimes been trimmed by collectors and dealers. A study based on a selection of 40 calligraphic works and paintings from the Tang to the Ming dynasty (1368–1644) in the collection of the Palace Museum, Beijing presents a preliminary list of the dimensions of the standard sheet in dynastic order: Tang paper (25–7 cm × 30 cm); Song paper (30–55 cm × 80–95 cm); and Yuan and Ming paper (30–50 cm × 100–150 cm).[86]

## PREPARATION OF THE SUPPORT

Generally, the support had to be treated in some way before the actual painting process began, and as elsewhere, the predominant methods for Chinese artists were the application of a preparatory layer and compaction by burnishing or by pounding or hammering. The purpose of the preparation was both physical and aesthetic, the physical being to prepare the silk or paper to hold the paint (the flexibility of silk and paper necessitated a thin, pliable preparatory layer), while the aesthetic was to control the surface texture of the painted image and the absorbency of the support. After the late sixteenth century, however, some artists avoided treating the support entirely, a deliberate decision based on aesthetic considerations.

One of the earliest support treatments in China was the application of a preparatory layer that could fairly be described as a 'ground'. Between the fourth and seventh centuries, some hemp paper was coated overall with a uniform layer of inert solids (gypsum, chalk or lime) suspended in liquid starch. However, after the seventh century this method was no longer common practice, and

FIG. 21
Pigment shop from *Prosperous Suzhou*
(detail of cat. no. 76)

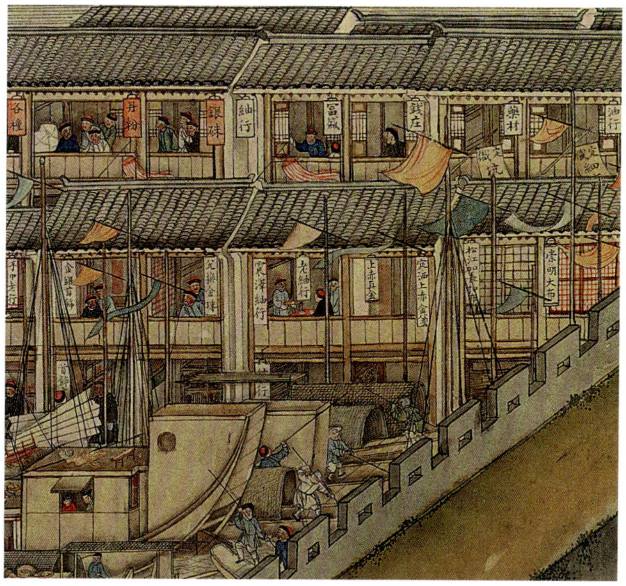

was only employed for certain types of decorative paper.[87] This type of preparatory layer was gradually abandoned altogether as it became important that the paintings could be moved frequently and this layer did not allow flexibility, and thus did not protect against damage such as flaking and loss of paint. Its replacement was a thin layer of starch paste employed as a size, which during the Tang period was in turn gradually abandoned in favour of a solution of glue and alum. This simply filled the interstices in the support,[88] and has become the standard treatment for a silk or paper support ever since.

In the case of silk, evidence suggests that artists have always treated it with a glue-alum size prior to painting. Sizing a silk support would have involved a special type of frame to hold it, as discussed above (fig. 18; see also page 30). As for paper, in the late fifteenth and sixteenth centuries, some artists who preferred a natural and spontaneous effect began to experiment by working directly on the raw paper instead of applying a conventional polished finish. These pioneering artists, who were all active in the south, are considered to be Shen Zhou (cat. no. 57), Chen Chun (1484–1544) and Xu Wei (1521–93).[89] Their success, and the popularity of this new aesthetic, led to raw paper gradually becoming the dominant support among scholarly artists, although sized papers were still used for works that required refined lines, subtle shading or soft, overlaid washes. One of the unfortunate consequences of their accomplishments is a popular, but historically inaccurate, generalization that the paper support used for paintings in China is typically unsized.[90]

## THE PAINT LAYER

*Pigments*

The range of pigments, or palette, used before the twentieth century was very limited when compared with that available today. Painters were responsible for binding the pigments together with a medium to make paint, and may even have produced several pigments themselves. A number of tenth-century account books among the surviving documents from Dunhuang record that local temples often paid painters for pigments with wheat or millet.[91] Most pigments, however, were typically obtained from market traders; the same temple account books mention pigments so purchased, including lead white, azurite, malachite, cinnabar and silver powder.[92] There is little evidence to indicate when the first artists' colourmen came into being, but in the thirteenth century, Wu Zimu records a shop called Qi Baiyi lang trading pigments in the market area of the Southern Song capital, Hangzhou.[93] In eighteenth-century Suzhou, 33 colourmen's names are recorded on a stone stele.[94] Visual evidence of such shops is provided by the handscroll *Prosperous Suzhou* by Xu Yang (1712–c.1779), where a two-storey shop is shown in the city's buzzing commercial area, next to the western city gate, Changmen (fig. 21).

Some pigments, such as lead white, indigo and vermilion, were manufactured, while others, including dyestuffs and mineral and earth pigments, came from natural sources. One mineral pigment, ultramarine (*qingjinshi*), the rich purple-blue extracted from lapis lazuli, was known to Chinese painters before those in Europe, and was probably less expensive than in the West. This was due mainly to the fact that, until the discovery of the Americas, all lapis came from a group of mines centred on a single deposit in Badakhshan in Afghanistan, a region that lay on the Silk Route. Since painters in Dunhuang were well placed to obtain supplies, from the fourth to the fourteenth century ultramarine was often used on murals in the caves,[95] and has also been scientifically identified on some tenth-century painted silk banners.[96] Featured in the exhibition is a large lump of material consisting of a hardened mixture of ultramarine and chalk, which was also found in an artists' storeroom during an excavation in front of the cave temples in the 1950s (see fig. 14).[97]

Azurite, a copper ore, was found in several regions in China, and had different names depending on its source; *shiqing* is its generic term in modern Chinese. It has a greener hue than the purple-tinged ultramarine, and was the most widely used blue pigment. As such, it was so often used on the same paintings as malachite (cat. nos 23, 24, 52, 61, 72) that the combination gave rise to the name of a specific style of landscape painting, the so-called *qinglü shanshui*, or 'blue-and-green landscape'. Although it was less readily available than malachite, there were few alternatives to azurite as a blue pigment. It was only in the eighteenth and nineteenth centuries that its position was seriously challenged by smalt and Prussian blue from Europe.[98]

Malachite, or *shilü* in Chinese, came from the same sources as azurite, but was more abundant, which may explain why it was used more widely. The pigment was also more popular in China than in Europe, perhaps because it has fairly low covering power in oil, but in the aqueous medium its lean paint layer gives much greater opacity.[99]

Transparent greens and blues from various plant sources were also widely used. Formulas show that the dark blue indigo (*huaqing*) was derived from a plant called dyer's knotweed in China, or in earlier periods imported from India via Persia, and that vegetable greens could be made from Sophora flowers, or by combining indigo and the bright yellow gamboge (*tenghuang*). These blue and green colourants were important as either underlaid or overlaid washes when painting foliage, according to the painter Li Kan in his fourteenth-century book, *Manual of Bamboo Painting*.[100]

While the transparent, bright yellow gamboge was used throughout the period 700–1900, the main opaque yellow used in Chinese painting was the relatively dull iron oxide-based yellow ochre (*tuhuang*). It is frequently mentioned in another fourteenth-century treatise, the *Secrets of Portrait Painting*, as useful for combining with other pigments to make satisfactory colours for faces, clothing and other objects. These other pigments include the opaque bright red cinnabar (*zhusha*) and vermilion (*yinzhu*), and the organic red colourants lac dye (*yanzhi*) and red sandalwood (*tanmu*).[101] Among the reds, vermilion (prepared from cinnabar) had an unusually long-standing importance as a pigment.

By comparison with all coloured pigments, however, black ink (*mo*) is the single most important material used in Chinese painting. A painting might be on silk or paper and coloured pigments may or may not be used, but ink would certainly be employed for at least part of the work, if not for the entire painting. Chinese ink is essentially a mixture of fine carbon particles and animal glue. Since the animal glue was the same as that used as a binder for coloured pigments, and since ink was intended to be used with a brush, it could well be considered a black pigment. Indeed, the existence of black ink allows for a uniquely Chinese painting tradition, according to which there was no clear distinction between ink and paint, or between drawing and painting.

### Glue-size paint

Chinese painters used the most elementary water-based medium, glue size, on a silk or paper support; the pigments were simply combined with the same type of animal glue that was used to size the support. Paintings in glue size have a distinctive appearance. In the case of silk, since the technique did not involve priming (as in Western oil paintings), the pigment particles to some extent mingled with the fibres of the fabric. As a result, the fine-woven surface texture of the silk is visually prominent, and some paintings might even be mistaken for silk embroideries or tapestries. The support's sensitivity to, and retention of, moisture allowed a certain amount of blending of the brushwork, which enabled the painter to achieve subtle tonal transitions. The glue medium permitted extremely fine lineal details, which were rendered in a style of brush-work that resembles European pen work. The relatively vivid colourization and opacity of the pigments when combined with glue size could also result in good coverage with a lean layer of paint, an advantage if the painting was to be rolled and unrolled. Glue-size paintings were not varnished, which explains why the painted areas have a matt appearance.

Since they were left unvarnished and the glue medium remains soluble in water, glue-size paintings are extremely vulnerable to water and dirt. It has been said that the poor survival rate of glue-size paintings (distemper or *Tüchlein*) produced in fifteenth-century Europe is proof of this vulnerability.[102] By comparison, Chinese paintings dating to the same period or earlier have been very fortunate, due partly to the early adoption of the scroll format and rigorous display and storage practices. Vegetable gums, especially gum arabic, deserve a footnote here. It should be noted that gum arabic was not used as a binder in Chinese painting, and therefore Chinese painting should not technically be defined as watercolour in the strict sense.[103]

*Paint handling*

Painters developed conventions of paint application based on personal experimentation, the methods of local schools and the influence of other traditions. Although it is impossible to generalize the techniques used for glue-size paint throughout the period from the eighth to the nineteenth century, two distinct modes of application should be highlighted. The first, layering, involved the meticulous building up of layers of paint in stages, while the second, direct painting, lent itself to spontaneity in both design and brushwork. These methods were not necessarily exclusive; an artist might use both within a single painting.

There has been little analysis of paint layering in Chinese scroll paintings, at least using the same scientific techniques as for European easel paintings, such as microscopic examination of cross sections, because of the usually thin application of fine-particle paint and the complexity caused by the penetration of the paint into the structure of the silk or paper support. Thus our knowledge of glue-size painting techniques derives mainly from documentary sources, as well as the practical experience of contemporary copyists of classical paintings. Work typically began with some form of underdrawing on the prepared support in a light ink line. The entire composition was then developed in monochrome as an initial layer, before the artist built up the forms and details in colour. Li Kan's instructions on painting bamboo leaves in the fourteenth century are quite specific: first, washes of indigo should be used to create tones so as to differentiate light and shade, and front and back. After the indigo washes have been applied, malachite green should be added. In places where the indigo is heavy, the green should be applied more thinly, while in places where the indigo is light, the malachite must be applied a little more thickly. When the malachite is completely dry, an overlayer of grass-green wash composed of gamboge mixed with indigo should be added.[104] In the case of painting on a silk support, there is one more step: prior to the application of any layers of paint on the front, the painter applies a continuous layer of thick, opaque paint (usually white pigment) to the back. Since silk supports tend to be more or less transparent, the paint layer on the back is seen from the front – and therefore contributes to the design. This back-painting technique is found frequently in paintings from all the periods covered in the exhibition (cat. nos 34, 53).[105] It is called *beifen* in Chinese, a term that has been used since the twelfth century, if not earlier.[106] The exhibition also features a rare example of double-sided painting on banners; here, the back-painting technique is employed to replicate almost every detail shown on the front (cat. no. 6).

Direct painting refers to a group of related techniques whereby the artist did not envision every detail of the final result before commencing work. It includes using spontaneous brushwork that resembles accidental splotches or strokes when viewed up close, letting paint spread and run freely, and applying wet paint to the previous layers (wet-in-wet). Perhaps the most extreme technique is that of *pomo*, or 'splashing and smearing ink'; it was allegedly invented by Wang Mo (act. 785–805), who was noted for painting while drunk, by spilling ink onto a piece of silk and finishing the work with a few touches of the brush.[107] However, direct painting does not have to be impromptu. In *Flowers on the River* (cat. no. 74), Bada Shanren (1626–1705) has deliberately created a 'spontaneous' effect; in fact, a careful reading of the artist's colophon reveals that he worked in multiple sessions over a period of four months.

1 For the history of Nantong Museum, see Claypool 2005; for the Institute of Exhibiting Antiques, see Wang Cheng-hua, 'Imperial Treasures, Art Exhibitions, and National Legacy: The Institute for Exhibiting Antiquities in the 1910s', paper presented at Memory Links: To Self, Country, and Culture in Chinese History, East Asian Studies Center, Indiana University, 30 October–2 November 2003.
2 These are Chen Jinxin (act. before 840), Chen Jinyan (act. before 840), Cheng Xiuji (804–63), Lu Huang (act. before 840) and Lu Tingyao (act. before 840). For an English translation and annotation, see Soper 1958, pp. 223–5, 227–8.
3 Ibid., p. 222
4 Others painters are Li Zhen (act. late 8th century), Yin Lin (act. 2nd half 7th century) and Zhou Fang (act. 2nd half 8th century); see (847–60) in Lu 1993–8. For an English translation and annotation, see Acker 1954, pp. 264, 266.
5 Ibid., pp. 326–7
6 For the formats of banners, see Zhao 2011, pp. 50–4.
7 Multi-cultural influences on the formats of the Dunhuang banners were proposed especially by Robert Jera-Bezard and Monique Maillard; see Jera-Bezard and Maillard 1985, pp. 83–91.
8 For the use of the Dunhuang banners in religious ceremonies, see Jera-Bezard and Maillard 1989, pp. 57–67.
9 See Zhang 2007, pp. 91–7.
10 For studies of Chinese screens, see Sullivan 1965, pp. 239–54; Handler 1993, pp. 4–31; and Wang 2006.
11 Van Gulik 1958, p. 146
12 Soper 1958, p. 220
13 Ibid.
14 The size of the screen behind the throne has been studied by Ogawa Hiromitsu; see Ogawa 1981, p. 45.
15 Soper 1951, p. 63.
16 Ibid., p. 58
17 Ye (1128) 1984, p. 346
18 See Ogawa 1981, pp. 45–6, esp. fig. 14.
19 For a good introduction to the history of fans in China, see Toronto 2002; see also Qian 2004.
20 Toronto 2002, pp. 13–14
21 Qian 2004, p. 7
22 Lachman 1989, p. 53
23 Deng (1168–73) 1993–8, vol. 2, p. 723.
24 Ibid., p. 716
25 Wu (late 13th–early 14th century) 1984, p. 117
26 Zhou (c.1290) 1882, *juan* 2, fols 19–20; *juan* 3, fol. 1
27 Soper 1951, p. 92
28 Deng (1168–73) 1993–8, vol. 2, p. 716
29 Acker 1954, p. 200
30 Ibid., pp. 283–4
31 Soper 1951, p. 95
32 Ibid., p. 18
33 Törmä 2002, pp. 43, 95
34 Zhao 1995, p. 4; quoted in Wu 1996b, pp. 99–101
35 For a fine introduction to the development of Chinese book formats, see Li 1996. For the history of Chinese scrolls, see Wang 1991.
36 See Zhang (847–60) in Lu 1993–8, vol. 1, pp. 136–7.
37 Murray 1995, pp. 17–31
38 Bush and Shih 1985, pp. 151–2
39 Su (1082) 1986, vol. 4, p. 1735. An abbreviated version of the story is recorded in Deng (1168–73) 1993–8, vol. 2, p. 716.
40 See *Etymological Dictionary of Chinese Language* 1988, p. 651.
41 See Xu 1997; see also Xu 1994.
42 According to Xu Bangda, the scroll was remounted at the court of Emperor Huizong; see Xu 1981, p. 52.
43 Acker 1954, p. 200
44 As van Gulik has pointed out, the word in Zhang Yanyuan's text could mean either 'hanging' or 'screen', because in Tang literature the character 幛 ('curtain' or 'hanging') was sometimes indiscriminately written as 障 ('screen'), and vice versa; see van Gulik 1958, p. 160.
45 Wang 1991, pp. 17–18
46 Cao 1975
47 Luoyang shi di'er wenwu gongzuo dui 1992, pp. 37–51
48 Quoted and translated in van Gulik 1958, p. 197
49 Ibid., p. 6
50 See Kawai 2002
51 Quoted in Wang 1991, pp. 18–19
52 Anne Burkus-Chasson argues that there is no historical link between the butterfly-book and the album painting; see Burkus-Chasson 2005, p. 376.
53 Xu 1984; see also Sturman 1990.
54 For example, the entry on traditional art training in China in *Grove Dictionary of Art* 1998, vol. 7, pp. 147–9.
55 See Shan 2004, pp. 117–8.
56 See Lin 1985.

57 Chen 1984, pp. 204–6; Yu 2010, pp. 475–506
58 For research on the topic, see Jiang 1985, pp. 171–91; Ma 1997.
59 See Wen 2013, pp. 57–62; for recent Chinese annotation, see Wen 2008, pp. 68–76; for a textual history of the *Record of the Scrutiny of Crafts*, see Loewe 1993, pp. 24–32.
60 Huang 1985, p. 6
61 Jiang 1985; Ma 1997
62 Pan and Ma 1985, pp. 81–98
63 For a study of the location of Ningbo workshops, see Nara 2009, pp. 251–3.
64 See *Complete Collection of Chinese Architecture* 1996–2003, vol. 20, p. 16; vol. 21, p. 12.
65 For a general account of the status of court artisan-painters in the Tang period, see Jin 2004, pp. 24–43.
66 See Bush and Shih 1985, p. 49.
67 Chen 1984, appendix 1
68 They include *Examples of Refined Usage*, dating from the third century BCE; *Dictionary of Ancient Characters*, by the Han (206 BCE–220 CE) scholar Xu Shen (*c*.58–*c*.147); *Dictionary of Ancient Dialectal Terms*; and *Explanation of Words*.
69 They are the *Classic of Poetry*; *Book of Documents*; *Book of Rites*; *Classic of Changes*; and *Spring and Autumn Annals*.
70 Liu 1993
71 Wen, cited in New York 1987, pp. 5–6
72 Pan and Ma 1985, pp. 81–98
73 For a good introduction to the history of Chinese brushes, see Chang 1991.
74 See Sha 1987, pp. 204–6.
75 Li (1318–9) 1993–8, vol. 2, pp. 733–4; Zou (1758) 1993, p. 359
76 Ibid.
77 Acker 1954, p. 187
78 Sze 1978, pp. 45–6
79 Guo 2010, p. 40
80 For a general history of silk as a currency, see Peng 1988, especially pp. 240–6 and 318–22.
81 Zheng 1997, p. 16
82 Peng 1988, pp. 240–6, 318–22
83 Ogawa 2008, pp. 73–80
84 Zhou (1280–90) 1993, p. 213
85 Wu 2009, p. 116
86 Pan 1979, pp. 190–9
87 Ibid., pp. 64–5; Winter 2008, p. 79
88 Pan 1979, pp. 61–2, 81–2; Winter 2008, p. 78
89 Xu 1981, p. 45
90 For example, see James et al. 1997, p. 38
91 Zheng 2004, p. 115
92 Ibid.
93 Wu (late 13th century-early 14th century) 1984, p. 116
94 Jiangsu Provincial Museum 1959, p. 273
95 Wang 1996, pp. 77–99; for a general history of use, see Plesters 1993, vol. 2, pp. 39–41.
96 Giès et al. 1994, vol. 1, pp. 14–39; Brack 2010, p. 18
97 Wang 1996, p. 74
98 Winter 2008, pp. 29, 31–3
99 Ibid.
100 Li (*c*.1286), quoted in Yu 1988, pp. 62–3
101 Ibid., pp. 32–4
102 Dunkerton et al. 1991, pp. 187–8
103 Goldman 2006, p. 74
104 Li (*c*.1286), quoted in Yu 1988, pp. 178–9
105 Guo 2010, pp. 49–50; Winter 2008, pp. 102–3, 125
106 Deng (1168–73) 1993–8, vol. 2, p. 719
107 Soper 1958, p. 228

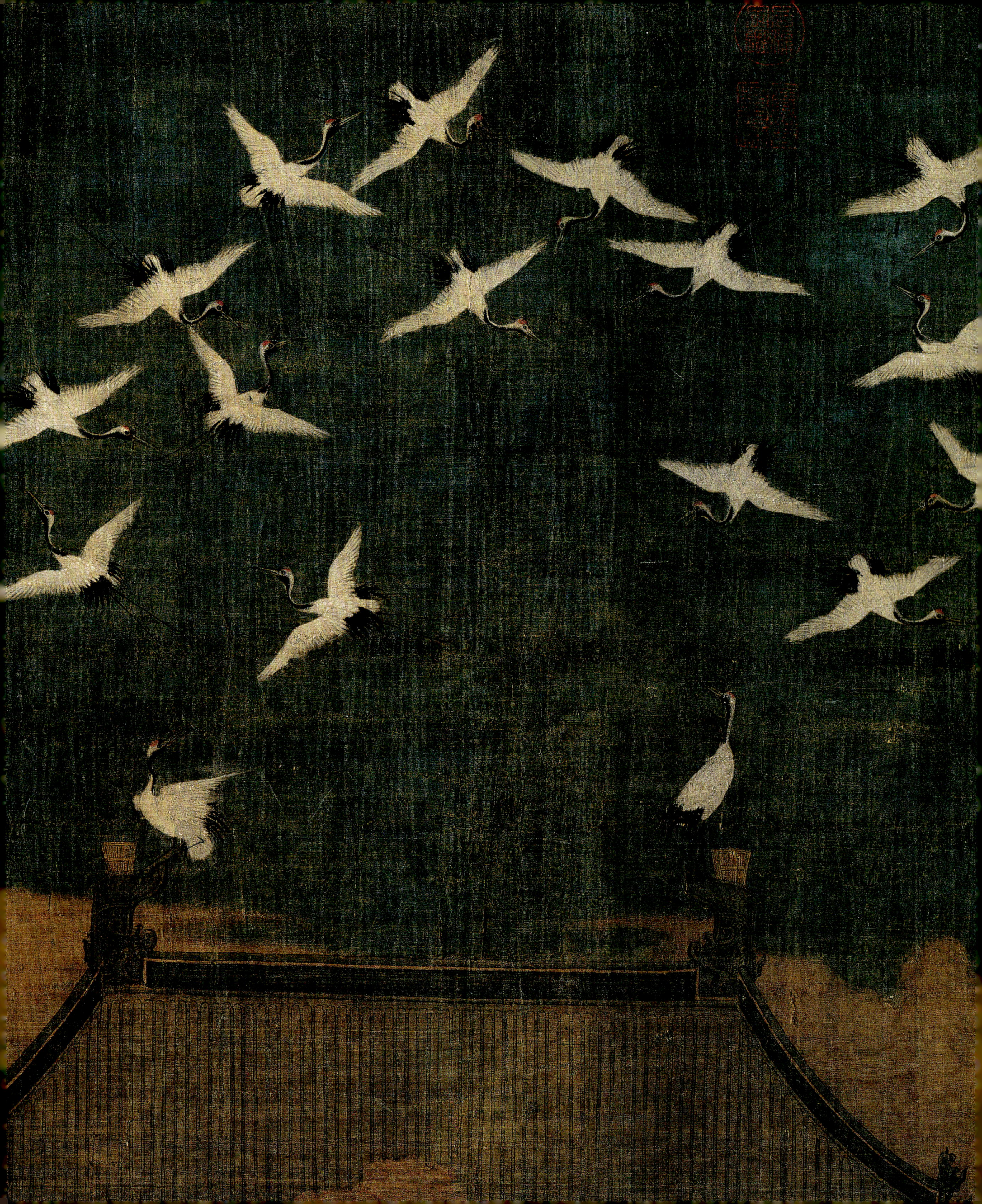

# CATEGORIES OF PAINTINGS IN CHINA

## GENRES AND SUBJECTS

Shane McCausland

### INTRODUCTION

In broad surveys, European paintings fall into five dominant genres: history painting, portraiture, landscape, genre scenes and still life.[1] While acknowledging real regional distinctions, we may observe that the experience of macro-historical changes underlying these categories was shared by people in China. So we should expect parallels, but also specific differences. This short essay is structured using three main headings: figure painting and portraiture; landscape and gardens; and flower-and-bird painting (and miscellanies).

Our knowledge about genres and subjects in China's painting tradition comes from two main sources. One is the material record, of which the subjects in the exhibition present a sample. The wider material record is itself comprised of what has been transmitted above ground or else discovered under it, as the essays on collections describe. What survives and the form it survives in also clearly have a bearing on how we understand genres.

A second source is China's long tradition of art criticism. To study painting subjects and genres is also to explore the shifting hierarchies constructed in critical writings to order and place them in the world.[2] Critical writings about paintings and catalogues of them powerfully shaped their reception.[3] Historically, these writings were familiar initially to critics and connoisseurs in manuscript and print form and, from the sixteenth century, to a broader public through wider printing. We may name a few of the monuments from the first millennium of the tradition.

An early one is the *Classified Record of Painters of Former Times* by the critic Xie He (act. 6th century), best known for its listing of the celebrated 'six laws' (or canons) of painting. These included the founding precept that good painting should have *qiyun shengdong*, or 'animation through spirit consonance', meaning that the figures rendered by the painter should come alive by resonating with the figures they represent in life.[4] A second text is the *Record of Famous Painters of Successive Dynasties*, written in 847–60 by the Tang dynasty (618–907) critic Zhang Yanyuan (815–76), which occupies a position in China's art history analogous to Giorgio Vasari's (1511–74) *Lives of the Most Excellent Painters, Sculptors, and Architects* in European art.[5] A third text is the imperial *Xuanhe Painting Catalogue*, compiled at court in about 1120 during the Xuanhe reign (1119–25) of the late Northern Song dynasty (960–1127) emperor Huizong (r. 1101–25), an aesthete and artist in his own right (see cat. nos 16, 17), which extolled close observation and representation of nature in painting.[6] The *Xuanhe Painting Catalogue* conveniently lists 10 genres deemed fit for the royal collection. Heading this list are Daoist and Buddhist subjects (the Emperor was a fervent Daoist), followed by figures. These are followed by the technically demanding genre of 'palaces and buildings', a new genre of 'barbarian tribes', and then 'dragons and fish', 'landscape', 'animals and beasts', 'flowers and birds', 'ink bamboo' and 'vegetables and fruits'. Chen Rong's (act. 1st half 13th century) *Nine Dragons* (cat. no. 38) is a tour de force of the 'dragons and fish' genre, another grouping with strong Daoist connotations. The scope of these genres and their focus on recording natural phenomena tally with an important proto-scientific principle of the time, namely that 'the investigation of things leads to the extension of knowledge' (*gewu zhizhi*).

This basic framework of genres envisioned in the *Xuanhe Painting Catalogue* continued to be used during the ensuing century and a half of China's political division into native and foreign regimes from 1127 to 1276, but the kind of natural philosophy behind it did not. Indeed, while the range of genres lasted into the fourteenth century, the uses and interpretations of particular subjects changed with the historical context. From the eleventh century on, scholar-painters became increasingly influential as critics. They included men like the Northern Song statesman and

cat. no. 17 (detail)

calligrapher Su Shi (1037–1101), the Yuan dynasty (1271–1368) polymath Zhao Mengfu (1254–1322) (cat. no. 46), the mid-Ming (1368–1644) doyen of brush art Wen Zhengming (1470–1559) (cat. no. 62), the late Ming statesman and artist Dong Qichang (1555–1636) (cat. no. 63) and the individualist monk-painter Shitao (1642–1707) (cat. no. 71).[7]

The ways critics and connoisseurs wrote about painting subjects – in books and notes, sometimes as appended colophons on the backing paper of scrolls of painting and calligraphy – can often provide an intrinsic starting point for our considerations, although not all formats or subjects were privileged enough to receive this special treatment. For example, most religious and vernacular paintings did not. In addition, the views of critics cannot be regarded merely as reflections of cultural attitudes any more than paintings can, but need to be understood as projections of ideas and values.

## Figure Painting and Portraiture

### STORY PAINTING

China's twin brush arts of calligraphy and painting first emerged during the long Period of Disunion (220–589) following the fall of the Han empire in 220, the result of technical advances in the manufacture of brushes and silk and the invention of paper. Leading calligraphers like the 'calligraphic sage' Wang Xizhi (303–65) and painters were recognized as artists, and critics began to evaluate their 'brush traces' (*biji*); at the same time, their peers – and soon also emperors – began collecting and emulating them. The exhibition contains a few examples of calligraphy in this classical tradition by members of the Song (960–1279) royal family (cat. nos 28, 29, 31, 32). As noted, the colophons to many handscrolls also consist of extensive calligraphic inscriptions. In the world of painting, the principal mode, inherited from the classical period, was didactic; embodying the early role of art as a tool of Confucian social transformation, the theme was inevitably something morally improving and beneficial to a stable social and political hierarchy.

The pioneers of the art of painting were Gu Kaizhi (*c*.344–*c*.406) and Lu Tanwei (act. *c*.450–90). No paintings by Lu Tanwei survive, but a remarkable copy of a scroll painting after Gu Kaizhi is extant. Known as the *Admonitions of the Court Instructress to the Palace Ladies* and held in the British Museum, it is an exemplar of an early copy (made in the late 6th to 8th century) that has chanced to survive (fig. 8).[8] Another painter sometimes grouped with Gu and Lu was Zhang Sengyou (act. 490–540); the painting *The Five Planets and Twenty-eight Constellations* in the exhibition (cat. no. 13) is believed to be a copy of an original work by Zhang.

The *Admonitions*, as it is known for short, embodies early painting – that is, figure painting. Originally comprising 12 individual scenes (of which nine survive), it presents both historical exemplars and more genre-like scenes of court ladies acting dutifully. The scroll illustrates a didactic text written in 292 (and inscribed on the scroll beside each scene) to improve moral standards at court, and thus confront political issues such as the royal succession, dynastic stability and the quality of kingship. Intended for use at court, this compelling painting was clearly done by a man of courtier status, not an artisan, whose art seems part of court life, with its witty and sometimes irreverent attitude toward convention, and its keen insights into the human psyche seen in the body language and facial expressions of the court ladies. See how the self-regarding beauty gets her comeuppance from the emperor, for example, in the 'rejection scene' (see fig. 8). Admonition is a fascinating form of political and social engagement, which both criticizes and proposes a solution at once. To cite exemplars is to draw on precedent, but there is also an allegorical implication – that the admonished person will reform his or her character in response to the exemplar, whether positive or negative. As such, admonition embodies China's ideals of statecraft: the duty of remonstration, moral self-cultivation and benevolence. Many later court paintings were done in this 'story painting' (*gushi hua*) mode, even as late as the eighteenth century, although from the eighth century it was largely superseded by other more fashion-conscious genres.

Historically, Gu Kaizhi was also believed to have painted long narrative scrolls illustrating another poetic text, the 'Goddess of the Luo River Ode', about a romantic encounter between the poet Cao Zhi (192–232) and a river nymph. Various Song dynasty copies show how the events could be elaborated and serialized in extended handscrolls, a 'strong' mode of narrative painting. Religious paintings like *Illustration of the Sūtra of the Contemplation of Buddha Amitāyus* (cat. no. 5) might belong in this category, as would Qiao Zhongchang's (act. late 11th–early 12th century) illustration of Su Shi's 'Red Cliff Ode' (cat. no. 19), one of the earliest extant scholar-paintings. Another narrative painting, *Sima Yu's Dream of the Courtesan Su Xiaoxiao* by Liu Yuan (act. 13th century) (cat. no. 37), however, reverts to the 'epitomizing', single-scene mode of narration found in the *Admonitions* scroll.

## GENRE SCENES

Following the reunification of China under the mighty Tang empire, there was less demand for the kind of didactic works seen in 'story painting'. With the spread of individualism and Buddhist thought came the growth of cities and cosmopolitan lifestyles, and as Tang emperors surveyed their position in the world, so emerged 'genre painting'. The Chinese term *fengsu hua* translates as 'paintings of customs and manners', but the category included all kinds of images of life. In the Tang it consisted mainly of court life, from banquets to the reception of ambassadors.

Works by the leading Tang figure painters, like Yan Liben (d.673) and Wu Daozi (c.685–758), are extraordinarily rare. We can get an idea of their art from the archaeologically recovered paintings of the seventh to tenth century, which depict ladies and musicians (see fig. 3). Early copies of Tang dynasty paintings supplement this knowledge, such as *Court Ladies Preparing Newly Woven Silk* (cat. no. 16), painted at Emperor Huizong's court.

Although genre scenes often celebrated imperial power, female beauty and fashion, they were not completely devoid of the moral content that critics deemed so important in painting. Indeed, the later scenes in the *Admonitions* scroll already foreshadow this development, with pictures of ladies at their toilette, the self-regarding beauty getting her comeuppance and the royal family living in harmony. In each case, the point of painting beautiful women performing everyday activities was to illustrate a moral. In the case of the toilette scene, the tract states that one should hone one's character to the extent that she or he decorates the body's outer form with fine clothes, coiffures and cosmetics. In the case of the several generations of the royal family seen together in a stable group, the court ladies are admonished to accept the rota system by which the emperor 'favours' them to maximize the royal progeny and guarantee dynastic succession (see fig. 3). As to preparing silk, this was perhaps not as innocent a subject as it might appear, since at the pinnacle of society China's rulers assumed gendered roles – the emperor as the agrarian society's first farmer and his empresses and court ladies as models of sericulture.

The later dynastic period saw more diverse types of genre scenes, including regional figures and beggars – subjects that could function as social commentary. Genre images such as *Qidan (Khitan) Falconer with Horse* (cat. no. 25) highlight prolonged interactions with other regional cultures, and remind us that China was not an isolated 'middle kingdom' but rather a polity in constant debate about its cultural traditions and their role in the region we know as East Asia. Occasionally genre and religious painting overlapped, for instance in Zhou Jichang's (act. 2nd half 12th century) *Luohans Bestowing Alms on Suffering Human Beings* (cat. no. 23), which pictures the arhat providing succour to starving people.

FIG. 22
Yan Liben (d. 673). *Thirteen Emperors* handscroll, c.650–700. Ink and colour on silk. Museum of Fine Arts, Boston (31.643)

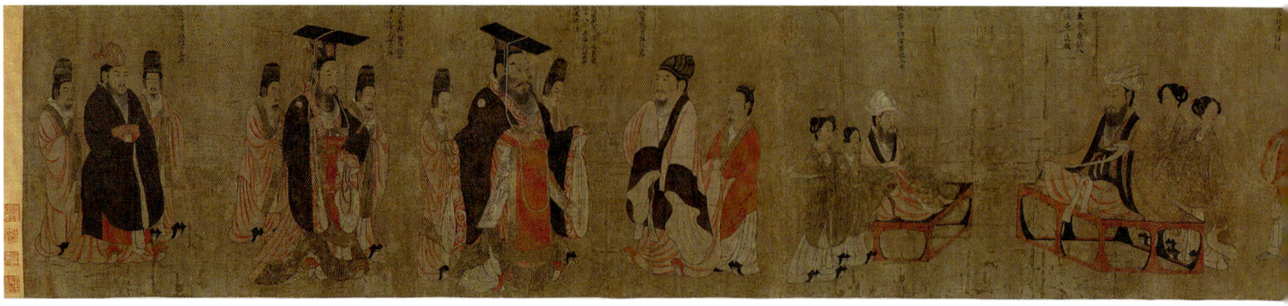

## PORTRAITURE

Portraiture was not defined as a genre in its own right by critics in China – it was regarded as a sub-genre of figure painting – but in practice specialist portraitists have worked uninterrupted, and often unremarked, since early times. Critical attention tended to focus on men like Gu Kaizhi, who was lauded for his inventive portraits, pictures that 'captured the spirit' (*chuanshen*) of the sitter rather than his or her actual appearance, perhaps by the addition of some distinguishing facial feature or placement in a particular setting. Ever the maverick, Gu Kaizhi quipped that the easiest subjects to paint were ghosts, because no one really knew what they looked like. The painting of ghosts and demons remained a niche subject down the centuries, as the *Ghost Amusement* scroll by Luo Pin (1733–99) (cat. no. 78), another eccentric, attests. Portraiture fulfilled another function in early painting – the anthropomorphism of natural phenomena such as planets and constellations, as in the work in the exhibition traditionally attributed to Liang Lingzan (cat. no. 13).

A strength of this exhibition is the view it affords of the development of figural painting and portraiture. In addition to the extremely rare transmitted scroll of portraits by Yan Liben, *Thirteen Emperors* in the Museum of Fine Arts, Boston (fig. 22), there are the mediaeval Buddhist materials discovered at and around Dunhuang. In particular, we may focus on two types of portrayal of figures in these Buddhist paintings. The figures of deities (including Buddhas and bodhisattvas) and their retinues, and of the donors (positioned below), are executed in a descriptive and realistic manner in the ink-outline mode, which is usually enhanced with colour wash. The portrayal of deities is necessarily imaginary (if conventional and iconographic), but the portrayal of donors varies. In contrast with standard commissions, which often portray the donors with merely generic features (cat. no. 12), some high-quality commissions contain an actual portrait of the donor's face attached to a generic ink-outline figure, whether male or female.[9] The survival of multiple sketches from life of heads of donors at different angles, as if the portraitist was looking for the most characteristic view, is evidence that specialist portraitists were employed by the various ateliers to record and then execute these portrait heads in the final banners.

When portraiture re-emerges as a major genre from about 1600, a stylistic disparity between facial and drapery techniques is still evident, even in the work of a specialist portraitist like Zeng Jing (1564–1647) (cat. no. 64). Specialist painters of heads, already familiar with existing shading techniques since the Song dynasty, quickly appropriated the new shading techniques appearing in China from Europe, while figure painters like Chen Hongshou (1598–1652), who ran a highly productive studio (cat. no. 66), continued to employ the ink-outline technique – as technically demanding as it was lyrical – for drapery. When these two types of artist collaborated, the contrast between shaded (Western-'influenced') heads and 'traditional' ink-outline figures was often stark.

In addition to depictions of deities, the Dunhuang materials contain depictions of eminent monks (fig. 23), a category known as *dingxiang hua* ('monk portraits') that lasted into the Song and Yuan dynasties. Paintings of various types by Chan (J. Zen) Buddhist monks of this period, including portraits of patriarchs and masters as well as spiritual encounters and transitions (cat. no. 41), were often inscribed by prominent Buddhist masters.[10] Eminent clerics moved in the same social circles as scholars, and scholar-artists like Zhao Mengfu may even have tried their hand at this genre.[11] Zhao Mengfu was an admirer of ancient painting, and in particular of Gu Kaizhi. His *Small Self-Portrait*, which appears to be the earliest dated self-portrait by a scholar-painter in China, draws on the tradition of carefully framing portrait figures in apt settings (fig. 24).[12] In Zhao's case, he stands in a bamboo grove, a potent image of virtue. In turn, Zhao Mengfu was a model to the literati (or scholar-) painters in Suzhou in the sixteenth century, including Shen Zhou (1427–1509) and Wen Zhengming. Shen Zhou, who worked in Suzhou, is himself the subject of a portrait in the exhibition

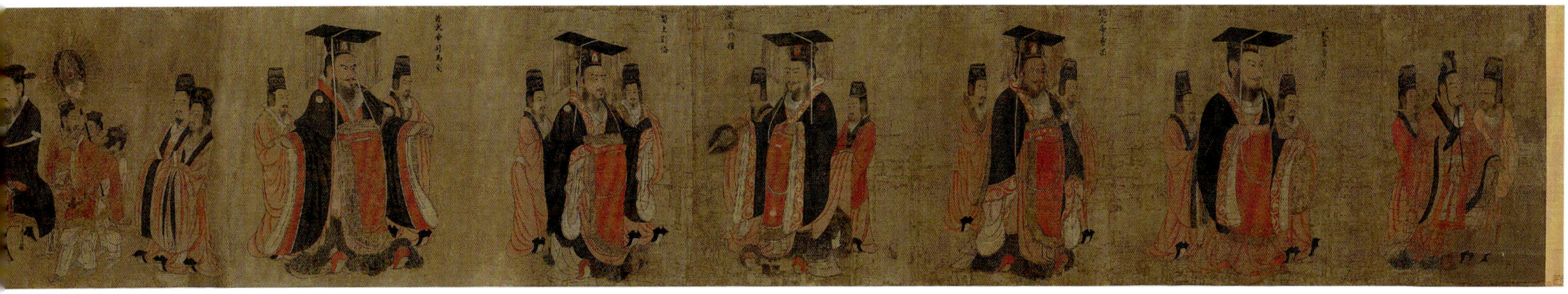

(cat. no. 58). Suzhou was the centre of a short-lived but fascinating mode, which we here include under the following section on landscape, known as 'alias painting' (*biehao tu*).

In the Qing period (1644–1911), arguably the 'evidentiary scholarship' and 'metal and stone studies' movements served to destabilize the established hierarchies of great names. Many of the later Qing painters revived less privileged genres, such as figures and horses, and also chose to develop non-canonical styles. Interest in both portraiture and self-portraiture hardly diminished from this period, however, as domestic and contemporary subjects tended to displace historical ones. Indeed, eccentric painters working in mercantile, urban circles during the eighteenth and nineteenth centuries delighted in producing bizarre and sometimes apparently unflattering portraits of

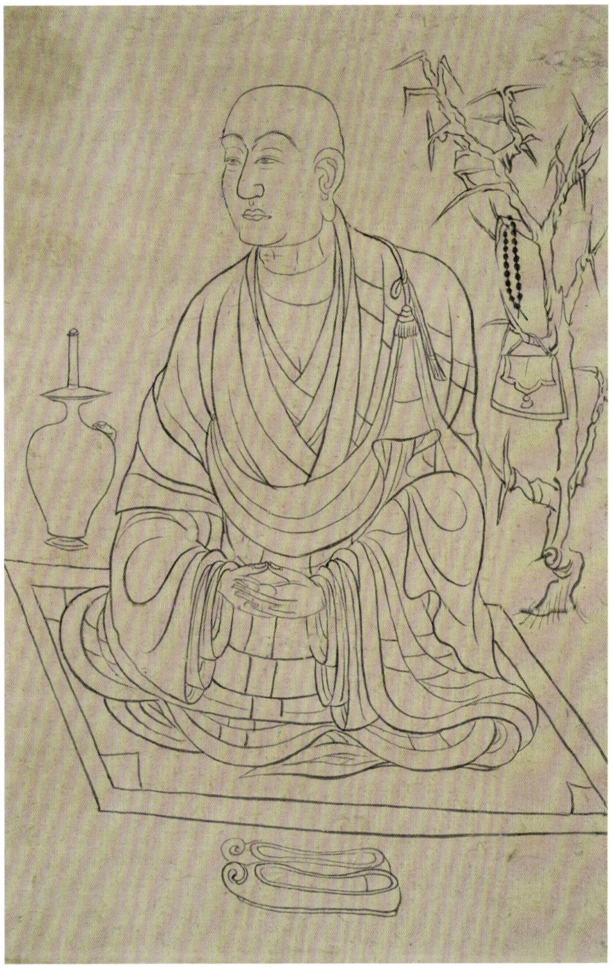

FIG. 23
Finely drawn portrait of a monk, c.851–950. Ink on paper. Excavated from Cave 17, Mogao Caves, Dunhuang. The British Museum, London (1919,0101,0.163)

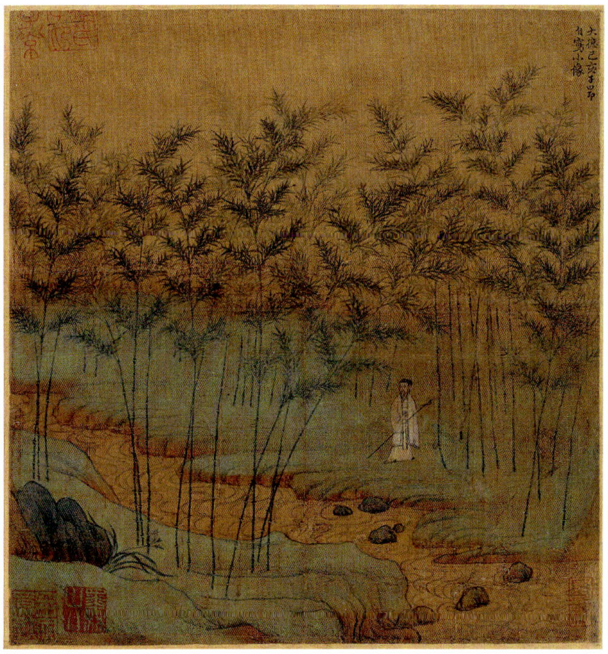

FIG. 24
Zhao Mengfu (1254–1322). *Small Self-Portrait* album leaf, 1299. Ink and colour on silk. The Palace Museum, Beijing

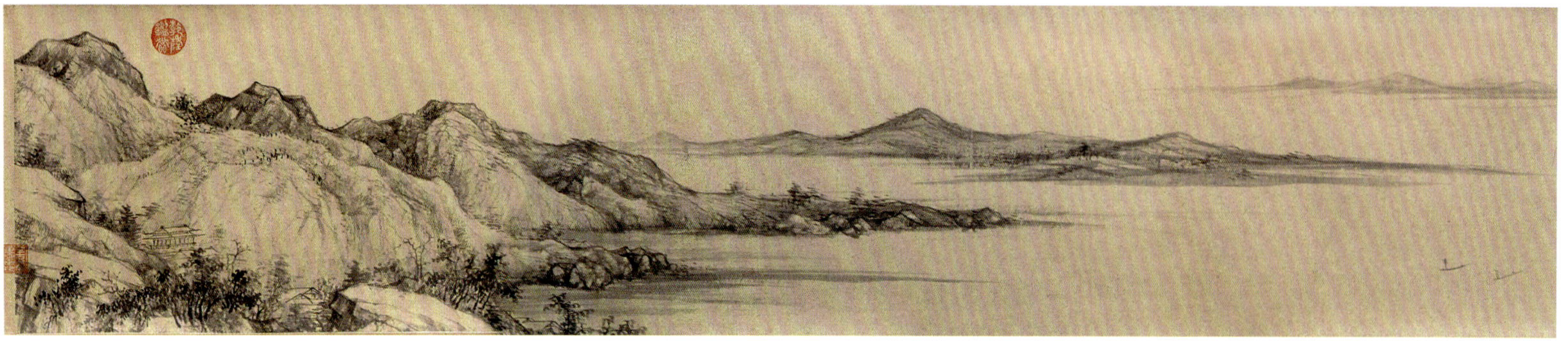

themselves, their friends and patrons, often contrasting historical stylistic referencing with contemporary descriptive vocabulary. The work of Yangzhou painters of the later eighteenth century like Jin Nong (1687–1763) and his follower Luo Pin, which treated genres such as figures, horses and ghosts, points to the independence and rich cultural life of the city and the region. These men seem to have had interests as varied as Chan Buddhism, the occult, Western science and learning, and 'metal and stone studies'. This last trend is seen in paintings in the new hard, flat quality of ink outlines, an echo of the prevailing interest in the calligraphy of ancient inscriptions cast in bronze vessels and engraved on to stone stelae, which have those qualities.

Ren Yi (1840–95), an admirer of both Luo Pin and Chen Hongshou, was an outstanding painter in late Qing Shanghai who preferred to paint sometimes disturbing portraits and figural scenes.[13] In Shanghai the effects of reinvigorated intellectual culture, including the 'metal and stone studies' movement and interest in photography and other technologies, can be seen in the qualities of his lineament and depiction. An admixture of traditional and modern effects and references suited the professional urban practices of Ren and his contemporaries. Theirs is a recognizably modern assertion of 'eccentric' identity and self in painting.

## Landscape and Gardens

Although it appeared earlier, landscape (*shanshui*; 'mountain and water') painting did not emerge as a genre in its own right until the transition from the Tang to Song empire in the tenth century, when Li Cheng (919–67), Dong Yuan (act. 930s–60s) and Fan Kuan (act. *c.*990–1030) were among the pioneering landscapists. Extant works by these men are again extraordinarily rare, but *Reading the Memorial Stele* (cat. no. 14), although not by Li Cheng, is an early painting in his distinctive 'wintry forest' mode of landscape. The *Wintry Forest* fan (now an album leaf, cat. no. 30), painted by a talented but unknown thirteenth-century artist in the same mode, is an artistic conceit designed to bring its user a blast of winter in the heat of summer. Yan Wengui (967–1030), painter of *Landscape with Pavilions* (cat. no. 15), is also sometimes included in this group. Landscape paintings done at the early Song court often served as images of universal cosmic harmony; soon, however, independent-minded men of the scholar class also used landscape types as forms, if not of dissent, then at least to distinguish their world views and values from those of the imperial agenda.

Despite its lowly position in the hierarchy of genres in the *Xuanhe Painting Catalogue* (6th out of 10), the landscape tradition came to dominate the field of painting following developments in the Mongol Yuan dynasty, notably by men like Zhao Mengfu and Ni Zan (1306–74) (cat. nos 46, 51), and with the establishment of the expression-oriented 'literati painting' movement in the Ming dynasty. Indeed, many of the paintings from 1400 to 1600 in the exhibition are types of landscape, although not all are by the literati. We may further discover what early Ming scholar painting looked like by considering the album leaves by Wang Lü (1332–*c.*1383) *Images of Mount Hua*, done in 1383, and the bucolic *Xiao-Xiang* handscroll (fig. 25), depicting the southern wilderness, of Wang Fu (1362–1416) and Chen Shuqi (act. 2nd half 14th century).

As the critical theories of Ming scholar-critics and collector-connoisseurs became distinguished from the court agenda, landscape became a critical battleground, as seen in such rivalries as that between the Zhe and Wu schools. Zhe refers to the province of Zhejiang, which includes Hangzhou, the former Southern Song (1127–1279) capital; Wu is an ancient name for the city of Suzhou, the cultural powerhouse of Ming China and spiritual home of scholar painting. The Zhe school, said to have been founded by Dai Jin (1388–1462), painter of *Spring Clouds in the Linggu Mountains* (cat. no. 52), comprised both professional and court artists – men of extraordinary technical

FIG. 25
Wang Fu (1362–1416) and Chen Shuqi (act. 2nd half 14th century). *Xiao-Xiang* handscroll (detail), c.1412. Ink and colour on silk. The Palace Museum, Beijing

skill and visual imagination like the bird-and-flower specialist Lü Ji (act. 1488–1505) (cat. no. 56). Zhe school painters active at court – some of whom held ranks in the imperial bodyguard unit (the Jinyiwei or Embroidered Uniform Guard) – were often brilliant performers, full of swagger and braggadocio, whose styles left the brush tip exposed to create sharp edges and points, with highly contrastive ink tones.[14]

The Wu school comprised Confucian-educated scholar-amateurs and 'men of culture' (*wenren*) of lofty character who created self-expressive paintings in ink on paper and were the heirs to the soft, dry brush modes of the Four Yuan Masters, such as Ni Zan (cat. no. 51), and to even earlier scholarly modes, like that of Mi Fu (1051–1107) and his son Mi Youren (1074–1151/1086–1165), who were famous for their cloudy mountainscapes (cat. no. 18). The leading scholar-painters, who either held or aspired to hold civil office or otherwise to live a life of public or civic service, lauded the restraint and modesty of *pingdan* ('mild, bland') brush techniques using a centred brush tip.

This division of painters into Zhe and Wu is both helpful and unhelpful. It makes some sense concerning painting subjects and stylistic modes: the Zhe school painters are rightly regarded as having revived native Chinese Song court subjects by artists like Ma Yuan (act. late 12th–early 13th century) and Xia Gui (act. 1180–1230, cat. nos 27, 28, 29), such as figures-in-landscapes and 'decorative' bird-and-flower subjects, although their paintings were much larger than Song ones. Zhe school painters also revived the wetter, slicker brush idioms of Song court artists and tended to paint in ink and colour on silk, a technically demanding ground. Still, there are numerous cases of artists who blurred these distinctions. Active in Beijing, Du Jin (act. c.1465–1509), painter of the *Court Ladies in the Inner Palace* handscroll (cat. no. 54), was a scholar turned professional. His art was influential on the figure painting of Tang Yin (1470–1523), a budding scholar-official from Suzhou, home of the Wu school, who was forced to turn professional after being embroiled in a civil service examination scandal. Tang's landscape paintings closely followed those of the professional Zhou Chen (c.1450–1535) (cat. no. 55), and also revived Southern Song court landscape painting. On commission, Tang Yin could paint garden or landscape scenes which illustrated or otherwise commemorated the aliases or literary names of his gentry patrons. The highly accomplished Qiu Ying (1494/5–1552), painter of *Saying Farewell at Xunyang* (cat. no. 61), was an out-and-out professional artist active in Suzhou who was drawn into these Wu school gentry circles, and sometimes illustrated texts transcribed by Wen Zhengming to create artworks comprising calligraphy and painting.

Various paintings in the exhibition belong in the sub-category of landscape known as 'alias painting', such as Zhou Chen's *Dwelling by the Stream in Spring* (cat. no. 55), in which the professional artist took the literary name of his patron, 'Chunquan' ('Vernal Spring'), and incorporated it into a rustic scene – an image of detachment and moral purity. The *Garden of the Inept Administrator* album by Wen Zhengming (cat. no. 62) might be included in this sub-genre as well in the sense that pictures of private gardens can also be seen as representing the 'inner person' of the owner.[15]

The Zhe-Wu rivalry underpins the significant critical formation of the early seventeenth century: the division of historical artists into an all-encompassing theory of Northern and Southern schools by the influential statesman-artist Dong Qichang (1555–1636). A historical rival of Zhao Mengfu, Dong refashioned the history of painting by tracing two lineages, Northern and Southern, based on China's Buddhist schools of thought and the ideas of gradual and sudden enlightenment. The southern lineage, ending with himself, comprised men who were typically scholar-amateurs, while the northerners were dogged, artisanal types. For Dong Qichang, in fact, calligraphy was a superior art to painting, and the abstract visual structures of that art lie at the core of his own landscape idiom, in which dynamic mountain forms abut one another like tectonic plates. painting. Entitled *Twin Marvels of Calligraphy and Painting* (cat. no. 63) it exemplifies this marriage of the two brush disciplines in literati art. Somewhat ironically, despite cherishing amateurism, Dong Qichang, like other 'men of culture', was under such social pressure to present his artworks as gifts or in exchange that he engaged a number of 'substitute brushes' (amanuenses) to paint landscapes and sometimes even to sign them on his behalf.

Whereas orthodox landscapists practised in a distinctive mode based on Dong Qichang's and often claimed to be painting after such-and-such an old master, some eccentrics and 'individualists' challenged the idea of painting after any kind of model. The Ming royal turned Buddhist monk turned painter Zhu Ruoji, also known by his monk's name Shitao (Stone Wave), boldly stated that the old masters should have seen his painting. He and Bada Shanren (1626–1705), another minor Ming royal who grew up as a refugee under the Manchu Qing dynasty, painted landscapes in the form of rural and suburban scenes such as cultivated fields and busy canals, as well as small scenes of figures-in-landscapes and plants like the lotus, a Buddhist symbol of purity rising out of the mire, often in eccentric, expressive styles (cat. nos 71, 74).

In terms of subjects and styles, paintings from 1600 to 1900 begin to look ever more familiar to the modern eye. In part, this is because European techniques of painting were gradually being appropriated by painters in China. Zhang Hong (1577–after 1652) (cat. no. 65) was among the first to study them carefully, most probably in engravings brought by missionaries. Later, baroque chiaroscuro and vanishing-point perspective were introduced first-hand by European Jesuits working at the court like the painter Giuseppe Castiglione (Ch. Lang Shining, 1688–1766) and his colleagues, and were disseminated to cities that enjoyed links with the court and that were forging civic identities through stylistic choices. The adaptation and incorporation of European painting techniques by artists in China was not an inevitable trend, nor is it the only story of painting in the 1600–1900 period: intellectual currents, notably scepticism and evidence-based learning in the eighteenth and nineteenth centuries, arguably played a far more powerful role in the story of Qing art.

Thus, where we see the landscape art and critical stance of Dong Qichang continuing into the Qing period, it is in the conservative court context. Dong's 'great synthesis' was adopted and made orthodox by the Manchu court, which was eager to co-opt the art of the Han-Chinese elite into the Qing polity. His followers, led by the so-called Four Wangs, occupied high ranks in Qing civil officialdom. The courtier-painter Wang Hui (1632–1717, cat. no. 67), for example, was charged with the politically significant painting projects, such as commemorating the Kangxi emperor's (r. 1662–1722) southern inspection tour in the 1690s. Two of the other Wangs – Wang Shimin (1592–1680), Wang Jian (1598–1677) and Wang Yuanqi (1642–1715) – are represented by landscapes in the exhibition (cat. nos 68, 75).

In the eighteenth century, the major cities of China, including Beijing, Yangzhou, Suzhou and, later, Shanghai, became distinctive centres of artistic production. The immense wealth generated by the salt merchants of Yangzhou fostered in and attracted to that city so-called eccentric painters like Zheng Xie (1693–1765), a specialist in 'bamboo and rocks' (cat. no. 77), which is sometimes regarded as a sub-genre of landscape. Although 'bamboo and rocks' had originally developed in the Song–Yuan period as the signature genre of the scholar-painter, Zheng Xie rode roughshod over the polite convention of not mentioning money by publishing his celebrated price list for his paintings.

The moneyed art patrons of Yangzhou had large mansions to furnish, judging by the scale of the landscapes by another Yangzhou professional, Yuan Jiang (act. *c.*1680–1730) – see his 1691 panoramic screen (cat. no. 72), a format referred to in Chinese as *tongjing*, 'continuous landscape', and depicting the old subject of opulent palaces among mountains. Note how Yuan Jiang matched this subject with the use of a parallel perspective system (in geometric terms, an axonometric projection), working essentially within China's tradition of architectural or 'ruled-line' painting (*jiehua*), which had peaked in the fourteenth century under Mongol rule (cat. no. 49). The appearance of these extensive landscape depictions in late seventeenth-century regional art flags up a new context, one in which major regional cities seemed to use landscape or cityscape painting modes to help define their distinctive urban identity and the nature of their ties to the court in Beijing.

We can explore this idea with reference to Xu Yang's (1712–*c.*1779) *Prosperous Suzhou* handscroll of 1759 (cat. no. 76). Xu Yang's period of activity coincided with a high point in the Qing imperial patronage of the arts. On the strength of impressive, lengthy cityscapes like *Prosperous Suzhou*, Xu was commissioned to execute a set of scrolls commemorating the Qianlong emperor's (r. 1736–96) historic 1751 inspection tour of south China – in the footsteps of Wang

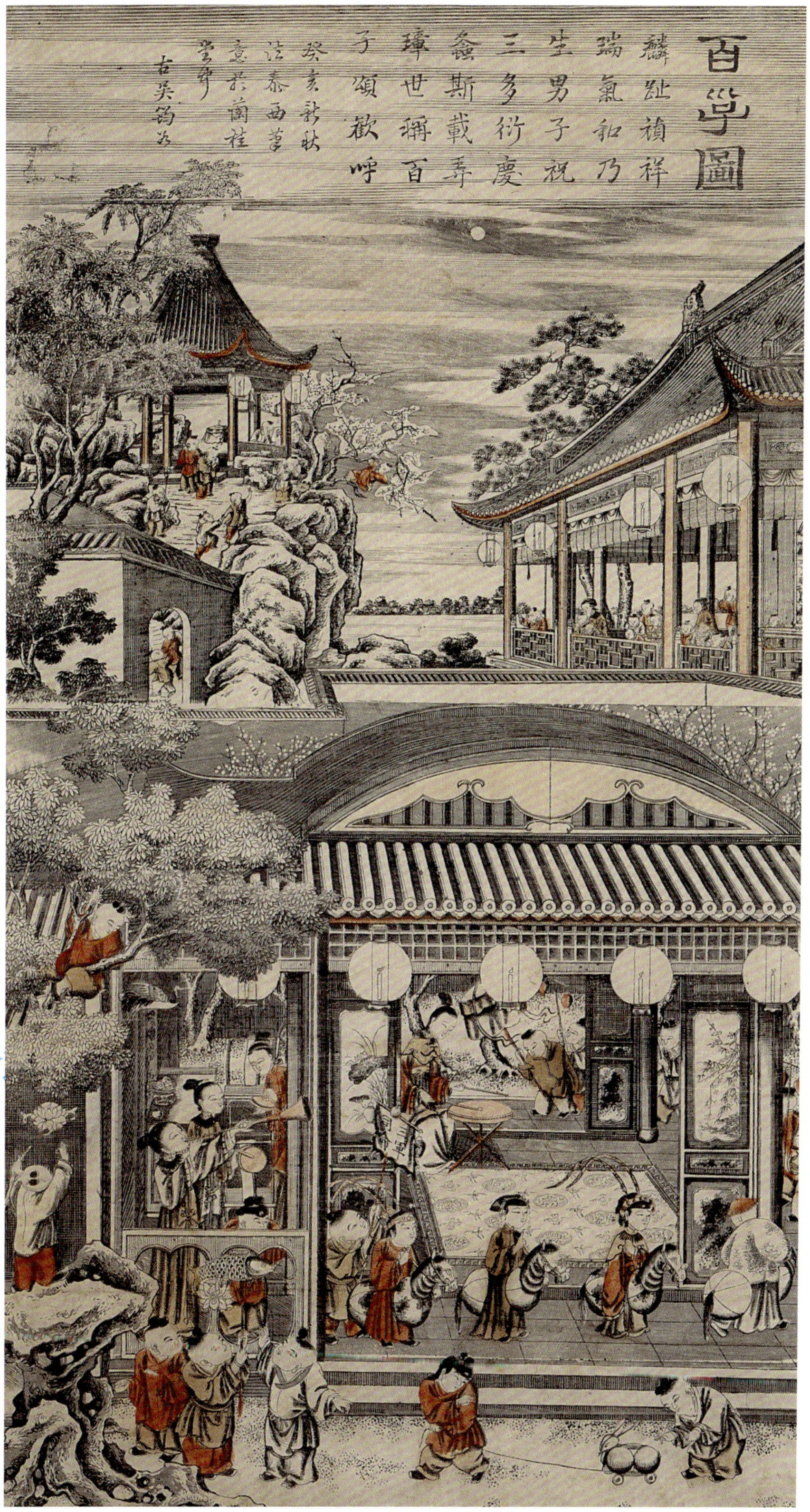


FIG. 26
Yungu and Zhang Xingju (act. 18th century). *One Hundred Children* hanging scroll, 1743. Hand-coloured woodblock print. The British Museum, London (1991,1031,0.1)

Hui, who had done this for the Qianlong emperor's grandfather, the Kangxi emperor, in the 1690s. From Xu Yang's set, the scroll depicting the Qianlong emperor's tour of Suzhou, dated 1770, now in the Metropolitan Museum of Art, New York, is just short of 20 metres in length, about as long as a handscroll can be. Xu's approach to depicting his city had strong local roots. Between around 1730 and 1750, in a printing boom, Suzhou was the production centre of fine woodblock-printed pictures depicting historical scenes, famous sites and cityscapes of Suzhou and Hangzhou, most of which were done using the baroque vanishing-point perspective system in vogue at court. Previously, painters like Zhang Hong and Gong Xian (cat. no. 70) had incorporated such European techniques into and tried out the European 'landscape' (horizontal) format for landscapes (whereas Chinese landscapes for display were usually in Western 'portrait' [i.e., upright] format), but they had never declared in inscriptions that their pictures were done 'following the Western brush mode' (*fa Taixi biyi*), as these Suzhou prints sometimes did (fig. 26),[16] or deployed vanishing-point perspective with such exactitude.

The term 'brush mode' (*biyi*) in this context is instructive. It indicates, for instance, how baroque optics were transformed as an idea in China into brush effects, underscoring the precedence of the performative brush in China's art over optical illusionism of representation. That this term appears on a woodblock print (which, needless to say, was carved rather than painted) also points to the source of this visual knowledge higher up the art hierarchy – in painting. In fact, the fascination with 'the Western brush mode' in Suzhou prints should be understood in the context of this competition among regional cities to give form to their close connections with the court. Suzhou artists sojourning in the imperial workshops in the Forbidden City in Beijing would have worked alongside men like Giuseppe Castiglione, the Qianlong emperor's favourite court painter and the leading purveyor of this mode. Later, with paintings like *Prosperous Suzhou*, the city's artists like Xu Yang could link Suzhou's commercial success and civic pride with a mode much admired by the Emperor, but carefully adapted to the Chinese format of the handscroll.

The vogue for the 'Western brush mode' in landscape painting passed, although landscapes of the orthodox type did continue on into the nineteenth century. Major innovations in styles and subjects were taking place at this time in other genres of paintings more attuned to life in the fast-developing global cities like Shanghai. One such development was the revival of paintings of figures and flowers.

## Flower-and-Bird Painting (and miscellanies)

One of the important original functions of painting, critics said, was to distinguish things one from another. Paintings of flora and fauna further became a way to order and categorize the world according to a particular world view. Various of the lesser genres in the partisan imperial text, the *Xuanhe Painting Catalogue*, for instance, would fall into this broad group, including 'dragons and fish', 'animals and beasts' and 'vegetables and fruits', as well as 'flowers and birds'. Emperor Huizong's painting *Auspicious Cranes* (cat. no. 17) demonstrates this Emperor's skill as a recorder of these natural phenomena such that they legitimized his rule. The appearance of the flock of auspicious birds over the palace here underscores what he saw as heaven's approbation of his kingship. In reality, he later lost half the Song empire and died in captivity. Nonetheless, in his reign, naturalism in painting – and especially in flower-and-bird painting – reached a new high-water mark, as court artists strove to translate the accurate observation of nature into representational realism.

Several examples from across the political spectrum of the Mongol Yuan dynasty demonstrate the range of interpretations of flora and fauna paintings. *Ink Orchid* (cat. no. 47), by the Chinese scholar Zheng Sixiao (1239–1316), was painted in the early Yuan, in 1306. Zheng Sixiao was a fervent loyalist of the recently defeated Song dynasty who, when his friend the Song royal Zhao Mengfu joined the Yuan government as a scholar-official, never spoke to him again. Although the ostensible subject of the painting is a wild orchid, a classical symbol of moral purity likened to the *junzi* or ideal gentleman, it is the way the orchid is framed in the picture that adds layers of nuance. First, it is an ink orchid – painted without colour in the signature mode of China's scholar-artists. Second, there is no ground because, it was said, the Mongols had stolen China away. The artist's chosen personal name, Sixiao (思肖), translates as 'yearning for the Zhao': 'xiao' (肖) is an element of the word 'zhao' (趙), the surname of the deposed Song royal family. Beyond this, the painter's literary name was 'Old Man Who Faces South' ('Suonan Weng'), which is to say he turned his back on the Mongol khans of China up in Beijing. Knowing this, it is hard to see this flower painting as anything but a righteous lament by a scholar who saw himself as a refugee in his own country.

The Mongols themselves, who have often lazily been portrayed as philistines, were in fact major patrons of flora and fauna paintings, such as images of fancy birds like pheasants and peacocks pictured in an elegant garden setting, all of which represented *wen*, or 'accomplishment'. They also fostered artists of high technical ability: the painter of *The Summer Palace of Emperor Minghuang* (cat. no. 49) was working in the shadow of acclaimed artists at the early Yuan court like Wang Zhenpeng (*c*.1280–*c*.1329), whose art marked a convergence of the scholar and court painting traditions.

Horse painting is another subject that flourished under the Mongols, a steppe people whose mastery of cavalry warfare underpinned the creation of their vast empire in Eurasia. *Emaciated Horse*, by another Song loyalist, Gong Kai (1222–1307) (cat. no. 44), symbolizes a neglected but unbowed Chinese living out his life under Mongol rule. By contrast, *Grooms and Horses* by Zhao Mengfu, his son and grandson (cat. no. 46), who all served in the Mongol government, represents another use of this subject. In an era notorious for corruption and nepotism, Zhao Mengfu was a lifelong advocate of appointment and promotion on merit. By convention, a painting of a horse being presented by a groom was a way of asking the question: is this horse (or would-be scholar-official) talented enough to merit patronage?

As subjects, flora and fauna continued to attract both painters of vaunted amateur status and court and professional artists. The Ming court, in particular, celebrated this topic, which significantly represented a revival of Song court art – Lü Ji's *Pomegranates, Autumn Mallows, Chrysanthemums, Blue Magpies and Rooster* is one example (cat. no. 56). A characteristic of the later painting tradition in China was the increasing use of numbered groupings, such as, in flower painting, the 'Four Gentlemen' and the 'Three Friends of Winter'. The 'Four Gentlemen' were orchid (spring), bamboo (summer), chrysanthemum (autumn) and plum blossom (winter). The term 'gentleman' comes from the Confucian classics, where it refers to a person of great cultivation and morality, as noted earlier; the great Song scholar Su Shi had famously referred to bamboo as 'this gentleman' (*cijun*). The 'Three Friends of Winter' are pine, plum blossom and bamboo (cat. no. 53).

## IN SUM

In about 1380, the influential Confucian scholar-official Song Lian (1310–81) wrote an essay entitled *The Origins of Painting*, in which he looked back at the early history of painting while seeking to define a new moral order for the fledgling native Chinese dynasty he served, the Ming.[17] He presented a radical overview of the categories of painting, their contents and phases, and sought to reassert the ancient moral justification for painting as an art which could illuminate the classic texts of China's Confucian humanist learning. The best of the ancients, he argued, had illustrated texts like the *Book of Odes*, the *Classic of Filial Piety*, the *Analects of Confucius* and the *Book of Changes*. These were paintings, in other words, which recorded great events and political affairs, the *gushi* (literally 'ancient matters' – and the modern word for 'story' [*gushi*]) which underpinned China's long and distinguished tradition of statecraft and the traditional emphasis on moral self-cultivation. Song Lian pointedly ignored Daoist and Buddhist paintings of the kind that today are indispensable for reconstructing the early history of painting. One of his chief arguments was that (Chinese) calligraphy and painting are two sides of the same coin: complementary arts of language and vision that coexist to distinguish things one from another, thereby promoting order and benefiting humanity.

The first major historical shift following the classical period, according to Song Lian, occurred with painters of the great Han empire and afterward (220 BCE–587 CE) who painted more in the way of historical subjects, although such topics were in his view still edifying, still qualified as 'story paintings', or *gushi hua*. Thereafter, he believed, painters had successively 'sullied their ambition painting frivolities such as horses, carriages and fine women [i.e., 'genre scenes']; dissipated their spirit painting the beauties of flowers and birds, insects and fish [i.e., flora and fauna]; and given free rein to their feelings in wildernesses of mountains, forests, streams and rocks [i.e., landscape]'.

Song Lian sounds like a dyed-in-the-wool Confucian who took an arch and long view of history. Yet, his approach to painting usefully highlights the long-term development of genres and subjects. Mirroring social changes over the mediaeval to early modern period, such as the spread of literacy and withering of sumptuary laws, genres did become less exclusively royal and more 'common' and domestic, less didactic and more overtly entertaining or pleasing to the eye, less religious and more secular. For the moralist, however, the bracing lessons of history still lurk in most of the genres, sober reminders of how sovereigns lose their realms because of beautiful women and how the integrity of statesmen is too soon compromised.

1 See, for example, 'Genre', in *Grove Art Online*.
2 See, for example, Ledderose 1973. Various essays in Powers and Tsiang (forthcoming) are also relevant to this essay, including ones by Richard Vinograd on genres, Peter Sturman on landscape, Dora C.Y. Ching on portraiture, Katherine R. Tsiang on Buddhist painting and this writer on figure painting.
3 Multiple-volume modern compilations of these historical texts like *Compendium of Writings of China's Calligraphy and Painting* are standard works of reference nowadays.
4 See, for example, Hay 1983.
5 For these early texts, see Acker 1954; Bush and Shih 1985.
6 Ebrey and Bickford 2006
7 Bush 1971
8 See McCausland 2003a and 2003b.
9 A nuanced study of this topic is Sha 2006.
10 A doctoral study by Malcolm McNeill on some of the text-image questions is currently under way at SOAS, University of London, entitled 'Narrative Agency in 13th–14th century Chan Figure Painting: a Study of Hagiography-Iconography Text Image Relationships'.
11 Brinker 1973–4
12 See McCausland 2011, fig. 4.11.
13 See, for example, Wue (forthcoming).
14 See New York and Dallas 1993.
15 On *biehao tu* see Liu 1990.
16 See further von Spee 2010, cat. no. 22.
17 Song 1957, vol. 1, pp. 95–6

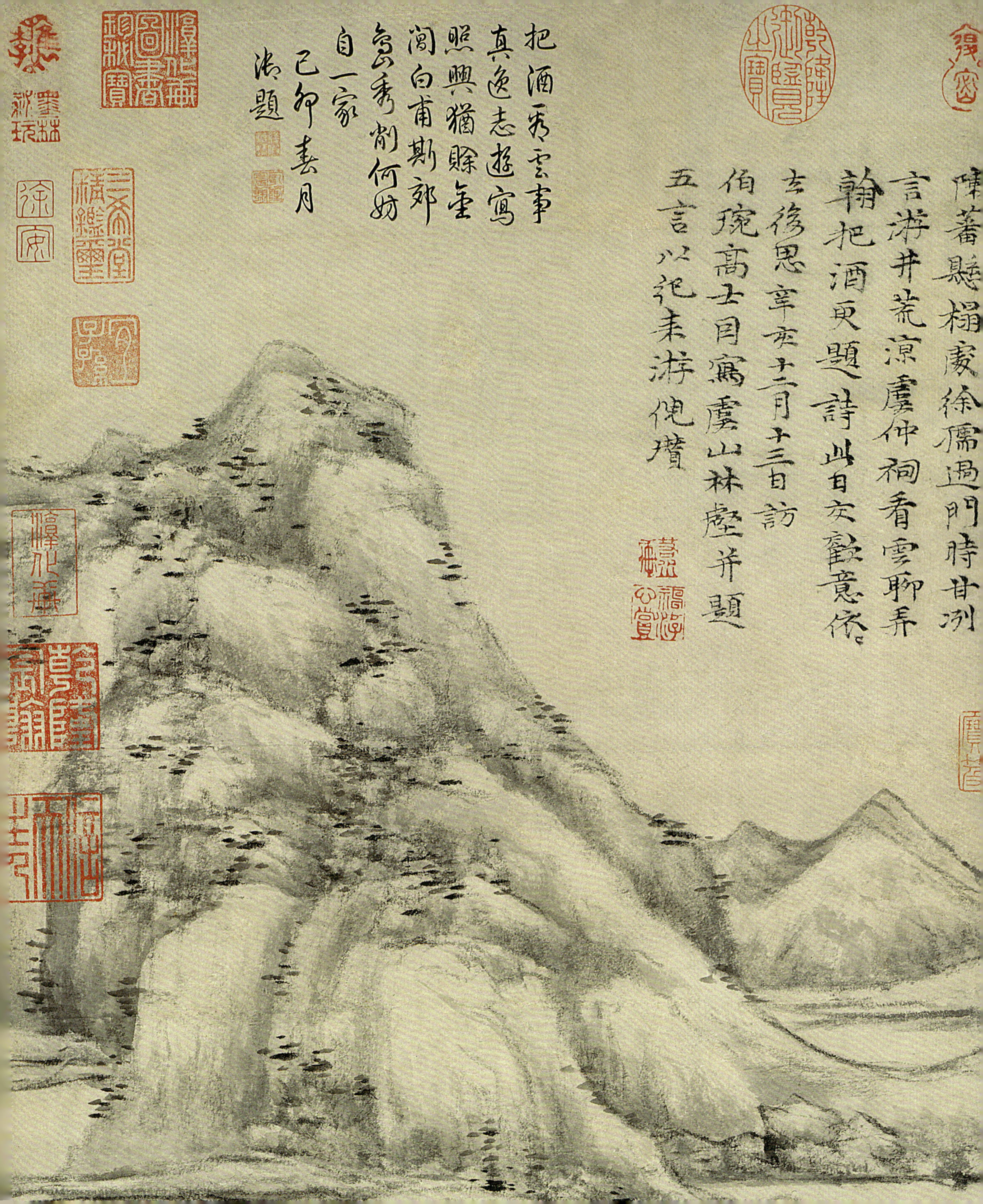
陳蕃懸榻處徐孺過門時甘洌言游井荒涼虞仲祠看雲聊弄翰把酒更題詩此日交歡意依依去後思辛亥十二月十三日訪伯琬高士因寫虞山林壑并題五言以紀來游倪瓚

# INSCRIPTIONS AND SEAL MARKS

Zhang Hongxing

Often, but not always, a true examination of a Chinese painting requires more than a scrutiny of the images. The inscriptions and seal marks also have a strong physical presence, both commanding the gaze and inviting closer inspection. Some inscriptions and marks intrude into the pictorial space, while others appear on the periphery, or in an appended frontispiece or a colophon. They were sometimes added at the time the painting was executed, either by the artist or by his contemporaries, and sometimes by those living in other times, the later additions in some cases stretching over many centuries. The inscriptions and seal marks provide a variety of useful information, including attribution, date, title, subject and the artist's thoughts and viewers' responses. Together, these highly relevant textual addenda embody a cultural practice predicated on a unique idea of the relationship between word and image that has evolved over a very long period, and in any serious engagement with Chinese painting, they should not be disregarded. This chapter aims to offer a general introduction to the major types of inscriptions and seal marks as an intrinsic part of a Chinese painting, according to their forms and content as well as the identities of their authors. It excludes those on the back or outside the painting itself, such as title slips and catalogue entries.[1]

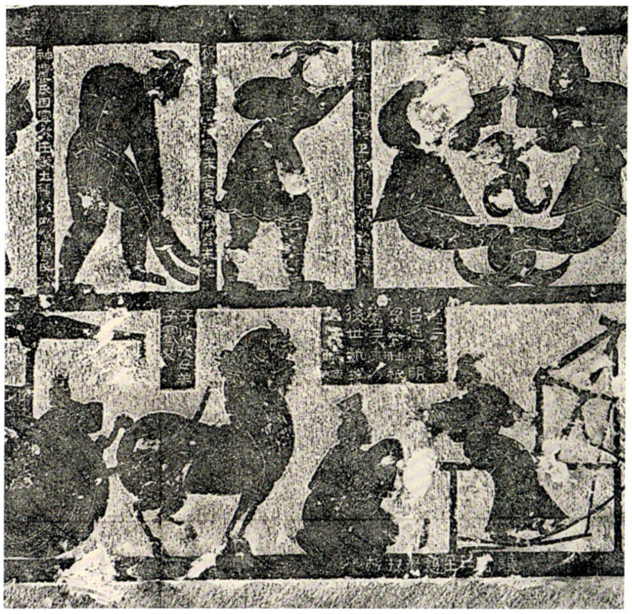

FIG. 27
Rubbing from the wall of Stone Chamber 3, Wu Liang Shrine, Jining, rubbing made before 1907. Princeton University Art Museum (2002.307.36)

## EARLY INSCRIPTIONS

The history of inscriptions on paintings originates with the rise in popularity of subjects with educational and didactic intent during the second half of the Han dynasty (25–220). Typically, these paintings were illustrations of Confucian moral tales and portraits of exemplars of wisdom and virtue, and were created, displayed and recycled in different media throughout the country as part of the imperial promotion of Confucian ideology. Texts were inscribed to accompany the images, in order to ensure their viewers would recognize the intended messages.

Few of these works have survived. However, based on murals in tombs and painted stone carvings at burial sites – the primary evidence for the pictorial art of the period – it is clear that the inscriptions were generally labels identifying the person or subject portrayed. The format of the inscriptions was not uniform, and depended much on the patron's taste and local artistic tradition. A short name label (*bangti*) was usually placed as near to the head of the figure as possible, while longer texts (*tiji*) could run up to two dozen characters and were sometimes arranged in several columns to form a rectangular block, with a four-character phrase in each column. Inscriptions were commonly enclosed within cartouches, although unframed inscriptions are often found as well (fig. 27).[2]

Through much of the period after the fall of the Han ruling house, when the country was divided into the Southern and Northern dynasties (420–589), the practice of inscribing paintings remained constant albeit with discernible changes and variations. In the south, the tradition of illustrating histories and the classics was upheld by the

Han-Chinese rulers. In his *Record of Famous Painters of Successive Dynasties*, Zhang Yanyuan (815–76) records in detail the scale of royal patronage under which such paintings were produced and collected. Emperor Gao (r. 479–82) of the Southern Qi dynasty (479–502), for instance, assembled 348 scrolls by 42 artists during his relatively short reign.[3] Although all the scrolls from the Southern dynasties were lost during the following centuries, there are a few surviving early copies, and these retain many elements of the originals. In the Song dynasty (960–1279) copy of the painting *Wise and Benevolent Women* in the collection of the Palace Museum, Beijing, by the great master Gu Kaizhi (c.344–c.406) of the Eastern Jin dynasty (317–420), which illustrates the Han dynasty (206 BCE–220 CE) compilation *Biographies of Exemplary Women*, the inscriptions are similar to those of the Han period: short labels to identify figures and long inscriptions to summarize stories. The long inscriptions are written on the painting as if to divide the scroll into a series of picture cells. This same pattern of text-image alternation can also be seen in other paintings, including *Admonitions of the Court Instructress to the Palace Ladies* (see fig. 8) and *The Goddess of the Luo River Ode* (fig. 9), the originals of both of which were also attributed to Gu Kaizhi.

In the north, by contrast, the politics and culture had drastically changed: the rulers were non-Han nomads from the steppes beyond the Great Wall, and Indian Buddhism had replaced Confucian ideology and become the new state religion. Despite lavishing resources on the decoration of Buddhist temples, however, the northern rulers did not completely cut themselves off from the Chinese tradition. Rather, they sought to promote their regime as a 'sinicized' government by adopting aspects of Han-Chinese culture, especially from the mid-fifth century on. Hence, paintings such as that on the lacquer screen from Sima Jinlong's tomb in Datong, which dates from before 484 (fig. 28), continue the Han tradition in both content and style. Like Gu Kaizhi, the northern painter of this screen, who lived almost a century later, has illustrated stories of virtuous women

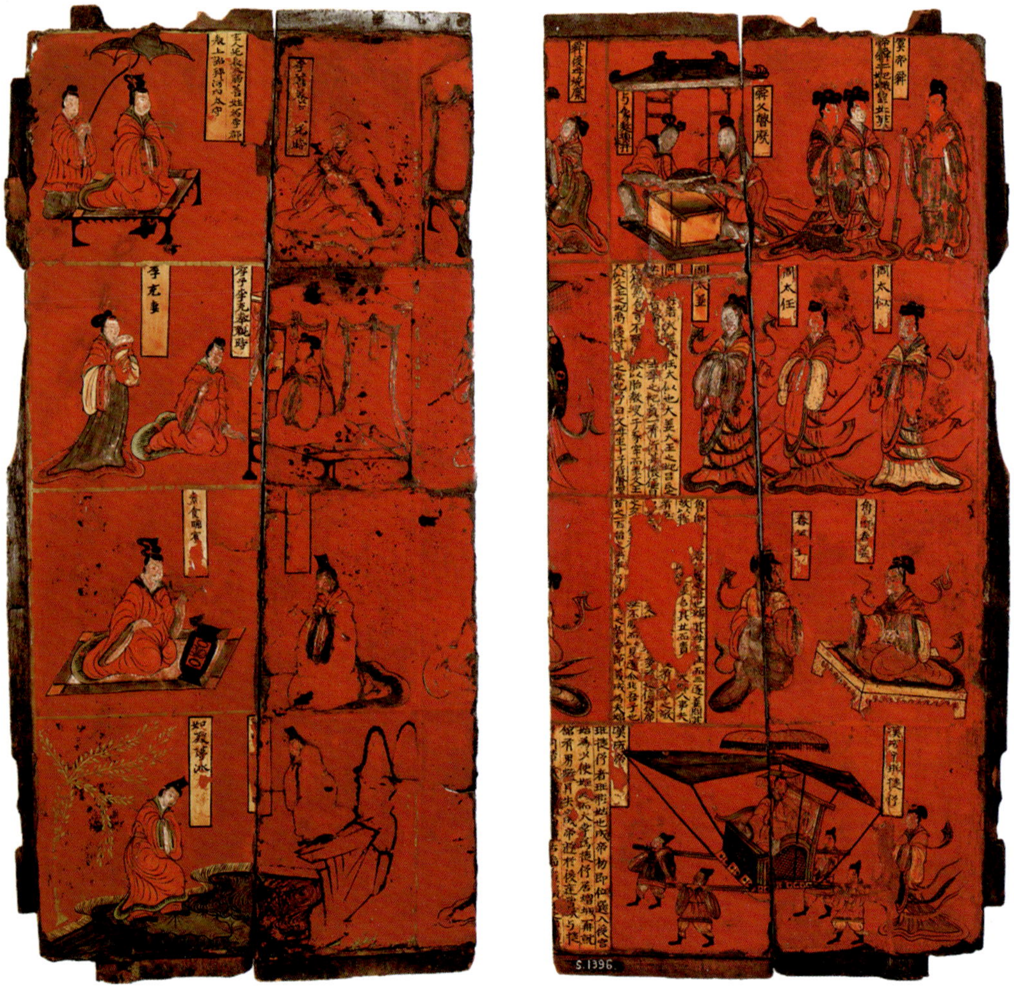

FIG. 28
Painted laquer screen showing scenes from the *Biographies of Filial Sons* and *Biographies of Exemplary Women*, before 484. Excavated from Sima Jinlong's tomb, Datong. Datong Museum

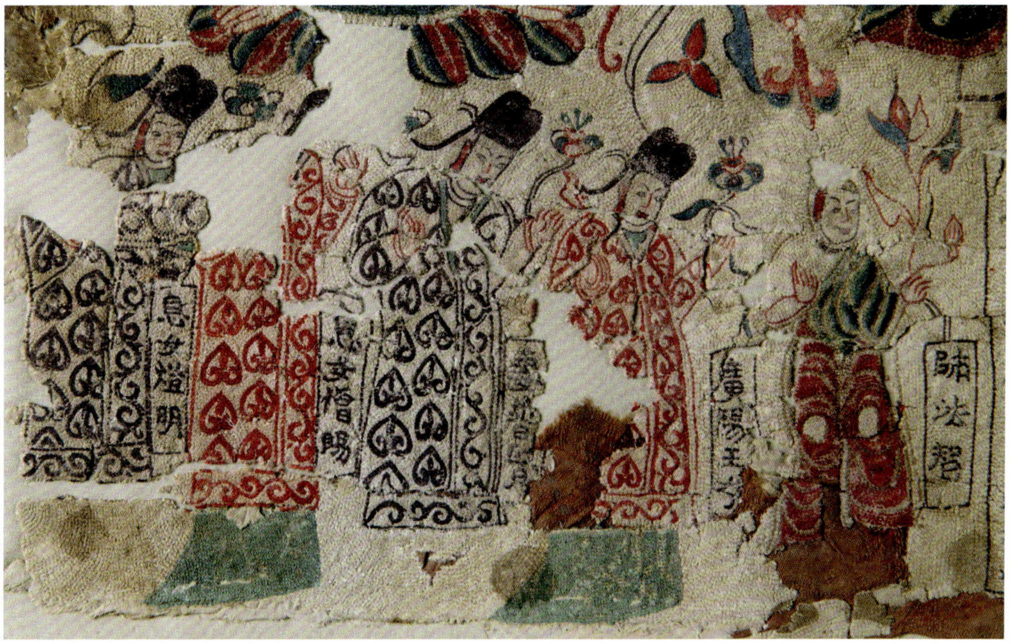

FIG. 29
Embroidered devotional image showing donors, 5th century. Excavated from Caves 125–6, Mogao Caves, Dunhuang. Dunhuang Academy

selected from the Han source book, *Biographies of Exemplary Women*. He has also used the same type of inscriptions, that is, name labels and long texts. He has, however, been more conservative than Gu Kaizhi, as here the inscriptions are even enclosed in hand-drawn cartouches, a feature of Han period inscriptional practice.

The most telling examples of the continuity of the Han inscriptional tradition in the north during this period, surprisingly, are not the Confucian didactic illustrations, but Buddhist images. In these early Buddhist icons and illustrated stories, the old practice of inscribing paintings was adapted to the images of another tradition: typically, name labels were employed to identify the Buddhist deities or donors portrayed, while long inscriptions were either brief synopses of a sutra or the donors' dedicatory texts (*yuanwen*). A cartouche was used in both cases. Early evidence can be found on murals in cave temples, such as the Mogao Grottoes in Dunhuang and the Bingling Grottoes in Yongjing,[4] whereas examples on early portable pictures are rare. An exception is a fragmentary devotional image in embroidery from Dunhuang, which dates from the fifth century. A dedicatory text in the form of a rectangle is placed in the centre, close to the lower edge of the picture; this is flanked by a row of donor figures on either side, with a name label identifying each person (fig. 29). Such a format is also commonly seen in extant Buddhist painted banners of later eras, such as those of the Tang (618–907) and Five Dynasties (907–60) periods found in Dunhuang (cat. nos 1, 10, 12). It would seem, then, that the ancient Chinese inscriptional tradition had been fully integrated into Buddhist image-making by the fifth century, and that in the process a new Buddhist inscriptional practice was developed. This practice was in turn respected by many later generations of Buddhist patrons and artists.

What holds true of inscriptions in Buddhist images also extends to those in non-Buddhist and non-didactic images throughout the Tang and Five Dynasties periods. In paintings such as *The Thirteen Emperors* (see fig. 22) attributed to Yan Liben (d.673) or *The Five Planets and Twenty-eight Constellations*, a work traditionally attributed to Zhang Sengyou (act. 490–540, cat. no. 13), for example, we can observe that the inscriptions are arranged in the same manner as in the past. Thereafter, with the decreasing popularity of religious and didactic subjects and the rise of other subjects such as genre painting, landscape and birds-and-flowers, this ancient form of inscriptional practice mostly fell into disuse.

## ARTISTS' INSCRIPTIONS AND SEAL MARKS

Signatures, inscriptions and seal marks by the artists themselves are rare in early Chinese paintings. However, artists did occasionally append their signatures in Tang dynasty murals, even including a self-portrait. For example, the Dunhuang painters Zhang Hong'en and An Cunli (both act. 10th century, fig. 30) depicted themselves among the standing donors in a mural in Cave 129 at the Mogao Grottoes, and inscribed their names in a cartouche beside their heads.[5] It was not until the eleventh and twelfth centuries that

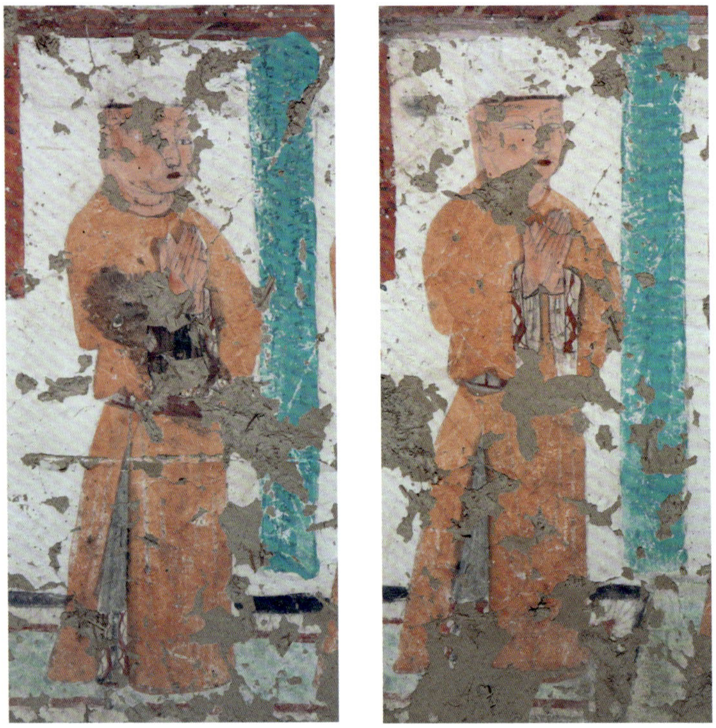

FIG. 30
Self portraits of Zhang Hong'en, far left, and An Cunli (both act. 10th century). Murals from Cave 129, Mogao Caves, Dunhuang

FIG. 31
Li Tang (*c.*1039–*c.*1130). *Whispering Pines in the Gorge* hanging scroll, 1124. Ink and colour on silk. National Palace Museum, Taipei

signatures and other artists' inscriptions began to appear more generally. They can clearly be seen in the work of many Song dynasty painters, like Cui Bai (act. 2nd half 11th century, fig. 20), Fan Kuan (act. *c.*990–1030), Yan Wengui (967–1030) (cat. no. 15), Guo Xi (*c.*1000–*c.*1090), Liang Shimin (act. 2nd half 11th century), Hu Shunchen (act. early 12th century) (cat. no. 20), Li Gongnian (*c.*1049–1106) (cat. no. 21) and Li Tang (*c.*1039–*c.*1130, fig. 31).

Artists' signatures (*kuan*) were executed in a simple manner, being generally limited to an autograph, sometimes with a name seal added underneath. It was also not unusual for a court painter to add 'Your Subject' (*chen*) or a similar designation before his name to indicate his courtier status. In *Landscape with Pavilions* by Yan Wengui in this exhibition, for instance, the artist's signature includes his official title at the Hanlin Academy (cat. no. 15). Occasionally, the date of execution would be included before the name and designation, with the reign name, *ganzhi* year (in a calendar system based on a 60-year cycle) or both being used. For example, in *Whispering Pines in the Gorges* by Li Tang, the artist gives the date as 'spring of the Jiachen year of the Xuanhe reign', or 1124 (fig. 31).

Another general characteristic of artists' signatures in the eleventh and twelfth centuries is that they are discreetly inscribed on the surface of the picture, usually appearing in small script at the bottom or near an edge. In some cases they are even integrated into a painted area such as a tree trunk or rock in a landscape, in order not to interfere with the viewer's appreciation of the painting; later connoisseurs called this cautious practice the 'hidden signature' (*cangkuan*). In the hanging scroll *Whispering Pines in the Gorges* by Li Tang, the signature is placed on a distant peak in the background. While at close quarters it appears to be engraved on the rock, when viewed from a distance it merges with the brushstrokes describing the rock's surface texture and is almost invisible.

It is important to be aware that the signing of a work by the artist was part of a series of fundamental changes to the concept of painting taking place during the Northern Song period, the most important of which were the notion of a painting as a product of an artist's personality and the popular perception of painting as silent poetry and poetry as painting without form. These new ideas had originated in the mid- to late Tang period, but it was not until the Northern Song, with their strong promotion by leading scholars such as Su Shi (1037–1101) and Huang Tingjian (1045–1105) as well as the imperial court, that they took hold and began to make a significant impact on artistic practice. For many painters during this period, especially those who specialized in landscapes and birds-and-flowers, to create a poetic meaning now became the ultimate goal. Guo Xi, one of the most celebrated painters of landscapes at court in the second half of the eleventh century, in his later years remarked to his son that in his free time he used to draw inspiration for his work from the great poems of the past, saying that 'among them were beautiful lines that gave full expression to the feelings that

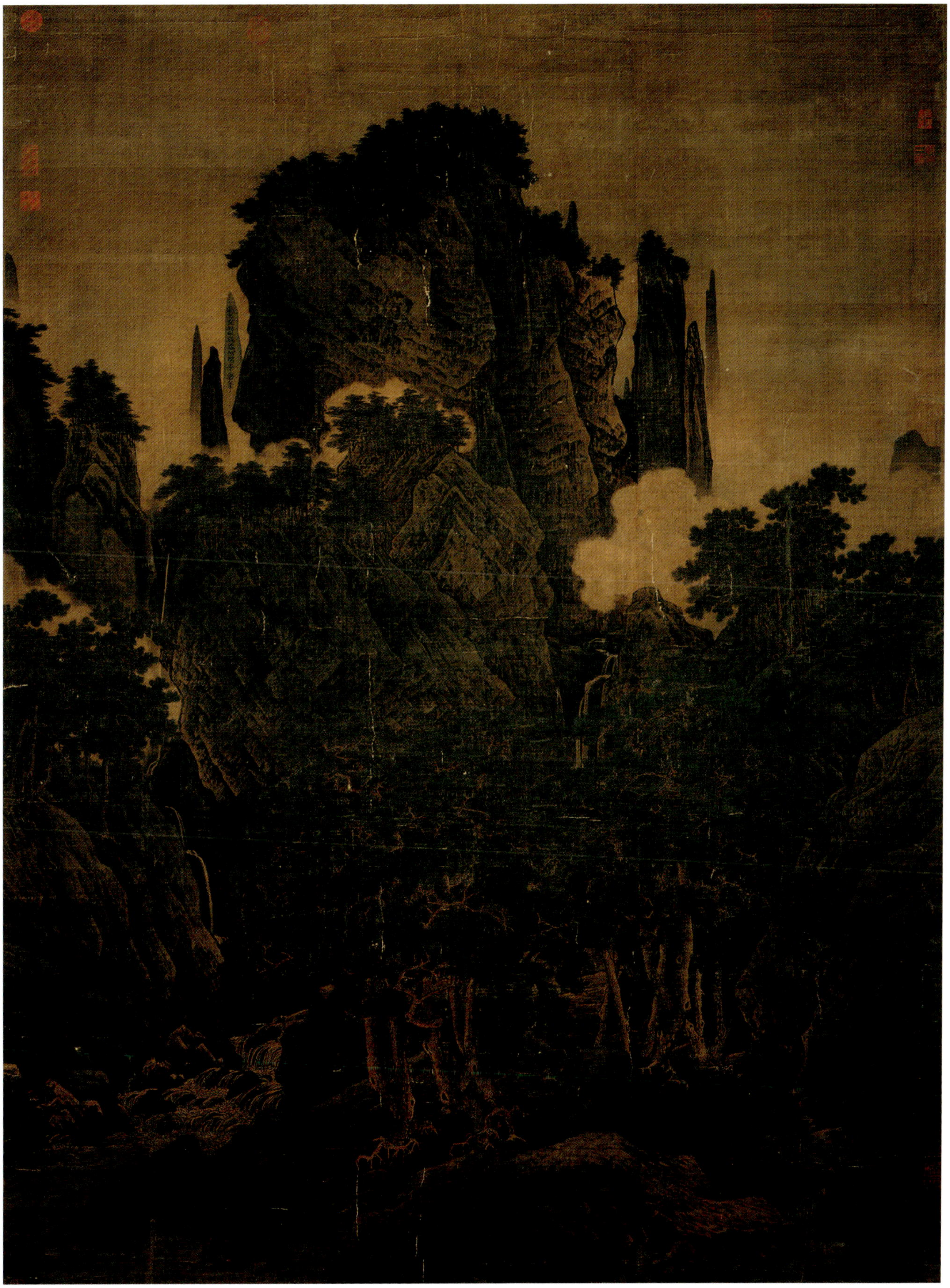

pass through men's hearts and the scenes before their eyes'.[6] In the early twelfth century, poetry education was introduced into the national School of Painting founded by Emperor Huizong (r. 1101–25); the students were given lines of poetry in their examinations, and required to turn them into subtle pictorial 'ideas'.

This general emphasis on poetic meaning in painting gave rise to a new kind of inscriptional practice, in which a poetic title, usually consisting of four characters, was given to a work, and more importantly, a long poetic text was sometimes juxtaposed with the picture. Thus, to his painting of a snowy river in the Palace Museum, Beijing, the early twelfth-century court painter Liang Shimin added the four-character title *Reeds along the Snowy Bank* above his name, while early examples of lengthy poetic artists' inscriptions include those by Hu Shunchen, Mi Youren (1074–1151/1086–1165) and Yang Wujiu (1097–1169). The work by Hu Shunchen in this exhibition (cat. no. 20), with a date of 1122, is thus one of the earliest extant paintings to bear a poem inscribed by the artist.

The emergence of lengthy poetic inscriptions in painting during the late eleventh and early twelfth centuries is significant in that, while the signature and title were discreetly integrated into the pictorial space, the poetic inscription, being relatively large, had an obvious tendency to subvert the painting's pictorial autonomy. However, evidence suggests that in general, Song dynasty painters laid emphasis on a work's pictorial integrity and were extremely careful with regard to inscriptions. In fact, during this period unsigned works still outnumbered signed ones, and among the signed works, artists seem to have preferred short, succinct inscriptions to long texts. In the late thirteenth and the beginning of the fourteenth centuries, however, the situation gradually changed, and from then on inscriptions were not only widely accepted, but had become the norm. By the end of the seventeenth century, artists' inscriptions were so popular that there was hardly a painting without one.

In the fourteenth century, many new inscriptional practices came into existence, pioneered by the literati-painters working in the lower Yangzi river delta. Being accomplished calligraphers and poets as well as painters, they had no hesitation in incorporating texts into their paintings. In the hanging scroll *Woods and Valleys of Mount Yu* by Ni Zan (1306–74) (cat. no. 51), the artist has placed his six-line text conspicuously in the expanse of the sky in the upper part of the picture. One may speculate that, rather than viewing it as an intrusion, the artist might have considered the text a necessity whereby it formed an integral part of a composite work of art in which image and text coexist, in addition to enriching the meaning of the painting. An extreme example of this image-text symbiosis can be found in the painting *Ink Orchid* (cat. no. 47) by Zheng Sixiao (1239–1316), which is dated to 1306: here, the minimal depiction of the orchid surrounded by the dense texts makes it difficult to classify the work as a painting, poetry, or both.

During this period, literati-artists increasingly used their paintings as a vehicle for social intercourse with other members of their class, which fuelled the popularity of another new element in inscriptions: dedications. In *Grooms and Horses* by Zhao Mengfu (1254–1322), his son Zhao Yong (1289–after 1360) and grandson Zhao Lin (act. 2nd half 14th century) (cat. no. 46), Zhao Mengfu's dedicatory sentence reads: 'On the tenth of the first lunar month in the second year of the Yuanzhen reign era [11 February 1296], I painted this *Groom and Horse* for Surveillance Commissioner Feiqing's pure enjoyment. Zhao Mengfu of Wuxing inscribed this'. The use of dedications already had a long history in painting; as discussed above, dedicatory words were usually seen in Buddhist painted banners of the Tang and Five Dynasties periods, and occasionally also appeared in inscriptions on paintings by twelfth-century artists, such as Hu Shunchen, Mi Youren and Yang Wujiu. However, in the fourteenth century they acquired a new, succinct form, and became part of the artist's signature. In traditional connoisseurial terminology, this type of signature consists of 'upper' and 'lower' elements, the upper element, or *shangkuan*, referring to the name of the dedicatee, and the lower element, or *xiakuan*, to the dedicator. The dedication of a fourteenth-century literati painting also differed from a ninth- or tenth-century painted Buddhist banner in that while the Buddhist dedication was a symbolic gesture, the dedication of a literati painting involved a real transferral of ownership from artist to recipient.

In the late thirteenth and fourteenth centuries, the use of seals also became part of the artist's common practice, and there was hardly a literati painter who did not add seal marks to his work. Typically, a fourteenth-century painter had two or more seals engraved with his personal name, courtesy name (*zi*), literary name (*hao*) or studio name (*shiming*). These seal marks customarily appear below the signature, but they could also be placed at a distance, as in *Emaciated Horse* by Gong Kai (1222–1307) (cat. no. 44). Apart from the various name seals, painters also began to use on their works so-called 'phrase seals' or *xianzhang*, a type of seal bearing no association with an artist's names but rather with mottoes, phrases or poetic lines somehow special to the artist. Qian Xuan's (*c*.1235–before 1307) *Doves and Pear Blossoms after Rain* (cat. no. 45), for example, bears the seal mark *han mo yae xi* ('brush and ink play'), and paintings by Wang Mian (1287–1359, cat. no. 48), Gong Kai and Zheng Sixiao (cat. no. 47) are also impressed with this type of seal. In Zheng Sixiao's *Ink Orchid*, the seal comprises a total of four phrases and sixteen characters, making it one of the longest inscriptions in the history of phrase seals.

While it is easy to identify innovations in the use of inscriptions and seals in the fourteenth century and earlier, it is not so simple later on. From the fifteenth century on, painters used the same basic types – short or long forms of signatures, poems or prose, and name or other seals – all of which had already been established by the fourteenth century. On the other hand, fashions, professional traditions and individual artists' intentions inevitably varied over such a long period, and differences and changes can be discerned in the ways in which these inscriptions and seal types were used. While artisan-painters working for the imperial court or for private clients in society, such as Dai Jin (1388–1462), Qiu Ying (1494/5–1552), Zeng Jing (1564–1647) or Ren Yi (1840–95), continued the pre-fourteenth century tradition, typically using the short form of inscriptions, the more elaborate style of inscription developed around the fourteenth century was popular among literati-painters. During the fifteenth and sixteenth centuries, long inscriptions in hanging scrolls were usually written in a blank area in the upper part of the painting, while in handscrolls they were added at the far end of the scroll; in the case of albums, they were placed on the pages facing the picture. Seal impressions generally appeared beneath the artist's signature. From the seventeenth century on, however, long inscriptions were more often placed inside the pictorial space, and their location within the painting became much more flexible. In albums, such as *Landscape Album* by Gong Xian (*c*.1619–89), the separation of painting and inscription is no longer seen, and inscriptions appear on the same pages as the images (cat. no. 70). The artist Zheng Xie (1693–1765) seems to have considered his inscriptions and seal marks to be a compositional element of the painting; in his hanging scrolls, the text is often either squeezed into blank areas in the lower part, or 'suspended' from the top edge (cat. no. 77).

From the fifteenth century, the sheer number of inscriptions and seal impressions also grew greatly. While poetic inscriptions continued to be used to enhance the meaning of the subject depicted, prose was favoured by literati-artists, through which medium they touched on a wide range of topics from artistic theory and the circumstances under which their painting were created to pertinent art-historical issues. The interest in art history was especially evident during the seventeenth century, when many literati painters were involved in passionate discussions concerning the Chinese painting tradition. The inscriptions in paintings by Dong Qichang (1555–1636), for example, were typically commentaries on the historical origins of painting styles (cat. no. 63). In later periods, individual artists also tended to give themselves more literary and studio names, which they used to sign their works and carve their seals. Bada Shanren (1626–1705), for instance, adopted about 20 different literary names in his life. While in his early Buddhist years he used the formal Buddhist name 'Chuanqi', after abandoning the monastic life he signed his work with other names, for the first four years using literary names such as 'lu' ('donkey') and finally, in 1684 at the age of 58, taking the name 'Bada Shanren', which he used for the remainder of his life.[7]

These extremely content-rich inscriptions and seal marks added to paintings by artists undoubtedly provide invaluable information for studying their lives and the evolution of their artistic ideas and styles. On the other hand, they sometimes present challenges, as the identity and exact meaning of some artists' seals can remain elusive. Bada Shanren's enigmatic 'slipper' seal, for example, was used frequently in his later career, but a conclusive reading has yet to be made.[8]

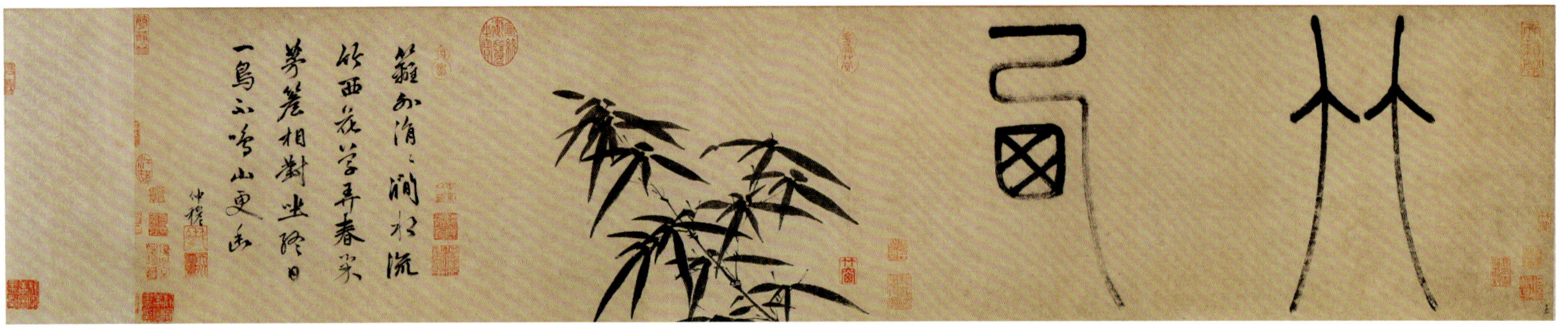

CONTEMPORARY AND LATER ADDITIONS

During the periods covered by this exhibition, it was not only the painters themselves who customarily inscribed and marked their work. In many cases, the artists' contemporaries (fellow artists, friends, clients and patrons), and most significantly, later generations of collectors and connoisseurs, all played their part in adding inscriptions and seal marks. Historically, the inclusion of inscriptions and seal marks by people other than the artists in fact predates their addition by the artists themselves, as even before painters enjoyed a status equal to poets, their work was admired, collected and catalogued.

Evidence suggests that the inscription of collectors' and connoisseurs' names on paintings seems to have been a standard practice from the fifth century.[9] According to Zhang Yanyuan in his *Record of Famous Painters of Successive Dynasties*, connoisseurs in charge of scroll conservation at the Tang imperial court were required to write their names on newly mounted works; such signatures were typically added at the end of the picture as *bawei* ('colophons').[10] A rare survival of the Tang signature-colophon can be seen at the end of Han Gan's (act. 742–56) *Night-Shining White* in the Metropolitan Museum, where Zhang Yanyuan's own name appears. Apart from the signature-colophon, the addition of a 'picture title' (*biaoti*) to paintings had also been an established practice for the imperial collections from very early on. The earliest surviving examples appear on works from the Tang and Five Dynasties periods, such as *Night-Shining White* and Zhao Gan's (act. mid-10th century) *Along the River at First Snow* (National Palace Museum, Taipei); in both cases, the picture title, written by the Southern Tang dynasty (937–75) emperor Li Yu (r. 961–75), appears in the upper right corner.

By the eleventh century, signature-colophons had gone out of fashion, to be replaced by colophons in the forms of poems and prose exploring and interpreting a particular image or theme. When these poem- or prose-colophons were first employed by poets and writers in the eleventh and twelfth centuries, it was in relation to the new interest among the literati in the ancient tradition of *tihua shi* or 'poems on paintings' (*ekphrasis*) as a sub-genre of poetry, which in turn was closely associated with the new intellectual trend that sought to promote the connection between poetry and painting. In 1187, during the reign of Emperor Xiaozong (1163–89), the first anthology of poems on paintings, *A Collection of Sound Paintings*,[11] was compiled by a scholar called Sun Shaoyuan (act. 2nd half 12th century); it comprised over 800 poems on paintings, some of which were evidently written as colophons. From then on, poem- or prose-colophons were no longer inscribed on the picture itself, as were the Tang signature-colophons. Instead, they were written on a separate sheet of paper, and then, in a mounting studio, attached to the end of the picture as part of the same scroll. This practice of separating colophon and picture gradually became a tradition and was continuously respected, as illustrated by a number of scrolls across the period covered by the exhibition.

After the twelfth century, two new elements adopted in the inscriptions on scroll paintings were the *yinshou*, or 'frontispiece', and *shitang*, or 'poetry hall'. The former, attached to the beginning of a handscroll and typically consisting of a four-character poetic phrase, is thought to have first appeared in the early fifteenth century; however, its origins can be traced back to the fourteenth century, as seen in *Thatched Cottage to the West of the Bamboo Grove* by Zhao Yong (1289–after 1360) (fig. 32).[12] The poetry hall was probably also invented at some point during the Ming dynasty (1368–1644),[13] with the aim of providing an alternative space for colophons on hanging scrolls; it was attached above and/or below the picture later on, after the work was completed. A good example in the present exhibition is *Fragrant Snow at Broken Bridge* (cat. no. 48) by Wang Mian, in which two poetry halls bear inscriptions by a late fifteenth- and a twentieth-century collector, respectively. When a hanging scroll did not have such a 'poetry hall', the colophon would simply have been written on the (usually damask) mount, as

FIG. 32
Zhang Wo (act. 1336–c.1364) and Zhao Yong (1239–after 1360). *Thatched Cottage to the West of the Bamboo Grove* handscroll (detail of the frontispiece by Zhao Yong), 14th century. Ink and colour on silk. Liaoning Provincial Museum

FIG. 33
Possibly Emperor Huizong (1082–1135). *Hibiscus and Golden Pheasant* hanging scroll, c.1101–25. Ink and colour on silk. The Palace Museum, Beijing

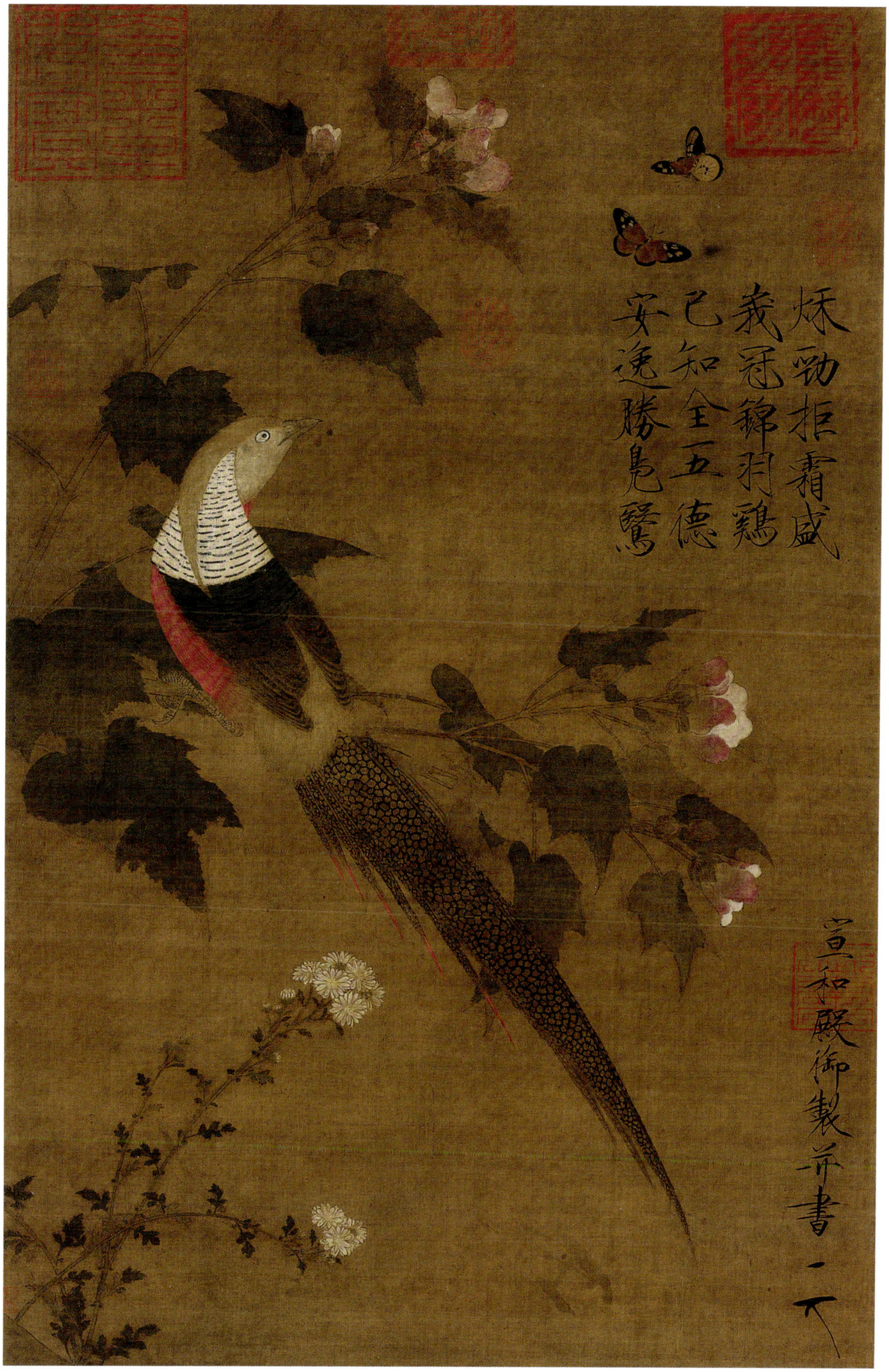

is the case in *Clouds and Mist in the Mountains* by Fa Ruozhen (1613–96); in this painting, the collector Wu Cizhi (act. mid-19th century) has composed a short biography of the artist on the mounting strip on the left (cat. no. 73).

Historically, there were a small number of inscribers whose approach was distinctively different from those discussed above. Rather than on the periphery of the painting, they placed their inscriptions – usually poems – on the painting surface proper, an area conventionally reserved for the painter. Pioneered by the Northern Song emperor Huizong (fig. 33), these inscribers included several Southern Song (1127–1279) emperors and their consorts, thirteenth- and fourteenth-century Chan monks and literati, and above all, the Qing dynasty (1644–1911) emperor Qianlong (r. 1736–96). In the case of the Song dynasty emperors and their consorts, the addition of such inscriptions was part of the imperial commission: probably, a poem or couplet was first given to the court artist, based on which he produced a painting; then after the painting had been submitted, the poem was inscribed by the imperial hand onto a designated space within the painting. Several paintings in the present exhibition (cat. nos 28, 29, 31, 32) were certainly the result of this system of commission, although their inscriptions appear beyond the painting itself. The same system must also have been adapted by the Chan monks and literati, judging by the vast space reserved for their inscriptions in the upper part of the painting (cat. nos 43, 50). The case of the Qianlong emperor is strikingly different, for not only did he place his long inscriptions on paintings by his court artists, but also on works in his collection by ancient masters – and in so doing, unintentionally changed the original composition of the paintings (cat. no. 51).

Apart from inscriptions, seal marks were also added by people other than the artist, especially collectors and connoisseurs. From the early twelfth century on, imperial collectors characteristically used sets of seals for the paintings in their collections, and devised various patterns for their placement. For instance, Emperor Huizong typically marked his handscroll painting collections with seven seals, four at the corners of the painting surface proper and the remaining three on the mount; all of the seals but one were impressed at joins. Such seal marks were therefore known as 'bridging seals' (*qifeng yin*). This set number and pattern invented by Huizong was followed by the Jin dynasty (1115–1234) emperor Zhangzong (r. 1190–1208) for his collection, and the painting *Court Ladies Preparing Newly Woven Silk* in the present exhibition is one of the rare works demonstrating the standard placement of his seals in the corners and on the mount (see fig. 34). The Qianlong emperor in the eighteenth century normally used five seals for his painting collection, but there are also many examples where the number is greater, especially when he had inscribed his own poems

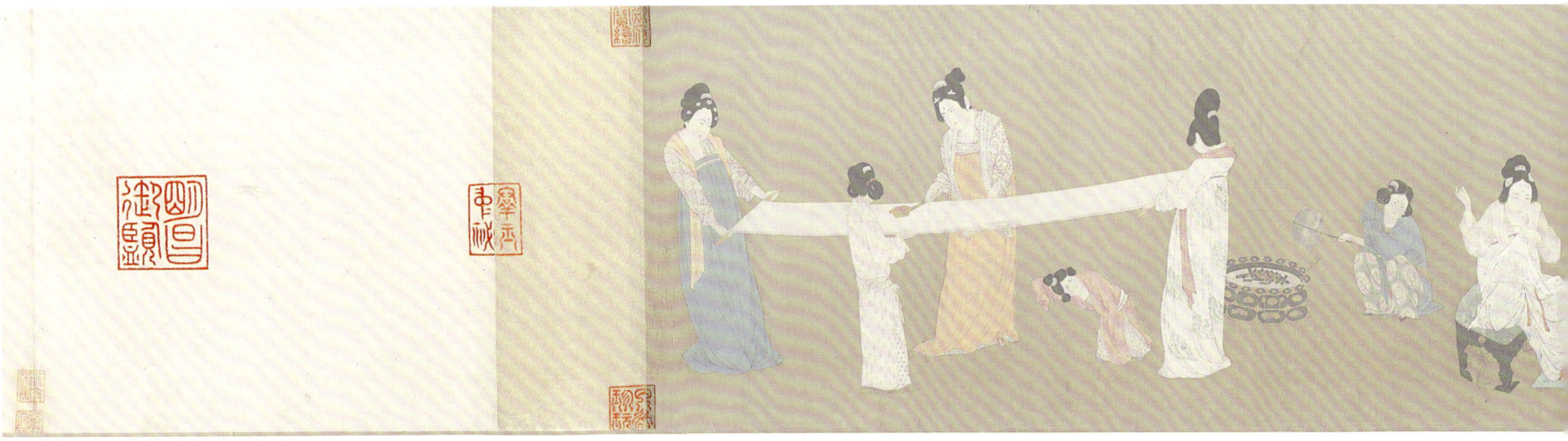

on a work. Generally, the Qianlong emperor's seal marks appear near the upper edge of the painting surface proper. By contrast, the seals of private collectors, such as Xiang Yuanbian (1525–90), Liang Qingbiao (1620–91) and An Qi (1683–1742), were usually clustered around the lower corners (see cat. no. 51).

In conclusion, the use of inscriptions and seal marks in Chinese paintings from the period surveyed in this exhibition was subject to modification, with a general tendency towards an increase in quantity and variety. At the same time, the continual tension between word and image should not be overlooked. The artist's sensitivity to the autonomy of the pictorial space, combined with the gradual expansion of literati culture, were probably the most important factors behind the changes. While a study of inscriptions and seal marks can provide invaluable insights into the worlds of artists and their viewers, it would be misleading to be overly insistent on their importance – a masterpiece such as *Flowers on the River* (cat. no. 74) by Bada Shanren, for example, bears no Qing imperial inscriptions or seals. Being a descendant of the royal family of the fallen Ming dynasty and a stubborn loyalist, it is not surprising that his art was not appreciated by the new dynasty and that his works did not enter the Qing imperial collections. Indeed, one may argue that the lacuna is significant in itself.

1 A detailed narrative of inscriptions and seal marks in Chinese painting has yet to be written. This author has benefited from the existing scholarship, particularly New Haven 1977, pp. 179–89; Xu 1981, pp. 29–41; Murck and Fong 1991; and Xu 2000. See also Zhang 2005.
2 Ouyang 2008
3 Acker 1954, pp. 118–19
4 He 1998, p. 181
5 Ma 1997, p. 27
6 Bush and Shih 1985, p. 158
7 See Wang in New Haven 1990, pp. 30–2.
8 See Washington 2003, p. 25.
9 Acker 1954, p. 216
10 Ibid., pp. 222–30
11 Sun (1187) in Lu 1993–8, vol. 2, pp. 360–427.
12 For different views on the origin of the *yinshou* in paintings, see Xu 1981, p. 35; New Haven 1977, p. 185.
13 See Zhou (1650–1) 1993.

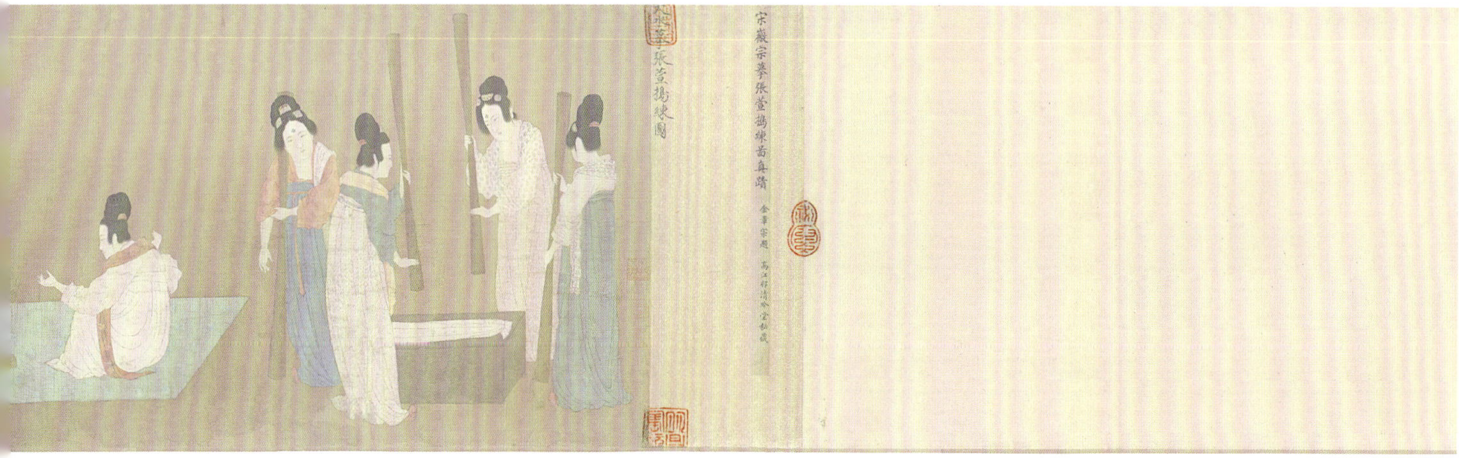

FIG. 34
*Court Ladies Preparing Newly Woven Silk* (cat. no. 16), showing Emperor Zhangzong's seals

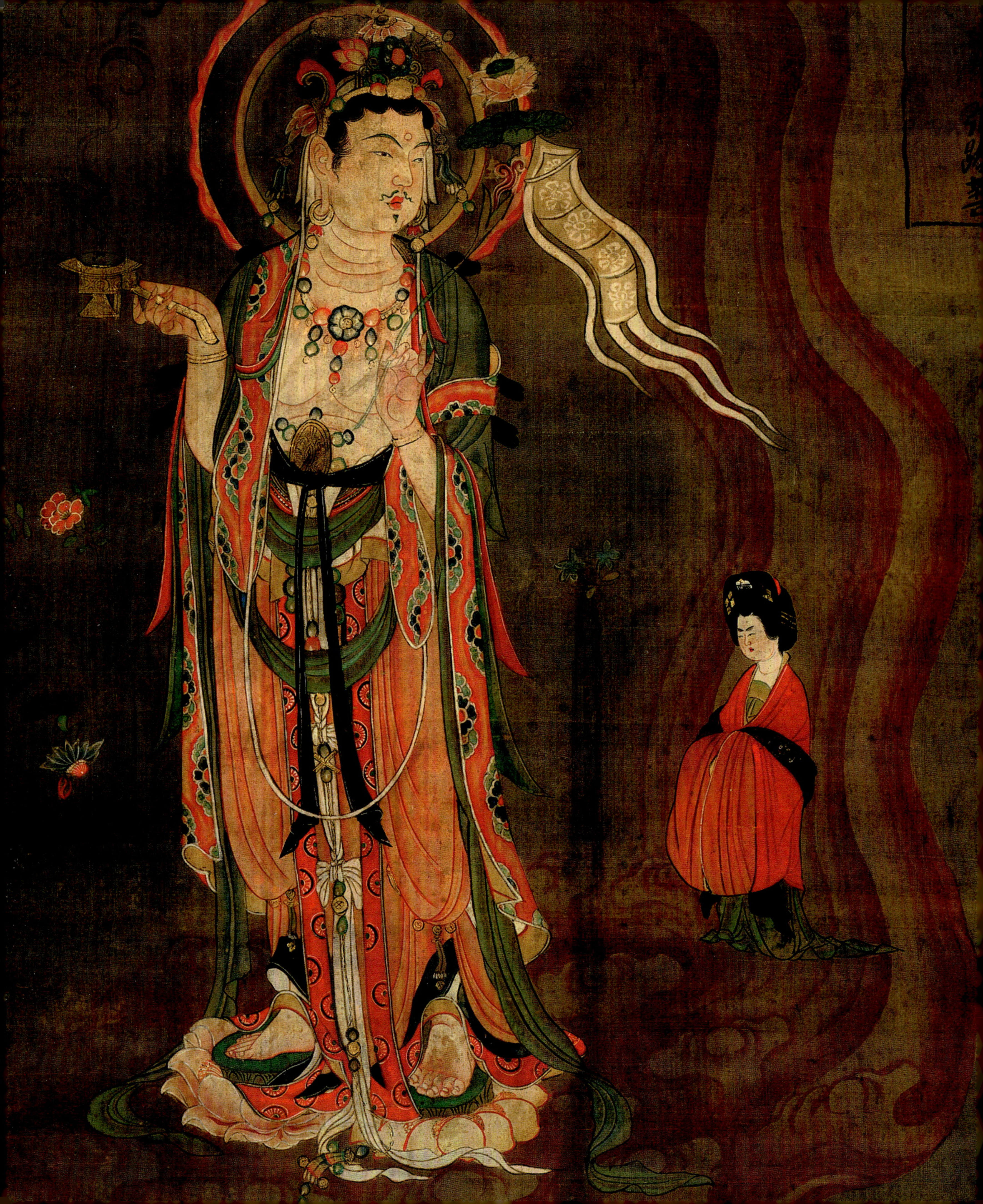

# SETTING MILESTONES

## COLLECTING CLASSICAL CHINESE PAINTINGS IN EUROPE

Clarissa von Spee

Chinese paintings have entered European collections since the sixteenth century, a time when Europe had established maritime trade connections with China. Classical Chinese paintings, however, that is paintings which were primarily produced for a Chinese or an Asian audience, were not systematically collected in Europe until the end of the nineteenth century.[1] The story of collecting Chinese paintings in Europe is a complex topic, and a complete overview is beyond the scope of this essay. Due to limitations of length, it will focus on developments in Britain, France and Germany, while collecting activities in countries such as Sweden, Switzerland, Italy, Russia, Poland and the Czech Republic will be discussed only marginally or not at all. The essay will present some major acquisitions of paintings that were integrated into museum collections in Europe from the sixteenth to the mid-twentieth century. By reconstructing the circumstances of these acquisitions, the author hopes to be able to identify some key players and to explore the understanding of these works within their time.

### PAINTINGS AS DIPLOMATIC GIFTS AND OBJECTS OF SCHOLARLY CURIOSITY

From the sixteenth to the mid-eighteenth century, Chinese paintings seem to have entered European collections primarily to satisfy their owner's curiosity about foreign lands or for use as diplomatic gifts. In 1565, the Bavarian court official Samuel Quiccheberg (1529–67) in Munich referred to the royal cabinet of curiosities there as a *theatris sapientiae* – a 'theatre of wisdom'.[2] In his opinion, objects and pictures from all fields of knowledge and all parts of the world could say more than could a thousand words. Pictures and paintings were therefore ideal media for teaching and educating the princes at court, giving them a comprehensive knowledge of the known world. Inventories of the cabinets of curiosities ('Kunst- und Wunderkammern') in Munich and Dresden in Germany and elsewhere in Europe list paintings from Japan and China as early as the sixteenth and seventeenth centuries.[3] The best known are probably a set of four Chinese paintings on silk in hanging scroll format from the estate of Archduke Ferdinand II (1529–95) of Austria from the House of Habsburg, which have been preserved in the collection of Ambras Castle in Innsbruck since 1596 (fig. 35).[4] While the exact circumstances of the acquisition are unclear, the four scrolls were presumably presented to the Archduke as diplomatic gifts, perhaps through Ferdinand's cousin, Philip II of Spain, who maintained territories and trade connections in East Asia. In China, such decorative paintings featuring architecture in landscape settings, figures and birds-and-flowers embellished the interiors of larger residences. Bird-and-flower paintings were often presented as gifts to express auspicious wishes for a birthday, success in an examination or retirement from an official career. In another instance, an inventory book of 1640 from the court of Dresden registers an 'Indian' – that is a Chinese or Japanese – 'picture album'. This picture album and a scroll, both painted on paper, were part of a series of diplomatic gifts that were exchanged along with other objects from Asia, including a group of Chinese ceramics, between the Grand Duke Fernando I of Medici in Florence and the court in Dresden in the 1580s and 1590s, to reaffirm their political alliance.[5]

The activity of collecting foreign objects and pictures to educate and teach the curious viewer about foreign civilizations remains relevant during the Age of Enlightenment in the seventeenth and eighteenth centuries. An album with fish collected by Sir Hans Sloane (1660–1753), the founding father of the British Museum, illustrates this attitude (fig. 36). Trained both as a botanist

cat. no. 9 (detail)

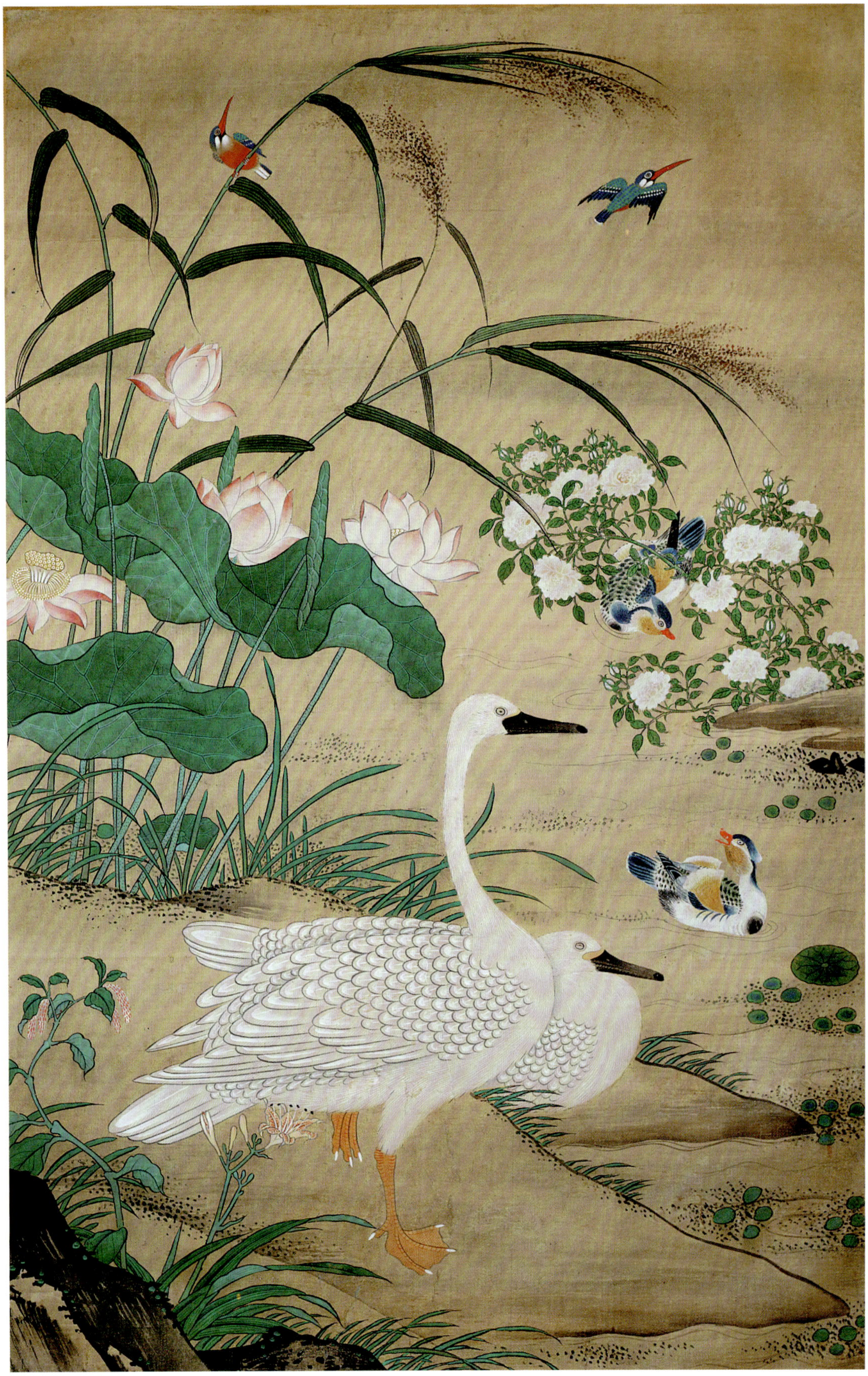

FIG. 35
Birds and Flowers hanging scroll, 16th century. Ink and colour on silk. Kunstkammer Kunsthistorisches Museum, Vienna (KK–8912)

FIG. 36
Yuan Shijing (act. 17th century). *Fish*, 17th century. Leaf from an album of 11 leaves. Ink on paper. The British Museum, London (1928,0323,0.43.1–11)

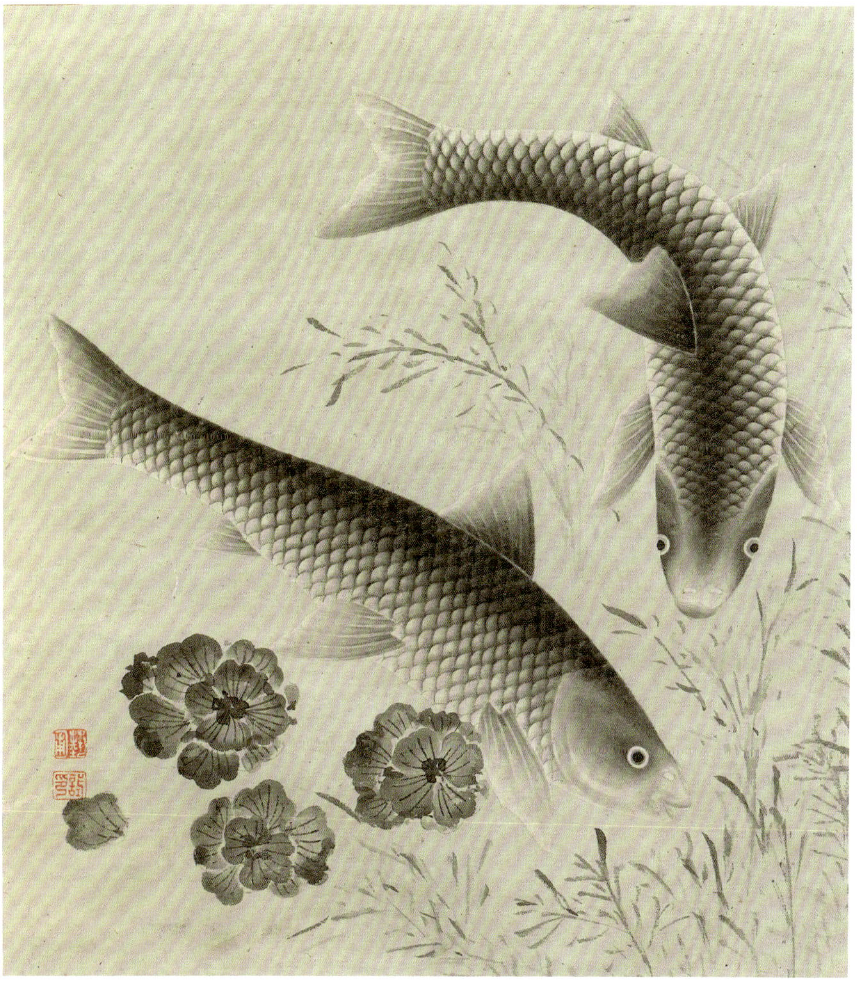

and as a physician, in which capacity he had served the royal household in England, Sloane acquired prints and drawings from all over the world to serve his scientific and scholarly interests.[6] While on a 15-month stay in Jamaica, he recorded and collected the local Caribbean flora and fauna, and during his lifetime assembled one of the largest collections of antiquities, sculptures, books and manuscripts, stuffed animals, minerals and plants of his time. Upon his death in 1753, Sloane bequeathed his collection to the British nation, a legacy which formed the founding collections of three national institutions: the British Museum, the Museum of Natural History and the British Library. The album in the British Museum presents 11 different kinds of fish. A seal reading *yi pu* impressed on each page identifies the artist as Yuan Shijing (act. 17th century) from Zhejiang Province, who had a reputation for painting flowers and plants.[7] In China, fish are associated with prosperity and abundance. They are also part of the daily diet, and watching fish is traditionally associated with a famous dispute between the philosophers Zhuangzi (or Zhuang Zhou, *c.*369–286 BCE) and Huizi (or Hui Shi, 380–305 BCE).[8] Hans Sloane, who acquired the album from a certain Mr Butler, was probably unaware of either its auspicious and possible philosophical connotations or the artistic qualities for which it would have been appreciated in China. However, the accurate portrayal of various species of fish would have satisfied his scientific interest and curiosity.

Another fine painting in the British Museum collection, *Fascination of Nature*, is – in a strict sense – believed to be the first classical Chinese painting to have reached Europe (fig. 37).[9] Whereas the paintings previously mentioned, namely the set of four decorative scrolls from Ambras Castle and the fish album from the collection of Hans Sloane, were presumably produced for sale on the open market either to Chinese or some rare foreign clients, *Fascination of Nature* was clearly made with the educated Chinese elite in mind. The silk painting in its distinctively Chinese handscroll format is signed and dated, and bears a calligraphic title and colophons by contemporaries of the artist. Interestingly, the scroll is inscribed on the inside wrapper with the name of its former owner, 'William

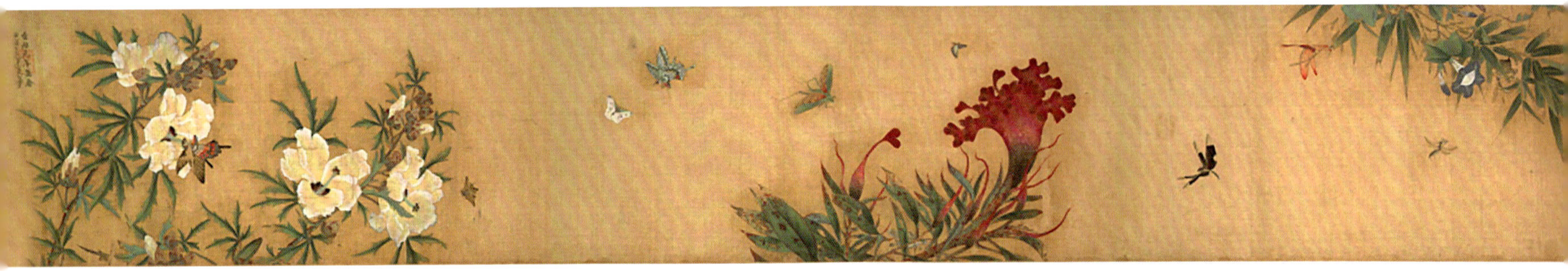

FIG. 37
Xie Chufang (act. 14th century). *Fascination of Nature* handscroll (detail), 1321. Ink and colour on silk. The British Museum, London (1998,1112,0.1.CH)

Butler', and the year '1796'.[10] William Butler (1748–1822) from Bristol was a writing master who taught young ladies in the East End of London. While it is not known how the scroll came into his possession, it is possible that the painting was brought to Europe by a member of the first embassy sent to China from Britain in 1792 under the direction of Lord Macartney (1737–1806). Although politically unsuccessful, the embassy had been invited by the Qianlong emperor (r. 1736–96) to attend his 80th birthday celebrations in his summer retreat, the Bishu shanzhuang, in Chengde, north of Beijing. Dated 1321, this painting is the only work by the Yuan dynasty (1271–1368) artist Xie Chufang (act. 14th century) known to survive. It portrays with breathtaking delicacy and accuracy a detailed drama of the natural world. In one scene, a mantis grapples with a cicada. In another, a procession of ants carrying parts of a dismembered butterfly is watched by a toad which lies in ambush under a cabbage leaf, waiting to pick them off. This struggle for survival together with a reading of the inscriptions has been convincingly interpreted by Roderick Whitfield as a possible allusion to the struggle for survival of the Chinese educated elite under the foreign Mongol government during the Yuan dynasty.[11]

## THE FIRST GENERATION OF COLLECTORS AND JAPAN

As previously mentioned, it was not until the nineteenth century that classical Chinese paintings began to be collected systematically in Europe. As the majority came initially from Japan, it is therefore necessary to turn our attention first to that country, where Chinese paintings had been collected since the fifteenth century, during the Muromachi period (1336–1573), and earlier.[12] Paintings of the Southern Song dynasty (1127–1279), Zhe school paintings from the Ming dynasty (1368–1644) and scrolls by other professional painters had been taken to Japan by Japanese monks and merchants, where they were studied and held in high esteem. However, Ming dynasty Wu school paintings and those by the Four Wangs of the Qing dynasty (1644–1911) rarely entered Japanese collections before the late nineteenth century. The Chinese artist Dong Qichang's (1555–1636) theory of the inferiority of Southern Song and Zhe school painters was not shared in Japan; in fact, Southern Song and Zhe school paintings had a major impact on Japanese art. The popularity of Chinese paintings in Japan also attracted numerous workshop copies of the Ming dynasty, while Chinese paintings were copied there as well, in particular by artists of the Kano school.

The study of Chinese and Japanese art history in Japan was further stimulated by the aesthetic theories of Ernest F. Fenollosa (1853–1908) from America and his student Okakura Kakuzo (1862–1913) in the early Meiji period (1868–1912). Fenollosa had graduated from Harvard University, and went to Japan in 1878. He taught philosophy at the Imperial University of Tokyo, and began collecting paintings two years later.[13] Fenollosa ranked painting as the highest artistic expression in Asia.[14] Since China's defeat by Japan in the First Sino-Japanese War in 1895, the Japanese government aimed to present Japan as the leading cultural nation in Asia. Fenollosa's disrespect for the tradition of literati painting of the Ming and Qing dynasties as practised by the leading Chinese elite supported the Japanese government's policy of creating the image of a weak China. This, in turn, influenced the perception of early Western collectors. In his *Epochs of Japanese and Chinese Art* (completed in 1908), Fenollosa writes:

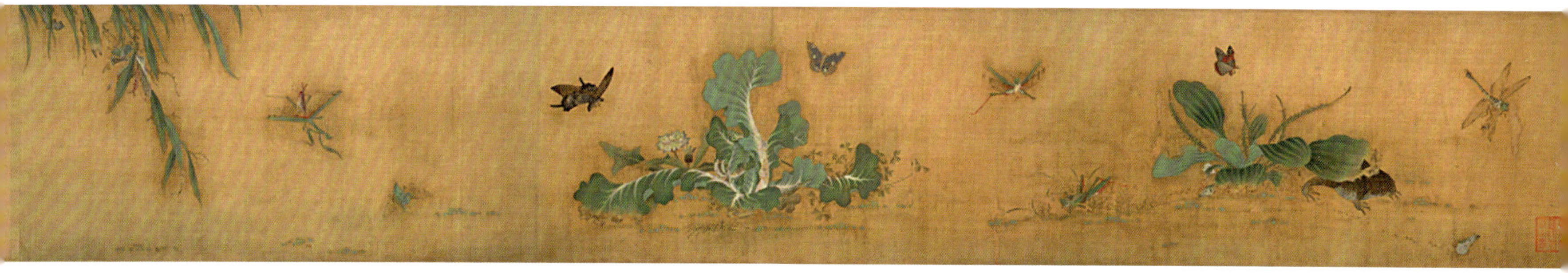

> The decay of modern Chinese art already foreshadowed by the middle of the Ming dynasty, is most conspicuous in pictorial art ... The modern Confucian government is a government of corrupt puritans ... The enormous evil of the impudent 'bunjinga' [Ch. *wenrenhua*; 'literati painting'] hypothesis, that soon stamped itself as orthodox in the belief of all China scholars, was a degeneration of art so rapid that by the end of the Ming hardly a respectable piece of work could be done.[15]

In Japan, the destruction of Buddhist temples and changes in the social order during the Meiji restoration caused Chinese and Japanese paintings from temples and private collections to become available on the market. Japan's opening and the call for Westernization by the government brought foreigners to the country, who began to collect art.

William Anderson (1842–1900) from Britain was one of the first to be invited to Japan. He went there in 1873. Anderson was employed at the Japanese Naval Medical hospital in Tokyo, and spent six years training Japanese physicians. During his stay, Anderson assembled over 2,000 mostly Japanese paintings, including some 114 Chinese scrolls. This was the first group of classical Chinese paintings to be acquired by the British Museum. They entered the collection in 1881.[16] Without any study or publication in a Western language available, many of Anderson's Chinese paintings bear false attributions to old masters or are in fact copies of Chinese paintings by Kano school artists. Most of them are hanging scrolls. The Anderson collection also reflects the lack of literati school paintings in Japan.

Likewise an amateur, Henri Cernuschi (1821–96), who came from a wealthy family in Milan, left Italy after his involvement in revolutionary activities and struggles for democracy and independence in 1848.[17] He made his career as an economist and banker in France, and then left Europe to travel to Japan and China, where he stayed from 1871 to 1873. Cernuschi assembled an impressive collection of Chinese bronzes and ceramics, as well as a few paintings, which was put on display in Paris in the Palais de l'Industrie as early as 1873–4. Upon his death in 1896, Cernuschi bequeathed his mansion and around 5,000 artefacts from Asia to the city of Paris. The Musée Cernuschi opened two years later, in 1898. Among the few paintings then in the collection and possibly on display was a striking finger painting by Gao Qipei (1660?–1734) featuring the auspicious motifs of deer and pine trees (fig. 38).[18] Gao's subtle use of colours in this work is particularly noteworthy.

Finger-painting was revived and practised by bannermen during the Manchu Qing dynasty in opposition to the orthodox literati tradition practised by the Chinese elite.[19] Encouraged by the Shunzhi (r. 1644–62), Kangxi (r. 1662–1722) and Qianlong emperors, finger-painting reached its highest artistic level in the eighteenth century. Finger paintings must still have been popular and available on the open market in north China during the nineteenth century, as Cernuschi acquired a number of them.[20] Mostly figurative, hardly any of them feature a landscape, a subject so important to the Chinese connoisseur. Finger paintings by Gao Qipei and by his follower Fu Wen (act. 1744–65) were on display in the Louvre in 1904 and at the Musée Cernuschi in 1912.[21] However, the genre did not regain scholarly attention in Europe until Klaas Ruitenbeek organized the exhibition *Discarding the Brush. Gao Qipei (1660–1734) and the Art of Chinese Finger Painting* at the Rijksmuseum in Amsterdam in 1992.[22]

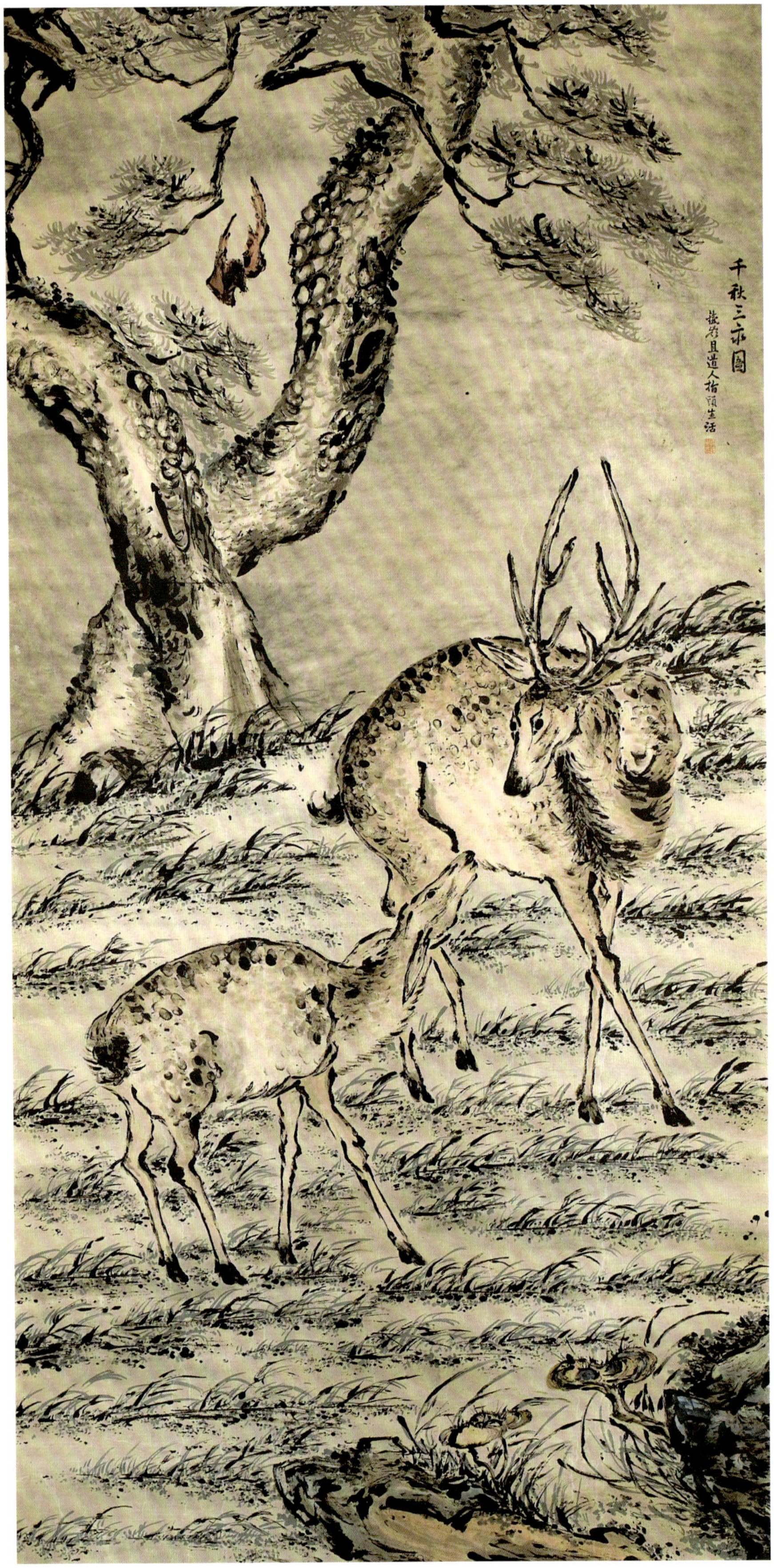

FIG. 38
Gao Qipei (1660?–1734). *Painting of 1,000 Autumns* hanging scroll, late 17th–early 18th century.
Ink and colour on paper.
Musée Cernuschi, Paris (MC 4463)

FIG. 39
*Beggar-Singer with Hound* hanging scroll, 14th century. Ink and colour on silk. Museum of East Asian Art, Cologne (A2)

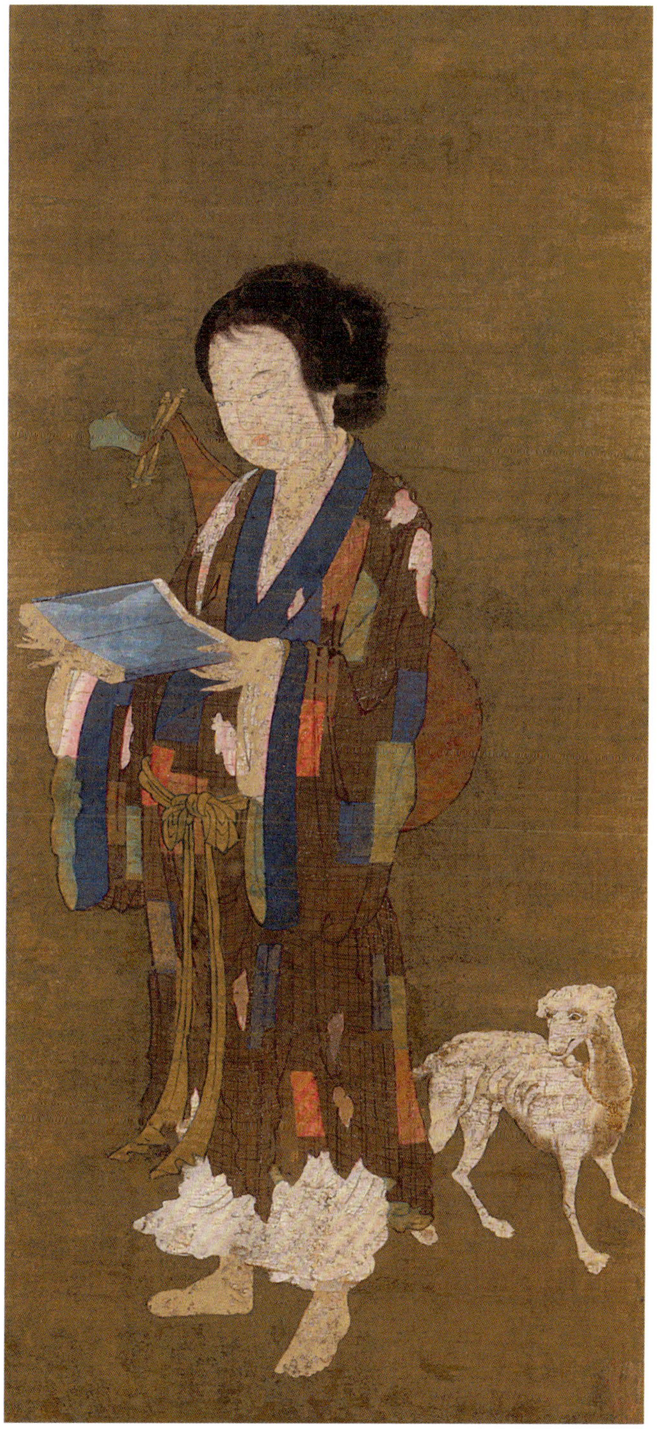

The German couple Adolph and Frieda Fischer (1857–1914) likewise acquired a number of finger paintings during their 10 years of travels in Asia between 1897 and 1907.[23] After completing his education in Switzerland, Adolph Fischer joined one of his father's businesses in Vienna and Prague. Finding this conflicted with his 'artistic soul', however, he then decided to become an actor, and eventually, like so many of his contemporaries, left Europe to travel the world. He spent some years in Berlin, where he developed the idea of founding a museum devoted exclusively to the high arts of China, Korea and Japan. Once in East Asia the couple studied collections in Japanese temples and museums, embarked on adventurous journeys into the Chinese countryside, and acquired art from dealers and agents in Beijing, Tokyo and Kyoto. Whenever Fischer purchased a work of art, he would look for a comparable piece in a temple or museum collection. Fischer developed a remarkable eye for quality. The Chinese paintings he acquired for the Museum of East Asian Art in Cologne remain highlights of the collection.[24] Among them are the two anonymous Yuan dynasty paintings *Beggar-Singer with Hound* (fig. 39) and *Lotus*. Another is a monumental Zhe school masterwork, *Two Men Conversing Beneath Cliffs*, which Richard Barnhart has attributed to Li Zhu (act. 1st half 16th century). Fischer's plans to found a museum of East Asian art were eventually approved by the authorities of the city of Cologne in 1906. The museum opened in 1913.

## RELIGIOUS PAINTINGS AND EXPLORERS IN CENTRAL ASIA

Another museum founder, the French industrialist Émile Guimet (1836–1918), arrived in Japan in 1876.[25] Guimet bought a great number of Buddhist works of art, particularly sculpture. It was his intention and mission to gather objects with a religious function in order to deepen the understanding of Asian religions in Europe. In 1879, Guimet presented his collection of Asian art to his hometown of Lyon, where it was housed in what became the first museum in Europe to specialize in Asian culture.[26]

The Musée Guimet in Paris was founded 10 years later, in 1889, with the transfer of the collection to the capital. Guimet's mission to further the appreciation of Asian religions in Europe also led the French scholar Paul Pelliot (1878–1945) in 1900 to acquire 33 Daoist and Buddhist paintings of the fifteenth century in Beijing (fig. 40).[27] In 1908, Pelliot returned to Paris with more religious paintings, this time mostly Buddhist paintings from the cave site of Dunhuang in north-west China (for example cat. nos 2–12). These silk paintings and banners from the so-called 'library cave' also entered the collections of the Musée Guimet.[28]

One year earlier, in 1907, Aurel Stein (1862–1943) had passed through Dunhuang on his second Silk Road expedition.[29] On his arrival, Stein negotiated with the local caretaker at the site, Wang Yuanlu, and persuaded the monk to allow him to view the cave's manuscripts and paintings. Stein eventually removed part of the contents in return for a small sum to help Wang Yuanlu fund the restoration of the caves. He shipped manuscripts, paintings, printed materials and textiles to London, where they arrived in 1909.[30] The material came to be divided between the British Museum, the National Museum in New Delhi, the Victoria and Albert Museum and the British Library. Over 300 silk paintings and banners remain today in the British Museum (cat. nos 1, 9). In 1910, together with the Anderson collection and the *Admonitions of the Court Instructress to the Palace Ladies* scroll acquired in 1903,[31] the paintings from Dunhuang were shown at the British Museum for the first time.[32] In 1914, paintings collected by Stein were again on display. In the same year, another religious scroll with a Daoist theme, *Deity with Phoenix*, was exhibited at the British Museum for the first time (cat. no. 59).[33] Meanwhile, just a few years earlier in 1907, the expeditions to Turfan and Kizil in Central Asia undertaken by Albert von Le Coq (1860–1930) and Albert Grünwedel (1856–1935) had brought impressive wall painting fragments to Berlin.[34]

These important collections of religious paintings in Paris, London and Berlin form a unique group of early material for the study of the history of painting and religions in Asia. The paintings were acquired at a time when China was experiencing military confrontations with foreign powers followed by humiliating concessions for peace. China's military inferiority eventually resulted in nationalistic, anti-foreign movements that were supported in part by the Qing government. In addition to these circumstances, civil war in China made travel in the country particularly challenging.

## CHINESE PAINTINGS COLLECTED BETWEEN THE WORLD WARS AND BEYOND

During the nineteenth century, the world expositions in London in 1851, in Paris in 1867 and in Vienna in 1873 offered first encounters with the craftsmanship and culture of Japan and China. It is important to note that the first European collectors of Chinese paintings, such as Anderson from England, Cernuschi from France and the Fischers from Germany, were hardly familiar with either the Japanese or Chinese language.[35] They chose to travel first to Japan, and acquired Chinese paintings primarily in the Japanese taste.

Two outstanding representatives of the next generation of scholars to collect Asian art were the previously mentioned Paul Pelliot from France and the German Otto Kümmel (1874–1952).[36] Kümmel was a university professor and the first director of the Department of East Asian Art at the State Museums in Berlin. While Pelliot was fluent in Chinese, Kümmel was confident in Japanese. Both men set high academic standards, and shaped a new generation of scholars in the field of Asian art.[37] The systematic collection of Chinese paintings in Berlin began in 1906 with the establishment of the Department of East Asian Art and Kümmel's subsequent appointment as its director. Like the American Fenollosa, Kümmel considered painting to be the highest form of art in East Asia. His prime criterion for the selection of a work was its aesthetic and artistic quality, and he aimed to represent the arts of China, Japan and Korea on an equal basis. Before the First World War, Kümmel acquired most of his paintings in Japan. Among the more important examples is an album with 12 works by masters of the Song (960–1279) to the Ming dynasty,

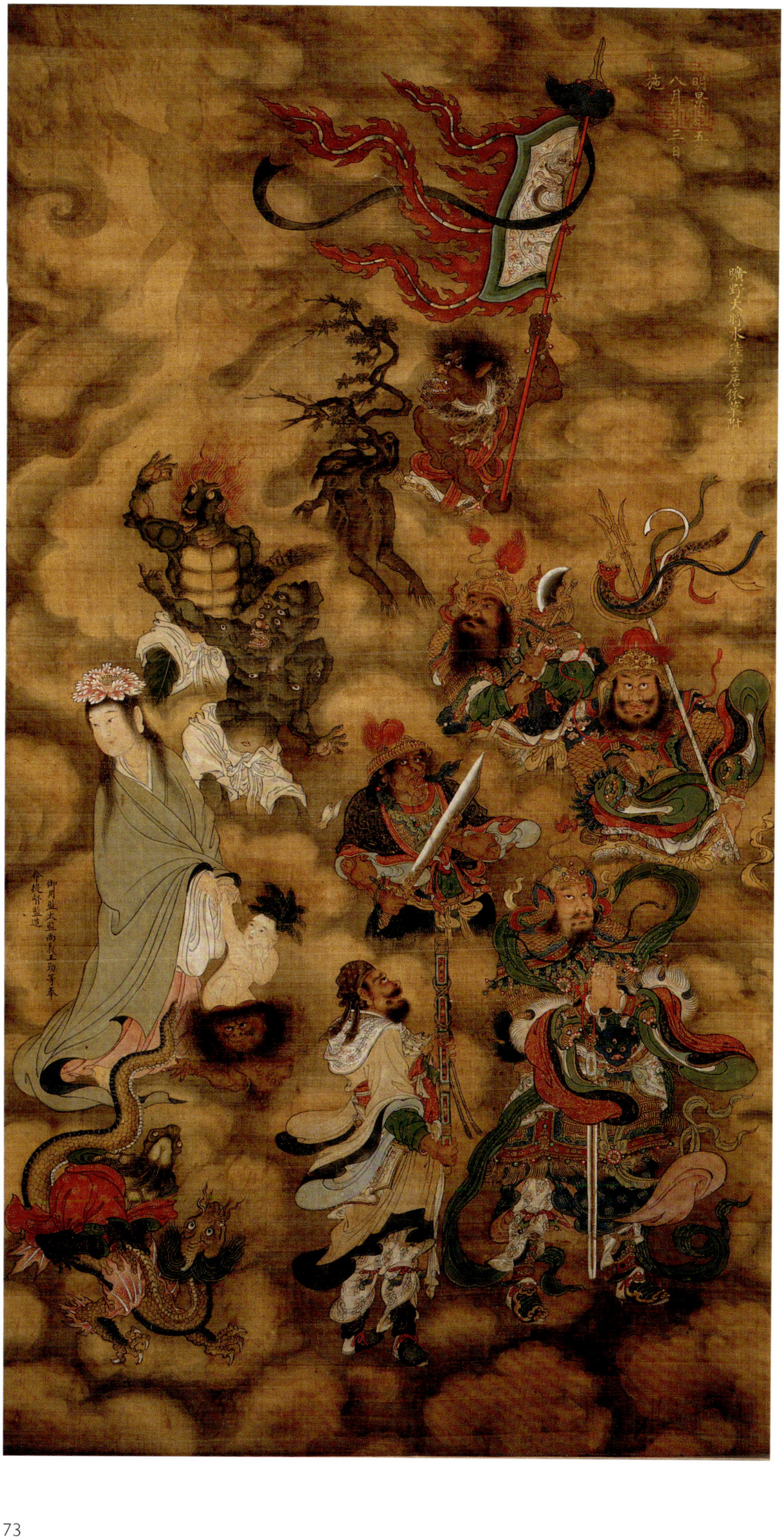

FIG. 40
*Great Generals of the Deserts and the Spirits of Grasses and Trees who Dwell in the Void of Water and Land* hanging scroll, 1454. Ink, colour and gold on silk. Musée Guimet, Paris (Pelliot Collection, EO 684)

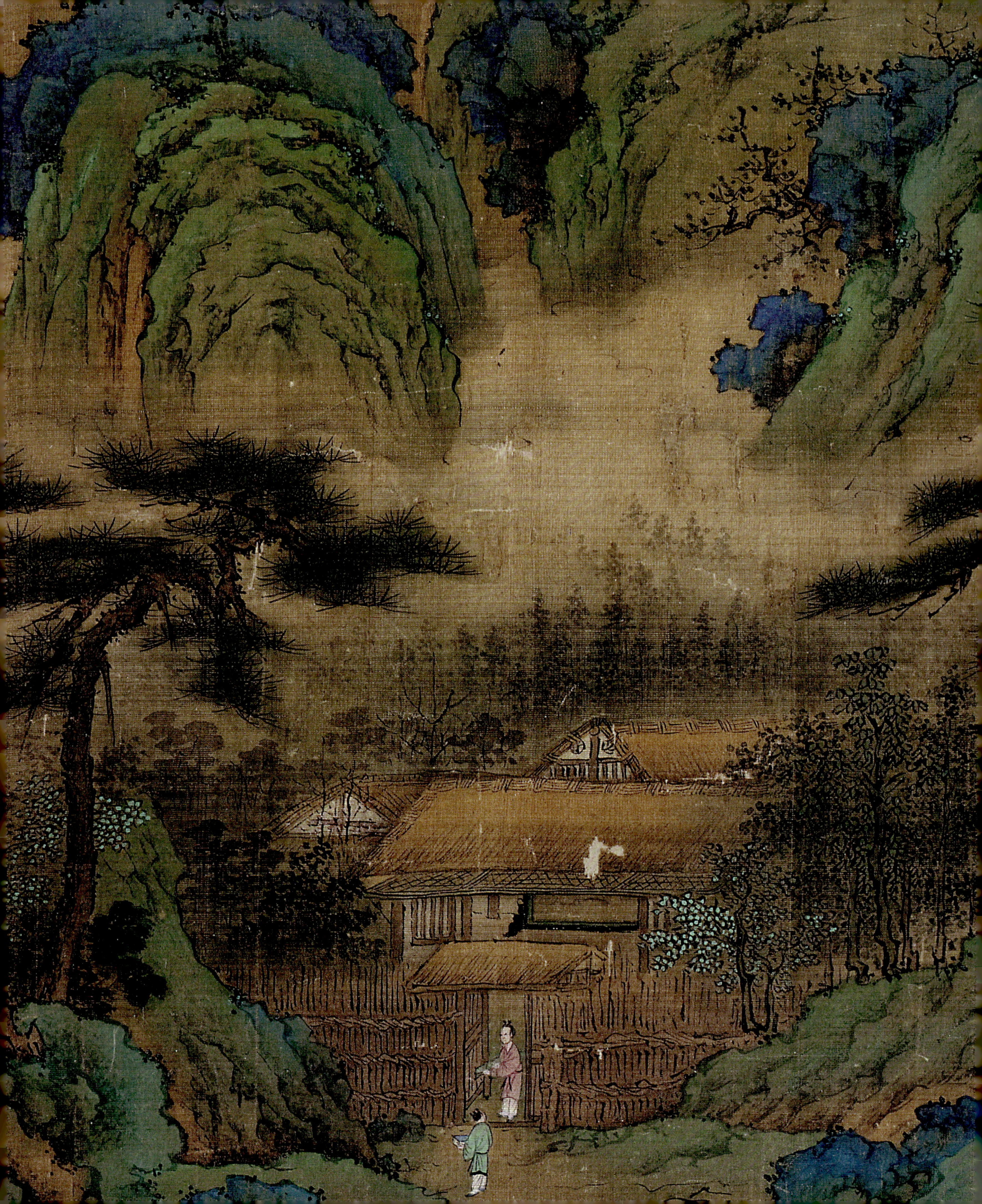

cat. no. 52 (detail)

acquired from the great collector Kuwana Tetsujo in Kyoto in 1907.[38] Between the two world wars, from 1918 to the late 1930s, Kümmel bought important Chinese paintings of the Ming and Qing periods in China. At a time when Song and Yuan or even Tang dynasty (618–907) paintings were still considered in the West to be the height of artistic achievement, in 1927 Kümmel had already purchased a painting by Dong Qichang in Beijing.[39] From the same collector, a certain General Wang, Kümmel also obtained *Yangzi Riverscape* by Fan Qi (1616–after 1694), perhaps the best work the artist ever produced (cat. no. 69). In 1927, he further acquired Dai Jin's (1388–1462) *Spring Clouds in the Linggu Mountains* in Beijing, from the collection of the late connoisseur Shao Songnian (cat. no. 52).[40]

According to Lothar Ledderose, by the end of World War II Kümmel had acquired a fine group of about 50 Chinese paintings, which in terms of aesthetic and artistic quality were among the best in Europe at the time. Kümmel had also established the best research library in the field of East Asian art in Europe. Tragically, in February 1944, the library burned down after an Allied bomb attack. The collection of East Asian art was dispersed after 1945, and 90 per cent of its holdings were lost. Kümmel, who had dedicated his entire career to building up a collection of East Asian art in Berlin, wrote to a friend: 'I can sum up my life with the word: FINIS [The End].'[41] In 2001, however, directors from the State Museums in Berlin were granted access to storage areas in the Hermitage Museum in St Petersburg, Russia.[42] Much of the inventory and many art treasures from Berlin were rediscovered. They had been transferred by the Soviet army from Berlin to Russia after the end of World War II in 1945. Both countries have been in dialogue since the 2001 visit.[43]

International exhibitions of Chinese art between the two wars – the earliest in Amsterdam in 1926, followed by exhibitions in Berlin in 1929 and London in 1935–6 – changed the perception of China and the field of academic studies in Europe.[44] The British exhibition of 1935–6, initiated and organized by the renowned collector Sir Percival David (1892–1964), was particularly successful. Although Percival David had gained his reputation as a collector of Chinese ceramics, he also greatly appreciated Chinese paintings.[45] David's collection featured prominently in the 1935–6 exhibition, and it was then that he began to acquire paintings. The greatest work in his collection was the famous horse painting *Night-Shining White*, attributed to the Tang dynasty artist Han Gan (act. 742–56). This iconic work and the *Admonitions of the Court Instructress to the Palace Ladies* scroll were the most important paintings collected in Europe at the time. However, *Night-Shining White* was purchased by the Metropolitan Museum of Art in 1977, and has been in the United States since then. Another individual that actively collected Chinese paintings between the two wars was Osvald Sirén (1879–1966), who acquired works for the National Museum in Stockholm between 1928 and 1944. A professor of European art history, Sirén committed himself increasingly to the study of Chinese art after visits to the United States between 1914 and 1917.[46] His interest was stimulated in particular by an encounter with the paintings of *luohans* ('arhats') in the Museum of Fine Arts, Boston (cat. nos 23, 24). Sirén's publications on paintings, such as *A History of Later Chinese Painting* (1938) and *Chinese Painting: Leading Masters and Principles* (1956–8), in 10 volumes, are important and still relevant in the field. Sirén obtained most of his paintings in China around 1929 and 1935. Among his most successful acquisitions is the hanging scroll *Clouds and Mist in the Mountains* by Fa Ruozhen (1613–96), which he obtained in Beijing between 1929 and 1930 (cat. no. 73).

Perhaps the most prominent representatives spear-heading the third generation of European experts in classical Chinese paintings were Jean-Pierre Dubosc (1903–88) from France and Victoria Contag (1906–75) from Germany, both pioneers in their field. Dubosc and Contag belonged to the first generation of European scholars to share the Chinese high appreciation of Ming and Qing literati painting, through direct contact and friendship with Chinese collectors. Victoria Contag had been an assistant to Otto Kümmel in Berlin and lived for over 10 years in China, from 1934 to 1946. During her stay in Shanghai, she joined the group of Chinese experts commissioned to authenticate and select paintings for the 1935–6 *International Exhibition of Chinese Art* in London. Contag was the only foreigner and the only woman on the team. With the support of Ye Gongchuo (1881–1968) and Wu Hufan (1894–1968), in 1936 she also teamed up with C.C. Wang (1906–2002) to compile the seal dictionary *Ming Qing huajia yinjian/Sammlerstempel der Ming und Ch'ing Zeit*, published in Shanghai in 1940. This was the first seal dictionary with photographically reproduced, life-size seals. The same year, Contag also published *Die Sechs berühmten Meister der Ch'ing Dynastie* (1940), which later appeared in English as *The Six Masters of the Qing Dynasty* (1970). This was the first Western monograph with a focus on masters of the Qing Orthodox school. Under the guidance of Wu Hufan, Contag collected 118 classical Chinese paintings during her stay in China.[47] Since German museums after the war were not in a financial position to make major purchases, Contag's collection, known as the 'Nüwazhai collection', was sold in the United States in 1958. Museums acquiring major parts of the collection included the Nelson-Atkins Museum of Art, Stanford University Art Museum and the Cleveland Museum of Art.

While Contag wrote pioneering books on the Qing orthodox masters, Jean-Pierre Dubosc promoted Ming and Qing literati painting by organizing exhibitions and selling high-quality works to Western museums. There is hardly a museum with a Chinese painting collection in Europe or the United States that has not acquired a Ming or Qing dynasty painting from Jean-Pierre Dubosc (see cat. no. 61). The French government alone purchased 50 works from his collection after an exhibition of his paintings in Paris in 1937.[48] Dubosc organized the exhibition *Great Chinese Painters of the Ming and Qing Dynasties* in the Wildenstein Gallery in New York in 1949. This exhibition, and his article 'A New Approach in Chinese Painting' (*Oriental Art*, vol. 3, no. 2 [1950], pp. 50–7), were a breakthrough for the perception and appreciation of Ming and Qing literati paintings in the West. A son-in-law of the famous Chinese art dealer C.T. Loo in Paris, Dubosc had also helped to build the collection of Dr Franco Vanotti in Switzerland, which was acquired by the Museum of East Asian Art, Berlin in 1987.[49]

In spring 1935, Wu Hufan noted in his diary about Victoria Contag:

> The German Mrs Contag came with Calligraphy and Paintings of the Palace Museum Collection, in 45 volumes, and asked me to point out the genuine and the false, the good and the lesser works. We went through the volumes, image by image. She was delighted. Mrs Contag is the most outstanding among the foreign women who study Chinese traditional paintings nowadays. Among Chinese women, there is likewise nobody with such talent. Jingshu asked her to stay and have chicken-and-shrimp noodles with us, we all enjoyed it. Mrs Contag is not like a [common] foreigner and has very Chinese manners.[50]

In 1937, Wu had this to say about Dubosc:

> Jiang Gusun accompanied the French Mr Du Bosi [Dubosc]. He is the one with whom I made an appointment the day before to look at paintings in my collection. Jean Pierre Dubosc is Secretary at the French Embassy and very fluent in Chinese. He has a considerable foundation of knowledge in ancient paintings, and is completely different from the bookish, superficial foreign dealers. After all, he is a scholar, a student of Bo Xihe [Pelliot] and cannot be compared with the dealers.[51]

To conclude, Chinese paintings entered royal and public collections in Europe from the sixteenth to the eighteenth century. During these early years, Chinese paintings were exchanged as diplomatic gifts, or were used to satisfy the viewer's curiosity about and scholarly interest in foreign civilizations. It was not until the nineteenth century that Chinese paintings were collected systematically and with a view to understanding their iconography and indigenous aesthetic and artistic qualities. Through three generations of collecting activity and travel in East Asia, European scholars gradually achieved an understanding of classical Chinese paintings that could be shared with Chinese collectors.

1 I would like to thank Minna Törmä, and Zhang Hongxing for valuable comments. This essay differentiates between classical Chinese paintings and so-called trade paintings, and focuses on classical paintings. Trade paintings are usually seen as a commodity made for export, and were mostly mass produced in various media and formats. Their rarity in collections in China has led to the questionable conclusion that they were produced exclusively for foreigners. The advent of trade paintings in Europe has been discussed elsewhere.
2 Wappenschmidt 2007, p. 9
3 Ibid., p. 17
4 Partly reproduced in Whitfield 1976
5 For the painting and picture album, see Marx 2007–8, p. 65. The group of ceramics is reproduced and discussed in Ströber 2004.
6 On Sloane and the founding of the British Museum, see MacGregor 1994 and Griffiths 1996.
7 *Dictionary of Chinese Artists* (1924) 1980, p. 755
8 The dispute evolved around the happiness of fish. Zhuangzi and Huizi were strolling along the dam of the Hao Waterfall when Zhuangzi said: 'See how the minnows come out and dart around where they please! That's what fish really enjoy!' Huizi said: 'You're not a fish – how do you know what fish enjoy?' Zhuangzi said: 'You're not me, so how do you know I don't know what fish enjoy?' Huizi said: 'I'm not you, so I certainly don't know what you know. On the other hand, you're certainly not a fish – so that still proves you don't know what fish enjoy!' Zhuangzi said: 'Let's go back to your original question, please. You asked me *how* I know what fish enjoy – so you already knew I knew it when you asked the question. I know it by standing here beside the Hao.' (Watson 1968, pp. 188–9; punctuation modified and romanization changed to *pinyin*)
9 For a comprehensive discussion of this painting, see Whitfield 1993.
10 It is not clear whether it is the same Mr Butler from whom Sloane acquired the fish album.
11 Whitfield 1993, p. 34
12 On collecting Chinese paintings in Japan and the first generation of European collectors, see Itakura in this volume; Nishida 2000; Miyazaki 2011; Yamaguchi 1993.
13 Yamaguchi 1993, p. 66
14 On Fenollosa's impact on European collecting, especially in Germany, see Ledderose 1998.
15 See Fenollosa 1912, vol. 2, ch. XV, pp. 141–2, 146–7.
16 The collection of over 2,000 Japanese and Chinese paintings assembled by William Anderson during his residency in Japan from 1873 to 1880 is published in Anderson 1886. See also Huang 2010b.
17 On Henri Cernuschi and the history of the museum, see Béguin 2000 and Maucuer 2011.
18 For the collecting history of Chinese paintings at the Musée Cernuschi, see Paris 2009, pp. 11–14 and 77–81.
19 On finger-painting, see Amsterdam 1992.
20 See the three finger paintings by Gao Qipei (1660–1734) and Fu Wen (act. 1744–65) reproduced and discussed in Paris 2009, nos 25, 28, 29. A fourth finger painting by Fu Wen is reproduced in Chavannes and Petrucci 1914, pl. XLVIII. This was the catalogue to a painting exhibition held at the Musée Cernuschi from April to June 1912.
21 Chavannes 1904; cited in Paris 2009, p. 11. For the 1912 exhibition, see the previous note.
22 Paris 2009, p. 11
23 On Fischer and the founding of the Museum of East Asian Art in Cologne, see Schlombs 2009.
24 See von Spee in Cologne 2010, in particular nos 2, 8, 19.
25 On Émile Guimet and the museum, see Macouin 2009.
26 See Ledderose 1998, p. 10
27 Pelliot had been sent to Beijing to acquire books, manuscripts and works of art for the library and the establishment of the École Française d'Extrême-Orient (EFEO). He arrived during the Boxer Rebellion (20 June–14 August 1900). The paintings he acquired are partly reproduced by Stpehen Little in Chicago 2000, nos 79–81, 84, 91.
28 See Giès et al. 1994.
29 On Aurel Stein, see Whitfield 2004.
30 On Stein's finds from the Silk Road, see Whitfield and Farrer 1990 and Whitfield 1982–5.
31 On the *Admonitions* scroll, its provenance and acquisition, see Zhang 2003. A letter in the British Museum from the previous owner, Captain C. Johnson, dated 7 January 1903, suggests that the museum had agreed to purchase the scroll. Captain Johnson had been in Beijing during the Boxer Rebellion, but the circumstances of how the scroll came into his possession are not known at present. Today, the *Admonitions* scroll is mostly considered to be a sixth to eighth century copy of the lost original work by the court artist Gu Kaizhi (c.344–c.406).
32 See London 1910.
33 The exhibition was held in the newly opened King Edward VII Gallery (today, The Joseph E. Hotung Gallery); see London 1914a and 1914b.
34 See National Museums of Berlin 2012.
35 It is said that Anderson began to learn Japanese during his stay in Japan.
36 On Otto Kümmel, see Ledderose 1995 and 1998; see also Klose 2009.
37 See, for example, Pelliot's substantial research and his excellent reviews on new publications in *T'oung pao* and his use of primary source material from Asia.
38 Reproduced in Ledderose 1998, no. 4
39 Today, the scroll's authenticity is questioned; ibid., p. 19
40 Reproduced in ibid., nos 11 and 24
41 Ibid., p. 24
42 See Veit 2001.
43 See National Museums of Berlin 2009.
44 Early European exhibitions between the wars devoted to classical Japanese and Chinese paintings took place in Munich (Museum für Völkerkunde, 1930), Stockholm (National Museum, 1930), Vienna (Albertina, 1932), London (Yamanaka & Co., 1932), Milan (Castello Sforzesco 1931–2) and Paris (Musée du Jeu du Paume, 1933).
45 See Pierson 2011, p. 133.
46 On Sirén, his career, scholarship and collecting activity, see Törmä (forthcoming); 2006–7; 2007.
47 On the Nüwazhai collection, see Sullivan 1967; von Spee 2012.
48 Bellec in Paris 2006, p. 137
49 See Eskenazi 2012, p. 105. A Dealer's Hand: The Chinese Art through the Eyes of Giuseppe Eskenazi, in collaboration with Itajni Elias. London 2012
50 See von Spee 2008, p. 58.
51 Ibid., p. 75

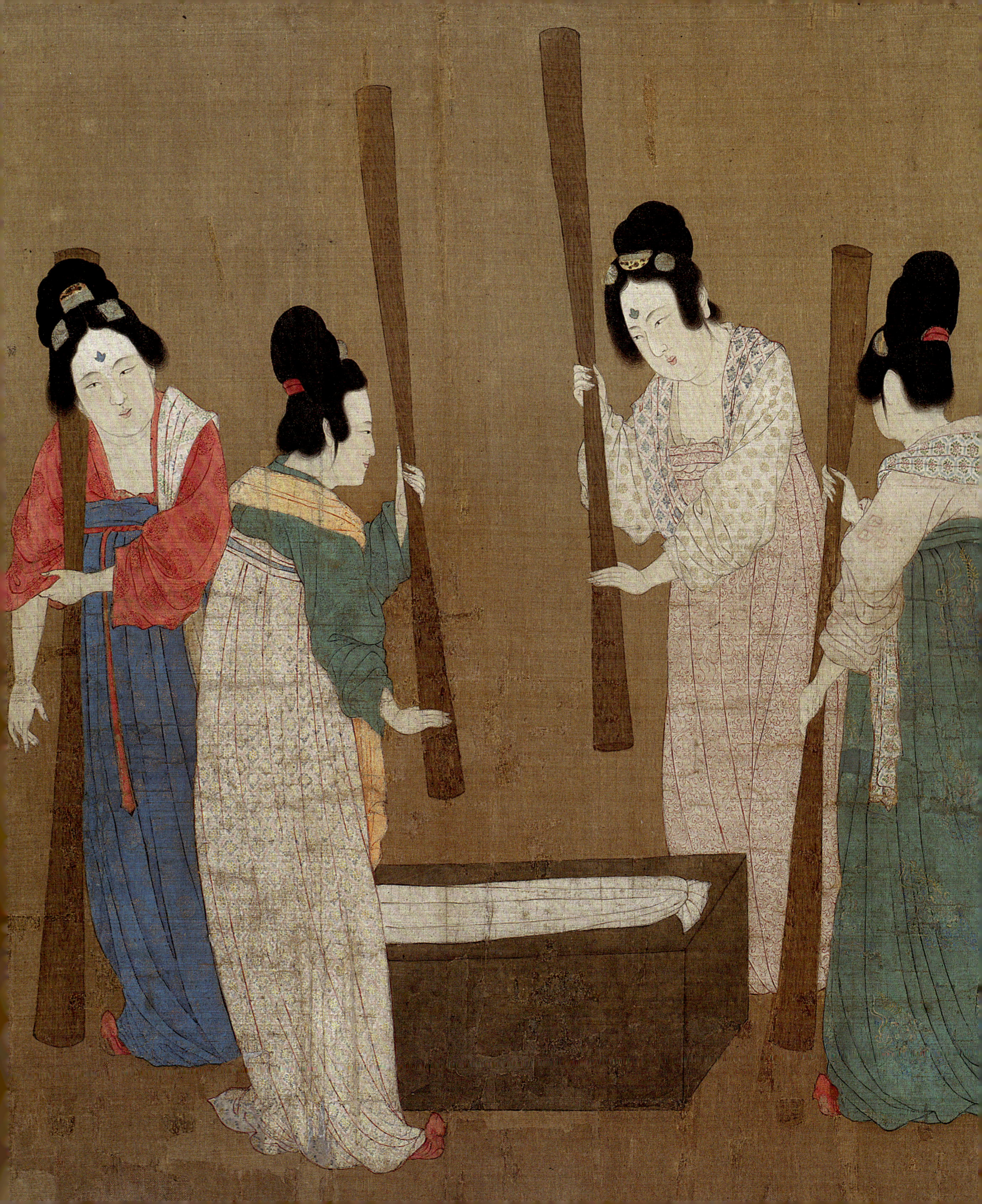

# COLLECTING CHINESE PAINTINGS IN THE UNITED STATES

Charles Mason

At the beginning of the twentieth century, Chinese paintings were little appreciated and scarcely collected in the United States. By the end of the century, however, America was home to some of the greatest museum and private collections of Chinese paintings in the world. This remarkable evolution was made possible by a unique convergence of historical forces. On the one hand, decades of political, economic and social turmoil in China forced large numbers of Chinese paintings out of private collections and onto the international art market. On the other hand, decades of relative prosperity and stability in the United States, combined with increasing expertise and popular interest in Chinese art and culture, resulted in many of those paintings going to America. While this unprecedented transfer undoubtedly helped to preserve many treasures that might otherwise have been lost, it also constituted a serious loss of patrimony for China. The odd reality is that there are now better collections of Chinese paintings in Cleveland and Kansas City than in many museums in China.

The history of collecting Chinese paintings in the United States can be divided into three major chronological periods: 1784 to 1894, 1894 to 1945 and 1945 to 1999. By focusing on five great American public collections – at the Museum of Fine Arts, Boston, the Freer Gallery of Art in Washington, DC, the Metropolitan Museum of Art in New York, the Nelson-Atkins Museum of Art in Kansas City and the Cleveland Museum of Art – we can trace an essential outline of how the United States became a major world repository of traditional Chinese paintings.

## 1784–1894

Before the American colonies declared independence in 1776, they were forbidden by British law to trade directly with China. However, there was a thriving market in the colonies for Chinese goods – especially tea, porcelain and silk – and so after the War of Independence was concluded, American merchants began extending their business networks into China. The first American ship to set sail for the Middle Kingdom was the *Empress of China*, which departed from New York on 22 February 1784, bound for Canton with a cargo of American ginseng and silver.[1] The *Empress of China* reached Canton in August that year, and despite the unfamiliar Chinese trading system, successfully exchanged its cargo for a shipment of Chinese goods, which it took back to New York on 11 May 1785. Within that shipment was a folding fan decorated with a painting of Western ships at anchor in Whampoa harbour.[2] Executed by a Chinese artist in a hybrid style that combines Chinese and Western elements, the fan from the *Empress of China* cargo may have been the first Chinese painting imported into the newly formed United States.

In the late eighteenth and early nineteenth centuries, as American trade with China steadily increased, more Chinese paintings filtered into the United States. Like the fan that arrived on the *Empress of China*, most were created specifically for export to the West. Stylistically, the work was a blend of native Chinese commercial painting traditions and aspects of Western art learned from prints and other images that were taken to China for artists to copy. Popular subjects included portraits, ships, nature studies and genre scenes that emphasized different aspects of Chinese life, such as clothing, household furnishings, occupations and even forms of punishment. Because the paintings had some familiar Western features while being also distinctly Chinese, American viewers accepted and enjoyed them as exotic curiosities. However, on the rare occasions they encountered paintings made for the

cat. no. 16 (detail)

Chinese domestic market, the Americans were much less favourably impressed. In 1820 Robert Waln, a Philadelphia merchant who visited China many times during the early nineteenth century, wrote the following about what was presumably an ink painting seen on one of his trips: 'To the eye accustomed to the vivid beauties of a [Benjamin] West or the proportioned excellence of a [John] Trumbull, the whole appears a mass of black marks, representing nothing.'[3]

Most Americans in the nineteenth century did not have access to paintings made for the Chinese domestic market, let alone the ability to understand them. One exception was Nathan Dunn, a Philadelphian who lived in China for extended periods during the 1820s and '30s. In the course of his various business dealings, Dunn became acquainted with Chinese government officials – as well as merchants – and developed a more nuanced understanding of Chinese life and culture than was usual for most Western traders. Determined to share this knowledge with his fellow countrymen, he spent US $50,000 acquiring examples of Chinese costume, household furnishings, religious sculptures and other objects, which he took back to the United States and installed in a museum in Philadelphia in 1838.[4] Dunn's Chinese museum remained open for three years, and attracted tens of thousands of visitors. The displays included a number of figure and bird-and-flower paintings, which William Langdon, the cataloguer of the exhibition, praised as having been done 'with great correctness and beauty'.[5] Unfortunately, most of Dunn's collection was destroyed in a train crash while touring England and Scotland in the 1840s, so we cannot be sure what the paintings in his exhibition actually were, but it seems probable that Dunn's museum provided the first widespread exposure to non-export Chinese paintings in the United States.

After Commodore Matthew Perry opened trade with Japan in 1854, American commercial and cultural interests in Asia began to shift away from China. Although there was a significant display of Chinese arts and crafts at the Centennial Exposition in Philadelphia in 1876, it was overshadowed by the much larger Japanese display.[6] We know from photographs that the Chinese gallery at the exposition included a wall of Chinese figural, landscape and bird-and-flower paintings, but apparently they did not make much impact on visitors, and little more is known about them. Except for porcelain, interest in Chinese art continued to wane during the 1880s, and because of anti-Chinese immigration laws passed by the American Congress, China was scarcely represented at the 1893 World's Fair in Chicago. Then, in December 1894, an exhibition opened at the Museum of Fine Arts in Boston that radically changed American perceptions of Chinese painting. It would spark a new era of collecting that lasted until the end of the Second World War.

## 1894–1945

The 1894 exhibition at the Museum of Fine Arts, Boston featured 44 Song dynasty (960–1279) Chinese Buddhist paintings from the collection of the temple Daitoku-ji in Kyoto. The exhibition was organized by Ernest Fenollosa (1853–1908), a Harvard-trained scholar who went to Japan in 1878 to teach philosophy and political economy, but quickly turned his attention to Japanese art and was eventually appointed head of the Imperial Museum by the Meiji government.[7] Fenollosa's government connections allowed him to meet and learn from leading Japanese scholars and connoisseurs, and gave him access to the most important private and temple-owned art collections in Japan, many of which contained Chinese paintings as well as Japanese art. Fenollosa maintained his contacts with collectors in Japan after he returned to the United States in 1890, and used them to arrange numerous acquisitions and exhibitions primarily for the Museum of Fine Arts.

The Daitoku-ji scrolls had been painted in the late twelfth century by professional artists active in or around the port of Ningbo in south-east China, and were exported to Japan soon afterward. In the sense that they were commercial paintings exported to another country, there were some parallels between the Daitoku-ji scrolls and the Chinese export paintings that Americans already knew.

However, the great age of the Daitoku-ji paintings, their religious subject matter and the high quality of their workmanship put them in a class above any Chinese paintings Americans had seen before, and they quickly became a sensation. No less imposing a figure than the renowned art historian Bernard Berenson praised them effusively: 'They had compositions of figures and groups as perfect and simple as the best we Europeans have ever done.'[8] The monks of Daitoku-ji had sent the paintings to America as part of an effort to raise money for desperately needed repairs to the temple. When Fenollosa saw the positive reaction to the paintings, he took advantage of the monks' financial need and pressured them to sell 10 of the scrolls. Five were acquired directly by the Museum of Fine Arts (cat. nos 23, 24) and five by one of the museum's leading Asian art patrons. Those acquisitions marked the start of serious Chinese painting collecting in the United States, and established the Museum of Fine Arts as the nation's leading institution in the field.

Boston's acquisition of the Daitoku-ji scrolls illustrates the importance of three conditions that were vital to the subsequent history of Chinese painting collecting in the United States: expertise, means and opportunity. The Museum of Fine Arts had expertise in the person of Ernest Fenollosa, and soon added to its capabilities in that area by hiring two scholars from Japan – Okakura Kakuzo (1862–1913) and Tomita Kojiro (1890–1976) – whose knowledge of and access to Chinese painting collections in Japan and China far exceeded Fenollosa's. The museum had the means to collect Chinese paintings through its own endowment funds as well as through its patrons, including two men in particular: Denman Waldo Ross (1853–1935) and William Sturgis Bigelow (1850–1926). Ross and Bigelow both came from wealthy families, and were avid collectors of Japanese art. They became interested in collecting Chinese paintings after seeing the 1894 Daitoku-ji exhibition (Ross bought the five scrolls that did not go directly to the museum), and with guidance from Okakura and Tomita, went on to acquire many important early Chinese paintings that remain stars of the Boston collection today (cat. no. 36). Finally, the Museum of Fine Arts had opportunities to collect, not only through Fenollosa's, Okakura's and Tomita's connections, but also because of the decline and fall of the Chinese Qing dynasty (1644–1911). The collapse of China's political, economic and social order forced many affluent families to sell treasures from their art collections to make ends meet, and during the first two decades of the twentieth century, many great old paintings came onto the market in this way. Some of those paintings went into other Chinese collections, some went to Japan, and some went to Europe or the United States. The Museum of Fine Arts was especially well positioned to take advantage of this situation, and acquired many of its finest early Chinese paintings in the years between 1908 and 1917 (cat. no. 16). Although Boston continued to add to its holdings in later decades, the Tang (618–907), Song and Yuan (1271–1368) dynasty paintings for which the museum is best known were mainly acquired in the first few decades of the twentieth century.

Although the Museum of Fine Arts formed the first great collection of Chinese paintings in America, other museums and private collectors soon began to follow suit. After Boston, unquestionably the second most important collection of Chinese paintings to be assembled in the United States in the early part of the twentieth century was that of Charles Lang Freer (1854–1919). A railroad magnate from Detroit, Freer began collecting Asian art in the 1880s, and eventually made it his goal to establish a national museum of Asian art in Washington, DC.[9] Freer knew Fenollosa and Okakura, and took some early direction from them when it came to collecting Chinese paintings. (Freer purchased two additional scrolls from the Daitoku-ji set, which had somehow remained with Fenollosa after the exhibition was returned to Japan.) However, Freer also developed his own network of dealers and advisers in the United States, Europe, Japan and China, who helped him acquire some of the paintings that became available as a result of the instability in China.[10] Ever the savvy businessman, Freer was most active as a collector of Chinese paintings between 1915 and 1919, when the First World War in Europe distracted many would-be buyers on that continent and temporarily drove down Chinese painting prices. Whereas the Boston collection of Chinese paintings was heavily influenced by Japanese

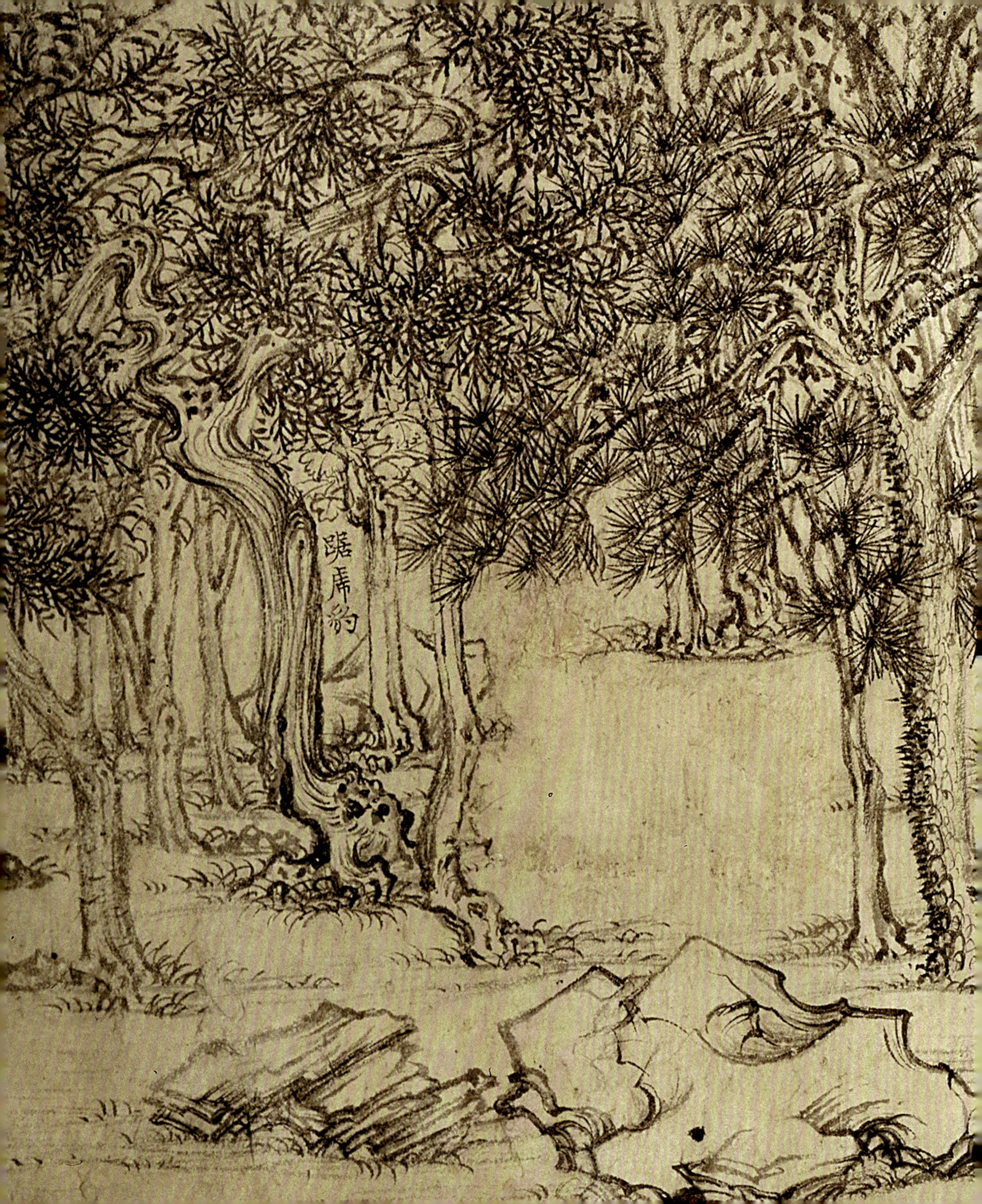
踞虎豹

cat. no. 19 (detail)

preferences, Freer acquired many works from Chinese dealers, such as C.T. Loo, Wang Jiantang and Li Wenxing, who supplied landscapes and figure paintings that were more in line with Chinese literati tastes. As a result, even though Freer also favoured paintings from the Tang to Yuan dynasties, his collection had a somewhat different character from the one in Boston. Freer died in 1919, four years before his national Asian art museum opened in Washington. The museum has continued to add to Freer's collection since his death, but as with Boston, the character of the Freer Chinese painting collection remains strongly rooted in the early twentieth century.

When the trustees of the Metropolitan Museum of Art in New York learned of the Chinese painting collections that were being formed in Boston and Detroit, they decided it was time to build their own. Since the museum lacked any curatorial expertise in Asian art, the American missionary-turned-diplomat John C. Ferguson (1865–1945) was hired as their buying agent in China.[11] Ferguson had lived in China since 1887; he spoke Chinese, and was familiar with many influential political and social leaders. When the Qing dynasty collapsed in 1911, he proposed to use his cultural knowledge and connections to acquire rare art treasures for the Metropolitan Museum. Accordingly, in 1912, the Metropolitan trustees advanced Ferguson US $50,000 for the purpose of buying Chinese paintings. Ferguson soon spent this amount and requested more funds, but the trustees wanted to see his first purchases before committing any more money. Ferguson, however, was impatient, and believed he would miss too many opportunities if he waited, so continued purchasing scrolls with his own money, eventually to amass a collection of more than 200 works. These supposedly ranged in date from the ninth to the nineteenth century, and many bore the names of famous masters, but when Ferguson shipped the paintings back to New York it quickly became apparent that few were what they purported to be. Ferguson had relied on his reputation and experience as an 'old China hand' to gain access to important collectors and dealers, but apparently those credentials were not enough to prevent those collectors and dealers from taking advantage of him. Although the Ferguson purchases did establish the Metropolitan Museum as a third centre of Chinese painting collecting in the United States, it would be many more years before the collection became a true rival of Boston and the Freer.

Other museum collections of Chinese paintings were being formed in the early twentieth century in Philadelphia, Detroit, Chicago, Cleveland and Kansas City. However, after the initial flood of paintings that came on the market in the years just before and after the fall of the Qing dynasty, it became much more difficult to find good examples, and none of the other museums were able to build extensive holdings. A combination of the Great Depression and the outbreak of war in Asia and Europe further dampened collecting activities. When World War II ended, however, America once again benefited from a convergence of expertise, means and opportunity that allowed it to resume acquisitions of Chinese paintings on an unprecedented scale.

## 1945–1999

In terms of expertise, post-war American efforts to collect Chinese paintings were aided by a new generation of academically trained Asian art experts, many of whom had gained first-hand experience with Asian cultures and art forms through serving in the military. Moreover, changes to the nation's immigration laws allowed greater numbers of Chinese and Japanese scholars and collectors to move to the United States, bringing with them knowledge and contacts beyond those of many American-born collectors and curators. The means to collect Chinese art were supplied by the profits from America's industrial and agricultural economies, which had been built up to fuel the war effort and were still running strong to stimulate reconstruction. Civic pride and a growing awareness of America's global power inspired many wealthy philanthropists to support the collection of Asian art in their local museums, even if they were not especially knowledgeable about the field themselves. Finally, the devastation wrought by the war in Europe and Asia created many new opportunities to collect. Paintings that had remained in China or gone to collections in Japan and Europe were drawn back onto the market and often acquired by American collectors. Still more paintings went to the United States with collectors fleeing the Communist takeover of China in 1949. Some of those collectors – including C.C. Wang (1906–2002), Zhang Daqian (1899–1983) and Wango Weng (b.1918) – became major sources of Chinese paintings for American museums and private collectors, and helped make the later twentieth century a golden age for collecting Chinese paintings in the United States.

One of the first places to emerge as a centre for collecting after World War II was the Nelson-Atkins Museum of Art in Kansas City. The main reason for this rise in prominence was the involvement of Laurence Sickman (1907–88), a trained sinologist who had lived in China during the 1930s and acquired some important works of art – including paintings – for the museum at that time.[12] Sickman served in India and China during the war, and afterwards in the Pacific section of the Monuments, Fine Arts and Archives (MFAA) division of the US Army, which was created to safeguard cultural property in occupied countries after the war. His experiences in Asia before, during and after the war gave Sickman an extraordinary depth of knowledge and breadth of contacts that he put to good use at the Nelson-Atkins, building one of America's great Asian art collections. In the area of Chinese paintings, Sickman began acquiring major works in 1946, and steadily added to the collection until his retirement in 1977 (cat. no. 19, opposite). He developed a collection that was remarkably balanced, with major works from the Song to Qing dynasty and representing virtually every important genre. Sickman's achievements as a collector are all the more impressive because his acquisitions came from an extraordinarily broad range of dealers and collectors in China, Japan, Europe and the United States, proving he was truly a master of the new, post-war Asian art world.

A second American museum that also built a great collection of Chinese paintings after World War II was the Cleveland Museum of Art. The growth of Cleveland's holdings of Chinese paintings was led by Sherman Lee (1918–2008), another trained art historian who had served in the Pacific MFAA division and who had worked as a curator at the Seattle Art Museum before going to Cleveland in 1953.[13] In Cleveland, Lee was supported by a Chinese-born curator, Wai-Kam Ho (1924–2004), and a healthy acquisitions fund that allowed him to purchase some of the best Chinese paintings to reach the market between the 1950s and 1970s. The collection Lee and Ho developed is especially strong in Chan (J. Zen) Buddhist paintings and Ming (1368–1644) and Qing dynasty 'literati' paintings (cat. no. 57). Lee and Ho were also leaders in organizing exhibitions, including *Chinese Art under the Mongols* (1968), *The Colors of Ink* (1974) and *Eight Dynasties of Chinese Painting* (1980). Those exhibitions, along with the enormously influential 1961 *Chinese Art Treasures*, an exhibition of works from the National Palace Museum in Taiwan, helped build popular awareness of and interest in Chinese painting and provided inspiration for many other museums and private collectors across the United States.

As it had after the fall of the Qing dynasty, the Metropolitan Museum wanted to take advantage of the opportunities that were created in the Asian art market after World War II, so in 1947 curator Alan Priest arranged to buy 142 Chinese paintings from the dealer A.W. Bahr.[14] Unfortunately, Priest lacked the necessary expertise to evaluate the paintings, and most turned out to be second-rate. The Metropolitan's Chinese paintings collection continued to languish in mediocrity for several decades, until in 1971 a Chinese scholar named Wen Fong (b.1930) joined the museum staff. Also a professor at Princeton,

Fong brought expertise and connections that quickly transformed the Metropolitan Museum into a major force in the area. Backed by some of the museum's most important trustees – including especially Douglas Dillon (1909–2003) – Fong began making major purchases in 1973, and over the next 25 years proceeded to build a truly important collection of Chinese paintings and calligraphy in New York (cat. no. 18). Fong's successes attracted the interest of other collectors, most notably John M. Crawford, Jr. (1913–88), who had formed one of the most important private collections of Chinese paintings after the war and donated it to the Metropolitan Museum in stages beginning in the 1980s (cat. no. 46). By the 1990s, the Metropolitan Museum had finally assumed its long-desired position as a major institutional collector of Chinese paintings in the United States.

The Museum of Fine Arts, Boston, the Freer Gallery, the Metropolitan Museum of Art, the Nelson-Atkins Museum of Art and the Cleveland Museum of Art may have built the best collections of Chinese paintings in America, but there are significant collections in other museums as well, from Chicago, St. Louis and Cincinnati to San Francisco, Phoenix and Los Angeles. There are also impressive collections of Chinese paintings in many American academic museums, including especially Princeton, Yale and the University of California, Berkeley. Such is the depth of all the Chinese paintings holdings in the United States that it would be possible to illustrate nearly the entire history of Chinese painting using works from US collections alone.

## CONCLUSION

The golden age of Chinese painting collecting in America began to wane in the 1990s, and might be said to have ended in 1999 when Christie's auction house stopped holding dedicated sales of Chinese paintings in its New York galleries. What brought this remarkable period to a close was not a decline in expertise, since American universities continue to turn out many well-qualified experts in Chinese painting every year. Nor was it a decline in means, since American collectors have money for many other types of art, including Asian art. Rather, the end of the golden age of Chinese painting collecting in America was mainly caused by declining opportunity. Many great Chinese paintings have by now been locked up in museum collections, and those that are still in private hands are attracting much more attention from China, where newly affluent collectors have been aggressively buying and repatriating China's cultural heritage. Still, while America's best days as a leading centre for collecting Chinese paintings may be past, the legacy of the earlier periods will remain. And while it may seem strange for America to possess such substantial holdings of Chinese paintings, it is not entirely inappropriate, for America is a land of immigrants and multicultural influences; as the number of Chinese Americans and Chinese influences in America continues to grow, Chinese painting will surely become an integral part of America's cultural history as well.

1 Washington 1984, pp. 18–20
2 The fan is in the collection of the Historical Society of Pennsylvania. For an illustration see ibid., p. 18.
3 Cohen 1992, p. 8
4 Philadelphia 1984, pp. 11–19
5 Cohen 1992, p. 11
6 Pitman 2002–3, pp. 35–73
7 Chisholm 1963
8 Boston 1997, p. 160
9 Lawton and Merrill 1993
10 Daisy Yiyou Wang, 'Mammon and the Muse: International Art Dealers and Charles Lang Freer', lecture at the Frick Collection symposium *The Dragon and the Chrysanthemum: Collecting Chinese and Japanese Art in America*, 16 March 2012
11 Lara Netting, 'All of the Best Collections of Individuals in China', lecture at the symposium *The Dragon and the Chrysanthemum*, 15 March 2012
12 Jason Steuber, 'Laurence Sickman: Pioneer and Connoisseur of Chinese Art', lecture at the symposium *The Dragon and the Chrysanthemum*, 16 March 2012
13 Cohen 1992, pp. 174–80
14 Maxwell K. Hearn, 'East Asia and the Encyclopedic Art Museum', lecture at the symposium *The Dragon and the Chrysanthemum*, 15 March 2012

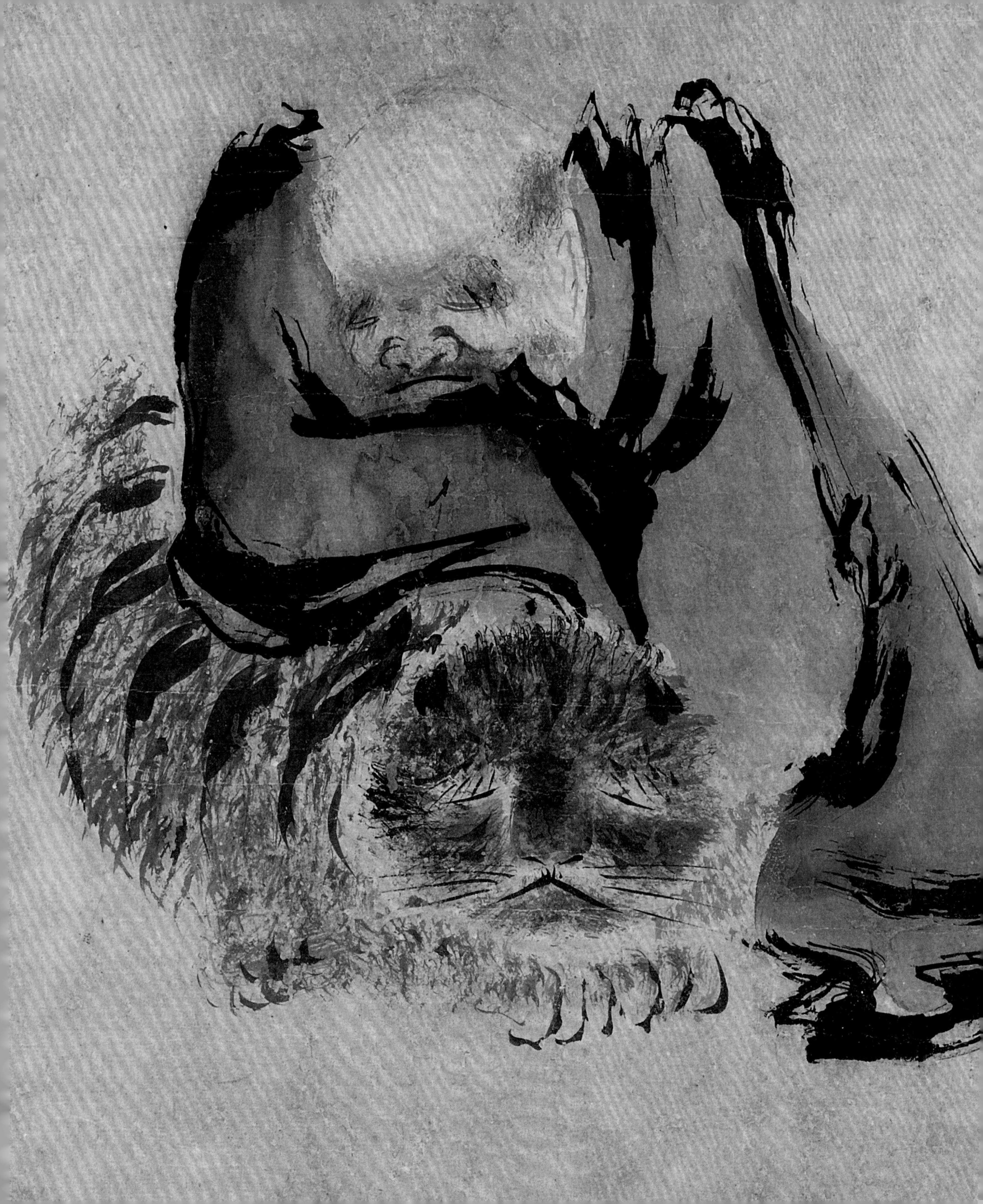

# CHINESE PAINTINGS THAT CROSSED THE SEA

## THE DEVELOPMENT OF CHINESE ART COLLECTIONS IN JAPAN

Itakura Masaaki

It is well known in East Asia that the art of China has consistently been an important source of inspiration for Japanese art. However, the accumulation of Chinese art, for members of the Japanese ruling elite, was not motivated simply by a love of the art itself. As well as embodying the art trends of the time, such collections, as assemblages of 'prestige goods', functioned as symbols of power and authority.

### THE SHŌSŌ-IN AND COLLECTIONS IN TANG CHINA

The best example of a very early imperial collection in Japan is the treasures housed in the Nara period (710–94) repository Shōsō-in at the temple Tōdai-ji in Nara. Since inventories of the collection have existed since its establishment, we know much about the objects and the circumstances of their inclusion.[1] The collection originated with the donation to Tōdai-ji of items owned and treasured by Emperor Shōmu (r. 724–49) following his death, and continued to grow with various additions made over a period of years.

In 756, the 49th day after his death, more than 600 of Emperor Shōmu's cherished possessions as well as 60 kinds of medicine were donated by his consort, Empress Kōmyō (701–60), in his memory. Two years later, in 758, the Empress donated a handscroll by the Chinese calligrapher Wang Xizhi (303–65) and his son Wang Xianzhi (344–86). The handscroll was described as 'a rare and precious thing transmitted through many generations; something that gave the late Emperor pleasure', and had been used by Shōmu as a calligraphy model. In 950, utensils and other objects were also moved from another repository at Tōdai-ji, in the sub-temple of Kensaku-in, to the south section of the Shōsō-in, and became part of its established group of treasures. These treasures were known as the 'Shōsō-in *hōmotsu*'.

As the state religion at the time, Buddhism played an important role in national security, and thus it is not surprising that Buddhist-related objects bequeathed by relatives of the deceased, as well as items used in Buddhist ritual, were well represented in the collection from the time of its formation. The act of making donations should be understood, first of all, in a Buddhist context. Important in this regard is Emperor Ashoka (r. c.269–232 BCE) of India, who was considered an ideal ruler according to the Buddhist tradition. His devotion to Buddhism and his practice of almsgiving served as a model for Buddhist emperors in China, such as Emperor Wu (r. 502–49) of the Southern Liang dynasty (502–57), who renounced the world and became a monk.[2]

We find early rulers in Japan also involved in the practice. Emperor Tenji (r. 668–71) dedicated precious objects to Hōkō-ji (Asukadera) in Nara in 671, and Emperor Tenmu (r. 673–86) in 685. Copies of the *Avatamsaka* (J. *Kegon-kyō*) and other sutras were donated, along with ritual banners (*kanjōban* and *dōjōban*), to various imperial temples on behalf of Empress Genshō (r. 715–24) in 722. Empress Kōmyō, moreover, presented offerings not only to Tōdai-ji, but to 18 major temples inside and outside Nara, including Hōryū-ji and Konkōmyō-ji. The Shōsō-in, then, was just one of the institutions among which the offerings were divided.

The precious objects collected in the Shōsō-in also include works of art not produced in a Buddhist context.[3] As we have seen, examples of those where the artist is known are calligraphies by the aforementioned father and son, Wang Xizhi and Wang Xianzhi of the Chinese Jin dynasty (265–420). Additionally, 20 scrolls of copies of Wang Xizhi's calligraphy are listed in the *Record of Rare Treasures of the Nation*. These scrolls, representing just one part of what was originally a 60-volume set, include volumes 1–10, 51–6 and 58–60, as well as a scroll of calligraphy on fans. The *Inventory of Screens, Rugs and Other Items* also lists a 12-panel screen bearing the calligraphy of

cat. no. 39 (detail)

Ouyang Xun (557–641) of the Chinese Tang dynasty (618–907) and a 12-panel screen of calligraphy after Wang Xizhi. Having been dispersed during the Heian period (794–1185), however, none of these works are in the Shōsō-in today.

Among extant calligraphies that were possibly once in the ancient Shōsō-in collection are early Tang period tracing copies of two pieces by Wang Xizhi, the *Note of Distress and Indignation* (Museum of the Imperial Collections, Sannomaru) and *Letter to Kong* (Maeda Ikutokukai Foundation). A square relief seal reading *Enreki chokutei* appears on both works. Taking 'Enreki' as the equivalent of 'Enryaku', we can conclude that the seals were affixed in the Enryaku era (781–806), during the reign of Emperor Kanmu (781–806). The two pieces correspond to a section torn off from scroll 7 in the set of 20 scrolls of copies of Wang Xizhi's calligraphy. Further, the letter known as *Meizhi Tie* (J. Maishi-jō) (private collection) and the recently rediscovered *Dabao Tie* (J. Taihō-jō) (private collection) are stylistically similar enough to the *Note of Distress and Indignation* and other letters, even in the condition of the paper, that it is highly likely that they, too, are early Tang copies of Wang Xizhi.[4] These historical documents indicate Wang Xizhi to be the earliest known Chinese artist in Japan, and we can say that it was with him that the Japanese appreciation of Chinese painting and calligraphy began.[5]

The majority of paintings in the Shōsō-in, not counting those decorating objects, were probably folding screens, judging from the inventory *One Hundred Imperial Screens* in the *Record of Rare Treasures of the Nation*,[6] and it seems that screens in large format in fact constituted the heart of the painting collection. A number of these works are now lost, and though their subject is known, the artists are not. They include depictions of palaces and famous sites in Korea and China; however, in some cases, their country of origin is somewhat unclear. The extant *Screen with Ladies under Trees* (fig. 41), for example, although Chinese in style, is believed to have been produced between 752 and 756 in Japan, a conclusion based on the use of feathers from a native Japanese bird, the copper pheasant, and the date inscribed on a scrap of paper attached to the back of one of the screen panels.

While there are no extant folding screens among the objects handed down from the Tang or earlier in China, recently a series of archaeological excavations has led to the discovery of a large number of multi-panelled screens, as well as murals imitating them.[7] In 1989, a mural representing a six-panel folding screen was excavated from the

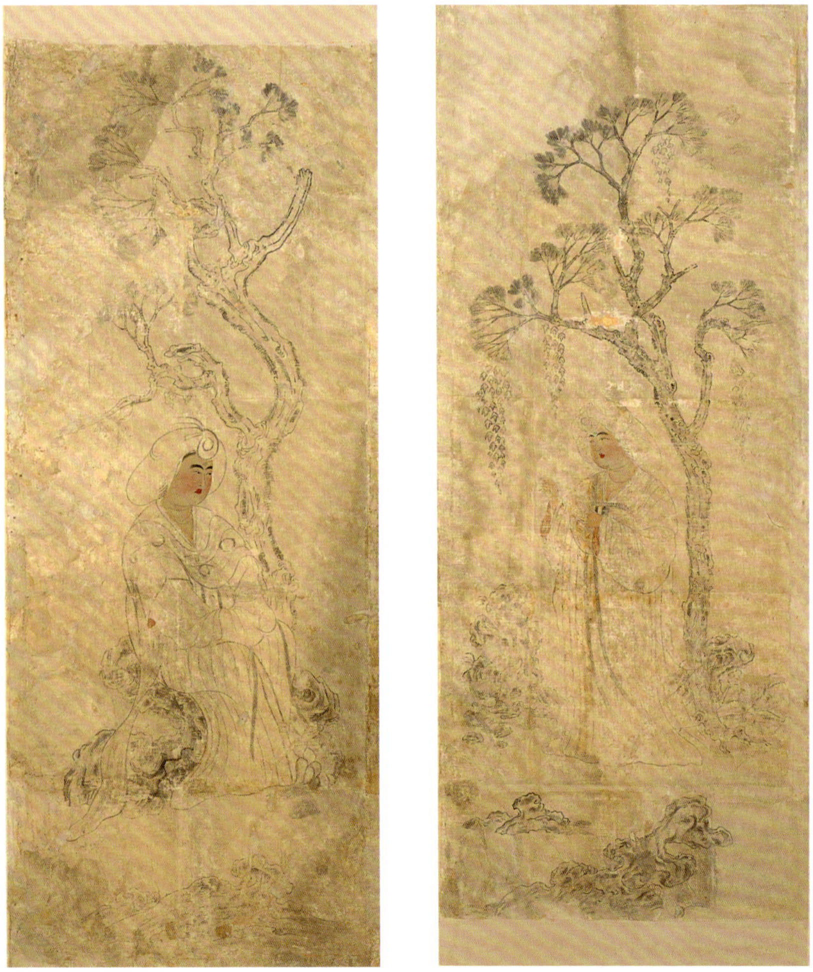

FIG. 41
*Screen with Ladies under Trees*, c.752
Two panels from a set of six, ink and colour on paper.
Shōsō-in, Nara

Wei family tomb in Nanliwang Village, Chang'an County, Shaanxi Province. The screen was painted on the south section of the west wall of the burial chamber, and depicts beautiful court ladies beneath trees. Each panel features one woman and her attendant, a configuration that is basically the same as that of the Shōsō-in's *Screen with Ladies under Trees*. It is clear, then, that the Japanese screen was the direct successor to a format and composition popular in Tang China, although the motif itself can be traced back to India and denotes holiness. For the screen's original owner, Emperor Shōmu, the work was perhaps all the more admirable as an immediate link to a land that held for him a particular fascination.

The Japanese imperial collection of painting and calligraphy in this period clearly evoked the character of the Tang Chinese collection, with the ranking of calligraphy above painting reflecting the state of these arts during the Tang dynasty. The reverence accorded Wang Xizhi in Japan also echoes Tang taste. In 639, the Tang emperor Taizong (r. 627–49) commanded that all calligraphy by Wang Xizhi be brought to him. Since he was willing to pay a high price, he was able to gather excellent examples from every part of China. When the history of the Jin dynasty was compiled, the Emperor himself wrote the entry on Wang Xizhi. He even requested that on his death, Wang's *Preface to the Poems of the Orchid Pavilion Gathering*, which he had finally obtained, should be buried with him.

## EMPEROR GO-SHIRAKAWA AND EMPEROR HUIZONG

In the Heian period, *karamono*, or 'Chinese things' in general, were highly prized. Beginning in the tenth century, they were distributed by the emperor to the empress, the empress dowager, the grand empress dowager, the crown prince and the royal regents and advisers. For the aristocracy, who were supported through networks of gift-giving, the possession of *karamono* had a direct bearing on their political power.

Treasured items and valuable books associated with the Heian emperors were generally placed for safekeeping in the storehouses and libraries of the imperial palace.[8] It is known that inherited treasures (*rekidai hōmotsu*) were stored in the Gyōden, general imperial treasures (*kōrei no gyobutsu*) were placed in the Kyōshoden and Ryōkiden, and other imperial items were housed in the Keihōbō and Ranrinbō. Among the treasures stored in the Gyōden were calligraphies by Wang Xizhi, possibly moved there from the Shōsō-in.

There are also cases of a retired emperor, after his abdication, placing treasured items and books in temple and palace storehouses associated with him. During the Insei era, or period of 'cloistered rule' (1086–1192), for example, Retired Emperor Go-Shirakawa (r. 1155–8) built a repository for his possessions at the Rengeō-in (popularly called Sanjūsangendō) on the grounds of his Hōjū-ji-*dono* palace.[9] Although the contents of the Rengeō-in treasure house are not fully known, various documents can assist us in reconstructing them, and it is clear that books and other writings, Buddhist paintings, illustrated handscrolls, musical instruments, costumes and weapons formed the core of the assemblage. Also known to have been included in the collection are examples from the new wave of Chinese painting, such as *Mandala of Kujaku Myōō*, from the text *Compilation of Kakuzen*. The assemblage in the Rengeō-in represents a shift in focus from calligraphy, which dominated the Shōsō-in collection, to painting (illustrated handscrolls and Buddhist works), a crucial change that characterizes the collections of the aristocracy as well. The transformation can be seen as a response to the increasing importance of painting in the collection of the Northern Song dynasty (960–1127) emperors in China.[10] Since Go-Shirakawa was well aware that art collections functioned as symbols of royal power, it was only natural, perhaps, that he turned his gaze towards the Chinese emperor Huizong (r. 1101–25), who had a passion for collecting both painting and calligraphy (cat. no. 17).[11]

## THE ADORATION OF ALL THINGS CHINESE AND THE HIGASHIYAMA GYOMOTSU

From the end of the Heian period on, the passion for *karamono* and *kara-e* ('Chinese pictures') took hold in Japan and spread throughout the country, with Buddhist temples and monasteries becoming centres for the new current.[12] In Kyoto, the monk Shunjō (1166–1227) founded the Zen Buddhist temple Senryū-ji, and Myōe (1173–1232) took Chinese Song period (960–1279) iconographic drawings and Buddhist paintings to Kozan-ji. Tōfuku-ji in Kyoto and Enkaku-ji in Kamakura were also among the temples that played a major role in Zen, which had spread to Japan from China, where it developed in the sixth century. The interest in things Chinese continued through the rise of the samurai and the establishment of the Kamakura shogunate, the military government that ruled Japan from 1192 to 1333. Its Kanazawa Hōjō clan, who were the real power-holders in the late Kamakura, accumulated a large number of Chinese artefacts, which they placed both in the Wakamiya and Tsurugaoka storehouses of the Tsurugaoka Hachimangū shrine in Kamakura, and in the library Kanazawa Bunko in Yokohama, a section of which is still in existence today.

The third shogun of the Muromachi period (1336–1573), Ashikaga Yoshimitsu (r. 1368–94), was very much aware of the collection of the Song emperors, and with the Chinese assemblage in mind, gave a more definite form to the Japanese collection and its display. Yoshimitsu, who acted as a unifier during the Nanbokuchō period (1336–92) of the Muromachi, used a vigorous adoption of Zen to increase his political and military power. In imitation of Daxiangguo Temple ('Great Shōkoku-ji') in the Northern Song capital Kaifeng, he had the Zen temple Shōkoku-ji built; he also organized the major temples in Kyoto and Kamakura according to the Gozan (Ch. Wushan; 'five mountains') system of administration of Chinese Chan (J. Zen) temples during the Northern Song.[13] After becoming a monk at age 38, Yoshimitsu moved to a country estate, the Kitayama dai. (The villa became the temple Rokuon-ji, popularly known as Kinkaku-ji, after his death.) He played a leading role in the arts of the period, his residence in the northern hills of Kyoto giving its name to the lively 'Kitayama' culture (*bunka*).

*Portrait of Ashikaga Yoshimitsu* (1408) by the Muromachi painter Tosa Yukihiro (act. 1st half 15th century), housed at Rokuon-ji, was handed down to his son, the fourth shogun Yoshimochi (r. 1394–1423). Yoshimochi displayed the portrait at the Buddhist memorial service for his father marking the 49th day after Yoshimitsu's death, held on the 25th day of the 6th month of 1408. The upper part of the scroll carries an inscription by Yoshimochi, in which he states that as all material things are illusion, the body also has no real substance. Even the mind was absent from the beginning, he writes, and sin and good fortune alike will flow away. Yoshimochi never praises his father, but rather emphasizes the differences in their chosen paths. The passage in the inscription was taken from the beginning of a Buddhist teaching given by the Chinese Chan master Dahui Zonggao (1089–1163) on the third anniversary of Huizong's death.[14] In using it, Yoshimochi was probably referencing his father's passion for cultural objects, drawing a parallel to Huizong's grand collection. It indicates Yoshimitsu's awareness of the Northern Song emperor, and is evidence of the part played by Huizong in the Japanese imagination during the Muromachi.

The Muromachi shogunal collection of *karamono* is generally known as the 'Higashiyama *gyomotsu*', or the Higashiyama Treasures, 'Higashiyama' being a reference to the mountain retreat of the eighth shogun, Ashikaga Yoshimasa (r. 1449–73). One source of knowledge about the paintings in the collection is *Tōhaku's Explanation of Painting*, consisting of comments by the Momoyama period (1573–1615) painter Hasegawa Tōhaku (1539–1610). 'In the Higashiyama palace are a huge number of decorations,' reads one passage. 'They are hung everywhere, up even to the eaves of the roof. The Chinese paintings [*kara-e*], all the Higashiyama palace treasures, are a magnificent sight.' Thus, by the Momoyama period, the Chinese paintings in the Higashiyama Treasures collection were legendary, and as masterpieces of Chinese painting, had a well-established value.

Documentary evidence and extant works indicate, however, that the core of the collection was not the objects brought in by Yoshimasa himself, but those collected by Yoshimitsu and the sixth shogun, Yoshinori (r. 1428–41), with the main part consisting of the Chinese paintings assembled by Yoshimitsu.[15] One of the documents is the inventory of Chinese paintings in the Ashikaga collection known as the *Catalogue of Imperial Paintings* (Tokyo National Museum and others), attributed to Nōami (1397–1441). The scrolls are listed in sets of three related works, presumably to emphasize the impression the viewer receives when seeing them displayed together and to make their exhibition more memorable. Chinese artists are placed in general categories, which include monk-artists like Muxi (d. *c.* 1281) and Yujian (act. 2nd half 13th century); court painters such as Xia Gui (act. 1180–1230) (cat. no. 28, 29) and Liang Kai (act. late 12th–early 13th century); and professional Buddhist painters like Zhang Sigong (act. late 12th–early 13th century) (cat. no. 36) and Jin Dashou (act. late 12th–early 13th century).

The *Record of Decorations on the Occasion of an Imperial Visit to the Muromachi-dono Palace* (Tokugawa Art Museum,

Nagoya), also compiled by Nōami, documents the appearance of the reception room at Yoshinori's residence on the occasion of a visit there by Emperor Go-Hanazono (r. 1428–64) in 1437. This record allows us to know which works were considered most important in Yoshinori's time. Also helpful in understanding the history of the collection is the presence of collection seals: the square relief seals of Yoshimitsu, *Tenzan* and *Doyu*; Yoshinori's intaglio seal *Zakkeshitsu-in*; and a gourd-shaped relief seal, *Ze'a*, indicating that the work was in the shogunal storehouse when it was under the management of Zen'ami (act. 2nd half 14th century), around the time of Yoshimitsu.[16] *Kara-e* that appear in the *Record of Decorations* are primarily Southern Song period (1127–1279) paintings of the imperial academy and Buddhist paintings, especially those related to Chan.[17] The reason the Muromachi shoguns did not collect works from the contemporaneous Ming dynasty (1368–1644), but were infatuated with the older Southern Song and Yuan dynasty (1271–1368) paintings, was not merely a question of taste. While it can be termed anachronistic, the desire for Southern Song objects can be seen as arising from the parallel roles Zen and Chan served in the construction of culture in Muromachi Japan and Southern Song China, respectively. For example, a standard work by the mid-Southern Song academy painter Ma Yuan (act. late 12th–early 13th century), the pair of hanging scrolls entitled *The Priest Qingliang* and *The Priest Yunmen* (figs 42–3), would probably have been stored either in the shogunal palace, as part of the Higashiyama Treasures, or in a Zen temple in Kyoto affiliated with the Ashikaga. This is a work, then, that can be seen as uniting the concepts of 'court painting' and 'Chan Buddhist painting'. Both scrolls have inscriptions by Empress Yang (popularly known as Yang Meizi; 1172–1232), the consort of the Southern Song emperor Ningzong (r. 1195–1224). The presence of imperial inscriptions makes it clear that while the theme of the work

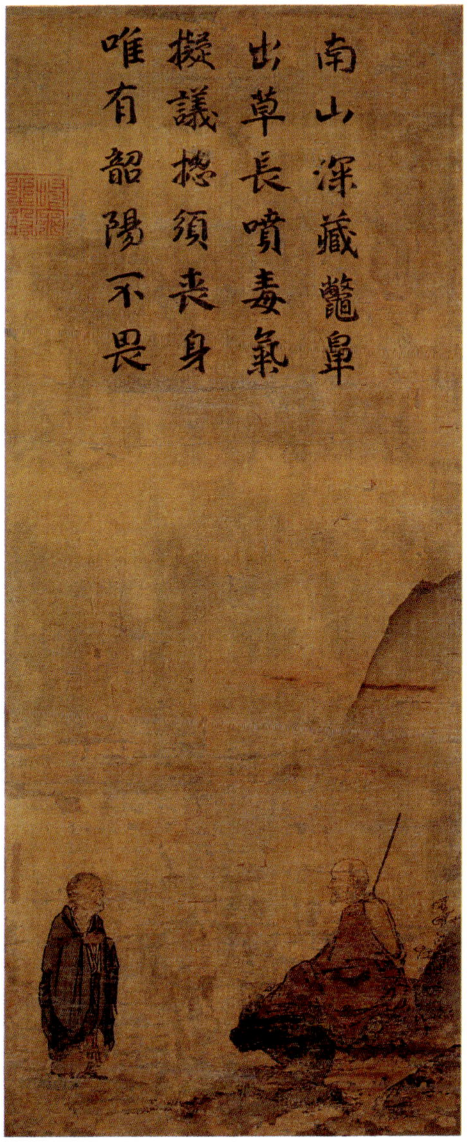


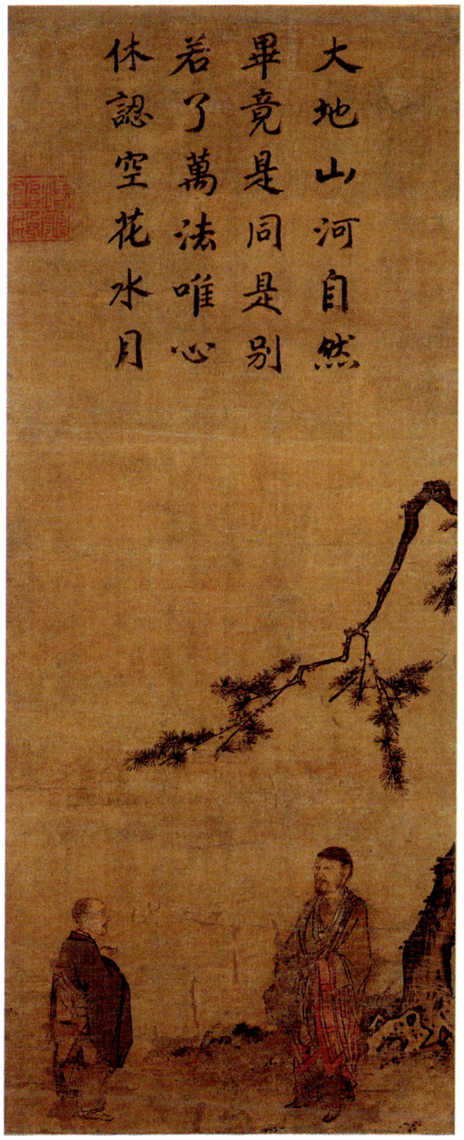


FIG. 42
Ma Yuan (act. late 12th–early 13th century). *The Priest Qingliang* hanging scroll, 13th century. Ink and colour on silk. Tenryū-ji, Kyoto

FIG. 43
Ma Yuan (act. late 12th–early 13th century). *The Priest Yunmen* hanging scroll, 13th century. Ink and colour on silk. Tenryū-ji, Kyoto

is Chan, the calligraphy and painting belong to the realm of the ruler and court painter. Even among the great Southern Song paintings collected from this time, *The Priests Qingliang and Yunmen* can be regarded as a masterpiece.

The Northern Song period *Peach Blossom and Dove* by Huizong and the Southern Song work once attributed to him, *Landscapes of the Four Seasons (Summer, Autumn, Winter)* (Kuon-ji and Konchi-in, Kyoto), provide a direct connection between Huizong and Yoshimitsu, and the presence of these scrolls in Yoshimitsu's collection holds important symbolic meaning. *Peach Blossom and Dove* is central to the image of Huizong in Japan even today. Yoshimitsu's collector's seal *Tenzan* appears at the lower left, and the title written by Sōami (d.1525) is attached. The 'slender gold' style of calligraphy and the style of the painting are characteristic of Huizong. *Landscapes of the Four Seasons (Summer, Autumn, Winter)*, on the other hand, listed in the fourth volume of the *Catalogue of Imperial Paintings* as 'Landscape, Emperor Huizong', is now known to be not of Huizong's period, but from the early Southern Song. It is, however, considered to be one of the highest-quality landscape paintings produced by the Southern Song academy.

The majority of works known through the *Catalogue of Imperial Paintings* to have been collected by Yoshimitsu are Chan paintings by the Chinese monk-painter Muxi, who was active at the end of the Southern Song and the beginning of the Yuan.[18] Muxi was born in Shu (modern Sichuan Province), and studied Chan with a high-ranking monk also from Shu, Wuzhun Shifan (1178–1249). Among those who practised Chan under Wuzhun were a number of Japanese monks, including Enni Ben'en (1202–80), the founder of Tōfuku-ji. Muxi was the equivalent of their fellow student. Much about Muxi's life is unknown. It is not clear at what point he left Shu for Hangzhou, though we do know that afterwards he went to live at Liutong Temple on the shores of the West Lake, an ancient temple dating back to the Five Dynasties period (907–60). He died during the Zhiyuan era (1264–94) of the reign of Kublai Khan (1260–94).

The most famous of Muxi's paintings in East Asia believed to be from the hand of the artist himself – *White-robed Guanyin, Crane and Gibbons* (Daitoku-ji, Kyoto), *Arhat* (Seikadō Bunko Art Museum), *Laozi* (Okayama Prefectural Art Museum) and *Eight Views of the Xiao and Xiang* – were all collected during the time of Yoshimitsu. *Slumbering Budai* (cat. no. 42), is also attributed to Muxi. One cannot say that Muxi was highly esteemed in his own country, as China was dominated by literati painting at the time. It was very likely the extraordinary regard in which Muxi was held in Japan, however, that strengthened the appeal of Southern Song Chan Buddhism in the Kamakura period, especially from the establishment of the Higashiyama Treasures onwards.

The Higashiyama Treasures were overseen by a class of shogunal attendants known as *dōbōshū*, or 'companions'.[19] This group had a variety of duties, primarily within the palace, and appeared as part monk, part layman, displaying the shaved head of a priest but carrying a sword – an image that comes from the handscrolls *Pilgrimage of the Shogun to the Rokujō Hachimangu Shrine* (Rokujō Hachimangu, Kyoto) and *History of Jūnen-ji Temple* (Jūnen-ji, Kyoto).[20] The *dōbōshū* responsible for the decoration of the large rooms used for gatherings and entertainments had special skills. The so-called 'Three Amis', Nōami, Gei'ami (1431–85) and Sōami, were in charge of the collection, authentication, display and repair of works of art, the equivalent of the curatorial staff of a museum today. They were known, moreover, as leading artists in their own right and as part of the wider intellectual community. Nōami's masterpiece *Screens of Birds and Flowers* (Idemitsu Museum of Arts) allows us a glimpse of how his direct experience with the Higashiyama Treasures worked to create a consensus between the connoisseur and the maker of art.

The *dōbōshū*, with their finely developed sensibilities, controlled the connoisseurship of Chinese painting, and part of their appreciation involved the cutting up, joining together, reworking and revising of the artworks under their management. A typical example of the breaking up of a handscroll concerns *Eight Views of the Xiao and Xiang* by Muxi.[21] There is a record of Yoshimitsu dividing Muxi's handscroll into the eight paintings and mounting them as separate hanging scrolls, then displaying them side by side in the reception room. The Eight Views theme expresses the subtle variations in light and atmosphere that occur as early evening passes into night. In Muxi's rendering, one finds a wide range in expressive effect, from the dramatic contrasts of light and dark in 'Fishing Village in Sunset Glow' (Nezu Museum) and the fierce wind and slashing rain of 'Returning Sails off Distant Shores' (Kyoto National Museum), to the lightly brushed birds of 'Wild Geese Descending to a Sandbar' (Idemitsu Museum of Arts) and the soft mists of 'Evening Bell from a Distant Temple' (Hatakeyama Memorial Museum of Fine Art), in which temple and foliage appear and disappear.

Similarly, Yoshimasa is described in *Tōhaku's Explanation of Painting* as cutting up Yujian's *Eight Views of the Xiao and Xiang*. However, in the *Record of Decorations* there is mention of Yujian's painting displayed in the palace as separate scrolls, which suggests that the work must have been made into eight hanging scrolls earlier, at least by the time of Yoshinori in the fifteenth century. Documents such as the *Record of Yamanoue Sōji* and *Tōhaku's Explanation of Painting* make it clear that the paintings later became very highly valued in the tea world. Nevertheless, the works now considered part of Yujian's *Eight Views* did not originally comprise a set: 'Returning Sails off Distant Shores' (Tokugawa Art Museum, Nagoya) was painted on Japanese mulberry paper, which is different to that used for the two other extant scenes, 'Mountain Market in Clearing Mist' (Idemitsu Museum of Arts) and 'Autumn Moon over Lake Dongting' (Japanese Agency for Cultural Affairs).

While the techniques used in mounting artwork are generally different in China and Japan, the origins of what may be thought of as the distinctly Japanese use of long narrow hanging strips of cloth called *fūtai* (Ch. *Jindai*) in fact can be found in Song China. It can be seen in the hanging scroll depicted in a painting from *Five Hundred Arhats* by the Southern Song painters Lin Tinggui (act. 2nd half 12th century) and Zhou Jichang (act. 2nd half 12th century, cat. nos 23, 24), and in another painting from *The Four Pleasures: Music, Chess, Calligraphy and Painting* (cat. no. 53) traditionally attributed to the Yuan dynasty artist Ren Renfa (1255–1327). In addition, Chinese paintings of the period in Japan are known to have been mounted luxuriously in gold brocade, a silk fabric that sparkled where the pattern was picked out in gold thread. This extravagant mounting was called 'Higashiyama mounting', and one can suppose it was used on many of the Higashiyama Treasures.[22]

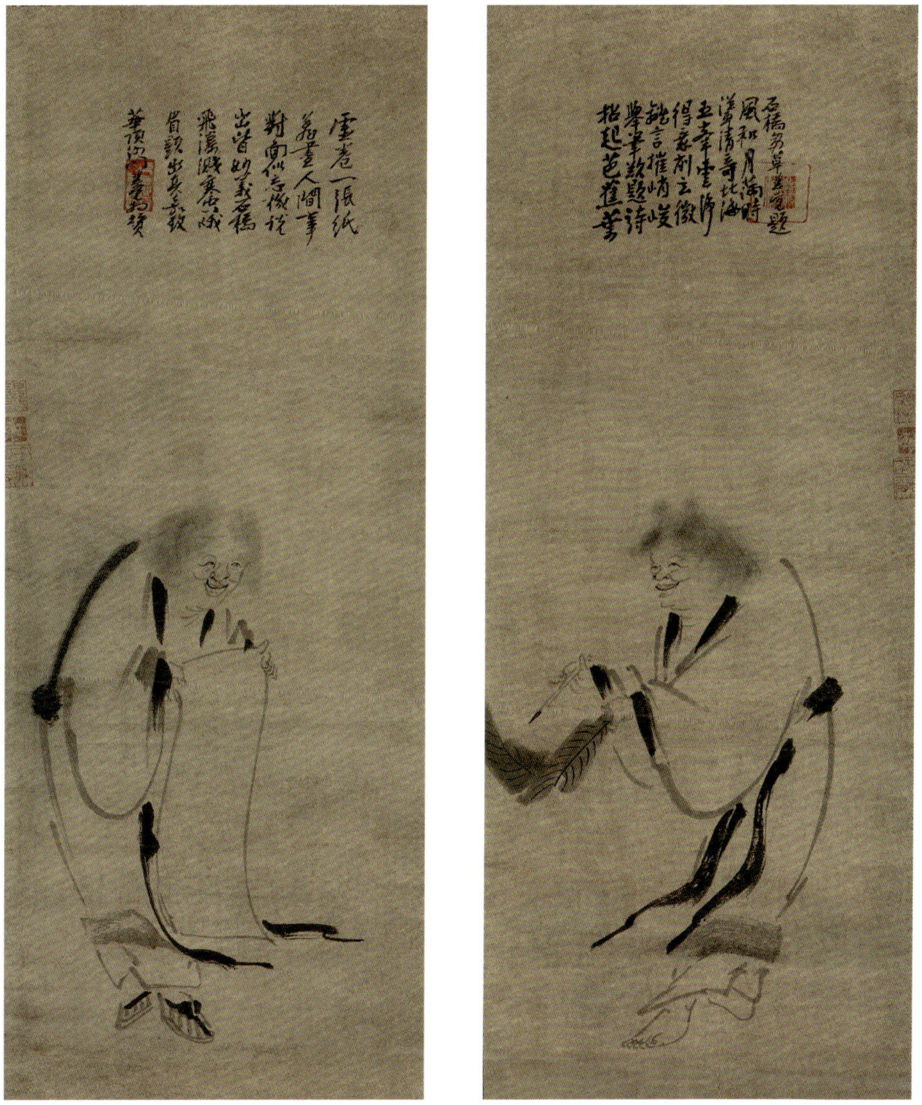

FIG. 44
Attributed to Yintuoluo (act. 2nd half 14th century). *Hanshan and Shide* hanging scrolls, 14th century. Ink on paper. Tokyo National Museum (TA–139)

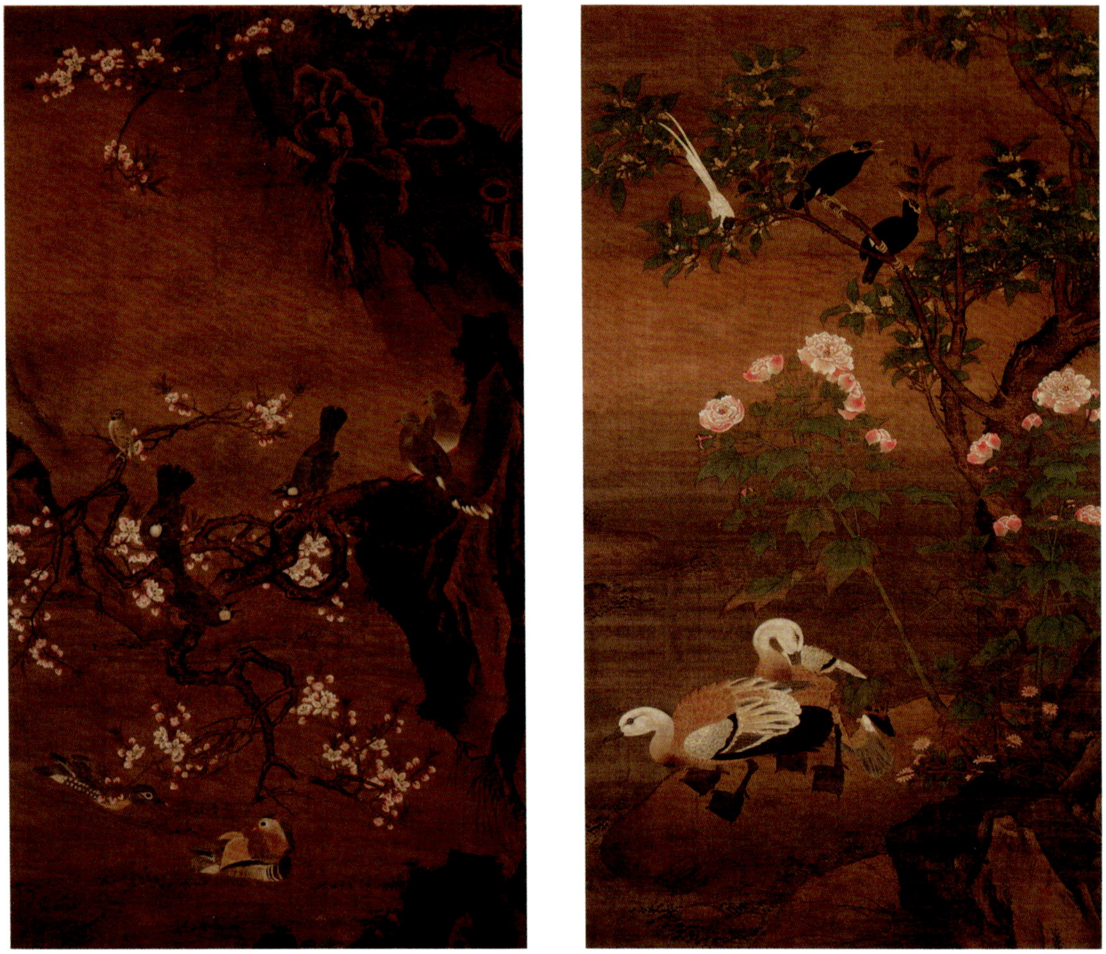

FIG. 45
Lü Ji (act. 1488–1505).
*Birds and Flowers of the Four Seasons*
hanging scrolls, 15th–16th century.
Two scrolls from a set of four,
ink and colour on silk.
Tokyo National Museum
(TA-163)

## DIFFERENCES BETWEEN CHINESE AND JAPANESE TASTES IN PAINTING

From the Muromachi period onward, China and Japan followed very different paths. Beginning in the Yuan dynasty, China was dominated by a view of painting history that put literati painting at the centre, and the literati became primarily responsible not only for the production of art, but also for its collection and assessment. In Japan, Zen monks were the intellectual elite of the day, and as such, took on the role of the literati in China. We find a huge gap between the tastes of Chinese and Japanese painting circles in this period, and a particular Japanese aesthetic preference is evident in the type of work collected. In China, the Yuan artists referred to as the 'Four Yuan Masters' and held in highest esteem were all literati-painters: Huang Gongwang (1269–1354), Wu Zhen (1280–1354), Ni Zan (1306–74) and Wang Meng (c.1308–85). By contrast, Yuan dynasty paintings collected in Japan reflected the preferences of Zen monks.

Representative of this taste is *Hama and Tieguai* (Chion-ji, Kyoto) by Yan Hui (act. early 14th century), an artist active in the early Yuan who specialized in painting religious figures. This is a type of highly coloured figure painting associated with China that had been known in Japan since the mediaeval era. Five segments from *Deeds of the Chan Masters* by Yintuoluo (act. 2nd half 14th century) of the Yuan are designated National Treasures: *Hanshan and Shide* (fig. 44), *Danxia Burning Buddhist Statues* (Ishibashi Museum of Art), *Budai and Jiang Mohe* (Nezu Museum), *Zichang and Courtier Libo* (Hatakeyama Memorial Museum of Fine Art) and *Priest Zhichang* (Seikadō Bunko Art Museum). These paintings have been highly esteemed ever since the time of Ashikaga Yoshimochi.

Chan paintings employing the techniques of 'ink play' associated with literati works were also present in large numbers in Japan. These include *Bamboo and Orchid* (Imperial Household Agency, Sannomaru) by the Yuan artist Xue Chuang (act. mid-14th century) and *Withered Trees* (private collection), a pair of hanging scrolls by Ziting Zubai (act. mid-14th century), also of the Yuan.

Little importance would have been attached to such paintings in their homeland, where the premier position in painting history was given to literati painting.

The situation is similar for Ming dynasty art. Few good works by the Wu school of literati painting, dominant at the time in China, were collected in Japan; rather, it is high-quality paintings by artists of the Zhe school active at the imperial court that were transmitted in large numbers. Examples include *Phoenix* by Lin Liang (c.1416–c.1480) (Shōkoku-ji, Kyoto) and Lü Ji's (act. 1488–1505) *Birds and Flowers of the Four Seasons* (fig. 45). During the Japanese Edo period (1603–1868), the disparity in taste in China and Japan is reflected in the vogue for a type of Song-Yuan manner seen in the work of such Qing dynasty (1644–1911) Chinese artists as Shen Quan (1682–c.1760). In early Qing China, the Four Wangs were dominant, and, in bird-and-flower painting, Yun Shouping (1633–90). Although Yun became popular later in Japan, the difference is immediately apparent between his elegant style, with its delicate colours, and that of Shen Quan, characterized by bright colours and meticulous detail.

Painters who travelled to Japan during the Edo and took with them such styles of painting that were somewhat marginal in the Qing art world were known as *raihaku gajin*. Most of Shen Quan's known masterpieces, for example, are extant in Japan. A number of his works were secured in a daimyo collection in the Edo period; among the most prominent was *Cat Trying to Catch Insects* (Seikadō Bunko Art Museum).

Another route by which Chinese culture entered Japan during the Edo was through the Huangbo (J. Obaku) sect of Chan Buddhism. Along with Huangbo paintings, works such as the huge *Nirvana of the Buddha* with the signature of the late Ming Eccentric Wu Bin (act. late 16th–early 17th century) (Sōfuku-ji, Nagasaki) came in that way.

These Chinese paintings served as an inspiration to Edo artists, and their impact was enormous. Colourful literati paintings of the late Ming/early Qing were also imported, and were behind the development of new artistic trends in the Edo period. Important among these paintings was *Autumn Landscape* (Seikadō Art Museum), part of a set of twelve hanging scrolls by Lan Ying (1585–c.1664). Multiple copies of the work are extant from the latter part of the Edo period, indicating that it was used as a model.[23] One also finds the work of Fujian artists, including that of Zhang Ruitu (c.1570–1641) and Wang Jianzhang (act. mid-17th century), who were highly regarded in their own country.[24] As the political situation in Qing China deteriorated, works from all periods were imported into Japan in large numbers. They became the foundation for the collections amassed by early modern industrialists: the Abe Collection in the Osaka City Museum of Fine Arts, the Seikadō collection of the Iwasaki family and the Sumitomo family's Sen'okuhakkokan collection are examples.[25] The general preference for Southern Song painting, however, remained strong, and the system of evaluation in which the Higashiyama Treasures represent the highest achievement in painting is still very much in place today. Shared and disparate tastes in both countries directly affected the type of artwork desired and its availability for collecting, and so guided the formation and development of Chinese art collections in Japan. Each age saw certain artworks become 'classics' and the rise of different concepts of beauty. Works painted in Japan in the Chinese mode came to be called *kara-e* or *kanga*, the same terms used to refer to Chinese paintings themselves. One finds that the distance between China and Japan expanded and contracted as aesthetic tastes and collecting practices converged and diverged through the ages.

1 Hashimoto 1997; Yoneda 1998a, 1998b and 2000; Sugimoto 2008
2 I am grateful to Inamoto Yasuo of Kyoto University Social Sciences Research Institute for calling my attention to the importance of Ashoka.
3 Yoneda 1998a
4 Tokyo 2013
5 Itakura 2013
6 Matsushima 1976
7 Itakura 2002
8 Tajima 2004, 2006a and 2006b
9 Takei 1998
10 Tsukamoto 2011a, 2011b and 2012
11 Ihara 2004; Ebrey and Bickford 2006
12 Seki 2002; Kawazoe and Minagawa 2011
13 Nishiyama 2011
14 Takagishi 2004 and 2011
15 Tokyo and Nagoya 1976; Baker 1993; Shimao in Tokyo 2004; Nagoya 2008
16 Yamamoto in Nagoya 2008
17 Shimao 1989; Hata 2004; Shimao 2006; Takagishi 2011
18 Toda 1973, Tokyo 1996a
19 Shimao 1994; Ietsuka 1997, 1998, 2001, 2009 and 2010
20 Shimosaka 2003
21 Takagi 1935; Tsukahara 1991; Tokyo 1995; Tokyo 1996a
22 Tokyo 2000
23 Kōno 2001 and 2002; Itakura 2012a
24 Kyoto 2006; Itakura 2012b
25 *Changes, Images and Fashion* 2008; Society for the Research of Collections 2012; Harada 2012

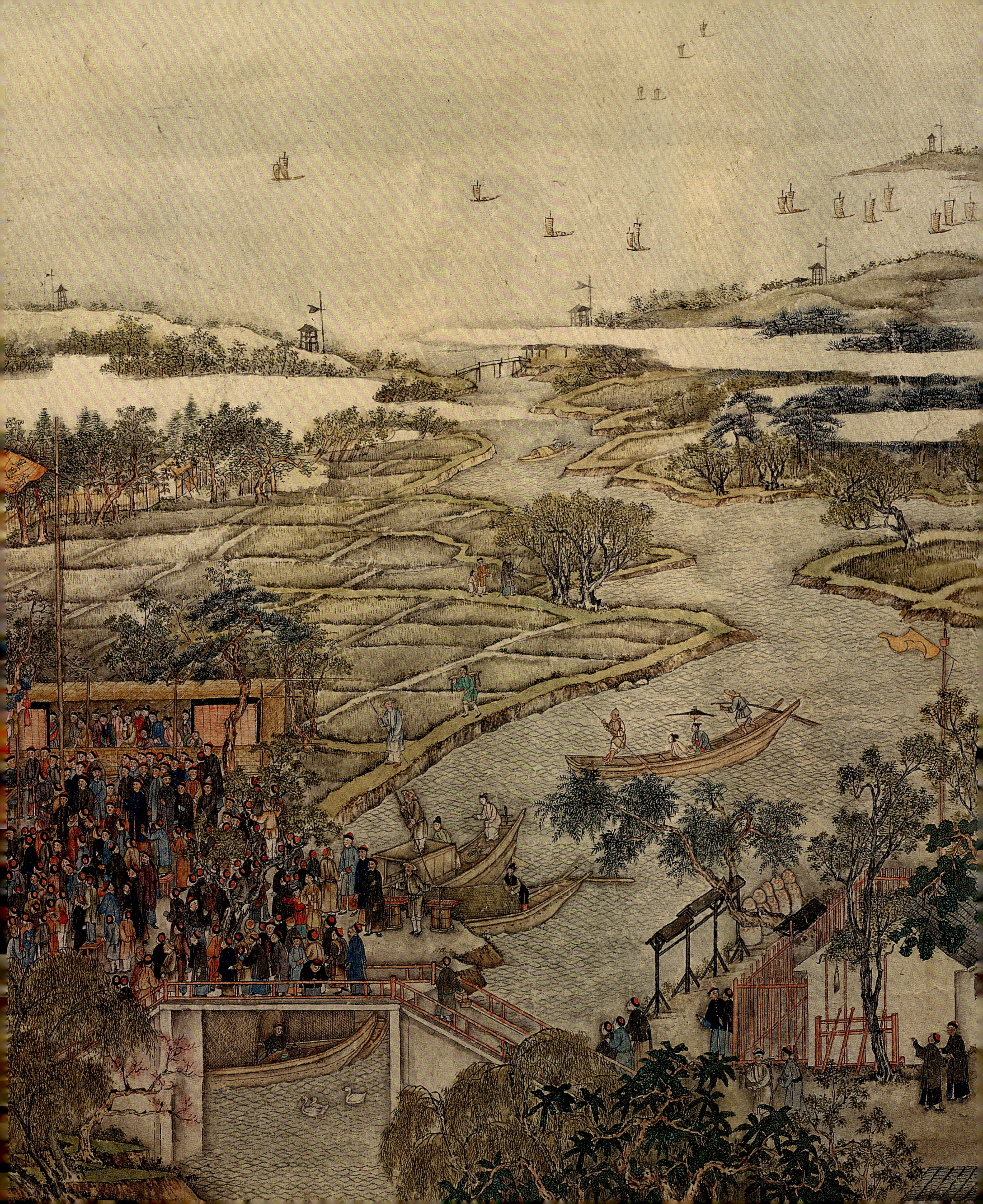

# A BRIEF HISTORY OF COLLECTING PAINTINGS IN CHINA

Ling Lizhong

Paintings, calligraphy and other types of artworks have seen a very long history of collecting in China. Both government and private collections of paintings had their true beginnings as early as the Six Dynasties period (220–589), when scroll paintings began to be produced in some quantity. Such works have thus clearly been a source of fascination in their homeland for over 1,500 years.

From the Six Dynasties through the Sui (581–618) and Tang (618–907) periods, the role of the collector or connoisseur evolved in line with changes in the role of painting itself. Initially, painting had essentially served to glorify the governance of the emperor, to promulgate the state religion and to indoctrinate the people, and examples were found mainly on the walls of the imperial palace and religious sites such as temples. As scrolls of paintings and especially calligraphy became more popular, they also featured in the imperial collection. Notable imperial collectors of painting and calligraphy mentioned in contemporary sources include Huan Xuan (369–404) of the Jin dynasty (265–420); Emperor Gao (r. 479–82) of the Qi (479–502); Emperor Yang (r. 605–16) of the Sui; and Emperor Taizong (r. 627–49), Empress Wu Zetian (r. 690–705) and Emperor Xuanzong (r. 712–55) of the Tang – in fact, these were main collectors in this era. At the same time, private collectors and connoisseurs also began to appear, most of them art critics or artists and calligraphers themselves, such as Gu Kaizhi (c.344–c.406) of the Eastern Jin dynasty (317–420) and Zhang Huaiguan (c.704–c.763) and Zhang Yanyuan (815–76) of the Tang, whose collections were acquired either by direct purchase or as gifts bestowed upon them either by the imperial family or by the emperor himself. As with the imperial collections, by the Tang dynasty collectors' seals or signatures were being added to works in private collections; for example, the Eastern Jin anonymous calligraphic work *Elegy for Cao E* (Liaoning Provincial Museum) bears the signatures of collectors from the Northern and Southern Dynasties (420–589), Sui and Tang periods. A number of works also found their way to Japan at this time, such as an early Tang period tracing copy of Wang Xizhi's (303–65) *Note of Distress and Indignation* (see page 87), which was owned by the Japanese emperor Kammu (r. 781–806) of the Enryaku era (781–806), and bears a square relief seal of the era reading *Enreki chokutei*.

As the Tang and Song (960–1279) dynasties unfolded, paintings came to be more greatly appreciated and enjoyed; however, large-scale imperial collections remained predominant, reaching a peak during the Northern (960–1127) and Southern (1127–1279) Song. The imperial court of the Northern Song emperor Huizong (r. 1101–25), for example, amassed a total of 1,248 works of calligraphy and 6,390 scroll paintings from the Six Dynasties to the early Song period. Huizong's inventory of the imperial collection, the *Xuanhe Painting Catalogue* contained records of the paintings, among which were *The Five Planets and Twenty-eight Constellations*, traditionally attributed to Zhang Sengyou (act. 490–540) (cat. no. 13), and Zhang Xuan's (act. 714–42) *The Picture of Pounding*. The above figures did not include works produced by painters in the imperial painting academy or by Huizong himself, such as *Auspicious Cranes* (cat. no. 17) and the copy of Zhang Xuan's *The Picture of Pounding* entitled *Court Ladies Preparing Newly Woven Silk* (cat. no. 16), the majority of which (over 1,100 works) were later pillaged by Emperor Zhangzong (r. 1190–1208) of the Jurchen-ruled Jin dynasty (1115–1234) and entered the collection of the Jin imperial court. Emperor Zhangzong's mother was in fact a daughter of the Song emperor Huizong, and Zhangzong was thus an ardent admirer of Han-Chinese art. Zhangzong also wrote in a hand similar to Huizong's 'slender gold' (*shoujin*) style of calligraphy (fig. 47), as in the title-inscription written by Zhangzong on the 'separator' (*geshui*) of the copy of Zhang

cat. no. 76 (detail)

FIG. 46
Zhang Zeduan (act. early 12th century). *Along the River during the Qingming Festival* handscroll (detail), early 12th century. Ink and colour on silk. The Palace Museum, Beijing

Xuan's work. His seven seals stamped on the scroll also imitate Emperor Huizong's seven Xuanhe reign (1119–25) imperial seals (see also fig. 34).

The imperial collections of the Southern Song dynasty are best exemplified by that of its first emperor, Gaozong (r. 1127–62), who established his capital in the city of Hangzhou. As the political climate began to stabilize, the Emperor sought to obtain the paintings that were being dispersed from the former Northern Song capital, Bianliang (today's Kaifeng in Henan Province). The Southern Song imperial collections were also derived from other sources, such as confiscation of the estates of Jia Sidao (1213–75), a chancellor known for his corruption and incompetence. All of these works were stamped with the confiscation seal *Taizhoushi Fangwu didangku ji* ('The Storeroom of Confiscated Estates, the City of Taizhou'). The Huizong painting academy's copy of Zhang Xuan's *Lady Guoguo on an Outing*, now in the Liaoning Provincial Museum, is one such work.

Significantly, the wave of private collections that started in earlier dynasties grew much bigger in the Song. While the main activity was still centred on the court, now collectors emerged among the aristocracy and high-ranking officials as well as among the artists themselves, and a number of works also began to circulate amongst the wealthy, thus marking a major transition in the history of art collecting in China. One such collector was the scholar-official Su Yijian (958–97), who was sent by the Northern Song emperor Taizong (r. 976–97) to seek out calligraphies and paintings from the former court of Li Yu (r. 961–78) of the Southern Tang dynasty (937–75); returning with some 1,000 masterpieces, he received 100 in reward, which remained in his family for four generations.
Other influential collectors included the above-mentioned Southern Song chancellor Jia Sidao, who rose up through the ranks as a result of his family connections, and at the height of his power had amassed an art collection comparable to that of the emperor. The British Museum's *Admonitions of the Court Instructress to the Palace Ladies* scroll (fig. 8) was part of Jia's private collection. Among other notable collectors were the well-known scholar-artist Mi Fu (1051–1107), the poet Su Shi (1037–1101) and the

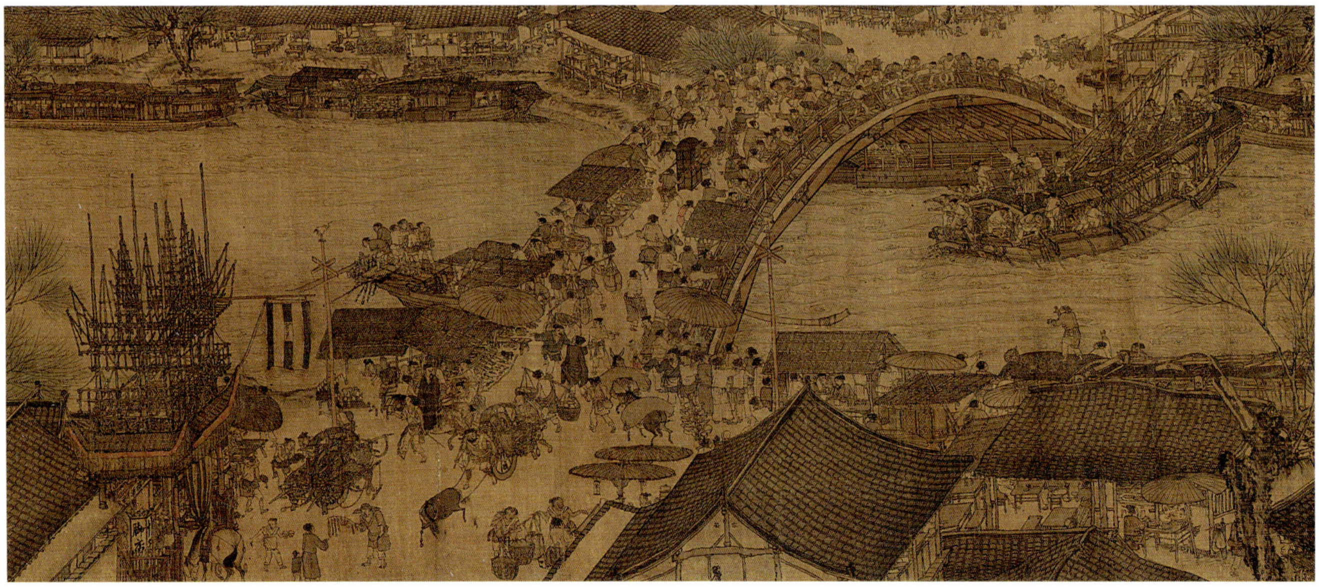

FIG. 47
Calligraphy from *Auspicious Cranes*
(detail of cat. no. 17)

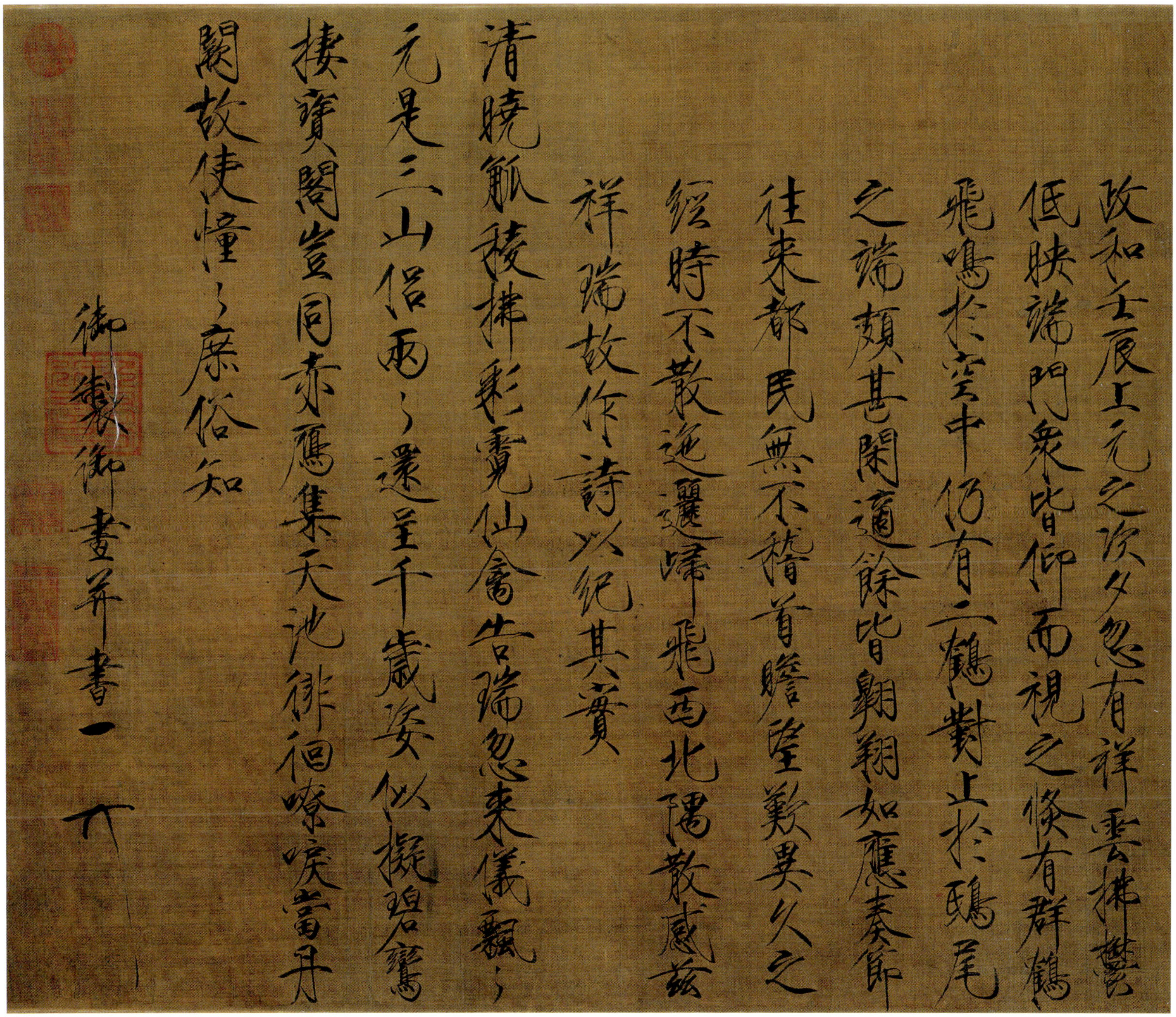

painters Li Gonglin (*c.*1049–1106) and Wang Shen (1048–1104) – all seasoned connoisseurs who had in their possession a wealth of artworks. Mi Fu owned over 60 works of calligraphy and paintings from the Six Dynasties to the Five Dynasties (907–60) period. During the Southern Song dynasty, Yan Wengui's (967–1030) *Landscape with Pavilions* (cat. no. 15) was in the private collection of Zhao Zishu (1089–1142), an official in Xiuzhou at the start of the Shaoxing reign period (1131–62), and the work bears his two seals. In the same vein, Hu Shunchen's (act. early 12th century) *Farewell to Hao Xuanming, Envoy to Qin* (cat. no. 20) of 1122 was amongst his friend Hao Xuanming's (act. early 12th century) most prized possessions, and Qiao Zhongchang's (act. late 11th–early 12th century) *Illustration to the Second Prose Poem on the Red Cliff* (cat. no. 19) entered the collection of Liang Shicheng (*c.*1063–1126), one of Emperor Huizong's favourite courtiers, and bears his three seals. Liang also excelled in emulating Huizong's 'slender gold' style of calligraphy, and history has it that this ability led to his forging an imperial edict, for which crime he was ultimately sentenced to death by Emperor Qinzong (r. 1126).

From the Yuan dynasty (1271–1368) on, 'literati paintings' gradually became the dominant trend in painting, and collectors were divided into two major groups that would persist throughout the Ming (1368–1644) and Qing (1644–1911) dynasties: the imperial and the literati. The literati, or 'scholar-officials', historically included those public officials who became politicians through academic achievement, displaced scholars, and merchants living according to Confucian ethics.

All in all, the imperial court of the Mongol Yuan dynasty showed less interest in collecting paintings, giving ample opportunity to Song loyalists to obtain artworks as they became available on account of the political turmoil. According to Zhou Mi (1232–98), an art connoisseur active at the start of the Yuan, collectors like Qiao Kuicheng (act. late 13th century), Guo Tianxi (1244–1302), Zhao Mengfu (1254–1322), Ke Jiusi (1290–1343), Zhang Yan (act. late 13th–early 14th century), Xianyu Shu (1246–1302) and Zhao Lanpo (act. late 13th century) had in their possession great works from the Six Dynasties to the Song, including paintings that came to light after the collapse of the Jurchen Jin dynasty. The copy of Zhang Xuan's *The Picture of Pounding* (cat. no. 16), for example, was once owned by Zhang Yan, who was known to collect only the finest works, and bears his seal, while Qian Xuan's (*c.*1235–before 1307) *Doves and Pear Blossoms after Rain* (cat. no. 45) was once examined and inscribed by Ke Jiusi (1290–1343). Artists in this exhibition such as Zhao Mengfu, Zhao Yong (1289–after 1360), Zhao Lin (act. 2nd half 14th century) and Ni Zan (1306–74) were also known for their rich collections of paintings as well as for their creative prowess; for example, Gong Kai's (1222–1307) *Emaciated Horse* (cat. no. 44) was owned by Ni Zan, whose seals were likewise indicative of the highest artistic quality. The daughter of the Yuan emperor Chengzong (r. 1295–1308), Shanga Lagyi (*c.*1283–1331), was another avid collector, and was thus one of the few known collectors of calligraphy and paintings in the Yuan imperial family. She communicated regularly with contemporary connoisseurs such as some of those mentioned above, with whom she exchanged news and discussed findings and opinions on various works.

Whereas during the Tang and Song dynasties the court was at the forefront of the collecting arena, by the Ming private collectors had become the major players, and especially scholar-officials and the literati in southern China. A particular feature of art collecting at this time was that a great many eunuchs, distant members of the imperial family and rich merchants also became keen competitors. However, neither imperial nor private collections were in fact pursued very actively at the start of the Ming, due largely to fears over the political situation and frequent transitions of power, and those who continued to collect did so mostly in secret. The situation changed somewhat in the Yongle (1403–24) and Xuande (1426–35) reign periods, but a genuine shift came only in the middle of the dynasty, when the emperor turned away from politics and the court was under the control of the eunuchs. For example, there seems to have been no collecting activity for Zheng Sixiao's (1239–1316) *Ink Orchid* (cat. no. 47) for the 60 years or so after being inscribed by Han Yi (1334–1406), who was active at the time of the Yuan–Ming transition, until Zhu Yunming (1460–1526) added his inscription in the mid-Ming; and the case is similar for Qian Xuan's *Doves and Pear Blossoms after Rain*, Gong Kai's *Emaciated Horse* and Hu Shunchen's *Farewell to Hao Xuanming, Envoy to Qin*.

Towards the end of the Chenghua reign (1465–87) in the mid-Ming, the eunuch Qian Neng in Nanjing is known to have had his minions remove two cases of historical paintings and calligraphy from the imperial palace every five days, while Sima Yin, the imperial censor at the time, stood by and watched. These stolen pieces were reputed to be primarily by renowned artists of the Six Dynasties, Tang and Song periods, with works from the Yuan deemed of little value. The entire collection of the Mu family (stemming from Prince Qianning, the posthumous title of Mu Ying [1345–92], who conquered the region of Yunnan), was also taken by Qian Neng, including Xia Gui's (act. 1180–1230) fan painting *Sailboat in Rainstorm* (cat. nos 28, 29), and the eunuch's collection grew to a size unmatched by that of any other contemporary collector. The collections of the prime minister Yan Song (1480–1567) and his son later on in the Jiajing reign (1522–67) were comparable to Qian's, however; their estates were eventually subjected to an official search, in which an astounding 3,302 paintings and calligraphic works from the Six Dynasties, Tang and later periods were discovered, including the Song dynasty masterpiece *Along the River during the Qingming Festival* (fig. 46) now in the Palace Museum, Beijing. Although they were taken into the custody of the authorities, Duke Chengguo Zhu Xizhong (1516–72) and others colluded with the court eunuchs to host a public auction of the works and at very favourable prices, reasoning that the proceeds would add to the state treasury. Ultimately, this led to the dispersal of even more scrolls from the imperial storerooms.

Literati and art connoisseurs active in the middle and late years of the Ming in fact constituted the main body of collectors in the dynasty overall. Notable figures from this group included Shen Zhou (1427–1509), Zhou Ding (1401–87) and Shi Jian (1434–96) (this trio once joined forces in an appreciation of Hu Shunchen's *Farewell to Hao Xuanming, Envoy to Qin*); Hua Xia (act. 2nd half 15th century); Wen Zhengming (1470–1559); Xiang Yuanbian (1525–90), whose collection boasted Gong Kai's *Emaciated Horse* (cat. no. 44), Qian Xuan's *Doves and Pear Blossoms after Rain* (cat. no. 45) and *Auspicious Cranes* (cat. no. 17); Han Shineng (1528–98), who owned *The Five Planets and Twenty-eight Constellations* (cat. no. 13); and Dong Qichang (1555–1636), who once examined Yan Wengui's *Landscape with Pavilions* (cat. no. 15). A number of works also found their way into Japan during this period, among which were Chan (J. Zen) paintings from the Southern Song dynasty such as Liang Kai's (act. late 12th–early 13th century) *The Sixth Patriarch Cutting Bamboo*, Yujian's (act. 2nd half 13th century) *Autumn Moon Over Lake Dongting* and Muxi's (d.c.1281) *Slumbering Budai* (cat. no. 42). These came to be included in the collections of the Tokugawa and Ashikaga shogunates, most notably that of Ashikaga Yoshimitsu (r. 1368–94).

Collectors of painting in the Qing period prior to the reign of the Qianlong emperor (1736–96) could be said to be similar to Ming collectors in consisting primarily of members of the literati, painters and calligraphers. Their activity was greatest at the start of the dynasty, with professional art dealers such as Gui Xizhi, Jiang Mengming, Wu Qizhen (c.1609–c.1678), Wang Yueshi, Wu Sheng (c.1639–c.1713) and An Qi (1683–1742; owner of Wen Zhengming's *Garden of the Inept Administrator* (cat. no. 62) rivalling the literati as collectors. The influence of these art dealers was entirely unprecedented in Chinese history.

On the cusp of the Qing, a great many works began to pour into north China from the south, and the north became the centre for art collecting. At this time a large number of collectors emerged among the high-ranking officials residing in the capital at Beijing, who took advantage of their official visits to the south to seek out great works. Among these were Zhang Yingjia (act. 2nd half 17th century), an official from Shandong Province; Li Zongkong (1618–1701) of Guangling (present Yangzhou), a counsellor at the imperial court; Xu Qianxue (1631–94) of Kunshan, a scholar of the imperial cabinet; Zhou Lianggong (1612–72) from Xiangfu (present Kaifeng), vice minister of the Ministry of Finance; the imperial censor Cao Rong (1613–85) of Jiaxing; and the grand secretary Li Wei (1625–84) of Gaoyang. Some, such as the Manchu grand secretary Songgotu (1636–1703), even commissioned connoisseurs to act on their behalf, and thus became great collectors in one fell swoop. There are records indicating that works were so procured and later entered the collections of officials in the capital; besides Songgotu, these included Sun Chengze (1592–1676), a previous owner of Dai Jin's (1388–1462) *Spring Clouds in the Linggu Mountains* (cat. no. 52); Liang Qingbiao (1620–91), a former owner of Qiao Zhongchang's *Illustration to the Second Prose Poem on the Red Cliff* (cat. no. 19); Song Luo (1634–1713); Gao Shiqi (1645–1703) and Zhang Chunxiu (1647–1706); Wang Hongxu (1645–1723); and Bian Yongyu (1645–1712). These individuals played a key role in the relocation of works of art to the north and into the imperial palace. For example, through the dealings of Shen Deqian (1673–1769), almost all of An Qi's collection entered the imperial court during the Qianlong reign, such as *The Five Planets and Twenty-eight Constellations* (cat. no. 13), and *Reading the Memorial Stele* attributed to Li Cheng (919–67) and Wang Xiao (act. 1st half 10th century) (cat. no. 14). Other works also ultimately found their way into the imperial court, like Zheng Sixiao's *Ink Orchid* (cat. no. 47), which was owned by Song Luo, and Gong Kai's *Emaciated Horse* (cat. no. 44), owned at this time by Gao Shiqi. Although collecting outside of the court was on the decrease in general, antique markets like Beijing's Liulichang began to flourish and were especially vibrant during Qianlong's reign, providing ample opportunity for the literati to expand their collections. Among them were Bi Long (1733–97) and Ruan Yuan (1764–1849), who purchased Qian Xuan's *Doves and Pear Blossoms after Rain* (cat. no. 45). As for the imperial collection, a very few works were bestowed upon members of the imperial family or ministers as gifts; for example, the Jiaqing emperor (r. 1796–1820) gave Han Gan's (act. 742–56) *Night-Shining White* (now in the Metropolitan Museum of Art) to Prince Cheng, Yongxing (1752–1823), and the Daoguang emperor (r. 1821–50) gifted Chen Rong's (act. 1st half 13th century) *Nine Dragons* (cat. no. 38) to Prince Gong, Yixin (1833–98).

As the Qing dynasty drew to a close, this relatively centralized type of collection came to an end, and from 1840 on, due to the corruption of the imperial court and frequent wars, works from the imperial collection once again found their way into the hands of the populace. Many pieces also went into public and private collections overseas, including Japan, the United States, Britain and other European countries.

In 1860, British and French allied troops invaded Beijing and sacked the Yuanming Yuan, the old summer palace on the outskirts of the city. The Yuanming Yuan was set ablaze, and some 200 historical paintings and calligraphies were destroyed or sold off. In 1900, the Eight-power Allied Forces again stormed the city, the same year in which the so-called 'library cave' at the Mogao Grottoes in Dunhuang, which contained vast quantities of paintings and documents and had been sealed for nearly 1,000 years, was discovered when the local Daoist monk Wang Yuanlu asked a Mr Yang to copy inscriptions from the wall paintings. In 1907, Aurel Stein (1862–1943), a British explorer of Hungarian roots, went to Dunhuang and carried more than 45,000 manuscripts and printed documents and almost 400 paintings away from the cave, which eventually entered the collections of the British Library, the British Museum and the National Museum in New Delhi. The Frenchman Paul Pelliot (1878–1945) likewise obtained 6,000 paintings and scriptures from the cave, while others were removed by S.F. Oldenburg (1863–1934) of Russia.

The greatest depletion of paintings from China in this era, however, would take place between 1922 and 1945, when the former Xuantong emperor, Puyi (r. 1908–11), the last emperor of China, abdicated the throne. While exercising his power of 'special rights of the Qing imperial family', Puyi bestowed artworks on his courtiers and servants at will, appropriating more than 1,200 paintings and calligraphies from the palace. Most of the fine works found in public and private collections in Europe, America and Japan came to be there because of Puyi, including *Reading the Memorial Stele* attributed to Li Cheng and Wang Xiao (cat. no. 14), *Court Ladies Preparing Newly Woven Silk* (see cat. no. 16) and *Auspicious Cranes* (cat. no. 17). There are a few exceptions, however, such as *Five-coloured Parakeet* by Huizong's painting academy, which was sold by Prince Gong, Yixin, to raise funds in preparation for war.

Another major transfer of art from the imperial palace

took place as a result of the Sino-Japanese War (1937–1945). To save the remaining artefacts in the palace from being destroyed, in 1933 the Nationalist government (or Kuomintang, active in mainland China from 1912 to 1949) had them transferred to the south, and in 1948, President Chiang Kai-shek (1887–1975) ordered nearly 600,000 pieces to be shipped to Taiwan. These included more than 8,000 paintings and works of calligraphy, which now form part of the permanent collection of the National Palace Museum in Taipei.

Of the more than 1,200 paintings and calligraphies removed by Puyi, a number were in turn stolen and sold off by members of the national army, and some were irrevocably damaged or destroyed. Most were sold in cities like Tianjin, where art dealers were able to buy them off the streets. One such work is Zheng Sixiao's *Ink Orchid* (cat. no. 47), which was sold by Puyi in Tianjin to the Japanese collector Abe Fusajiro (1868–1937), whose collection was later donated to the Osaka City Museum of Fine Arts. The port of Hong Kong served as a transfer station for these works, becoming an important source of paintings and calligraphies for public and private collections in Europe, the United States and Japan. A number of notable collectors emerged during this period, such as Zhang Boju (1898–1982); Wanyan Jingxian (1875–1931), who owned works like *The Five Planets and Twenty-eight Constellations* (cat. no. 13), *Sailboat in Rainstorm* (see cat. no. 28, 29) and *Reading the Memorial Stele* (cat. no. 14); Wu Hufan (1894–1968); Pang Yuanji (1864–1949); Hui Jun (1902–79); Tan Jing (1911–91); Wang Nanping (1924–85); and Zhang Daqian (1899–1983), whose *The Colours of Mount Taihang* by Wang Hui (1632–1717) can be seen in the exhibition (cat. no. 67).

Works sometimes changed hands several times. For example, the Shanghainese merchant Tan Jing bought Ni Zan's *Woods and Valleys of Mount Yu* (cat. no. 65) from Zhang Boju, which then passed to Zhang Daqian and C.C. Wang (Wang Jiqian, 1906–2002), thus going via Hong Kong to the United States and eventually ending up in the Metropolitan Museum of Art. *Zhao Yu's Pacification of the Barbarians* from the Jurchen Jin dynasty was sold to the Nelson-Atkins Museum of Art via a dealer in Hong Kong, and Zhang Daqian acquired Guo Xi's (c.1000–c.1090) *Old Trees, Level Distance*, which went to the American collector John M. Crawford, Jr. (1913–88) and then entered the Metropolitan Museum. Crawford also bought Qiao Zhongchang's *Illustration to the Second Prose Poem on the Red Cliff* (cat. no. 19) from Wang Zheng (1887–1963) in Hong Kong, and sold it to the Nelson-Atkins Museum of Art in 1983. Of the 27 paintings and calligraphic works from the Qing imperial palace in the permanent collection of the Metropolitan Museum of Art, 25 were purchased by C.C. Wang. One such work is *Grooms and Horses* (cat. no. 46), painted by three generations of the Zhao family, which was purchased by Wang Enqing from members of the Chinese Nationalist Army in the city of Changchun and resold to Jin Bosheng in Beijing; it then passed through Hong Kong to the United States, where it entered Crawford's collection and was ultimately gifted to the Metropolitan Museum.

This type of occurrence is described by Liu Cha in his 1954 inscription on Du Jin's (act. c.1465–1509) *Court Ladies in the Inner Palace* (cat. no. 54):

> Comparing it with *The Nine Songs* (fig. 48) and *The Poet Tao Yuanming Wandering with a Stick*, which have been in the collections of Yan Huiyu [1895–1968] and C.C. Wang, it is certain that this is by the hand of Gukuang [Du Jin]. Zhou Wenju's [act. 961–75] masterpiece *Court Ladies in the Inner Palace*, for 100s of years secreted away in the imperial court, was stolen and has gone overseas; it is now in the British Museum. The dispersal of such relics really makes me sigh! Ten years ago I came across a Japanese publication of a copy by [the] Song [emperor] Huizong, which was of the highest standard. This picture [by Du Jin] is the only version I have seen in China; its value cannot be estimated.

*The Nine Songs* referred to is in fact Zhang Wo's (act. 1336–c.1364) work of this name, which is presently in the Cleveland Museum of Art. *Court Ladies in the Inner Palace* attributed to Zhou Wenju is now part of the permanent collection of the British Museum (under the name *Women and Children on Garden Terrace*).

FIG. 48
Zhang Wo (act. 1336–c.1364) and Chu Huan (act. c.1361). *The Nine Songs* handscroll (with detail), 14th century. Ink on paper. The Cleveland Museum of Art, Cleveland

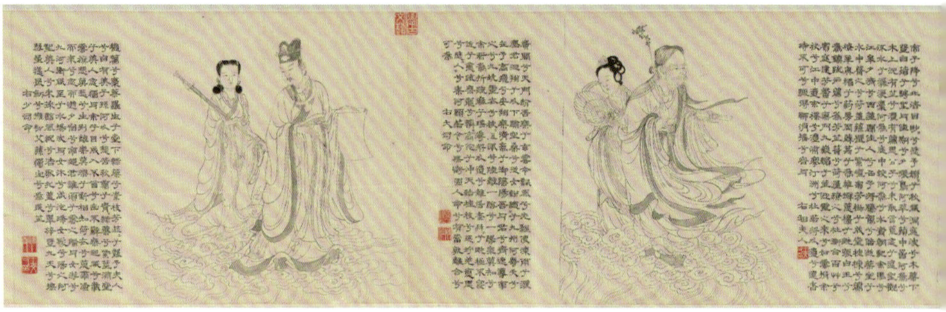

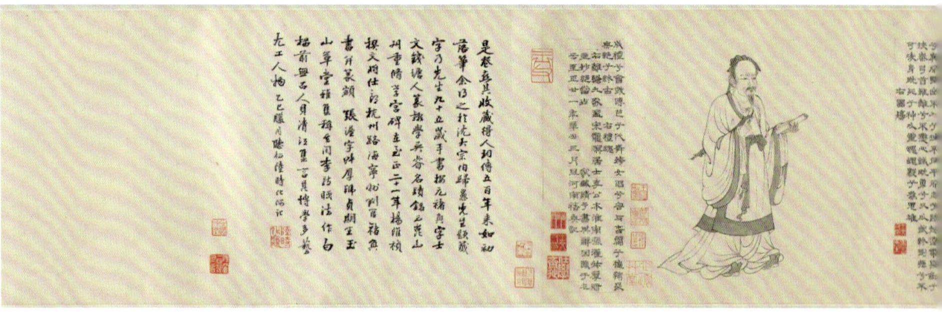

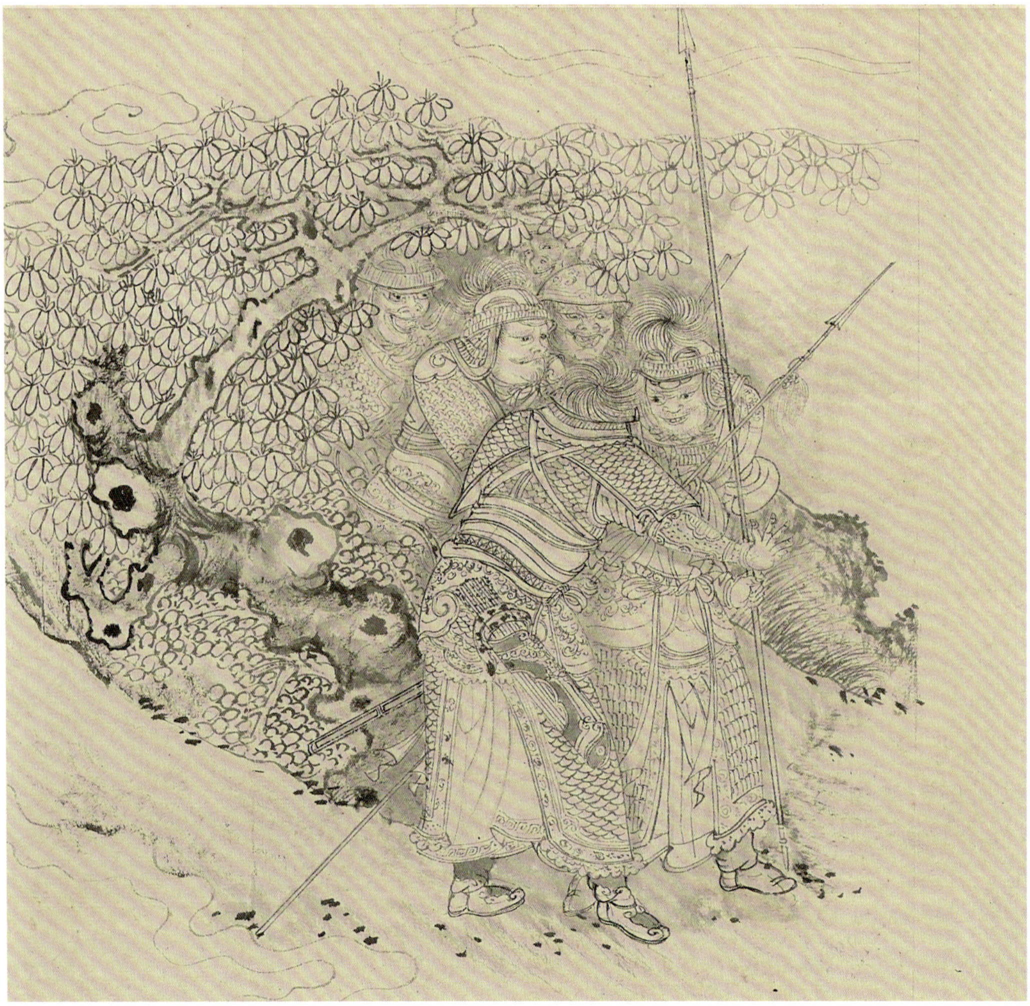

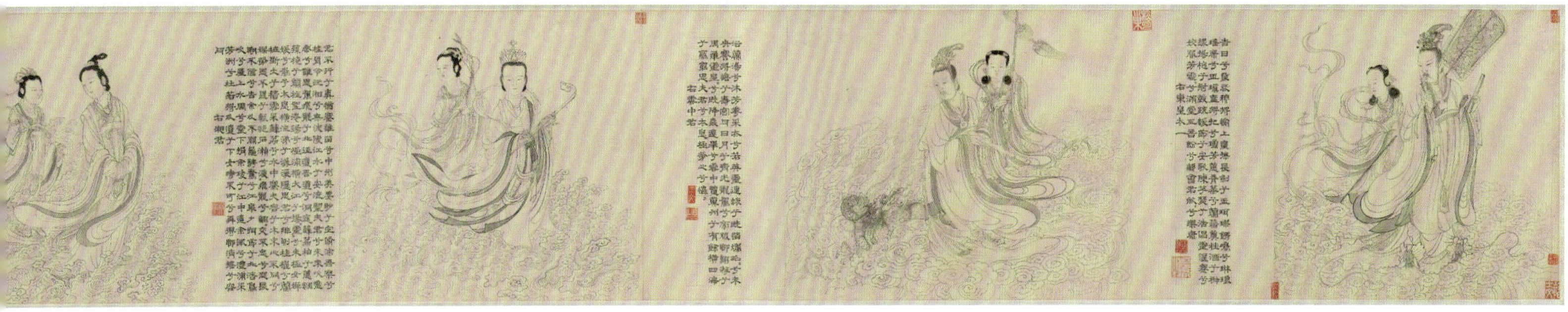

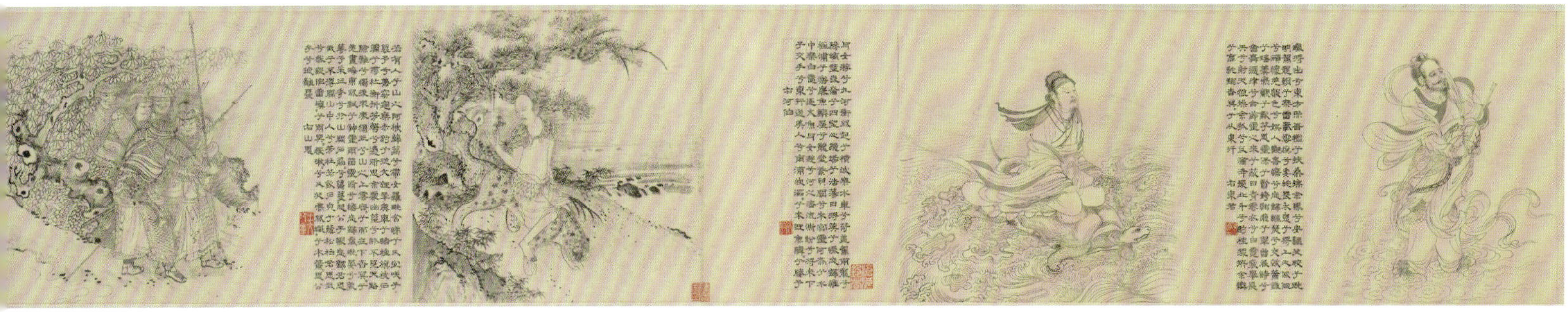

After the founding of the People's Republic of China in 1949, museums throughout China made it a priority to track down the paintings from the imperial collection that had not gone abroad. The Shanghai Museum, for example, purchased Zhao Kui's (1186–1266) *Picturing the Poetic Feelings of Du Fu*, Li Song's (1166–1243) *West Lake*, Sun Wei's (act. 2nd half 9th century) *Portrait of Gao Yi* and Liang Kai's *Eight Eminent Monks*, from such collectors as Pang Yuanji, Wu Hufan, Hui Jun and Jin Bosheng. A substantial number of the works in the Palace Museum in Beijing (including Zhang Zeduan's [act. early 12th century] *Along the River during the Qingming Festival* (fig. 46) and Zhou Chen's [c.1450–1535] *Dwelling by the Stream in Spring*, cat. no. 55) and in the Liaoning Provincial Museum (for example, Xu Yang's [1712–c.1779] *Prosperous Suzhou*, cat. no. 76) were also part of the former Qing palace collection.

The scope and quality of the holdings of China's museums today are a direct result of the extensive redistribution of artefacts since the late Qing. Apart from the Palace Museum, where a large number of works from the former imperial collection are preserved, the other institutions derive their collections from a number of different sources, including gifts from major collectors, purchases, and personal donations from the artists. For example, the Shanghai Museum received in the year 2000 a donation of 230 paintings and calligraphies from the Ching family in the Philippines, and has bought works from the collections of Gu Wenbin (1811–89), Liu Jingji (1902–97) and Qian Jingtang (1907–83). Paintings and calligraphic scrolls have also been found in archaeological excavations, including the Ming tombs in Huai'an County, Jiangsu Province (which yielded nearly 20 works, among them *Lilies* by Li Zai [d.1431]), Astana in the Xinjiang Uyghur Autonomous Region and Yemaotai in Liaoning Province.

The above discussion presents an overview of the history of collecting Chinese paintings in China, and examines the provenance of a number of works that have made their way abroad. The artworks presented in the current exhibition include a wide range of examples, giving testimony to the different categories of collectors considered and their traits.

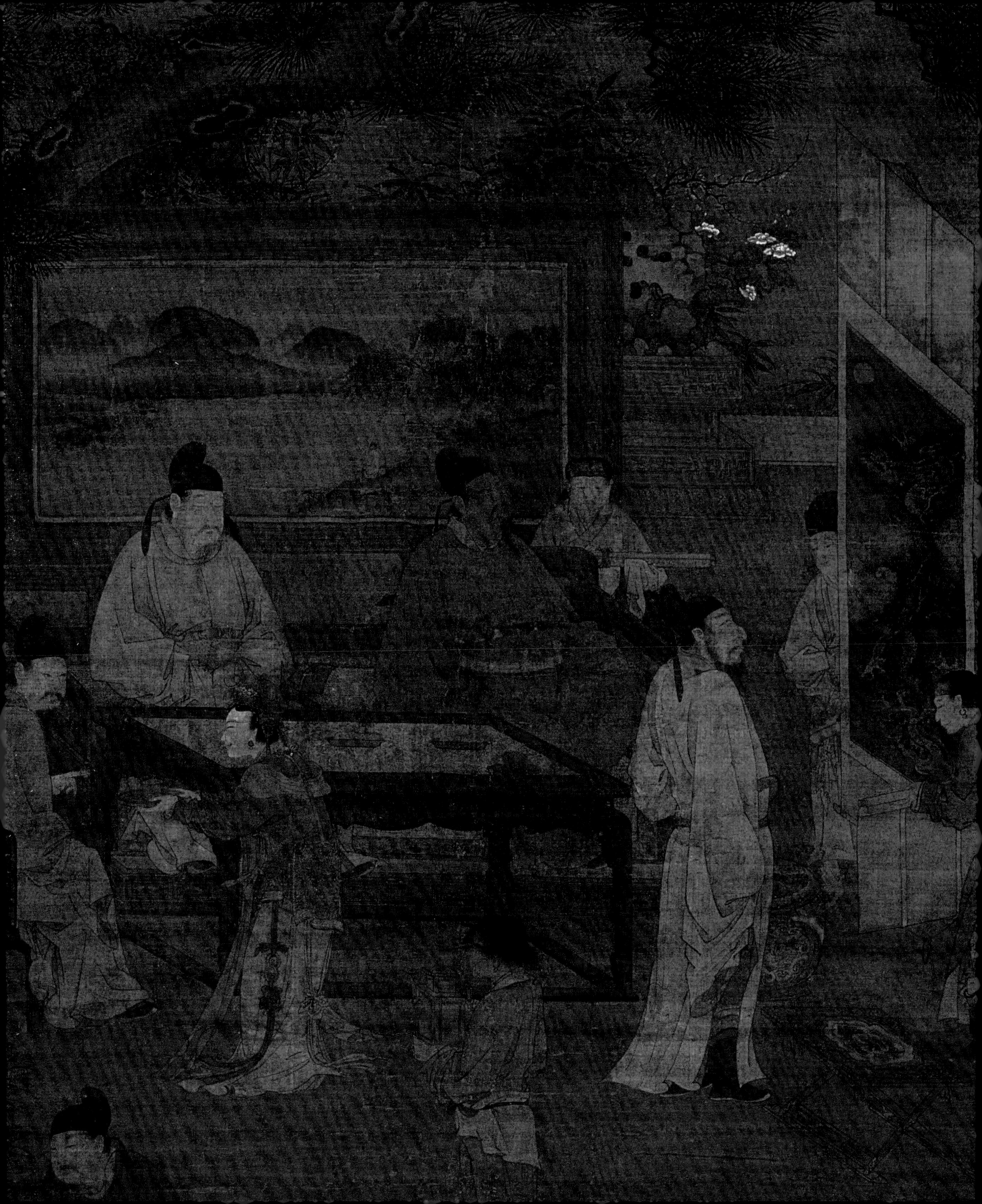

# THE PRESENTATION AND PRESERVATION OF CHINESE SCROLL PAINTINGS

Camille Schmitt

Most Chinese paintings appear as scrolls, a format that helped to conserve the painting by protecting it with several layers of silk and paper. They were never intended for permanent exhibition. Although countless early scrolls have been lost, so that it is difficult to reconstruct a complete history of their mounting, the numerous descriptive texts that survive provide important information on mounting materials and techniques, which can occasionally be corroborated by surviving examples.

Chinese scroll paintings have their origin in books. Until the third century BCE, most written texts were made up of narrow bamboo or wooden slips bound together with cords, a format called *jiance*. They could be rolled up, like a bamboo place mat, except that the slips were about a centimetre wide and 30 centimetres or more in length. This was also the format for texts written on fabric (*bo*) or on silk (*juan*).[1] From the first century CE, works on paper and silk coexisted. Over time, various techniques were developed to ensure that these essentially fragile materials could be preserved.

Works on paper were typically dyed yellow with the bark of the Amur cork tree (*Phellodendron*; *bo*), a treatment that both prepared the surface and conserved the substrate. This treatment is evident on a scroll dated 506 from Dunhuang,[2] and its use is still apparent in the ninth century. The term *huang*, referring in particular to dyeing paper yellow but also to dyeing procedures in general, was mentioned for the first time between 194 and 203 by the classical scholar Liu Xi.[3]

Writing at the beginning of the sixth century, the scholar-official Jia Sixie in his book *Principal Techniques for the Welfare of the People* devotes a chapter to 'methods of dyeing in yellow and treating books'.[4] From his work, we learn that by his time dyeing was done in a procedure known as 'treating books' (*zhishu*). In the treatment, the sheets of paper[5] were joined end-to-end for assembly as a horizontal scroll either before or after they were dyed.[6] Then one or two sheets of blank paper were added at the beginning (the right) to prevent the paper of the text from tearing – the ancestor of the frontispiece. Further to the right might be an additional 'protective cover' (*biao* or *biaoshou*) of brocade (*jin*), plain silk (*juan*), gauze (*luo*) or damask (*ling*). On this would be inscribed the title of the work (and a number if the work comprised several scrolls). A ribbon and fastening pin were usually attached to the middle of the bamboo splint[7] at the beginning of the scroll. Examples from Dunhuang show that the last sheet of the scroll (on the left) was trimmed on both edges at 45 degrees and inserted through a slit in a wooden rod, then pasted to hold it in place.[8] The ends of this rod might be lacquered or ornamented with ivory knobs. Thus, on the eve of the Tang dynasty (618–907), the basic techniques of mounting were already being practised.[9]

Zhang Yanyuan (815–76), an official, scholar and private collector, in his famous work *Record of Famous Painters of Successive Dynasties*, is the first to have discussed the mounting of calligraphy and paintings.[10] For Zhang, the arts of mounting and preservation (referred to as *zhuang*, *bei*, *zhuangchi*, *zhuanghu* and *zhuangbei*)[11] were important. He differentiates between paintings done on silk with mineral pigments (*juansu caise*) and those outlined in ink on paper (*zhishang baihua*).[12] He describes paste, working tables and mounting tools in some detail,[13] and draws attention to the correct choice of paper for lining, advising in particular against lining works with sized (or prepared) paper 'since it is sure to wrinkle up' and recommending the use of large sheets of untreated paper that are white, smooth and fine.[14] Moreover, he notes that the lining paper should not be joined where there are figures on the front of the work, and that the joins must be staggered so that they do not align when the work is rolled up.

cat. no. 53 (detail)

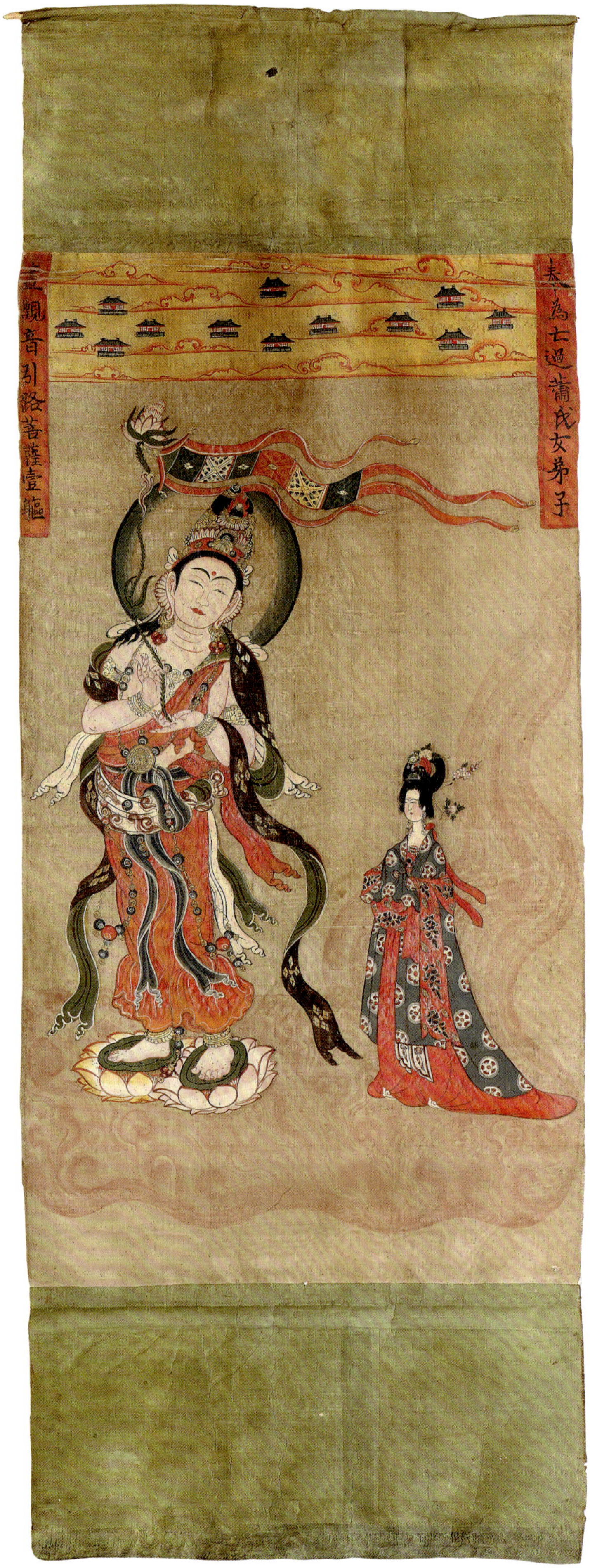


FIG. 49
*Guanyin Showing the Way* mounted as a hanging scroll, 10th century. Ink and colour on silk. Musée Guimet, Paris (MG 26461)

Although he gives precise tips on preservation, Zhang does not discuss methods of assembly. Like earlier writers, however, he gives detailed information about the different kinds of wood used for the roller and end knobs. For the roller, he relates that the best woods are white sandalwood and Cunninghamia (*Cunninghamia lanceolata*; *shamu*). The knobs should be of eaglewood (*Aquilaria agallocha*; *chentan*) or tortoiseshell, or set in gold; for small scrolls, he says that white jade is best, then rock crystal, and finally amber, while for large scrolls, he recommends lacquering the ends of the roller.

The earliest physical evidence of mounted scroll paintings comes from the tenth century. The painting *Guanyin Showing the Way* (fig. 49) from Dunhuang, mounted as a hanging scroll, raises many interesting points. Two panels of silk are sewn on above and below the painting, the lower one slightly shorter than the one above; there are no silk borders to the right and left. The top stave is made of wood, and there is a pocket at the bottom that once held a wooden roller. In spring 1974, two silk paintings mounted as hanging scrolls (figs 52–3) were discovered in an early Liao dynasty (907–1125) tomb (dated by the excavators to between 959 and 986)[15] at Yemaotai in present-day Liaoning Province. Although they had fallen down, they were originally hanging opposite one another.[16] The top stave is of bamboo while the upper and lower panels are of silk taffeta, beige in colour on one painting and a faded yellow on the other. The upper panel is longer than the lower one, and again there are no borders. The bottom roller has ivory knobs.

While a good number of scroll paintings have survived from the Song dynasty (960–1279), no Song mounts have survived. We also have few precise descriptions of the mounts used in the Northern Song (960–1127). However, successive emperors placed great emphasis on art-collecting, and the Hanlin Academy (the institution to which painters working for the court were attached) included dedicated studios for the mounting of their collections. From the Southern Song (1127–1279) onwards, mounting materials are well described. According to the texts, the silk and paper factories at the time produced materials of extremely high quality.

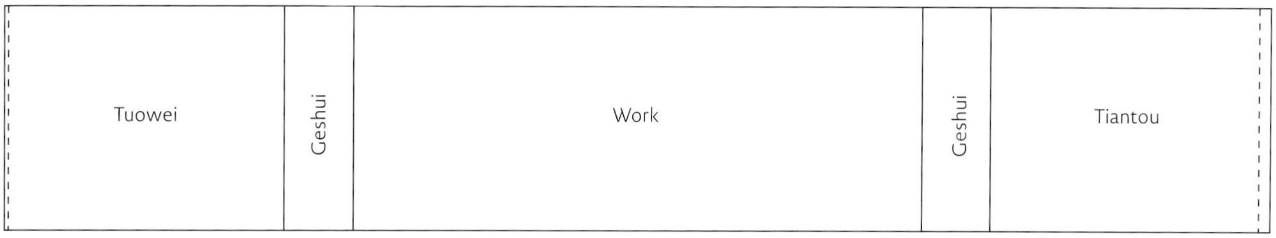


FIG. 50

The texts distinguish between mounts of 'Xuanhe style' (from the reign name Xuanhe [1119–25]) in the Northern Song and those of 'Shaoxing style' (from the Shaoxing [1131–62] era of the reign of Emperor Gaozong) in the Southern Song, but the exact differences are not made explicit.[17] In general, for horizontal scrolls, the standard elements of the mount (from right to left) were as follows (fig. 50). First, a headpiece (*tiantou* [heaven]) in a dark shade of damask; the writer Tao Zongyi (1316–1403) lists over 20 damask motifs.[18] Then between the headpiece and the work came a separator (*geshui*) of yellow silk in the Xuanhe style, and of white damask with a pattern of clouds and pheasants in the Shaoxing style. Attached to the end of the work is another separator of the same kind of silk or damask, followed by the endpiece (*tuowei*) in paper.[19] The roller ends, in white jade, agate or ivory, projected beyond the scroll, and the stave was in sandalwood – which repelled insects.[20]

In the case of hanging scrolls (fig. 51), the upper and lower pieces (*tiantou* ['heaven'] and *ditou* ['earth']) and the borders were in damask. The separator between the work and *tiantou* above, and between the work and *ditou* below it, was usually also of damask with pheasant motifs. There were vertical 'brocade strips' (*jindai*)[21] on *tiantou* which were attached by slitting the cover, probably just below the top stave.[22] The knobs were in white jade, agate or ivory, and the roller was again in sandalwood. The painter and calligrapher Mi Fu (1051–1107) recommended sandalwood (hollowed out to reduce the weight), paulownia (*tongmu*) and sappanwood (*Caesalpinia sappan*; *sumu*) for ordinary scrolls.[23] He advised against knobs in gold and silver (vulgar and tempting to thieves), rock crystal (too heavy) and horn (which might attract insects).

After the final Mongol overthrow of the Song dynasty in 1279, the new ruler of the Yuan dynasty (1271–1368) appropriated the imperial collections, and had 646 scrolls of calligraphy and painting remounted by professionals from Hangzhou. The annals describe the materials needed for this huge enterprise.[24] By comparing this list with that provided by Tao Zongyi, some important facts come to light. Most of the mounts – the majority of which were for hanging scrolls – were to be in brocade and damask. The brocade, with a pattern of pheasants and magpies (*luanque*), was ordered together with a very large quantity[25] of sky-blue damask (there is no information on the pattern of the latter), and various dyes: two kinds of vegetable yellow, a mineral yellow, blue and two kinds of lamp black. There was also a request for 'blue bands' (*lanqingtiao*) and several kinds of ribbons (*dai*), according to the size of the works or their mounts.[26] The knobs were most often

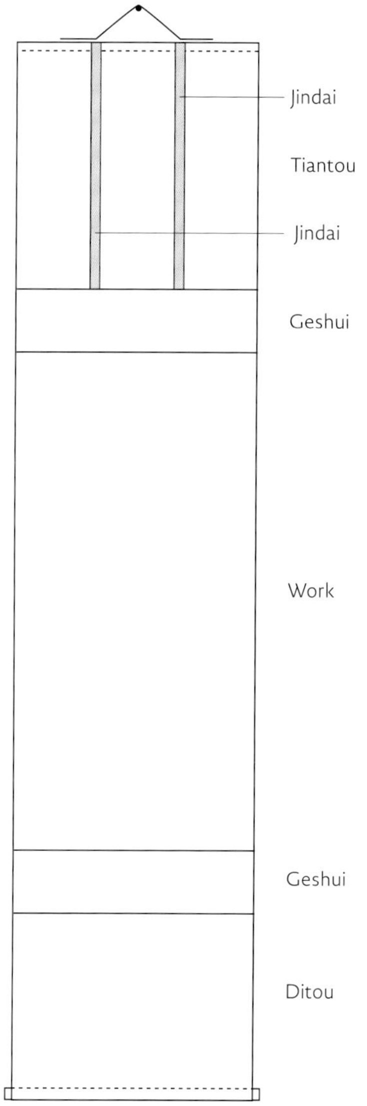


FIG. 51

FIG. 52
*Sparrows in Bamboo and Two Rabbits* hanging scroll, 959–86. Ink and colour on silk, excavated from the Yemaotai Tomb, Faku County. Liaoning Provincial Museum

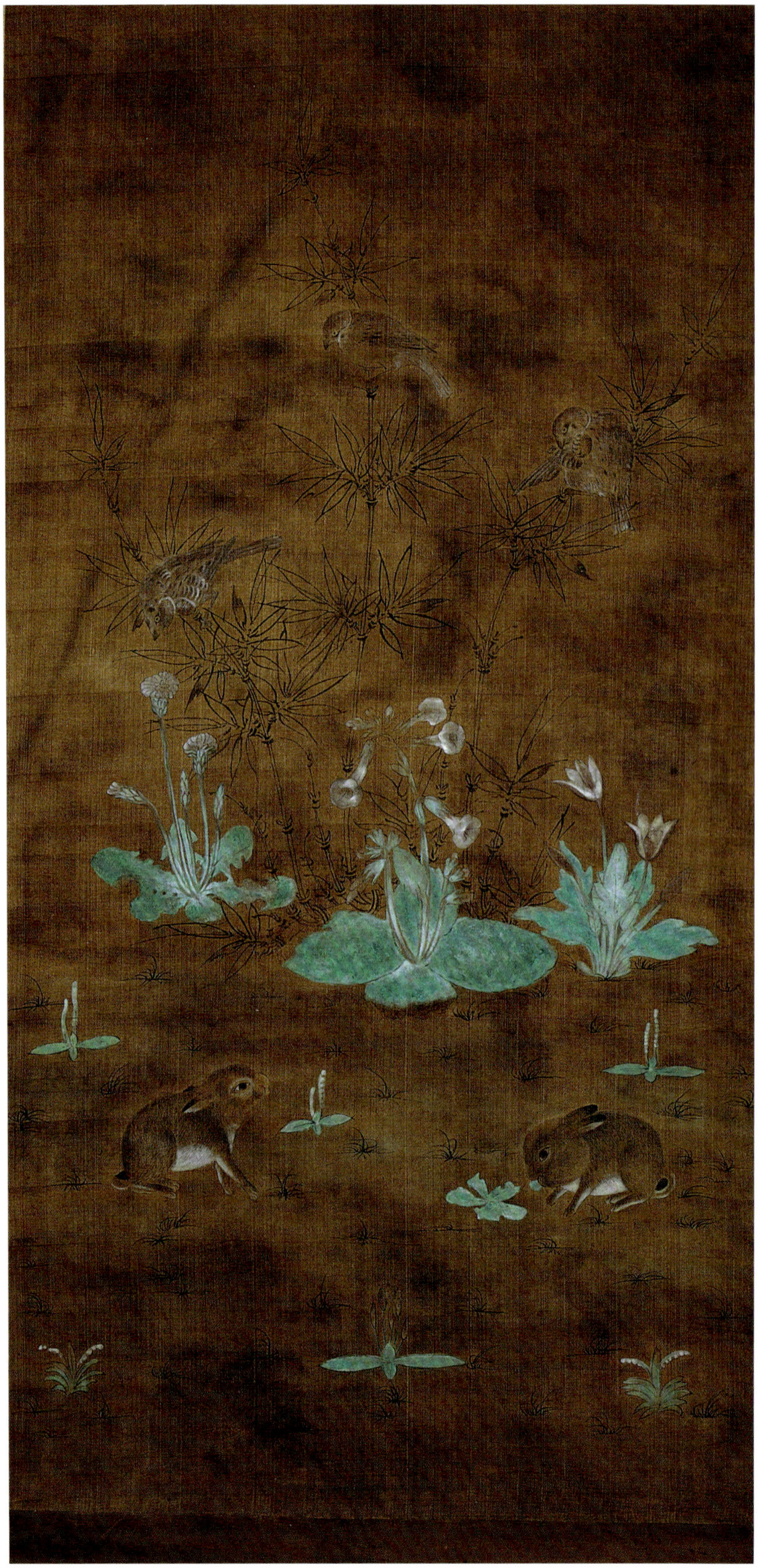

made of ivory, and the staves were all in *luo* wood (*Cyathea spinulosa*; *luomu*).

Numerous texts have come down to us from the Ming dynasty (1368–1644), evidencing the intense activity of private collectors at that time. Among the texts on mounting and the profession of the mounter, we can distinguish between those which simply copied earlier works and those which diverged from them or provided new details, bearing witness to changes in aesthetics or responding to new demands. One such text is the *Treatise on Mounting* by Zhou Jiazhou (1573–1620), a late Ming writer from Yangzhou in Jiangsu Province. The methods he lays out are still influential in the mounting studios in China today.[27]

According to the *Treatise*, the Ming mounters kept to the measurements and materials for handscrolls used in the Song dynasty, but modified some of the terms used to describe mounts[28] as well as some of the presentational details. For example, a sheet of sized and/or decorated paper (*yinshou*) on which a title or preface could be written appears between the silk beginning of the scroll and the first separator. Elsewhere, we have more details on the silk mount: for instance, if a work was somewhat narrow, the scholar and painter Wen Zhenheng (1585–1645) recommended framing it with a single length of silk (a technique called *waqian*, 'inlay').[29] The strips of chestnut-brown paper pasted along the edges of handscrolls were also the subject of debate in the Ming: should they be in silk, or in paper as was usual under the Song?[30] For the cover, the brocade pattern that Wen Zhenheng considered to be the best of those used in the Song was that of flowers falling on water (*luohua liushui*).[31] Apparently, the Ming silk factories were producing brocades with copies of popular Song designs, such as cranes in flight or tortoiseshell patterns on a stippled ground (*fanhong guiwen sudi dengjin*). Also in the Ming, the knobs of handscrolls, which hitherto had projected, became flush with the rolled-up scroll.[32]

Some pre-Ming handscrolls have been discovered buried with their owner, as in the tomb of Zhu Tan (1371–90), the tenth son of the Ming founder, in Shandong Province.[33] Unfortunately, the archaeological reports neglect to mention the original mounts. Evidence was also

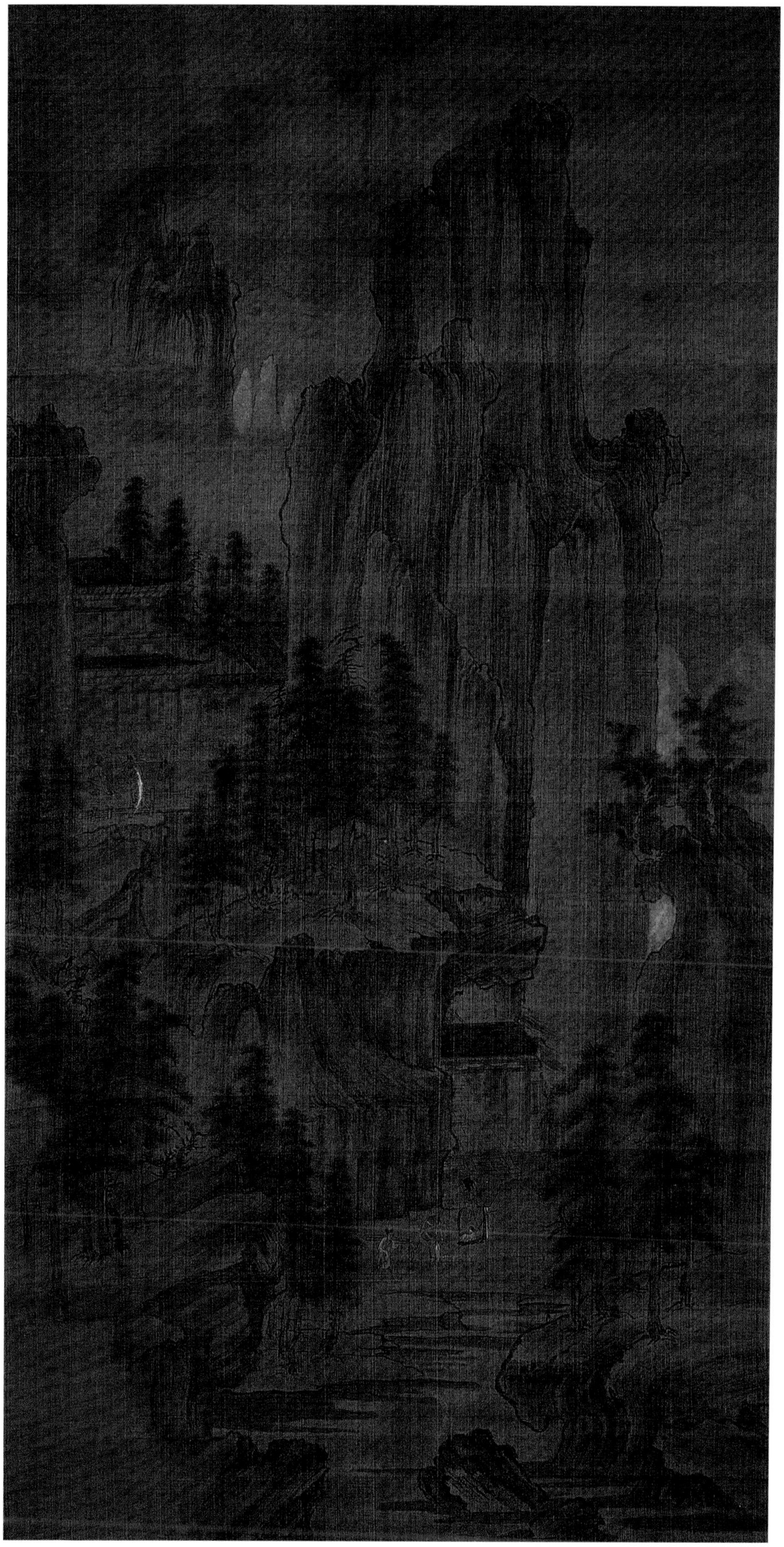

FIG. 53
*Playing Chess in Remote Mountains*
hanging scroll, 959–86. Ink and colour on silk, excavated from the Yemaotai Tomb, Faku County. Liaoning Provincial Museum

lost when contemporary handscrolls found in Wang Zhen's tomb in Jiangsu were immediately remounted.[34]

Texts on hanging scrolls from the end of the Ming period differentiate between those inspired by the Song dynasty and those that followed contemporary fashion. The conservative connoisseur and collector Wen Zhenheng distinguishes mounts of the Xuanhe style from those in the Ming mode by their having narrow brown edges, or edges of white damask if the works were large; in the latter case, an inscription (*tishi*) would be added above the work.[35] When a Ming collector acquired a work, they very often had it remounted. While the original silks or parts thereof were sometimes retained, most of the time everything, including the first lining (*mingzhi*; 'paper of vital importance'), was replaced.

It seems that in the late Ming, silk and damask were preferred as materials in general. Wen Zhenheng reverts to the earlier custom, recommending the use of a dark silk, while Zhou Jiazhou contends that although a dark damask for 'heaven' and 'earth' makes for an ancient and elegant style, dark colours do not stand the test of time and the silks easily fray, so he prefers pale or dark blue.[36] Other sources confirm the popularity of pale colours (pale blue, pale green, white or ivory) for both damask and silk mounts. It seems that the choice of colour was also made in regard to the pictorial genre: a highly coloured work would be mounted with an ivory silk, but is also recorded with silks of very pale blue, or with damask for 'heaven' and 'earth'. Fewer designs were in use than earlier, dragons, phoenixes and clouds being the most common.

The origin of the two vertical strips on 'heaven' is unclear. Prior to the Ming, they probably hung free; in the Ming dynasty they were strips of silk, perhaps emphasized with black edging,[37] and by the fifteenth century they were evidently pasted down, as we can see in cat. no. 53 (see detail p.106). The materials used for knobs in the Ming were very varied: while jade, rhinoceros horn, ivory or carved buffalo horn provided a more classical effect, more frequently employed were red sandalwood (*Pterocarpus indicus*; *zitan*), fragrant rosewood (*Dalbergia odorifera*; *huanghuali*), cloisonné, various kinds of bamboo, and lacquer speckled with gold or silver in the Japanese style.

During this period, scholars paid attention to the quality of the lining paper more than ever before,[38] and the two layers of paper on the back of both the work and its mount served for preservation. An examination of the measurements of different sections as given in three textual sources reveals that mounts became longer from the fifteenth and sixteenth centuries on.[39]

A long, narrow hanging scroll format known as *dantiao*[40] made its appearance in the Ming, along with paired scrolls (*duizhou*) and 'hanging screens' (*guaping*), all with very narrow borders or none at all (cat. no. 53). Although disparaged by the more conservative connoisseurs, these formats represent the first instance of scrolls in sets, which would eventually evolve into the format of 'continuous landscape screen' (*tongjingping*, cat. no. 72). The fascination with sets of paintings, and especially series of four, which made their appearance in interiors during the Ming, was reinforced by the rules of good taste then proliferating in guidebooks on household management.

The new rulers of the Qing dynasty (1644–1911), once installed in their capital at today's Beijing, strove hard to recreate and establish an imperial collection worthy of the name. Many craftsmen were recruited from the south, where mounting and restoration workshops had been renowned since the Song dynasty, and the great majority of the works from the imperial collections to which we have access today were remounted during this period. In private workshops, however, particularly in the south, the Qing period gave rise to many new fashions, such as mounts in three parts as well as mounts half in paper – for 'heaven' and 'earth' – and half in silk damask. It was very popular to have brocade borders above and below the work for emphasis.[41]

Following his predecessors, for hanging scrolls the writer Zhou Erxue (1650–?) recommends damasks decorated with a small repeat pattern of clouds and phoenixes, dyed black for 'heaven' and 'earth', or in sky blue. He innovates here with porcelain knobs. There were also fanciful decorations, such as motifs cut out from the ends of the heaven strips (*jingyan*, namely *jindai*). From this time on, hanging scrolls had covers in pale silk rather than brocade. The fastening braid was in silk or damask that matched the mount, and was sewn on.[42]

The Qing dynasty did not see any fundamental modifications to the traditional structure of the scroll. The materials for Qing handscrolls were on the whole identical with those of earlier dynasties (notably in the production of traditional mounts of Xuanhe style), but differed in some respects. Zhou Erxue[43] describes the attachment of a chestnut-brown border along the edges (a technique now known as 'turned borders' [*tongbian*] using treated paper with long fibres, or a very dense and fine silk), and states that a jade fastening pin was placed at the end of the ribbon (made of old brocade). Ribbons with the Buddhist 'eight-treasures' pattern (*babao dai*)[44] began to be used at court probably in the Qianlong period (1736–96). During the Qing, it was also thought necessary to match the fastening pin and the knobs. Zhou Erxue[45] draws attention to the need for suppleness in handscrolls, recommending a single layer of *liansi* paper rather than a thicker paper.

In the Qianlong period also, works in the imperial collection benefited from the use of top-quality materials made expressly for the court. Typical of these were the silk damasks patterned with small flowers from Suzhou, although there were numerous other designs, such as large and small cranes-and-clouds motifs, phoenixes-and-clouds and dragons-and-clouds.[46] Some materials were specially created for certain sets of paintings at the imperial court, as in the case of the paintings used for the Buddhist 'Water and Land' ritual (*shuiluhua*), which feature orange and blue damasks with a geometric ground.

Several variations of yellow can be observed in the damask mounts in some imperial works. Other colours are common as well, such as a very pale green (*huse*), off-white (*mise*) and white. The most beautiful mounts were created in the extensive workshops of the Institute of Indulgences (Ruyi guan; a branch of the Palace Workshops – Zaoban chu), sited within the Forbidden City, where the finest craftsmen in the country worked. Its teams had the expertise to tackle truly exceptional tasks, such as the mounting of the very long handscroll by Xu Yang (cat. no. 76), which required great skill.

We have seen above that in the earliest times, the mounting of scrolls – which then mainly bore written texts – was functional, and served merely to protect and classify them. With the development of paintings on silk, however, scrolls acquired the status of works of art; their mounts became a 'costume', for which the knobs and silk borders were the principal ornaments. Under the Song dynasty, the scroll's structure and the techniques of mounting and restoring, which had evolved in response to the need to protect and enhance the artistic value of works collected by the emperor or by scholars, became more or less fixed. On the other hand, the surviving literature reveals that aesthetically, the scrolls we are acquainted with today have their roots entirely in the Ming dynasty, as does the practice of the professional mounter.

1 Wang 1991, p. 4
2 Whitfield 1982–5, vol. 1, pl. 2 and p. 295
3 Liu Xi (act. late 2nd–early 3rd century), *Explanations of Names* (*Shiming*) http://www.gucn.com/Info_KnowLedgeList_Show.asp?Id=12537 (accessed 7 May 2013)
4 Jia (6th century) 1998, pp. 110–11
5 Sheets of paper at this time were between 41 and 49 centimetres long. See Wang 1991, p. 5.
6 Drège 1981, p. 309; Wen, Pu and Yang 2008, p. 98
7 Whitfield 1982–5, vol. 1, p. 297: 'Numbers of covers have . . . been preserved separately; they may be made of stouter paper or of a doubled sheet of the same quality as used in the manuscript itself and attached by paste to the first sheet of the manuscript, with a narrow bamboo splint pasted in at the beginning. The fastening tape (one example is a narrow strip of silk cut across the weave and folded lengthwise three times) is ingeniously attached by piercing the paper just behind the splint. The tape passes once around the splint and back through the same pierced hole, and through a slit in the tape itself. About 2 cm of the tape is left inside and may be pasted down. The result is a very simple but secure fastening, which remains quite flat and cannot come away from the cover.'
8 Ibid., pp. 295–6, pls 5–6
9 Wen, Pu and Yang 2008, p. 103
10 Zhang Yanyuan (815–76), *Record of Famous Painters of Successive Dynasties* (*Lidai minghua ji*), ch. III, sec. III 'On mounting, backing, ornamental borders and rollers', translated in Acker 1954, pp. 242–53
11 Acker 1954, pp. 203, 210–11, 242–3, 245–6
12 Zhang says: 'Pound [the paper] with a stone', Acker 1954, p. 248.
13 Zhang recommends making a lacquered table (*an*; the same word is used today) and using a wooden ruler (*mujie*). Acker (1954, p. 249), following a variant in the text, has 'vermilion boundary lines', which is unlikely.
14 Acker 1954, p. 247
15 Yang 1975, p. 37
16 Ibid.
17 One handscroll in the Palace Museum, Beijing, *Reeds along a Snowy Bank* by Liang Shimin (act. 2nd half 11th century), although probably remounted in the Qing dynasty (1644–1911), is thought to retain the appearance of a Xuanhe mount. See Wang 1991, p. 21.
18 Tao (1360–8) 1963, pp. 329–31
19 Wang 1991, p. 20
20 Vandier-Nicolas 1964, p. 114; Van Gulik 1958, p. 190
21 Zhou Mi (1232–98), quoted in Wang 1991, p. 26
22 For the stave, See van Gulik 1958, p. 190; see also Hung 2007, p. 93
23 Vandier-Nicolas 1964, p. 115
24 Tao Zongyi (1316–1403), (*Notes on the Pictures and Statues of the Yuan Period* (*Huasu ji*)). For a full translation, see van Gulik 1958, p. 227.
25 Over 7,000 metres for the 646 works, which comes out to about 10 metres for each. There is no explanation for this enormous quantity.
26 There were four times as many medium-sized formats ('double mounts'; *shuangfu*) as large formats ('triple' or 'quadruple mounts'; *sifu sanfu*) or handscrolls (*shoujuan*), and five times as many small ones ('single mounts'; *danfu*).
27 Zhou (1650–1) 1993. For a detailed study of this indispensable text see Schmitt 2011.
28 See Schmitt 2011, pp. 123–33.
29 Wen (1637) 1987
30 Apparently, the preference in the Ming was to have these in silk, a practice that is strongly criticized by Zhou Jiazhou, according to whom the paper edges of the Song were stronger than the silk ones used in his time (Zhou [late 16th–early 17th century], 1988, p. 84). It should be noted that nowadays the preference is for silk. See also Hung 2009, p. 101.
31 Wen (1637) 1987
32 This is criticized by Wen Zhenheng. See Schmitt 2011, p. 131.
33 See Shandong Provincial Museum 1972, p. 25; Liu 1972, p. 64; Yang 1980, p. 70.
34 The remounting was done in a Suzhou workshop. See Jiangsu sheng Huai'an xian bowuguan 1987, p. 1.
35 Wen (1637) 1987
36 Zhou (late 16th–early 17th century), 1988, p. 83
37 These black borders are found on a work in the Palace Museum, Beijing (Fu 2005, p. 114).
38 Zhou Jiazhou recommends the use of paper of the highest quality, especially *liansi* (Zhou [late 16th–early 17th century], 1988, p. 85).
39 Specifically, in the texts by Zhou Mi (repeated in Cao [14th century] 1986), Wen Zhenheng and Zhou Jiazhou.
40 Wen (1637) 1987, vol. 872 ; Gao (1591000), in QDSKQS 1986, vol. 871
41 Fu 2005, p. 114
42 Zhou Erxue (1650–?), *Records of Prolonged Gratification of the Simple Heart* (*Shangyan suxin lu*), Records of Prolonged Gratification of the Simple Heart, 1734, in van Gulik 1958, pp. 328–30
43 Van Gulik 1958, pp. 328–30
44 Houng 2010, p. 104, no. 321
45 Van Gulik 1958, p. 331
46 Fu 2005, p. 114–15; Lu 1997, pp. 93–4

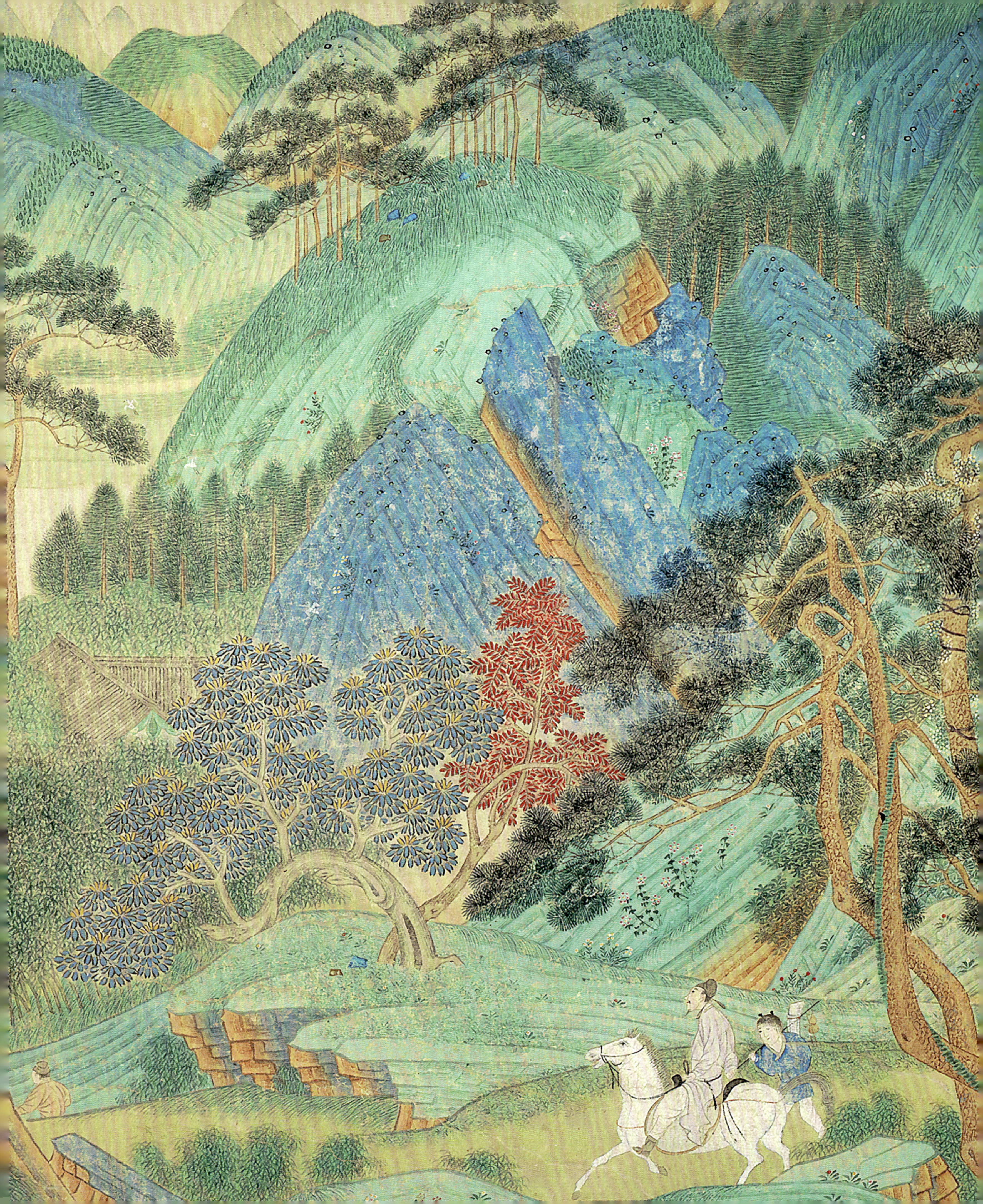

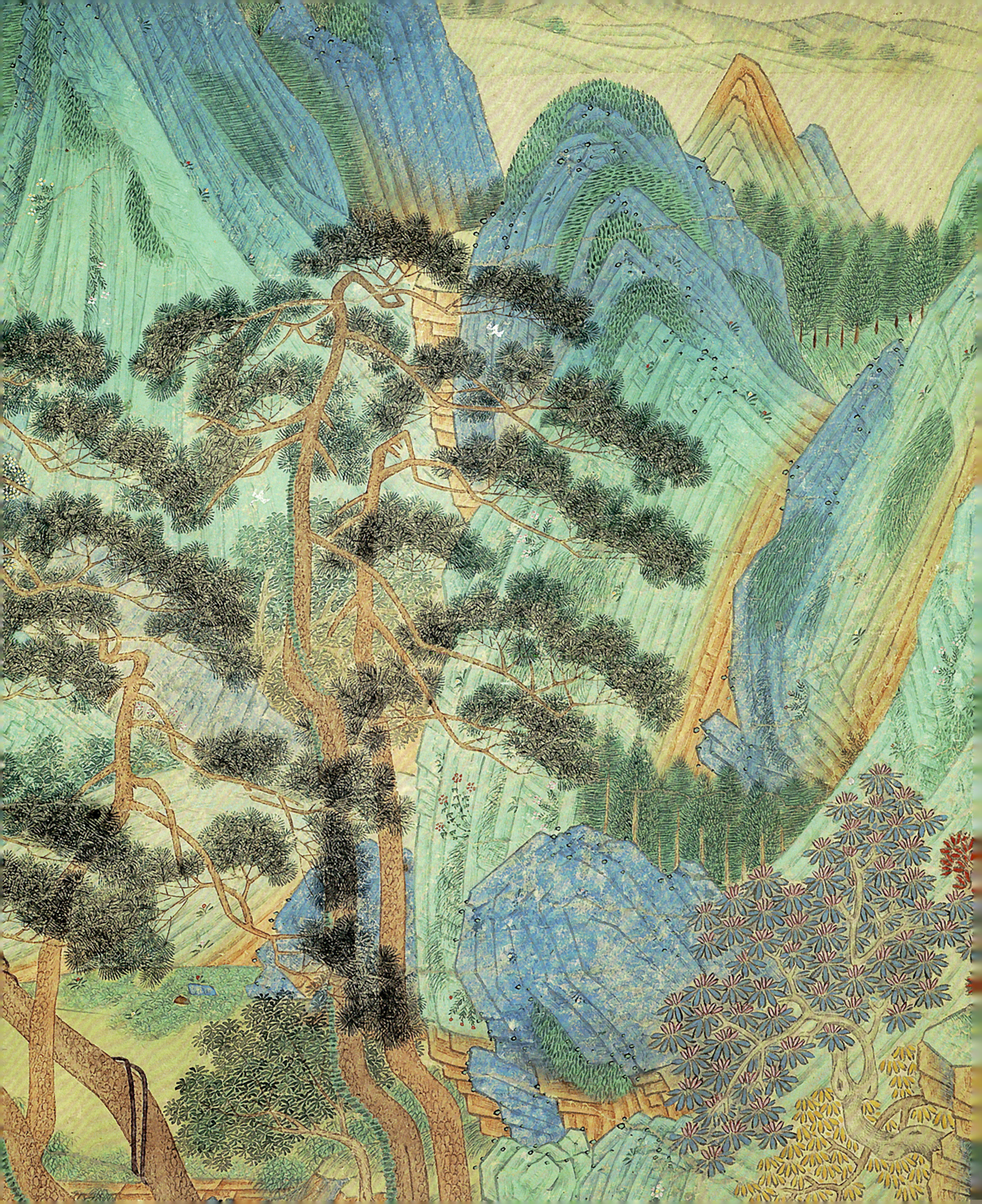

# Introduction to the catalogue

Roderick Whitfield

The invention of ink, brushes and silk and paper enabled the Chinese to create a unique artistic tradition whose history can be traced back to the pre-Han period (206 BCE–220 CE). From the sixth century onwards, numerous writings on aesthetic theory inform us of how the Chinese themselves viewed their art. Early writers stressed the importance of portraiture to teach moral values by example, providing models both to emulate (as with sages and exemplars of filial piety) and to avoid (in the case of villains and scoundrels). This native tradition of narrative painting was greatly enriched with the introduction of Buddhism in the early centuries CE. Yet at the same time, painting was highly regarded for its ability to depict scenes from the natural world, majestic mountains and rivers, within a small space. No doubt the inherently fine quality of silk itself and the delicate effects that could be obtained with brushes of carefully selected animal hairs, gathered at a time of year when the fur was in top condition, encouraged this miniaturization. Especially, *shanshui*, 'mountains and water', the term used for landscape, embodied the workings of the universe in accordance with the theory of the five elements (wood, metal, water, fire and earth) and yin and yang, the basic female and male principles whose interactions were held to govern the seasons and all natural phenomena. Officials posted to distant provinces had plenty of opportunity to record their observations of the changing landscape on their lengthy and time-consuming journeys to and from the capital, such as Lu You's (1125–1210) account of his journey from east to west China.[1] The writer Jing Hao (c.870–c.930) eloquently described the way in which a noble pine tree resembled the *junzi*, or accomplished gentleman, in its relation to the other trees and landscape elements around it; some 100 years later, Guo Xi (c.1000–c.1090), whose own paintings were highly favoured by Emperor Shenzong (r. 1068–85), noted the changing aspects of landscape, and especially mountains, throughout the four seasons, and proposed a theoretical sequence of compositional formulae, *pingyuan* ('level distance'), *shenyuan* ('deep distance') and *gaoyuan* ('high distance'). All three 'distances' had in fact already been practised since the eighth century under the Tang dynasty (618–907), but it was in the tenth and eleventh centuries that they were used in subtle combination to achieve unprecedented effects of scale, enabling the portrayal of human figures, trees and rocks, vast open spaces and massive or lofty mountains, creating landscape masterpieces that still astonish us today.

From the twelfth century onwards, but especially from the thirteenth and fourteenth centuries, calligraphy brought an extra dimension to painting, complementing and enhancing it in a variety of ways, whether as signatures or inscriptions by the artist or his contemporaries, or as colophons and seals added later by connoisseurs to show their appreciation and understanding of the work. Familiarity with brush and ink since earliest childhood meant that all literate persons were potential painters as well: in China, writing and painting were held to stem from the same origin. Above all, brush techniques of line and different types of modelling stroke, and the myriad tones of ink and ink wash, were of prime importance in defining outlines and creating textures. Chinese painters were not concerned with observing the play of light and shade on surfaces, but with understanding and revealing the life principles within every object, animate or inanimate. They sought to capture growth and decay in trees and plants, behaviour in animals, character in portraiture, solidity and fluidity in rocks and water. Ironically, this intense observation, particularly keen during the Northern Song dynasty (960–1127), meant that often they created prototypes that were then copied time and again throughout successive dynasties. This abundance of copies and imitations has been seen, particularly by students outside China, as an obstacle to understanding, but in pre-modern China they were indeed the only means by which the achievements of great masters could become better known. Our privilege in this catalogue is to be able to view some of the best examples in context, and thereby to enjoy the true qualities of brush and ink.

1 Watson 2007

## CONTRIBUTORS TO THE CATALOGUE

| | |
|---|---|
| NB | Nancy Berliner |
| MH | Maxwell Hearn |
| YH | Yin Hwang |
| KR | Kure Motoyuki |
| LLZ | Ling Lizhong |
| CL | Cary Liu |
| LL | Ling-en Lu |
| MM | Malcolm McNeill |
| KR | Klaas Ruitenbeek |
| MS | Mette Siggstedt |
| HS | Hou-mei Sung |
| SY | Szeto Yuen-Kit |
| TM | Tsukamoto Maromitsu |
| CVS | Clarissa von Spee |
| RW | Roderick Whitfield |
| JW | Jennifer Wong |
| CY | Chia-ling Yang |
| YT | Yumino Takayuki |
| VZ | Valerie Zaleski |
| ZH | Zhang Hongxing |

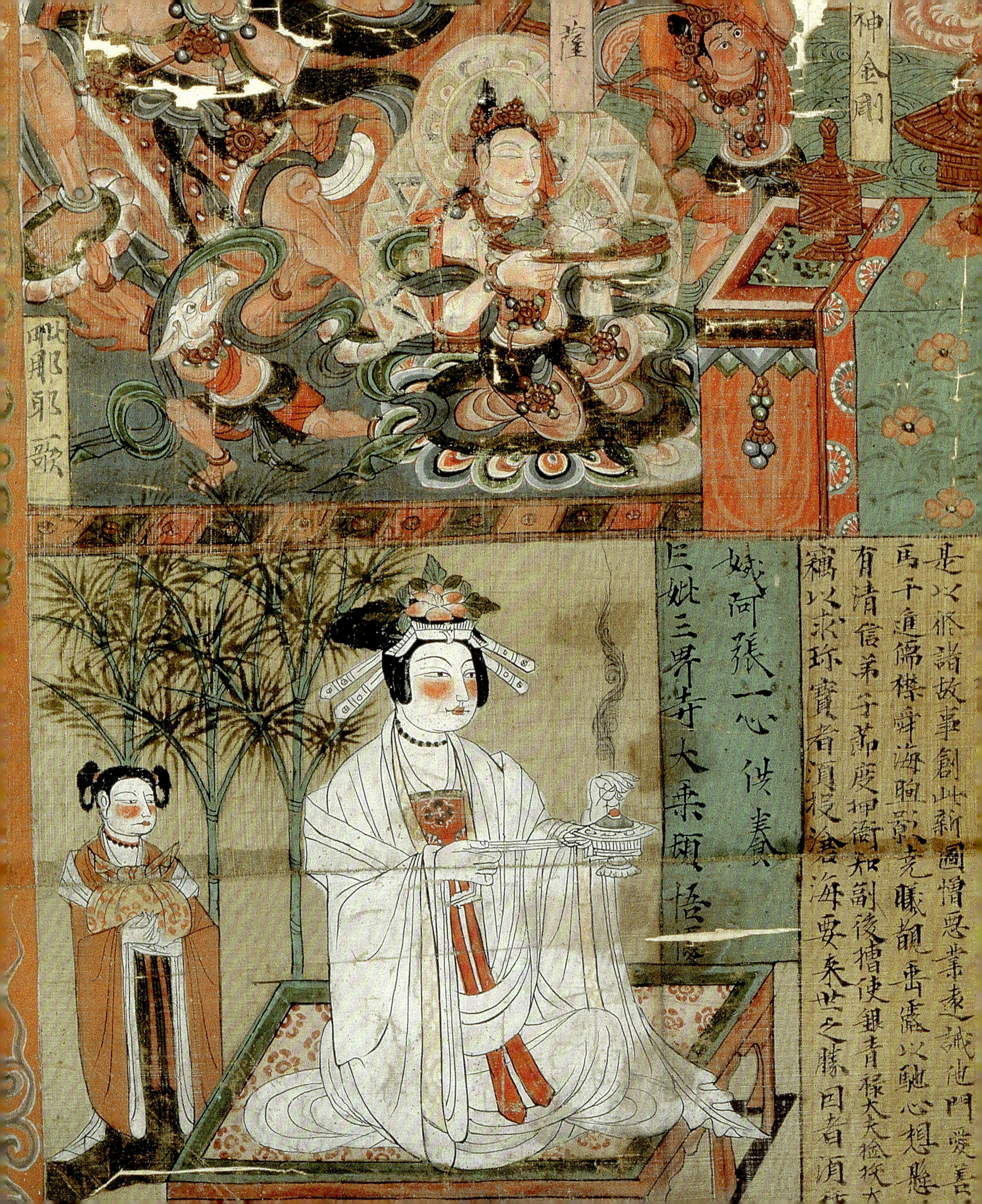
薩
神金剛
娘阿張一心供養
巨姚三界寺大乘頓悟
是以依諸故事創此新圖惜惡業哀誠他門受善
焉千道脩樓舜海睥睨充賤韻盡處以馳心想懸
有清信弟子節度押衙知副後槽使銀青祿大夫檢校大
竊以求珎寶者須投滄海要來世之勝因者須

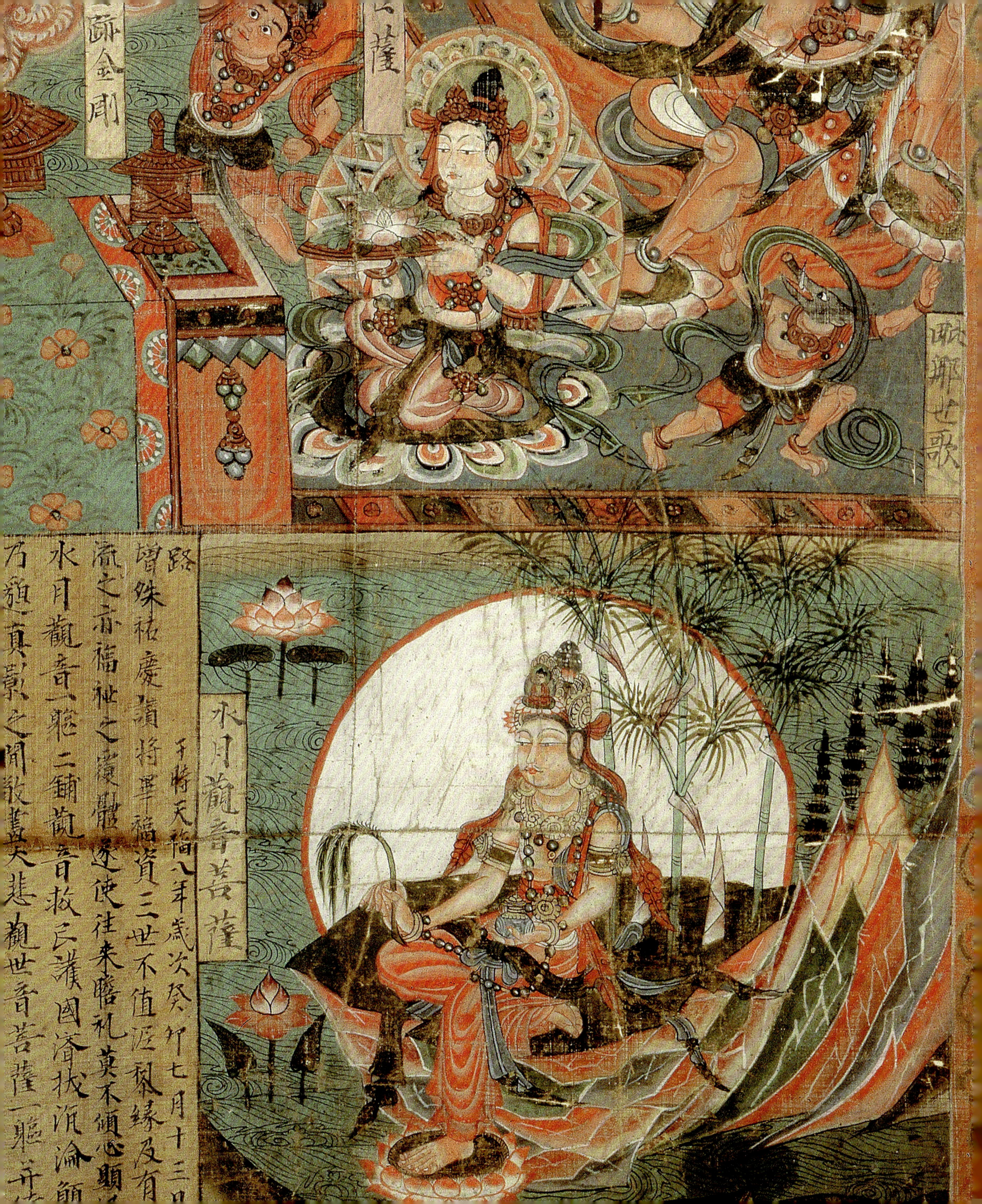
跡金剛
水月觀音菩薩
于時天福八年歲次癸卯七月十三
路
增殊祐慶讃將畢福資三世不值泥犁緣及有
流之亦福祉之護體遂使往來瞻礼莫不傾心
水月觀音一軀二鋪觀音救苦護國濟拔沉淪
乃顯真顏之間敬畫大悲觀世音菩薩一軀

# Paintings 700–950

Commensurate with the military and political achievements of the Tang empire (618–907), written records such as Zhang Yanyuan's (815–76) *Record of Famous Painters of Successive Dynasties* of 847–60 testify to the immense stature of figure painters such as Yan Liben (d.673) and Wu Daozi (c.685–758), whose works adorned the walls of great monasteries in the Tang capitals Chang'an (modern Xi'an, Shaanxi Province) and Luoyang (in Henan Province). Already endangered and indeed destroyed in Zhang Yanyuan's own time by the Buddhist persecution of 842–5, none of these murals survive today, but some handscrolls are still associated with their painters: the late Ming (1368–1644) connoisseur Dong Qichang (1555–1636), for instance, regarded the handscroll *The Five Planets and Twenty-eight Constellations* (cat. no. 13) as being by none other than the great Wu Daozi himself. Nevertheless, archaeological excavations of princely tombs of the eighth century have provided abundant evidence of figural compositions, sometimes, as in the tombs of Prince Zhang Huai (706) and Prince Yide (706), depicted in landscape or architectural settings. Such scenes, of hunting or polo playing, of guards and personal attendants, show large numbers of figures in vigorous activity, with a great variety of characters and a clear sense of space.

Similar characteristics can be observed in the treatment of figures in the Buddhist paintings on silk discovered at the beginning of the twentieth century in a sealed cave, originally a small chapel commemorating the eminent monk Hongbian (d.862), at Mogao near the garrison town of Dunhuang, which controlled access to the trade routes across Central Asia. Despite the great difference from the subject matter of the tomb murals, silk paintings from Dunhuang such as *Buddha Preaching the Law* (cat. no. 1) reveal a comparable mastery of spatial arrangement and ability to portray differences of age and character in groups of figures. Buddhism and Buddhist iconography had originally reached China from India via Central Asia, but in the late seventh and early eighth centuries, the main focus of creativity in Buddhist art was no longer in the west, but in the Tang capitals, Chang'an and Luoyang. Thus, it is possible that some paintings like this had been executed in those cities and sent to Dunhuang as models for the murals adorning the scores of cave temples that were cut during the Tang dynasty. Both the silk paintings and the murals served to earn merit for the donors and especially for their deceased parents, securing their rebirth in the Buddhist Pure Lands.

Because they often portrayed the donors themselves, Buddhist paintings from Dunhuang also display the changing tastes in fashion in metropolitan China, as well as allowing a glimpse of what the works of renowned landscape painters active in the eighth century such as Li Sixun (653–718) and Wang Wei (699–759/701–61) might have looked like. The favoured technique of composition involved tall mountain peaks set close together, allowing a view between them to extensive plains beyond, often with a river zigzagging into the far distance. Human activities could be shown in the foreground, or negotiating cliff-side paths. All these features can be seen in the anonymous painting (long associated with Li Sixun and his son Li Zhaodao) *Emperor Minghuang's Flight to Shu* (National Palace Museum, Taipei). For Buddhist narratives, successive scenes were set one above the other, separated by oblique slopes and accompanied by alternating cartouches, so as to fill the available space, right up to a very high horizon. Such narrative scenes could take the form of narrow silk banners with a triangular top, or appear in the margins of larger rectangular banners or murals, on either side of representations of the Buddhist Pure Lands, whose buildings, incidentally, also reflect the architectural features of the lost monasteries of Chang'an and Luoyang (cat. no. 5).

While the majority of narrow banners portrayed individual bodhisattvas and guardian figures (cat. nos 3, 4, 6, 7, 10, 11), there is one very different figure, that of a travelling monk (cat. no. 8). Apart from the intrinsic interest of the subject, no doubt inspired by Xuanzang's 16-year journey to India to bring sutras, images and relics back to China, this painting illustrates a new technique, seen in several paintings of the 980s,[1] namely the application of small diamonds of cut gold leaf to the dark bands between the patches of the monk's robe. This technique, and the realism of the monk's facial features, quite different from the idealized features of the monks in *Buddha Preaching the Law* (cat. no. 1), are new elements that look forward to the paintings of the next period.

1 Giès et al. 1994, vol. 1, pls 60–2; Whitfield 2011

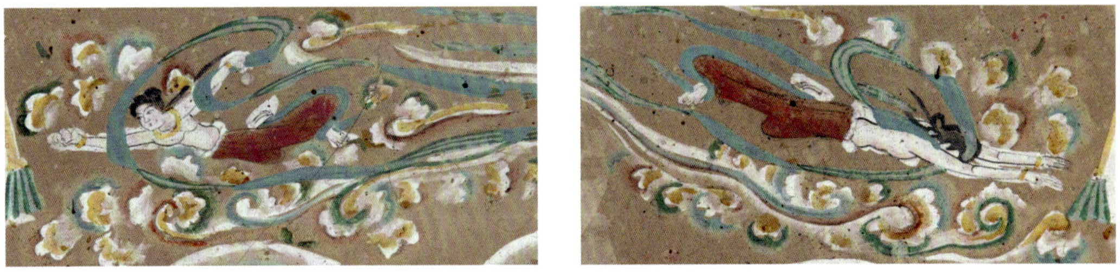

1

UNIDENTIFIED ARTIST

## Buddha Preaching the Law

唐 佚名 樹下說法圖

c.700, banner mounted as a panel, ink and colour on silk, 139 × 102 cm
The British Museum, London
(Stein Collection, 1919,0101,0.6)

Although it has been stretched on a panel, this painting remains an archetypical example of the Buddhist paintings from the 'library cave' at Dunhuang. Such paintings were not mounted as scrolls: instead, a border of silk or hemp cloth was sewn to all four edges, with loops at the top edge so that they could be hung from a rod of bamboo or wood. Tang dynasty (618–907) silks were woven on looms that were all of similar size, producing standard lengths of silk with a uniform width of about 56 centimetres. Smaller votive paintings were painted on a single width of silk, while the largest could encompass three whole widths, sewn together. In this painting, there is a single length of silk in the centre; a second length of silk was divided lengthwise into two halves, and these were sewn on to the sides of the first length, selvedge to selvedge, with very fine stitches. Surface abrasion along the seams means that they can be clearly seen. The borders, a few centimetres wide, were folded lengthwise and sewn on so as to sandwich and protect the cut edges of the painting silk on all four sides. When found, most of the paintings in the library cave had simply been folded up, and the older ones had often sustained losses, such as are seen here in the lower right and upper left.

This type of assembly means that the painting can be as wide as two complete widths of silk with no central seam to impair the depiction of the central figure. Here, this is Śākyamuni, the historical Buddha, seated, with his hands in *dharmacakra* mudra, the gesture of teaching. Seated on an elaborately decorated lotus throne and sheltered by a similarly decorated canopy, he is surrounded by four bodhisattvas, two seated and two kneeling, and six monks with shaven heads. While the Buddha is depicted frontally, the two principal bodhisattvas are in three-quarter view, and the monks are concealed to varying degrees behind the other figures. In this way, the unknown painter has achieved a strong sense of three-dimensionality, which is reinforced by the two apsarasas riding multi-coloured clouds above the two bodhi trees behind the Buddha. One, damaged, descends while the other ascends, and the clouds on which they are borne weave past other clouds which may also have carried smaller figures. In the lower part of the painting, two donors were originally depicted. The female figure, in the fashionable early Tang costume of a short jacket and a high-waisted skirt, kneels in demure fashion, holding a lotus (another lotus is judiciously placed to set off her black hair). The male figure is missing, but incense smoke can be seen rising, so he would have been holding a censer. It is not clear, however, if the painting was actually used as a votive offering, since there is no inscription on the panel between the donors. This panel is unusual, as it takes the form of a stone tablet, with a space for a title in the top centre, supported on a turtle base (the hexagonal pattern of the upper shell can be made out, as well as a single eye). The turtle-supported tablet, of a type well known in the capital Chang'an (present Xi'an), may be a clue that the painting was executed there and taken to Dunhuang, perhaps as a model.

Similar multi-coloured clouds are found in several of the caves at Dunhuang, all dating to the early Tang period, between 618 and 710. Some of the best examples are in Cave 321, which has three groups of a Buddha preaching, located on the east wall above the entrance to the cave, making the same teaching gesture, and with similar colouring and highlighting of the facial features (fig. 55). Perhaps because of the limited space above the entrance, this preaching scene has no apsarasas above the Buddha; however, they are present in a very similar group on the entrance wall of another early Tang cave, Cave 329 (fig. 54). Other figures, and indeed whole Buddha groups, are seen riding multi-coloured clouds on the ceiling of the main niche of Cave 321: all can be dated to the early Tang, most probably during the reign of Empress Wu Zetian (690–705), for whom Dunhuang held special significance as the site where several auspicious signs had been observed. RW

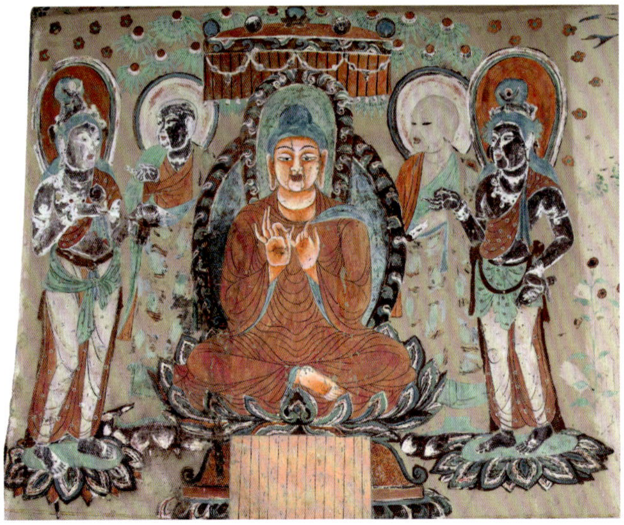

FIG. 54 (above)
*Apsarasas*, c.700. Mural from Cave 329, Mogao Caves, Dunhuang

FIG. 55 (left)
*Buddha Preaching*, late 7th century. Mural from Cave 321, Mogao Caves, Dunhuang

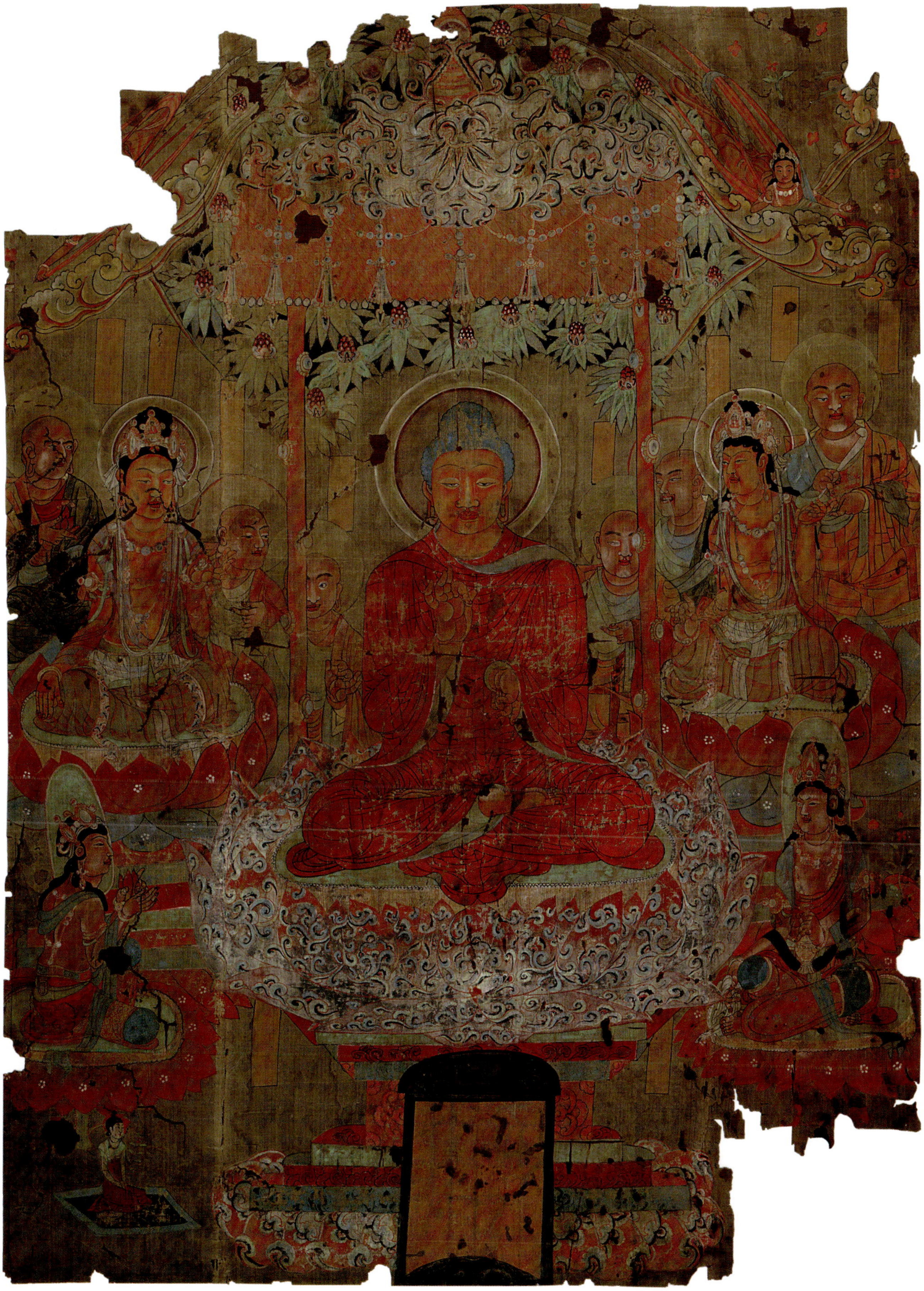

2

UNIDENTIFIED ARTIST

## Apsaras

唐 佚名 飛天

late 7th–early 8th century, banner fragment, ink and colour on silk, 50.2 × 33 cm
Musée Guimet, Paris (Pelliot Collection, EO 1155)

REFERENCE LITERATURE

Giès et al. 1994, vol. 2, pl. 86; London 1936, no. 646; Whitfield 2003; *Chinese Cave Temples: the Mogao Caves at Dunhuang* (1983) 1987; Sun and Sun 2001, pl. 98; Liang 1996, pls 62–5

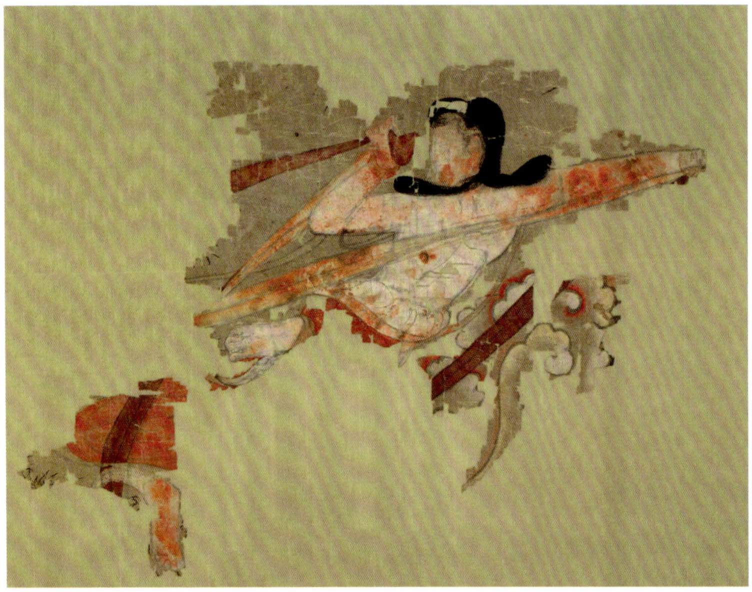

FIG. 56
*Apsaras* fragment of a Pure Land painting, late 7th century. Ink and colour on silk, mounted. Excavated from Cave 17, Mogao Caves, Dunhuang. The British Museum, London (1919,0101,0.345)

This fragment of a splendid apsaras descending on multi-coloured clouds is one of the most celebrated paintings from the Pelliot collection.[1] In 1935–6, it was one of a very limited selection of paintings from Dunhuang shown in the *International Exhibition of Chinese Art* at the Royal Academy in London.

Apsarasas, known in Chinese as *feitian* or 'flying heavenly beings', are typically depicted as a pair, in contrasting poses high above and on either side of the Buddha: one such apsaras is visible in the painting *Buddha Preaching the Law* (cat. no. 1). This fragment, therefore, was originally part of a much larger painting. As this apsaras is larger than its counterpart in *Buddha Preaching the Law*, presumably the whole painting must also have been larger than the latter. Another fragment of the same work, unpublished until recently, confirms this assertion.[2] Part of the Stein collection in the British Museum, it is another apsaras (fig. 56).

Equally lively in movement, this second figure turns away from the viewer but has the same flying scarves of *zhusha* red, lined with *zhubiao* orange-red (these are different grades of the same cinnabar vermilion), and the same drawn-up left leg and extended right foot. The preliminary drawing in ink is clearly visible in both fragments, owing to the loss of colours applied to the surface, and both figures are lightly supported on clouds depicted with the kind of brilliant colouring and confident brushwork seen in the early Tang period (618–907) wall paintings in Cave 220, dated 642, at Dunhuang.[3] Both fragments also show leaves and stems of bamboo, stunningly executed in very fine black ink in the *shuanggou* or 'double-outline' technique, probably the earliest surviving appearance of this distinctive Chinese method. The two flowers that emerge from a crown of longer and wider leaves (originally green) at the upper left of the Pelliot fragment can be identified as being part of a bodhi tree, similar to the bodhi trees behind the Buddha in *Buddha Preaching the Law*.

The two fragments are linked not simply by these similarities in subject matter, artistic skill and use of ink and pigments, but also and crucially by the silk support on which they are both painted. Most of the silk paintings from Dunhuang, including *Buddha Preaching the Law*, are painted on silks that show a clear distinction in thickness between the warp and weft threads. Their warp threads are much thinner, and paired, with a slightly wider spacing between adjacent pairs, while the weft threads are thicker and evenly spaced. In the present case, however, both warp and weft are evenly spaced, giving a much denser picture surface for the painter to work on. This type of silk is used in no other paintings from Dunhuang. Not only does this confirm that the two apsarasas come from a single painting, it also strongly suggests that this work was originally painted not at Dunhuang, but in metropolitan China. Numerous sutras written under imperial auspices in the 670s were among the manuscripts found in the so-called 'library cave'

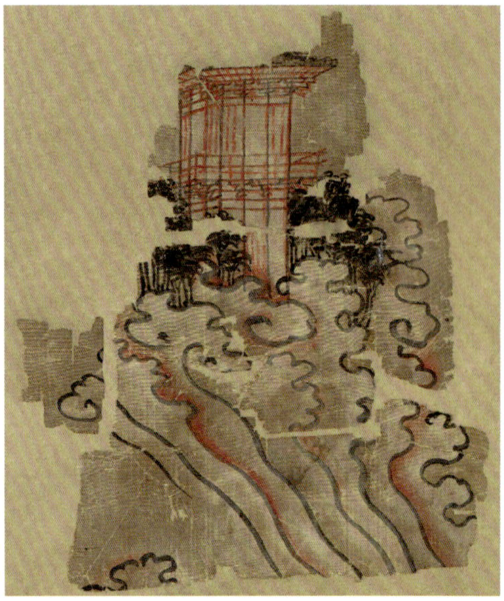

FIG. 57
*Heavenly Pavilion* fragment of a Pure Land painting, late 7th century. Ink and colour on silke, mounted. on silk. Excavated from Cave 17, Mogao Caves, Dunhuang. The British Museum, London (1919,0101,0.352b&c)

at Dunhuang. At this time, the Tang capital Chang'an (present Xi'an) was a Buddhist centre of great importance; both manuscripts and silk paintings were easily transported to Dunhuang, where they served as models of subject matter, style and composition for wall paintings. Other fragments of this same painting include a horse seen in back view, a small fragment of landscape with trees, a donor holding a lotus bud and a section of the original broad ink border. Among them, a tall tower, slenderly built, is surrounded by trees and supported on a dense cluster of clouds (fig. 57). It matches well with the cloud-borne pavilions and other paradise buildings seen in the Amitābha paradise on the north wall of Cave 321 at Dunhuang, dated around 695.[4]

For the purposes of dating, several considerations apply: the brilliance of the pigments used and the skill of brush and ink, comparisons with wall paintings still in situ at the Dunhuang caves and the fragmentary condition of the painting itself, since the relative age of the paintings when they were stored away in the library cave was a crucial factor in their state of preservation when they emerged some nine centuries later – some were almost new, others already centuries old. These considerations suggest that the painting originated in Chang'an in the late seventh century, during the reign of Empress Wu (690–704). RW

1 Giès et al. 1994, vol. 2, pl. 86
2 Whitfield 2003
3 *Chinese Cave Temples: the Mogao Caves at Dunhuang* (1983) 1987; Sun and Sun 2001, pl. 98
4 Liang 1996, pls 62–5

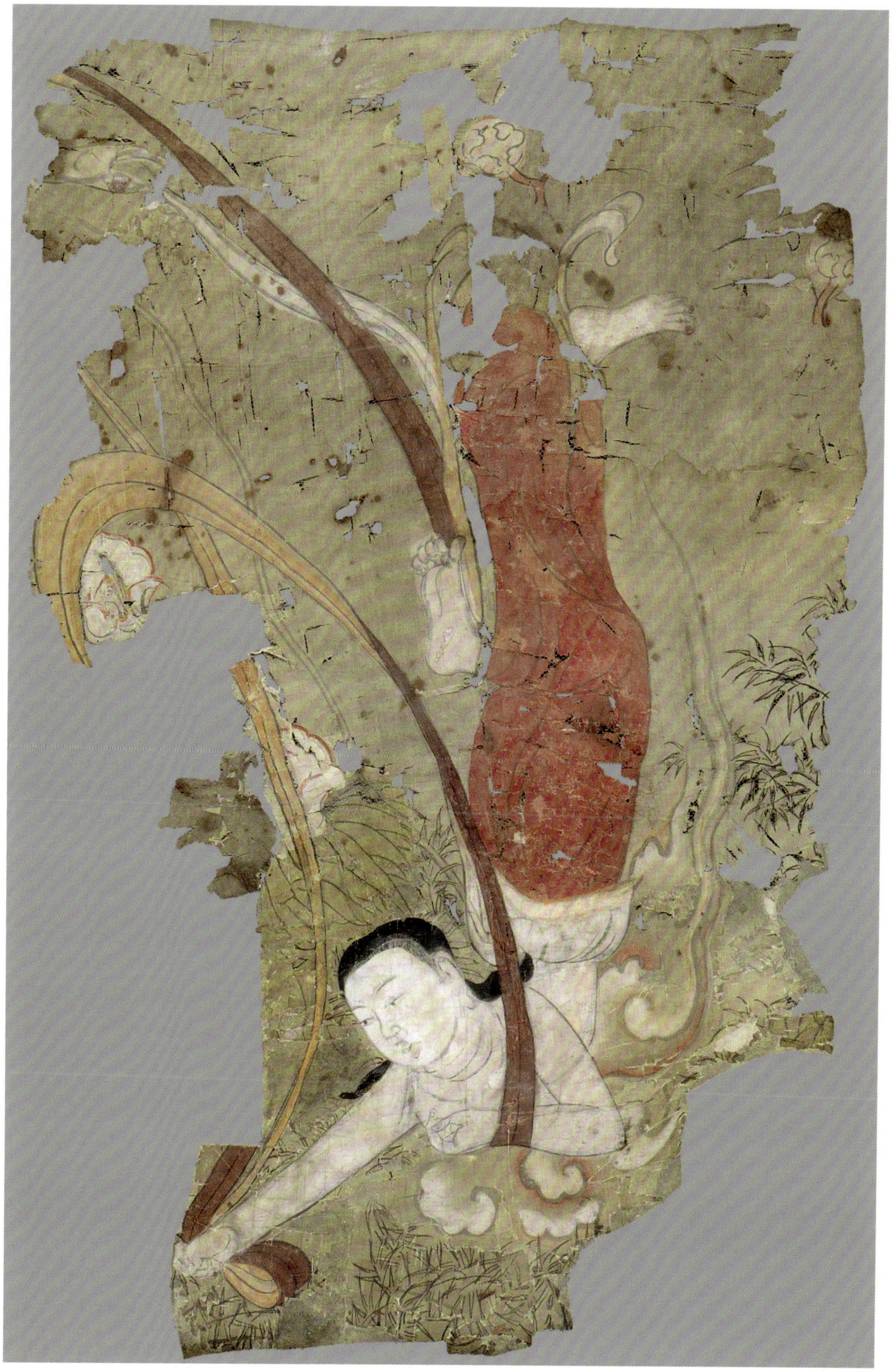

3

UNIDENTIFIED ARTIST

## Guardian King of the North, Pishamen-Vaiśravaṇa

唐 佚名 毗沙門天王立像

2nd half 8th century, banner fragment,
ink and colour on silk, 44 × 13.5 cm
Musée Guimet, Paris (Pelliot Collection, EO 1190)

REFERENCE LITERATURE

Vandier-Nicolas 1974–6, pp. 365–6, pl. XVI, 1;
Giès 1996, vol. 2, p. 310, pls 74 and 189

This martial figure, his feet supported by a figure of whom only the chest and head are visible, illustrates the journey of Buddhist images and concepts to China from Central Asia. The figure is Vaiśravaṇa (Ch. Pishamen), the *lokapāla* or guardian king who protects the north, standing on the earth goddess Pṛthivī (Ch. Ditian) – an iconographic association of these two divine Buddhist protectors that was particularly favoured in the kingdom of Khotan, where Vaiśravaṇa was regarded as the protector of the state and its rulers and venerated as a royal ancestor. According to legend (recorded by the monk-pilgrim Xuanzang in his *Records of the Western Regions*), Vaiśravaṇa granted the king of Khotan a son, who was then suckled by the earth goddess. The worship of this guardian figure, who emerged from the Gandhāran composite depictions of Pharro-Pāñcika-Kubera-Vaiśravaṇa, and was known as Vrēšaman in the Sogdian pantheon further west, seems to have been brought to Khotan by the Kuṣāṇas, whose protector he was. He is shown on Pṛthivī's shoulders in the late sixth or early seventh century in Khotan, as well as in the monastery of Rawak to the north-east of Khotan and at Dunhuang in north-west China, from where his iconography spread as far as Japan.

Vaiśravaṇa is said to have been given the task of protecting Buddhism in the northern regions at the time of the Buddha's passing, and was the ruler of the area north of Mount Meru, where the ground was said to be full of treasure. Lord of the *yakṣas* or nature spirits, he is also linked to Kubera, god of wealth and guardian of the north in the Hindu tradition. He is the most important of four the guardian kings.

Seen here from the front, in the guise of a general armed with a sword and dressed in a suit of scale and lamellar armour, he wears a three-pointed crown and the wide trousers of west Central Asia. In accordance with canonic prescriptions, he holds a three-pointed lance and a stupa, symbolizing the Buddha. However, in contrast to earlier depictions in the Dunhuang caves, stylized flames burst from his shoulders, which did not appear in Dunhuang until the early Tang period (618–907).

Certain stylistic details, such as the treatment of the goddess's eyes, the lower strip of foliate scrolls and the treatment of the jewellery (necklace and bracelets with cabochons), link this painting to a banner from Dunhuang portraying the bodhisattva Samantabhadra that is estimated to date to the mid-eighth century (Pelliot Collection, EO 1210). They reflect the custom, at least at this time, of depicting venerated beings on banners in place of the earlier decorations of geometric motifs, as seen particularly on paintings depicting Yinlu pusa ('the bodhisattva who leads the way', see cat. no. 9). VZ

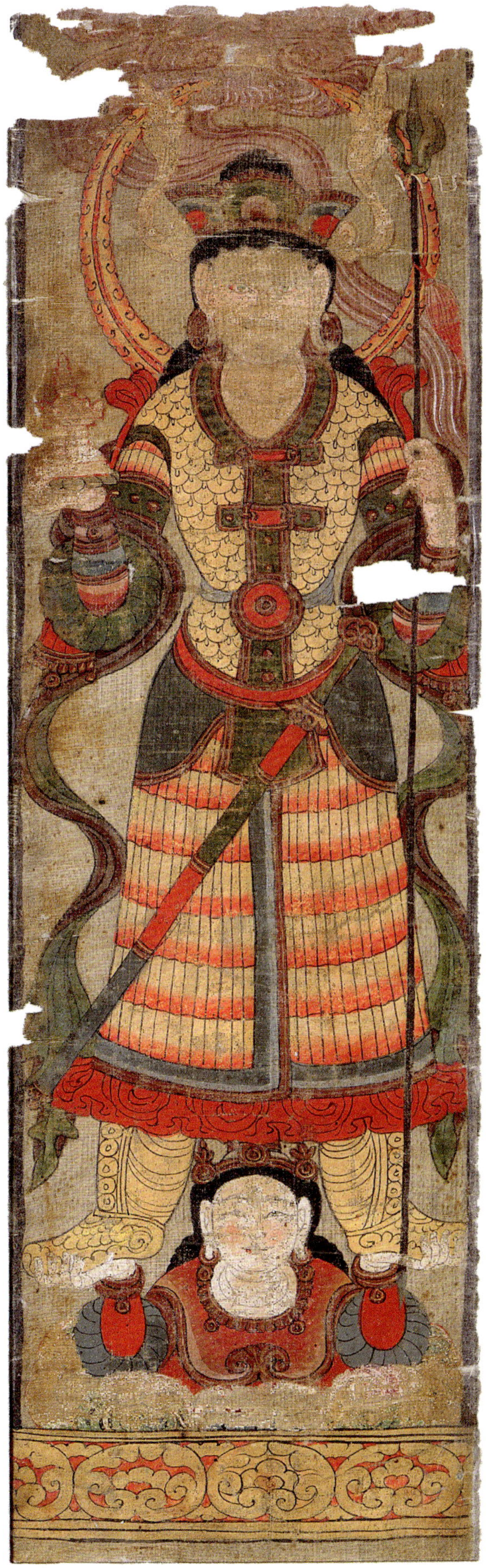

4

UNIDENTIFIED ARTIST

## The Bodhisattva Dizang (Kṣitigarbha)

唐 佚名 地藏菩薩像

729, banner fragment, ink and colour on silk, 62 × 27 cm
Musée Guimet, Paris (Pelliot Collection, MG 17658)

REFERENCE LITERATURE

Hackin 1923, p. 47; Matsumoto 1932; London 1936, no. 758; Monod-Bruhl 1939, p. 126, no. 145; Paris 1947, p. 28, no. 105; Vandier-Nicolas 1974–6, vol. 2, pp. 401–2, pls XVIII and 209; Paris 1995–6, no. 120; Giès 1996, vol. 2, p. 300, no. 59

Visible behind this fragment of a painting showing a haloed monk on a flower-strewn ground is an earlier painting of a face seen from the front, revealing two different stages of the painting or perhaps a pentimento brought to light by time. However, the identity of the monk, who holds a sistrum (S. *khakkhara*) in his right hand and a rosary in his left, remains uncertain, as he has sometimes been identified as Mahākāśyapa (the aged disciple of the Buddha) and sometimes as the bodhisattva Kṣitigarbha (perhaps initially sketched from the front and then drawn in three-quarter profile). Nevertheless his open garment, which leaves his right shoulder and torso bare and reveals the undergarment edged with a staggered row of beaded roses, is a monk's robe or *kaṣāya* dotted with blue and green striped with black, similar to those depicted on other images identified as Kṣitigarbha.

Furthermore, above him, and perhaps also originally above another representation next to him, is a cloud with a small haloed 'transformation-body' (Ch. *huashen*; S. *nirmānakāya*) Buddha which, together with the wisps of vapour escaping from the hand holding the rosary – possibly signifying the 'Six Paths' of rebirth – and the last two characters of a *pusa* ('bodhisattva') inscription, supports an identification as Kṣitigarbha.

The inscription in the cartouche to the right of the figure, reading 'Given with all her heart by Zhang, wife, in the 17th year of the Kaiyuan era', dates the painting to 729, in the Tang dynasty (618–907), revealing it to be the oldest dated portable painting found in the 'library cave' at Dunhuang.

From a stylistic point of view, the skilled and individualized treatment of the anatomy and face, as well as the fluidity of the drawing of the drapery, sets this painting apart from Indian and Central Asian models, and places it within the great tradition of the Chinese painting of the Kaiyuan (713–41) and Tianbao (742–55) eras of the Tang, so that it has been compared to the work of one of the contemporary painters known for his powerful portraits, Wu Daozi (*c*.685–758). However, other representations on the walls of the Dunhuang caves (such as that of Vimalakirti in Cave 103) suggest that there may in fact have been a local school during the Kaiyuan era, perhaps even founded by masters from Central Asia. VZ

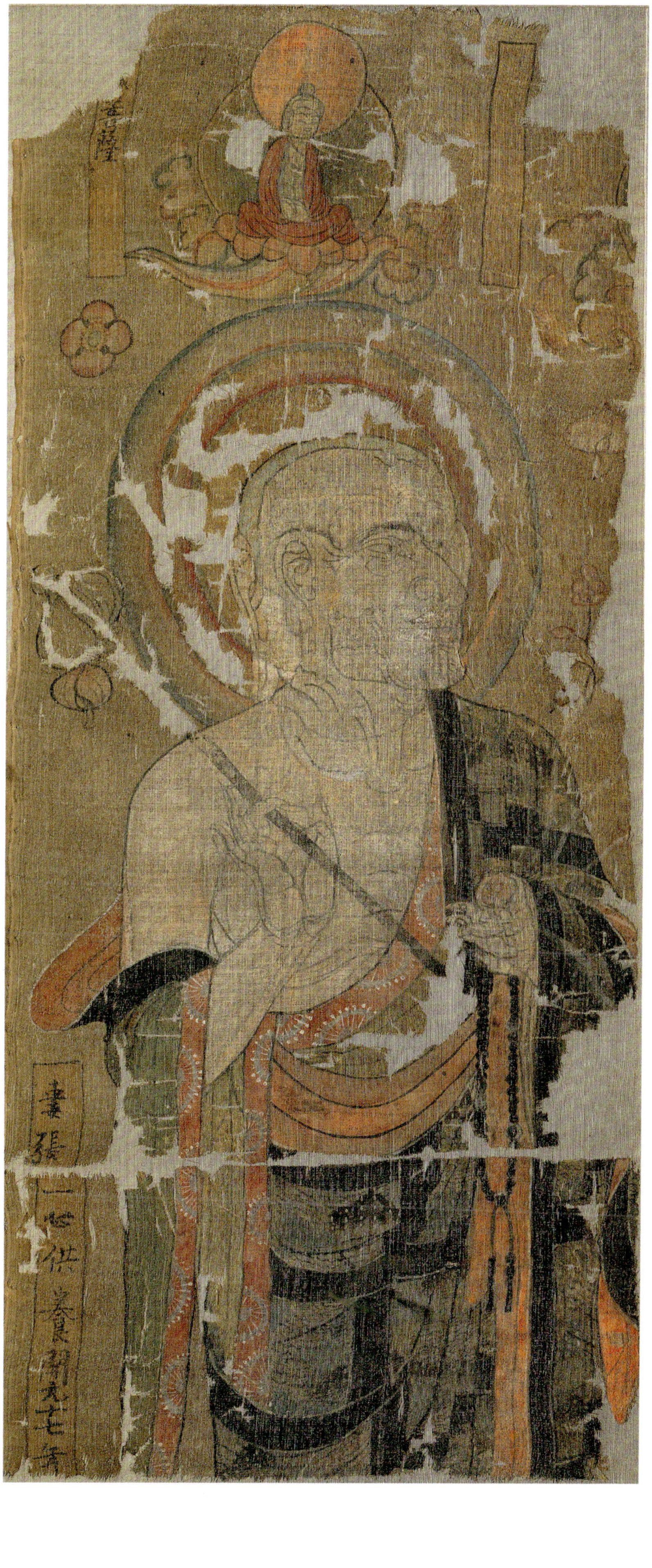
菩薩
妻張一心供養開元七年

5

UNIDENTIFIED ARTIST

## Illustration of the Sūtra of the Contemplation of the Buddha Amitāyus

唐 佚名 觀無量壽經變

1st half 9th century, banner mounted as a panel, ink and colour on silk, 171 × 118.2 cm
Musée Guimet, Paris (Pelliot Collection, EO 1128)

REFERENCE LITERATURE

London 1936, no. 2385; Paris 1947, p. 38, no. 166; Vandier-Nicolas 1974–6, pp. 33–7, pl. 19; Paris 1976, pp. 59–60, no. 166; Paris 1995–6, no. 244; Giès 1996, vol. 1, pp. 317–9, pl. 16, figs 10–13; Tokyo 1996b, no. 197; Yamabe 2012

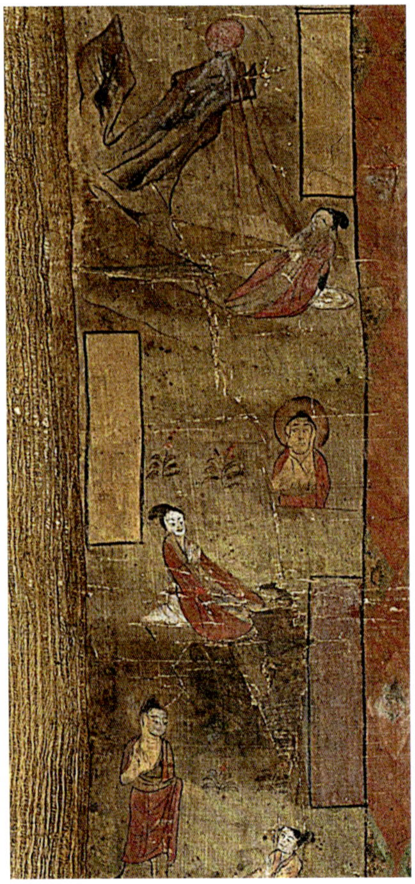

This painting shows the Pure Land of Amitābha, named Sukhāvatī, which became a favourite theme in Tang period (618–907) Dunhuang and was depicted in large wall paintings, notably in Caves 220, 172, 320, 112 and 12 (as well as Cave 25 at Yulin), and on the portable paintings in the Musée Guimet and the British Museum.

Descriptions of the fabled Pure Land, where those who have faithfully prayed to the Buddha Amitābha may be reborn, feature in the longer and shorter *Sukhāvatīvyūha* sutras, taught by the historical Buddha Śākyamuni to his disciples Ānanda and Śāriputra, respectively, and which exist in several Chinese translations.[1] However, another description of Amitābha's Pure Land is given in a third text, the *Amitāyurdhyāna Sūtra* ('on the contemplation of Buddha Amitāyus', another form of Amitābha). This sutra was translated into Chinese in the fifth century, and an important commentary was written on it in the seventh century by Shandao (613–81), to whom tradition also attributes the execution of around 200 paintings.

The sutra was taught by Buddha Śākyamuni to Queen Vaidehī, who had been imprisoned for secretly feeding her incarcerated husband King Bimbisāra by their son, the usurper Ajātaśatru. It teaches her how to visualize the Pure Land and how to be reborn there through the 'Sixteen Contemplations'.

This painting provides a complex but typical depiction of the Pure Land or paradise of Amitābha and the visions usually associated with him in the iconographic tradition related to the *Amitāyurdhyāna Sūtra*. Amitābha, attended by the bodhisattvas Avalokiteśvara and Mahāsthāmaprāpta (undifferentiated here other than by the bell held by Avalokiteśvara), is shown teaching in his palace, surrounded by 22 bodhisattvas. Before him is a pool overlooked by terraces intended for its contemplation, on which sit two other Buddhas (perhaps two other forms of Amitābha, manifesting his omnipresence), each accompanied by a bodhisattva. An orchestra of musicians playing *sheng* (reed instruments reminiscent of the south-east Asian *knene*), *di* (flutes) and *pipa* (lutes) on one side, and *paiban* (clappers), *sheng* and *qin* (zithers) on the other, accompanies a dancer. From the waters filled with heavenly beings, *kinnara* (here conventionally portrayed as half human, half bird) and *haṃsa* (wild geese), lotus flowers emerge and open to reveal the reborn souls of the elect as naked babies. Four miniature Buddhas in the sky, seated in meditation on clouds emerging from pavilions at the side, may evoke the other pure lands where beings may be reborn according to their progress along the Path.

As on other portable paintings (MG 17672 and MG 17673 in the Musée Guimet; Stein paintings 35 and 70 in the British Museum) and on the wall paintings in Caves 172 and 320 at Dunhuang and 25 at Yulin, the story of Bimbisāra and the visions of Queen Vaidehī unfold on either side of the Pure Land (here to the left and right, respectively). Two other scenes preceding the story of Bimbisāra also appear here, showing Bimbisāra's murder of a hermit and his soul's escape in the form of a hare, both apocryphal episodes from Shandao's commentary.

In the lower section, depicting five of the Seven Jewels of the Universal Monarch, a large blank dedicatory cartouche and traces of the images of donors indicate that the painting was intended as an offering for the salvation of the deceased.

Several elements of the painting have been linked to the paradise of Bhaiṣajyaguru in Cave 112 at Dunhuang, which dates to the period of Tibetan occupation in the late eighth to early ninth century. These include the appearance of the central Buddha and the small meditating Buddhas emerging from the pavilions, the two octagonal pavilions containing a bell and drum, and the two conical banners behind the palace that are ornamented with a lozenge pattern and surmounted by a fringed canopy. VZ

1 Samghavarman's translation of the former (T 360) and Kumārajīva's of the latter dated 402 (T 366) seem to be most frequently used.

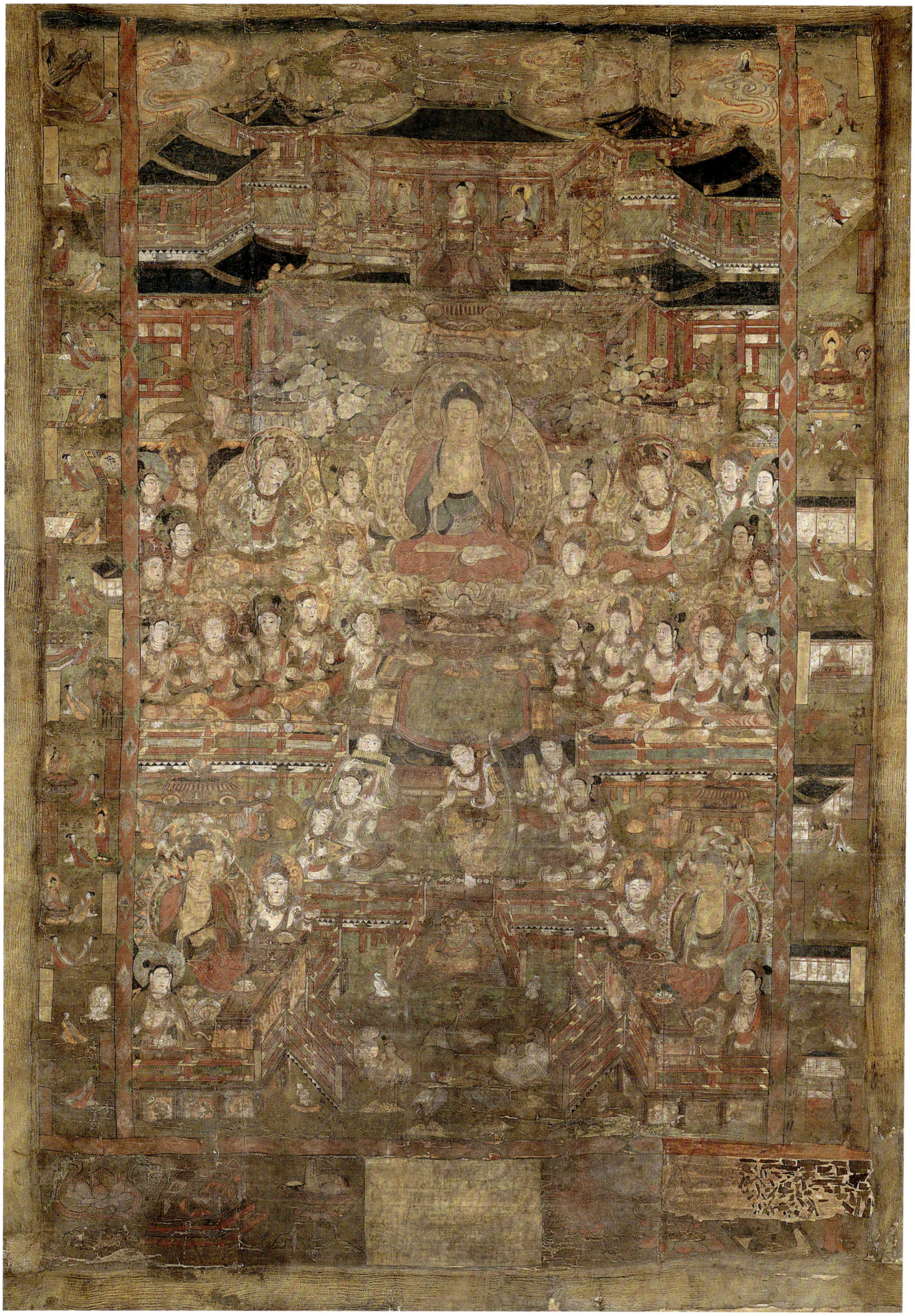

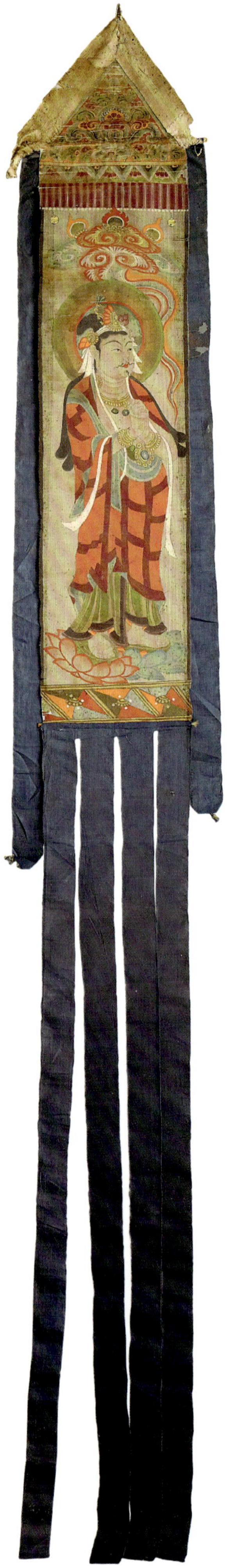

6

UNIDENTIFIED ARTIST

## Bodhisattva in Monastic Dress Standing at Prayer

唐 佚名 身著袈裟菩薩立像

late 9th–early 10th century, banner,
ink and colour on silk, 67 × 18 cm
Musée Guimet, Paris (Pelliot Collection, MG 22797)

REFERENCE LITERATURE

Venice 1954, no. 722; Vandier-Nicolas 1974–6, vol. XIV, pp. 309–10 and vol. XV, pl. 150; Giès 1996, vol. 2, p. 292, pl. 33

The double-sided painting on this banner shows an unusual image of a standing bodhisattva in three-quarter profile. In addition to his joined hands with fingers interlaced, the bodhisattva wears jewellery, yet is dressed in the monastic *kāsāya* worn by the bodhisattva Dizang (S. Kṣitigarbha) on other banners, but without the requisite shaved head of a monk. As in other images of Dizang, his feet rest on two separate lotus flowers and a cloud curls in wreaths (here yellow, orange, vermilion, blue-green and white) above his halo. The cloud is surmounted by three flaming jewels, recalling those of the cloud in another image of Dizang (cat. no. 10) and, more generally, those decorating most of the jewelled canopies depicted on banners, so that these clouds have been interpreted as substitutes for a canopy.

Meanwhile, the tile decoration on the lower band, the ruffled and tasselled lambrequin hung with two small bells, and the flower decorating the triangular headpiece all seem very similar to those on another banner depicting Dizang in the Tokyo National Museum (TA 158), which itself is the mirror image of yet another representation of this bodhisattva (MG 22798).

We may then wonder whether the bodhisattva shown here, combining monastic and princely features in the manner of Dizang, might not have been individualized due to his iconographic particularities.

In the light of representations of the bodhisattva Maitreya known in Gandhāra, where he accompanies the Buddhas of the past, we could also see this image as Maitreya, adorned with jewels and with his hair dressed in the princely chignon but wearing the monastic robe of the Buddha he will become, as he almost certainly appears on another banner in the Pelliot collection (EO 1225). However, on the latter, the bodhisattva holds the vase of water and his left hand is open, palm down, whereas here the bodhisattva's hands are joined in prayer. Moreover, no depictions of the bodhisattva and Buddha of the future Maitreya are attested on any banner or other auxiliary votive painting.

Unless, reflecting both the Indian and Chinese (or Central Asian) traditions, this is a representation of Dizang as at once a bodhisattva, whose jewels and hairstyle he has retained, and a monk, though as yet he wears only the *kāṣāya*. His gesture of homage might then indicate that this banner accompanied an extensive paradise of Maitreya, a Buddha with whom Dizang is sometimes associated.

The banner itself has retained its complete original mount, with the triangular headpiece edged in white damask, the trapezoidal bamboo board decorated with paintings forming the counterweight and the ribbons on the side and lower edge in blue taffeta with rolled edges ending in tassels. VZ

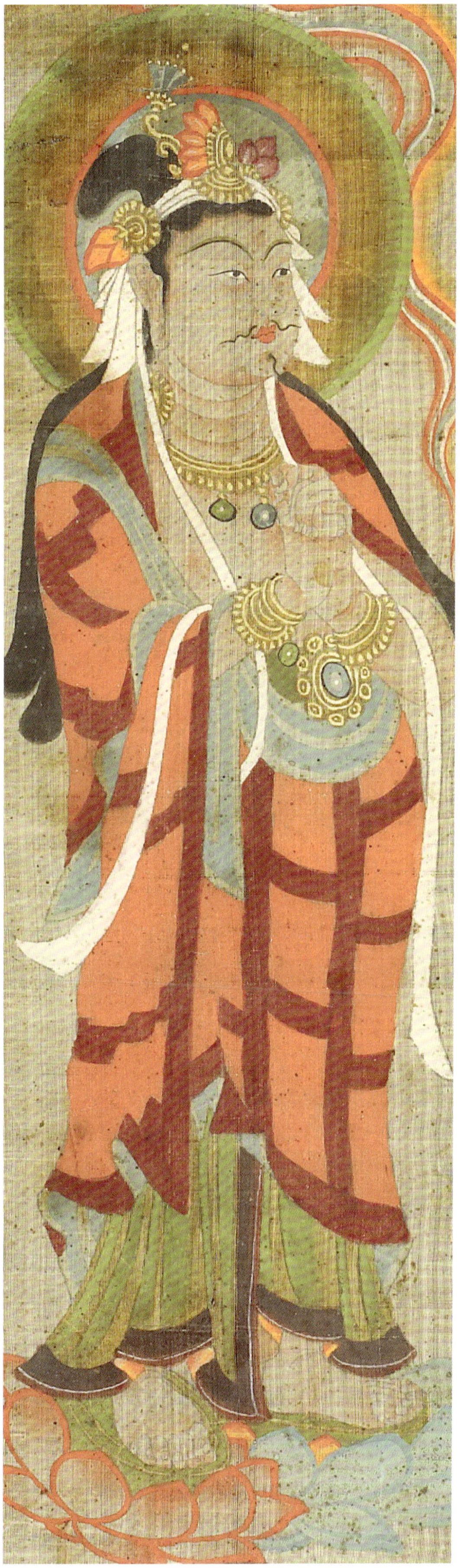

(detail)

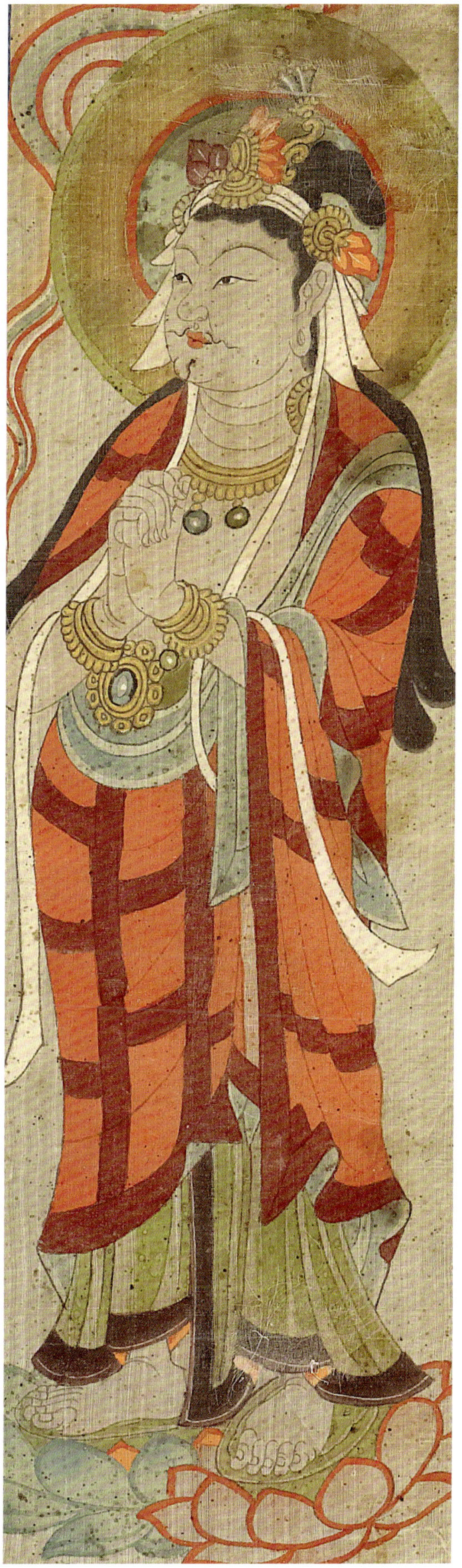

(reverse)

7

UNIDENTIFIED ARTIST

## Bodhisattva Presenting a Cup of Flowers

唐 佚名 手托花盤供養菩薩立像

8th–9th century, banner fragment, ink and colour on silk, 80 × 28 cm
Musée Guimet, Paris (Pelliot Collection, MG 17650)

REFERENCE LITERATURE

*Paintings of the Musée national des arts asiatiques-Guimet*, Paris 1968, p. 170, pl. 90; Vandier-Nicolas 1974–6, vol. XIV, p. 301, pl. 145; Giès 1996, vol. 2, p. 287, pl. 14; Paris 1995–6, no. 13

The princely figure shown here is a bodhisattva, who stands in three-quarter profile on the pericarp of a lotus. With his right hand he makes the gesture of argument, *vitarka* mudra, and with his left, offers flowers in a stem-cup. As the cartouches are blank, however, a precise identification is difficult.

The bodhisattva's hair is arranged in a chignon, with long tresses trailing down on either side, and he wears a red dhoti and scarves (one green with blue lining, the other white and tied around his waist), necklaces with cabochons and pendants, and a wrought-gold diadem with lotus flowers and white ribbons, one of which hangs in a long loop at the front. This style of dress, although depicted in a conventional, even stereotypical way, places this banner among a group representing unidentified bodhisattvas who are nonetheless clearly differentiated by their position, expression or attributes, from a pink lotus flower to a jade ring, censer or glass bowl. However, the scarf with S motifs on the torso also links him to another banner (Musée Guimet, EO 1399), which itself has a double that is identical in design (MG 17651), so that it seems certain that these figures were produced using a pattern.

The face in three-quarter profile with thin moustache and 'mouche' beard, in the tradition of the faces of bodhisattvas at various sites in Central Asia (and notably the remains of carved or painted bodhisattvas at Kizil, Kucha, Kumtura, Dandan Uiliq, Ming-Oi and Shorchuk), appears on another set of banners (Musée Guimet, EO 1399; MG 17769; TA 159; and EO 1414). These depict figures that seem slightly schematic or simplified (dressed less richly in plain cloth, with ruffles on their feet), for which patterns were undoubtedly also used.

While it remains impossible to establish a precise chronology for this type of production, which has been variously dated, sometimes to the ninth century and sometimes in connection with bodhisattvas depicted at Dunhuang at the height of the Tang period (618–907) (Caves 199, 217, 328 and 194), this figure represents an archetype that existed from the eighth century, and which persisted at least during the Tibetan occupation in the ninth (Dunhuang Cave 112; Stein painting 3) and even later (Stein painting 5). It also illustrates the existence of serial production, made using either variations on a particular model or patterns (the use of which has been demonstrated elsewhere for the mural paintings in Dunhuang). It was designed to be mounted as a banner, and was probably hung from a pole for use in ceremonies. VZ

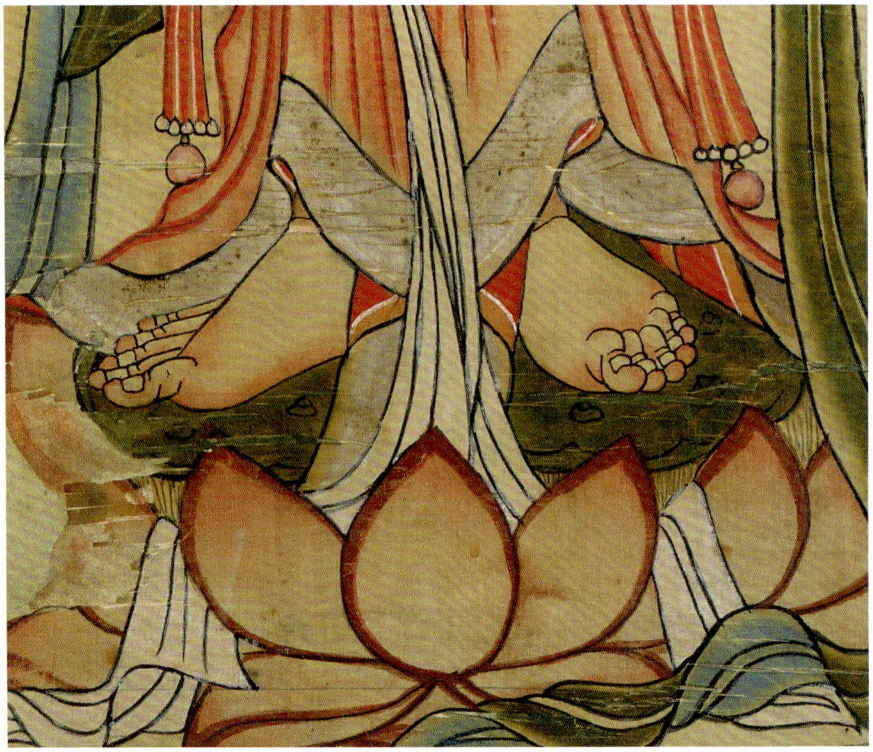

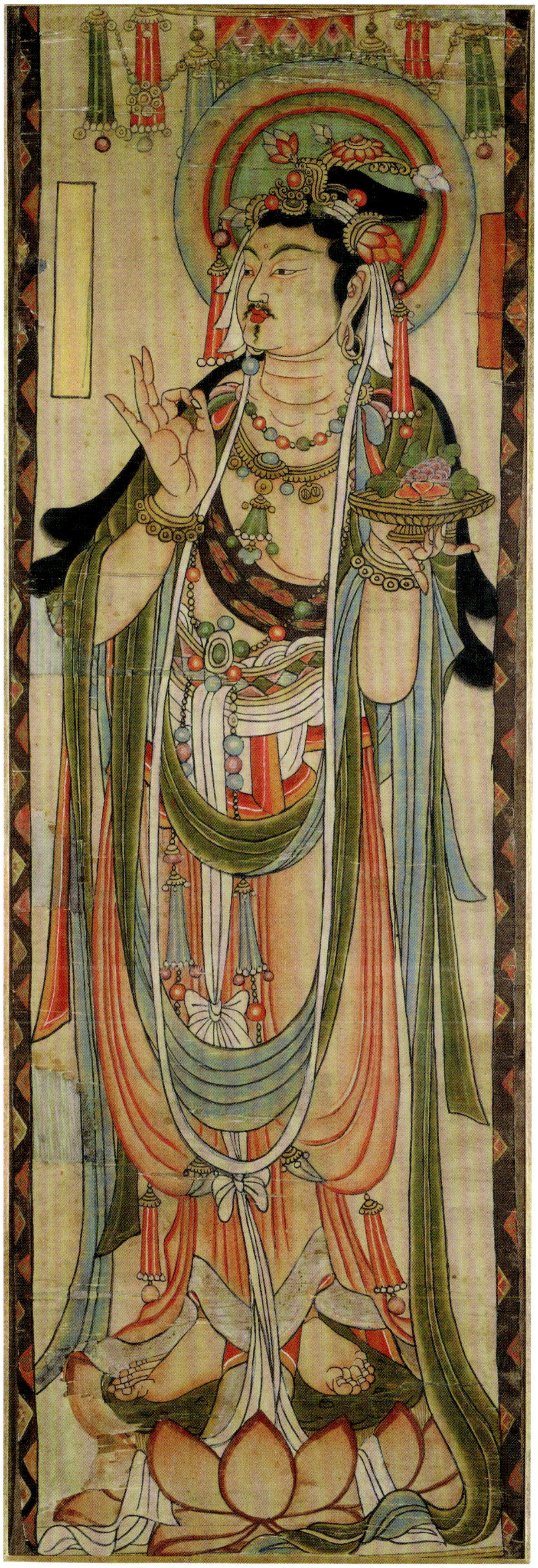

8

UNIDENTIFIED ARTIST

## Itinerant Monk Accompanied by a Tiger

唐 佚名 寶勝如來像

9th century, banner mounted as a panel, ink and colour on silk, 80 × 54 cm
Musée Guimet, Paris (Pelliot Collection, EO 1141)

REFERENCE LITERATURE

Akiyama 1965, pp. 163–76; *Paintings of the Musée national des arts asiatiques-Guimet, Paris* 1968, p. 171, pl. 95; Vandier-Nicolas 1974–6, vol. XIV, pp. 397–8, pl. 207; Lyons and Paris 1991, p. 1, pl. 3; Giès 1996, vol. 2, p. 317, no. 88; Hong Kong 1997, p. 107, no. 201, Thote 1997, pp. 43–4, fig. 4; Nara 1999, no. 201; Paris 2002, p. 161, no. 122

This votive painting showing an itinerant monk has long been a source of fascination – as well as puzzles. The monk carries a basket from which a cloud-like swirl ascends, no doubt emanating from the sacred Buddhist texts within (part of the Buddhist canon, as indicated by the inscription). Other known depictions of such monk-pilgrims include two painted on silk, some 10 ink drawings on paper and a few on the walls of the caves at Dunhuang (Caves 306, 308 and 363) and Yulin (Cave 2), but few have been precisely identified.

These monks, who are usually preceded by a Buddha meditating on a cloud (Ch. Baosheng; S. Ratnasambhava), are sometimes thought to be Dharmatrātā (as in Dunhuang Caves 306 and 308) – one of the 18 arhats or Buddhist saints, who is always accompanied by the tiger he subdued – and sometimes the Buddha of Meditation himself, Baosheng or Ratnasambhava, as the truncated dedication here indicates. However, particularly in the Japanese tradition, these images are also thought to commemorate the famous Chinese pilgrim Xuanzang (629–45), under Ratnasambhava's protection.

The shaven-headed figure shown here wears a monk's robe, or *kasāya*; in his hands are a fan and a dragon-headed stick, and he carries scissors, phials and a sutra table. Hatless, he looks more Chinese than 'barbarian'. As such, the depiction seems to fit well with the latter hypothesis, if we accept that the painters of the western regions did not portray the figure of Xuanzang with an Indian or Serindian appearance until later on.

The halo, a mark of his deification corroborated by the addition to his legend of supernormal feats and other signs of predestination, would thus seem to establish him as one of the protectors of the Buddha's teachings, in accordance with his status as a collector of sacred writings. The presence of the tiger would stem from the fact that, as the instigator of the worship of the Buddhist saints in China by virtue of having translated a text on the Sixteen Arhats, Xuanzang had been absorbed into their pantheon, eventually to become the eighteenth among them.

Whatever its interpretation, this painting is undoubtedly symbolic of the role of itinerant monks as propagators of the Buddhist doctrine. By the fifth century at the latest, these collectors and translators had begun to seek out the sources of Buddhist texts, travelling across Chinese Central Asia all the way to India via the inland branches of the Silk Road. VZ

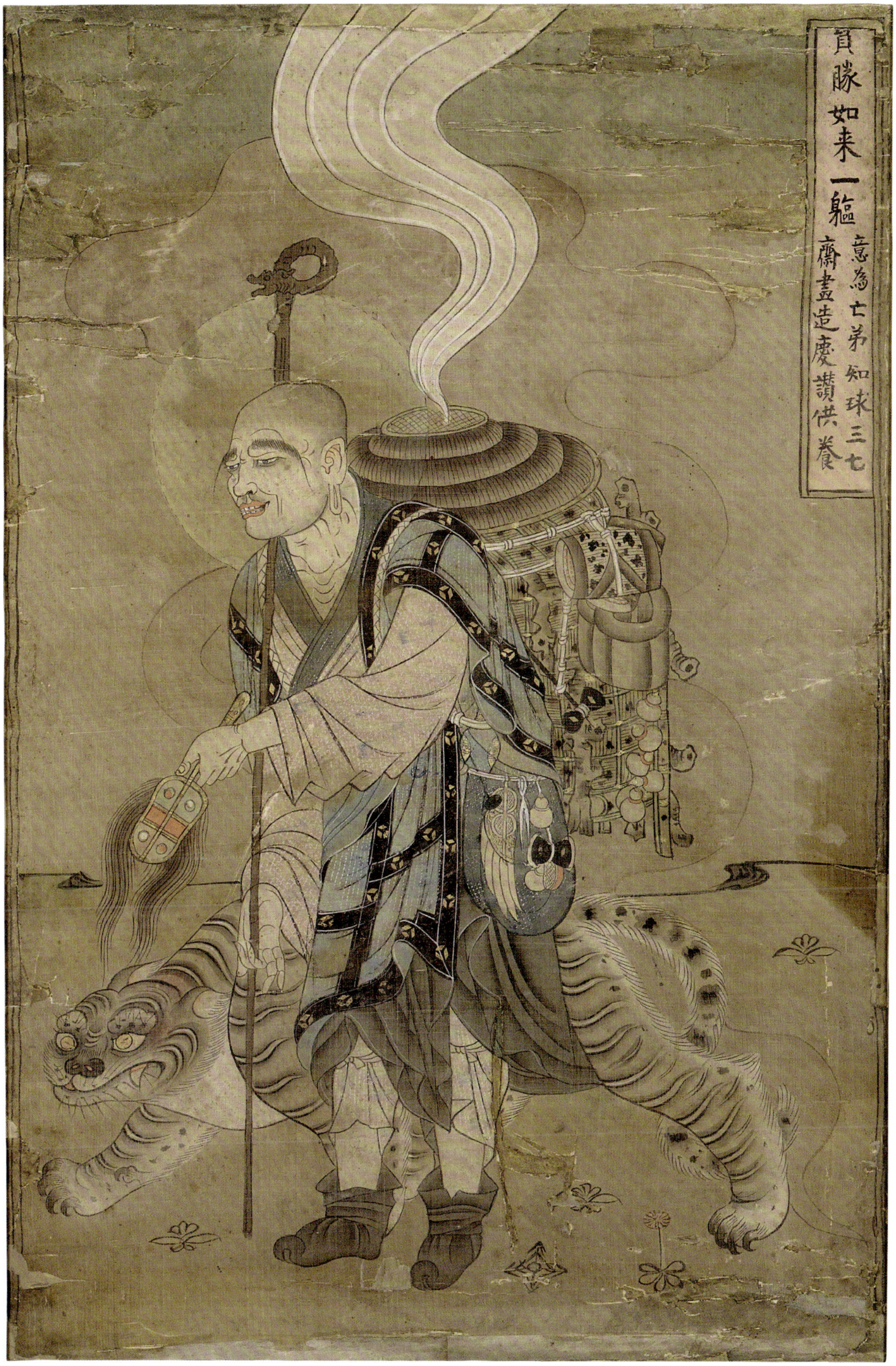
寶勝如来一軀
意為亡弟知球三七
齋畫造慶讃供養

9

UNIDENTIFIED ARTIST

## Bodhisattva as Guide of Souls

唐 佚名 引路菩薩

2nd half 9th century banner mounted as a hanging scroll, ink and colour on silk, 80.5 × 53.8 cm
The British Museum, London (Stein Collection, 1919,0101,0.47)

This painting characterizes the format known in Chinese as *fan* and in English as 'banner'. Above all, the term is often applied to the kind of banner carried by the large bodhisattva in this painting, consisting of a triangular headpiece, square panels making up the main part, and side and tail streamers. There is at least one mention, in an Esoteric Buddhist sutra translated in 709, of *zhufopusa fan* ('Buddhas and bodhisattvas banners'), *jin'gang zhi fan* ('diamond banners', probably representing *lishi* or 'guardians'), *tianwang fan* ('heavenly kings banners') and *zhushen fan* ('many deities banners'), with instructions to hang them in pairs, on either side of doorways, as *zhuangyan*, appropriate ornament in worship.[1]

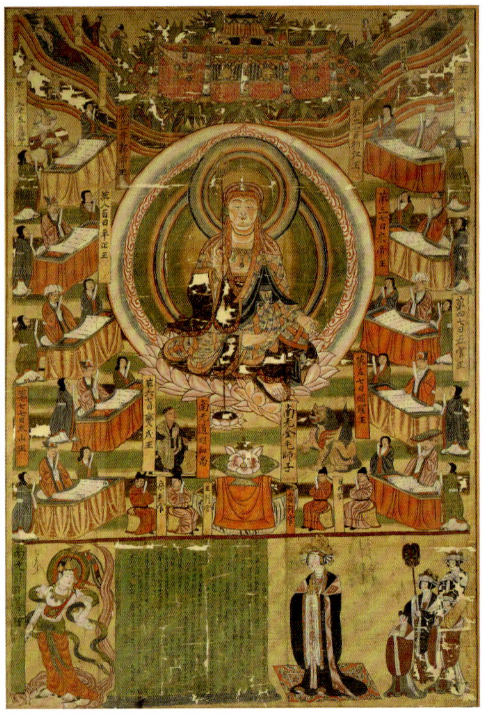

FIG. 58 *Bodhisattva Kṣitigarbha and the Ten Kings* banner, 983. Ink and colour on silk. Musée Guimet, Paris (Pelliot Collection, MG 17762)

Banners showing a single bodhisattva standing alone, most often in *anjali* mudra, with the palms pressed together in a gesture of worship, are extremely frequent among the paintings on silk and hemp cloth from Dunhuang. They are different from those that, like this one, show a cloud-borne heavenly bodhisattva leading a smaller lay person towards a palatial building in the sky above. Three characters in the cartouche read *yinlu pu[sa]* ('bodhisattva who leads the way', or 'bodhisattva as guide of souls'). Wang Huimin of the Dunhuang Academy has pointed out 11 examples in all, including just two examples as wall paintings in Cave 176, dating from the Song dynasty (960–1279).[2] Two of those in the Pelliot collection bear votive inscriptions, in which reference is made to a *yinlu pusa*. Although this term does not occur in the sutras, there is therefore no doubt that this is the correct designation.

This subject originates in Pure Land belief, signifying the devotee's wish to be reborn in the Pure Land – *jingtu*, or paradise – of a Buddha, most commonly Amitābha, whose Pure Land is in the west. Such paintings were often commissioned and offered (*gongyang*) on behalf of a deceased parent; both the donor and his or her deceased relative would earn merit as a result. In this example, the deceased person is an upper-class lady clad in the fashion of the late Tang dynasty (618–907), fuller of figure than the kneeling devotee (who probably also represents a deceased parent) in *Buddha Preaching the Law* (cat. no. 1). Although her demeanour is suitably reverential, she is wearing expensive ornaments such as a golden comb and hairpins, so there is no doubt about her status.

A painting dated 983 in the Pelliot collection (fig. 58), which must have been sealed away barely 20 years after it was created and so is in very good condition, shows the bodhisattva leading the way as part of a much larger composition. The chief figure here is Kṣitigarbha, whose function is to rescue souls who have already fallen into hell. Here he is flanked by the Ten Kings, each depicted as a judge sitting at a tribunal assisted by two officials, before whom the deceased's soul should appear (at 7-day intervals until the 49th day, thereafter at the 100th day, and the 1st and 3rd anniversaries after death) to determine in which of the 'Six Ways' he or she should be reborn. The soul in this instance is shown at the bottom on the right, standing on a richly decorated carpet wearing her full bridal regalia, and holding a golden vase; behind her are female members of her household.

The bodhisattva who leads the way, standing on a purple cloud, and identified as such in a separate cartouche at the left, turns towards her and makes a gesture of blessing with his free hand (in his right hand, he holds the staff from which a banner hangs in the wind). The descendants who dedicated this fine painting on behalf of the lady were seeking a double reassurance for her future rebirth by invoking Kṣitigarbha (who is very often paired with Avalokiteśvara) as well as the bodhisattva who leads the way. The bodhisattva's appearance is generally similar to that of Avalokiteśvara, the bodhisattva of compassion, though without the distinctive seated Buddha in his headdress. A correspondence between the bodhisattva who leads the way and Avalokiteśvara is, however, suggested by two more paintings from the Pelliot collection (MG 22795, 22796),[3] each with a bodhisattva (with seated Buddha in the headdress) carrying a banner suspended from a staff, while male and female devotees are depicted underneath, on a very small scale. Yet another banner from the Pelliot collection (MG 17657) invokes the bodhisattva who leads the way in the dedicatory inscription, written by a woman, surnamed Kang, on behalf of her deceased husband. These banners all testify to the same belief in a salvationist being who will guide the deceased to rebirth in a Buddhist paradise. RW

1 One-word Buddhoṣnīṣa-Wheel-turning King sutra (T 951.19.0249a20–4)
2 Wang 2010a
3 Giès et al. 1994, vol. 2, pls 70–1

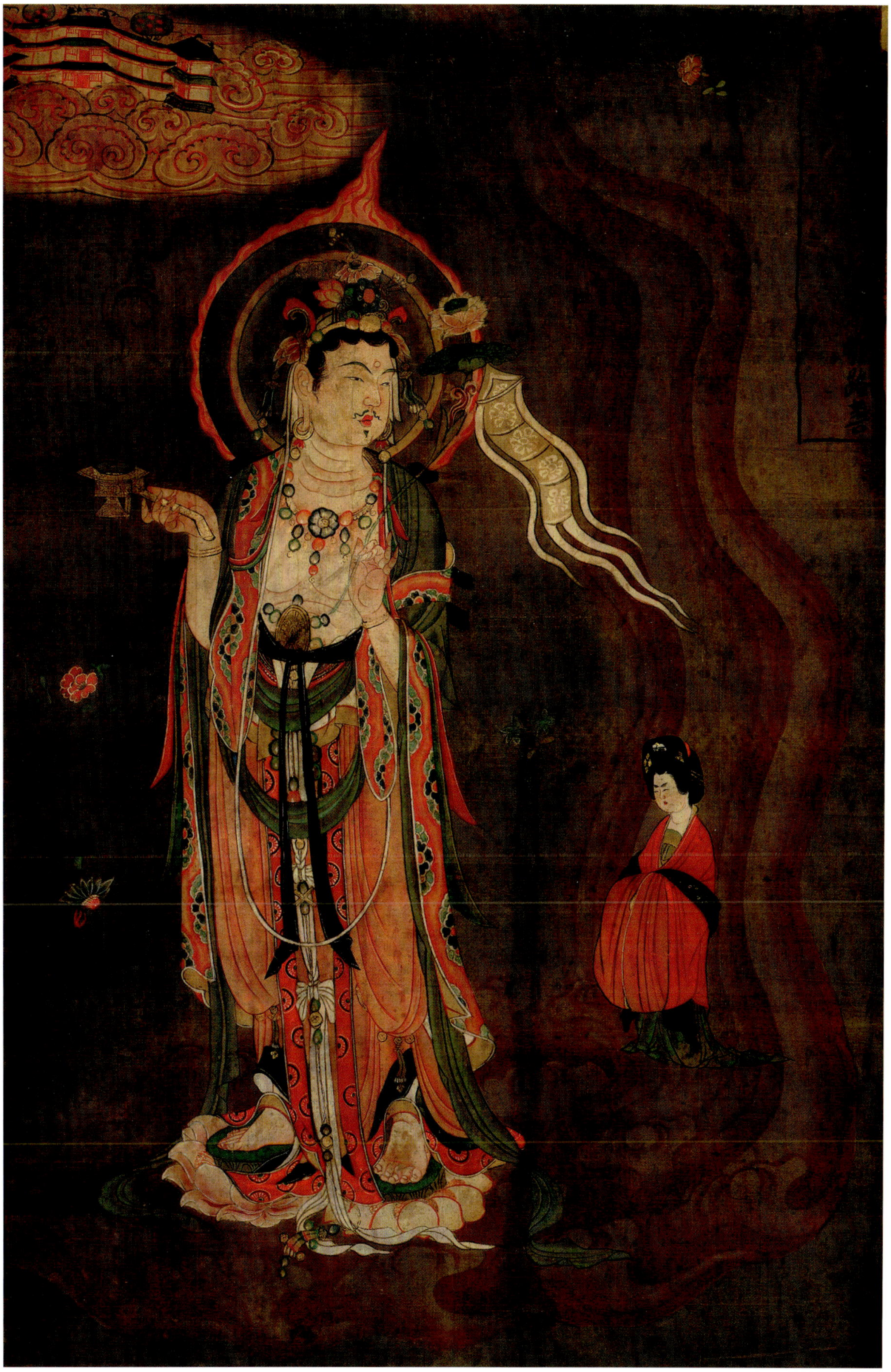

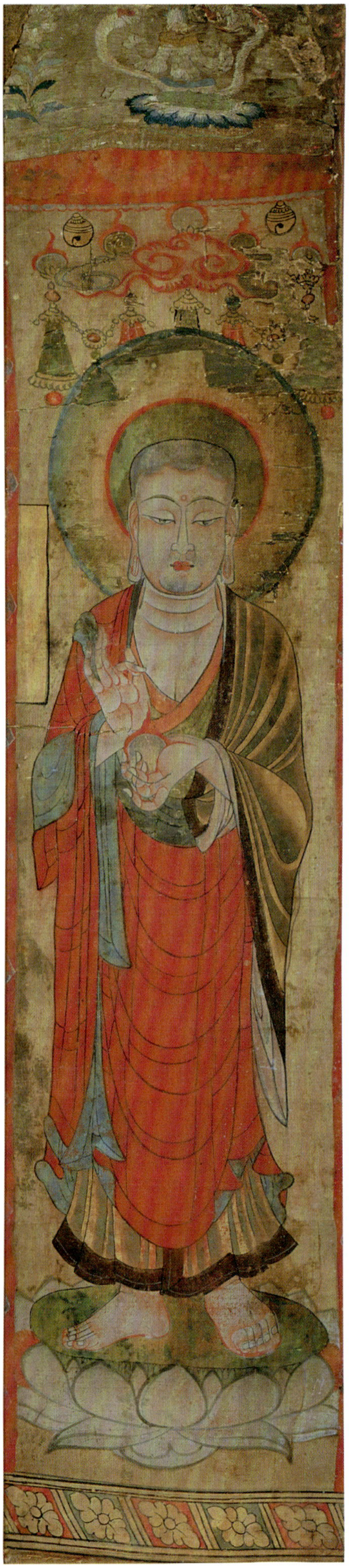

10

UNIDENTIFIED ARTIST

## The Bodhisattva Dizang (Kṣitigarbha)

唐 佚名 地藏菩薩立像

780–840, banner fragment, ink and colour on silk and embroidery, 73 × 16.5 cm
Musée Guimet, Paris (Pelliot Collection, MG 17768)

REFERENCE LITERATURE

Paris 1947, p. 28, no. 107; Vandier-Nicolas 1974–6, vol. XIV, p. 229, pl. 108; Giès 1996, vol. 2, p. 298, pl. 52; Paris 1995–6, no. 150; Tokyo 1996b, no. 120

The being venerated here is shown with a halo beneath a canopy-like cloud hung with bells and pendant jewels wreathed in cloud, but is depicted standing and has the vermillion *kasāya* or robe and shaven head of a monk. Although there is no inscription, among all the bodhisattvas and devotional figures in the Buddhist pantheon this would seem to be a depiction of Dizang (S. Kṣitigarbha), who is described and represented as a monk, standing and occasionally walking.

With his right hand he makes the gesture of argument (S. *vitarka* mudra), his left hand holding the wish-fulfilling flaming jewel (S. *cintāmaṇī*) that is said to 'illuminate the paths of illusion' and the dark paths of hell. As in other ninth-century banners he does not hold the monk's sistrum (S. *khakkhara*), which became usual in images from the tenth century on, where Kṣitigarbha appears as Master of the 'Six Paths' of rebirth, seated among the Ten Kings of Hell and wearing a shawl. However, unlike similar ninth-century depictions, which he otherwise greatly resembles, he has no jewellery and his forehead is marked with the *ūrṇā* (a tuft of hair between the eyebrows, one of the marks of an enlightened being). Also, like another bodhisattva of uncertain identity (cat. no. 6), rather than a canopy he has a cloud above him, studded with flaming jewels and pendants, which may evoke the Six Paths of rebirth but which could also be seen as an intermediate stage between the representation of a canopy and a cloud, or the beginnings of the replacement of the canopy with a cloud.

Devotion to Kṣitigarbha and belief in his powers of intercession are thought to have developed in Central Asia or in China, when he was associated with the salvation of the dead in apocryphal texts whose seventh-century Chinese translations established his popularity in the ninth and more particularly the tenth centuries. The *Mahāvaipulya Daśacakra Sūtra* (Ten Wheels sutra, translated by Xuanzang in 651) is thought to be one of the earliest describing Kṣitigarbha as a *śramaṇa* or monk.[1]

In addition to its format and painted red borders with grey-blue diamonds, the fragment sewn at the top, and the remains of a triangular headpiece embroidered with a blue lotus and other flowers, indicate that the painting was (originally or intended to be) hung as a banner. It would have accompanied a larger image used in worship such as an illustration of a Pure Land (or paradise) of a Buddha, though the empty cartouche indicates that it was not yet dedicated. VZ

1 The Sutra of Bodhisattva Kṣitigarbha's Fundamental Vows (T 412) is thought to have been based on the Ten Wheels sutra (T 410 and T 411).

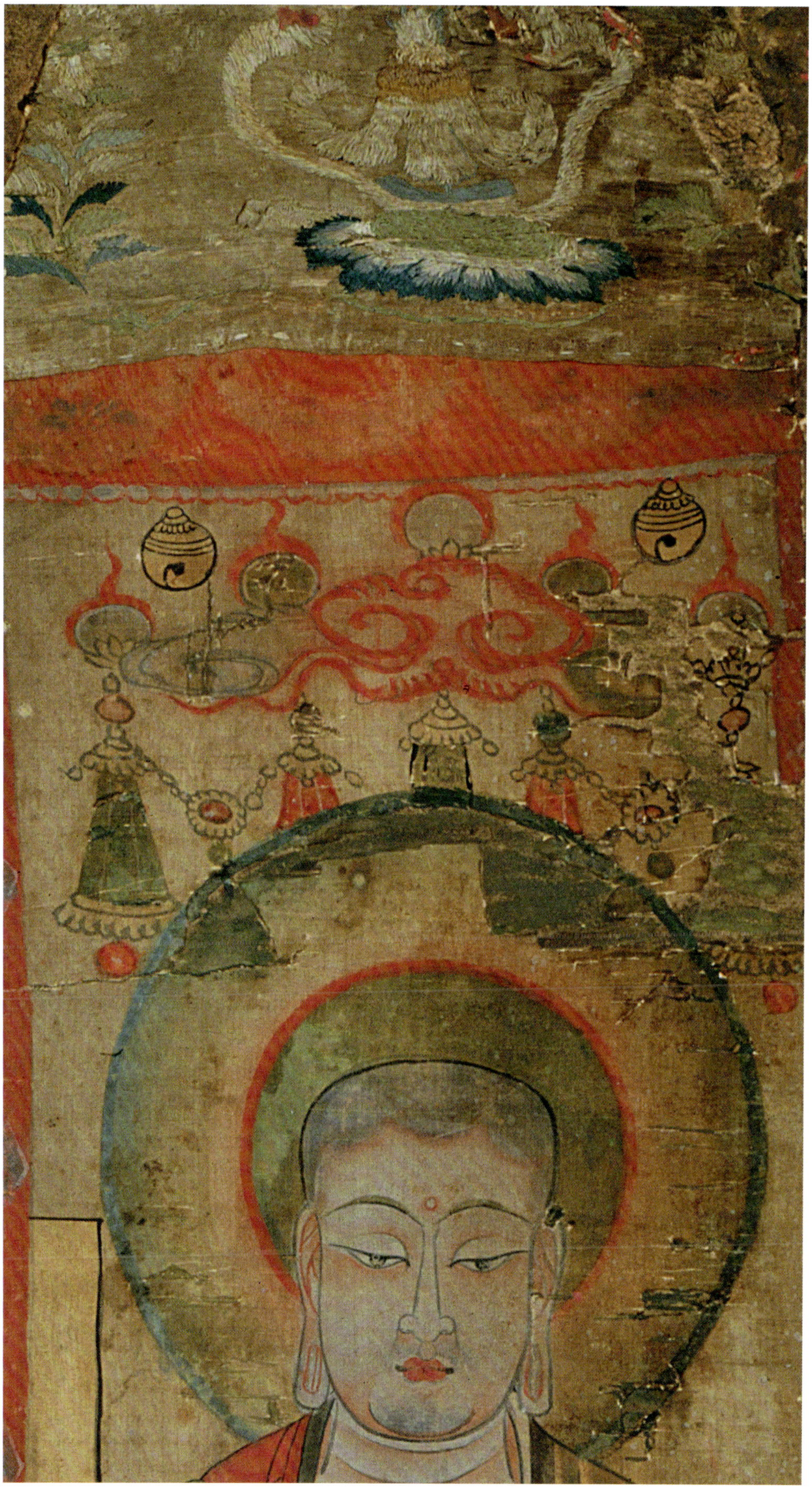

11

UNIDENTIFIED ARTIST

## The Bodhisattva Guanyin Carrying a Banner

五代 佚名 觀音菩薩持幡立像

907–60, banner, ink and colour on hemp, 161 × 53 cm
Musée Guimet, Paris (Pelliot Collection, MG 22796)

REFERENCE LITERATURE

Los Angeles 1957, p. 34, no. 12; Riboud 1970, p. 353, pl. 81; Vandier-Nicolas 1974–6, pp. 283–4, pl. 135; Paris 1995–6, no. 241; Giès 1996, vol. 2, p. 309, pl. 71; Tokyo 1996b, no. 194

This banner, identifiable as such by its format and loops, shows an apparently conventional depiction of the bodhisattva Guanyin, seen in three-quarter profile standing on two lotus flowers. He is depicted with a halo and a manifestation of the Buddha Amitābha in his diadem, which ornaments long hair styled in a chignon and complements his other jewellery and princely attire (red scarf and *paridhāna* [undergarment], overlaid with a green, flounced dhoti). He also has a thin moustache and a 'mouche' beard, and makes the gesture of argument (S. *vitarka* mudra) with his left hand. The lower register, which forms a predella, shows three women with pins in their hair, and three men in the winged headdresses of civil servants and accompanied by a child, kneeling and presenting offerings on either side of cartouches that remain uninscribed.

The bodhisattva featured here is unusual in holding a standard in his right hand, as does another bodhisattva depicted on a very similar banner, but facing the other way and holding a censer as well (Pelliot Collection, MG 22795). These two paintings may possibly have formed a pair, being of the same size, painted in a similar style and colours, and mirror images. They are thought to have been placed on either side of a central image, where they would have illustrated two manifestations of Guanyin or the 'Great Compassionate One' or two specifically Chinese manifestations of the bodhisattva Yinlu, 'who leads the way', here identified by his standard, which is found in association with a censer in other images of Yinlu that can be identified by their dedications.

However, whether this is the specific bodhisattva Yinlu or a particular aspect of Guanyin 'who shows the way', the fact that this bodhisattva might then, unusually, have been a secondary figure and the absence of any dedication in the cartouches counter the likelihood of these being two complementary banners. Rather, it suggests that they may simply have been works in a series, in which the figures were shown in different positions, with different attributes or small variations in their clothing, as in many banners painted on silk (see cat. no. 7).

This banner has no mount, and was apparently intended to be hung directly. It is among the few found in the 'library cave' at Dunhuang that – starting in the second half of the tenth century, to judge from dated examples – no longer followed the traditional design with its triangular headpiece, which was still present, however summarily, on earlier hemp banners. VZ

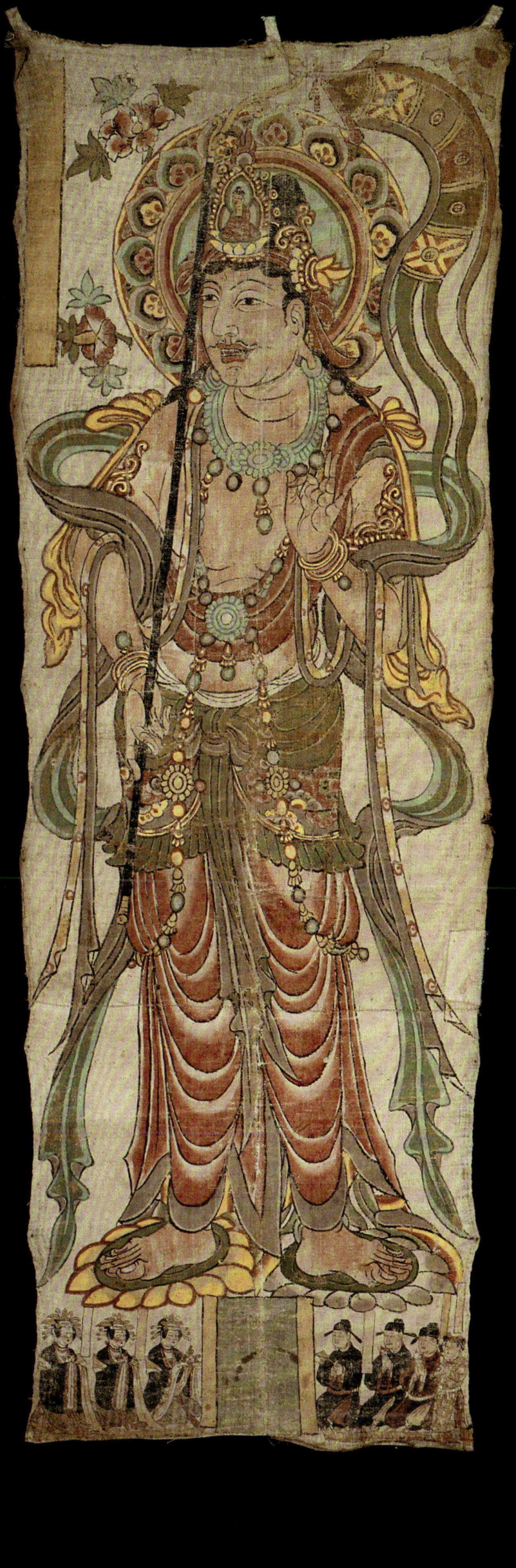

12

UNIDENTIFIED ARTIST

## Guanyin of the Thousand Hands and Thousand Eyes

五代 佚名 千手千眼觀音經變

943, banner mounted as a panel, ink and colour on silk, 123.5 × 84.3 cm
Musée Guimet, Paris (Pelliot Collection, MG 17775)

REFERENCE LITERATURE

Vandier-Nicolas 1974–6, pp. 198–203, pls IX and 101; Yü 1994, p. 155, fig. 49; Giès 1996, pp. 359–61, no. 96, fig. 39; Tokyo 1996b, no. 218; Paris 2004, p. 149; Paris 1995–6, pp. 372–4, no. 268

This votive painting depicting two manifestations of the bodhisattva Guanyin (S. Avalokiteśvara) reflects the popularity in Dunhuang of two forms of this enlightened being that were often linked and almost certainly embraced starting from the Tang period (618–907), one Chinese in origin and the other deriving from tantric Buddhism, or *vajrāyana*.

The central image represents the principal form of Guanyin of the Thousand Hands and Thousand Eyes (Ch. Qianshou Qianyan Guanyin; S. Sahasrabhuja-sahasranetrāvalo-kiteśvara), whose worship is attested in China from the first half of the seventh century.[1] Surrounded by his attendants and spotlighted by a canopy with pendants, he is seated in *vajrāsana* on a lotus throne and wears a diadem featuring a manifestation of the Buddha Amitābha. The bodhisattva is encircled by a moon disc, the space within filled by his many hands, their open palms each marked with an eye, signifying his infinite compassion and the light of his wisdom protecting beings everywhere.

Of the 42 hands shown in the foreground in accordance with the texts, eight principal hands either hold the stem of a lotus – symbol of the bodhisattva in his aspect as Padmapāṇi – or make esoteric mudras. The others also hold attributes, some with tantric associations.

The central Guanyin is attended by 14 divinities, identified by inscriptions in cartouches. Some of these are reversed, including those near the canopy identifying the *lokapāla* or guardians of the south and west, Virūḍhaka and Virūpākṣa (the latter is also shown with the diadem more usually worn by Vaiśravaṇa, the guardian of the north), while others include errors, such as those of the two *nāga* kings in the pool, Nanda and Upananda (Ch. Nantuo and Banantuo), who support the bodhisattva's moon disc and are here named 'Great Deva Vajra' and 'Secret Traces Vajra'.

On either side of the aureole are the divinities from the substratum of Brahman usually associated with this form of Guanyin. Sarasvatī (Ch. Dabiancai tian nü), goddess of eloquence, here offering the *cintāmaṇi* (wish-fulfilling gem), is opposite the ascetic Vasu (Ch. Posou xian). Below are two fierce, six-armed esoteric divinities, 'Blue Poison Vajra', a form of blue-throated Vajrapāṇi who 'keeps poisons away' (an echo of Śiva Nīlakaṇtha?), and 'Fire-Head Vajra', a form of Ucchuṣma as protector of the dharma, thwarting two *vināyaka* (at once demons and obstacles), one with the head of a boar, the other with the head of an elephant.

In the foreground two praying divinities, identified by their inscriptions as the two bodhisattvas 'Sun Receptacle' (Ch. Rizang pusa) and 'Moon Receptacle' (Ch. Yuezang pusa), personify the sun and moon in place of the usual Sūrya and Candra and reinforce the symbolism of light initially conveyed by the Buddha, but which also became characteristic of this type of manifestation of the bodhisattva.

As noted in the large cartouche in the centre of the lower register predella, dated the eighth year of the Tianfu reign (943), the painting was consecrated during the rite of intercession for the dead and had been commissioned for that occasion by one Ma Qianjin for his late mother, a faithful devotee.

This dedication is flanked by the portrait of the rite's beneficiary accompanied by a servant and an image particular to Chinese Buddhism of the bodhisattva Shuiyue Guanyin, 'Water-Moon Avalokiteśvara' or 'Reflection of the Moon in Water'. Shuiyue Guanyin appeared in the eighth century and also occurs at Dunhuang (notably in Cave 2, where his image is associated with that of the pilgrim Xuanzang, see cat. no. 8). He is seated here on an allegorical mountain and holds a flask and the willow branch of an 'easer of pain'. He is also characterized by the moon disc surrounding him and by the presence of bamboo and the sea, their exoticism reflecting the legendary Mount Potalaka in the seas south of India, where he is said to dwell. The image of the reflection, perhaps evoking the empty, illusory nature of phenomena according to the doctrine of the Mādhyamika school of Buddhism, is thought to refer to the bodhisattva's capacity to bring illumination. VZ

1 The translations of most of the sutras mentioning this manifestation of the bodhisattva date from the Tang period (618–907), notably Paramit's version of the *Śūrangama Sūtra* ('of the heroic march'; T 945) and those of the *Mahā Karuna Dhāranī Sūtra* (Dhāranī sutra of great compassion) by Zhitong (T 1057), Bhagavat-dharma (T 1060), Bodhiruci (T 1058) and Amoghavajra (Ch. Bukong) (T 1113b).

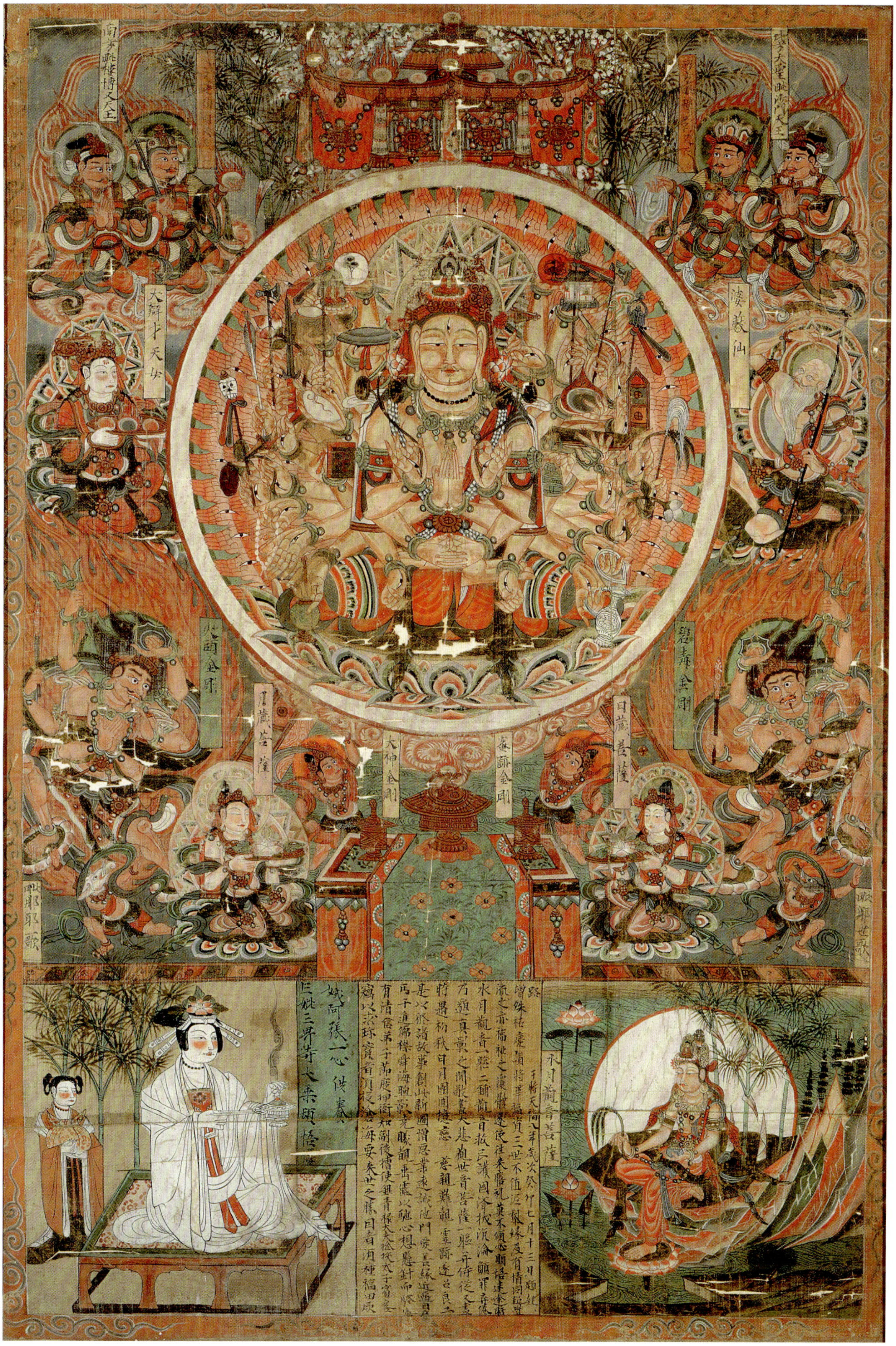

13

UNIDENTIFIED ARTIST; traditionally attributed to ZHANG SENGYOU (act. 490–540)

## The Five Planets and Twenty-eight Constellations

唐／宋 傳張僧繇 五星二十八宿神形圖 卷

960–1127, or earlier, handscroll, ink and colour on silk, 27.5 × 489.7 cm
Osaka City Museum of Fine Arts (42,1-121)

REFERENCE LITERATURE

Harada 1939; Yashiro 1944; Osaka and Shanghai 1994; Meng 2000; Yumino in Shanghai 2010; Tsukamoto 2011a

The Five Planets (Ch. Wuxing) are part of a universal order expressed in the principle of yin and yang and the five elements (or phases). Included in the group are Jupiter (Ch. Suixing), corresponding to the element wood; Mars (Ch. Yinghuoxing), to fire; Saturn (Ch. Zhenxing), earth; Venus (Ch. Taibaixing), metal; and Mercury (Ch. Chenxing), to water. The Twenty-eight Constellations stay fixed as the sun, moon and Five Planets orbit the sky. It was believed that the position of the constellations and planets foretold a person's destiny and could divine lucky and unlucky omens. In the scroll, they are depicted in anthropomorphic form. Images of all five of the planets are extant, as are 12 of the constellations: Horn, Neck, Root, Chamber, Heart, Tail, Winnowing-basket, Dipper, Ox, Woman, Emptiness and Rooftop.

The image of Mars, for example, shows a deity with the head of a horse, sitting cross-legged on a horse's back, and with six arms, each of which holds a weapon. All the paintings are consistent in style, the figures outlined in fine, wire-like brushstrokes and embellished with colours that are clear and brilliant, even today. Each illustration is preceded by a passage written in seal script relating the attributes of the stellar deity portrayed. At the end of the scroll are three seals, indicating that the work was once part of the Song (960–1279) emperor Huizong's (r. 1101–25) collection.

There are various theories about the identity of the artist. A work with the title *The Five Planets and Twenty-eight Constellations* and attributed to Zhang Shenyou appears in the inventory of Huizong's collection, the *Xuanhe Painting Catalogue*. The theme itself is an ancient one, however, and the entry may not refer to the painting under discussion. The presence of Emperor Huizong's imperial seals on the painting probably contributed to its identification on the label slip attached to the scroll as '*The Five Planets and Twenty-eight Constellations*, a true painting from the brush of Monk Zhang of the Southern Liang dynasty'. In the Tang period (618–907) compilation *Record of Famous Painters of Successive Dynasties*, the author Zhang Yanyuan (815–76) describes Zhang's style, which matches well the strength of the brushed line seen in the scroll.

A second theory gives the creation of the painting to Liang Lingzan (d. 720s?) of the Tang dynasty, according to an inscription in clerical script at the beginning of the scroll, which can be read as follows: 'Submitted by Court Gentleman Consultant, Administrative Aide of Longzhou, Expectant Official of the Academy of Scholarly Worthies and also Grand Astrologer Liang Lingzan'. There is also a Yuan dynasty text, *The Precious Mirror of Painting* (preface dated 1365) by Xia Wenyan (c.1312–c.1357) that mentions a scroll with the same title. The oldest secure documentation of the present handscroll is in *The Great Vista of Artworks* (preface dated 1712), which gives credence to this attribution. Also significant is a colophon of the scroll written by An Qi (1683–1742) of the Qing (1644–1911), which makes it clear that he regards the scroll as a work by Liang Lingzan.

At the end of the scroll is another colophon dated 1636 by Dong Qichang (1555–1636) of the Ming dynasty (1368–1644), however, attributing the work to Wu Daozi (c.685–758). The entry on Wu Daoxuan (Wu Daozi) in the *Xuanhe Painting Catalogue* mentions an 'image of the Five Planets', a 'Five Planets painting' and an 'image of the Twenty-eight Constellations'. The *Great Vista of Artworks* also mentions Wu Daozi in conjunction with a handscroll of this title.

Yet another painter, the Tang dynasty artist Yan Liben (d.673), is credited in a colophon by Chen Jiru (1558–1639). That Yan was also associated with the subject can be seen in the entry on that artist in the *Xuanhe Painting Catalogue*, where 'image of the Five Planets' appears. A painting of the Twenty-eight Constellations by Yan Liben is further recorded in such works as *Colophons on Painting* (c.1125) by Dong You (c.1079–c.1140).

There is no way to know definitively who produced the scroll, and the various theories dating it to the Tang period or earlier based on its archaic style are somewhat confused. Certain aspects, such as the disorder in the layout planning and execution of seal-script characters, moreover, point to its being a version of a later date. Most recently, Meng Sihui fruitfully investigated the iconographical sources of the extant 12 constellations, such as the Buddhist astrological work *Xiu and Planet Sūtra* translated by Bukong (S. Amoghavajra) in 759, and proposed that the images date to the mid-eighth century, hence potentially supporting the attribution to Liang Lingzan. Nevertheless, it is extremely valuable as one of the few examples of early images of popular gods. YT

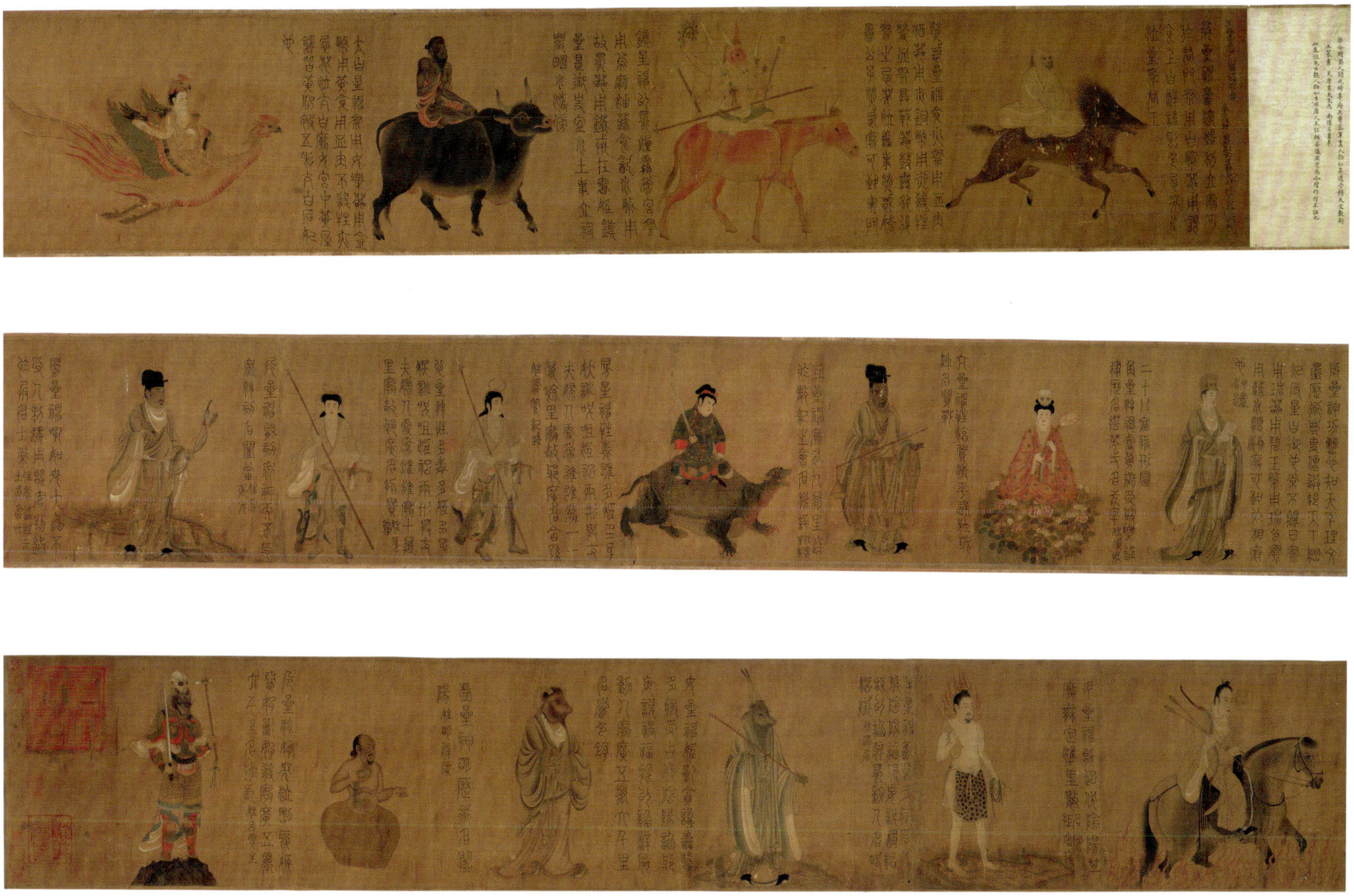

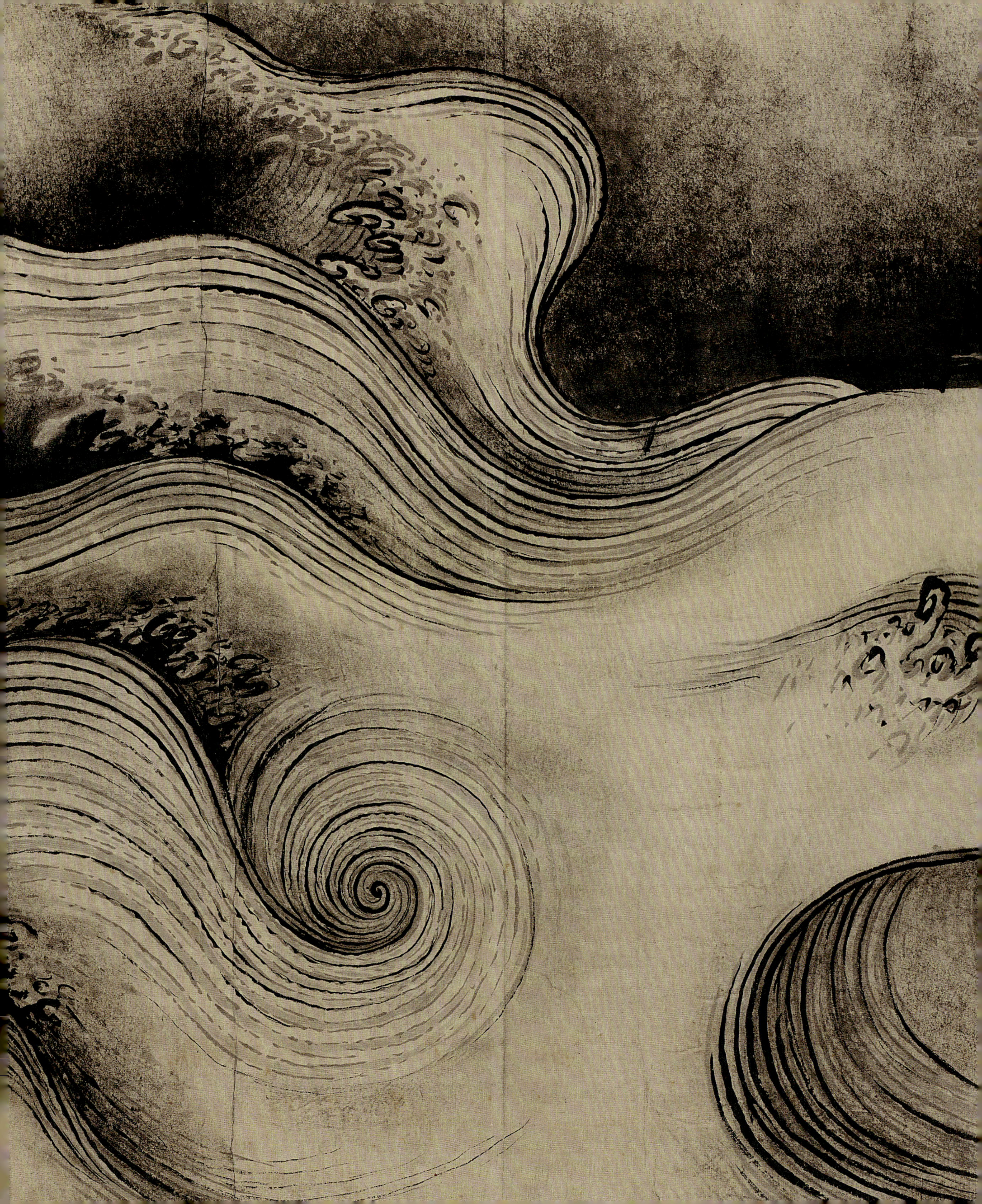

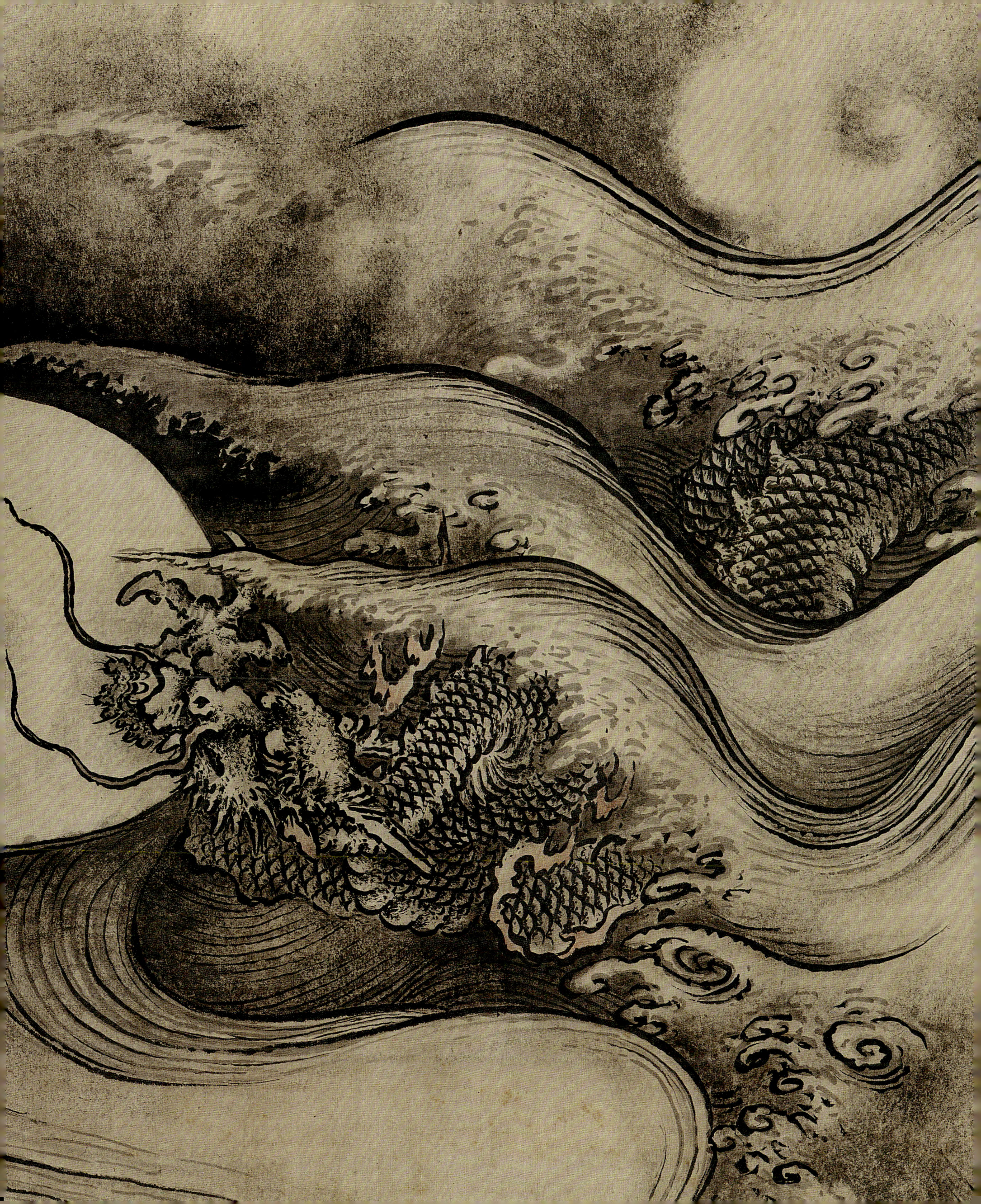

# Paintings 950–1250

With the fall of the Tang dynasty (618–907), China was split up into a succession of smaller courts, in the period known as the Five Dynasties (907–60). However, painting continued to flourish in the individual courts, and from this period onwards, landscape appears as a subject in its own right: in *A Note on the Use of the Brush* by Jing Hao (c.870–c.930), an old hermit advises a young painter to make sketches from nature.[1] The great masterpieces of this period and of the Northern Song (960–1127) are the fruit of such close observation of the natural world. Rocks and mountains embody the yang or male principle, complemented by water, in the form of lakes, rivers and waterfalls, or simply as mist and clouds, as the yin or female principle. Guo Xi (c.1000–c.1090), highly favoured by Emperor Shenzong (r. 1068–85), wrote about the changing appearance of landscape elements, especially trees and plants, throughout the four seasons. A sense of how contemporary Chinese appreciated landscape can be seen in the handscroll by Qiao Zhongchang (act. late 11th–early 12th century) *Illustration to the Second Prose Poem on the Red Cliff* (cat. no. 19), where the painter provides a narrative illustration of a famous poem, written in 1082 by Su Shi (1037–1101). Following an alfresco meal in the company of friends, the protagonist eventually senses the other-worldly nature of the mountains when he reaches a place where eagles nest and cranes fly, evoking the sensation that he is intruding into a Daoist realm, so that he hastily retreats.

The figures in *Illustration to the Second Prose Poem on the Red Cliff* are commensurate with the size of the landscape features, but more often, in comparison with the colossal scale of the mountains and forests, human figures are tiny and it often takes a close inspection of the work to reveal them all, as in the handscroll *Landscape with Pavilions* by Yan Wengui (967–1030) (cat. no. 15), which portrays both ordinary fishing villages and lofty temples, alike dwarfed by the scale of the mountains and valleys around them. As Richard Barnhart has observed, this work shows that the techniques of creating the illusion of space and distance had already been highly developed well before 1000.[2] The timeless, indeed cosmic nature of such themes, seen in Li Gongnian's (act. early 12th century) *Winter Evening Landscape* (cat. no. 21), a work in the mode of Li Cheng (919–67) and Guo Xi, has ensured their survival in greater numbers than those showing urban surroundings, such as Zhang Zeduan's (act. early 12th century) *Along the River during the Qingming Festival* (fig. 46): nevertheless, the latter displays the same attention to verisimilitude in the depiction of figures from all walks of life, boats and carts, and the accurate representation of architectural features, as seen in paintings of landscape proper.[3] Painters of this period paid close, almost scientific, attention not merely to the physical appearance of their chosen subjects, but also to details of animal behaviour, as with Cui Bai's (act. 2nd half 11th century) *Magpies and Hare* (fig. 20), where the artist has captured a moment on a windy winter's day; yet, far from being frozen in time, the scolding magpies appear to be in the very act of arriving in the greatest of haste, while the hare leisurely turns its head through 180 degrees for a moment before lolloping off to resume its browsing.

In the case of handscroll paintings, their great length means that the viewer experiences them over a certain time, a characteristic that offers the artist a chance to depict, not only distance and height, but the changing time of day as well. This sense of the passing of time alerts us to the fact that for both handscrolls and hanging scrolls, the viewer is not intended to grasp the whole scene at once, but to explore it at their own pace. According to Guo Xi, 'there are those [landscapes] through which you may travel, those in which you may sightsee, those through which you may wander, and those in which you may live. Any paintings attaining these effects are to be considered excellent, but those for traveling and sightseeing are not as successful in achievement as those suitable for wandering and living'.[4] More often than not, one discovers hitherto unsuspected details every time one revisits such paintings.

At the very end of the Northern Song, during the reign of Emperor Huizong (r. 1101–25), the Emperor himself prescribed the subjects to be painted, and the artists of the imperial academy vied with each other in the pursuit of perfection. Huizong's large album leaf (now mounted as a handscroll) *Auspicious Cranes* (cat. no. 17), complemented by an inscription in his distinctive 'slender gold' calligraphy, is a model of the effect that was sought by them. The paintings in the imperial collection were classified by subject matter, implying that individual painters specialized in particular subjects; as a result, the paintings of the Song dynasty (960–1279) set standards for the depiction of those subjects that were seldom exceeded thereafter.

The tradition of a painting academy was continued under the Southern Song (1127–1279), after the Northern Song capital was routed by the Jin (1115–1234), with whom Huizong had unwisely formed an alliance against the Liao (907–1125). The court took refuge in Lin'an (present-day Hangzhou) in the south. The hardships of the journey and a memory of the rugged northern landscape they had left behind, with precipitous tracks and mountain inns (and sometimes a watermill as well), are perhaps evoked in paintings such as *Bullock Carts Travelling over Rivers and Mountains*, attributed to Zhu Rui (act. 1st half 12th century) or a follower (cat. no. 22). Hangzhou in the thirteenth century, on the other hand, was the epitome of cultivated and educated living. Its West Lake, with the palace and the city on one bank and Buddhist monasteries on the other, inspired poets and painters alike. Compared to the north, the great difference in climate and scenery was soon reflected in paintings of a more intimate and lyrical nature, such as those by or attributed to Ma Yuan (act. late 12th–early 13th century) and his contemporaries. Many were originally painted to ornament fans, made of silk stretched over a slender bamboo frame, with a painting on the front complemented by calligraphy on the back. Ma Yuan's *Bare Willows and Distant Mountains* (cat. no. 27) depicts a scene not unlike one that we can discover near the beginning of Yan Wengui's *Landscape with Pavilions*, but in a gentler manner and employing Ma Yuan's characteristic 'one-corner' composition, with the smooth outlines of the distant mountains echoing the graceful branches of the foreground willows. Ma Yuan's elegant compositions are complemented by the more watery or rainswept scenes depicted by his contemporary Xia Gui (act. 1180–1230) (cat. nos 29, 30), while at the same time Chen Rong's (act. 1st half 13th century) *Nine Dragons* handscroll (cat. no. 38) exploits all the possibilities of ink, from ink washes of every tone to the driest of brush-strokes, to portray the elemental forces of nature, perhaps inspired by storms raging above the hills on the far shore of the West Lake.

A separate development under the Southern Song was a flourishing school of professional painters based in the port city of Ningbo and specializing in religious paintings, often in large sets, such as depictions of the Ten Kings of Hell sitting in judgement on the souls of the deceased. Such paintings, including those of an even larger set of 100 each showing 500 *luohans* ('arhats': awakened disciples of the Buddha charged with protecting the Buddha's teachings) (cat. nos 23, 24),[5] have survived in considerable numbers, having been acquired by Japanese monks embarking at Ningbo after studying Buddhism in China, and ever since kept safely in the treasuries of their home monasteries. The figures in such paintings exhibit considerable realism in the portrayal of race and character and in the vivid description of the landscape settings: they also allow us to imagine the colourful style of mural painting once found in countless contemporary Chinese monasteries.

1 Munakata 1974
2 Barnhart 2012, p. 123
3 For the latest, and brilliant analysis of this now world-famous painting, see Chen 2013.
4 Bush and Shih 1985, p. 151
5 Nara 2009



cat. no. 19 (detail)

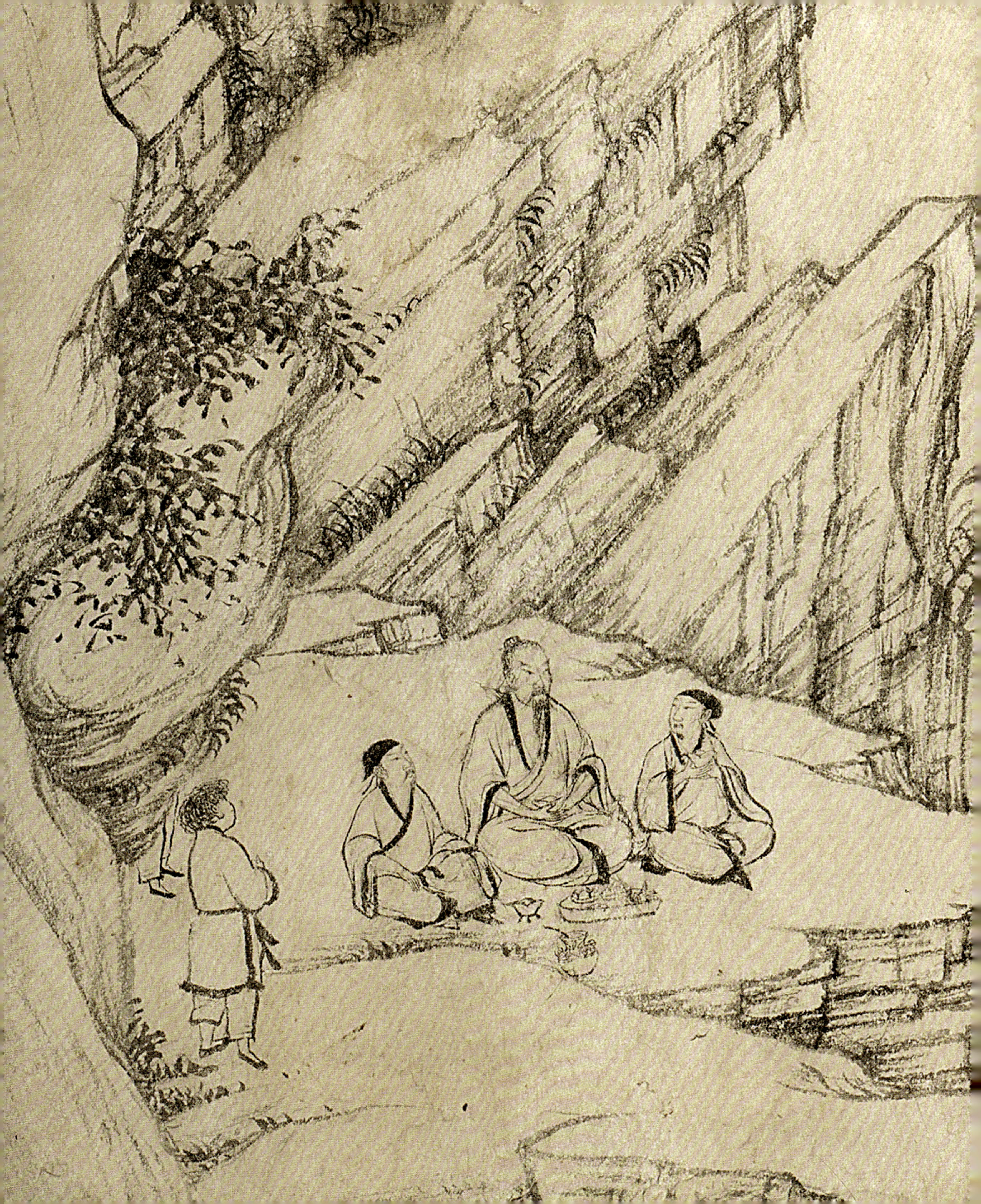

14

UNIDENTIFIED ARTIST; traditionally attributed to LI CHENG (919–67) and WANG XIAO (act. 1st half 10th century)

## Reading the Memorial Stele

宋 傳李成 王曉 讀碑窠石圖 軸

14th century or earlier, hanging scroll, ink and light colour on silk, 126.3 × 104.9 cm
Osaka City Museum of Fine Arts (42,1-12)

REFERENCE LITERATURE

Ise 1930; Suzuki 1981; Osaka and Shanghai 1994; Sturman 1995; Nara 2008; Yuimino in Shanghai 2010

The subject of the painting is regarded generally to be based on a historical event concerning the warlord Cao Cao (155–220) (posthumously titled Emperor Wu of the Wei dynasty, 220–80) and his attendant Yang Xiu (175–219).[1] Two figures have stopped at the base of a stele dedicated to Cao E, a famous filial daughter of the Eastern Han dynasty (25–220). On the back of the tablet is written 'huangjuan youfu, waisun jijiu'. Yang Xiu understood the meaning of the inscription at once. 'Huangjuan' ('yellow silk') denotes coloured thread ('sesi'; 色絲), which combines as the single character 'jue' (絕), meaning 'utterly'; 'youfu' is 'young woman', so putting together the character for 'little' or 'few' (少) [years] and that for 'girl' (女) creates the character 'miao' (妙), meaning 'lovely'; 'waisun' is 'maternal grandson', or 'the son of a daughter' (女)(子), and so becomes 'hao' (好), or 'wonderful'; 'jijiu' is to taste something sharp or spicy, so becomes the character 'ci' (辭), meaning 'speech or words'. Thus, the original phrase on the stele is transformed into 'juemiao haoci', or 'utterly lovely, wonderful speech', a line praising the majesty of the epigraphs compiled by Handan Chun (act. *c.*220). It took Cao Cao longer to fathom the meaning than Yang Xiu, but after travelling on for 30 leagues, Cao finally understood. The story appears in a number of sources, including *New Tales of the World* by Liu Yiqing (403–44).

In the centre of the painting, on one side of the stele, is an inscription reading 'figures [by] Wang Xiao; trees and rocks [by] Li Cheng'. Little is known about Wang Xiao, other than that he was a contemporary of Li Cheng who came from Sishui in present-day Shandong Province. He was said to be excellent at painting birds and animals, and shrubs, among other subjects, and also skilful at figures, evoking the flavour of the ancients.

Li Cheng was originally from Chang'an (present Xi'an in Shaanxi Province). The Li family was part of the Tang (618–907) imperial clan, and boasted generations of Confucian scholars. With the fall of the Tang dynasty, they were forced to flee the capital, and the artist's father and grandfather settled in Yingqiu (present Shangdong Province). Li Cheng himself was blessed with tremendous talent, and excelled especially at composition. He was open-hearted and had high aspirations, but ended his life without high rank or fortune, having spent his energies in poetry, drinking and painting.

*Reading the Memorial Stele* utilizes the perspective known as level distance, in which the viewer looks out across a landscape where space does not extend indefinitely, but where, in the Chinese phrase, 'a thousand miles is expressed in a square foot of space' (*chichi qianli*). The ink dabs used to depict the sharply pointed leaves are called *zanzhen*. On the left side of the composition are placed a hillock and wintry trees; in the centre are the stele and the figures gazing up at it; and on the right stretches an expanse of sky and a view over the flat land. Especially prominent are the branches, which resemble crab claws. The painting is a very important one for conveying Li Cheng's style, but glimpses here and there of mannered curlicue strokes indicate that it may in fact be a later work in his style. From this and the treatment of the hillock and trees, the work is thought probably to date from as late as the fourteenth century in the Yuan period (1271–1368).

Li Cheng was described as unmatched as a landscape painter, but secure works by him are extremely rare. Even his near contemporary, the Northern Song (960–1127) painter Mi Fu (1051–1107), said that after a thorough search, he could find only two genuine scrolls, leading him to propose that there were no true paintings by Li Cheng at all. YT

1 For an alternative interpretation, see Sturman 1995, pp. 85–8.

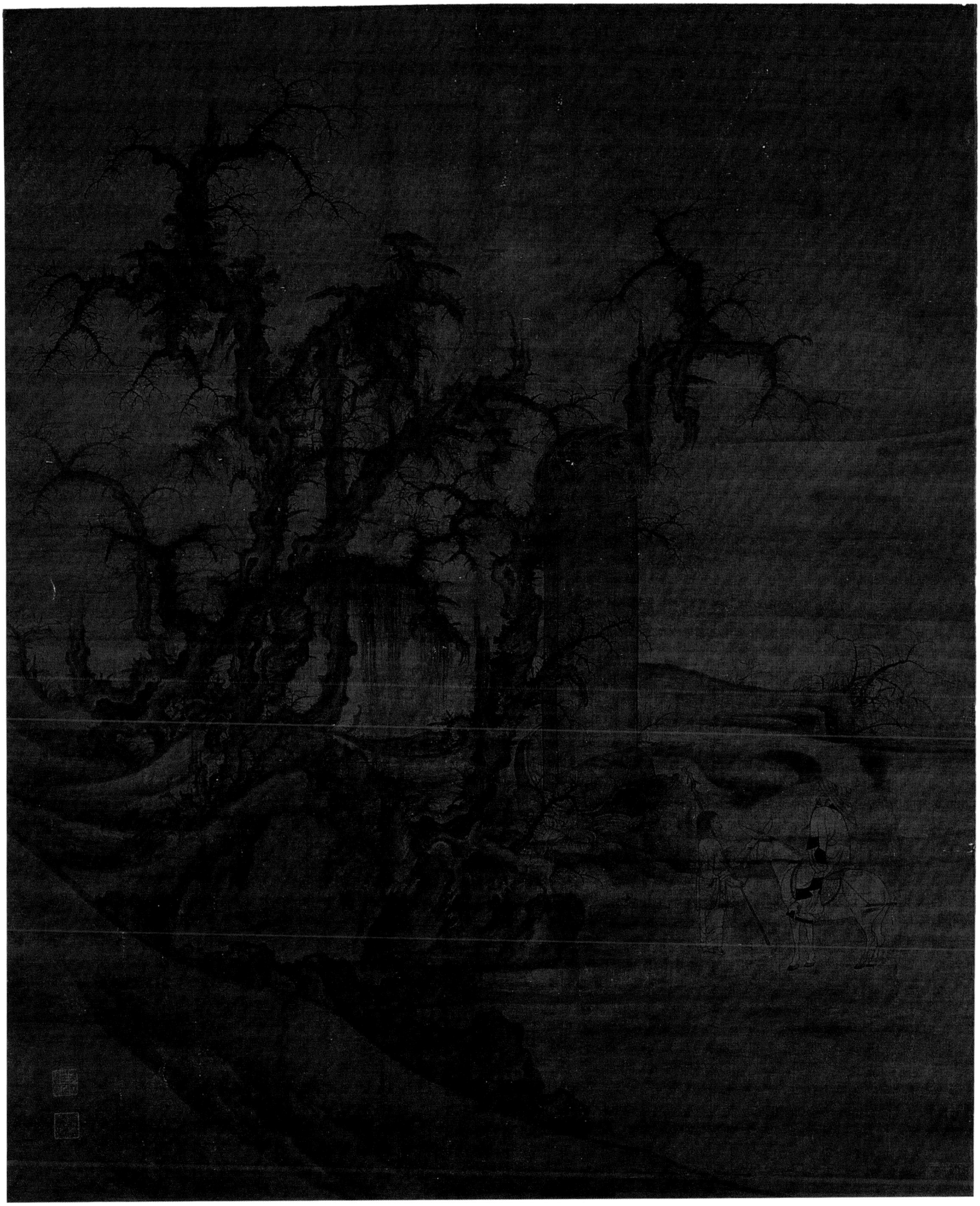

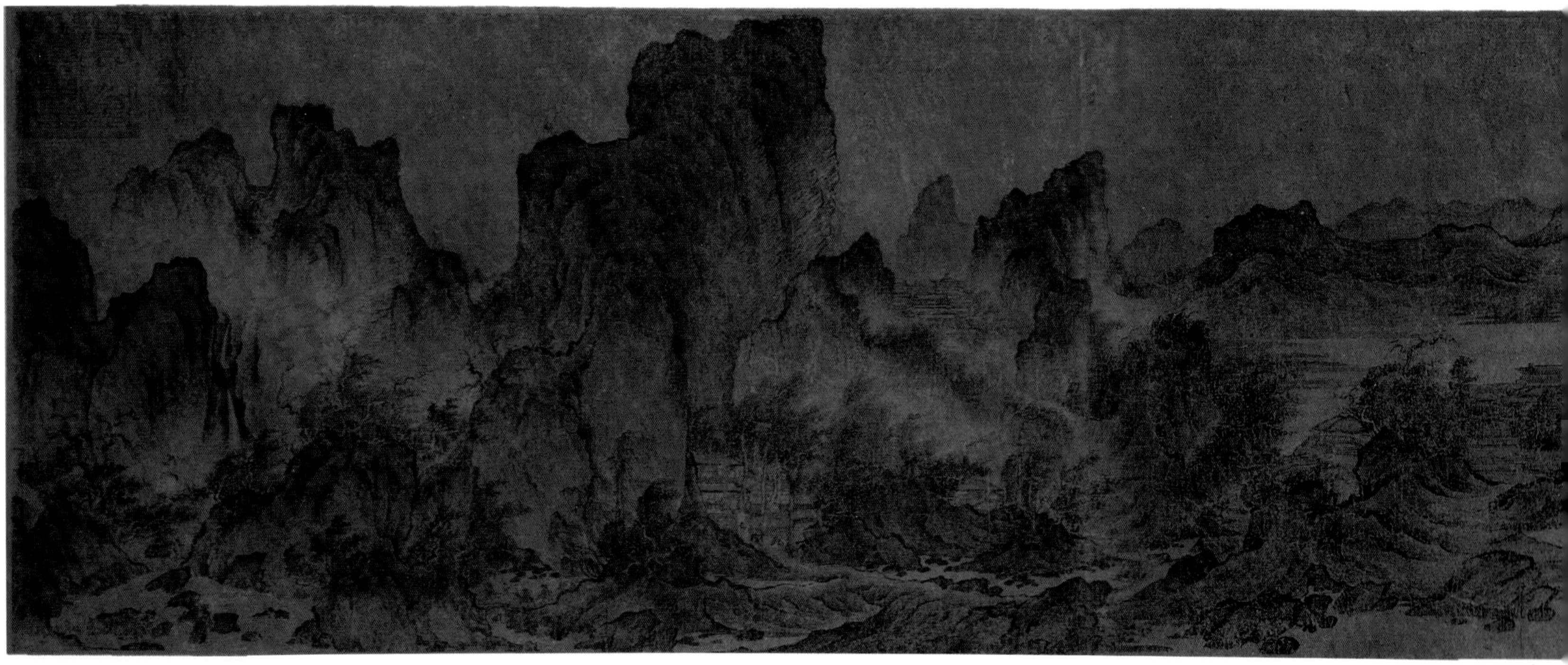

15

Possibly YAN WENGUI (967–1030)

## Landscape with Pavilions

宋 燕文貴 江山樓觀圖 卷

early 11th century, handscroll, ink and light colour on paper, 32 × 161 cm
Osaka City Museum of Fine Arts

REFERENCE LITERATURE

Ise 1930; Toda 1967; Tsuruta 1971; Suzuki 1978, vol. 2; Shimada 1976; Sofukawa 1977; Suzuki 1981; She 1988; Fujita 1989; Ogawa 1990; Osaka and Shanghai 1994; Takenami 1998; Nara 2008; Yumino in Shanghai 2010

In this scroll a vast landscape unfolds, beginning with a river stretching far into the distance and ending with a view over towering mountains. The sky is dark and leaden; clouds and mist hang over the valley. As one moves towards the last section, the mountains become increasingly steep and rugged; a swiftly moving stream appears, and bent trees tell of the power of the wind and rain.

The work is signed 'Secretary of [...] Prefecture [and] Treasurer of [...] County, Yan Wengui'. Although one might doubt the authenticity of the signature, the painting is generally believed to date from the period. In this context, attention should be paid to the two seals that appear at the end of the scroll: a large square seal pressed at the top of the paper and a rectangular seal at the edge. These read *Xiuzhou guan guancha shi yin* ('Surveillance Commissioner of Xiuzhou') and *Chonglan Guan* ('Chonglan Hall'), respectively, and belonged to Zhao Zizhou (1089–1142), a member of the Song dynasty (960–1279) imperial family. If these are genuine, it means that the work could have been done no later than the early Southern Song (1127–1279).

A native of Wuxing (present Zhejiang Province), Yan first served as a military official. He studied painting with Hao Hui of Hedong, and became especially skilled at landscapes and figural subjects. When Emperor Taizong (r. 976–97) acceded to the throne, Yan left for the capital at Bianjing (now Kaifeng, in Henan Province), where he made his living selling his

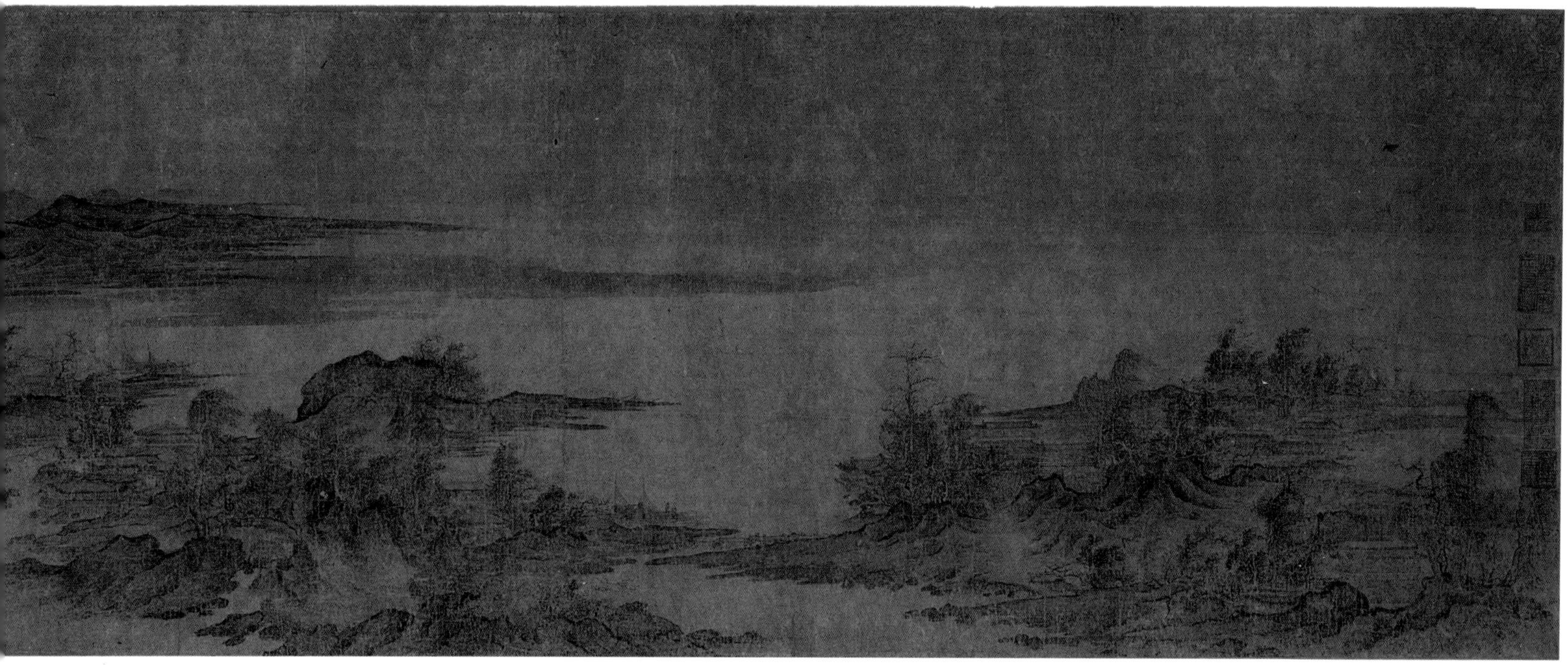

paintings. He was discovered by Gao Yi (act. late 10th century), a court painter holding the rank of *daizhao* (first secretary in waiting), and was invited to participate in the painting of murals at Xiangguo Temple. Afterwards, Yan served in the imperial painting academy. Judging from the use of the title *daizhao* in his signature, Yan also rose to that rank.

In both the *Evaluations of Song Dynasty Painters of Renown* (1086–94) and *Experiences in Painting* (1070s), Yan was said to have opened up new expression in landscape painting. It was also pointed out that Yan combined the northern style of such artists as Li Cheng (919–67) and Fan Kuan (act. c.990–1030) with the southern style of Dong Yuan (act. 930s–60s) and others. Certainly, the massive central mountain composed of richly layered peaks recalls Fan Kuan's *Travellers amid Streams and Mountains* (National Palace Museum, Taipei), while the composition, with its movement from foreground to far distance through a series of overlapping forms, is reminiscent of *Wintry Groves and Layered Banks* (Kurokawa Institute) attributed to Dong Yuan.

The painter's distinctive scenes were termed 'Yan-style views', and they initiated a new trend in academic painting from the mid-Northern Song period (960–1127) on. His finely detailed figures and grand vistas are described in the first scroll of the *Evaluations*: 'in one roll no bigger than a square foot, the ship is like a leaf and the figures are like seeds of millet … A thousand miles in a single foot – such was his subtlety!'

In the centre of the composition is a village beside a bay where, here and there, fishing boats are moored. We see fishermen with their nets, men riding donkeys along a plank road, and other figures carrying umbrellas, hurrying home. YT

1 Translation borrowed from Lachman 1989, p. 53

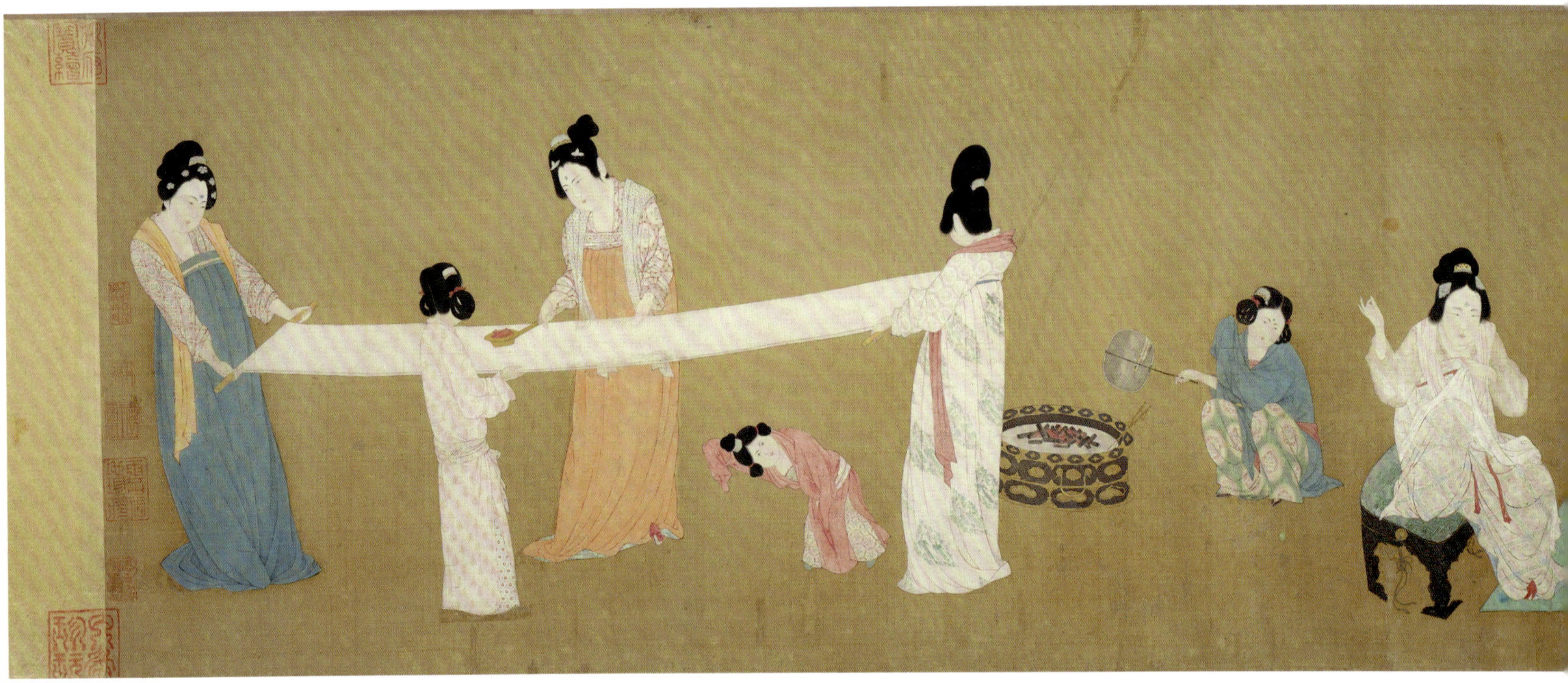

16

Possibly EMPEROR HUIZONG
(1082–1135; r. 1101–25)

## Court Ladies Preparing Newly Woven silk

宋 徽宗 搗練圖 卷

early 12th century, handscroll, ink,
colour and gold on silk, 37.1 × 145 cm
Museum of Fine Arts, Boston
Special Chinese and Japanese Fund, 1912
(12.886)

PROVENANCE

Wanyan Jingxian (1875–1931) in 1912

REFERENCE LITERATURE

Museum of Fine Arts, Boston 1944; Paine 1964; Whitehill 1970; Gomi 1971; Boston 1973; Museum of Fine Arts, Boston 1975; Jin 1982; Museum of Fine Arts, Boston 1982; Hay 1985; Tomita 1990; Museum of Fine Arts, Boston 1991; *New Trends in Art* 1992; Rogers and Wohlauer 1996; Wu 1996a; Yokohama 1996; Barnhart et al. 1997a; Nagoya and Boston 1999; Törmä 2002; Zhou 2003; Sofukawa 2006; Ebrey 2008; New York 2008c; *A Compendium of Song Paintings* 2008; Boston 2010, pp. 254–83

The Song dynasty (960–1279) emperor Huizong was renowned for his devotion to the arts – a major art collector and patron with particular interests in bronzes, paintings and rocks, he was also a calligrapher who finessed his own style of calligraphy (called 'slender gold' and distinguished by delicate lines and resemblance to gold filaments), a painter, poet, musician and garden aficionado. He had a large court atelier with numerous painters, some of whom were engaged in copying masterworks in the imperial collection. Among the books the Emperor commissioned were inventories of two of his collections, the *Xuanhe Painting Catalogue* and the *Xuanhe Bronze Catalogue*. The *Xuanhe Painting Catalogue* records that a painting by the Tang dynasty (618–907) court artist Zhang Xuan (act. 714–42) entitled *The Picture of Pounding* was in Huizong's collection. It is this work that scholars and collectors have suggested was the model for the current painting. There is no artist's inscription, seal or signature on the present work, and while most scholars agree that it dates to the twelfth century, some have suggested that the painting was actually done by one or two copyists in Huizong's court rather than by the Emperor himself.[1]

Huizong's passion for the arts and subsequent neglect of his responsibilities to the country has been blamed for the weakening of his government and the overthrow of northern China by the Jurchen nation from the north. In that conquest of 1127, Huizong and his son, and most of the imperial family, were captured and taken to northern Manchuria. Huizong lived for another eight years, dying in captivity at the age of 53.

The earliest attribution of *Court Ladies Preparing Newly Woven Silk* to Huizong is the inscription by an emperor of the Jurchen Jin dynasty (1115–1234), Zhangzong (r. 1190–1208), himself also a renowned calligrapher and collector, born over three decades after Huizong's death. Zhangzong's inscription reads: 'Tianshui mo Zhang Xuan *Daolian tu*' ('Zhang Xuan's *The Picture of Pounding* copied by Tianshui [Huizong]'). The words articulate that the painting was believed to be a copy of Zhang Xuan's work and that it was executed by Huizong. The name 'Tianshui' was posthumously given to Huizong by the Jurchens in 1141. Moreover, the inscription by Zhangzong suggests that the Jurchen had seized the painting during their conquest of the Northern Song (960–1127), most probably along with many other treasures of the Song imperial collection. Zhangzong would have inherited the collection from his forebears.

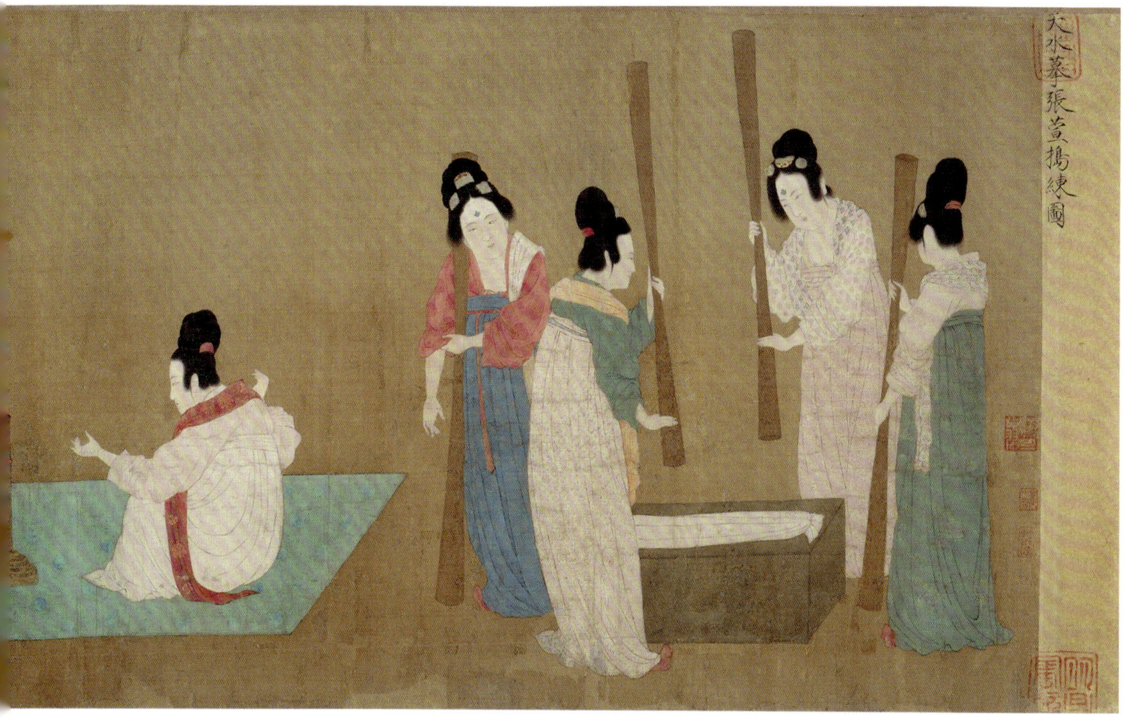


The painting depicts three groups of women (nine court ladies with a child and two girls, most likely servants). Each group is engaged in a distinct task related to silk production and preparation: pounding, sewing and ironing. These are, of course, only some of the many complex processes involved in the manufacture of silk. The exquisite patterned silk textiles worn by the women indicate their status as court ladies. (The English title *Court Ladies Preparing Newly Woven Silk* was first applied to the painting only in 1912 when it was acquired by Okakura Kakuzo for the Museum of Fine Arts. The name *Daolian tu*, given by Zhangzong, endures in Chinese.)

The painting may have been a representation of 'palace sericulture' (*gongcan*), an annual ritual in which the empress and other palace women took part in the many silk-making procedures to ensure a year's plentiful production. The painting could in that manner be compared with a work in the Palace Museum, Beijing depicting the Qing dynasty (1644–1911) emperor Yongzheng's (r. 1723–35) symbolic ploughing of the fields at New Year.

The original painting by Zhang Xuan disappeared long ago, but the question of how close Huizong's work may be to the original has persisted. The luxurious costumes worn by the court women in the painting do not resemble those depicted in Tang tomb murals, and instead probably reflect Song styles. Likewise, the style of the landscape painting on the round fan held by one of the servant girls is decidedly characteristic of the Northern Song, lending further evidence to the probability that the Song work was a modified version of the Tang painting. Some scholars have wondered if Huizong only borrowed part of what was a larger, more thorough, composition.

Going beyond past approaches to this work, recent scholars have proposed new interpretations. Lara C.W. Blanchard, for instance, comparing the painting's imagery with traditional erotic poetry in her article 'Huizong's New Clothes', presents an argument that the painting may be a visual trope affirming the Emperor's mandate from heaven by depicting women's devotion to an unpictured man, for whom they are creating new clothes.[2] NB

1 Bickford 2006
2 Blanchard 2006

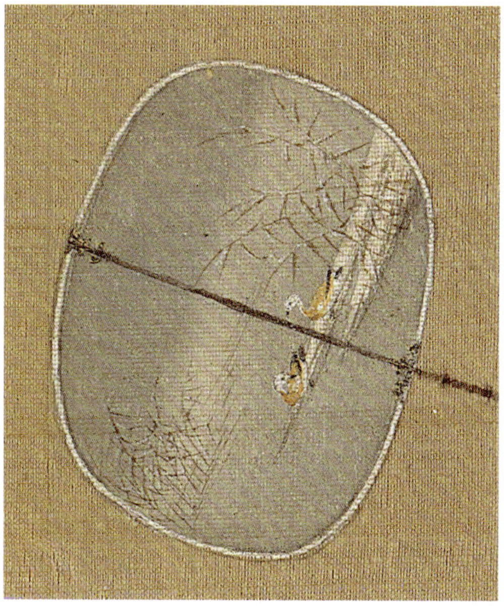

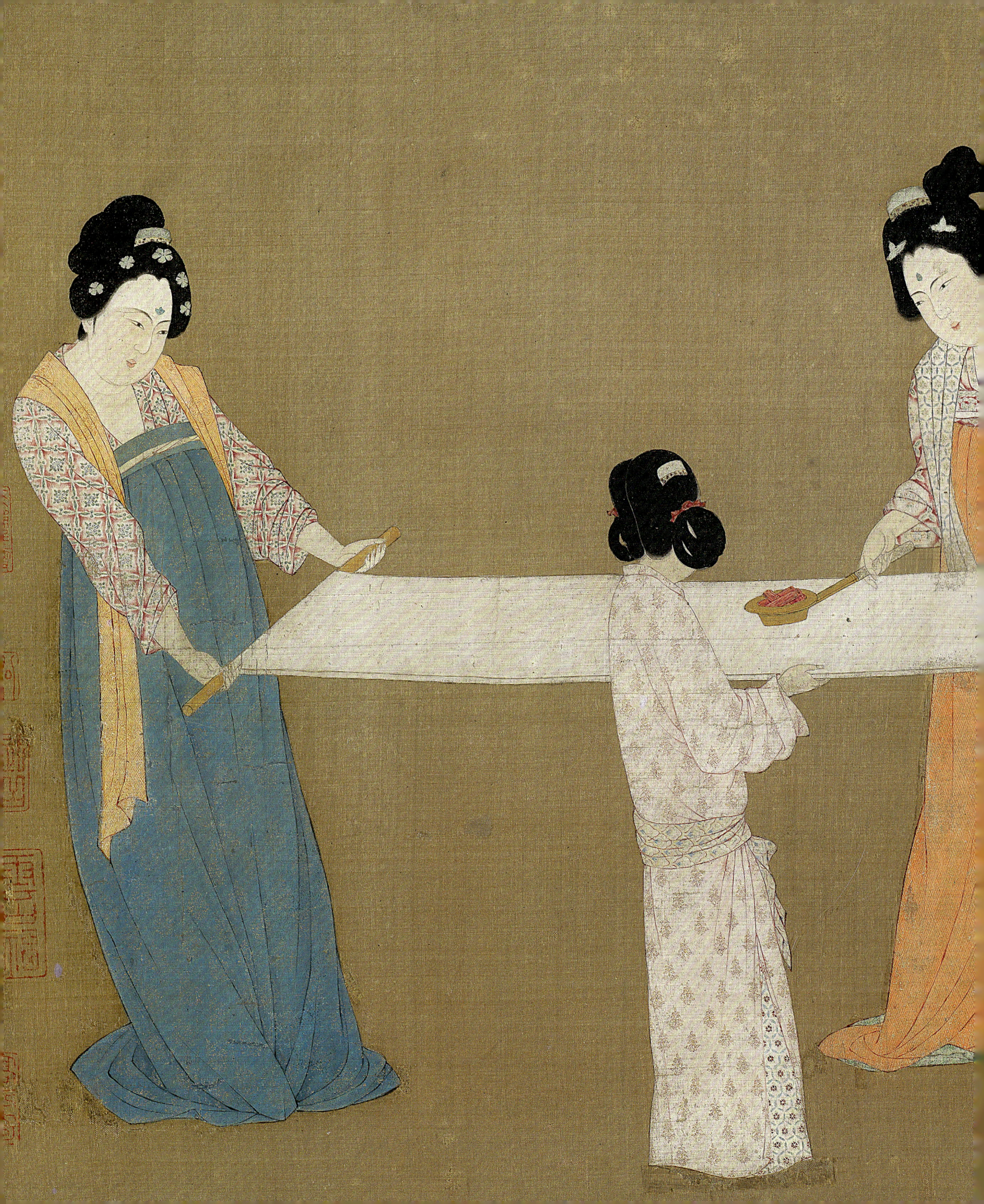

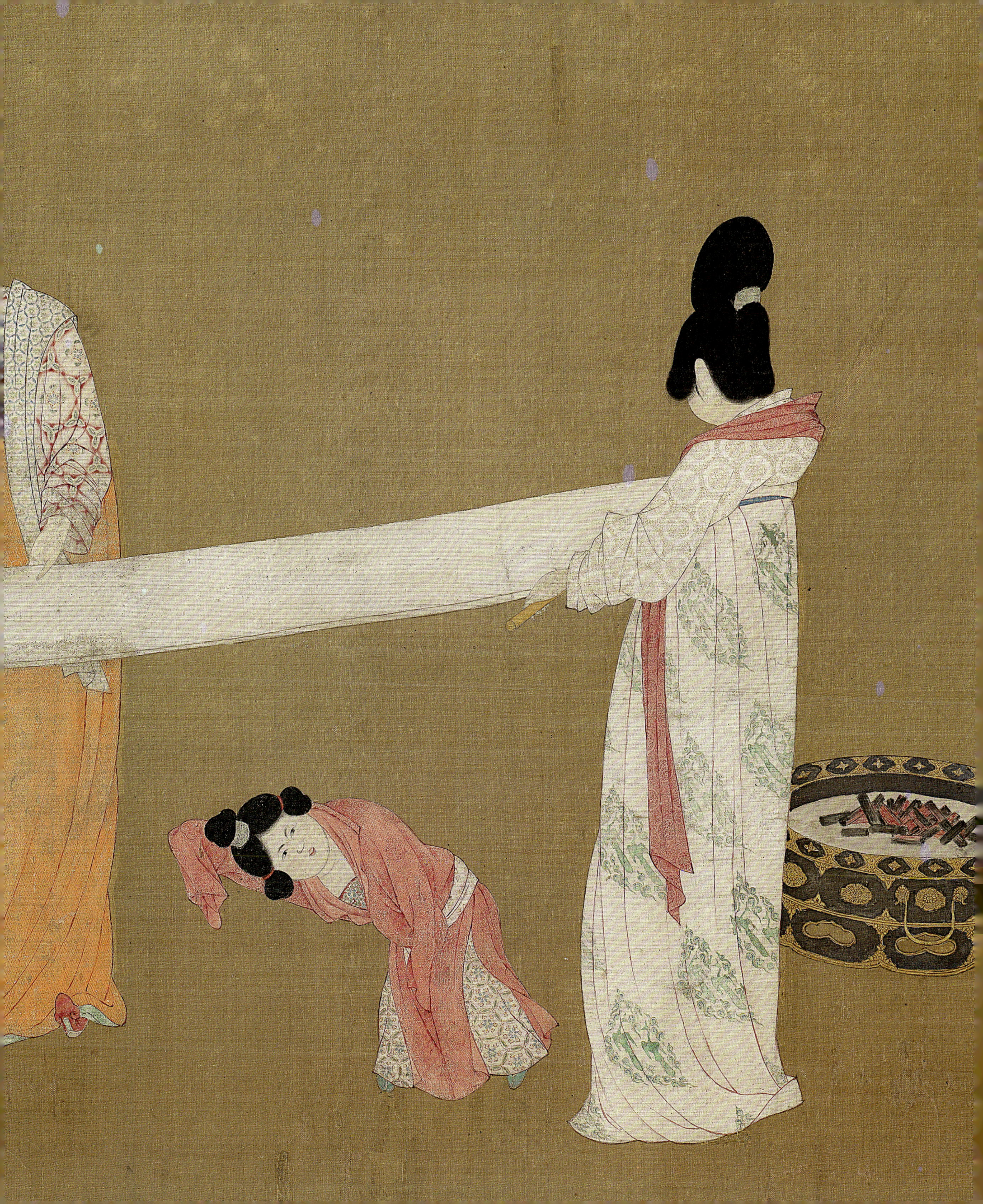

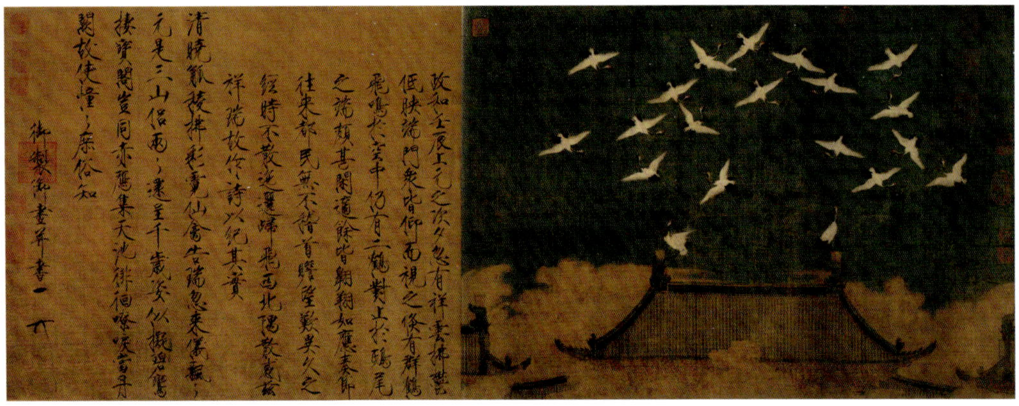

17

Possibly EMPEROR HUIZONG (1082–1135; r. 1101–25)

## Auspicious Cranes

宋 徽宗 瑞鶴圖 卷

c.1112, album leaf mounted as a handscroll, ink and colour on silk, 51 × 138.2 cm
Liaoning Provincial Museum (ZONG 4848 SHU 150)

REFERENCE LITERATURE

*Complete Collection* 1988, vol. 5, p. 1915; Ecke 1972; Xu 1979 and 1984; Huang 1986; Fu 1988, no. 47; Xie 1989, no. 2; Sturman 1990; Ogawa 1996; Bickford 2002–3; Ebrey and Bickford 2006

This short handscroll is one of the most mesmerizing Chinese paintings to survive today, and displays the richest self-documentation among the works associated with Emperor Huizong. From his inscription written in 'slender gold' calligraphy, we know precisely how the painting came to be made (see the appendix). On the evening of the second day of the Lantern Festival (the festival marking the end of the New Year celebration) in 1112, in the Northern Song dynasty (960–1127) capital Kaifeng, miraculous clouds descended on the Xuande Gate of the imperial palace and then a flock of 20 Manchurian cranes appeared in the sky, two perching atop the 'owl-tail' roof ridge and the others hovering gracefully. The residents of the capital all looked up in amazement and then bowed in reverence. Moved by this scene, Huizong writes, he painted this picture and composed a eulogizing poem to record the sudden appearance of the cranes as a good omen.

From historical sources and other paintings attributed to Huizong, it is also almost certain that the painting was originally mounted as a large album leaf, accompanied by the inscription on another sheet, and that it was part of *The Xuanhe Reign Album of Sagacious Viewing*, a vast imperial art project to record a wide range of auspicious creatures and phenomena sighted by officials across the empire. According to the writer Deng Chun's (c.1109–79/83) *Painting Continued* of 1168–73, when the project was completed it consisted of 1,000 volumes in total, each containing 15 paintings,[1] although only three survive today: the other two are *Five-coloured Parakeet* in the Museum of Fine Arts, Boston and *Auspicious Dragon Rock* in the Palace Museum, Beijing.

Whether or not the painting was in fact executed by Huizong or by one of his favourite court painters is an intriguing question. Based on Huizong's biographical information that when he was a prince he had studied under the court painter Wu Yuanyu (act. c.1080–1104), who specialized in painting birds and flowers in a meticulous style, and above all the specificity of Huizong's signature on the picture: 'imperially composed, imperially painted and written', it seems reasonable to conclude that Huizong painted it himself. On the other hand, the enormous stylistic differences between the paintings attributed to Huizong make it difficult to believe that they were all painted by a single person.[2]

The most intriguing feature of the painting, however, is the imagery itself. Although by this time three-dimensional effects had been achieved and had come to be preferred by many artists, the painter of this scroll strangely departed from this naturalistic trend, embracing flatness instead. Here all the flying cranes are rendered with spread wings as if performing a synchronized dance. The clarity of the silhouettes is reinforced by the flat blue background, which evokes the sky, complementing the white tonality of the birds. As a result, the entire painting brings to mind embroidery or silk-tapestry pictures, as Tseng Yu-ho Ecke has observed (fig. 59),[3] which were in fact elevated by Huizong as an integral part of pictorial art.[4] Further investigation is necessary in order to reveal the whole significance of the striking resemblance between this painting and textile art. ZH

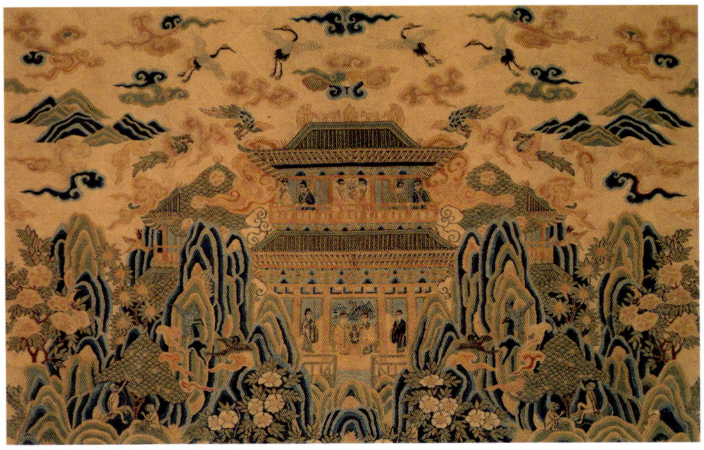

FIG. 59
*Immortals in a Mountain Pavilion*, early 12th century. Silk tapestry from an album of 12. National Palace Museum, Taipei

1 Deng (1168–73) 1993–8, vol. 2, p. 704
2 See Xu 1979 and 1984, pp. 217–33.
3 Ecke 1972, pp. 125, 182–3; see also Bickford 2002–3, p. 83.
4 For Huizong's patronage of textile art, especially embroidery pictures, see Huang 1986, p. 10.

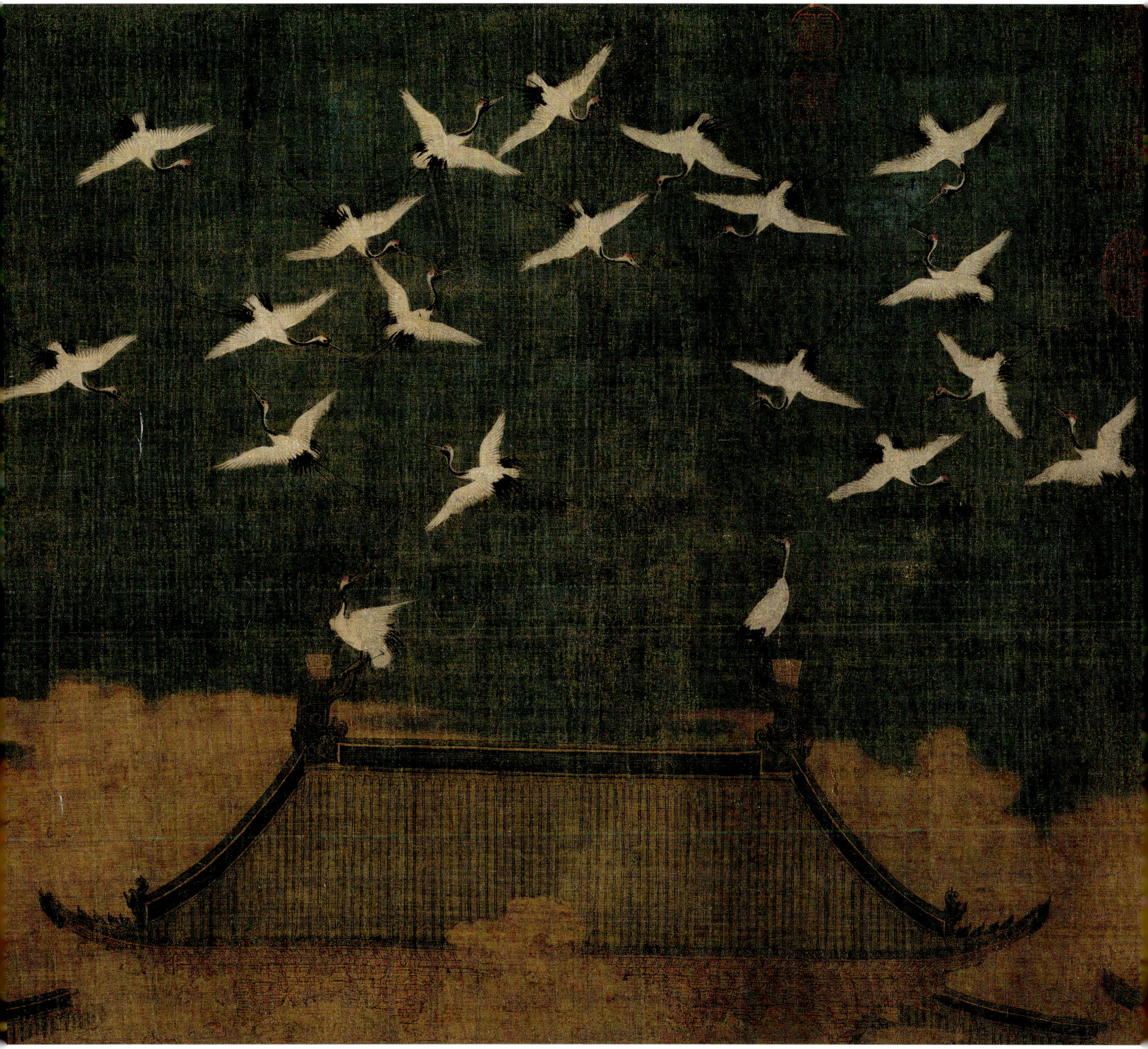

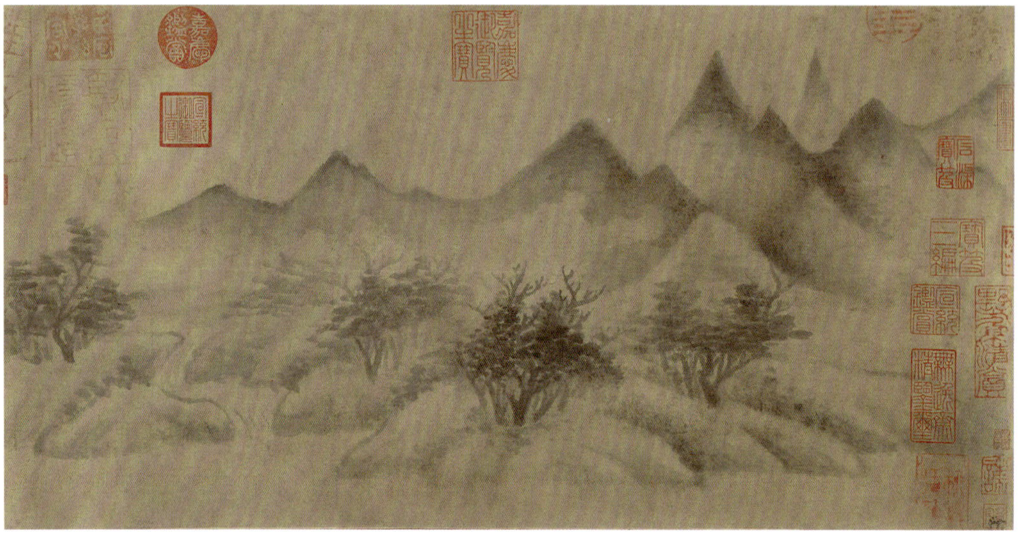

18

MI YOUREN (1074–1151/1086–1165)

## Cloudy Mountains

宋 米友仁 雲山圖 卷

1140s, handscroll, ink on paper, 27.6 × 57 cm
The Metropolitan Museum of Art, New York
Purchase, Gift of J. Pierpont Morgan,
by exchange, 1973 (1973.121.1)

PROVENANCE

C.C. Wang Family

REFERENCE LITERATURE

Xie 1957, pl. 58; New York 1962a, pp. 24–5, no. 4; Sun 1962, p. 600, pl. 9; *Complete Collection* 1988, vol. 9, pp. 1452–4; Hu (1816) 1972; New York 1973, pp. 62–4, 74–5, 141–2, no. 6; Barnhart, Iriya and Nakata 1977, pp. 76, 145–6, pl. 59; Lee and Ho 1980, no. 80, pp. 101–57, no. 80; Nakata and Fu 1981–3, vol. 2, pp. 143–4, pls 36–7; Boston 1983, pp. 45–6, fig. 11; Sturman 1989, vol. 3, pp. 616, 618, figs 3.1, 3.3; Fong 1992, pp. 162–8, pl. 21; Weitz 2002, p. 267, no. 1.163, fig. 23

The son of the renowned scholar, calligrapher and connoisseur Mi Fu (1051–1107), Mi Youren was himself an accomplished scholar-artist, a high official – he rose to the position of vice president of the Board of War – and the leading connoisseur of his time, often acting as the authenticator of ancient paintings for Emperor Gaozong (r. 1127–62) of the Southern Song dynasty (1127–1279).

The style of simplified, blurry mountain forms that Mi Youren inherited from his father (there is no longer any reliable example of the older Mi's painted work) marks a significant break from the Northern Song (960–1127) courtly tradition of highly detailed landscapes. Referred to by scholar-artists of the time as 'ink play', this non-representational manner of wet ink brush marks (called 'Mi dots') suggests a preference for self-expression over descriptive realism, thereby raising the status of painting to a level equal to that of poetry and calligraphy.

In this work, Mi Youren has radically simplified the complex vision of nature that had characterized tenth- and eleventh-century landscape painting, reducing mountains and trees to their iconic minimum by rendering them as pictographic abstractions with mountains envisioned as triangular peaks, trees simplified to a few branches and horizontal foliage dots, and foreground embankments defined by layered arcs.

The esteem in which later admirers have held this painting is attested by the numerous seals impressed on its surface and its borders as well as by its colophons – the poems or commentaries inscribed on the mounting following the painting. The painting was executed in the 1140s, and the earliest colophon is dated 1200; the most recent seals date to the late twentieth century. By reading the colophons and deciphering the collectors' seals, we can reconstruct something of the scroll's 800-year transmission and provenance.

One colophon by the celebrated calligrapher and scholar Xianyu Shu (1246–1302) evidences the major revival of Mi's distinctive 'scholarly' idiom during the early Yuan dynasty (1271–1368):

> Poetry critics say that if one has ten ideas but puts into words only three, one may then compare with the *Li sao* [Encountering sorrow] by Qu Yuan (343–278 BCE) and the *Ya* [Book of odes]. I say the same is true with painting. An artisan's painting is short in ideas but long on representative likeness, but the opposite is true with the works of lofty souls and superior scholars. The paintings by the two Mis are of the latter kind. In this piece of paper, if one speaks of clear delineation then anyone can do it. But in describing the trees, sloping bank, and grasses mixed with the earth, all with the ideas of a choice stretch of river shore lying far beyond the actual brushwork, then no one can match this.[1]

MH

1 Translation from New York 1973, p. 63

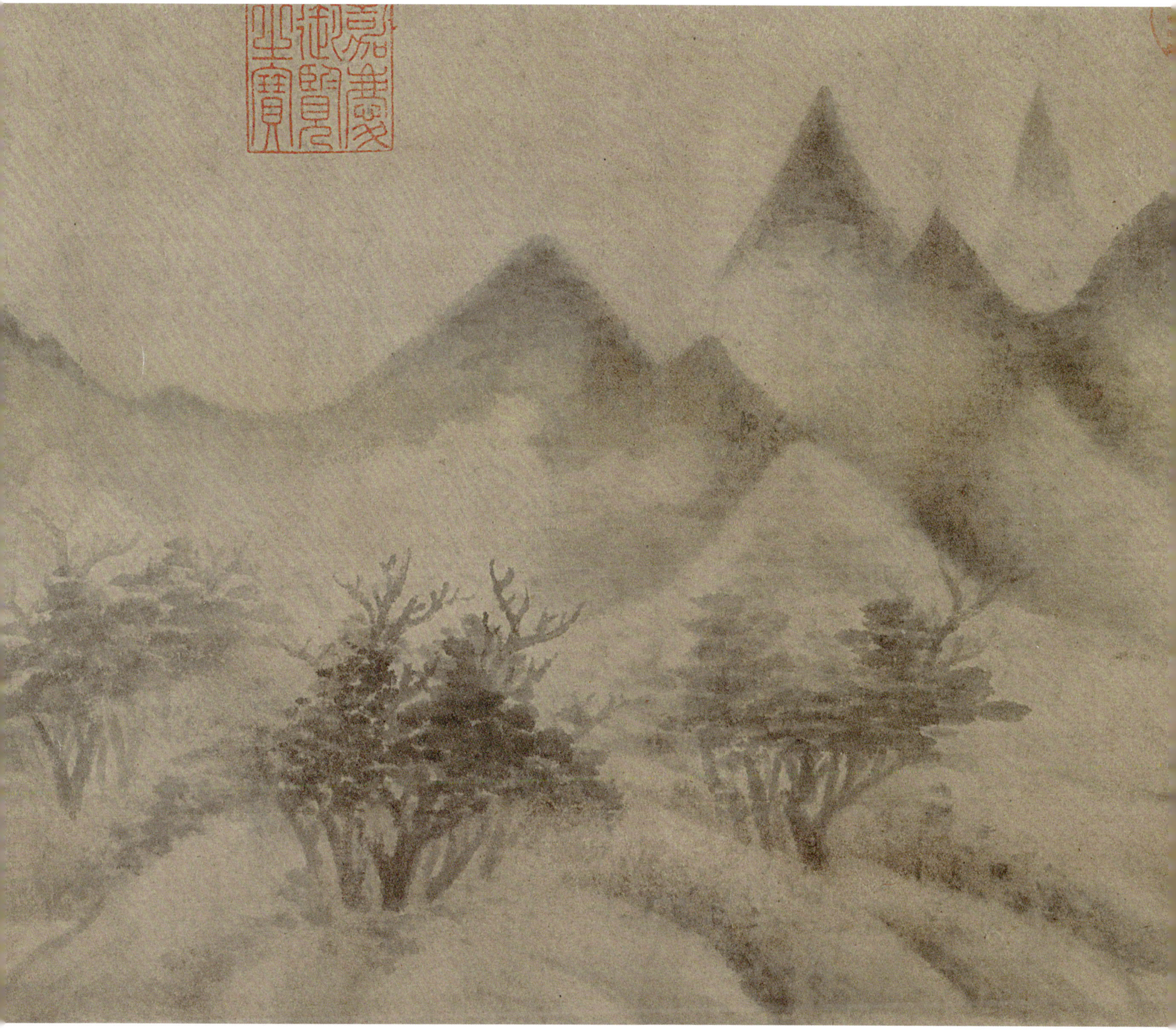
嘉慶御覽之寶

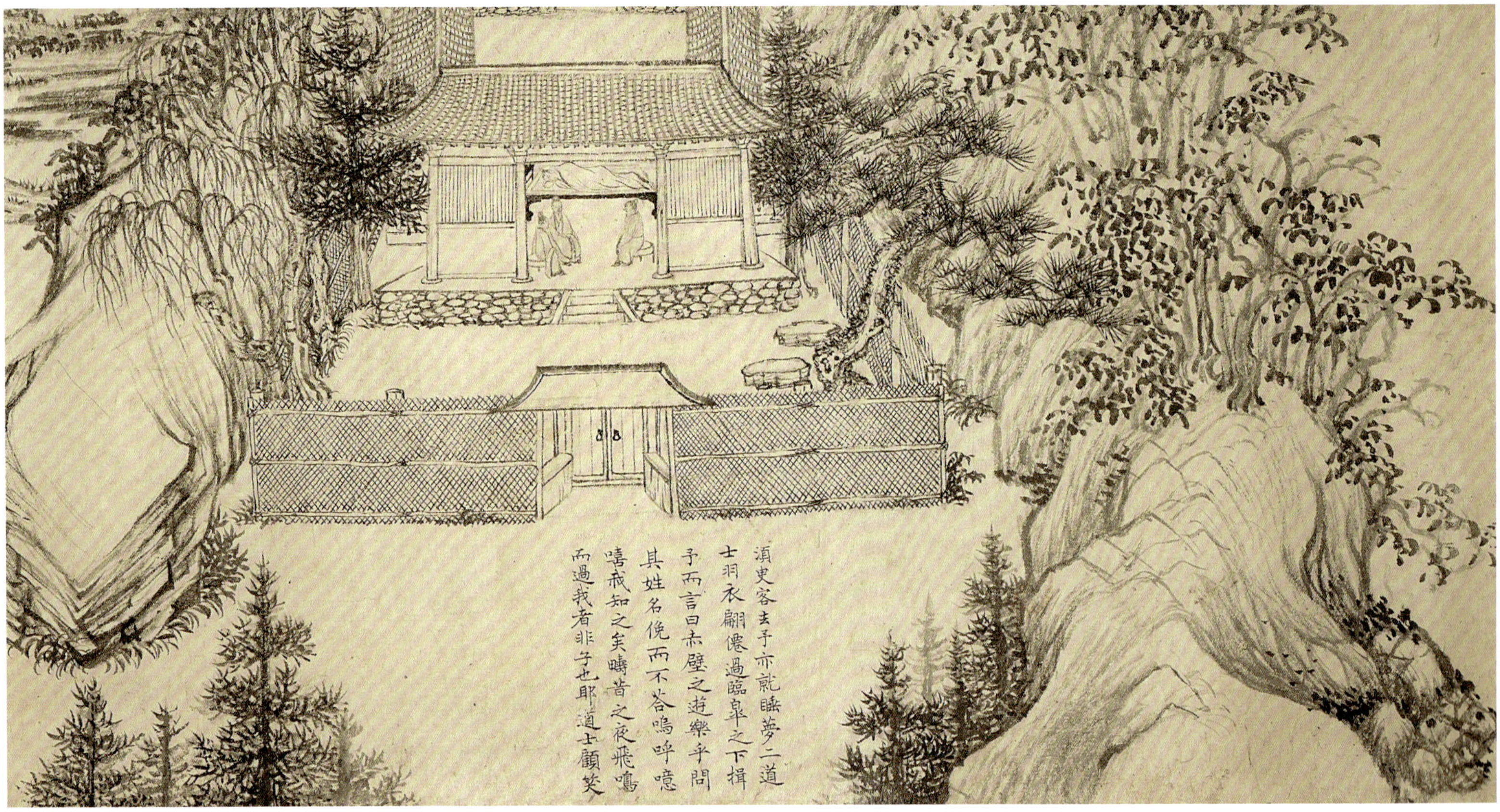


19

QIAO ZHONGCHANG
(act. late 11th–early 12th century)

## Illustration to the Second Prose Poem on the Red Cliff

宋 喬仲常 後赤壁賦圖 卷

early 12th century, handscroll, ink on paper, 30.48 × 566.42 cm
The Nelson-Atkins Museum of Art, Kansas City (F80-5)

PROVENANCE

John M. Crawford, Jr. (1913–88)

REFERENCE LITERATURE

*Complete Collection* 1988, vol. 2, pp. 968–9; Cahill in New York 1962b, pls 15, 16; Wilkinson 1981; Altieri 1983; Ward with Rowlands 1987, pp. 56–7, no. 19; Li 1990, figs 2a–d; Ding 1991; Silbergeld 1995; Itakura 2001; Kent 2001; Yi 2001, figs 1–8; Taipei 2006, pp. 166–9, no. 25; Itakura 2008; Shanghai 2012, pp. 93–109, no. 5; Zhang 2012, ch. 15

The painting illustrates the second of the two famous prose poems by Su Shi (1037–1101), one of China's most celebrated literary talents and a leading figure of literati culture. In 1082, when Su was exiled to a small town in Huangzhou, he twice visited the Red Cliff on the Yangzi River, and wrote a prose poem inspired by each visit. A great naval battle was known to have taken place in 206–7 at a site named Red Cliff, but the actual location remained uncertain. The two poems Su wrote about the visit, representative of works written in his most vital years, made the Red Cliff in Huangzhou the culturally accepted site. The two poems became the inspiration for many paintings, decorative arts and plays produced in later centuries.

Painted two decades after Su Shi's death, this scroll is the earliest extant work to illustrate the poems. *Second Prose Poem* is fully pictured in a long, continuous narrative that comprises eight scenes, each inscribed with a stanza from the poem. It begins with a chilly evening. The trees are bare, and the moon casts shadows on the ground. Su and his two friends, having obtained food and wine, depart for their outing to the Red Cliff. After the meal, the poet ascends the cliff on his own, but trembles when he senses the power of nature's ability to change. He returns to set sail on a skiff with his friends on the windless Yangzi, but a lone crane passing emits a piercing cry that shatters the tranquillity. Returning home, Su dreams that two Daoists come to visit him, and learns that the crane was a Daoist immortal in disguise. After he wakes up, Su attempts to search the for Daoists, but realizes they were only in his dream.

What is revolutionary in the painting is the use of an expressive ink style, not only to illustrate Su Shi's journey, but also to evoke the psychological intensity of his engagement with the Red Cliff. The style is commonly known as *baimiao* ('plain outline'), which entails the use of a variety of dry or moist ink strokes without colour or wash. Here, the brushwork is so remarkably built up with shades of ink tones that it can be appreciated for itself. With its

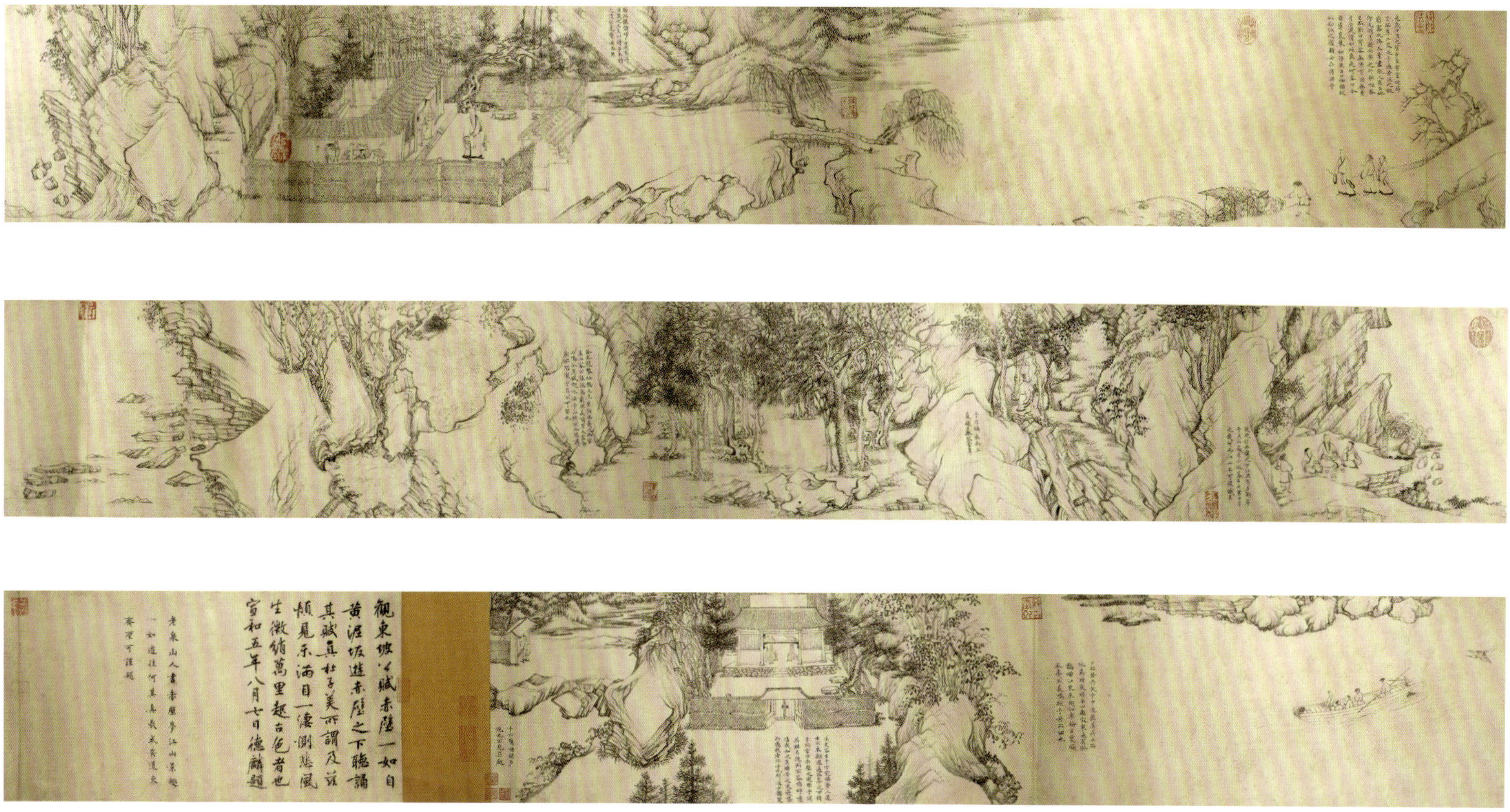

avant-garde style and literary theme, this painting is considered to be the pioneer of the literati paintings that came to be significant in succeeding centuries. Yet despite the new approach, the depictions of figures and landscape elements still rest in the realistic painting tradition of the Northern Song dynasty (960–1127), and the juxtaposition of text and image recalls antiquity.

A closer inspection finds the painting evocative in the way that it conveys – beyond the matching of words – Su Shi's inner state. While the solitary poet faces the transience of nature in the fourth and fifth stanzas, he disappears from the painted scenes. Instead, the dense woods, bizarrely shaped boulders and churning water crashing against the cliff represent his struggle in the face of change and his inner battle with his harsh exile. Intensifying the turmoil, the forms and perspectives are rendered with brushstrokes that are almost abstract in nature. Viewed from Su's intellectual and religious life, the moon, the crane and the dream, which are faithfully depicted in the painting, may be seen as symbols of enlightenment, or as representing the duality between constancy and the illusoriness of nature.

Little is known of the life and works of the painter on record, Qiao Zhongchang. The attribution of the painting is recorded in the catalogue *Treasured bookcases of the stony moat* in 1745, when it was admitted to the imperial collection during the reign of the Qianlong emperor (1736–96). The attribution was based on an unsigned colophon that was cut away from the scroll sometime in the early twentieth century. Qiao was reportedly related either to a student or to a young relative of Li Gonglin (c.1049–1106), a legendary artist who associated with Su Shi and who made *baimiao* a respected form of painting. If this account is true, Qiao may have been a member of Su's social circle.

The date of this scroll is affirmed by the collection seals of the court minister, Liang Shicheng (c.1063–1126), and the colophon of the imperial prince, Zhao Lingzhi (1061–1134). Both are known to have been sympathetic to Su Shi. After the scroll left the former palace collection in the early twentieth century, a few centimetres in the opening of the painting were trimmed, and the frontispiece of the Qianlong emperor and several other colophons were removed. Since the painting was taken to America, its significance has been much discussed in Chinese and Japanese as well as English publications. LL

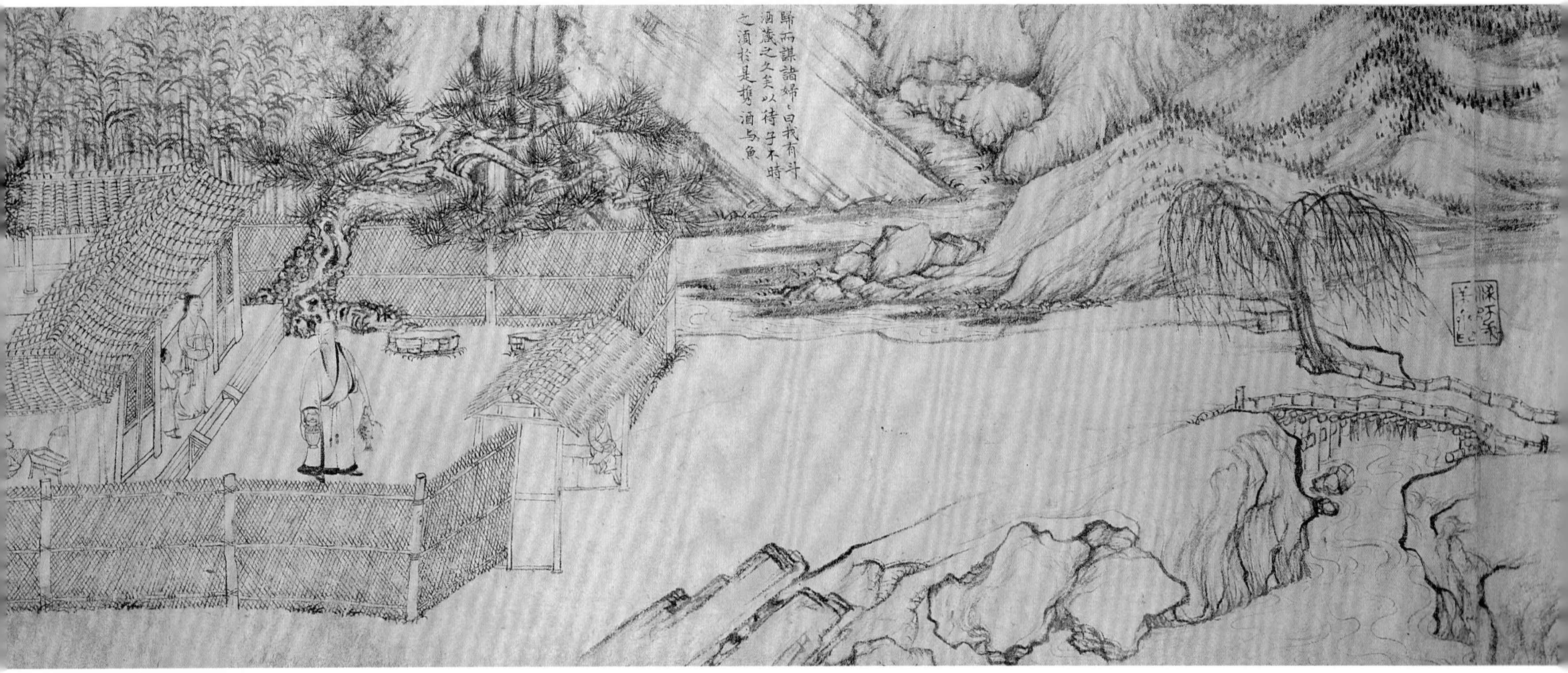
歸而謀諸婦、曰我有斗
酒藏之久矣以待子不時
之須於是携酒与魚

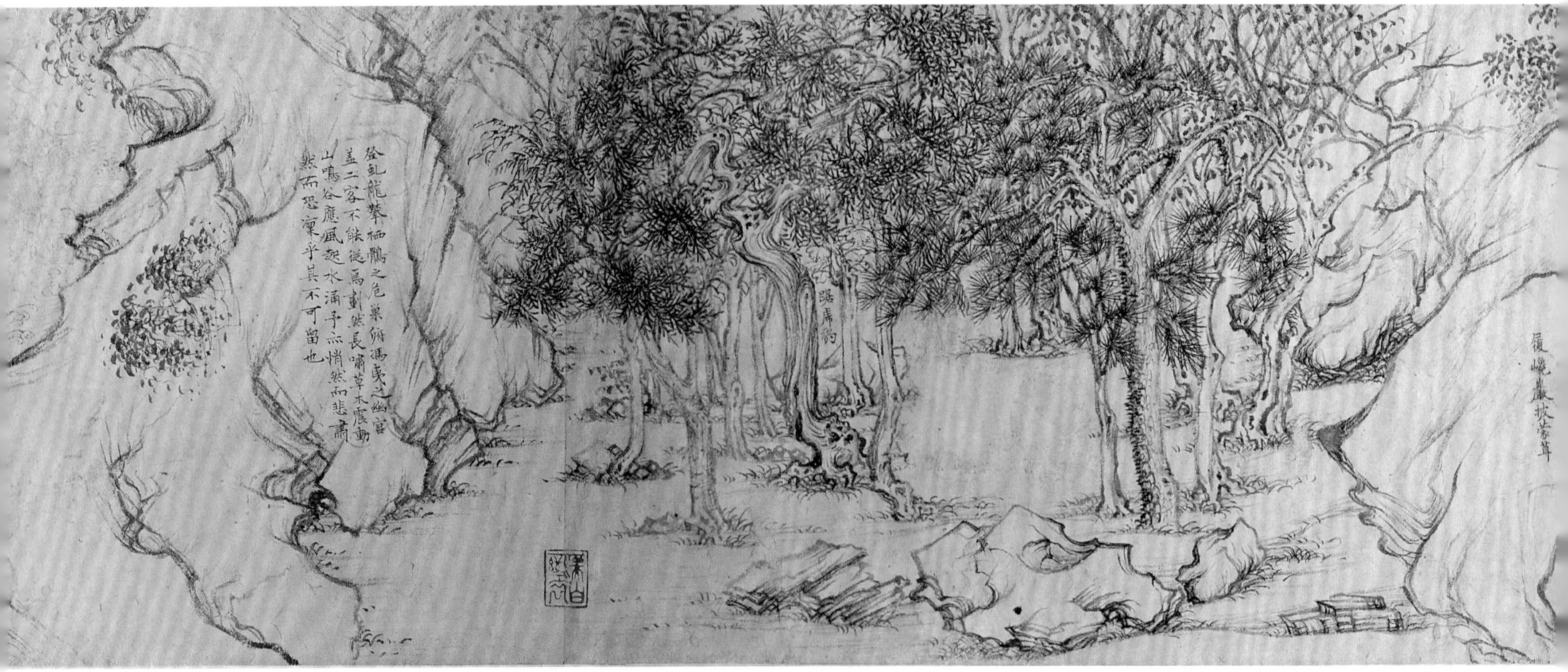
登虬龍攀栖鶻之危巢俯馮夷之幽宮
蓋二客不能從焉劃然長嘯草木震動
山鳴谷應風起水涌予亦悄然而悲肅
然而恐凜乎其不可留也
踞虎豹
履巉巖披蒙茸

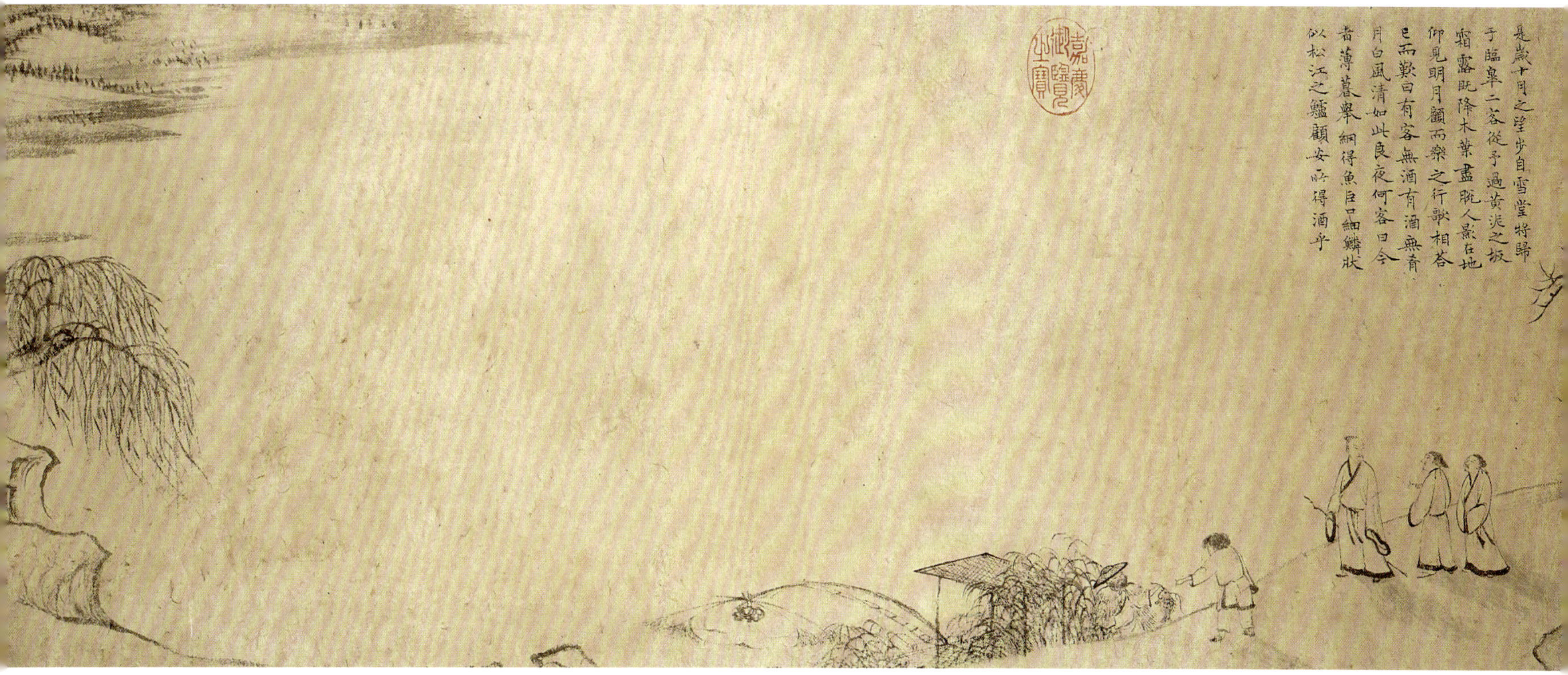
是歲十月之望步自雪堂將歸
于臨皋二客從予過黃泥之坂
霜露既降木葉盡脫人影在地
仰見明月顧而樂之行歌相答
已而歎曰有客無酒有酒無肴
月白風清如此良夜何客曰今
者薄暮舉網得魚巨口細鱗狀
似松江之鱸顧安所得酒乎

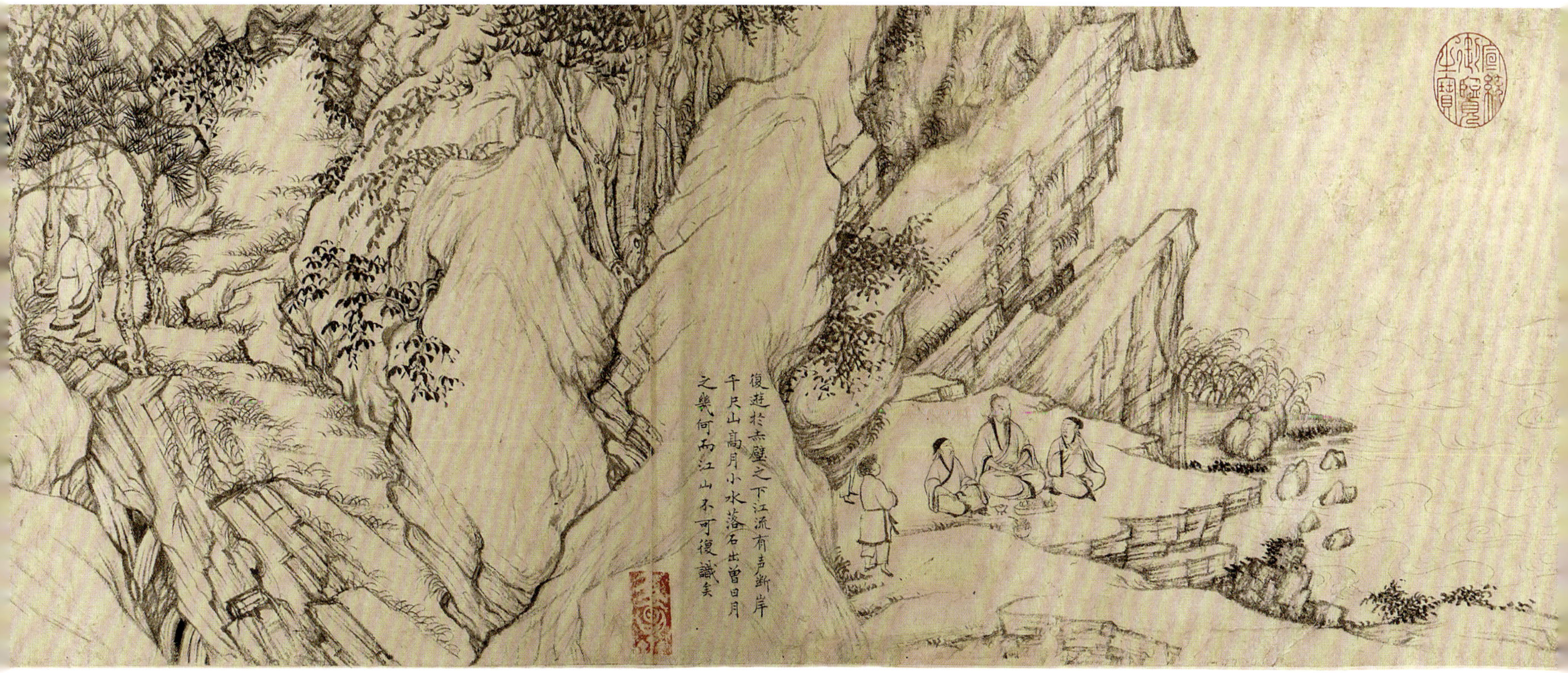
復遊於赤壁之下江流有声斷岸
千尺山高月小水落石出曾日月
之幾何而江山不可復識矣

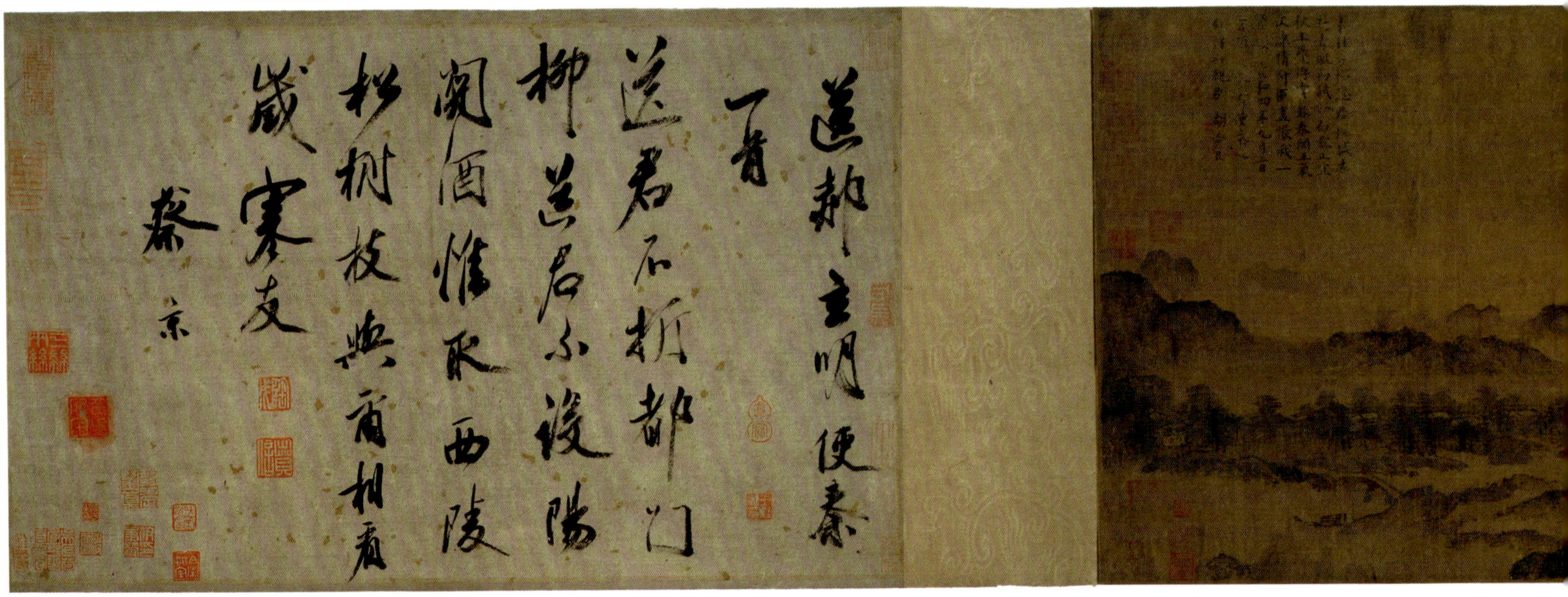

20

HU SHUNCHEN
(act. early 12th century)

## Farewell to Hao Xuanming, Envoy to Qin

宋 胡舜臣 送郝玄明使秦圖 卷

1122, handscroll, ink and light colour on silk, 30 × 111 cm
Osaka City Museum of Fine Arts (42, I-127)

REFERENCE LITERATURE

Harada 1939 and 1940; Suzuki 1985; Fujita 1989; Osaka and Shanghai 1994; Brotherton 2000–1; Chen 2004; Tokyo 2004; Itakura 2006; Nara 2008; Yumino in Shanghai 2010

Little is known about the painter Hu Shunchen. He is mentioned in Xia Wenyan's (*c.*1312–*c.*57) *Precious Mirror of Painting* (preface dated 1365) as a follower of Guo Xi (*c.*1000–*c.*1090). In the early Xuanhe era (1119–25) of the reign of Emperor Huizong (1101–25) of the Northern Song dynasty (960–1279), he was awarded the rank of *daizhao* (first assistant in waiting) at the painting academy, and then was reinstated at the beginning of the Shaoxing era (1131–62) in the Southern Song period (1127–1279) after the capital was moved to Lin'an (present Hangzhou). This painting is the only work by him that has come down to us.

Hu inscribed the painting with an eight-line, five-syllable poem. He then gives a brief account of the reason for the painting: 'On the second day of the ninth lunar month in the fourth year of the Xuanhe reign period, Hao Xuanming the Grand Councillor has received the assignment of envoy to Qin, and I have made this to commemorate his departure. Hu Shunchen.' On a separate sheet of paper attached to the scroll is a seven-line poem by the government official Cai Jing (1047–1126), Emperor Huizong's favourite official and his chief minister.

From the poems and inscription, we learn that Hao Xuanming, a high government official holding the title of vice-grand councillor, was being sent as an envoy to Qin (present Shaanxi Province), and that Hu Shunchen's painting and Cai Jing's poem were intended as a farewell gift. The figure of Hao Xuanming appears midway through the scroll, riding a donkey and accompanied by an attendant. They have passed through a low-lying village and over a bridge spanning a river (seen in the leftmost portion of the scroll), and are now following a mountain path which rises in front of them to the gate of Qin, visible ahead in the scroll's opening passage.

Assessments of the work's style in Chinese painting history can be roughly summarized as follows. Hu's portrayal of landscape as a grand vista where the viewer looks up at steep mountains in the first half of the handscroll (high distance) and then across low, horizontal hills in the last half (level distance) corresponds to the work of Guo Xi's leading disciples and shows the characteristics of the Northern Song. On the other hand, the diagonal division of the composition along lines moving from upper left to lower right in accordance with the mountain ridges anticipates the Southern Song academy style. YT

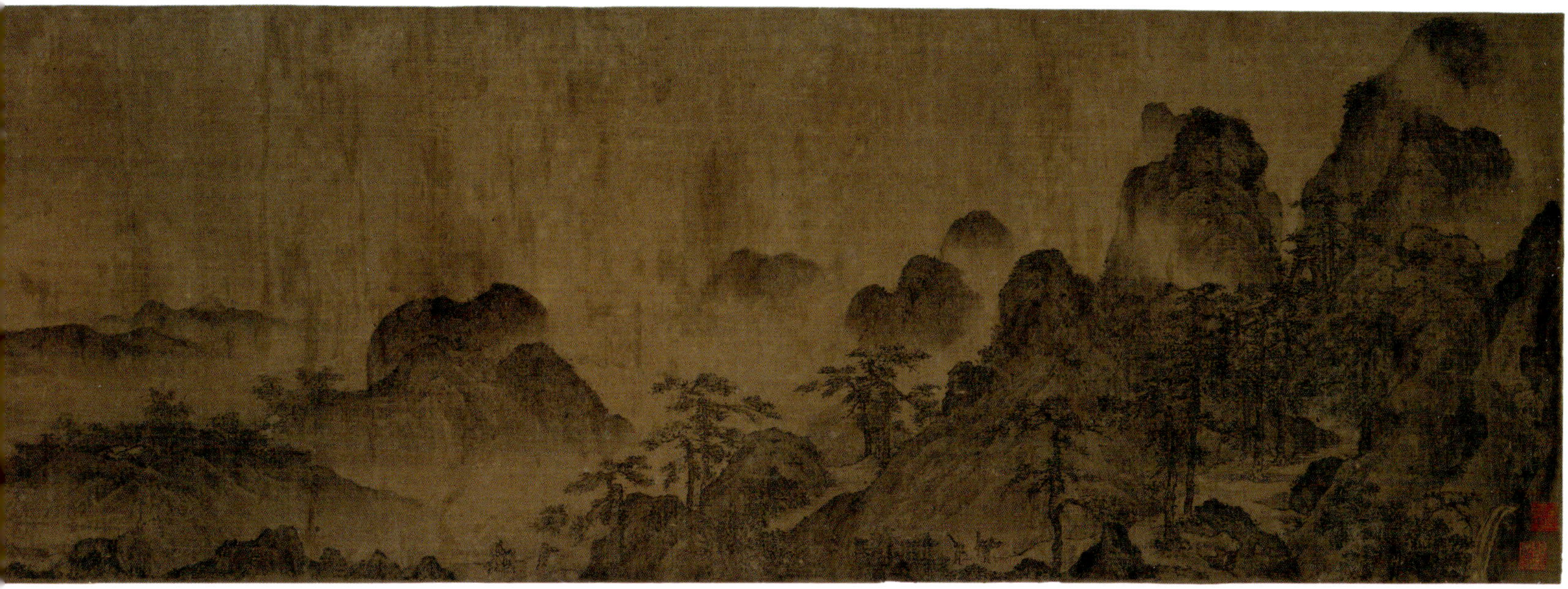

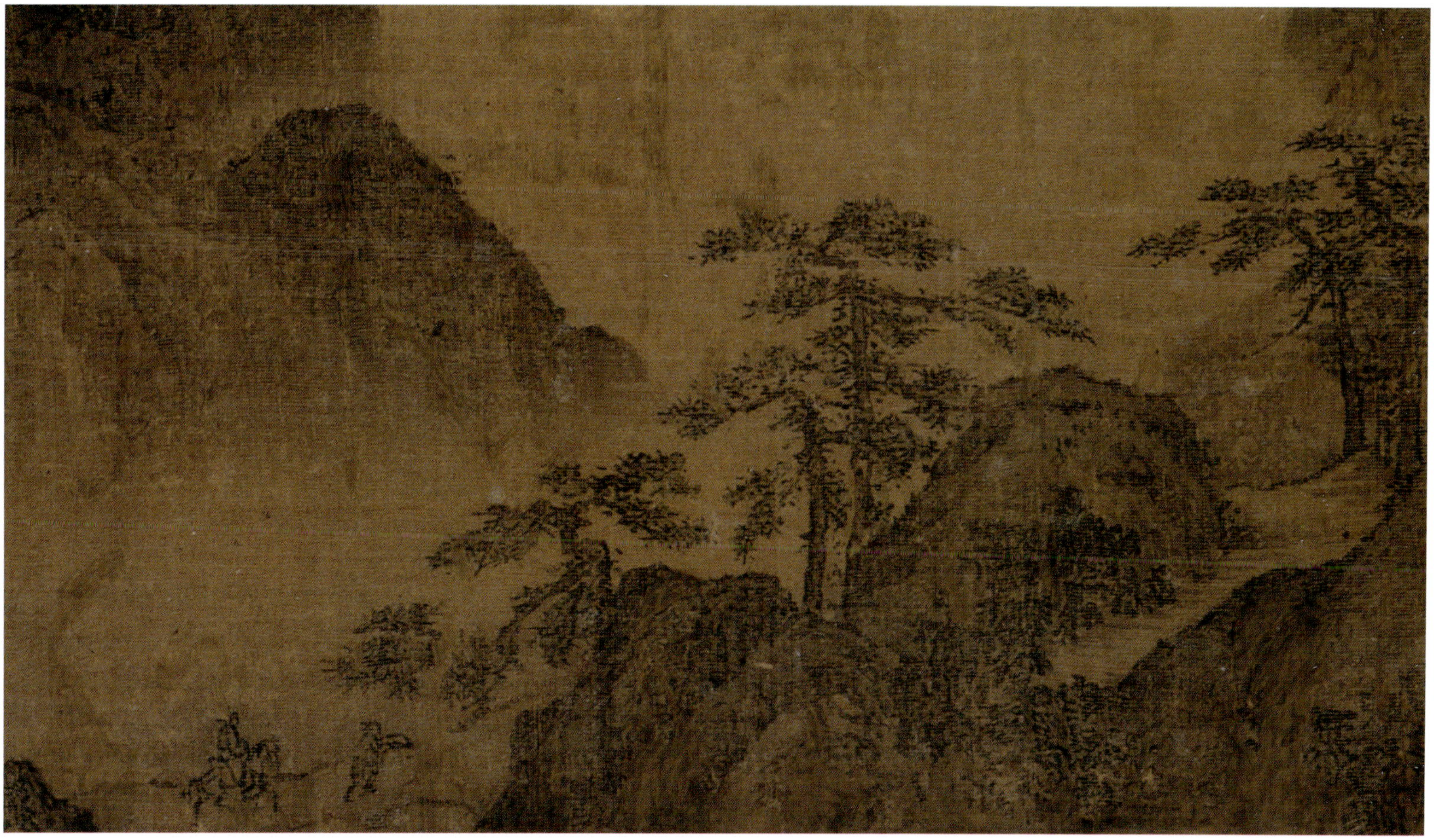

21

LI GONGNIAN
(act. early 12th century)

## Winter Evening Landscape

宋 李公年 冬景山水圖 軸

c.1120, hanging scroll, ink and light colour on silk, 129.6 × 48.3 cm
Princeton University Art Museum
Gift of DuBois Schanck Morris, Class of 1893 (Y1946–191)

PROVENANCE

DuBois Schanck Morris (1873–1956)

REFERENCE LITERATURE

London 1936, p. 47, no. 1115; Rowley 1947, pp. 103–4, pl. 24; New York 1962a, pp. 18–19; Suzuki and Akiyama 1973, vol. 1, p. 219, no. 5; Suzuki 1978, pp. 17, 156, no. 7; *Essence of Chinese and Japanese Literati Paintings* 1974–9, vol. 2, pp. 41, 219, pl. 32; *The Art of China* 1977–82, vol. 3, pp. 185–6, pl. 51; Suzuki et al. 1982–3, no. A16-012; Princeton 1984, pp. 53–4; *Chinese Art in Overseas Collections* 1985, p. 27, fig. 24; Ogawa 1997, pp. 9, 34, fig. 48; *New History of World Art* 1997–2001, vol. 5, pp. 58, 360, no. 44; Liu 2005, p. 150; Wang 2007, p. 477; *A Compendium of Song Paintings* 2008, vol. 6, pp. 112–14, 264, no. 25; *Princeton University Art Museum* 2007, p. 23; Takenami 2010, p. 61, fig. 6

The Northern Song (960–1127) imperial *Xuanhe Painting Catalogue* describes the scenery of Li Gongnian's sunrise and sunset landscapes as having 'shapes of objects appearing and disappearing in vast emptiness'.[1] In this painting, layered hills with desolate trees in the foreground lead back through mist-obscured mountain slopes to reach distant peaks rendered in black ink and blue wash. A river vanishes in the haze as it weaves from front to back, uniting the composition. Alone at upper right are the faint remaining colour traces of an evening sun or moon hovering over the chilly winter scene. Inhabiting the desolate wilderness, a man rowing a skiff is seen just about to drift behind a riverbank at lower left, while above in the middle distance, a young attendant waits beside another man seated on the shore. With his back towards us, he peers into the depths, possibly contemplating the empty pavilion set near the base of the far cliff. Such a forlorn building may be seen less as a landmark in the scenery than as a vantage point for the bleak views all around, perhaps paralleling the Northern Song literati's regard for moral rectitude in troubled times and providing visual resonance for the solitary wanderings of scholar-officials through a cold barren landscape.[2] The empty pavilion in *Winter Evening Landscape* anticipates the continued use of this motif; in particular one thinks of Ni Zan's (cat. no. 51) sparse landscapes with solitary pavilions, which became a model for later literati painters.

The desolate mood of mountains rising in a landscape filled with mist is reinforced by the gnarled, almost demonic, forms of the tree branches. These are rendered in the 'crab-claw' manner associated with the artist Li Cheng (919–67, cat. no. 14), whose style Li Gongnian is said to have followed. Lyricism expressed through 'pictorial conception' (*huayi*) was a keynote in landscape paintings of the eleventh and twelfth centuries, so this winter evening scene may originally have been meant to evoke a poetic line, such as 'Winter sun emerges from the lingering mist' (*hanri chu wuchi*), or complement a title, for instance *Sparse Trees in the Glow of the Evening Sun*. Both verse and title are mentioned in the *Xuanhe Painting Catalogue* manual in reference to Li's landscapes. Besides his skill as a painter, little is known about Li Gongnian's life. Also known as Li Changmao, he served in government office in Sichuan Province and as the Zhejiang judicial commissioner (*tidian xingyu gongshi*).[3] *Winter Evening Landscape* may be his sole surviving work; it is signed 'Gongnian' on the rocky outcrop beneath an overhanging cliff at right. Immediately below the signature are the faint traces of a seal, possibly the artist's.

Collectors' seals reading *Hu zhong tian* and *Lu shi Jidao* stamped on the painting indicate that during the early fourteenth century it was in the collection of Lu Xingzhi (1275–after 1349).[4] A calligrapher and painter, Lu resided in Suzhou and held a position in the Hanlin Academy. A heavily damaged seal below Lu's may indicate a previous owner. In the Ming dynasty (1368–1644), the painting probably entered the collection of Wang Xianchen (1473–c.1543), the owner of the *Garden of the Inept Administrator* (cat. no. 62) in Suzhou. His seal, reading *Wang shi cangshu zizi sunsun yong bao zang*, also appears on the scroll.[5] Afterwards, the painting's whereabouts are unclear until it was acquired by Dubois Schanck Morris (1873–1956), an American Presbyterian missionary based in Anhui Province. Morris returned to the United States in 1928 and deposited this painting and many others at his alma mater, Princeton University, until they were formally donated in the 1940s. It should also be noted that *Winter Evening Landscape* was one of two paintings from the Morris collection that were selected for display in the landmark 1935–6 *International Exhibition of Chinese Art* in London.[6] CL

1 *Xuanhe Painting Catalogue* (1120) 1964, p. 202; translation follows Princeton 1984, p. 53
2 Wang 2007, p. 477
3 Yu 1992
4 Also known as Lu Fuzhi (*zi* Jidao, *hao* Huzhong tian); for a short biography see the 1913 preface to his *Ci zhi* (On *ci* poetry) in Tang 1967, vol. 1, pp. 245–7. There is some confusion over his death date; some sources indicate that he served in office during the reign of the Ming dynasty (1368–1644) emperor Hongwu (1368–98).
5 From email correspondence of 6 June 2012 with Ho Chuan hsing, other paintings with Wang Xianchen's seals include the hanging scrolls *Joy in Fishing* attributed to Jing Hao (act. c.870–930) and *Sitting Alone by a Stream* attributed to Fan Kuan (act. c.990–1030), in the National Palace Museum, Taipei. The Ming dynasty artist Wen Zhengming (1470–1559) painted two albums depicting the Garden of the Inept Administrator as its subject. This suggests a close association between the two men and the likelihood that Wen Zhengming may have seen *Winter Evening Landscape*.
6 London 1936, p. 47, no. 1115

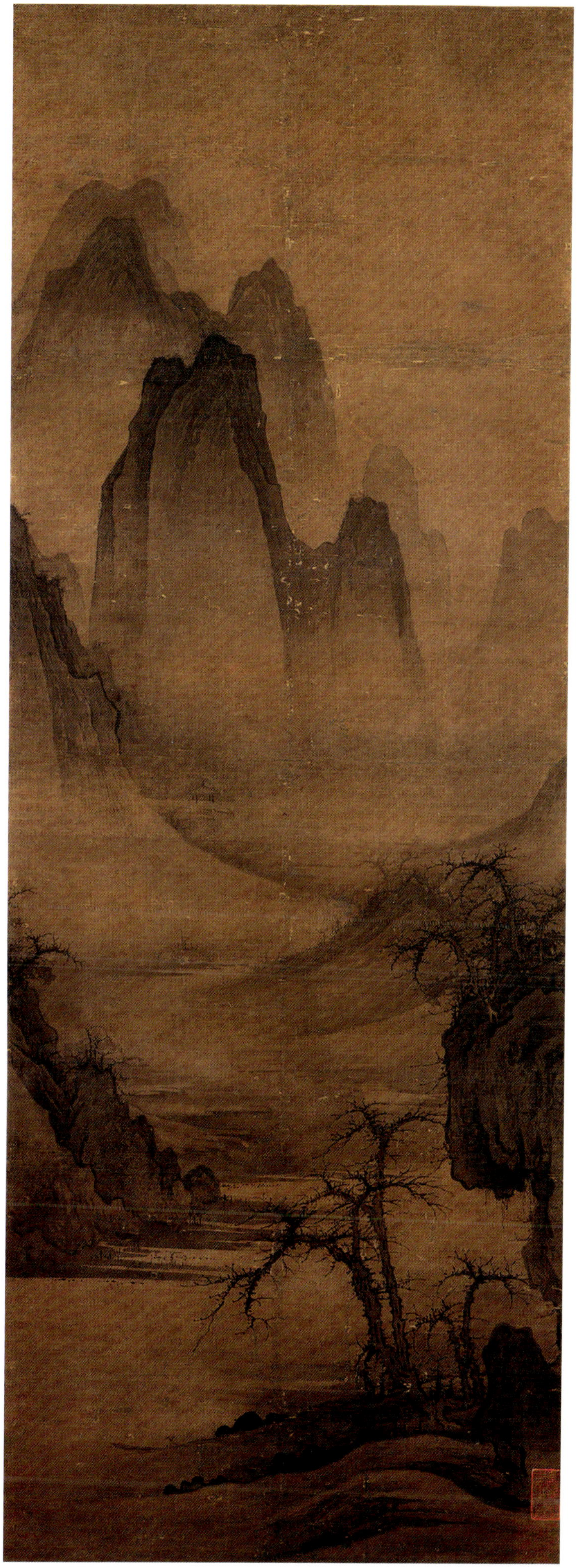

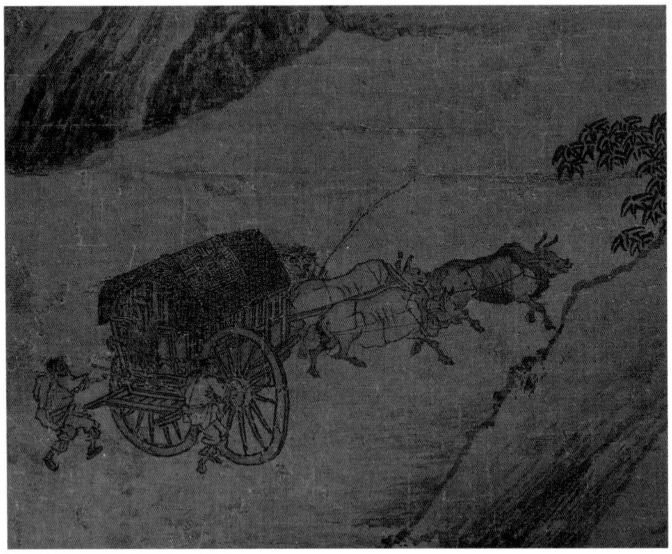

22

UNIDENTIFIED ARTIST;
traditionally attributed to ZHU RUI
(act. 1st half 12th century) or a follower

## Bullock Carts Travelling over Rivers and Mountains

宋 傳朱銳 盤車圖 軸

2nd half 12th century, hanging scroll,
ink and colour on silk, 104.2 × 51.4 cm
Museum of Fine Arts, Boston
Julia Bradford Huntington James Fund, 1908
(08.115)

PROVENANCE

Okakura Kakuzo (1862–1913)

REFERENCE LITERATURE

Museum of Fine Arts, Boston 1944; Wu 1996a; Yokohama 1996; Boston 1997; *A Compendium of Song Paintings* 2008

At the base of high cliffs, on a rocky mountain pass, small human figures and animals labour under the harsh conditions of their lives. Carts pulled by teams of oxen or donkeys are laden with immense wrapped packages, their owners leading from the front or goading with whips from behind. Some exhausted and almost emaciated 'beasts of burden' – camels – the bones visible through the hide of one, lie in front of an inn while their masters also take a rest. Through the open doors, the viewer notices that a tired patron has fallen asleep.

The monumentality of the landscape in this painting may at first suggest a Northern Song (960–1127) date (and the camels imply a north China setting), but the liveliness and dramatization of the details – from the animals hauling their heavy carts to the human figures relaxing at the inn – reveal the new aesthetics and sentiments that arose in the growing prosperity of the Southern Song period (1127–1279).

Zhu Rui was a painter in the imperial academy during the last decades of the Northern Song, and hailed from Hebei Province, 100s of miles to the east of the capital, Bianjing (present Kaifeng). He was known for his technique in painting landscapes, flowers and birds. It was during the last years of the dynasty, under the politically inept but culturally refined emperor Huizong (r. 1101–25), that the academy reached new heights. Huizong gathered the most talented artists in the country into his service, including painters such as Su Hanchen (act. mid-12th century), Zhang Zeduan (act. early 12th century) and Wang Ximeng (1096–1119). Zhang Zeduan was responsible for the much-celebrated scroll *Along the River during the Qingming Festival* (fig. 46) which depicts a wealth of human activity along the river and in the busy urban streets of the capital. The work is representative of the genre painting that had just begun to flourish at this time. Several years later, after the fall of the capital to the northern Jurchen, during the Southern Song dynasty based in Lin'an (present Hangzhou), affluent connoisseurs delighted in the human emotions expressed in the details of such genre paintings. Fuelled by their enthusiasm – and a growing disinterest in more political works illustrating social virtues – the popularity of genre paintings grew, resulting in such engaging images as the present work by an unknown artist.

A signature in the lower left corner, reading 'chen Zhu Rui gonghua' ('painted respectfully by Your Subject Zhu Rui'), points to the painting as a work of this artist of the Northern Song imperial academy. However, neither the calligraphy nor the grammatical construction of the phrase is in a style that would have been appropriate for the time or artist. The work may have been painted by a follower of Zhu Rui living in the Southern Song capital, and the seal appended at a later time by an owner hoping to increase its value and importance. For today's connoisseur, the fine workmanship and dynamism of the painting and its human details alone are enough to mark it – despite the ambiguous attribution – as a significant subject of focus. NB

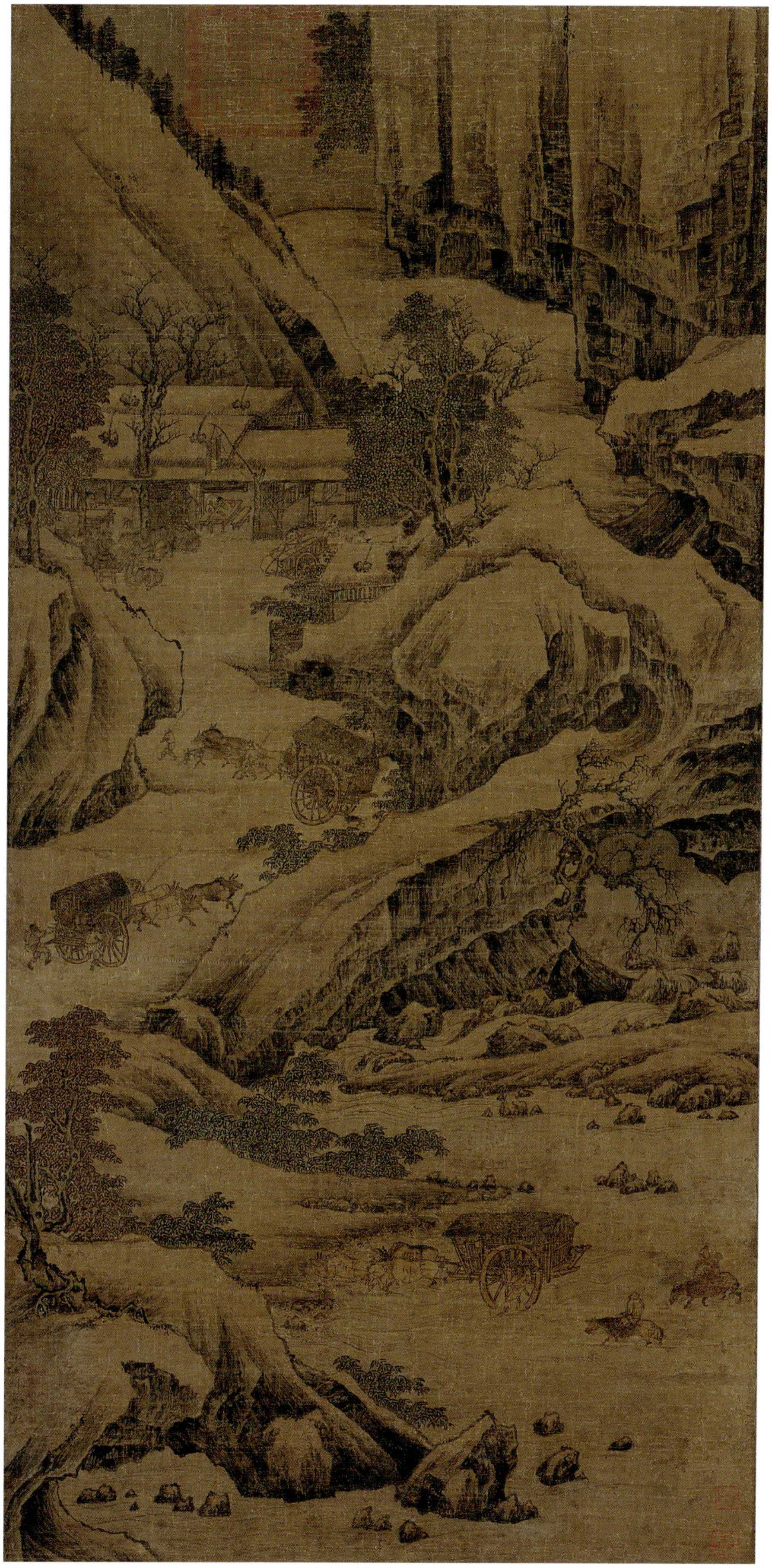

23, 24

ZHOU JICHANG
(act. 2nd half 12th century)

## Luohans Bestowing Alms on Suffering Human Beings

宋 周季常 五佰羅漢圖 軸 施財貧者

c.1184, hanging scroll mounted as a panel, ink, colour and gold on silk, 111.5 × 53.1 cm
Museum of Fine Arts, Boston
General Fund, 1895 (95.4)

PROVENANCE

Daitoku-ji, Kyoto, Japan

## Luohans in a Bamboo Grove Receiving Offerings

宋 周季常 五佰羅漢圖 軸 竹林致琛

c.1180, hanging scroll mounted as a panel, ink, colour and gold on silk, 113 × 51.5 cm
Museum of Fine Arts, Boston
General Fund, 1895 (95.5)

PROVENANCE

Daitoku-ji, Kyoto, Japan

REFERENCE LITERATURE

*Kokka* 1923; Museum of Fine Arts, Boston 1944; Whitehill 1970; Museum of Fine Arts, Boston 1975 and 1982; Tomita 1990; Museum of Fine Arts, Boston 1991; Wu 1996a; Yokohama 1996; Barnhart 1997; Boston 1997; *Song hua quanji* 2008; Jiang 2009

During the 10 years between 1178 and 1188, the pair of professional artists Zhou Jichang and Lin Tinggui (act. 2nd half 12th century) produced a set of 100 votive paintings depicting 500 *luohans* ('arhats'), or enlightened disciples of the Buddha. These 100 works were presented to the Hui'an Yuan (Monastery of Beneficent Peace), located to the east of the modern-day city of Ningbo in Zhejiang Province. Numerous donors from the region provided monetary offerings to pay for the production of the works in the hope of gaining merit, as evidenced by dated dedicatory inscriptions written in gold on many of the paintings by a supervisory monk named Yishao (act. late 12th century). The inscriptions, some of which have been damaged or rubbed away over the years, reveal that Zhou Jichang executed the majority of the works.

Ningbo was a major port for commercial trade as well as for Buddhist pilgrimages and exchanges between Japan and China. During the century following its creation, the set of paintings was transported from the Hui'an Yuan to the temple Jufuku-ji in Japan. (In 1386, the celebrated Japanese monk-artist Mincho [1352–1431] made a copy of the entire set – incorporating the 500 *luohans* into 50 paintings with 10 *luohans* each – which still exists today at Engaku-ji in Kamakura City.) From Jufuku-ji, the original set moved over the years from temple to temple, eventually arriving at Daitoku-ji in Kyoto.

In 1894, Daitoku-ji was in need of renovations and of funds to make the repairs. The Bostonian and Japanophile Ernest Fenollosa (1853–1908) arranged for 44 scrolls of the set to travel to the United States and be exhibited at the Museum of Fine Arts, Boston. While they were there, Daitoku-ji agreed to sell a number of the paintings as a way to raise further monies for its building renovations. Five of the 44 were purchased by the Museum of Fine Arts, five by the museum's trustee and benefactor Dr Denman Waldo Ross, who later donated them to the museum, and two by the Detroit collector Charles L. Freer, whose collection is now in the Freer-Sackler Galleries at the Smithsonian Institution in Washington, DC. The remaining paintings, less six that went missing, are still at Daitoku-ji today. The set is considered the oldest extant example of a work depicting 500 *luohans*.

The number of *luohans* depicted in Chinese Buddhist imagery has increased over the centuries. When the Tang dynasty (618–907) monk-artist Guanxiu (832–912) created his renowned set of portraits, he depicted 16 of these enlightened beings. Later artists often increased the number portrayed to 18, and by the Southern Song period (1127–1279), the cult of the *luohan* had become widespread and some devotees were depicting 500. Moreover, as can be seen in these works, instead of portraits of individual *luohan* almost filling a painting's surface for a contemplative image, artists had begun to locate multiple figures in a larger landscape or narrative context.

This set of paintings represents the largest body of work by such a small number of pre-Ming dynasty (1368–1644) artists, and are the only known works by Zhou Jichang and Lin Tinggui. Their names are not mentioned in any known historical texts or records.

In *Luohans Bestowing Alms on Suffering Human Beings*, five almost corpulent and colourfully clothed *luohans* floating in clouds before a waterfall drop a stream of coins to destitute, starving mortals dressed in patched and tattered clothes on a hillside below. Four of the eight unfortunates scramble to grab the money, dropping their broken baskets and slippers in their desperation. The image portrays both compassion and kindness for the impoverished of the world as well as concern and heed for the 'hungry souls' of those who have died without living family members to care for their spirits. Works depicting underprivileged members of society were a rare occurrence in Chinese painting during the Song period (960–1279), but Zhou has skilfully represented the misery and reality of poverty. To engender greater emotional response, Zhou has injected realistic details into his composition. One of the poor recipients of the *luohans*' generosity seems to be paralysed from the waist down, and moves with the aid of a seat-board clamped on to his hips and stirrup-like grasps in his hands for pushing himself along the ground.

*Luohans in a Bamboo Grove Receiving Offerings* depicts two non-Chinese men making offerings to the *luohans*, who stand and sit on in a rocky landscape surrounded by bamboo. One man kneels down as he presents a gift of a coral tree – one of the seven treasures in Buddhism – to the enlightened beings. On the ground are two elephant tusks, additional precious gifts to be presented. The costumes of these two men, including the fur-rimmed hats with red top ornaments and high boots, distinguish them as foreigners, probably Central Asians, as do their beards and exaggerated facial features. Again, such specific details add a level of realism to the paintings that would have impressed contemporary viewers and worshippers. NB

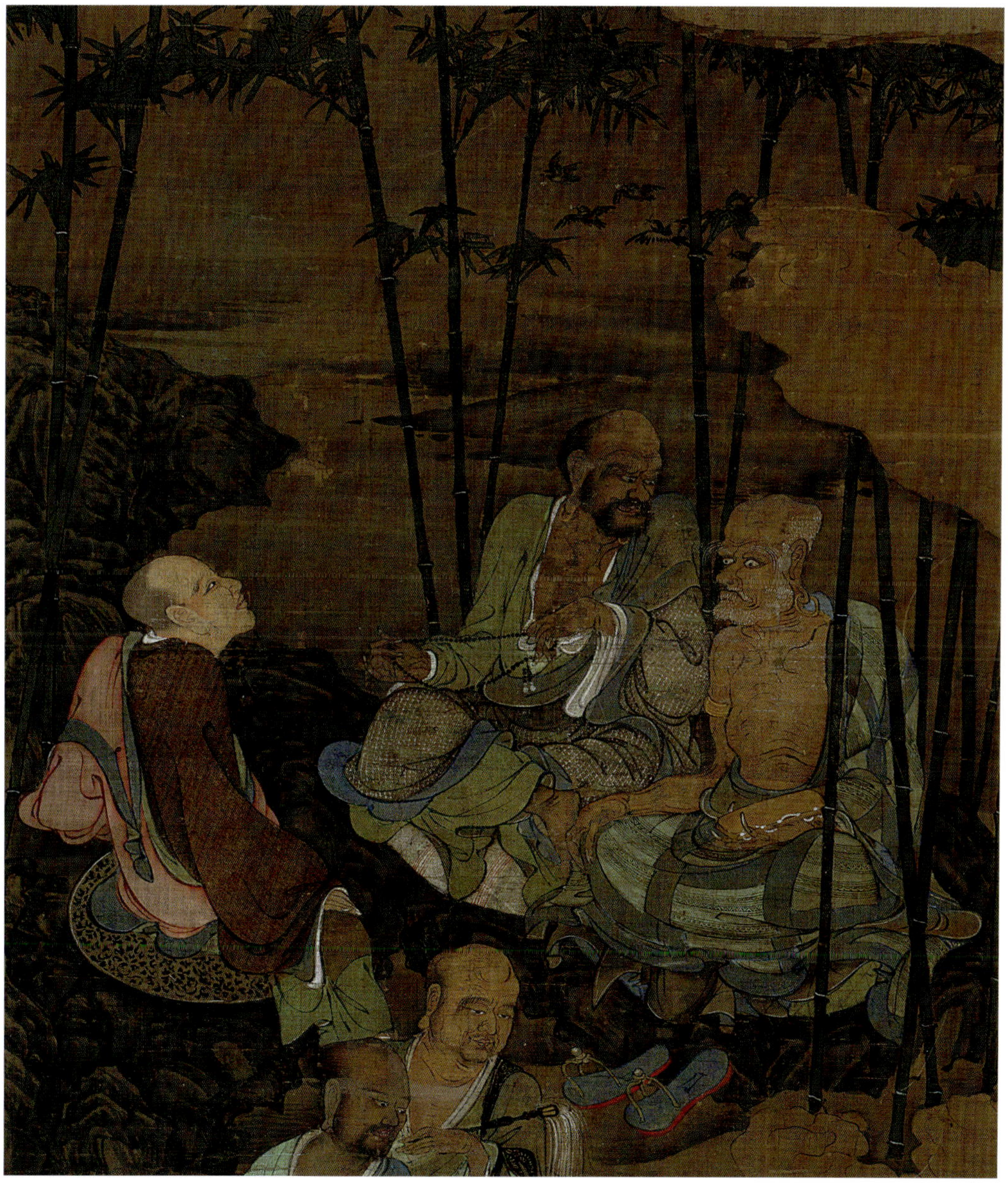

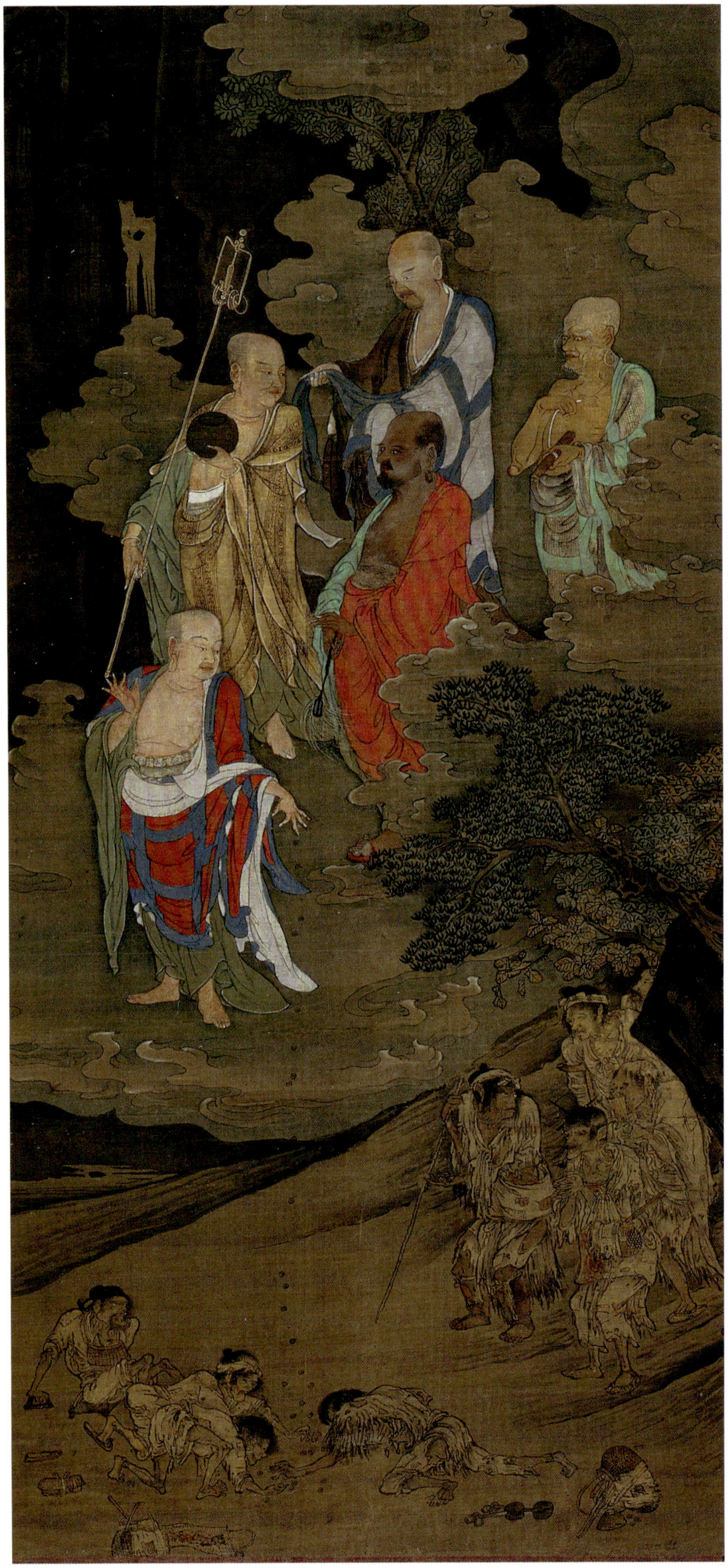

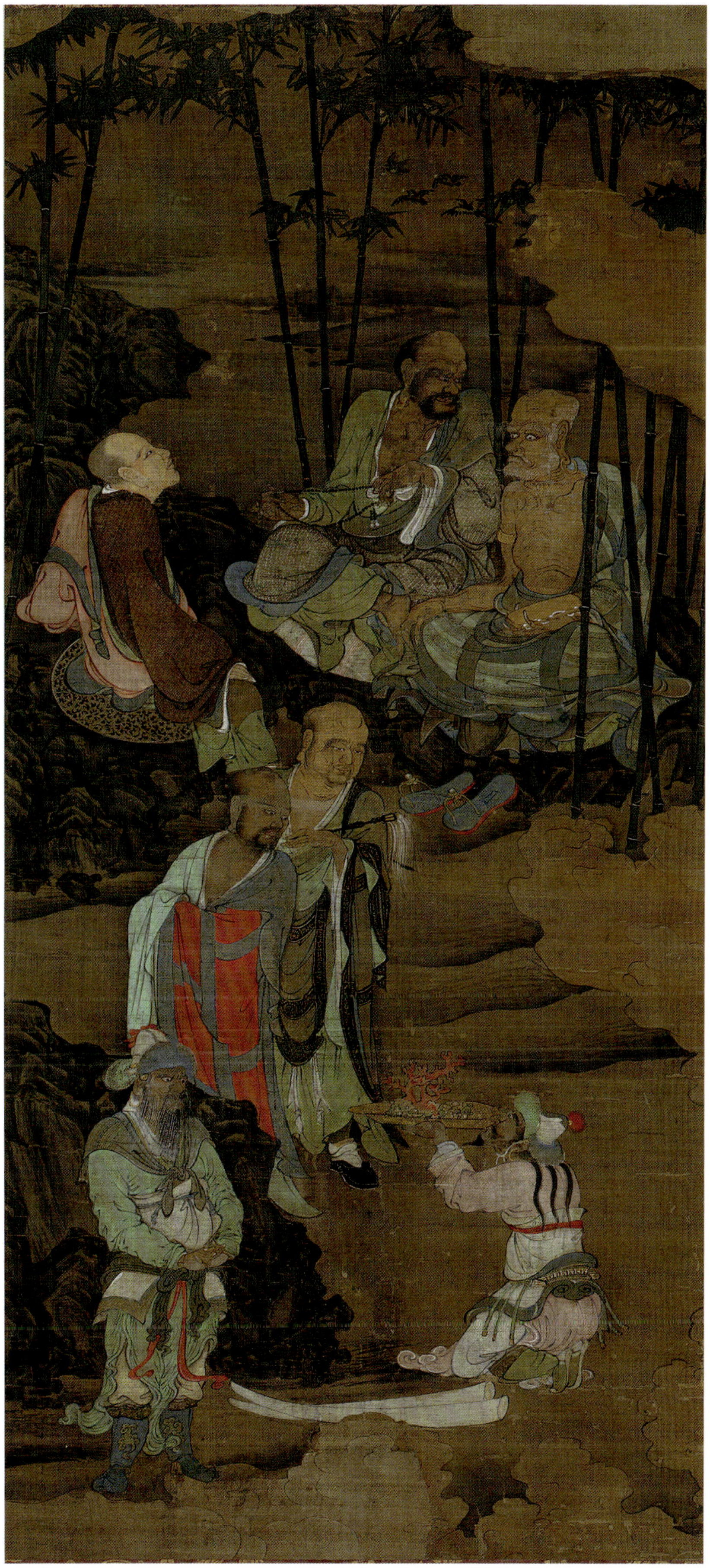

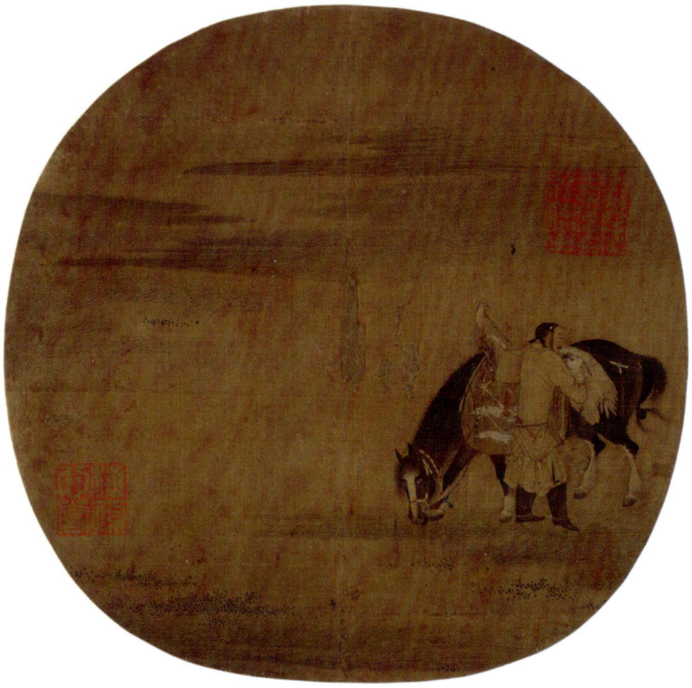

25

UNIDENTIFIED ARTIST;
traditionally attributed to HU GUI
(act. c.907–c.960)

## Qidan (Khitan) Falconer with Horse

宋 傳胡瓌 番馬圖 團扇

late 12th century, round fan mounted as an album leaf, ink, colour and gold on silk, 23.4 × 24.1 cm
Museum of Fine Arts, Boston
Special Chinese and Japanese Fund, 1912 (12.895)

REFERENCE LITERATURE

Sirén 1927; Tomita 1933; Museum of Fine Arts, Boston 1944; Wu 1996a; Yokohama 1996; Boston 1997; *A Compendium of Song Paintings* 2008

PROVENANCE

Wanyan Jingxian (1875–1931)

During the Song dynasty (960–1279), there was a growing fascination among the Chinese with the peoples to their north, an interest motivated by concerns over military threats and inspired by romantic concepts of the nomadic lifestyle and steppe landscape. The horses of the peoples of Central Asia – which at times were presented to Chinese emperors as tribute gifts and at others used to conquer Chinese territory – were favourite subjects in painting. Song connoisseurs also collected works by several artists from the north, among whom the Qidan (Khitan) painter Hu Gui was considered one of the finest. Hu's work sat side by side with the masterpieces in the important collection of the Song emperor Huizong (r. 1101–25). The poet Mei Yaochen (1002–60) once commented on this artist's work: 'So superb was Hu Gui's skill, who could ever fathom it?'.[1] This painting depicting a Qidan hunter with his horse and a falcon to assist in pursuit was most probably not done by Hu Gui; but the fine draughtsmanship and the subject have earned it an attribution to that tenth-century master.

Looking more closely at the painting itself, the one-corner composition quickly reveals it to be a work of the Southern Song dynasty (1127–1279), probably painted several centuries after Hu Gui's lifetime. However, the later date does not diminish the work. Fine brushstrokes delineate the details of the horseman's and horse's actions and accoutrements: a beautiful, textured blanket, decorated with imagery of two birds, to soften the impact of the saddle on the horse's back; gilt-metal hardware linking the leather strips on the bridle and flank straps; an embroidered roundel on the back of the horseman's robe; and the complex knotting of strings on which the horseman's attention is fixed to make sure his captured prey – a large white swan – is well secured for travel. The falcon perched at the front of the saddle also focuses its eyes back in the direction of the horseman's action. Moving to consider a wider view of the painting, the grasses in the foreground offer the viewer a foothold on which to stand within the composition, while the distant flat landscape of the steppes provides a sense of the vastness of the surroundings. The artist has also added a level of poetry with the repeated images of feathered beings – the alert falcon, the flying birds depicted on the saddle blanket, and the large and heavy deceased swan, freshly killed by the handsome hunter.

During the Southern Song, several Chinese artists worked in styles and subjects imitating the Qidan artists. Among them was the early thirteenth-century court painter Chen Juzhong (act. 1201–4), also a painter of horses in landscapes, one of whose works can be seen in the National Palace Museum in Taiwan. A comparison with the Chen Juzhong work begs the question: was Chen also responsible for this painting? NB

1 The commentary on Hu Gui entry is in the *Xuanhe Painting Catalogue*, the record of Emperor Huizong's (r. 1101–25) painting collection.

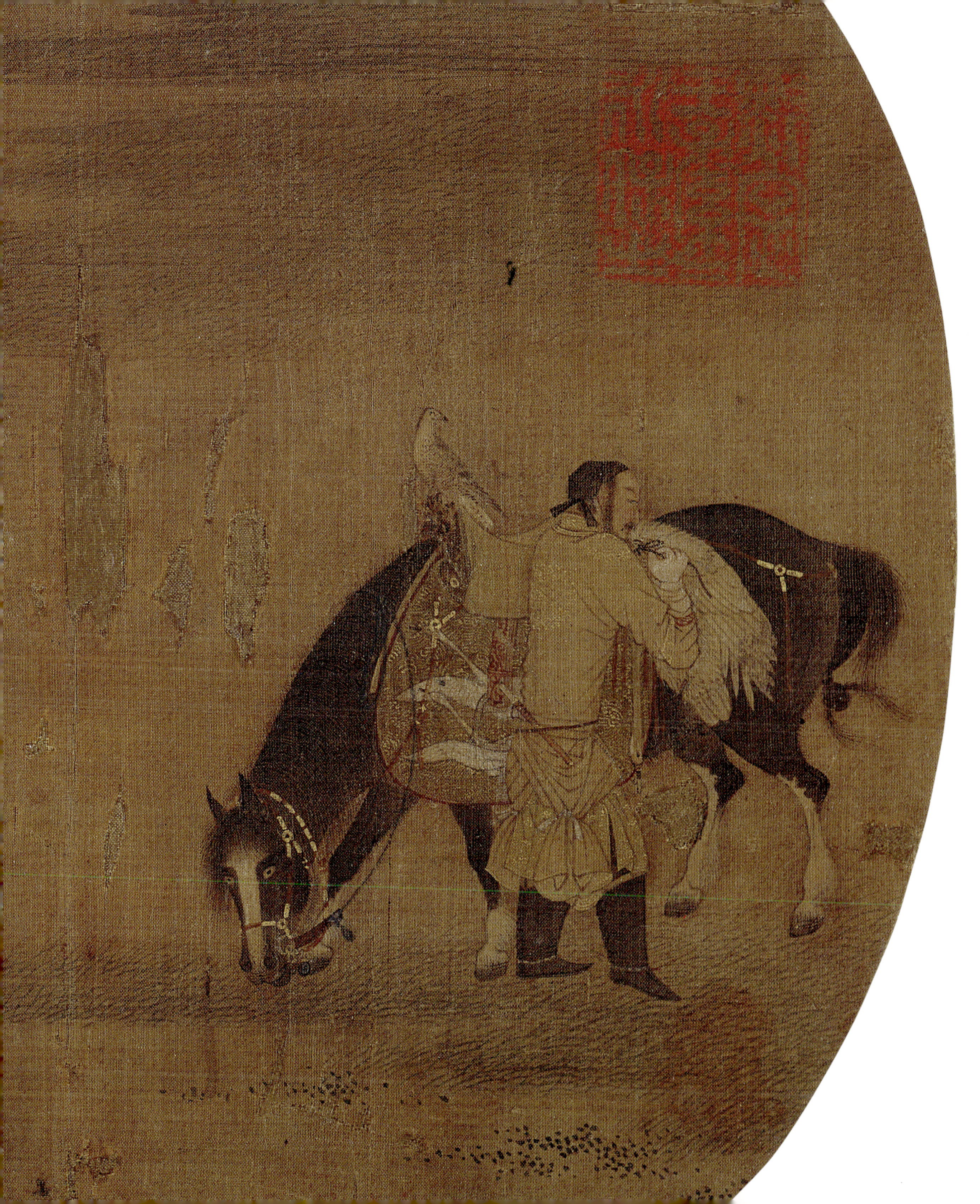

26

UNIDENTIFIED ARTIST

## Travelling Caravan in Snow

宋 口東 雪中行旅圖 軸

mid-12th century, round fan mounted as a hanging scroll, ink and light colour on silk, 23.5 × 25.3 cm
Private collection

REFERENCE LITERATURE

Tomita 1933; Osaka 1980; Fujita 1989; Itakura in Tokyo 2004

Delicate brushwork describes a caravan passing through a mountain canyon in clearing snow. This small, fan-shaped painting combines two themes, capturing both the stillness of mountains after a snowfall and the hurried pace of a journey through those mountains. The result is a work of great lyricism. On the earthen slope under the trees at right is a signature comprising two characters, the second of which is the character for 'east', *dong*. Stylistically, the painting can be described as being based on the landscapes of the Guo Xi school in the Northern Song academy, while at the same time exhibiting the highly detailed and precise depiction of natural form characteristic of the Southern Song academy.

The mountains through which the travellers thread their way are textured with *juanyun* strokes so that they resemble billowing clouds. Pale ink is subtly and harmoniously combined with red ochre on the face of the rocky cliffs, and small dots of black ink are placed here and there. There is a strong emphasis on the snow piled on the high, precipitous ridges and the deep shadows on the cliff walls. The trees are all bare, but are described in modulated brushstrokes that somewhat soften the harsh crab-claw form of the branches (see cat. no. 14). While in general the work preserves the type of rugged mountain scenery of northern China exemplified in the work of Guo Xi (*c*.1000–*c*.1090), the brushwork in the mountain masses and the trees is softer than usually seen in that style.

An example of a work on this theme in the Li-Guo style is *Travelling through Snowy Mountains* (The Palace Museum, Beijing). It utilizes the perspective of 'high distance', and purportedly dates from the Southern Song period (1127–1279). The painting, however, has a hardness of line that relates it to the Li-Guo school of the Yuan period (1271–1368), while the present work displays greater subtlety and delicacy in the texture strokes and the depiction of the trees. Small paintings in circular fan shape were produced in great numbers during the Southern Song, but as exemplified in the landscapes of Ma Yuan (act. late 12th–early 13th century) and Xia Gui (act. act. 1180–1230), the elements were commonly placed in one corner of the composition, with the other side opening up to a view over a river to vast space beyond. For that reason, this painting is noteworthy as an original interpretation of the Guo Xi style in fan format that preceded Ma Yuan and Xia Gui in the early Southern Song.

The forms of the figures and horses are captured in extremely fine line. While in style they follow those seen in Li Gonglin's (*c*.1049–1106) handscroll *Wei Yan's Herding Horses* (The Palace Museum, Beijing), they have been simplified. With the horses' bulging packs and the tradesmen huddled in their heavy coats, roundness informs every element of the painting. Another example of the caravan genre in the exhibition is *Bullock Carts Travelling over Rivers and Mountains* attributed to Zhu Rui (act. 1st half 12th century, or a follower) (cat. no. 22). In that work, the procession is shown in the lower part of the composition, moving on a slight diagonal. *Travelling Caravan in Snow*, on the other hand, utilizes the circular shape of the fan, with the line of men and horses arranged along the face of the mountain in an arc that goes from right to left. It is these figures that provide the focal point and guide the viewer's gaze through the composition. The result is a painting with a strong narrative component.

Also related is a close copy of *Travelling Caravan* made by Kano Tanyū (1602–79) in the early Edo period (1603–1868). It appears in his handscroll of sketch copies, now in a private collection. KM

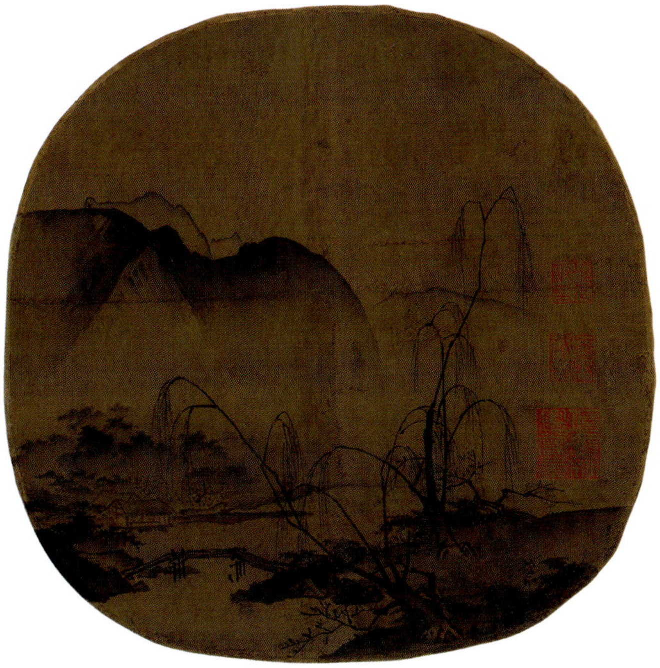

27

MA YUAN
(act. late 12th–early 13th century)

## Bare Willows and Distant Mountains

宋 馬遠 柳岸遠山圖 團扇

late 12th century, round fan mounted as an album leaf, ink and colour on silk, 23.8 × 24.2 cm
Museum of Fine Arts, Boston
Special Chinese and Japanese Fund, 1914 (14.61)

PROVENANCE

Koichi Hayasaki (1874–1956)

REFERENCE LITERATURE

Sirén 1927; Tomita 1933; Ruan (1791) 1854; Wang et al. (1708) 1969; Museum of Fine Arts, Boston 1982; Bian (1682) 1993–8; Museum of Fine Arts, Boston 1992; Wang (1643) 1993–8; Yokohama 1996; Boston 1997; Lee 2001; *A Compendium of Song Paintings* 2008

When the refugees from the Northern Song dynasty (960–1127) capital Bianliang (present Kaifeng) were forced to flee south after the city was taken by the Jurchen conquerors, they established their new capital in the idyllic city of Lin'an (today's Hangzhou), surrounding the island-sprinkled West Lake. The southern landscape, with its low hills, calm waterways and lush greenery, offered a refreshing calm for the displaced populace. In time prosperity came, and with it artworks painted to meet the demands of aspiring patrons and reflecting new visions and outlooks.

Since the fourteenth century, the artist Ma Yuan has been considered one of the 10 great masters of the Southern Song (1127–1279) imperial academy. The descendant of a family of painters who had originally resided in Bianliang and moved south with the court, Ma was well trained in the fine painting traditions. With their subtle washes and delicate brushwork, his paintings evoke the tranquil beauty of the southern scenery. Their intimate formats – often round fans or album leafs – and poetic expression are in sharp contrast to the monumental landscape paintings of the Northern Song. In 1190, Ma Yuan's talent and ability to resonate with the culture of the time were rewarded by his being accepted into the imperial academy.

Ma Yuan and his fellow artist Xia Gui (act. 1180–1230) together developed what became known as the Ma-Xia school of painting, characterized by meditative, lyrical landscapes, often presided over by foggy atmospheres and compositions weighted into one corner of the painting's surface. The style would soon have a deep impact on the aesthetics of Japanese art.

In this work, two large willows, in their winter form bare of leaves, dominate the composition rooted in the painting's bottom right-hand corner. To the right of the trees, a small figure with a pole over his shoulder can be seen heading towards a modest wooden bridge, which in turn draws the viewer's eye into the distance, to a waterside, thatched house and mountains in the mist beyond. Hui-shu Lee surmises that the scene is a specific location on the West Lake. Its quiet mood is characteristic of the sophisticated and poetically attuned culture of the Southern Song.

The painting has suffered some damage over the years, and some details have been lost. A now effaced spot next to the small figure may once have displayed an official riding a horse, the small figure therefore being a servant following his master. Also barely visible because of damage is the second character of Ma Yuan's signature. NB

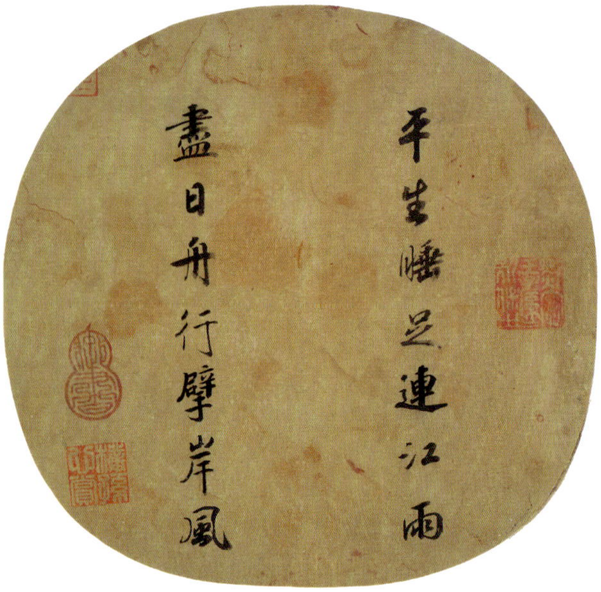


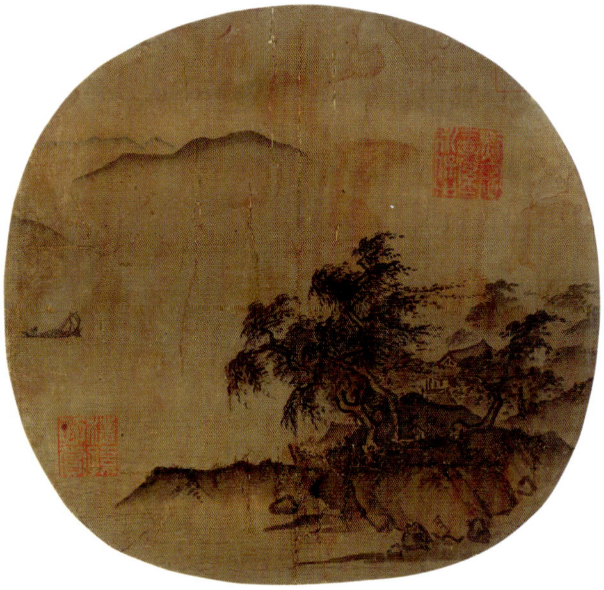

28, 29

XIA GUI (act. 1180–1230)

## Sailboat in Rainstorm

宋 夏珪 雨江舟行圖 團扇

c.1189–94, round fan mounted as an album leaf, ink and light colour on silk, 23.9 × 25.1 cm
Museum of Fine Arts, Boston
Special Chinese and Japanese Fund, 1912 (12.891)

PROVENANCE

Okakura Kakuzo (1862–1913)

EMPEROR XIAOZONG (1127–94; r. 1163–89)

## Calligraphy of Poem by Su Shi in Semi-cursive and Regular Scripts

宋 孝宗 書蘇軾七言聯 團扇

c.1189–94, round fan mounted as an album leaf, ink on silk, 23.9 × 25.1 cm
Museum of Fine Arts, Boston
Special Chinese and Japanese Fund, 1912 (12.892)

PROVENANCE

Okakura Kakuzo (1862–1913)

REFERENCE LITERATURE

Boston 1973; Fairbrother 1991; Wu 1996a; Yokohama 1996; Boston 1997; Lee 2001

These two round fans have most likely been together since at least the fifteenth century – as evidenced by the early Ming dynasty (1368–1644) collectors' seals of the Mu family on both works – and possibly even longer. One fan is a landscape by the renowned imperial academy artist of the mid-Southern Song dynasty (1127–1279), Xia Gui. The other features calligraphy – two lines of poetry describing a water scene inscribed by Emperor Xiaozong, the eleventh emperor of the Song dynasty (960–1279) and the second emperor of the Southern Song.

The inscribed poem was composed by the great Northern Song personage Su Shi (1037–1101). These fans, then, in the great Chinese literati tradition, bring together works by three prominent and influential men: Xia Gui, one of the most eminent artists of the Southern Song dynasty who, together with his contemporary Ma Yuan (act. late 12th–early 13th century), established the one-corner style of painting composition; Emperor Xiaozong, under whom prosperity and stability returned to the land controlled by the Song court, and the new capital city, Hangzhou (then called Lin'an), blossomed into a sophisticated cultural centre; and Su Shi – poet, writer, painter, calligrapher, art critic, gastronome and statesman – who was one of the great luminaries of Chinese history, influencing the direction of Chinese culture and intellectual thinking for generations.

The text and image in these works seem to complement one another. In the painting, Xia Gui has depicted the rocky bank of a waterway in the bottom right-hand foreground; a large leafy tree upon the rocks, its branches tossed by the wind; a temple or house in the hills beyond; soft mountains emerging from a haze in the distance; and a lone boat on the water far from shore. Su Shi's poem, selected and brushed by the Emperor, appears to be a poet's contemplation of the scene:

> The ceaseless river rain always lulls me
> to sleep,
> Winds beat the cliffs all day to move my
> boat along.

Some scholars have speculated that the Emperor may indeed have written the calligraphy in response to seeing the painting. However, this scenario would imply that Xia Gui in fact entered the academy earlier than has been thought.[1] During their eight centuries of history and ownership, the fans were, in the early nineteenth century, in the collection of the great connoisseur Ruan Yuan (1764–1849). Ruan Yuan believed that the artist of the calligraphy was Emperor Gaozong (r. 1127–62), who preceded Xiaozong as ruler of the Southern Song. It was Tomita Kojiro (1890–1976), formerly head of the Asiatic Department at the Museum of Fine Arts, Boston, whose investigations determined that the work was actually done by Gaozong's successor.[2] NB

1 Boston 1997, p. 178
2 Ibid.

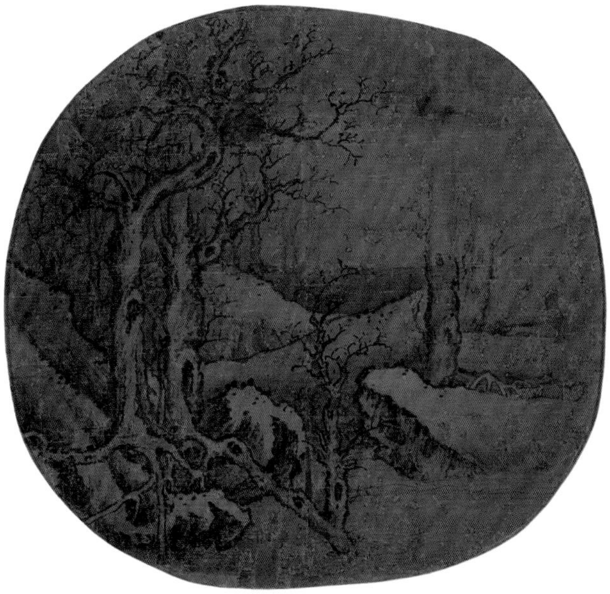

30

UNIDENTIFIED ARTIST; traditionally attributed to FAN KUAN (c.990–1030)

## Wintry Forest

宋 傳范寬 寒林圖 團扇

mid-12th century, round fan mounted as an album leaf, ink and colour on silk, 23.8 × 24.9 cm
Museum of Fine Arts, Boston
Special Chinese and Japanese Fund, 1914 (14.53)

PROVENANCE

Koichi Hayasaki (1874–1956)

REFERENCE LITERATURE

New York 1972; Wu 1996a; Yokohama 1996; Boston 1997

The wintry forest was a common theme in Chinese landscape painting during the tenth and eleventh centuries. The master landscape artists of that era – Li Cheng (919–67) (cat. no. 14), Fan Kuan and Guo Xi (c.1000–c.1090) – all portrayed in monumental scale the harsh effects of cold and snow on the natural world. Trees that in spring and summer flaunted lush green foliage appeared stalwart with naked branches in the chill air and blanketed with frigid snow. These wintry views would have been inspired by the similar poetic imagery created by writers of earlier times.

The Tang (618–907) poet Wang Wei (685–759) wrote 'Thoughts on a Winter Night', here in a translation by G.W. Robinson:

> The winter dark is cold and also long.
> The night clock strikes within the palace.
> Grass is white, clouded over with frost
> Trees are decayed, lit up by the clear moon.

The image of the ancient tree in the winter snow not only expressed a feeling of melancholy, but also came to represent the Confucian concept of the virtuous scholar or official capable of remaining upright and righteous in any challenging situation. As such, artists and poets continued to employ the theme for centuries. The stark ink portrayals of trees by waterways by the Yuan artist Ni Zan (1306–74) (cat. no. 51), for instance, were often given titles referring to the trees as 'gentlemen'.

Even within the small format of this fan, the artist was able to capture the penetrating chill of winter settling on the trees in the forest. Not only do the bare branches extend into the cold air, but the roots are likewise exposed to the extreme temperature. The composition of the fan, with the focused trees in the left foreground, the waterway flowing back into the woods and the hazy, cold hills in the background, is elegantly tight. Moreover, the same distinct brushstrokes that evoke the struggle of winter also express the calligraphic interest and skill of the artist. The art historian Max Loehr was deeply moved by the sensitivity expressed by this unknown artist's brushstrokes: 'If Song painting were to vanish and this small work alone to remain, it would still testify to the greatness and profound insight in the art of that period.'[1] NB

1 Quoted in Barnhart 1972, p. 3

31

EMPEROR LIZONG
(1205–64; r. 1225–64)

## Poem by Huangfu Ran in Regular Script

宋 理宗 書皇甫冉七絕 團扇

2nd quarter 13th century, round fan mounted as an album leaf, ink on silk, 24 × 25.6 cm
Museum of Fine Arts, Boston
Special Chinese and Japanese Fund, 1912 (12.890)

PROVENANCE

Wanyan Jingxian (1875–1931)

REFERENCE LITERATURE

Sirén 1927 and 1933; Tomita 1933; Museum of Fine Arts, Boston 1944; Wu 1996a; Yokohama 1996; Boston 1997; New York 2001; *A Compendium of Song Paintings* 2008

32

UNIDENTIFIED ARTIST;
traditionally attributed to FAN KUAN
(act. c.990–1030)

## Temple among Snowy Hills

宋 傳范寬 雪山蕭寺圖 團扇

early 13th century, round fan mounted as an album leaf, ink and light colour on silk, 24.7 × 25.5 cm
Museum of Fine Arts, Boston
Chinese and Japanese Special Fund, 1912 (12.889)

PROVENANCE

Wanyan Jingxian (1875–1931)

An oft-repeated legend tells of the renowned calligrapher Wang Xizhi (303–65) coming upon an elderly and poverty-stricken woman selling fans in the street. Grabbing the fans from her, he graced each one with his respected calligraphy. The woman was understandably angered until she realized that the artist's words had vastly increased the value and desirability of her fans. The story sheds light not only on the custom of decorating fans, but also on using fan surfaces for artwork of the highest order.

Connoisseurs and collectors have prized the images and calligraphy on the present two fans for centuries. Since at least the early Qing dynasty (1644–1911), they have been remounted together on album leaves. A review of the contents displayed on each fan suggests that a collector consciously paired the two.

On one fan, large wintry trees on a cliff by the bank of a waterway weight the right side of the foreground composition. Beyond is a high peak and, moving into the distance, a range of snow-covered mountains. A temple nestles against the peak. The careful viewer notices a boat pulled up along the shore, and a small human figure apparently struggling as he walks through the stormy environment with an umbrella. The artist Fan Kuan lived during the Northern Song period (960–1127), and painted monumental landscapes depicting the scenery

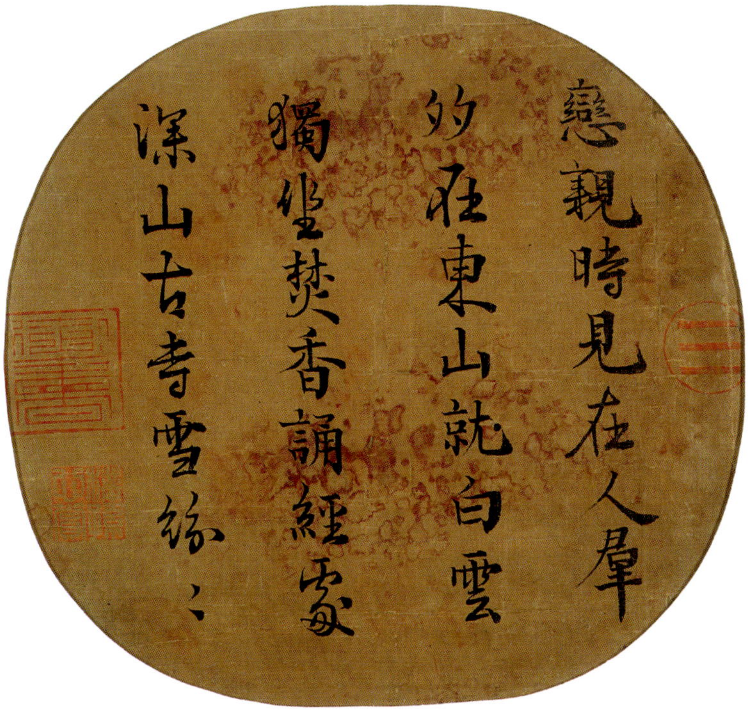

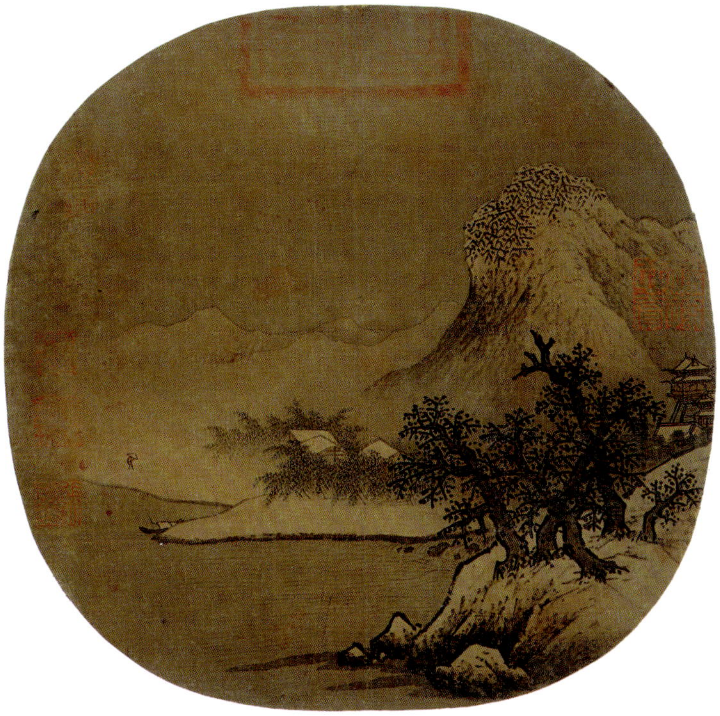

of northern China. A follower of the artist Li Cheng (919–67) (cat. no. 14), he later professed that nature was his teacher, and spent many years in the Qiantang mountains in Shanxi Province. Though the group of trees on the right side of the fan, with their thick trunks and sharp brushstrokes, as well as the depiction of the vegetation on the snow-covered summit, are reminiscent of Fan Kuan's manner of delineating trees, the single-corner composition immediately establishes the work as a product of the Southern Song period (1127–1279). The painting also reveals a tendency towards abstraction that contrasts with the Northern Song artists' interest in naturalism. The early misattribution to Fan Kuan has, however, never distracted connoisseurs from appreciating the painting, nor did it deter one collector from matching the work with calligraphy from an emperor's hand.

Lizong, the 14th emperor of the Song dynasty (960–1279) and the fifth emperor of the Southern Song based in Lin'an (present Hangzhou), reigned from 1225 to 1264, probably about the same time as the landscape fan was being painted. A descendant of the founder of the Song, Zhao Yun, as he was originally known, was not in direct line to inherit the throne, but was placed there as part of a larger political strategy orchestrated by the powerful minister Shi Miyuan (1164–1233). With little interest in politics, Lizong left much of the business of ruling to his ministers, including Shi, and pursued his own pleasures ranging from the arts and religion to prostitutes. His lack of attention to governmental affairs probably contributed to the weakening of the Southern Song dynasty and its eventual demise in 1279, when the country fell to the Mongols.

There are numerous extant examples of Lizong's elegant calligraphy, including four fans in the Metropolitan Museum of Art in New York.[1] The calligraphy on this fan is the Emperor's rendition of a poem by the Tang dynasty (618–907) poet Huangfu Ran (c.714–67) entitled 'Sent to Monk Zhen's Dwelling at the Temple of Non-Attachment', translated by Wu Tung as:

> Still I yearn to see my parents in every crowd.
> Here, white clouds always touch the eastern mountains.
> Sitting alone, I burn incense and recite sutras.
> The mountain is deep; the temple, ancient;
> and snow, everywhere.[2]

The poem describes the calm life of the monk high in the snowy mountains, who still misses his family. Hui-shu Lee has suggested that the fan may have been a gift for one of the Chan monks befriended by the spiritually inclined Lizong.[3] Others have noted that the poem may simply have resonated with the Emperor, taken from his family to the court at a young age.[4] Most striking is the harmony between the poem and the painting. The desolate and snowy scene of the temple in the mountains could easily have been an illustration for the poem, with its forlorn tone and endless snow.

The calligraphy on the fan was previously attributed by scholars reading the imperial seals to Emperor Ningzong (r. 1195–1224). However, after later scholars compared the calligraphy and seals with those of Ningzong's heir, Lizong, they concluded that the brushstrokes were those of the later emperor. NB

1 Fong 1992, p. 242
2 Boston 1997, p. 182
3 New York 2001, p. 100
4 Ibid.

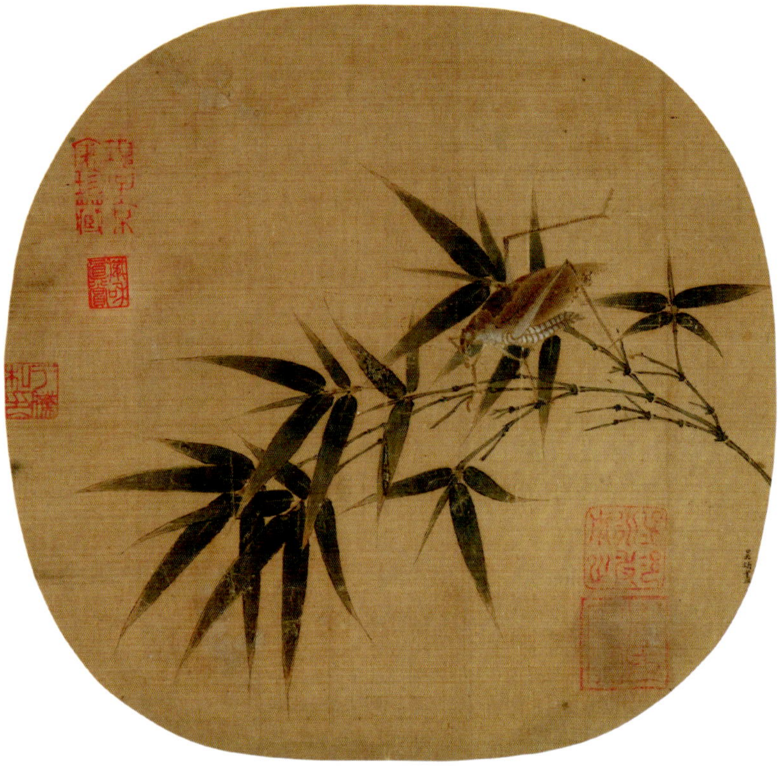

33

Possibly WU BING
(act. late 12th–early 13th century)

## Bamboo Twig with Grasshopper

宋 吳炳 竹蜢圖 團扇

late 12th–13th century, fan mounted as an album leaf, ink and light colour on silk, 23.8 × 24.8 cm
Museum of Far Eastern Antiquities, Stockholm (OM–1989–0063)

PROVENANCE

Donation of The Ernest Erickson Foundation

REFERENCE LITERATURE

Wirgin 1989, no. 63

The album leaf depicts a grasshopper on a twig of bamboo. The twig curves across the empty background – a favourite composition of artists in the Song (960–1279) painting academy. The brushwork is light; the contours of the bamboo are outlined in ink and filled in with different shades of green. The outline of the grasshopper is so lightly drawn that the insect almost seems painted in the *mogu* ('boneless') manner, in other words without outlines, its details very finely rendered despite the small format.

'Grass and insects' (*caochong*) was a minor genre in China, enjoying its popularity in part due to the Daoist classic *Zhuangzi*, traditionally ascribed to the philosopher Zhuang Zhou (c.369–286 BCE), where the world of insects is sometimes seen as mirroring that of man. In the *Xuanhe Painting Catalogue*, compiled at the imperial court during the early twelfth century, the genre of grass and insects is classified as a sub-genre under paintings of 'vegetables and fruit' (*shuguo*) at the very end of the catalogue. Despite its seemingly low status as a painting genre during the Song period, the artists excelled in these minute renderings of nature.

This album leaf is signed with the name Wu Bing – a *daizhao* ('first secretary in waiting') in the imperial painting academy during the early Shaoxi era (1190–4) of the Southern Song (1127–1279). He was favoured by Empress Li, the consort of Emperor Guangzong, and received the Golden Belt – the highest honour in the Song painting academy.

Wu Bing was a native of Piling (present Changzhou, Jiangsu Province). The painters of the so-called Piling school (also called Changzhou school or Wujin school) were especially famous for their renderings of plants and insects. This genre had been a tradition in the Piling region going back to the monk Juning, who was active in the Northern Song dynasty (960–1127).

The painting fits well with the style of the regional school of Piling, but whether it is an actual work by Wu Bing's hand is an open question. There are several paintings in the 'bird-and-flower' genre attributed to Wu Bing in existence today, but they do not form a consistent oeuvre. A few paintings belong to the genre of 'grass and insects', but are clearly not by the same hand; there are differences both in the brushwork and in the writing of the signature. As forged signatures were often added to genuine, unsigned Song paintings, today it is impossible to judge who was actually the master of this fan. MS

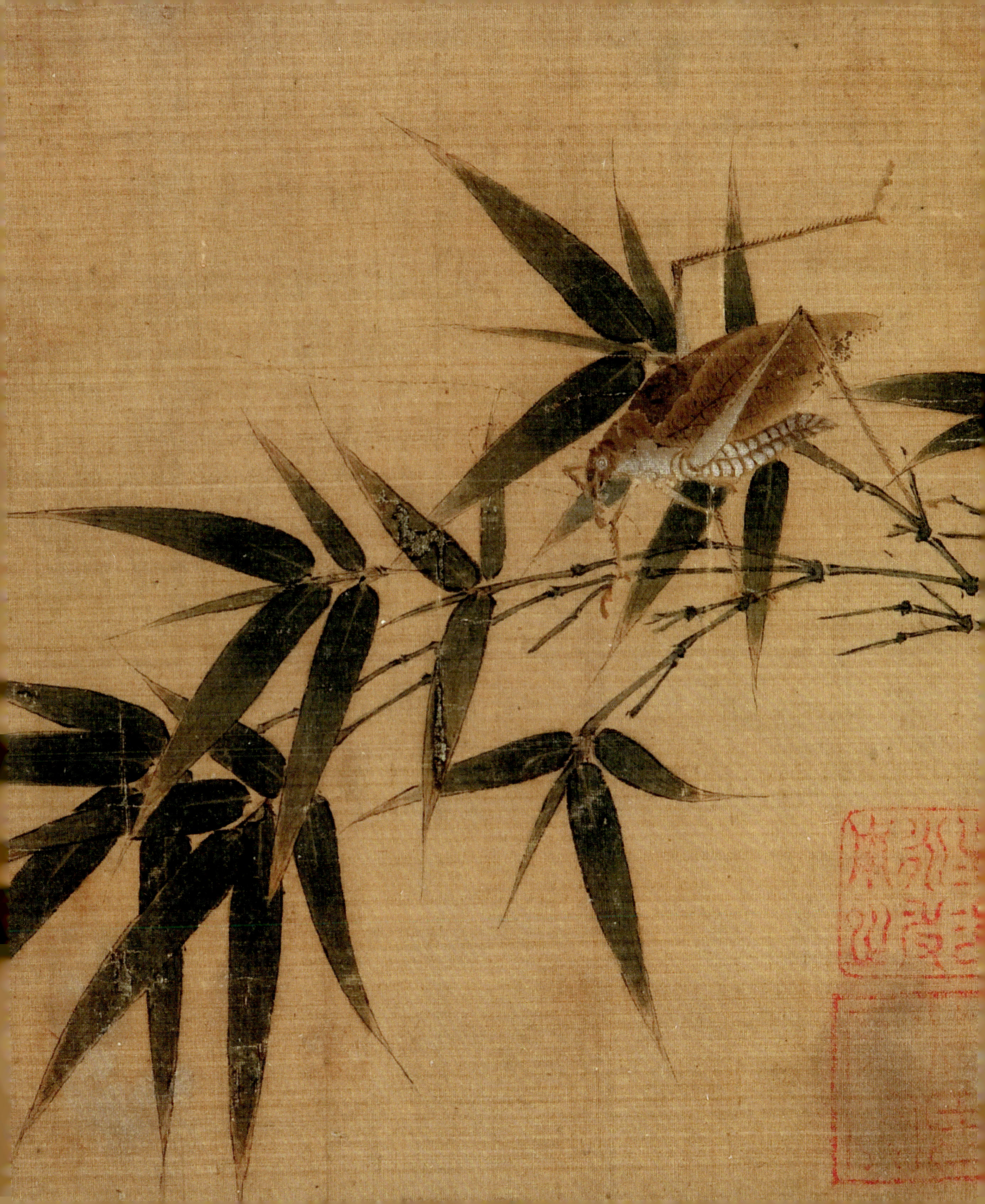

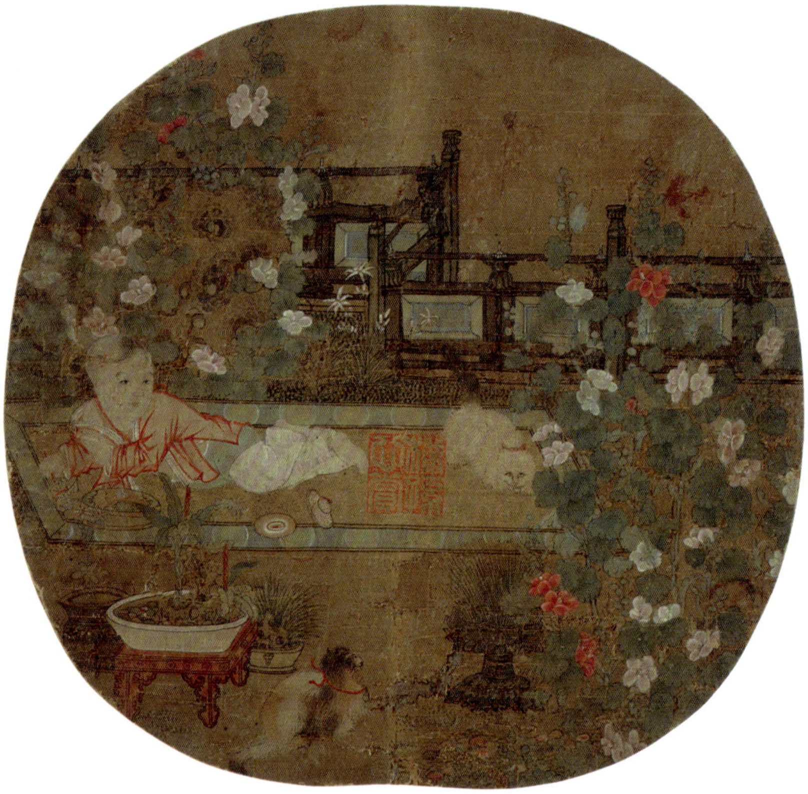

34

UNIDENTIFIED ARTIST; traditionally attributed to ZHOU WENJU (act. 961–75)

## Child with His Pets in a Flower Garden

宋 傳周文矩 貍奴嬰戲圖 團扇

13th century, round fan mounted as an album leaf, ink and colour on silk, 24.5 × 25.7 cm
Museum of Fine Arts, Boston
Special Chinese and Japanese Fund, 1912 (12.897)

PROVENANCE

Wanyan Jingxian (1875–1931)

REFERENCE LITERATURE

*Bulletin of the Museum of Fine Arts, Boston* 1912; *Kokka* 1912; Bell 1917; Sirén 1927; Tomita 1933; Museum of Fine Arts, Boston 1944; Tominaga 1974; Wu 1996a; Yokohama 1996; Boston 1997; *A Compendium of Song Paintings* 2008

The establishment of the capital in Lin'an (present Hangzhou) during the Southern Song period (1127–1279) led to new prosperity in the region, and the art of the time reflected the resulting new lifestyles. In this fan painting, a child plays on a mat in the luxurious surroundings of a well-appointed garden. Sprinkled around the boy are a few toys, including a pair of cymbals. A white cat rests contentedly on the mat beside him, while another multicoloured feline sits on the ground, ready for play. Both animals have red strings around their necks. Behind the child is a finely carved stone balustrade, indicating a pond or view beyond. Lilies grow out of the inlaid pebbled ground behind the mat. Between the child and the balustrade is a large ornamental garden rock – of the type that the early Song (960–1279) emperor Huizong (r. 1101–25) collected for his imperial garden in Kaifeng a century earlier – and a flowering hollyhock bush. In front of the boy are miniature landscapes (*penjing*; J. *bonsai*) and potted plants. One landscape, ina tray on a small, elegantly ornamented, red lacquered table, features a handsome rock and greenery planted in pebbles, while a pot on the ground holds grasses surrounding a rock. Another stem grows in an ancient – or reproduction – bronze vessel. On the right of the composition, ornamental grasses fill a raised stone pedestal-style container elaborately carved to echo the form of a lotus flower. The painting is a scene of summer leisure and plenitude. While the boy is outdoors and among natural elements, the entire scene – unlike a painting depicting a mountain range or waterways – reflects constructions and interventions formed by human hands, and affordable only to the urban well-to-do.

Paintings of children – happy, often chubby and well-indulged children – grew fashionable in the Southern Song dynasty. The theme, which reflects and expresses prosperity – or the wish for prosperity – became a common motif in Chinese visual imagery. Fine paintings, popular woodblock prints and even lithographed mass-produced posters of the late twentieth century all continued such portrayals. Zhou Wenju, a court artist of the Southern Tang (937–75) painting academy, to whom this work was once attributed, was known for his figure painting. The painter of this work, however, was more probably a disciple of the later artist Su Hanchen (act. mid-12th century), who was renowned for his depictions of children. The work's last private owner, Wanyan Jingxian, has left his seal at the centre of the picture. NB

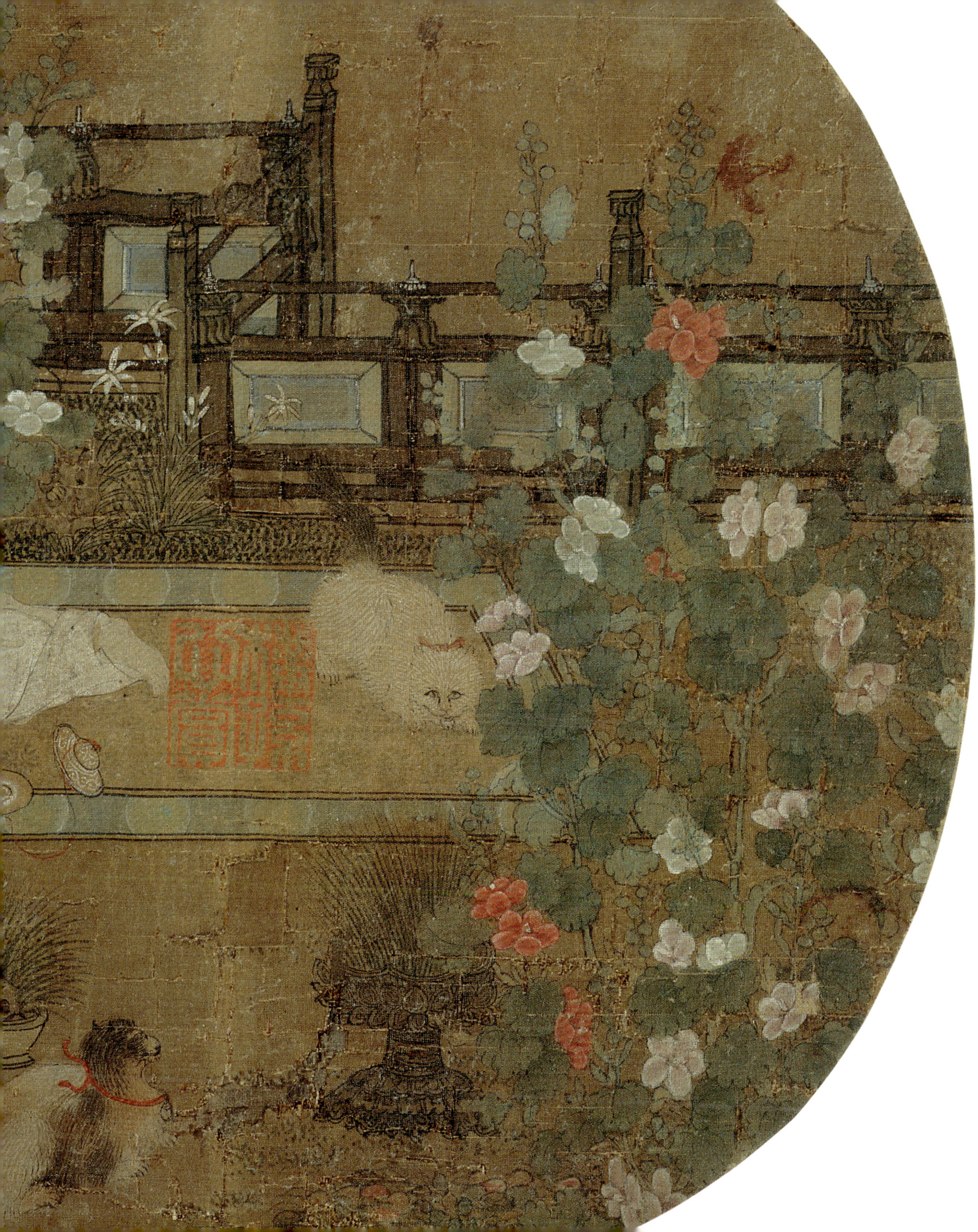

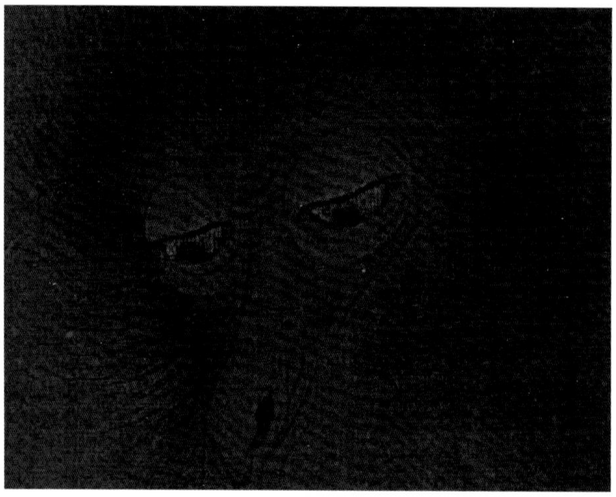

35

UNIDENTIFIED ARTIST;
traditionally attributed to MAO SONG
(act. 2nd quarter 12th century)

## Monkey

宋 傳毛松 猿圖 軸

2nd quarter 12th century, hanging scroll,
ink, colour and gold on silk, 47.0 x 36.5 cm
Tokyo National Museum (TA-297)

REFERENCE LITERATURE

*Kokka* 1918; Masaki 1933; Dōtani 1951; Nakamura in Tokyo 1962; Toda 1967; Tokagawa 1984; Toda 1988; Hata 1997; Ebine 2000; Yamashita 2000

This work is not simply a realistic depiction but a true portrait, a profound portrayal of an animal that has achieved the status of a masterpiece. The monkey appears as if descending into deep sadness, or perhaps deep thought. Only the animal itself is depicted, and one is left to imagine the narrative behind the image: is this a mother who has lost her child? A monkey separated from its family? The painting evokes a variety of emotions in the viewer.

What makes such a response possible is the high quality of the depiction. For the monkey's body, a light brownish-red undercoat was first laid down, and then the fur painted on strand by strand. The type of brushstroke differs depending on what area is being described: short, fine lines for the torso; thicker, softer strokes for the area of the elbow, and longer, sparser strokes for the top of the head. Vitality is expressed in every line, resulting in a portrayal that is full of life.

A close observation of the painting reveals that gold paint is mixed with ink in rendering the fur. This expression of colour through exquisite touches of gold, done without any loss to the naturalistic quality, is characteristic of Song period (960–1279) painting. Gold was also employed in the rendering of the monkey's eyes. Applied to the back of the silk, it shines through the material to give the eyes a brightness that enhances the sense of life. Perhaps because gold leaf was to be used on the back of the painting, the silk chosen has a rather loose weave. There is a vertical fold running through the material, which raises the possibility that the piece of silk was trimmed down and was once larger.

Accompanying the painting is a letter by Takeda Shingen (1521–73), a Sengoku period (15th–17th century) daimyo from Kai Province, which states that on the 19th day of the 7th month in 1570, he presented the work to Prince Kakujo (1521–1579) of the Manshu-in in Kyoto. The painting was handed down in that temple until it entered the collection of the Tokyo National Museum. Prince Kakujo was the third son of Emperor Go-Nara (r. 1526–57), and in 1570, he was installed as the head priest of the temple Enryaku-ji on Mount Hiei. Enryaku-ji is paired with the Shinto shrine Hiyoshi Taisha, which is associated with the monkey, and thus the painting could well have been presented to Kakujo as a congratulatory gift. The following year, 1571, Mount Hiei was set ablaze by the daimyo Oda Nobunaga (1534–82), and Kakujo fled, receiving protection from Shingen. Through Kakujo's intercession, Shingen gained the priestly rank of *Gon no sojo*, and until his death in Kai, the two enjoyed a very deep friendship.

The attribution to Mao Song was made by the painter Kano Tanyū (1602–74) in another letter in the work's storage box. Mao Song was an early Southern Song period (1127–1279) artist from Kunshan (present Jiangsu Province). He was said to excel at bird-and-flower painting, and like his father Mao Yi, also specialized in paintings of animals. In the fifteenth-century *Catalogue of the Shogunal Collection with Instructions for Display* (Kundaikan sōchōki) is the statement 'Mao Song: birds, flowers, monkeys, deer and scenery of the four seasons in colour'. Tanyū probably based the attribution primarily on knowledge of such appraisals by Japanese experts.

There is a story concerning this painting and the Shōwa emperor (r. 1926–89), who had an extensive knowledge of zoology. When he was crown prince, he was given a lecture on Chinese painting, and on viewing this work, exclaimed: 'That is a Japanese monkey!' It is true that Chinese paintings most often depict gibbons, which in Japan are known as 'Muxi monkeys' to distinguish them from the native macaque. If this work does indeed portray a Japanese monkey that does not inhabit China, it is possible that such a monkey was taken to China as an exotic animal, became the subject of a painting, and then went back to Japan in pictorial form. A deeper understanding of this issue, however, must await future research. TM

36

UNIDENTIFIED ARTIST;
traditionally attributed to ZHANG SIGONG
(act. late 12th century–early 13th century)

## The Planet Deity Shuixing (Mercury) Attended by a Monkey

宋 傳張思恭 猴侍水星神圖 軸

early 13th century, hanging scroll mounted as a panel, ink, colour and gold on silk, 121.4 × 55.9 cm
Museum of Fine Arts, Boston
Gift of William Sturgis Bigelow, 1991 (11.6121)

PROVENANCE

William Sturgis Bigelow (1850–1926)

REFERENCE LITERATURE

Museum of Fine Arts, Boston, 1944; Wu 1996a; Yokohama 1996; Boston 1997; *A Compendium of Song Paintings* 2008

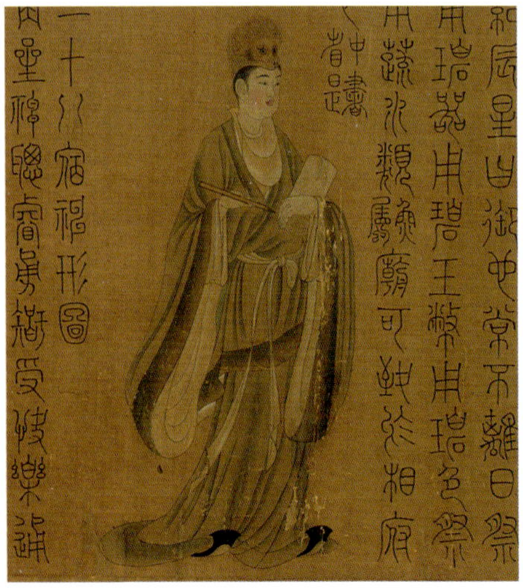

FIG. 60
Shuixing (Chenxing) from *The Five Planets and Twenty-eight Constellations* (detail of cat. no. 13)

A full female figure, elegantly robed and with a bejewelled crown, sits on a platform, a brush in her right hand and a sheet of paper in her left hand resting on her knee, as if about to begin writing. First, however, she glances down to her right, where a monkey is holding up an ink stone, offering her ink.

This impressive painting came to Boston from Japan in the late nineteenth century, and early cataloguers at the museum – influenced by the figure's posture and costume – believed the work to be a thirteenth-century image of a bodhisattva in the style of the artist Zhang Sigong. Later research and analysis, considering the accoutrements of the brush, paper, ink stone and monkey, led scholars instead to identify the work as a portrayal of one of the Five Planets or stellar deities, the Deity of Mercury, known first as Shuixing and later as Chenxing. These stellar deities were part of the Daoist pantheon. In the Tang dynasty (618–907), Mercury became associated with the Buddha of Blazing Light (Tejaprabha Buddha) in Esoteric Buddhism.[1] It was at the same time that the Tang court redesignated this deity as Chenxing. Stephen Little argues that the belief in these stellar deities may well have originated in ancient Rome and then spread to China with Buddhism.[2] Earlier paintings depicting Shuixing are recorded in Chinese sources. There was, for instance, one by the Liang period (502–57) artist Zhang Sengyou (act. 490–540) and another by the Tang artist He Changshou (act. mid-7th century). A lengthy scroll now in the Osaka City Museum of Fine Arts entitled *The Five Planets and Twenty-eight Constellations* (cat. no. 13, fig. 60) includes a standing female figure labelled as Chenxing and grasping a brush and paper.[3] Her headdress is in the form of a monkey. The inscription notes that she is in charge of writing, law and morality. These responsibilities thereby explain the presence of the brush and paper that were perhaps for recording the deeds of mortals.

The name of the artist Zhang Sigong, who was once associated with the present painting, is only found in Japanese historical records, and not in records from China. The Japanese records note that he excelled at figure painting and Buddhist images, and that he was a professional artist based in the Ningbo area. A large number of paintings originally attributed to Zhang Sigong have more recently been identified as Korean works, and Yang Siliang has suggested that Zhang Sigong himself may have been a Korean who worked in the style of the Ningbo professional artists.[4] The echoes between the Korean works of the Koryo period (918–1392) and Chinese Song dynasty (960–1279) Buddhist paintings are reminders of the full commercial and religious contacts between China and Korea at the time and the resultant mutual artistic influences.

Despite the early misattribution and the absence of any other artist's name, the sensitivity, flourishes and finely articulated brushstrokes in this painting work together to manifest the qualities expressed by the great religious paintings of the thirteenth century. NB

1 Boston 1997, p. 185
2 Little 2000, p. 132
3 Ibid. p. 132
4 Catalogue entry in Weidner 1994, pp. 229–30

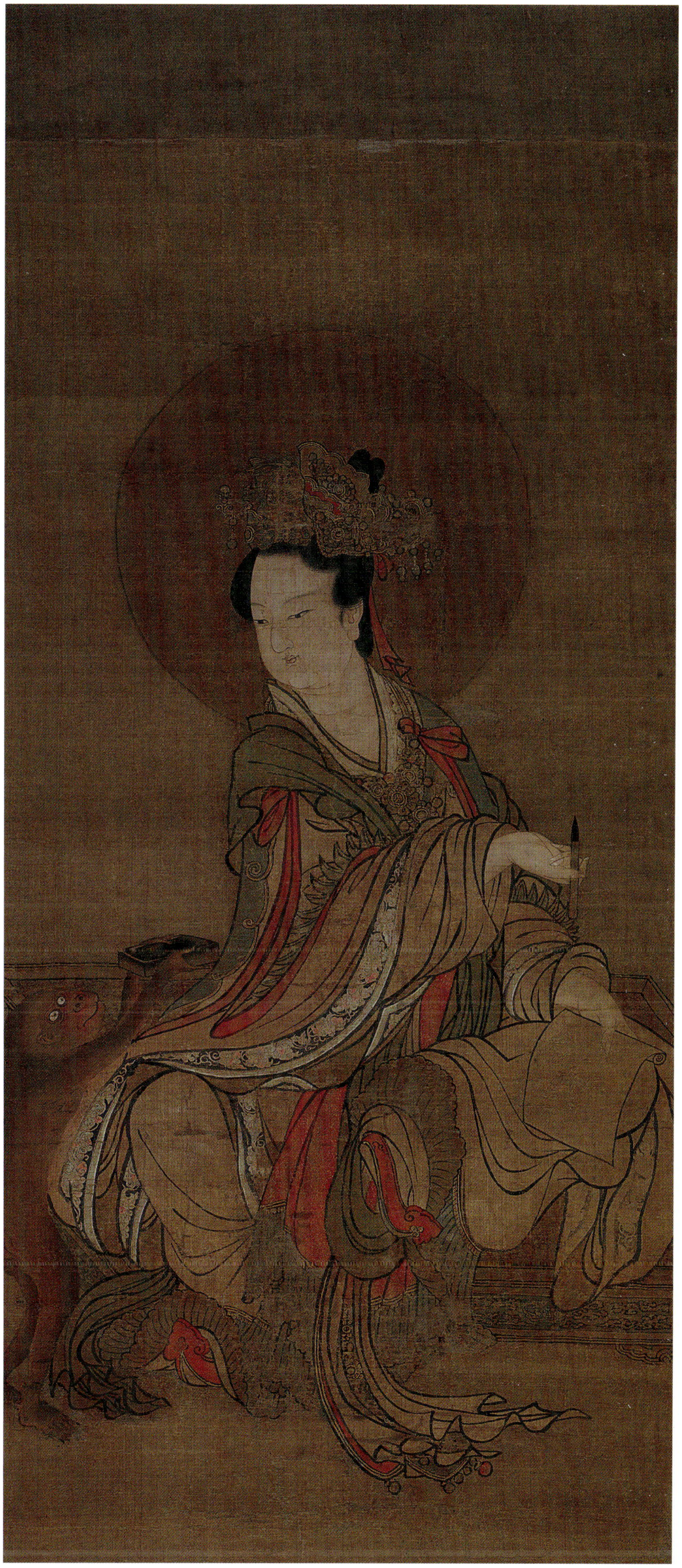

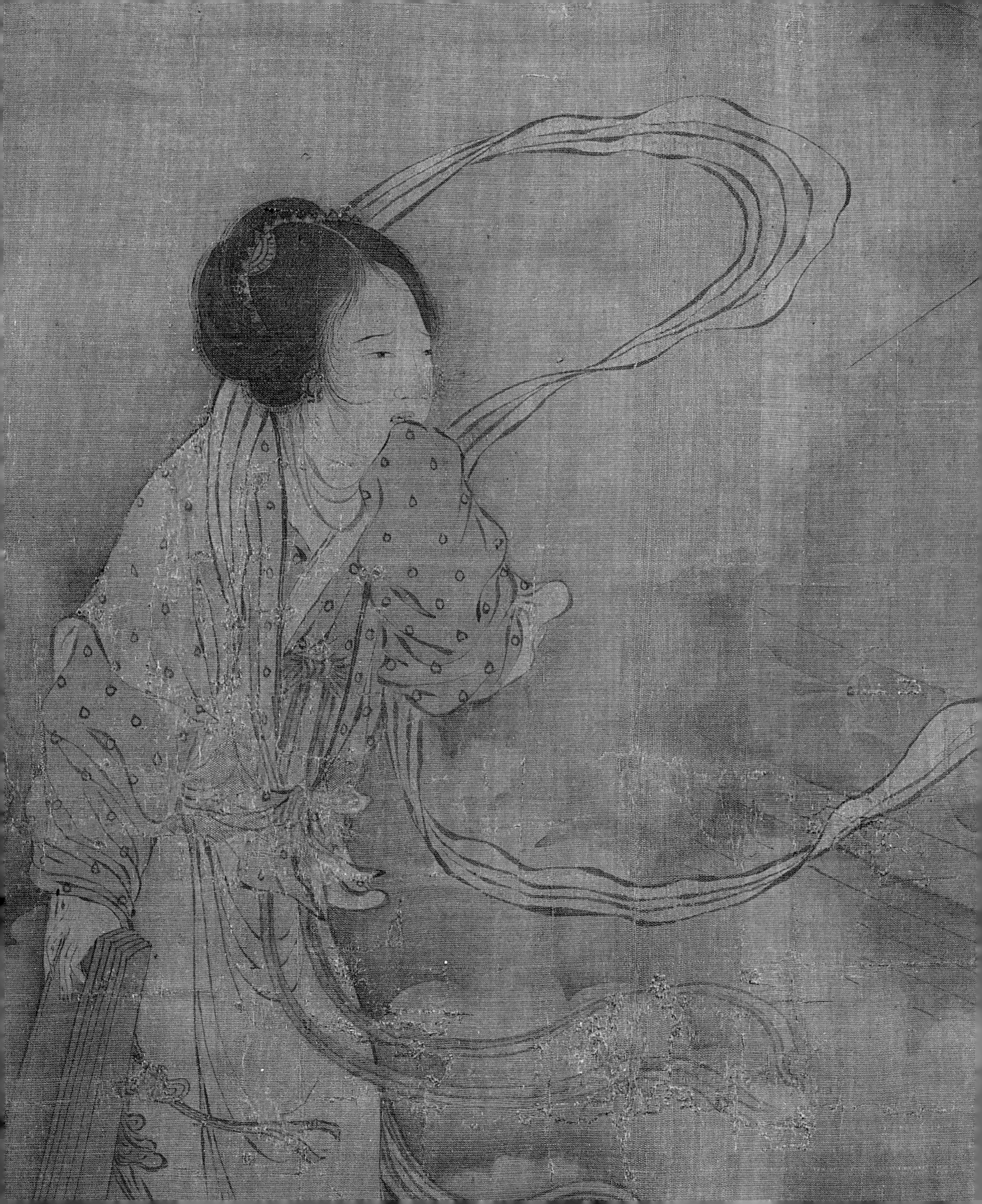

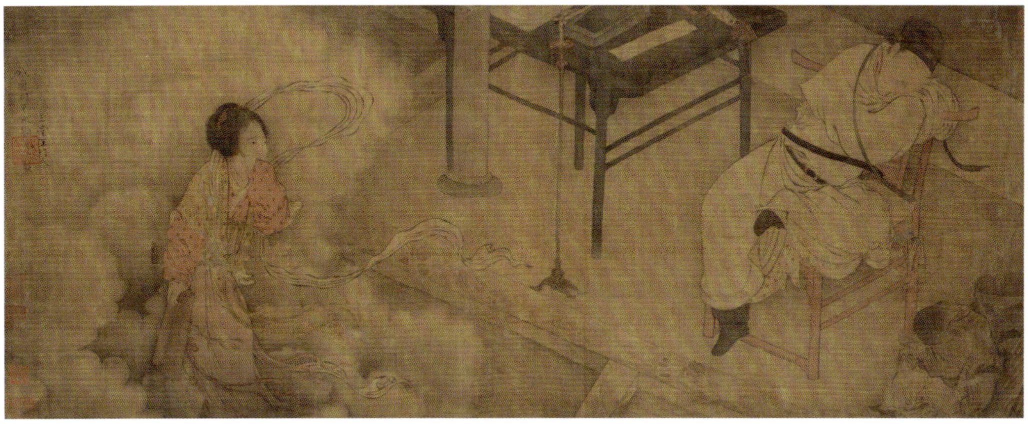

37

LIU YUAN (act. 13th century)

## Sima Yu's Dream of the Courtesan Su Xiaoxiao

金 劉元 司馬豫夢蘇小小圖 卷

early 13th century, handscroll,
ink and colour on silk, 29.2 × 73.6 cm
Cincinnati Art Museum,
John J. Emery Endowment (1948.79)

REFERENCE LITERATURE

Cleveland 1968; Avril 1997

This painting depicts the legendary love story of the Northern Song (960–1127) scholar Sima Yu and the spirit of the fifth-century courtesan, Su Xiaoxiao. Su was a renowned beauty and talented singer from Qiantang (present Hangzhou). The story soon evolved into a fascinating plot, and was adapted for many popular songs and dramas in the Yuan dynasty (1271–1368). The scene depicted here illustrates an episode that took place in Luoyang, where the singer appeared to the young scholar in a dream and sang:

> I used to live by the Qiantang River,
> The flowing years have passed by unnoticed,
> In the blooming and shedding of the flowers.
> Now springtime is carried away by the swallows once again,
> Then comes outside of my screen window
> The yellow-plum rain.

At the end of the song, Su told Sima that they would meet again on the bank of the Qiantang River. Five years later, when Sima became an official and was posted to Qiantang, he found Su's tomb right behind his official residence. The two then resumed their relationship in Sima's dreams. A few years later, after a final rendezvous with Su, Sima died in a mysterious boat accident, and presumably joined Su in the other world.[1]

The artist has created the dramatic scene by a diagonal division of the handscroll space into two realms. On the right, a tilted background affords viewers an intimate view of the interior of the study, where Sima Yu and his young attendant are asleep. The restful world contrasts sharply with the theatrical scene on the left, where the melancholy Su Xiaoxiao emerges from thick mists, holding a wooden clapper in her right hand and lifting her sleeved left hand to conceal her mouth. With an expression of endless yearning and regret, Su advances from the ethereal world to join her lover. The union of the two is gently suggested by the billowing long scarf looping high over her head and floating across the division of the two realms toward the sleeping scholar.

Little is known about the painter, Liu Yuan.[2] Based on the information provided in his inscription on this painting, Liu was from Pingshui (in present Shanxi Province) and served in the Jurchen Jin dynasty's (1115–1234) Crafts Office (Zhiying si), which was first established in 1196. Liu's inscription also mentions that he was a disciple of Santang Wang.[3] Despite the poor biographical information, this single extant work by Liu demonstrates the level of sophistication in Chinese figure painting developed at this time. The sensitive and realistic portrait of Su Xiaoxiao also reveals the strong influence of drama, which totally transformed the Chinese narrative depiction of women. HS

1 For a fuller version of the story of Sima Yu and Su Xiaoxiao, see Cleveland 1968, no. 199.
2 Liu Yuan is also the name of a famous sculptor of the Yuan dynasty (1271–1368), but he was recorded to be a native of Baodi, Hebei Province. See ibid.
3 The name 'Santang Wang' could be either an official name or a literary name. As a literary name, it would be translated as 'Wang of the Three Studios'; see Avril 1997, pp. 59–60, no. 28.

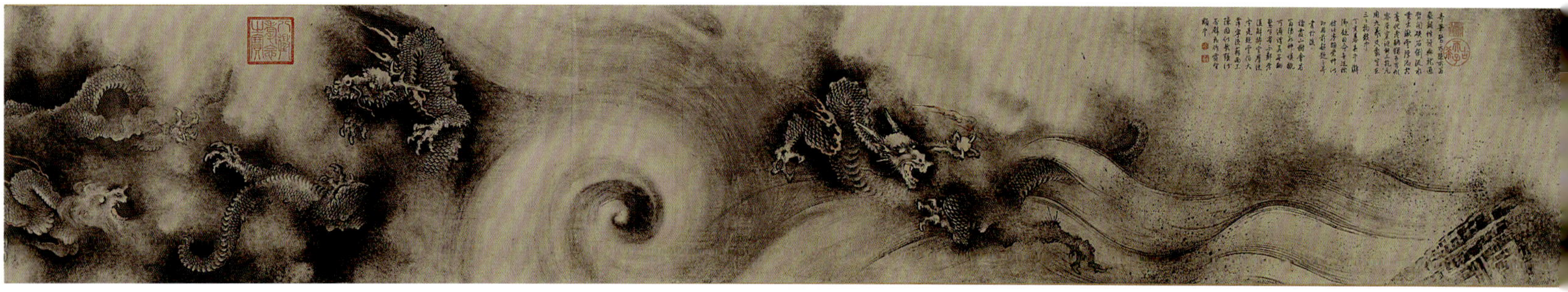

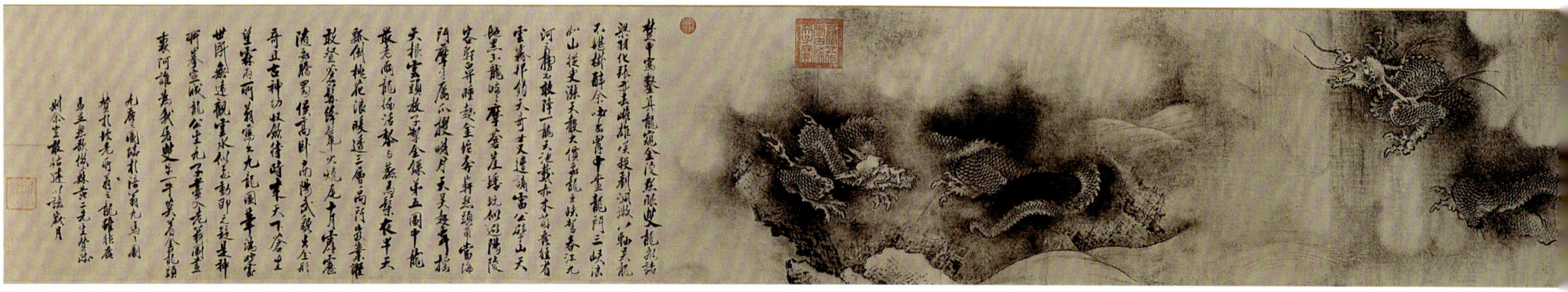

38

CHEN RONG (c.1189–c.1268)

## Nine Dragons

宋 陳容 九龍圖 卷

1244, handscroll, ink and touches of red on paper, 46.3 × 1096.4 cm
Museum of Fine Arts, Boston
Francis Gardner Curtis Fund, 1917 (17.1697)

PROVENANCE

Yamanaka and Co., New York

REFERENCE LITERATURE

Zhang 1744; *Bulletin of the Museum of Fine Arts, Boston* 1917; Sirén 1927; Tomita 1933; Museum of Fine Arts, Boston 1982 and 1992; Boston 1997; Zhang 2003, p. 278; Sung 2009; Li 2012

Along the length of some 10 metres of paper, nine vigorous dragons leap, tangle, contort, cavort and retreat among the dynamic whirls of clouds, waves and mountains of the universe. All of this multidirectional energy was summoned up through the skilled manipulation of a brush and ink. When the artist Chen Rong completed his *Nine Dragons* scroll in the year 1244, during the waning years of the Southern Song dynasty (1127–1279), he was so impressed with the result that he was inclined to credit an unearthly power. He inscribed the painting with a poem describing the process of his efforts, his intoxicated state while creating the work and a respectful awe: 'I have painted the picture of nine dragons, and the greatness that emerged from the tip of my brush cannot be found elsewhere in the world. At a distance, one feels as if the clouds and the waves were flying and moving. Viewed closely, one suspects that only a god could have painted these dragons.'[1] The artist's spontaneity and adaptability can be detected in areas of the scroll where he continued painting despite wrinkles and other defects in the paper's surface. Connoisseurs and collectors over many centuries have echoed his sentiments and added their praise of his extraordinary virtuosity, which can be read in the numerous colophons added to the scroll.

The painter of this masterpiece, Chen Rong, was an aspiring scholar from Fujian Province, who was unable to pass the *jinshi* civil service exams until 1235, when he was already in middle age. He was assigned to be a minor official in Putian, in his home province of Fujian, and never rose to great heights in the official hierarchies of power. In this rather impoverishing situation, he expressed his talents and sentiments through the arts of poetry, calligraphy and painting. The poem on this work is the only one by him known today. In addition to dragons, he was noted for his paintings of bamboo, pine trees and rocks, themes that continued to be characteristic of scholar-painters over the years.

The history of painting dragons stretches back at least to the third century. The first reference is to works by the third-century Cao Buxing and the sixth-century Sengyou in the *Record of Famous Painters of Successive Dynasties* by the ninth-century scholar Zhang Yanyuan (815–76). The Song dynasty (960–1279) emperor

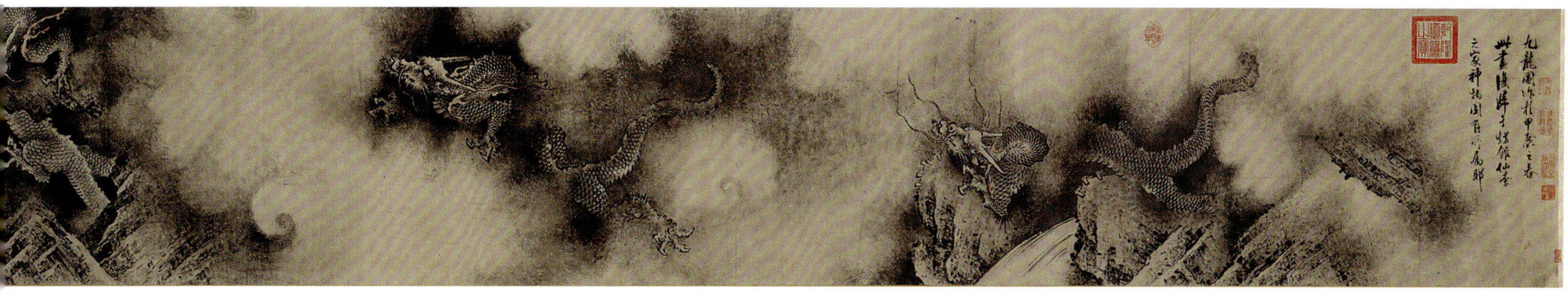

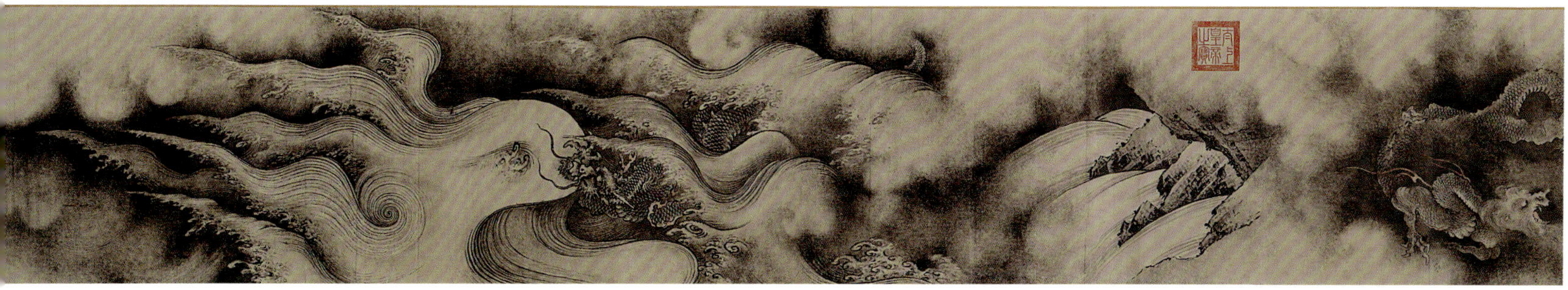

Huizong's (r. 1101–25) *Xuanhe Painting Catalogue*, the inventory of his imperial collection of paintings, also includes an entire section listing only paintings of dragons. However, Chen Rong notes in his inscription that his work was inspired not by previous dragon paintings of dragons, but by two works depicting other animal types: Cao Ba's (act. 8th century) *Nine Horses* and Huichong's (*c*.965–1017) *Nine Deer*. The present painting is today thought to be the oldest extant example of a dragon scroll, and is almost universally accepted as the finest.

The dragon has had two primary symbolic roles in the Chinese tradition over the past 1,000 years, representing the emperor and imperial power in national life and, in Daoism, embodying the forces of nature. In Chen Rong's painting, the nine dragons, each in a different position and posturing a different expression, romp and rove through clouds, waters and mountains manifesting the dynamism of nature and the Dao. Scholars have suggested that the whirlwind of a cloud approximately halfway through the scroll is a representation of the yin-yang symbol.[2] Daoist interpretations of the painting began shortly after the work was completed. Among the many colophons are a number by eminent early fourteenth-century Daoist scholars and priests noting the affinities between the work and Daoist belief systems. Wu Quanjie (1269–1346), for instance, in his colophon points out that the dragon is a symbol of Laozi, and that the number nine, like the dragon, embodies the yang element. The painting was for a time in the Qing (1644–1911) imperial collection, and likewise impressed the Qianlong emperor (r. 1736–96), who added his own colophon along with, over the years, 11 seals.

Despite over 700 years of interpreting, researching and extolling Chen Rong's dragons, scholars are continuing to shine new light on the work and its history. Researcher Li Song, for instance, has recently written that he believes that the painting is not by Chen Rong, but instead was created by his great-grandson Chen Yisuo (*c*.1263–?) one 60-year cycle later in 1304. NB

1 Boston 1997
2 Ibid., p. 199

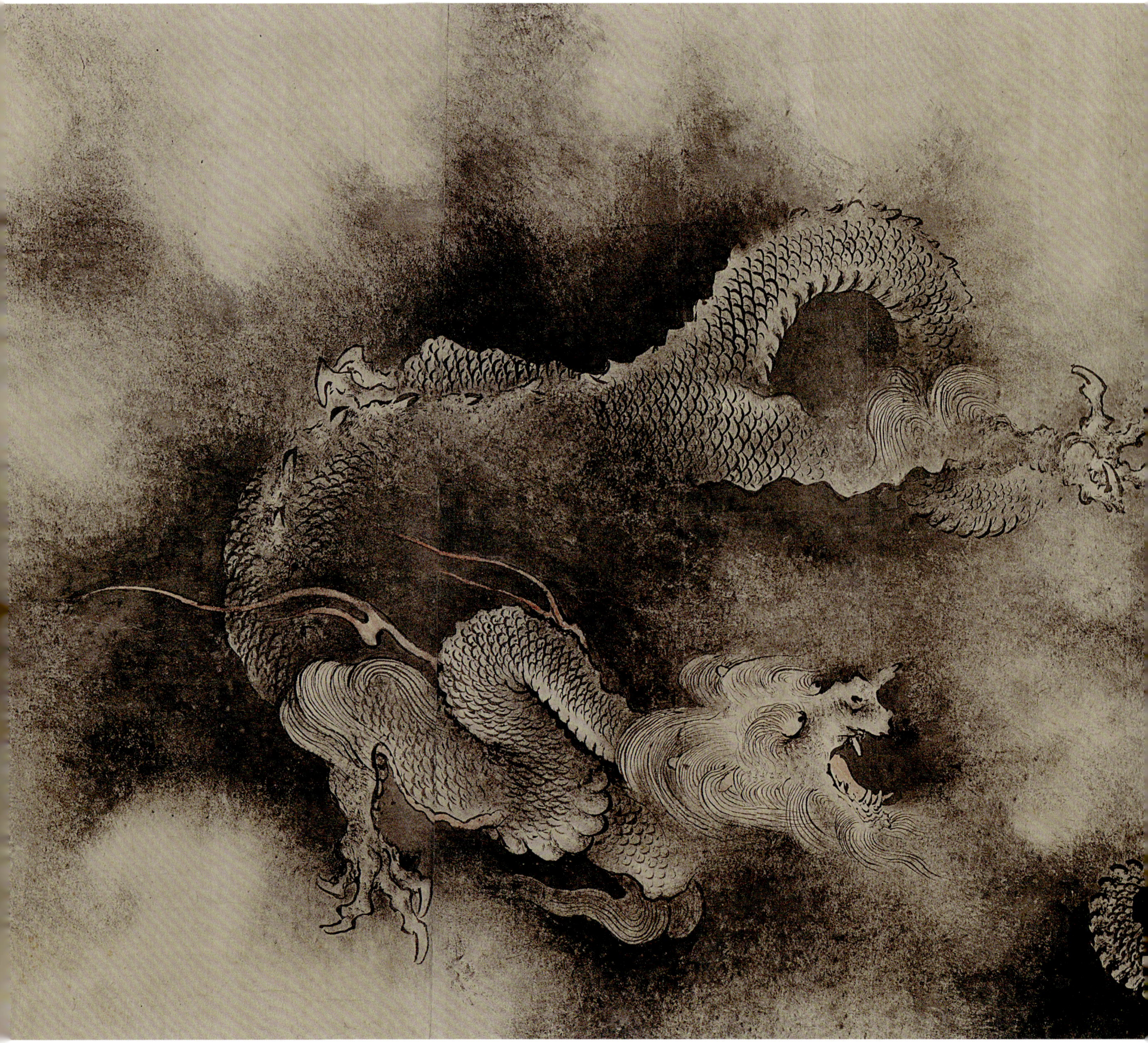

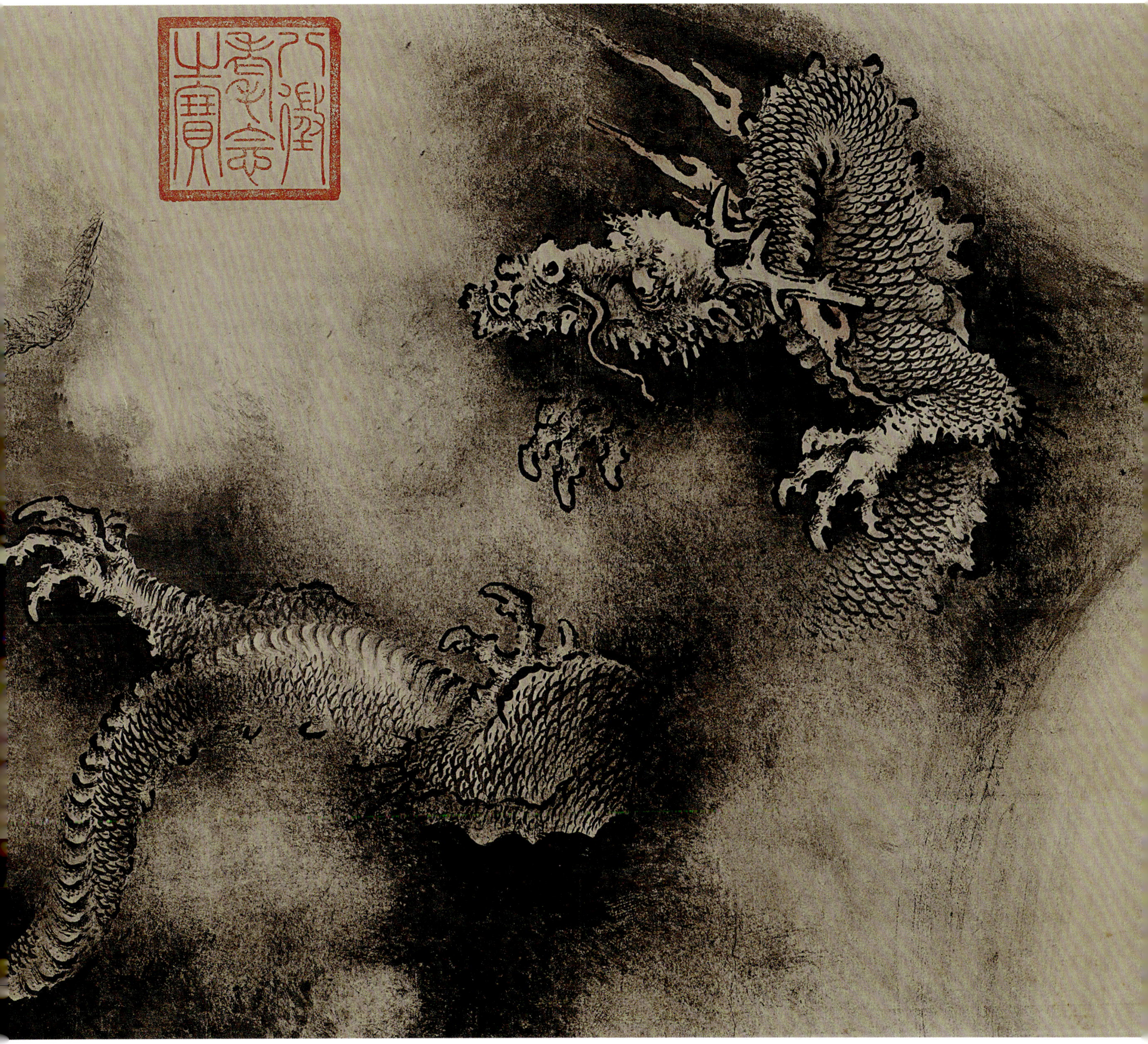

# Paintings 1250–1400

The Mongol conquest of China, overcoming the Jurchen Jin dynasty (1115–1234) in the north and finally demolishing the Southern Song (1127–1279), had effects that were felt in every sphere of life. Although north and south were reunited after the period of division between Jin and Song, travel between the two areas was not necessarily easy. One of the most famous paintings of the time, *Autumn Colours on the Qiao and Hua Mountains* (1295; National Palace Museum, Taipei), was painted, in a deliberately archaic style, by Zhao Mengfu (1254–1322) for his friend Zhou Mi (1232–98), who had no way to visit his ancestral homeland in Shandong Province, through which Zhao had travelled on his return from a journey to the Mongol capital Dadu (modern Beijing). Zhao himself came under attack for serving under the Mongol Yuan dynasty (1271–1368) instead of remaining loyal to the fallen Song dynasty (960–1279) by living in retirement, as Confucian ethics dictated for 'leftover' subjects like Zhou Mi, who had been in office under the Southern Song before the change of rulership. The keenness of their grief, far exceeding the nostalgia that the Southern Song had felt following the Jin conquest in 1127 for the loss of the former capital and territory in the north, is vividly depicted in Gong Kai's (1222–1307) *Emaciated Horse* (cat. no. 44). The black solemnity of the calligraphy in this handscroll matches the sentiments of the text, which relates the sorry state of a once proud and splendid steed, now reduced to a pitiful wreck on the verge of death from starvation. Qian Xuan (c.1235–before 1307) evokes a similar sense of loss in his subdued depiction *Doves and Pear Blossoms after Rain* (cat. no. 45).[1]

Contrary to what one might expect, however, the tragedy of the Mongol occupation gave rise to an extraordinary flowering of artistic talent, in both literature and the visual arts. The foremost intellectual of the time was Zhao Mengfu, mentioned above, whose calligraphy, fluent and disciplined, became the first (and only) style since the Tang dynasty (618–907) to be adopted as a standard for the writing of the regular style, and is still found in model books today. In painting, Zhao looked back to the ideals of the distant past, *fugu* ('return to antiquity'), but another source of inspiration, throughout the Song dynasty and into the Yuan, was the artistic and calligraphic friendships that the literati maintained with Chan Buddhist monks, who used free-flowing ink washes on paper rather than silk. Their subjects included Buddhist patriarchs (cat. nos 39, 40) and deceptively simple themes such as bamboo and mist-filled landscapes, symbolic of sudden enlightenment and the emptiness of nirvana, and shorn of all the trappings of traditional Buddhist iconography. Monk painters like Muxi (d.c.1281) (cat. no. 42) and Zhiweng (act. early 13th century) (cat. no. 41) painted in this carefree and totally unconventional manner, though often inscribed in elegant calligraphy that betrays their friendship with eminent scholar-calligraphers such as Zhao Mengfu. The secular heirs to these artistic friendships were the Four Masters of the Late Yuan, Huang Gongwang (1269–1354), Wu Zhen (1280–1354), Ni Zan (1306–74) (cat. no. 51) and Wang Meng (c.1308–85). In protest against Mongol rule, some of them never sought official employment, living instead in seclusion, but they nevertheless had the most profound effect on the literati painters of later dynasties. Like Chan monks, they painted predominantly in ink and exclusively on paper, and each of the four pioneered an individual and clearly recognizable brush style and subject matter. Above all, their paintings were expressions of their own views of the world: writing about landscape, Huang Gongwang characterized the methods of earlier masters, as well as advising artists always to carry brushes with them so as to make sketches of unusual scenes; Wu Zhen wrote poems in a special 'fisherman's ode' metre, and painted the solitary fisherman as an image of the recluse; Wang Meng used an amazing range of brush techniques and dense strokes, seen to perfection in his *Dwelling in the Qingbian Mountains* (1366; Shanghai Museum), while Ni Zan went to the opposite extreme, limiting both his use of ink and the elements in his compositions. All of them also wrote directly on their own paintings, opening the way for fellow artists and later connoisseurs or collectors to add their own inscriptions in the same manner. A different style entirely is seen in *The Summer Palace of Emperor Minghuang* (cat. no. 49), which, although bearing the signature of the tenth-century master Guo Zhongshu (d.977), is unmistakably in the same vein as the *jiehua* or 'ruled-line' paintings of Li Rongjin (act. 2nd half 14th century), whose mentor Wang Zhenpeng (c.1280–c.1329) pioneered a distinctive style of architectural painting at the Mongol court under Emperor Renzong (r. 1312–20).

1 Sung 2009, p. 99

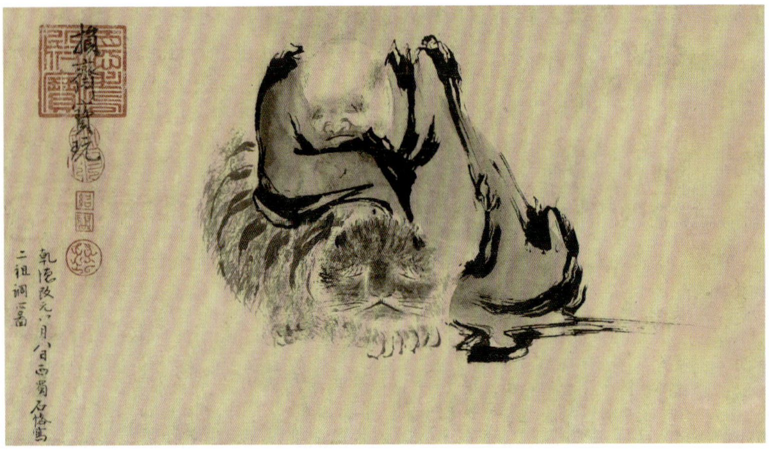

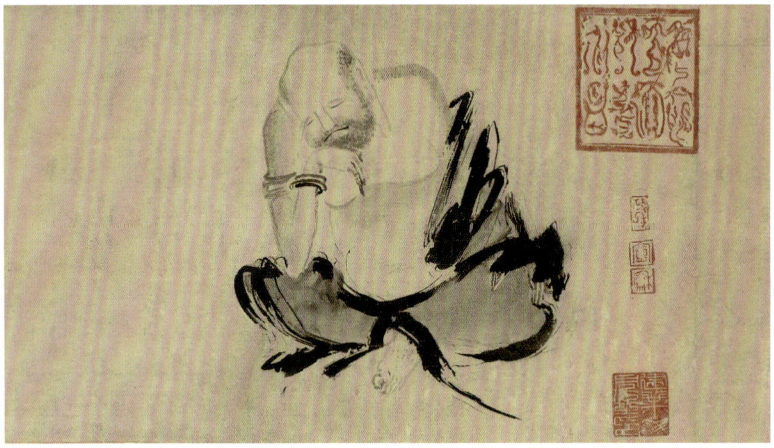

39, 40

UNIDENTIFIED ARTIST;
traditionally attributed to SHI KE
(act. 10th century)

## Two Chan Patriarchs Harmonizing Their Minds

宋 傳石恪 二祖調心圖 軸

13th century, pair of hanging scrolls, ink on paper, both 35.3 × 64.4 cm
Tokyo National Museum (TA-162)

REFERENCE LITERATURE

*Shinbi taikan* 1899; Tokyo 1929; Tanaka 1941; Okudaira in Tokyo 1962, p. 5; Tanaka 1944; Kakui 1984

The artist Shi Ke was born in Chengdu (in present-day Sichuan Province), and lived during the period of the Later Shu Kingdom (934–65). He studied under the master Zhang Nanben, and specialized in ink figure painting, wielding his brush freely and without care for what others might think. His use of fine lineation for the face and a broader, rougher brushstroke for the drapery suggests an affiliation with the painting style prevalent from the mid-Tang dynasty (618–907) onward that featured a similar type of roughly brushed line. The artist was involved in the production of many wall paintings for Chengdu temples, but after the fall of Shu, he travelled to the new capital at Kaifeng. There he worked on murals for the Xiangguo Temple, which had been expanded to serve as an imperial temple. Afterwards, although Shi Ke was invited to join the imperial painting academy, he declined, and instead returned to Shu.

One of the paintings is inscribed '1st year of Qiande, 8th month, 8th day; west Shu; painted by Shi Ke; second Chan patriarch in contemplation'. The date corresponds either to the year 919, during the Former Shu Kingdom (907–25), or to 963 in the Northern Song (960–1127). If this work was indeed done by Shi Ke, then 919 must be correct. It is the only work traditionally attributed to the artist that has come down to us. Current thinking, however, ascribes a later date to the painting, placing it around the time of the Southern Song.

The second patriarch of the Chan school of Buddhism was Huike (487–593). Stories of his daring, iconoclastic behaviour bear little relation to the two sleeping figures here. In addition, if one looks at the figure propping his head on his hand, there is evidence that the paper has been cut along the left edge of the body (as it faces the viewer), and another sheet attached. If a bag was originally shown resting on the ground behind this figure, then the image could well have been intended to represent Budai. That suggests that the depictions might be Budai with his sack and Fenggan with his tiger, raising the possibility that the images were taken from a larger work, probably a handscroll illustrating various religious figures. In Japan, long handscrolls and large-scale paintings were often cut up and made into smaller hanging scrolls to be displayed in a *tokonoma*, or alcove. These works may well have undergone such a transformation.

The manner in which the brush moves rapidly back and forth to create abbreviated form bears a close similarity to a hanging scroll of Fenggan (private collection) that bears an inscription by Siqiao Kexuan (act. early 13th century). TM

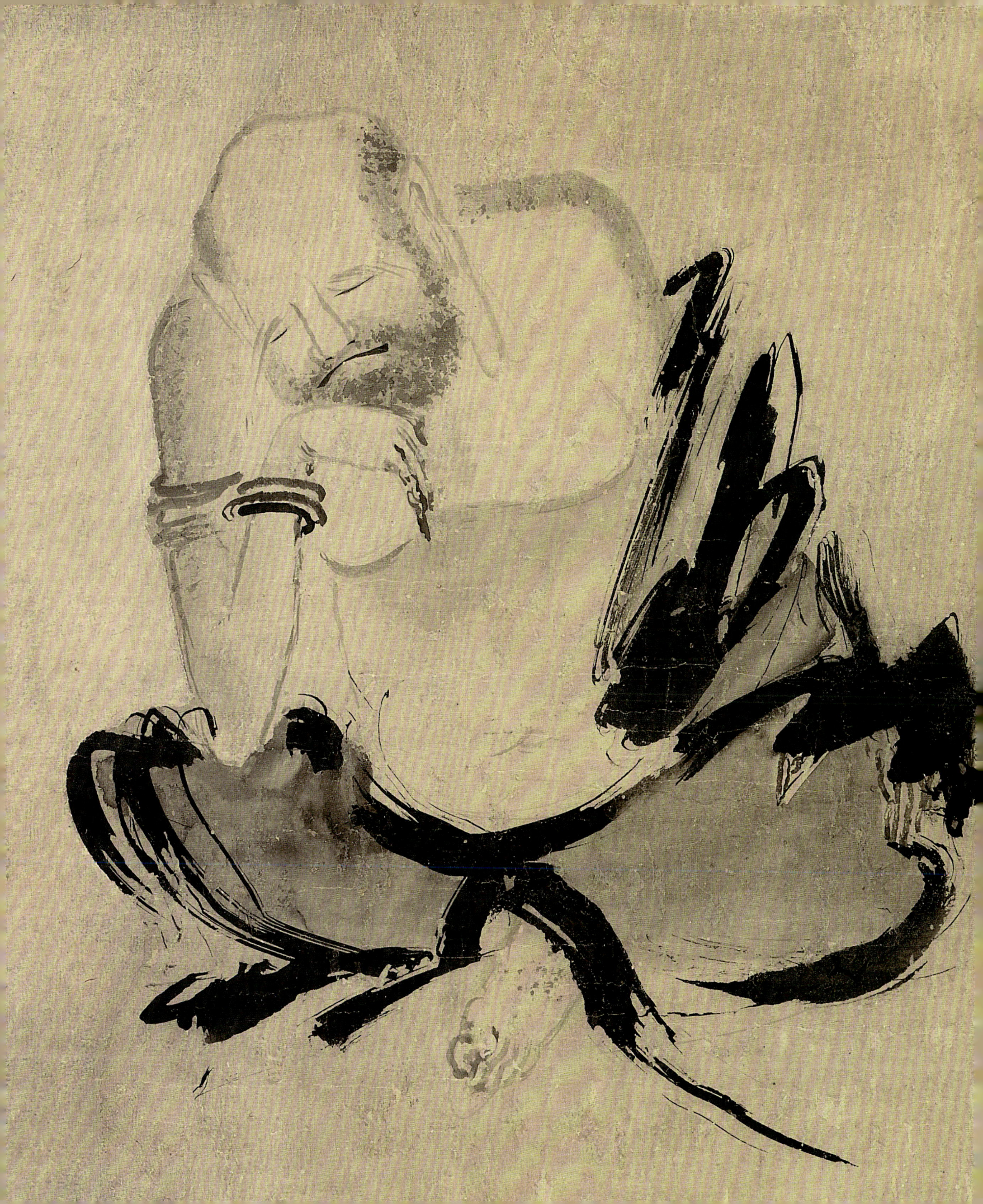

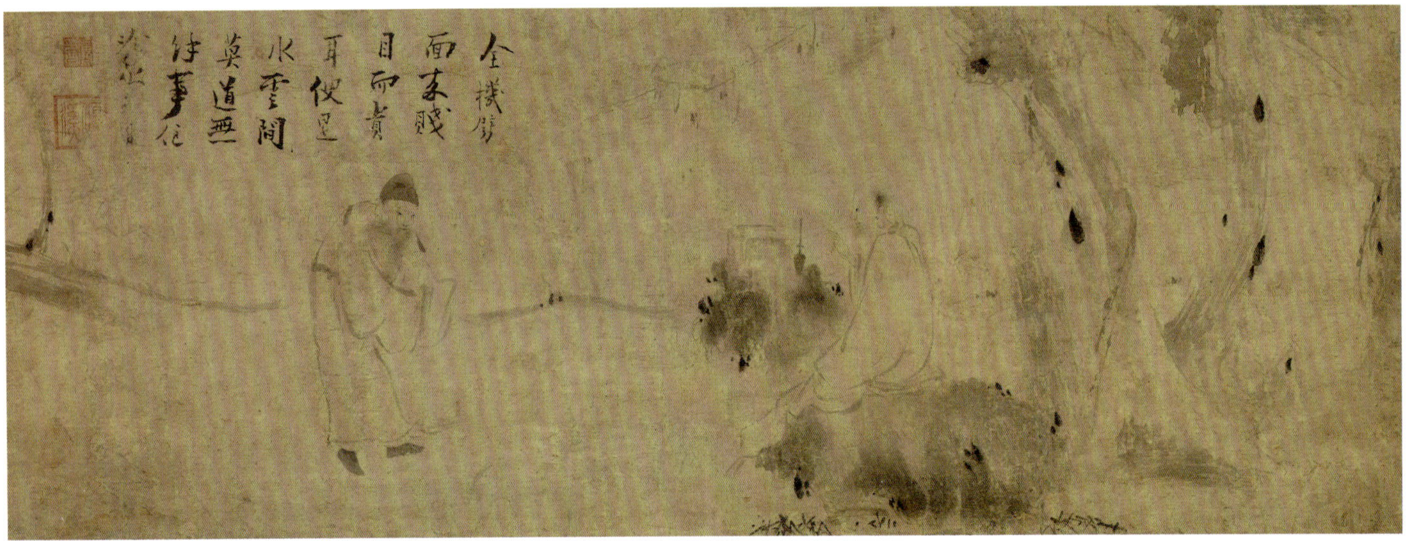

41

UNIDENTIFIED ARTIST
(mid-13th century); traditionally attributed to
ZHIWENG (act. early 13th century)

## Meeting between Yaoshan and Li Ao

宋 傳直翁 藥山李翺問道圖 軸

before 1256, album leaf mounted as a hanging scroll, ink on paper, 31.8 × 84.5 cm
The Metropolitan Museum of Art, New York
Edward Elliott Family Collection, Purchase, The Dillon Fund Gift, 1982 (1982.2.1)

PROVENANCE

Edward Elliott Family Collection

REFERENCE LITERATURE

Yonezawa 1963, p. 20; Awakawa 1971, pp. 60–1; Shimizu 1980, fig. 16; Fong and Hearn 1982, pp. 26–7, figs 15–16; Fong 1992, pp. 352–3, fig. 77; New York 2001, pp. 124–5, no. 34; Weidner 2001, p. 17, fig. 1.4; New York 2007, pp. 134–7 no. 25; New York 2008a, pp. 66–7, no. 13

Depicted here is a famous encounter between the Confucian scholar Li Ao, bowing reverently as he approaches, and the Chan (J. Zen) Buddhist master Yaoshan (both act. *c.*840). Hearing of the master's reputation, the scholar went to see him and, disappointed, remarked: 'Seeing your face is not as good as hearing your name.' The master replied: 'Would you distrust your eye and value your ear?' He then pointed up and down, thereby counselling Li Ao to trust his own experience by indicating that reality lies in what we can actually see – such as 'the clouds in the sky, and the water in a vase'.

The painting was subsequently inscribed by the Chan Buddhist priest Yanxi Guangwen (1189–1263) between 1254 and 1256, while he was abbot of Lingyin Temple in Hangzhou. His inscription may be translated as follows:

All moments of enlightenment come in
a flash,
Why distrust your eye and value your ear?
Just as between the water and the clouds,
Don't say there is nothing there.

The Chan master used riddles to sharpen a student's direct perception in the face of distracting hearsay, while the Chan painter employed a simple and spontaneous, albeit elusive, brush style to capture his fleeting vision of truth.

The painting is an important example of early Chan Buddhist 'apparition painting' (*wanglianghua*), so named because of its pale, sensitive brushwork. Like contemporary Song academy painters, the anonymous monk-artist has focused on a few picture elements set in a shallow foreground space, but he renders them with diffuse washes and pale brush lines that emphasize the illusory nature of human perception. In spite of this abbreviated style, the artist effectively evokes the rough bark of the trees, the fissured surface of the rocks and the heavy drapery folds of the figures. By adding his boldly brushed inscription directly onto the picture surface, Yanxi Guangwen pointedly refutes the illusionistic function of the painting.

Prior to this time, only emperors and their consorts customarily added inscriptions directly to their paintings or to those of their court artists – thereby enhancing their personal connection to works that were presented to loyal courtiers. The Chan monk's usurpation of this prerogative marks the beginning of a new tradition. In this case, the abbot undoubtedly presented this work to a worthy disciple as a kind of diploma that testified to the disciple's connection to his mentor. Not long after this, artists themselves began to add dedications to their paintings, making inscriptions an integral part of their compositions. In time, both recipients and later admirers and collectors felt free to add their poetic responses or seals of ownership on to a painting as evidence of their own connection to the work of art. MH

42

UNIDENTIFIED ARTIST;
traditionally attributed to MUXI (d.c.1281)

## Slumbering Budai

宋 傳牧谿 布袋圖 軸

mid-13th century, hanging scroll,
ink on paper, 77.1 × 30.9 cm
Kyoto National Museum (AK 673)

REFERENCE LITERATURE

Wakimoto 1934; Yonezawa 1954; Ebine 1976 and 1978a; Egiatsu in Tokyo 1996a; Ebine 2000; Itakura in Tokyo 2004, p. 161; New York 2007; Kihara 2007; Wu in New York 2007; Shiga in Nagoya 2008, p. 211; Li in Taipei 2010, p. 396

Budai (d. 916) is a partly historical, partly legendary Chan monk with the Buddhist name 'Qici', who came from the city of Mingzhou (present Ningbo in Zhejiang Province) and lived from the end of the Tang dynasty (618–907) into the Five Dynasties period (907–60). Having no permanent residence, he wandered through the countryside carrying everything he needed in a cloth bag. Because of his itinerant life and unorthodox behaviour he was called 'Cloth Sack Monk' ('Budai Heshang'), and in Chan Buddhism is highly revered as an enlightened master. Here we see the pot-bellied Budai falling asleep as he leans against his bag. The image is rendered in abbreviated brushwork, using primarily pale ink and a minimum of line.

There is no background – just the figure of Budai lying in the centre of the painting. Only his closed eyes and mouth are depicted in black ink, and his features are set in a good-humoured expression. His head, belly, torso and the bag on which he reclines are composed of a series of large and small circles, each carefully rendered in finely brushed line. In contrast, the lines that describe the robe wrapped around the figure were done with a straw brush and so are broad and rough. The body is executed in a ghostly pale wash, with the ink thickening as it details the clothing, the bag, the pole and the outline of the figure. The repetition of circular shapes and the alternation of coarse and fine brushwork and of light and dark ink allow for an expression that captures the figure of this extraordinary monk in very few brushstrokes.

The type of figure painting seen here is known as *wanglianghua* (J. *mōryōga*), or 'apparition painting', and is believed to have originated in the early Southern Song period (1127–1279) with the Chan monk-painter Zhirong (1114–93). It quickly gained popularity in the middle of the era, beginning with the Southern Song academy painter Liang Kai (act. late 12th–early 13th century). *Slumbering Budai* shows a sure and skilled hand, and so there is reason to ascribe it to the late Southern Song, after *wanglianghua* had become somewhat established. The painting, which was imported early into Japan, has long been attributed to the Chan monk-painter Muxi, active from the end of the Southern Song to the beginning of the Yuan dynasty (1271–1368). However, it bears no signature or seal of the artist. A gourd-shaped relief seal reading *Zen'ami*, purported to date from the fourteenth century, is in the lower right-hand corner.

The meaning of the *Zen'a* seal has been a matter of debate. Traditionally, it is believed to have belonged to Zen'ami (act. 2nd half 14th century), the gardener who served the eighth Muromachi (1336–1573) shogun Ashikaga Yoshimasa (r. 1449–73).

Also of interest is the luxurious mounting in gold brocade embellished with a double-vined peony arabesque pattern on a dark blue ground. The fabric is the same as that used for the mounting in the triptych by Liang Kai of two snowy landscapes and *Śākyamuni Descending the Mountain* (Tokyo National Museum). Also similar is the material in the tunic worn for performances of *bugaku* (court music and dance) handed down in the Amano-sha shrine on Mount Koya (now also in the collection of the Tokyo National Museum). Such gold brocades were probably 'Chinese things', or *karamono*, that were circulating at the end of the fourteenth century. In the note of provenance attached to the painting, *Slumbering Budai* is recorded as being the central image of a triptych, flanked by paintings of gibbons.

The scroll also has a connection with the daimyo Toyotomi Hideyoshi (1537–98). It was in Hideyoshi's possession, then passed to his brother-in-law Kinoshita Iesada (1543–1608), the elder brother of his wife Kōdai-in (Kita no mandokoro; 1547?–1624); to the temple Kōdai-ji in Kyoto, established by Kōdai-in in memory of Hideyoshi; to Nakagawa Denbei, and then into the Yoshikawa family. Incidentally, the artist Kano Tanyū (1602–79) made a direct copy of the hanging scroll in 1664, a work which accompanies the painting. KM

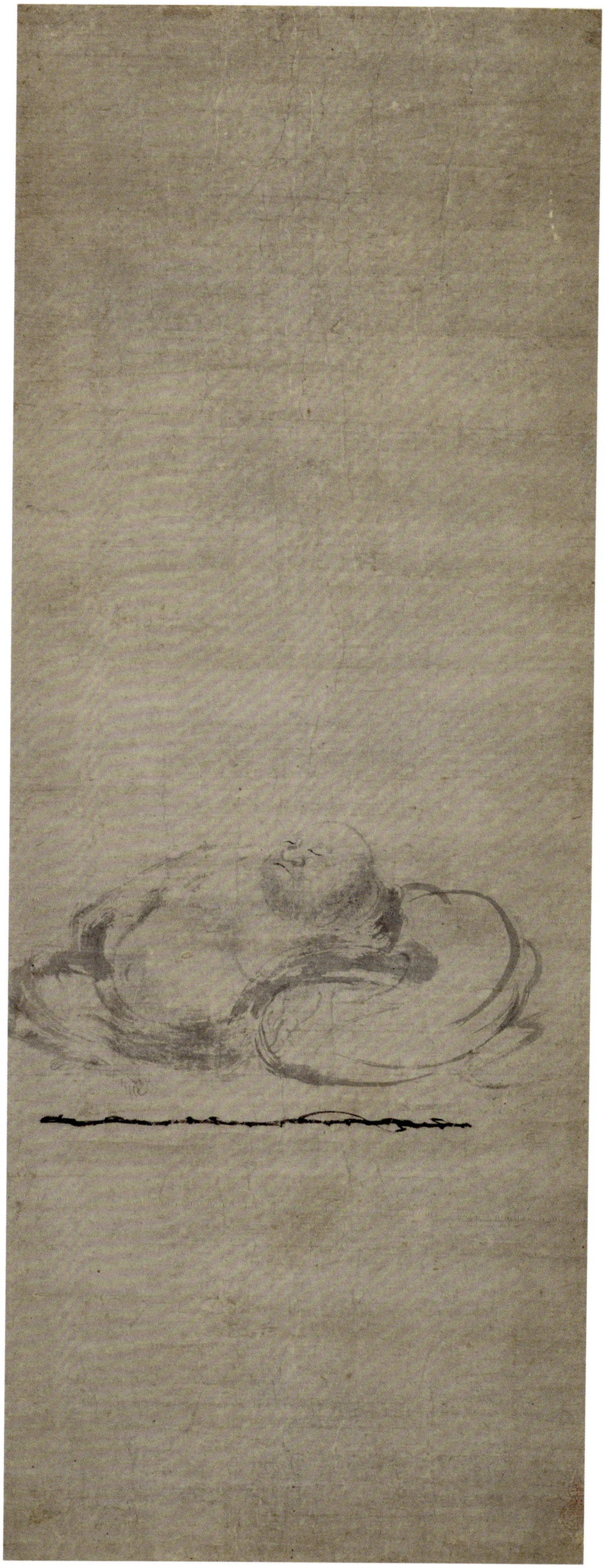

43

UNIDENTIFIED ARTIST;
traditionally attributed to MUXI (d.c.1281)

## Monk Mending Clothes in the Morning Sun

宋 傳牧谿 朝陽圖 軸

late 13th century or early 14th century, hanging scroll, ink on paper, 84.5 × 30.5 cm
Kyoto National Museum (AK 817)

REFERENCE LITERATURE

Sawamura 1916; Kinbara 1938; Tanaka, Akiyama and Tanaka 1938; Kohara 1967; Ebine 1971, 1977 and 1978b; Egiatsu in Tokyo 1996a; New York 2007; Shimizu in New York 2007

The theme of the painting, 'in the morning sun', is traditionally one of a pair, the other being 'in the moonlight'. Together they refer to the daily practice of the Buddhist monk, repairing his *kesa* (S. *kaṣāya*), or robe, in the morning, and reading sutras at night. The exact source is unclear, but the subject is possibly based on a Chinese poem by Wang Fengchen that reads: 'In the early morning sun I mend my ragged clothes; in the moonlight I read my sutra assignment.'[1] If indeed this painting was originally part of a diptych, the works became separated early on, as it is just the single scroll that has long been treasured in Japan.

The monk sewing his black *kesa* is shown in the lower part of the composition, seated on a rock beneath a pine tree. His right arm is outstretched, and with the other hand, he brings the garment to his mouth. Siting with his right leg bent vertically, he pulls a thread out from a wheel at his feet. The figure itself is described in fine, precise lines, while the drapery is deftly depicted with the type of relaxed, smoothly variegated brushstrokes known as *liuyemiao* ('willow-leaf lines'). In contrast, the pine and rock in the background are rendered in rough strokes of wet, pale ink. The artist has used primarily light ink in the work as a whole, and the dark accents provided by the black of the *kesa*, the tangle of vines in the pine tree, the edge of the rock and the foliage at its base create a rhythm in harmony with the pale washes. This is a classic example of *wanglianghua* (J. *mōryōga*), or 'apparition painting' (see also cat. no. 42).

The scroll is accompanied by an authentication written by Kano Tsunenobu (1636–1713), which judges the work to be 'a true painting by Muxi'. However, there is no signature of the artist, and while the style is lucid and elegant, there is a slight, but undeniable, sense of stiffness in the execution. Recent opinion ascribes the scroll to a Zen painter in Muxi's circle rather than to Muxi himself, and considers the traditional attribution probably to have been acquired after the painting's arrival in Japan.

The scroll bears an inscription by Dongsou Yuankai (act. 1314–40), a Chan monk. He was the disciple of Dachuan Puji (1179–1253), who was in the lineage of Zhuo'an Deguang (1121–1203), a student in the Dahui Zonggao (1089–1163) line of the Lingji (J. Rinzai) school of Chan Buddhism. The word 'yuji' in the inscription refers to the Jade Desk Pavilion at Ayuwang Temple, a famous site in Ningbo. Dongsou inscribed the painting around the time he was serving as the 48th chief priest of the temple.

*Monk Mending Clothes in the Morning Sun* is the first painting illustrating the theme known in Japan. There is a Japanese scroll close in composition in the Cleveland Museum of Art. Entitled *Priest Sewing under Morning Sun*, the work bears the seals *Ka'ō* and *Ninga*, and dates to the Nambokuchō period (1336–92). In addition, a copy exists in the Kano school collection of sketches after Chinese paintings, *Copybooks of the Kano School: Chinese Paintings* (scroll 17) (Tokyo National Museum).

As well as the authentication certificate written by the artist Kano Tsunenobu (1636–1713), there are accompanying notes by the sixteenth-century monk Sankyū Sōgen (dates unknown) of the sub-temple Shinju-an at Daitoku-ji addressed to Hariya Sōgen. They describe the scroll as having been in the possession of Hariya Sōshun, believed to have been a disciple of the Kyoto tea master Sen no Rikyū (1522–91). Sōshun displayed it during a visit by the daimyo Toyotomi Hideyoshi (1537–98) in the Momoyama period (1573–1615). KM

1 Translation taken from Princeton 1976, p. 42

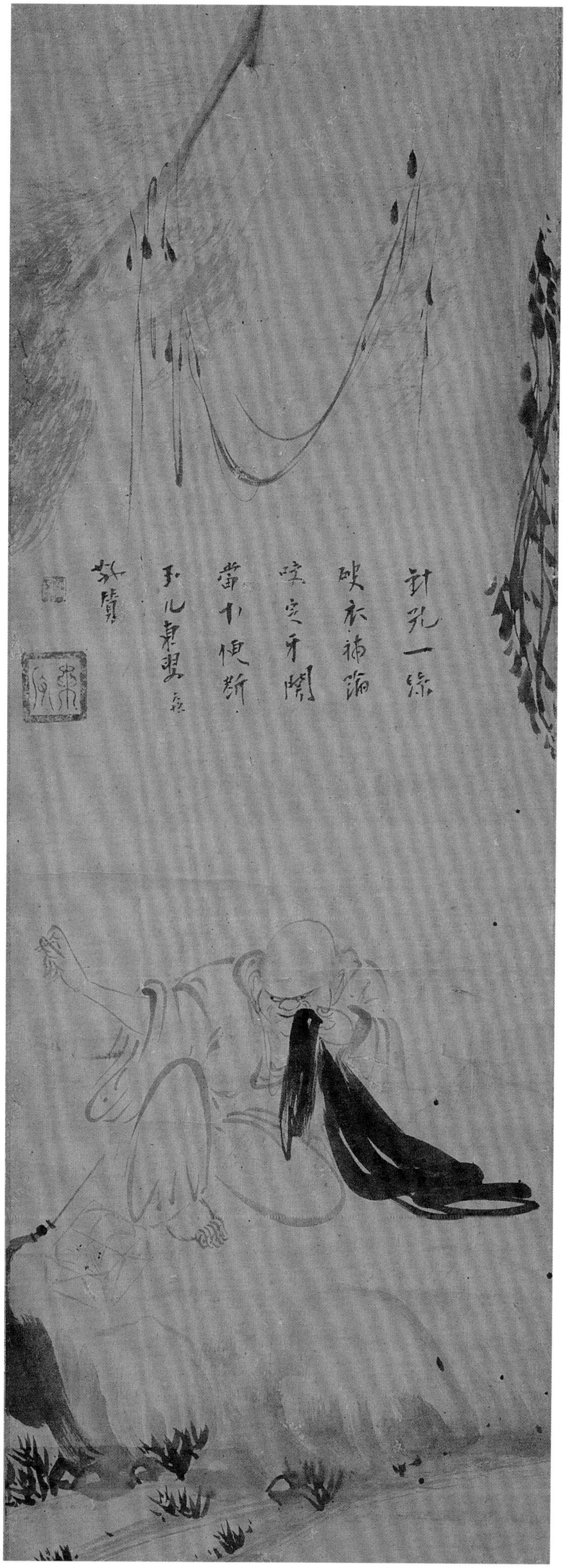

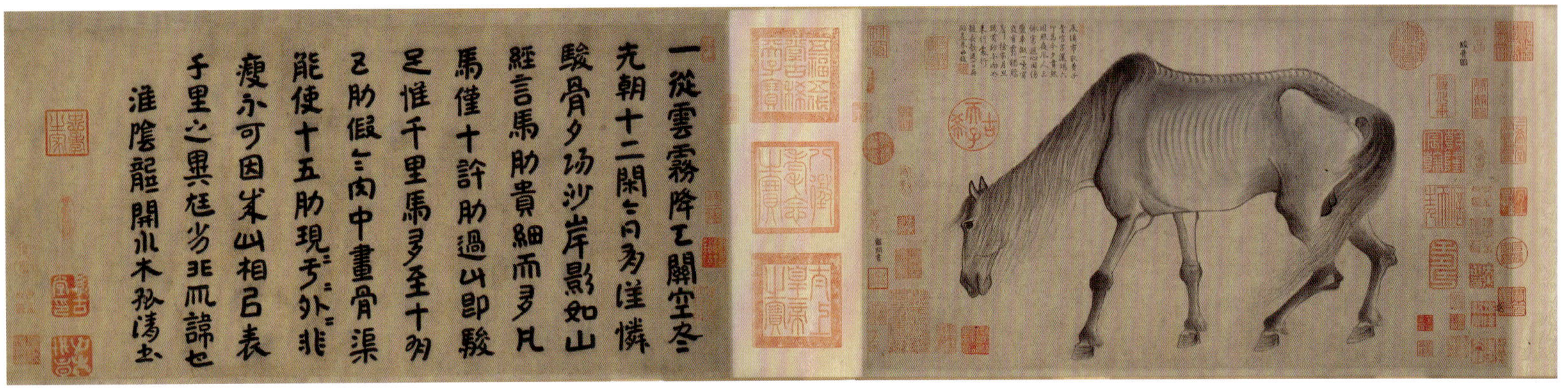

44

GONG KAI (1222–1307)

## Emaciated Horse

元 龔開 駿骨圖 卷

2nd half 13th century, handscroll, ink on paper, 29.9 × 56.9 cm
Osaka City Museum of Fine Arts (42, I-131)

REFERENCE LITERATURE

Ise 1930; Nakagawa 1983; Osaka and Shanghai 1994; Nara 1997; Itakura 1998; Takenami 2011

Born in Huaiyin (in today's Jiangsu Province), during the Song dynasty (960–1279) Gong Kai served as the state commissioner for the Lianghuai region, but lost the position with the establishment of the Mongol Yuan dynasty (1271–1368). Gong was learned, multi-talented and unconventional. A Song loyalist, he lived as a *yimin* ('leftover subject'), though he supported himself through the sale of his work. He was known as both a poet and a painter, and was said to have excelled at landscape, where he followed the style of the two Mis (Mi Fu [1051–1107] and Mi Youren [1074–1151/1086–1165]). For figures and horses, he admired Cao Ba (act. 8th century) of the Tang dynasty (618–907), although Gong's brush style was rather more rough. He delighted in painting ink demons and Zhong Kui, the Demon Queller of Chinese legend. His style was described as 'strange and wonderful, odd and extraordinary', and he was placed in a class of his own. Only a very few works by the artist have come down to us. In addition to the present painting, there is one other: *Zhongshan Going on Excursion*, in the Freer and Sackler Galleries in Washington, DC. *Emaciated Horse* is inscribed with Gong's own poem:

> Ever since the clouds and mist fell upon
> the Heavenly Pass,
> Empty have been the twelve imperial
> stables of the former dynasty.
> Today who will have pity for the shrunken
> form of his splendid body?
> In the last light of the setting sun, on the
> sandy bank, he casts his towering shadow –
> like a mountain![1]

With the complete destruction of the Song, the emperor's once grand stables are bare. The magnificent, 15-ribbed steed that could run a thousand leagues has now grown old. Emaciated and worn out, there is no one to pity him. For his composition, Gong Kai drew on the writings of the Tang poet Du Fu (712–70), who in 'Ballad of the Lean Horse' used the imagery of a horse to express his own unhappy circumstances. In Gong's painting, the horse is the artist himself, forced to live the life of a *yimin*.

The painting is followed by a great number of colophons and collectors seals. Also helpful is the fact that references to the work appear in various literary records. Not everything about the painting is secure, however: the colophons by Yang Weizhen (1296–1370) and Ni Zan (1306–74) are probably not genuine. YT

1 Translation by Wai-kam Ho, quoted in Cahill 1976, pp. 17–18

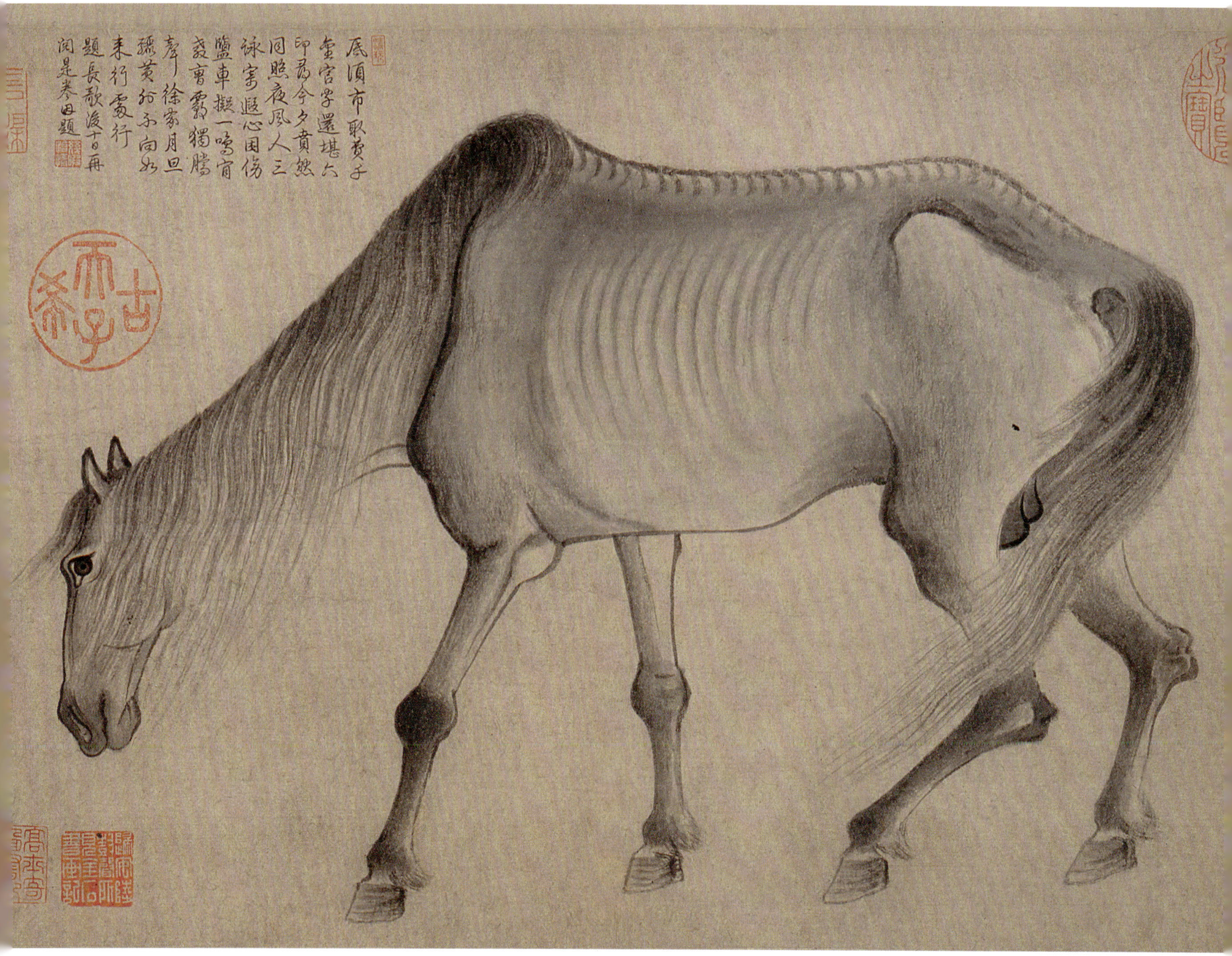
底須市取黄千
金宮字還堪六
印爲今夕貴然
同照夜風人三
詠寓遐心因傷
鹽車擬一鳴肯
羨曹霸獨騰
聲丨徐家月旦
議黄於不向如
來行處行
題長歌後十日再
閱是卷因題

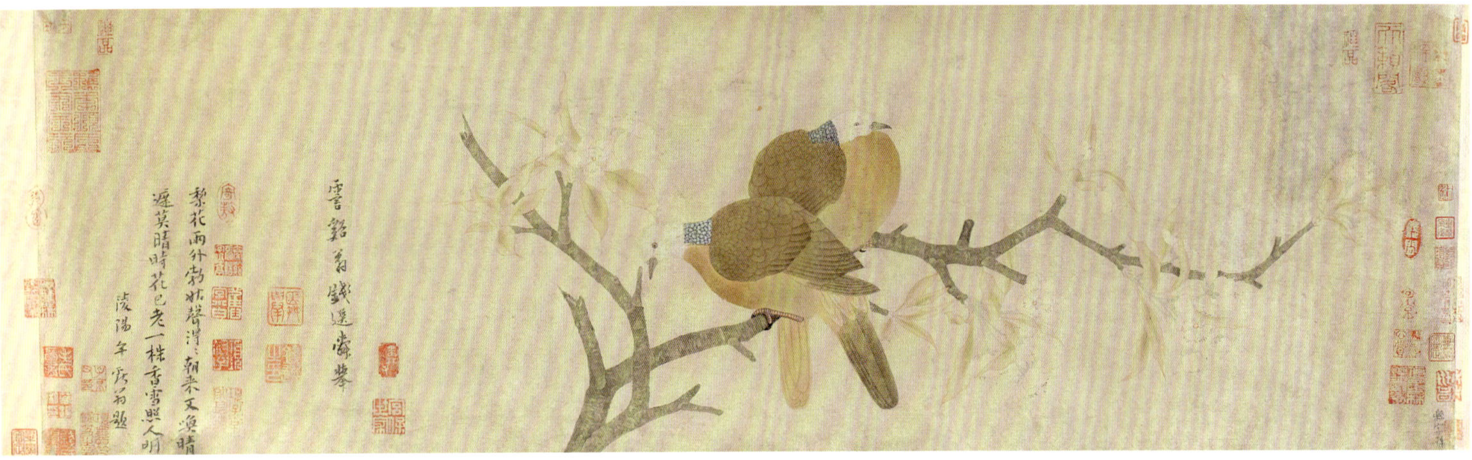

45

QIAN XUAN (c.1235–before 1307)

## Doves and Pear Blossoms after Rain

元 錢選 春雨鳴鳩圖 卷

2nd half 13th century, handscroll, ink and colour on powdered paper, 30.5 × 97.8 cm
Cincinnati Art Museum
John J. Emery Endowment (1948.80)

REFERENCE LITERATURE

Edwards 1953a; Cahill 1958; Fong 1960; Cleveland 1968; Wang, Li and P'an 1979; Robinson 1984; Shih 1984; Fong 1992; Avril 1997; Sung 2009

Qian Xuan was an accomplished scholar and painter of the thirteenth century, who witnessed the collapse of the Southern Song dynasty (1127–1279) and its replacement by the Mongol-ruled Yuan (1271–1368). The artist, then in his forties, renounced government service and dedicated the rest of his life to poetry and painting. He is especially known for his creative rendition of the traditional bird-and-flower themes.[1]

This painting, signed and marked with three seals by the artist, was also inscribed by Mou Yan (1227–1311), an older friend from Qian's native town, Wuxing, in present Zhejiang Province.[2] Attached to the work are numerous colophons by scholars of the Yuan and Ming (1368–1644) dynasties.[3] The painting depicts a pair of doves perched on a blossoming pear branch after rain. Although the depiction of doves and pear flowers first appeared in the tenth century, Qian has transformed the subject. The dampness of the branch and the softness of the blossoms are beautifully portrayed through Qian's conscious play with the flattened patterns. The faded shades of his subdued colours and deliberately geometric images of the placid doves perched against the equally unreal pear branch evoke neither the vitality of spring, nor the lyrical mood associated with spring rain as depicted in the Song works. Apparently, Qian was no longer interested in depicting the birds and flowers of spring as part of a cosmic pattern; rather, he was using the birds to portray his own state of mind as he confronted the alienation and isolation of his life as a Song loyalist. The style, often referred to as Qian's 'archaic manner', was his way of conveying his feelings of loss and nostalgia under Mongol rule.

After the Song dynasty, Chinese poets frequently referred to doves' singing as a prelude to the spring rain.[4] In the agricultural society of China, the spring rain, essential for the growth of the crops, had long been associated with 'blessings from heaven', and hence complimented the ruler (the 'son of heaven'). Thus, Qian's choice of the subject and his personal rendition of it were laden with layers of political and social meaning. Doves, as a traditional symbol of peace, express the wish for harmony and relief from the destruction of constant warfare and reprisal. The faded blossoms and the doves calling for spring rain may indeed have served as a metaphor for Qian's aspiration for the return of a benevolent Chinese ruler. HS

1 For research on Qian Xuan's (c.1235–before 1307) bird-and-flower painting, see Edwards 1953a; Fong 1960; Robinson 1984; Shih 1984; and Fong 1992, pp. 314–24.
2 For Mou Yan's (1227–1311) biography, see Wang, Li and P'an 1979, vol. 1, pp. 333–4.
3 For all inscriptions attached to the painting and their translation, see Avril 1997, pp. 61–4, no. 29.
4 See Sung 2009, ch. 5, pp. 96–101.

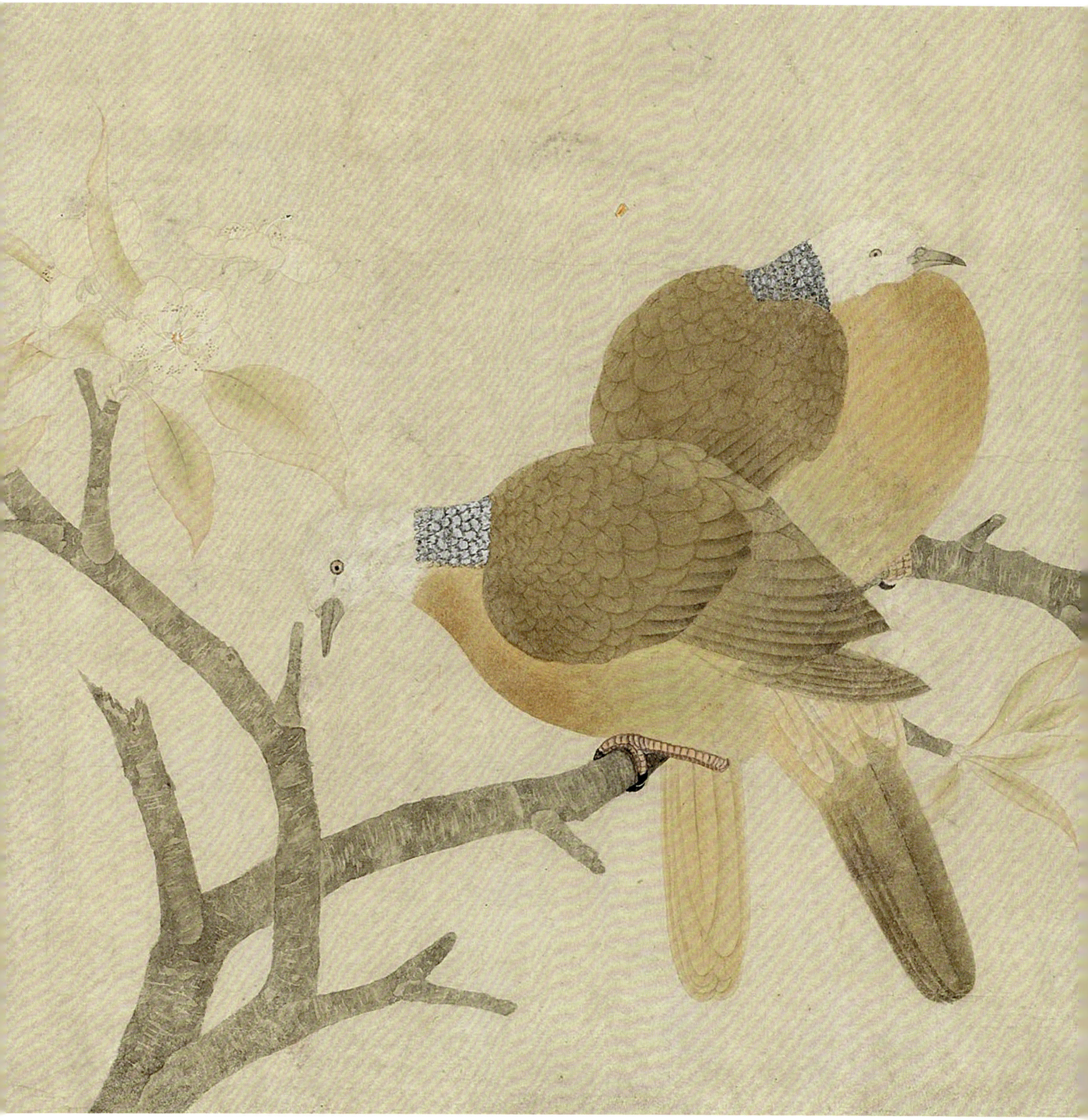

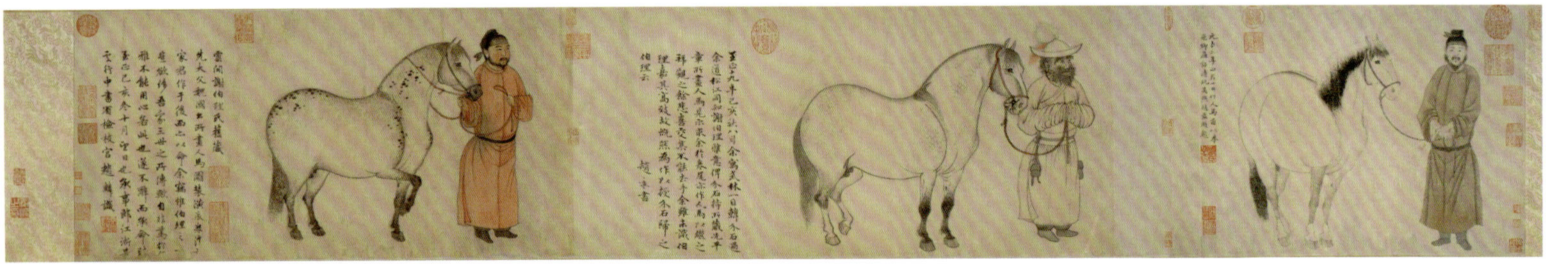

46

ZHAO MENGFU (1254–1322);
ZHAO YONG (1289–after 1360);
ZHAO LIN (act. 2nd half 14th century)

## Grooms and Horses

元 趙孟頫 趙雍 趙麟 三世人馬圖 卷

1296 and 1359, handscroll, ink and colour on paper, all three paintings 30.2 × 178.1 cm
The Metropolitan Museum of Art, New York
Gift of John M. Crawford, Jr., 1988
(1988.135)

PROVENANCE

John M. Crawford, Jr. (1913–88)

REFERENCE LITERATURE

Ruan (1791) 1854, vol. 4, pp. 6a-b; Xie 1957, no. 25, pls 95–7; New York 1962b, pp. 101–4, no. 43, pl. 28; Hay 1989, figs 1–4; Li 1991; Wang, Sun and Song et al. (1708) 1991, vol. 4, pp. 619–20; Fong 1992, pp. 432–3; Bian (1682) 1993–8, vol. 6, pp. 1080–1; Wang (1643) 1994; Zhang 1995; *A Collection of Paintings by Zhao Mengfu* 1995, pp. 6–10, 63–7, no. 2; Harrist 1997, fig. 15; New York 1997, pp. 88–9, no. 19; Cahill 1998, fig. 11; *A Compendium of Chinese Paintings* 1997–2001, vol. 7, *Yuan I*, p. 47, pl. 43 and vol. 8, *Yuan II*, pp. 12–13, 152, pls 12, 129; McCausland 2000, p. 114, fig. 1; Chen 2003, fig. 12; Li 2003; New York 2008a, pp. 10–13, no. 2; New York 2010, pp. 193–4, fig. 211

The imported 'celestial steed', treasured by early emperors and noble warriors, was a subject favoured by such leading painters as Han Gan (act. 742–56) and Li Gonglin (c.1049–1106). In the early Yuan period (1271–1368), when the ruling Mongols curtailed the employment of Chinese scholar-officials, the theme of the groom and horse – one associated with the legendary figure of Bole, whose ability to judge horses had become a metaphor for the recruitment of able government officials – came to be a symbolic plea for the proper use of scholarly talent. Zhao Mengfu painted the first part of this work for the high-ranking surveillance commissioner Feiqing, who may have been a government recruiter. Executed in early 1296, shortly after Zhao withdrew from civil service, the sensitively rendered groom may be a self-portrait.

The striking geometry of the composition, made up of a series of prominent arcs in the figures of the horse and groom, and framed by the level ground line and vertical inscription, appears to have been constructed with a compass and square. The Chinese term 'compass-square' (*guiju*) means 'regulation' or 'order'. Thus, the painting may also be read as a metaphor for good government and, by extension, a measure of the artist's moral rectitude.[1]

Some 63 years later, in 1359, Xie Boli, the associate magistrate of Songjiang, near Zhao's hometown of Wuxing in Zhejiang Province, showed the painting to Zhao Mengfu's son Zhao Yong and grandson Zhao Lin, each of whom, at Xie's request, added his own painting of a groom and horse. The scroll has since been celebrated as a work incorporating paintings by three generations of the Zhao family.

Zhao Mengfu's almost entirely white horse is defined by geometric, calligraphic lines. This stark abstraction of the horse's form combined with its dramatically foreshortened pose creates a bold contrast with the sensitively rendered groom, who faces directly forward, confronting the viewer with his gaze. The son's and grandson's paintings show nothing of this intensity. Zhao Yong's profile image of a piebald horse executed in emphatic outlines comes across as static, while the accompanying heavily bearded Mongolian groom is more caricature than portrait. Zhao Lin follows a similarly formulaic pose for his horse and attendant, although his Chinese groom is made more prominent through the use of bright pigments. All three artists are indebted to an earlier prototype – *Five Tribute Horses* by Li Gonglin (c.1049–1106) – but only Zhao Mengfu surpassed his model by reconceiving of the relationship of the groom, both with his horse and with the viewer. MH

1 See Hay 1989.

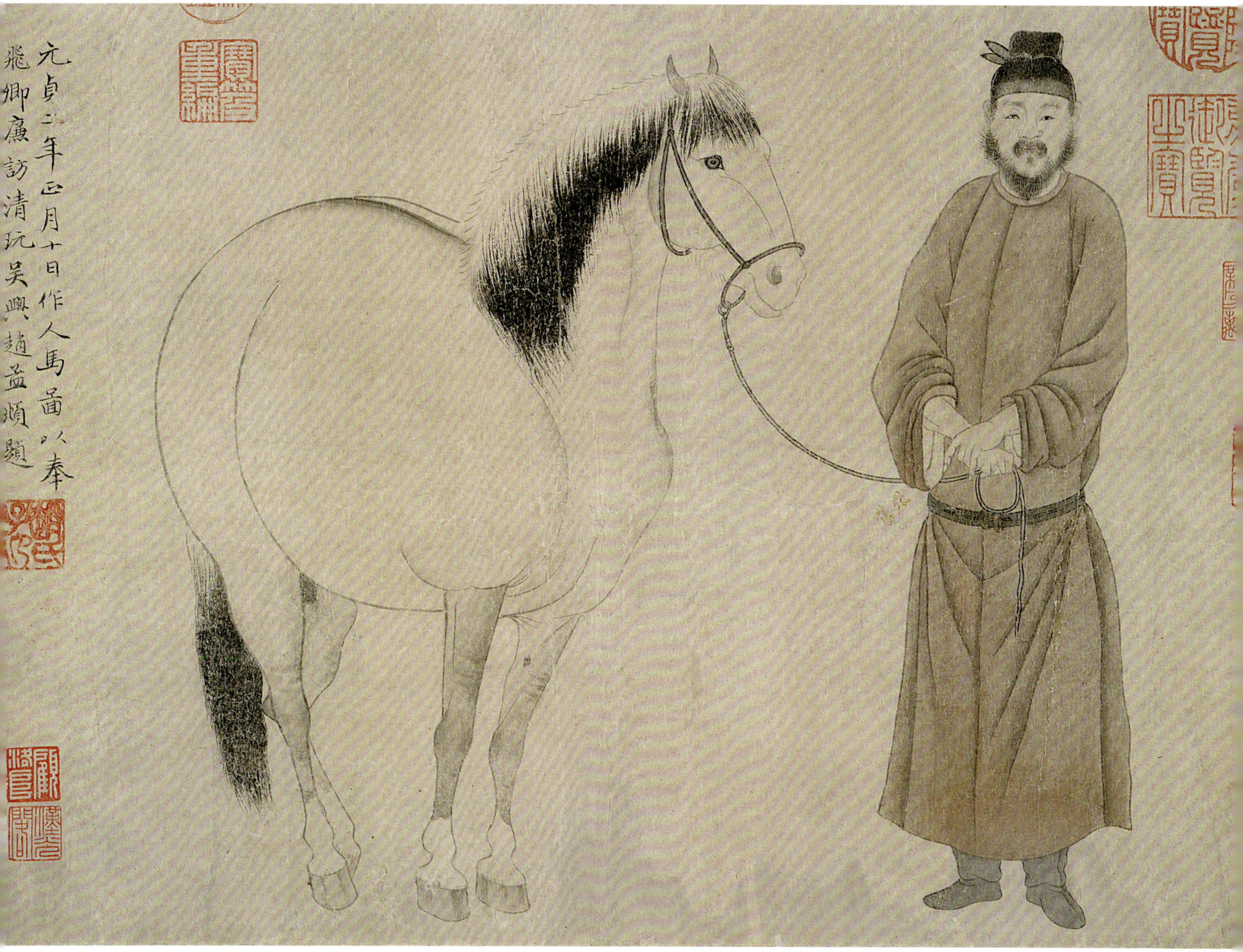
元貞二年正月十日作人馬圖以奉
飛卿廉訪清玩吳興趙孟頫題

47

ZHENG SIXIAO (1239–1316)

## Ink Orchid

元 鄭思肖 墨蘭圖 卷

1306, handscroll, ink on paper, 25.7 × 42.4 cm
Osaka City Museum of Fine Arts (42,1-132)

REFERENCE LITERATURE

Harada 1939; Yang 1977; Kyoto 1982; Osaka and Shanghai 1994; Nara 1997; Yumino in Shanghai 2010; Takenami 2011

Zheng Sixiao, courtesy name (*zi*) 'Yiweng', literary name (*hao*) 'Suonan', was a native of Lianjiang (in present-day Fujian Province). He attended the imperial university in the last years of the Song dynasty (960–1279), and was selected to enter for the 'erudite literatus' (*boxu hongci*) examination – a special civil service examination for men of exceptional literary talents – but with the collapse of the Song and the establishment of the Mongol Yuan dynasty (1271–1368), withdrew to a life of monastic reclusion in Pingjiang (present Suzhou). Vowing to have nothing to do with the conquerors from the north, he refused an invitation to serve at the Yuan court, and as a *yimin* ('leftover subject'), remained loyal to the fallen Song.

The name 'Sixiao' itself can be read as 'thinking of the Song imperial line': 'si' (思) signifies 'to think', and 'xiao' (肖) is the right-hand element of the character 'zhao' (趙), and can thus stand for the family name of the Song imperial clan. Likewise, the first character of Zheng's courtesy name, 'yi' (憶), 'to remember' and the second character of his literary name, 'nan' (南), meaning 'south', also convey loyalist sentiments.

Zheng Sixiao wrote many poems raging against Yuan rule. He collected a number of these in an anthology entitled *History of the Heart*, including 'A Brief Account of the Great Righteousness', his expression of yearning for the Song dynasty. In 1283, Zheng sealed the poetry collection in an iron box, and threw it into a well at Chengtian Temple in Suzhou. It was discovered some 350 years later, in 1638, at the end of the Ming dynasty (1368–1644), when Suzhou was experiencing a severe drought and the well ran dry. While dredging the well, one of the temple monks came upon the box in the muddy water. Consequently, the anthology has become known as the 'Iron Box History of the Heart'.

A great painter as well as a poet, Zheng used the orchid to express his bitter feelings about the devastation of his country. It was a subject he took very seriously. The leaves and flowers of his orchids are rendered in fluid, abbreviated strokes, and there are no roots to hold the plants securely in the ground. When asked about this, it is said that Zheng replied: 'The soil has been taken by the foreigners. Can you bear it?'

Brushed in light ink wash, it is pure and elegant in appearance. The poem inscribed in the upper right of the composition reads:

> I have been asking Xihuang [an ancient hermit] with my head bowed:
> Who were you – and why did you come to this land?
> I opened my nostrils before making the painting,
> And there, floating everywhere in the sky, is the antique fragrance undying.[1]

To the left of the image is an inscription giving the date. Only the characters for 'the first' and 'the fifteenth' designating the month and day were written with a brush; the other characters were printed with a woodblock. This suggests that in that year, Zheng was producing ink orchids in some number. Next to the date is inscribed a poem by his contemporary Chen Shen (1260–1344) written in cursive script. Another short handscroll of an ink orchid with the same poem by Chen Shen and an identical date is held in the Freer and Sackler Galleries in Washington, DC. YT

1 Translation by Wai-kam Ho, quoted in Cahill 1976, p. 16

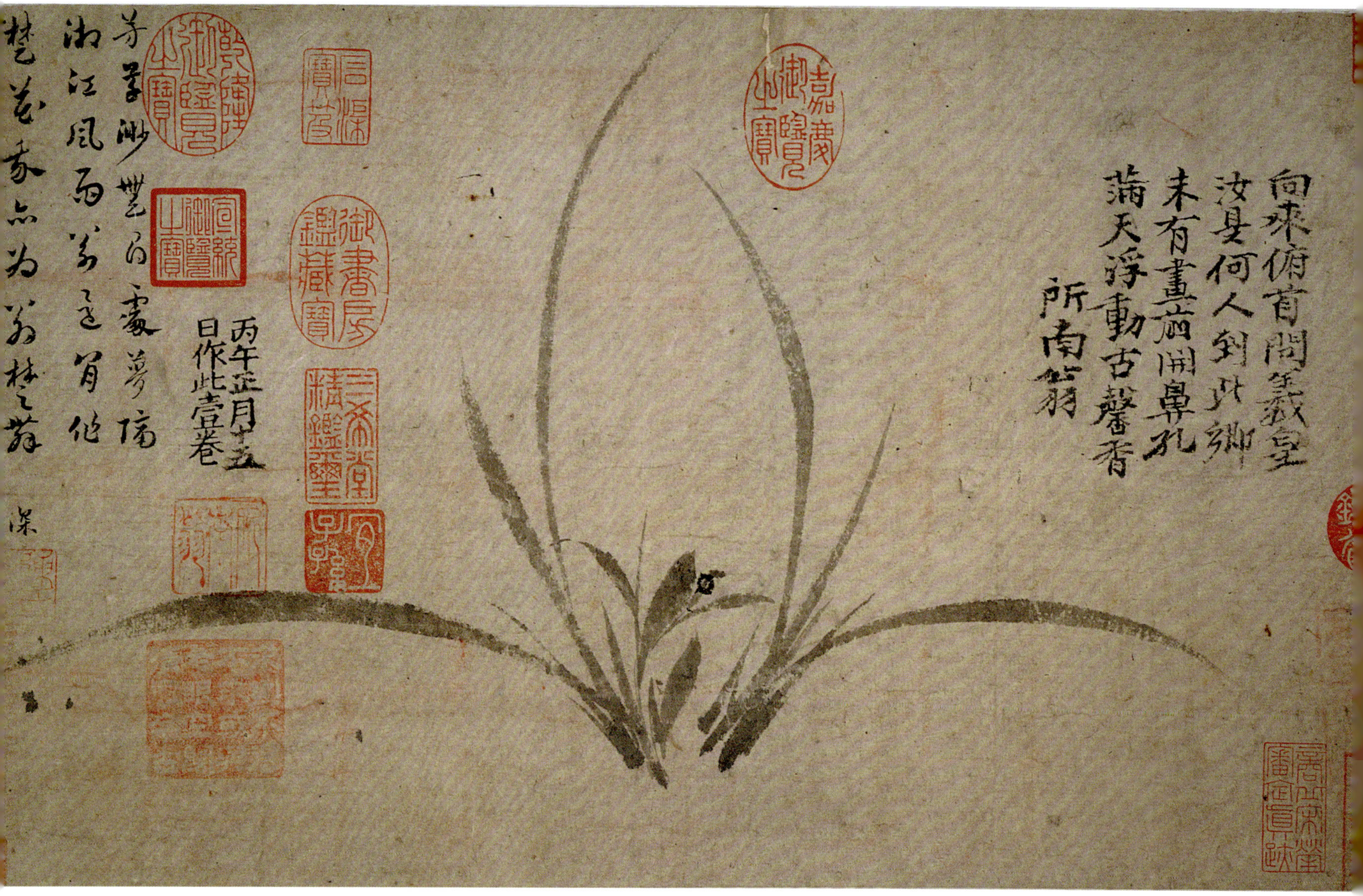
向來俯首問羲皇
汝是何人到此鄉
未有畫前開鼻孔
滿天浮動古馨香
所南翁
丙午正月十五日作此壹卷

48

WANG MIAN (1287–1359)

## Fragrant Snow at Broken Bridge

元 王冕 墨梅圖 軸

1st half 14th century, hanging scroll,
ink on silk, 113 × 50.2 cm
The Metropolitan Museum of Art, New York
Purchase, Gift of J. Pierpont Morgan,
by exchange, 1973 (1973.121.9)

PROVENANCE

C.C. Wang Family

REFERENCE LITERATURE

Cleveland 1968, pp. 49–50, 97–9, no. 250; New York 1973, pp. 131–3, 135, 151, no. 25; Barnhart 1983, pp. 142–3, fig. 65; Chi 1984a, pp. 37–58, 1984b, pp. 41–66, fig. 17 and 1985, pp. 29–51, reference p. 50; New Haven 1985, pp. 59, 78, figs 17 and 30, no. 14; Fong 1992, p. 392, fig. 87; New York 2000, p. 64, no. 4

Together with the pine and bamboo, the flowering plum was celebrated as one of the 'Three Friends of Wintry Weather', emblems of longevity, endurance and renewal. By the eleventh century, each had become an independent subject for painters, particularly scholar-artists, who reduced the complex forms of these subjects to calligraphic conventions. Blooming before all other trees, the plum was welcomed as the harbinger of spring, but by Wang Mian's time, under the impact of the harsh rule of the Mongol Yuan dynasty (1271–1368), the image of craggy plum trees blossoming through snow-covered branches had become a powerful symbol of purity and endurance in adversity.

Poet, painter, scholar and would-be military tactician, Wang Mian was determined to fulfil his responsibilities as a man of talent despite the frustrations and dangers of life under Mongol rule.[1] Born in Zhuji, in present Zhejiang Province, Wang received a Confucian education, but failed the civil service examination. Seeking advancement by other means, in the late 1340s he travelled to the Yuan capital (present Beijing), where he sought the patronage of the high official Tai Buhua (Tai Bukha; 1304–52). Sensing the imminent disintegration of Yuan rule, however, he returned to the south in 1348, living in reclusion in the Kuaiji mountains above Zhuji, planting plum trees and composing political treatises. Most of his plum paintings date from this period. In 1359, when Chinese troops under the future Ming (1368–1644) founder Zhu Yuanzhang (1328–98) laid siege to Shaoxing, Wang volunteered his services as a military strategist, but his plan for capturing the city failed. He died shortly thereafter.

Though he failed in his career ambitions, Wang established a lasting reputation as the quintessential painter of the blossoming plum. Here, Wang Mian brought into balance the expressive and representational elements of his subject. In depicting fragile blossoms a nd rough branches, he employed both the delicately descriptive techniques of his academic predecessors and the bold calligraphic brushwork of his literati contemporaries. The dramatic curving branches of the pendant bough powerfully evoke the force of the wind as it sweeps rightwards, carrying some of the petals with it. The arcing lines of the branches are a tour de force of brushwork, while the white of the blossoms and snow-caked bough is highlighted by covering the rest of the picture surface in a light grey wash.

According to Maggie Bickford, Wang Mian was the first plum painter to integrate poetry into his compositions, thereby establishing the principal model for all subsequent explorations of this theme.[2] Nested between the branches, the artist's inscription, written in a bold cursive script that echoes the drama of the painting, extends the meaning of his pictorial imagery:

> Chilly plum blossoms fill branches of
> white jade;
> Scattered by a warm breeze, [petals] flutter
> like snowflakes.
> The 'Recluse of Solitary Hill' [Lin Bu]
> remains true to himself,
> But who carries the song of reed pipes
> across Broken Bridge?

The image of scattering blossoms in both the painting and the poem evokes the fleeting transience of life, while the artist's firm resolve is conveyed through the painting's sturdy branches and the poem's invocation of the poet Lin Bu (967–1028). Lin maintained an unsullied existence living on Solitary Hill (Gu Shan), a small island in Hangzhou's West Lake, where he cultivated plum trees and styled himself as the Plum Blossom Recluse. However, the poem's final line heralds a possible end to reclusion as someone crosses the apparently 'broken' snow-covered bridge that connects Solitary Hill to the shore. Could it be a harbinger of change brought about by rebel forces challenging Yuan dynasty rule? MH

1 For a fuller account of Wang Mian's life and art, see Bickford 1996, pp. 203–17.
2 Ibid., p. 208

49

UNIDENTIFIED ARTIST;
traditionally attributed to
GUO ZHONGSHU (d.977)

## The Summer Palace of Emperor Minghuang

元 傳郭忠恕 明皇避暑宮圖 軸

probably 2nd half 14th century, hanging scroll,
ink on silk, 161.5 × 105.6 cm
Osaka City Museum of Fine Arts (42, I-13)

REFERENCE LITERATURE

Ise 1930; Maeda 1975; Ogawa 1980; Kyoto 1983; Osaka and Shanghai 1994; Ogawa 1994 and 1997; Nara 1997; Liu 2002; Nara 2008; Yumino in Shanghai 2010; Tsukamoto 2011a

Emperor Minghuang is the Tang period (618–907) ruler Xuanzong (r. 712–55). He restored the Sui dynasty (581–618) Renshou gong (The Palace of Benevolence and Longevity), located in the hills of present-day Shaanxi Province and renamed it Jiucheng gong (The Palace of Nine Perfections), moving there every summer to conduct affairs of state from the cool retreat (see cat. no. 72). The painting depicts the magnificent building and the grand landscape surrounding it. At the lower right is a signature reading 'Zhongshu', which would identify the painting as a work by Guo Zhongshu (d.977).

Guo was a native of Luoyang (in modern Henan Province). It is said that by the age of seven he was skilled at both reading and composing. He was well versed in philology, as well as gifted at calligraphy and painting. During the Guangshun era (951–3) during the Five Dynasties period (907–60), he was summoned to the imperial court as minster for imperial clansmen, serving at the same time as erudite of calligraphy at the National University. When he took the throne, the Northern Song (960–1127) emperor Taizong (r. 976–97) bestowed on him the title of recorder at the Directorate of Education. Guo also compiled a succession of etymological dictionaries and authored other scholarly works on etymology, including *The Origins of Characters* and *Small Seal Script*. In calligraphy he was known particularly for the excellence of his seal and clerical scripts, while in painting he was especially skilled in the finely detailed 'ruled-line' (*jiehua*) technique used for architectural structures, and showed a great talent for landscape depiction. He is in a rank of his own among the Song (960–1279) painters listed in the 'Palaces' category in the *Xuanhe Painting Catalogue*, where one finds a total of 34 works ascribed to him, including those with the title *The Summer Palace of Emperor Minghuang* and its variations.

The Song literatus Li Zhi's (1059–1109) *Evaluations of Painters from the Deyu Studio* contains this description of Guo's work: '[in his paintings] roof beams, girders, pillars and rafters are shown with open spaces between, through which one might move. Railings, lintels, windows and doorways look as if they could really be passed through, or opened and shut. A *hao* length [that is, ⅓ decimillimetre] is used to mark off an inch; a *fen* length [⅓ centimetre] to mark off a foot; and an inch to mark off 10 feet; increasing thus with every multiple, so that when a large building is drawn, everything is to scale and there are never even slight discrepancies.'[1] As Li states, here the entire architectural structure is rendered in extremely precise, fine line, a meticulously detailed and careful depiction that characterizes even the roof tiles and paving stones, as well as the furnishings and vegetation. It is certainly the kind of painting that draws the viewer in.

We enter through the gate at the bottom of the composition, move across a terrace to the pavilion in the centre, and proceed toward the main palace building in the upper part of the painting, encountering along the way a series of towers projecting out to the left. Moving through the painting creates the sensation of strolling through the huge palace. Figures abound, none of them identical: they lay out tableware, close curtains, hold scrolls of painting and calligraphy, and examine the fine utensils displayed on the table. Others are depicted in lively conversation. The human activity takes place against a background of lofty mountains wrapped in soft mists and soaring into the sky, and a river that flows swiftly down the left side of the painting. The juxtaposition of the strict, straight lines of the buildings and the presentation of the landscape embody the style for which Guo was rightly famous.

Since the signature appears to have been added later, however, a confident attribution to Guo Zhongshu is somewhat problematic. Certain elements of the painting, including the texture strokes used to define the distant peaks, have led to the current supposition that the work may be by a Yuan period (1271–1368) artist working in the Li-Guo tradition. Further, it is close in style to Li Rongjin's (act. 2nd half 14th century) *The Han Palace* (National Palace Museum, Taipei). The student of Wang Zhenpeng (c.1280–c.1329), who developed a particular style of architectural painting at the Mongol court, Li was highly skilled at this type of work. YT

1 Translation borrowed from Liu 2002, p. 566

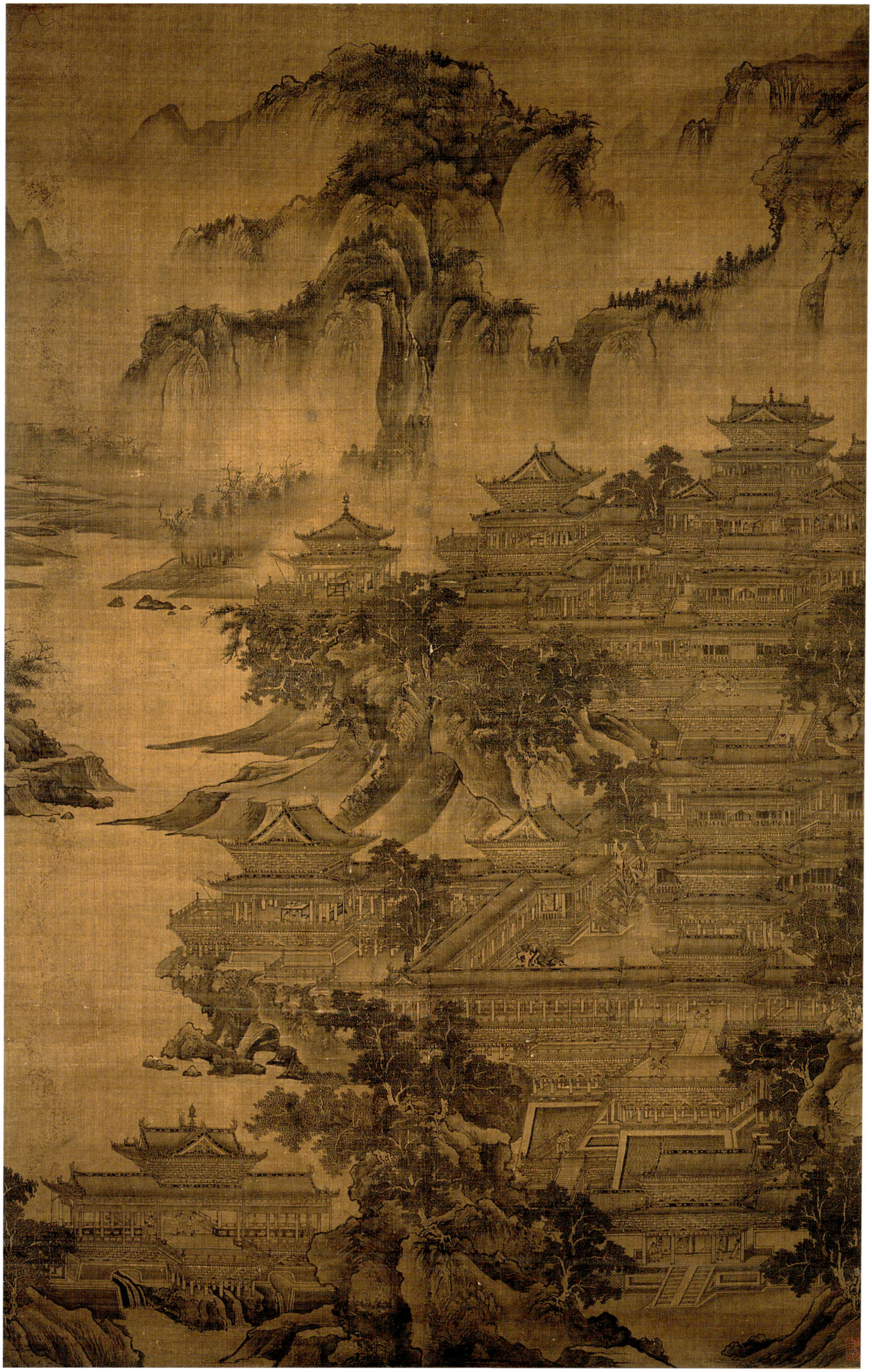

50

UNIDENTIFIED ARTIST
(act. 14th century)

## Bodhidharma Crossing the Yangzi on a Reed

元 佚名 達摩渡江圖 軸

before 1363, hanging scroll, ink on paper,
89.2 × 31.1 cm
The Cleveland Museum of Art
John L. Severance Fund (1964.44)

PROVENANCE

Purchased from N.V. Hammer, Inc., New York City in 1964

REFERENCE LITERATURE

Cleveland 1964, fig. 39; Lee 1972, p. 244, fig. 5; Zainie 1978, pp. 241–3, figs 2 and 10; Kansas City and Cleveland 1980, pp. 124–5; Cleveland 1986, p. 253

Bodhidharma, the First Patriarch of Chan (J. Zen) Buddhism, is shown miraculously crossing the Yangzi River on a reed. The text *The True Record of the Five Schools* (1254) tells us that after coming from India to China to teach the Chan doctrine, he travelled to the court of Emperor Wu (r. 502–49) of the southern Liang dynasty (502–57). When the Emperor failed to grasp the master's teaching, Bodhidharma headed north. Arriving on the bank of the Yangzi, '[Bodhidharma] then snapped a reed and crossed the [Yangzi] River; arriving at Shaolin, he faced a wall for nine years.'[1] In Bodhidharma's long biography this event marks a simple change of setting, yet this moment of transition was one of the most popular subjects of thirteenth- and fourteenth-century Chan iconography.

The popularity of this subject in painting can be explained by its combination of dramatic tension and powerful religious symbolism. It is both a physical and spiritual transition, as the master simultaneously crosses China's greatest river and moves from a life of teaching into nine years of reclusion. This association of religious hermits with a supernormal ability to cross water has a long history in China, seen in images of Daoist immortals traversing rivers and oceans.[2] As such, this painting casts Bodhidharma as an accomplished Chinese wonder-worker, in spite of his foreign origins.

This artist has also drawn on a specifically Chan style of depiction to reveal Bodhidharma's transcendence, known as 'apparition painting'.[3] This style's name derives from the illusionistic pale ink of the figure's body that appears to fade before the viewer's eye. In this work a handful of fast, undulating strokes shapes the patriarch's robe, varying the thickness of their line to imply his hunched shoulders and the clasped hands beneath his garment. His grim and resolute stare contrasts with the paleness of his body, emphasized by the dark ink of his pupils, eyebrows, nostrils and downturned mouth. This expression is framed by the thick wash of the master's beard, reiterating his foreignness. Highlighting Bodhidharma's origins in the lands from which Buddhism came to China lends greater weight to his spiritual authority, while also injecting a frisson of excitement at the combination of the sacred and the grotesque.

The Chan abbot Liaoan Qingyu (1288–1363) inscribed the painting with the following verse:[4]

> The reeds bloom, the wind rises, and the crests of waves are high,
> The Shaoshi cliff lies ahead, a far road to travel,
> Beyond the world of kalpas [an aeon in the Buddhist cycle of cosmic time], a single flower blossoms into five petals,
> My heels are now readied for the whipping of a rattan cane.[5]

Liaoan's inscription would have accompanied the giving of this painting to a disciple, recording the student's connection to his master. The poem makes explicit reference to this practice in the third line, borrowing the image of the flower blossoming into five petals from the third line of a verse in *The True Record of the Five Schools*, which marks the transmission of Bodhidharma's teachings and robe to the second patriarch, Huike.[6] Liaoan thereby connects the transmission of his own teachings back to Chan Buddhism's mythical founder. MM

1 Shao (1254) 1975–89, 1:0576b15
2 For example, see *Immortal Crossing the Waves*, in the style of Yan Hui (act. early 14th century); hanging scroll, ink and colour on silk, c.14th century. The British Museum, London (1881–1210–0.58.CH)
3 For a detailed discussion of apparition painting, see Lippit 2009.
4 Liaoan Qingyu (1288–1363), (Liaoan Qingyu Chanshi yulu) The Recorded Sayings of Master Liao Qingyu, lists only four inscriptions on images of Bodhidharma, this verse not among them; see *Supplement to the Manji Edition of the Buddhist Canon* 1975–89, vol. 71, no. 1414, 5:0351,c23-0352,a07.
5 Translation adapted from Wai-kam Ho in Kansas City and Cleveland 1980, pp. 124–5; and Chou 2012, provided by the Cleveland Museum of Art in personal correspondence with the author
6 Shao (1254) 1975–89, 1:0576b18

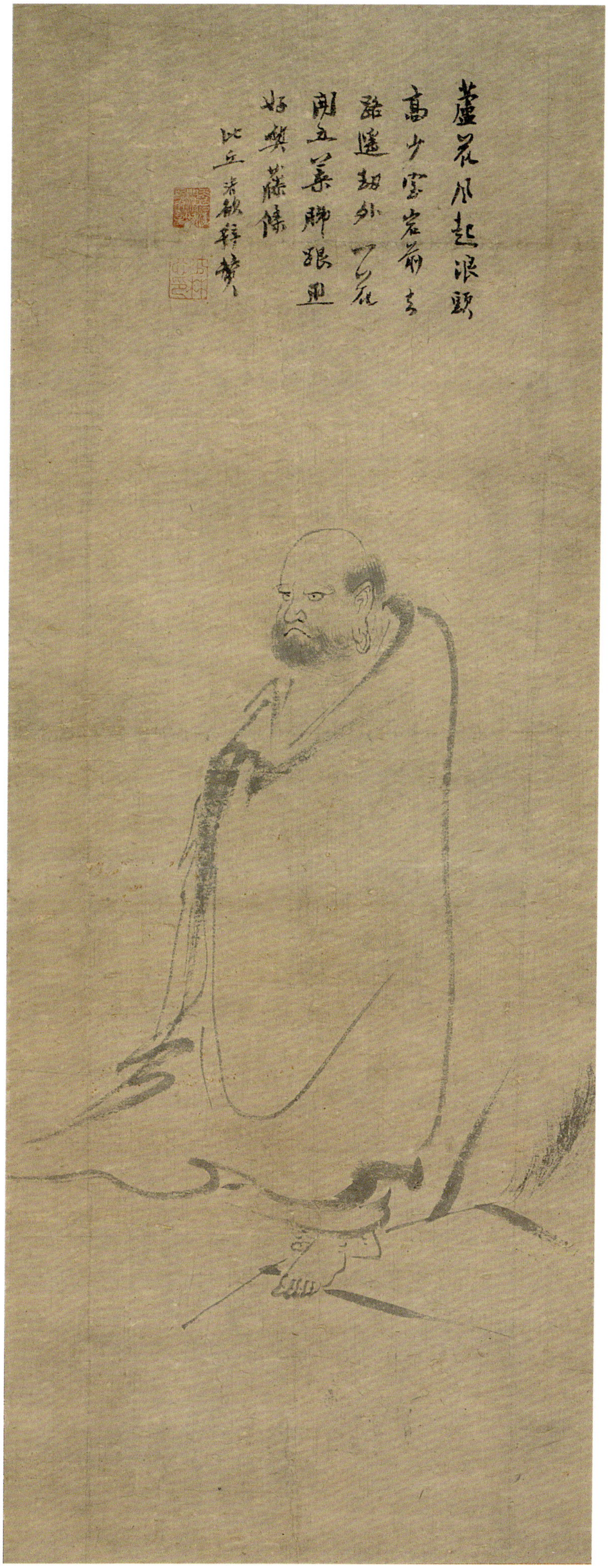

## 51

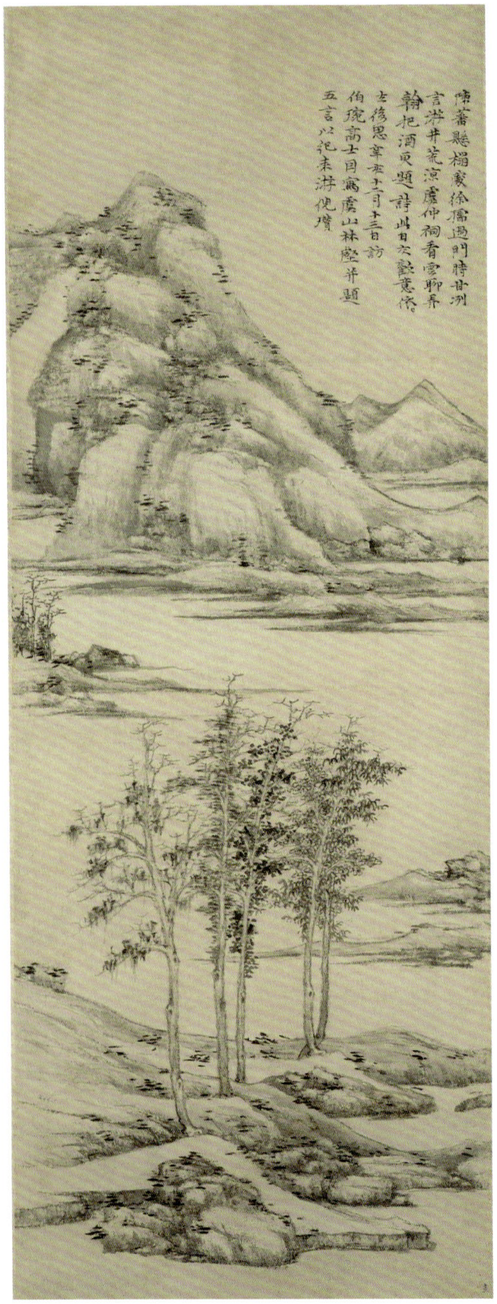

NI ZAN (1306–74)

### Woods and Valleys of Mount Yu

元 倪瓚 虞山林壑圖 軸

1372, hanging scroll, ink on paper, 94.6 × 35.9 cm
The Metropolitan Museum of Art, New York
Gift of the Dillon Fund, 1973 (1973.120.8)

PROVENANCE

C.C. Wang Family

REFERENCE LITERATURE

Zheng 1948, pl. 34; Zhu 1952, p. 109; Chen 1956, p. 41; Sirén 1956–8, vol. 4, p. 81; vol. 6, pl. 95; vol. 7, p. 128; Cahill 1960, pp. 111–12; Fong 1963; Wang 1967, pp. 26–7, fig. 14; Cleveland 1968, no. 253; New York 1973, pp. 110–14, 124, 149, no. 20; Xu 1974, p. 32; Zheng 1982, p. 28, fig. 6; New York 1983a, pp. 162–5, fig. 77; Princeton 1984, pp. 125–6, fig. 118; Fong 1992, pp. 490–6. fig. 118a,b; An (1742) 1993–8, vol. 10, pp. 380–1; Wu (17th century) 1994, vol. 8, p. 98; Wu (1713) 1993–8, vol. 8, p. 510; *A Compendium of Chinese Painting* 1997–2001, vol. 8, p. 125, pl. 107; Chen (1915) 2007, pp. 321–3; New York 2008a, pp. 100–5, no. 23

*(with collectors' seals and an inscription removed digitally)*

Ni Zan is celebrated as one of the Four Masters of the Late Yuan (1271–1368). His spare, dry-brush style featuring angular rocks and sparsely foliaged trees is one of the most iconic in all of Chinese painting, and had a lasting impact on later Chinese art.

A well-to-do landowner and dilettante in his early life, Ni was forced to abandon his comfortable lifestyle and flee his hometown of Wuxi, Jiangsu Province, to escape the extortionate tax collectors that emerged with the disintegration of Yuan dynasty rule in the 1350s. Between 1356 and 1366, Ni and his family became refugees, residing to the south-west of Suzhou at a place he nicknamed 'Snail's Hut'. This simple existence was disrupted in 1366 when Ni was again forced to abandon his home due to marauding soldiers. Even after the establishment of the Ming dynasty (1368–1644), Ni continued the life of a wanderer, visiting old haunts he had not seen in decades. According to his epitaph writer Zhou Nanlao (1308–83): 'In his late years, he became quieter and more withdrawn than ever. Having lost or given away everything he ever owned, he did his best to forget his worries. Wearing a yellow [Daoist] cap and country clothes, he roamed the lakes and mountains, leading a recluse's life.'[1]

Ni Zan painted virtually the same composition his entire life – a grove of trees on a rocky foreground shore juxtaposed with distant mountains – the subtle variation in each iteration revealing changes in his circumstances and state of mind. Always painting for a friend or close associate, his foreground trees were a metaphor for his tight-knit circle of like-minded colleagues. Almost always, this grove of trees is isolated from the distant mountains, whose promise of shelter and refuge lies beyond reach. Beginning sometime in the 1350s, Ni also ceased to add seals to his paintings – imparting a sense of incompleteness and impermanence to his works that mirrored his own lack of a settled existence. However, in *Woods and Valleys of Mount Yu*, executed in 1372, just two years before his death, it is clear that Ni had regained his equilibrium. The dry, softly rubbed brushwork is confidently and effortlessly applied. There is a tranquil, luminous quality to the painting that makes it one of the most fully realized works of the artist's later years. Ni's improved situation and spirits are apparent in the flourishing summertime foliage of his trees, where the rich complexity of the leaf patterns conveys a sense of energy and excitement. Likewise, the near-ground embankment and distant mountains – which now appear much closer to the foreground trees – show an increased substantiality that suggests a renewed feeling of security. The accessibility of the mountains is underscored by an intermediate shoreline that actually intersects with the trees' uppermost branches. Ni's accompanying poem expresses this same spirit of optimism and contentment in the life of a recluse. The poem ends with these lines:

> We watch the clouds and daub with our brushes;
> We drink wine and write poems.
> The joyful feelings of this day
> Will linger long after we have parted.[2]

MH

1 This account is drawn from Wen Fong's biography of Ni Zan in Princeton 1984, pp. 105–12. The quote is from page 112.
2 Translation from Fong 1992, p. 490

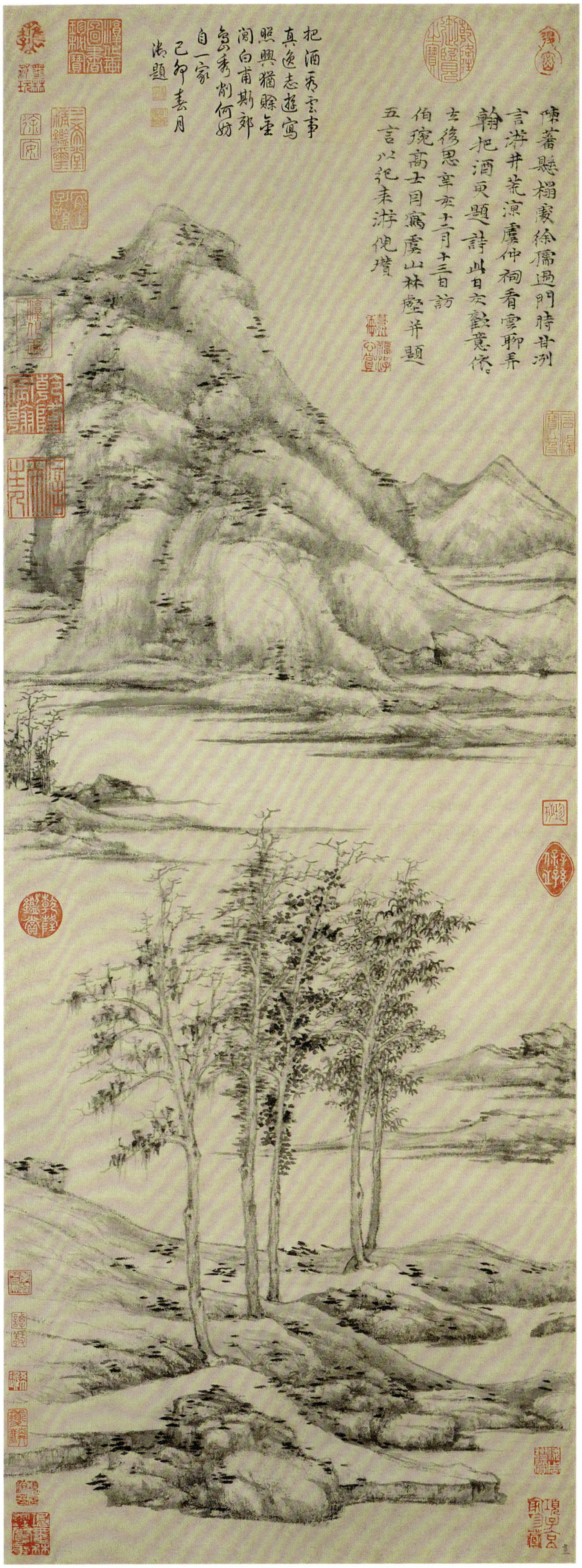

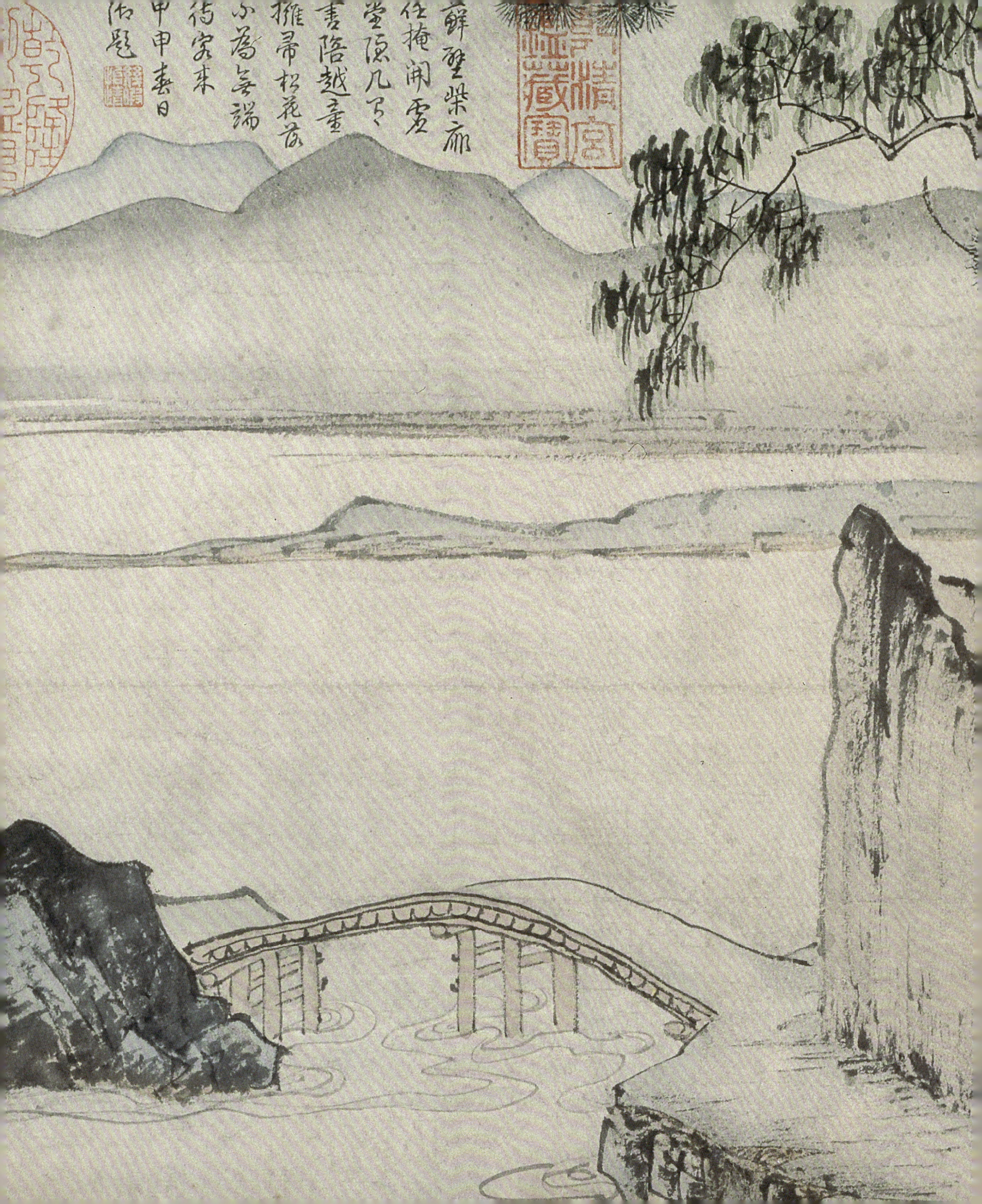

任掩閑雲
擁帚松花落
待客來
甲申春日
御題

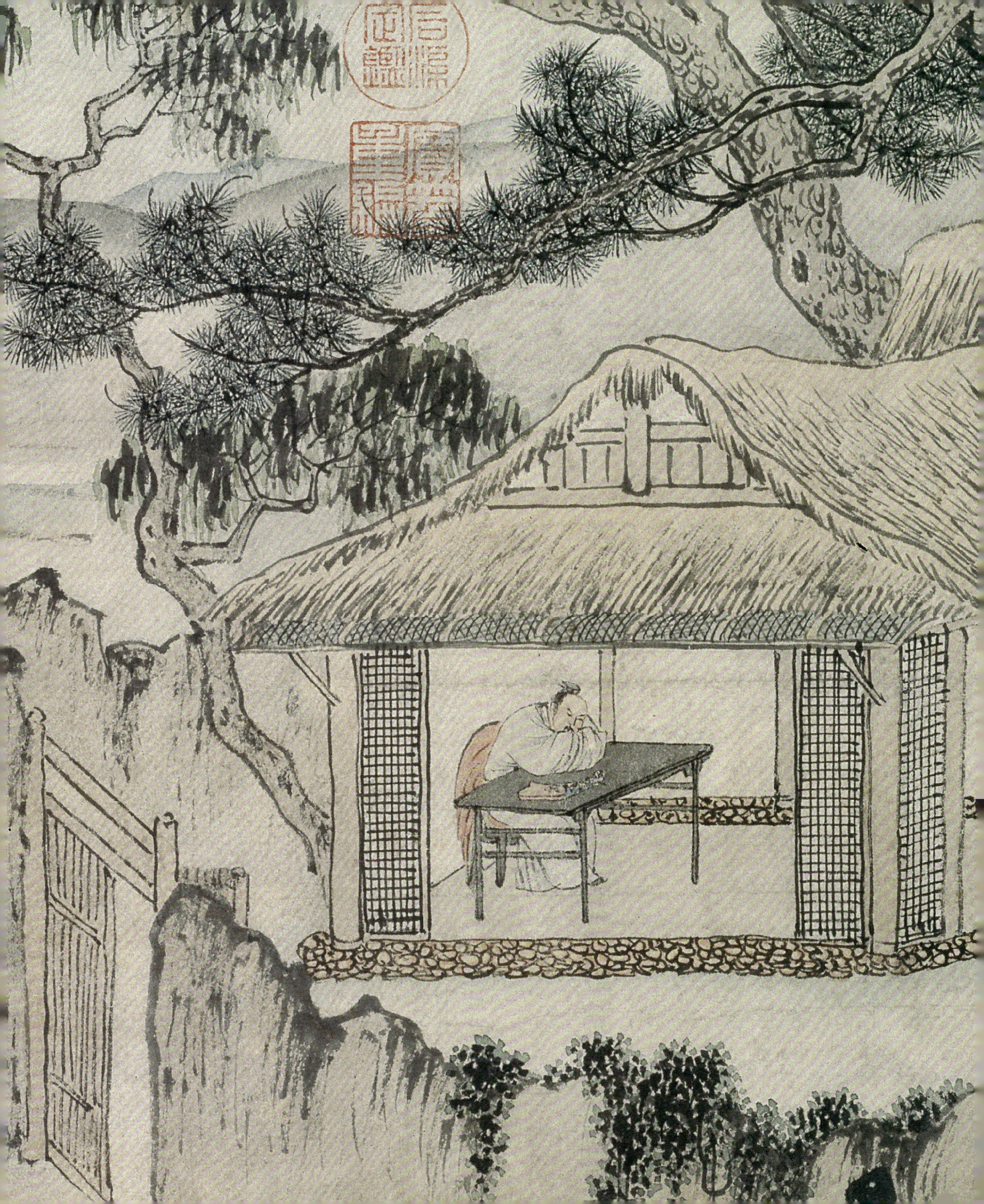

# Paintings 1400–1600

In 1368, Han-Chinese rule was restored by the first emperor of the Ming dynasty (1368–1644), Hongwu (r. 1368–98). It was further consolidated by his fourth son, Zhu Di, Prince of Yan, who usurped the throne (reigning as Yongle; 1403–24) and moved the capital to Yan (present Beijing) in order to secure the all-important northern frontier. In the arts, there was a conscious revival of indigenous Chinese themes, harking back especially to the glories of the Song dynasty (960–1279). There was an academy of court painters, but with a difference: they were given nominal ranks in the imperial guard, and were based inside the Forbidden City, in the Wuying dian or Hall of Martial Valour. A vast painting by Shang Xi (act. *c.*1430–40) in the Palace Museum, Beijing, displays the Xuande emperor (r. 1426–35) with his colourful entourage on an excursion to the imperial Shangxi Park, inhabited by cranes and other auspicious creatures, such as those portrayed among brightly coloured flowers and trees by Lü Ji (act. 1488–1505) (cat. no. 56); another, by Xie Huan (act. *c.*1426–52), in the Metropolitan Museum of Art, New York, depicts and identifies by name the most powerful officials of the time, one of whom, Yang Shiqi (1364–1444), kept his post in the Grand Secretariat for 43 years, serving under no fewer than four emperors.[1] Significantly, these grandees are shown not in the exercise of their government functions, but in the garden of another, Yang Rong (1371–1440), indulging in the sophisticated pastimes of the educated scholar-official, just like the gentlemen depicted in the set of *The Four Pleasures: Music, Chess, Calligraphy and Painting* (cat. no. 53). Despite the magnificence, the atmosphere at court was restrictive: Dai Jin (1388–1462), who initially served at court under the Xuande emperor, was driven out by intrigue, becoming the leader of the professional painters outside the court. His *Spring Clouds in the Linggu Mountains* (cat. no. 52), with a colophon inscribed by the recipient whose retreat it depicts, is a marvellous example of skill in the handling of colours on silk: the pine-tree clumps in the foreground recall the noble trees portrayed in the Song dynasty, but are enlivened by the floating greenery of their crowns and by the bright colours of the small-scale figures. Stretching Ma Yuan's (act. late 12th–early 13th century) 'one-corner' composition, Dai Jin cuts off the tops of the mountain peaks, depicted in the blue-green manner employed by Li Sixun (653–718) in the Tang dynasty (618–907), and adjusts the scale to achieve a vast expanse of water at the end of the scroll. The formula proved to be a popular one as scholars vied to display their country residences in idyllic surroundings.

Some scholars, however, gave up the idea of an official career, and followed the Yuan dynasty (1271–1368) painters in a life of chosen, rather than enforced, seclusion. Foremost among them, in both calligraphy and painting, is Shen Zhou (1427–1509). Not content with imitating their way of life, he also adopted the brush manners of not just one, but all four of the Yuan Masters, now one, now another, though with a marked preference in later life for the blunt ink idiom favoured by Wu Zhen (1280–1354). His large-character calligraphy, on the other hand, for which he was also renowned, is clearly related to that of the great calligrapher Huang Tingjian (1045–1105). Living in the pleasant town of Suzhou in Jiangsu Province, still famous for its gardens, Shen Zhou epitomizes the literati painter ethic, and his paintings often, as with *Twelve Views of Tiger Hill* (cat. no. 57), depict local sights and landmarks. On others he would add lengthy inscriptions that described the circumstances in which they were painted. His modest character, so evident in all his work, shines out in *Portrait of Shen Zhou at Age Eighty* (cat. no. 58), and also emerges in his studies of objects from daily life, like the animals and plants in a 16-leaf album in the National Palace Museum, Taipei, accompanied by a poem, the first couplet of which reads:

> Towards things that move and plants
> that grow
> I with my brush still may steal creation's
> secrets.[2]

Suzhou, also known as Wu Prefecture, gave its name to Shen Zhou's followers in the Wu school, chief among whom was Wen Zhengming (1470–1559), another brilliant calligrapher who took the examinations in the capital nine times but failed each time to match the exacting standards of the 'eight-legged essay' that was required; in 1523, he was nevertheless appointed to the Hanlin Academy, but resigned within a year. His difficulties on the long journey, and with the lack of money, are vividly recounted in a series of letters written to his sons Wen Peng and Wen Jia, along with instructions to study hard and look after their mother.[3] His contemporary, Tang Yin (1470–1523), also fell foul of the examination system, though in his case jealousy on the part of less talented but higher-class candidates may have played a part in his failure. *Dwelling by the Stream in Spring* (cat. no. 55), by his teacher Zhou Chen (*c.*1450–1535), exemplifies the idyllic surroundings in which these literati painters lived, while the title of Wen Zhengming's album *Garden of the Inept Administrator* (cat. no. 62) (a garden of this name still exists in Suzhou) makes clear the uneasy nature of their relationship with officialdom.

Counterpart to the Wu school was the Zhe school, named for the province of Zhejiang, from which many of the court painters were recruited. Their paintings, seldom adorned with more than a brief signature, favoured bold ink brushwork with none of the calligraphic restraint of the Wu painters; their subjects were often stirring tales from the turbulent period of the Three Kingdoms (220–80), or figures from mythology, such as *Deity with Phoenix* (cat. no. 59). From the viewpoint of the literati painters, the painters of the Zhe school were professionals, incapable of conveying the values inherent in calligraphic brushwork. So when Dong Qichang (1555–1636), whose influence was to prove inescapable in the succeeding centuries, inscribed Dai Jin's *Spring Clouds in the Linggu Mountains*, he determined that this was the work of an 'able' painter, outside the orthodox hierarchy of literati painting that he traced back through the fourteenth-century Yuan masters to Dong Yuan (act. 930s–60s) in the tenth century and eventually to Wang Wei (699–759) in the eighth.

Both schools continued to flourish in the sixteenth century, with descendants of Wen Zhengming particularly prominent in the Wu school. Suzhou, however, was also home to professional artists, among whom the foremost was Qiu Ying (1494/5–1552), who left a legacy of highly coloured and finely detailed works, often in the archaic 'blue-green' manner, such as *Saying Farewell at Xunyang* (cat. no. 61), the likes of which continued to be immensely popular until the end of the Qing dynasty (1644–1911).

1 This handscroll exists in two versions: Xie Huan's (act. *c.*1426–52) original executed for Yang Rong (1371–1440), in the Zhenjiang Museum, and an abbreviated version for Yang Shiqi (1364–1444), in the Metropolitan Museum of Art. See Hearn 1999.
2 Edwards 1987, p. 76
3 Translated in Ann Arbor 1976, pp. 86–93



cat. no. 61 (detail)

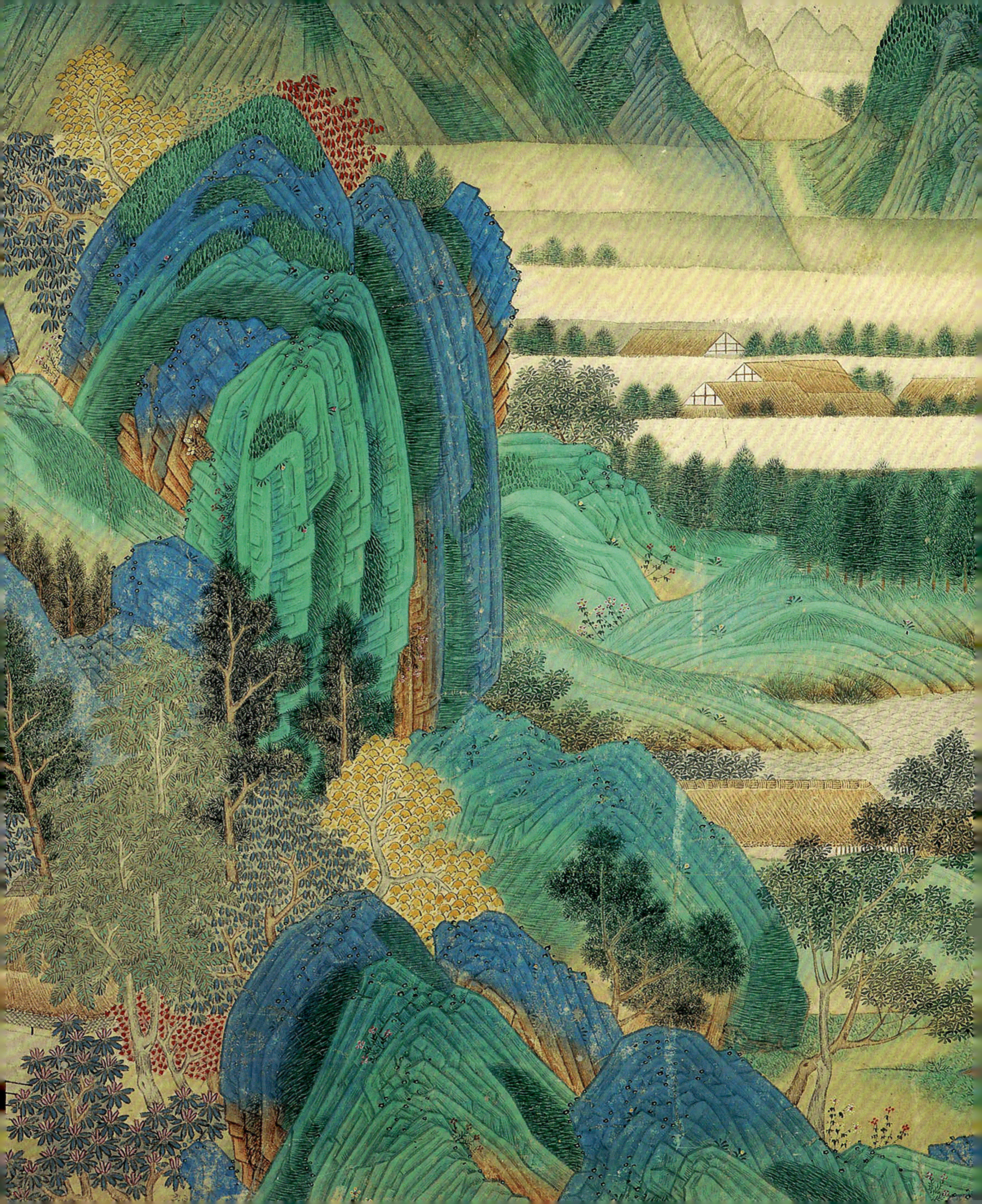

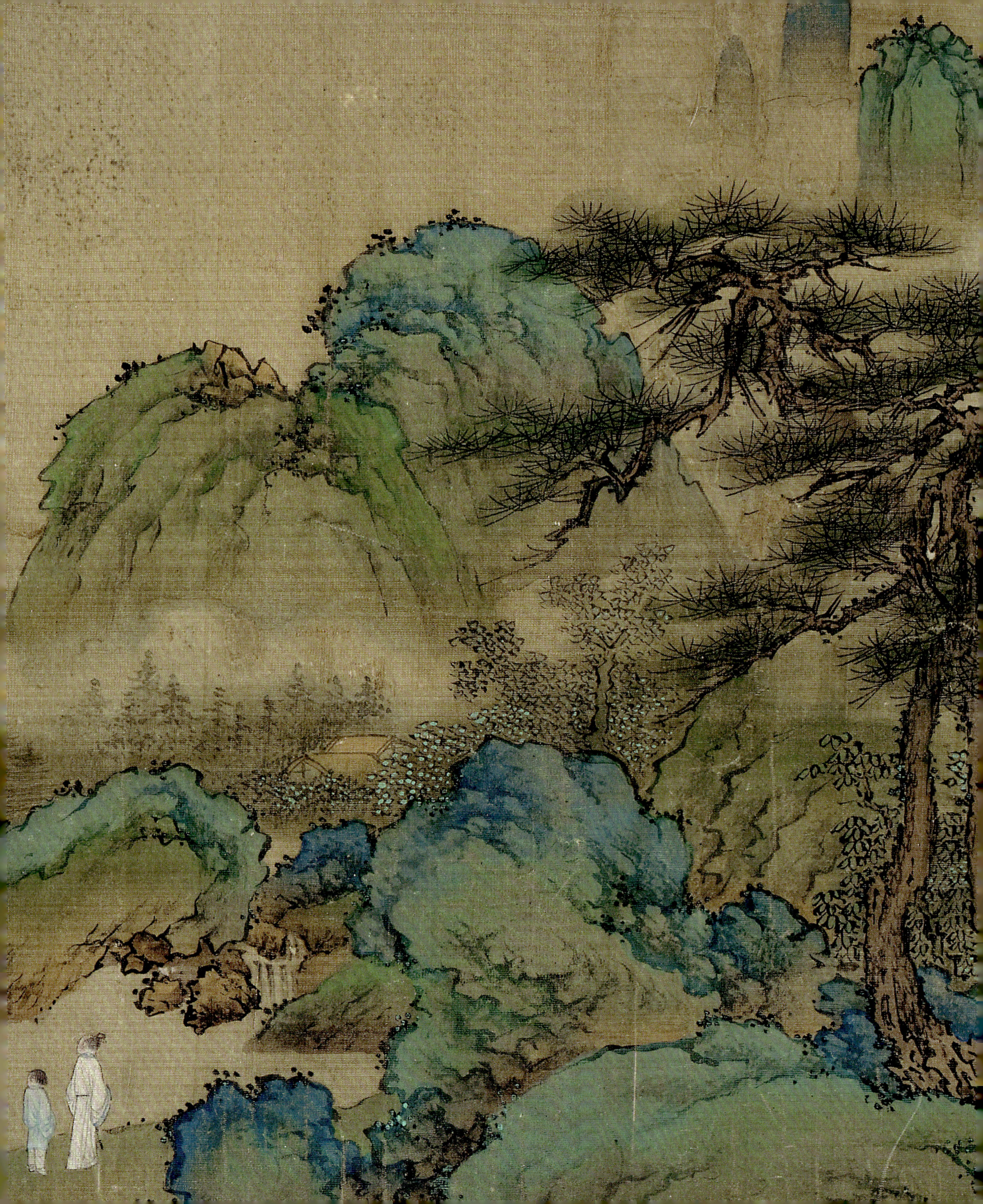

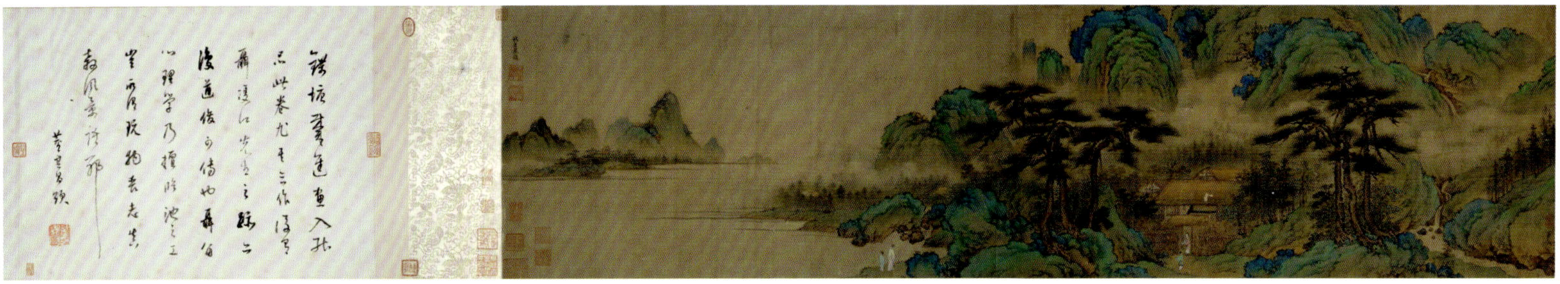

52

DAI JIN (1388–1462)

## Spring Clouds in the Linggu Mountains

明 戴進 靈谷春雲圖 卷

c.1440–62, handscroll, ink and colour on silk, 31.6 × 124.2 cm
Museum of Asian Art, Berlin (NR 5010)

PROVENANCE

Purchased in 1927 from the estate of Shao Songnian in Beijing

REFERENCE LITERATURE

Sun (1960) 1970, vol. 3, pp. 17–18; Rogers in New York and Dallas 1993; Veit in Ledderose 1998; Lu 2004

Dai Jin was the most important and famous Chinese painter of the first half of the fifteenth century. Many stories exist about his life, but it is hard to distinguish between fact and fiction.

What we do know is that he grew up in Qiantang, present-day Hangzhou, in a family of craftsman and artisan painters, and was already a highly respected artist by the time he went to the capital, today's Beijing, in 1428. Well received at the court initially, he failed to become an accredited court painter, and returned to Hangzhou. Around 1436 he again went to the capital, where he stayed for over 10 years. His last years were spent in Hangzhou.

Dai Jin worked in a characteristic new style that was prevalent in the fifteenth century, and which he was influential in creating. Its roots lay in the painting style practised at the Southern Song dynasty (1127–1279) court, with Ma Yuan (act. late 12th–early 13th century) and Xia Gui (act. 1180–1230) as representative masters, but which was now executed in a bolder manner and larger formats. Much later, around 1600, it was named Zhe school painting by the leading artist and theoretician Dong Qichang (1555–1636), after the province Zhejiang, where many of its representative painters were from. By Dong, Zhe school painting was regarded as craftsman-painting, much inferior to an idealized scholar-amateur painting he labelled Wu school, after Wu, an alternative name for the city of Suzhou.

*Spring Clouds in the Linggu Mountains* is a delicate painting in the blue-and-green (*qinglü*) style, named for the copious use of mineral blue and green pigments. This painting style was regarded as slightly solemn and archaistic, as it was associated with a number of early masters, primarily Li Sixun (653–718) and Zhao Boju (d.c.1162). Blue-and-green painting is rare in Dai Jin's oeuvre, but he uses it deftly here, without the stiffness it sometimes exhibits. The painting is a depiction of the Dongming studio near the Linggu mountains, not far from Linchuan in Jiangxi Province, about 100 kilometres south-east of the provincial capital, Nanchang. It was commissioned by the studio's owner, Nie Danian (1402–55), himself a famous poet, painter and calligrapher.

The studio is thatched, and is framed by two groups of three majestic pines in the foreground and towering mountains at the back. To the right is a stream and to the left are a lake, with the Linggu mountains in the distance, and a temple, most likely Daoist, as the Linggu mountains were a Daoist sanctuary. The painting fits exactly the description of the villa's surroundings given by Nie in his colophon, which he had probably given to Dai Jin beforehand. Two servant boys (they can be recognized as young boys by their hair tufts) stand at the entrance gate, one holding a zither, the other books. They seem about to bring these objects to a man standing with another servant at the lake's shore. His hair is done in a large topknot, in Daoist fashion, and he could well be waiting for a boat to take him to the temple.

At the end of his colophon Nie Danian writes that he had asked the artist, whom he had long admired, to paint the work for his son so that he would be more eager to travel home, where the painting should be treasured by future generations. It is clear that Nie Danian, himself an artist of no mean stature, had commissioned this painting from Dai Jin because he considered him a famous and important painter.

How ironic it is for his colophon to be followed by a text written about 150 years later by Dong Qichang, the man who had done everything to discredit Dai Jin as the great painter he really was: 'The paintings by Dai Jin of Qiantang may be classified as capable works, and this scroll does indeed live up to that description.' He continues by extolling the merits of Nie Danian's short calligraphical note: 'Moreover, it includes the handwriting of Nie Danian, which, vigorous and refined, is worthy to be transmitted. Nie studied Confucian metaphysics attentively, and practised calligraphy with great zeal. How could one say in his case: "He lost ambition by playing with trifles"? A truly unpleasant phrase here.' Did he perhaps mean Dai Jin?

*Spring Clouds in the Linggu Mountains* is a fine and characteristic work by Dai Jin, with an impeccable pedigree that can be followed through inscriptions and collectors' seals almost continuously from its creation to the date it entered the museum collection. The inscription by Dong Qichang, the man who coined the term 'Zhe school' with all its negative implications, gives it added importance. Its manifest qualities as a great work made it immune, however, to the criticism of a theoretician of art even as important as Dong. KR

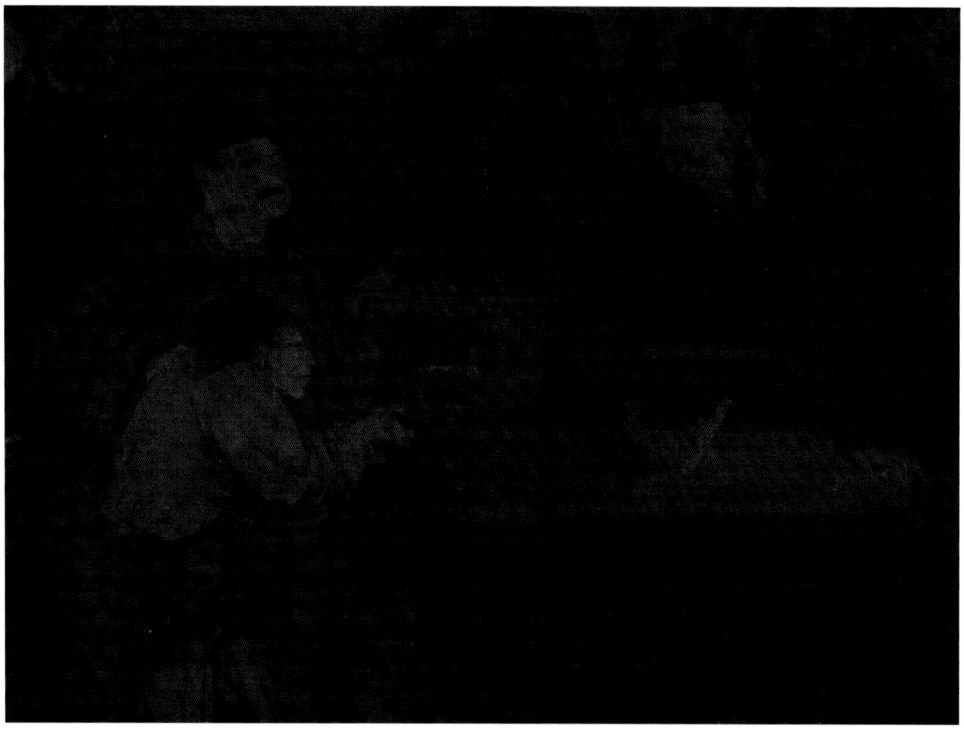

53

UNIDENTIFIED ARTIST; traditionally attributed to REN RENFA (1255–1327)

## The Four Pleasures: Music, Chess, Calligraphy and Painting

明 傳任仁發 四樂圖 琴棋書畫 軸

early 15th century, set of four hanging scrolls, ink and colour on silk, each scroll 172.8 × 104.2 cm
Tokyo National Museum (TA-106)

REFERENCE LITERATURE

Kitaura 1929; Tokyo National Museum 1979

Depicted here are scholars enjoying the 'four pleasures'. Proceeding from right to left, these are music, in the form of the *qin* (Chinese zither); chess, namely the board game *weiqi* (J. *go*); calligraphy; and painting. At the same time, the scrolls also represent the four seasons, with plum blossoms signalling spring; lotus flowers, summer; grapevines and chrysanthemum, autumn; and pine, winter.

The set opens with spring and the *qin*. A scholar plays the zither in the centre of the painting, and just beyond the partitioning screen is a lady with a *pipa* (lute). Beside the scholar are a youth holding the cloth covering for the *qin* and three close friends listening to the music. In front of this group, a figure burns sticks of incense and another approaches with a basket of large peonies. A flowering plum grows beside a garden rock in the foreground. In the background is a large broadleaf tree coming into bud – another indication of the season. Flowers are also present in the hair ornaments worn by the women. The scene is one of pleasure and delight. Painted on the screen is a depiction of gentlemen gazing at a waterfall.

The game of *weiqi* is the theme for the summer scroll. At the far left, three men sit at the game board, while another looks on. Perhaps because it is hot, they have loosened their collars, and the atmosphere is relaxed, with little sense of competition between the players or focus on the outcome of the game. Lotus flowers bloom in pots in the foreground and are being watered by a young boy, whose graceful gesture lends a refreshing feeling of coolness. On a small table nearby are various utensils. The green ceramic jar standing in the centre is of particular interest; it looks very much like the kind of wine container called *jiuhuihu* from the Longquan kilns in Zhejiang Province, popular during the Yuan (1271–1368) and Ming (1368–1644) dynasties.

Of especial interest is the fact that this summer scene is set during the mid-afternoon, at teatime. The foreground figure with a round fan offers a melon, while a half-eaten piece of peeled fruit rests on top of the scholar's desk at the centre of the composition. In the background stands a willow, with a crisp crape myrtle and a male and female figure holding a flute and *pipa* beneath its hanging branches. There is also a large *penjing* (J. bonsai), through which a dragon-shaped ornament appears to be climbing. The small banana tree depicted at the edge of the spring scroll has grown larger, indicating the passage of time.

At the centre of the painting illustrating autumn and calligraphy are a scholarly gentleman holding a brush and a servant grinding ink. Another figure carries books with a title slip reading 'Correct Interpretation of the *Five Classics*', suggesting that the source for the scene may be the image of the 'Eighteen Scholars of the Tang Dynasty'. In the foreground is a figure who has removed his cap and is washing his hands; the thin-faced servant standing nearby has a chrysanthemum inserted into his cap. In the background are ladies holding a *qin* and pan pipes and a figure with a ball, as well as a paulownia tree just beginning to change colour and a grapevine bearing fruit.

Winter is paired with painting, and in the centre of this work, four scholars gaze at a hanging scroll. Of particular interest is the style of the painting's mounting. The upper portion ('heaven') is of pale blue figured satin, while the horizontal sections just above and below the painting are of white figured satin. The two narrow vertical strips (J. *fūtai*) hanging from the upper rod (and seen also in the scroll being rolled up by the attendant) have been sewn flat to the upper section of the mounting. This is a different style to that seen in the mounting depicted in the Southern Song period (1127–1279) painting *Five Hundred Arhats* at Daitoku-ji, where the strips are shown hanging freely. The painting itself resembles Chen Rong's (act. 1st half 13th century) *Dragon* (Tokugawa Art Museum). In the foreground, a young attendant prepares tea, and a scholar, who appears intoxicated, leans heavily on another attendant's shoulder. In the background are depicted the so-called 'Three Friends of Winter': pine, bamboo and plum. The plum blossoms seen here are the same as those that appeared in the spring scroll, a testament to the cycle of the seasons.

Each scroll is signed 'Ziming' and pressed with a square relief seal reading *Renshi Ziming*, but it is difficult to ascribe the work to Ren with certainty. It is believed that pigment was originally applied to the reverse side of the painting in the rendering of the facial features and other elements, and the loss in the thickness of the colour is regrettable. The facial expressions of the women and the poses of the scholars indicate a familiarity with the murals at Shuishen Shrine in Guangsheng Temple, Hongdong, Shanxi Province, making it possible to hypothesize an early Ming period date for the painting. While the theme comes from Tang dynasty (618–907) literature, there are a number of paintings on the subject similar to the work under discussion, including two from the Ming dynasty, one in the National Palace Museum, Taipei, and the other in the Shanghai Museum.

The work has long been appreciated in Japan. The artist Kano Tsunenobu (1636–1713) wrote titles for the paintings. In addition, there are copies (by an unknown artist) now also in the Tokyo National Museum. Nemoto Yūga (1824–66), an official painter (*goyō eshi*) for the Tottori clan and a student of Oki Ichiga (1797–1855), painted a set of three hanging scrolls on the theme, in which the spring *qin* scene and the summer *weiqi* scene are combined in a single composition (Tottori Prefectural Art Museum). This work is of great interest in understanding the reception and circulation of copies of Chinese paintings in Japan. TM

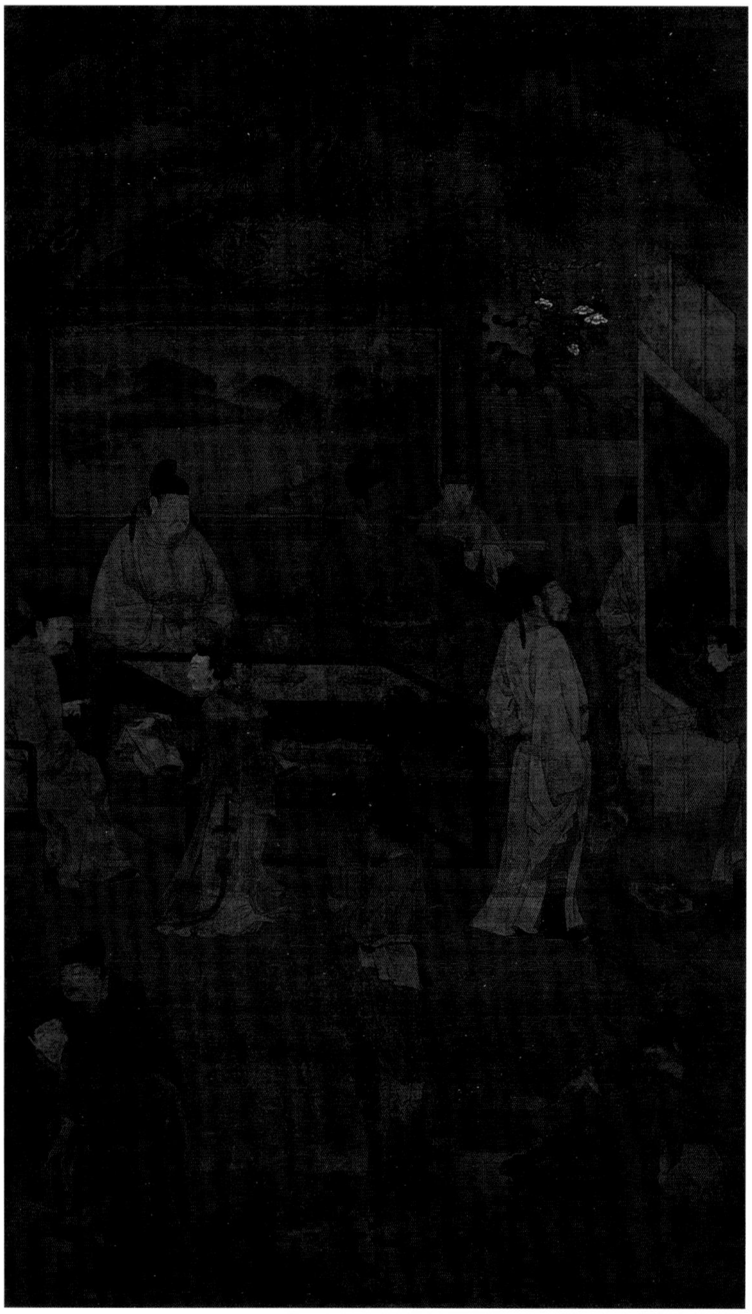

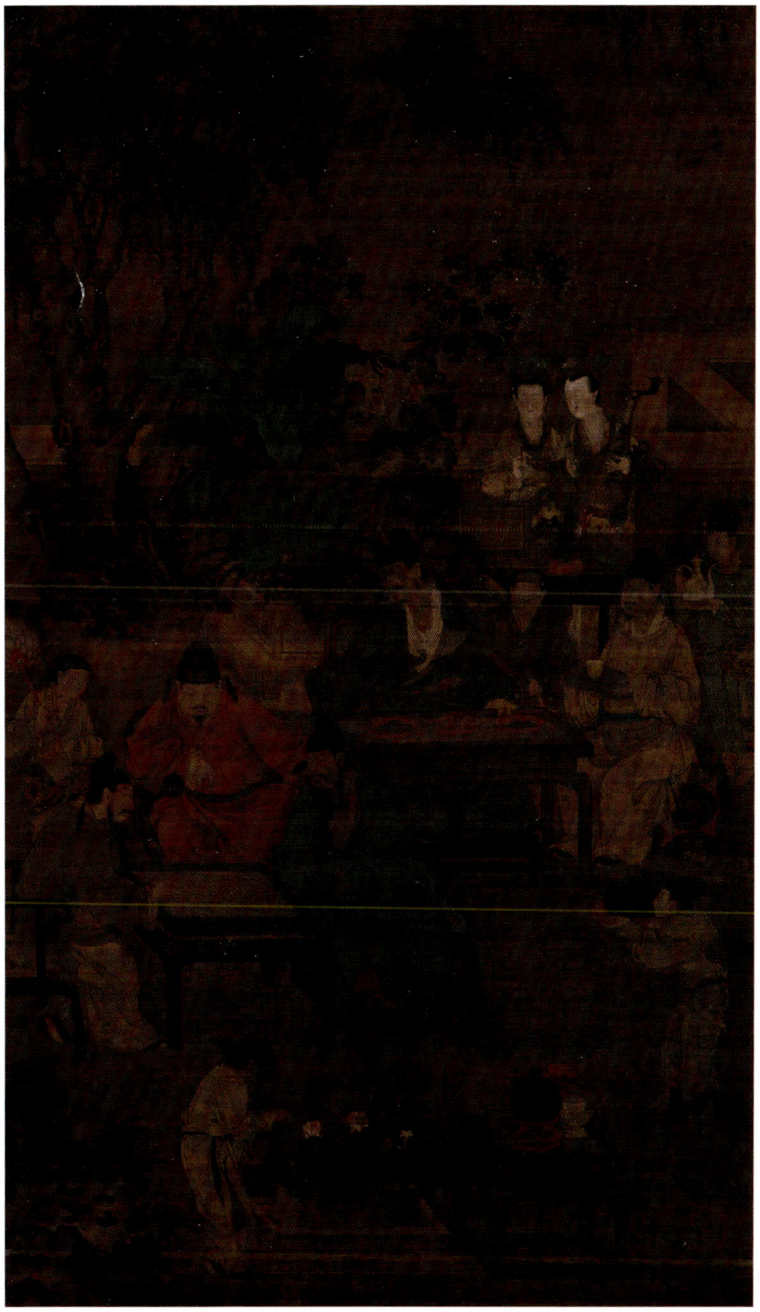
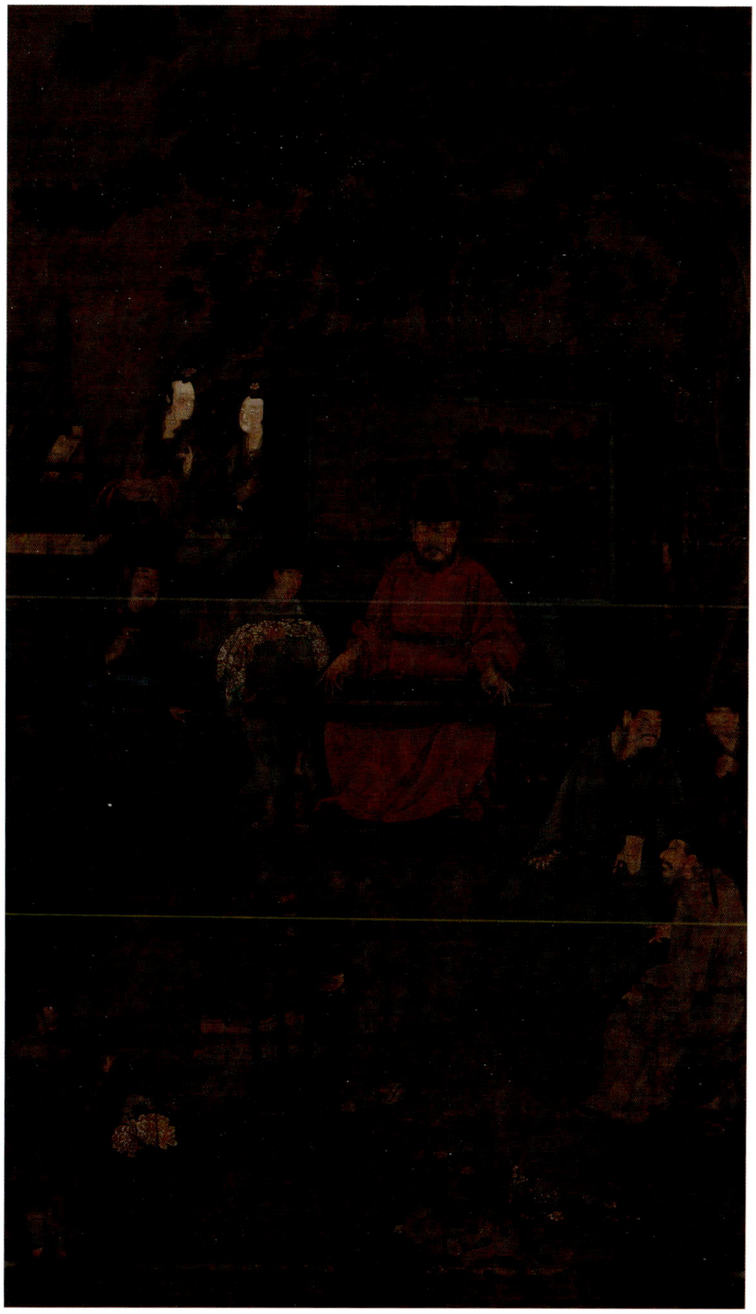

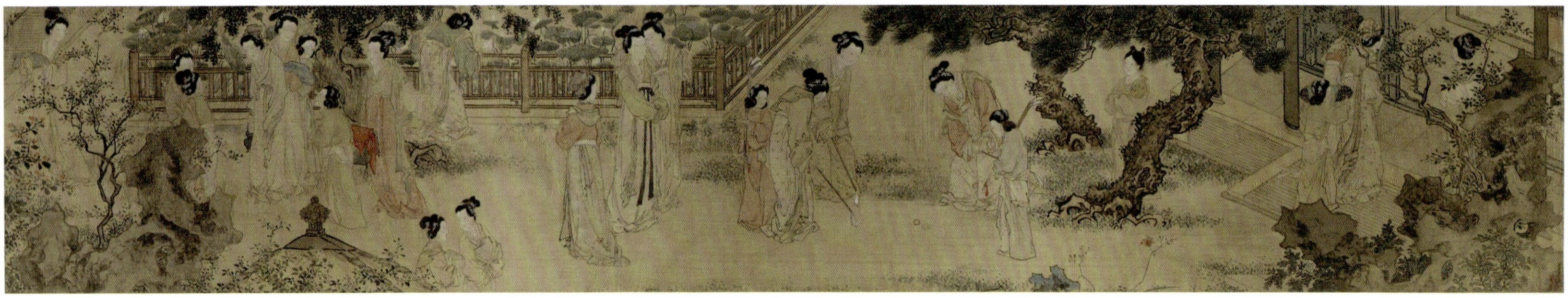

54

DUJIN (act. c.1465–1509)

## Court Ladies in the Inner Palace

明 杜堇 宮中仕女圖 卷

2nd half 15th century, one of a pair of handscrolls, ink and colour on silk, each section 30.5 × 168.9 cm, 167.8 cm, 173.5 cm, 175.1 cm, 152.8 cm, 169 cm
Shanghai Museum (31919)

REFERENCE LITERATURE

Zhongguo gudai shuhua jianding zu 1986–2001, vol. 2, pp. 245–8, Hu 1-0435; Cui 2000, p. 48, fig. 45; San Francisco 2008, pp. 231–4, no. 132; Shanghai 2008

Although the mid-Ming dynasty (1368–1644) *fugu* ('return to antiquity') literary movement was mainly concerned with the collation and revival of texts from earlier dynasties, it also led to a surge of interest in antiquarianism and the study of archaic artistic styles, especially among figure painters central to the Wu school. These artists used both literary and visual models from the past and created works that combined the meticulous brushwork of the professional with the expressiveness associated with the literati. Representative exponents of this 'new' style included Du Jin and Tang Yin (1470–1523).

Du Jin was a native of Dantu (present Zhenjiang, Jiangsu Province). An earnest student, he was well versed in the classics, history and philosophy. Du was resident in Beijing, but after failing the *jinshi* civil service examination, he abandoned all ambition of an official career. A poem by Tang Yin, written during his sojourn in the capital, describes him as elderly and destitute, with only a sack of books for company. Nevertheless, his wide circle of friends, fellow artists and patrons included Liu Jue (1410–72), Shen Zhou (1427–1509), Wen Zhengming (1470–1559) and Li Dongyang (1441–1516), several of whom were leading figures in the *fugu* movement. Wang Shizhen (1526–90) pronounced him the 'premier *baimiao* ["plain outline"] painter' of the period.[1]

Studies of Du Jin's surviving paintings (about 20), however, suggest a more diverse oeuvre that shows touches of individuality while referencing the Southern Song (1127–1279) academy, the Zhe school and works associated with Qiu Ying (1494/5–1552).[2] Not surprisingly, given his literary and aesthetic preferences, one of his literary names was 'Gukuang' ('Obsession with Antiquity').

The six scenes by Du Jin depicting activities of women in the imperial palace are mounted separately in two handscrolls, each comprising three sections (*duan*). The sections in the exhibited scroll include groups participating in *cuju*, or kickball, and *chuiwan*, a form of golf, as well as playing with a child. *Cuju* was first played in the Qi State during the Spring and Autumn period (c.771–c.476 BCE), and became very popular during the Tang (618–907). As the popularity of the game grew, the method of making the ball became increasingly sophisticated. By the Tang, a more spherical form had been achieved by sewing together octagonal pieces of leather. Instead of stuffing the ball with hair, the interior was lined with an animal bladder and air was blown in to make it lighter. This was the first ever use of an inflatable ball. Such a ball can be seen in the Du Jin painting. *Chuiwan*, which was played from the Song dynasty (960–1279) onwards, evolved from a game that resembled hockey.

Paintings of women playing *cuju* as well as polo had been known since the Tang period. However, by the Ming dynasty, elite women rarely participated in sport, as foot binding had become prevalent. Thus for Du's immediate audience, these scenes were clearly historical. As indicated by the colophons, the work is

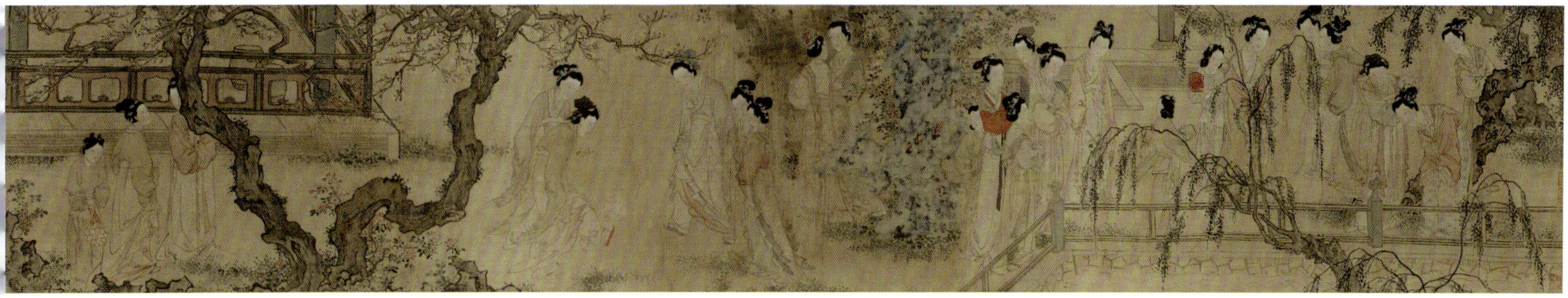

suggestive of models from the Five Dynasties (907–60), Song or Yuan (1271–1368) periods. Comparable scenes can be found in surviving fragments of a mid-twelfth century copy of a painting by Zhou Wenju (act. 961–75).[3] Archaistic flourishes can be seen in the 'nail-head' endings of the fluid, inky strokes used to render the garments. Traditionally, paintings of palace women were set against a blank background, as exemplified by *Court Ladies Preparing Newly Woven Silk* (cat. no. 16). Here, the subjects have been placed within a garden setting that allows the artist to show his skill in *jiehua* ('ruled-line') drawing and provides context for the viewer. The architectural elements serve not only to organize and frame the pictorial space, but the linearity of the balustrades also emphasizes the horizontality of the handscroll format. LLZ / YH

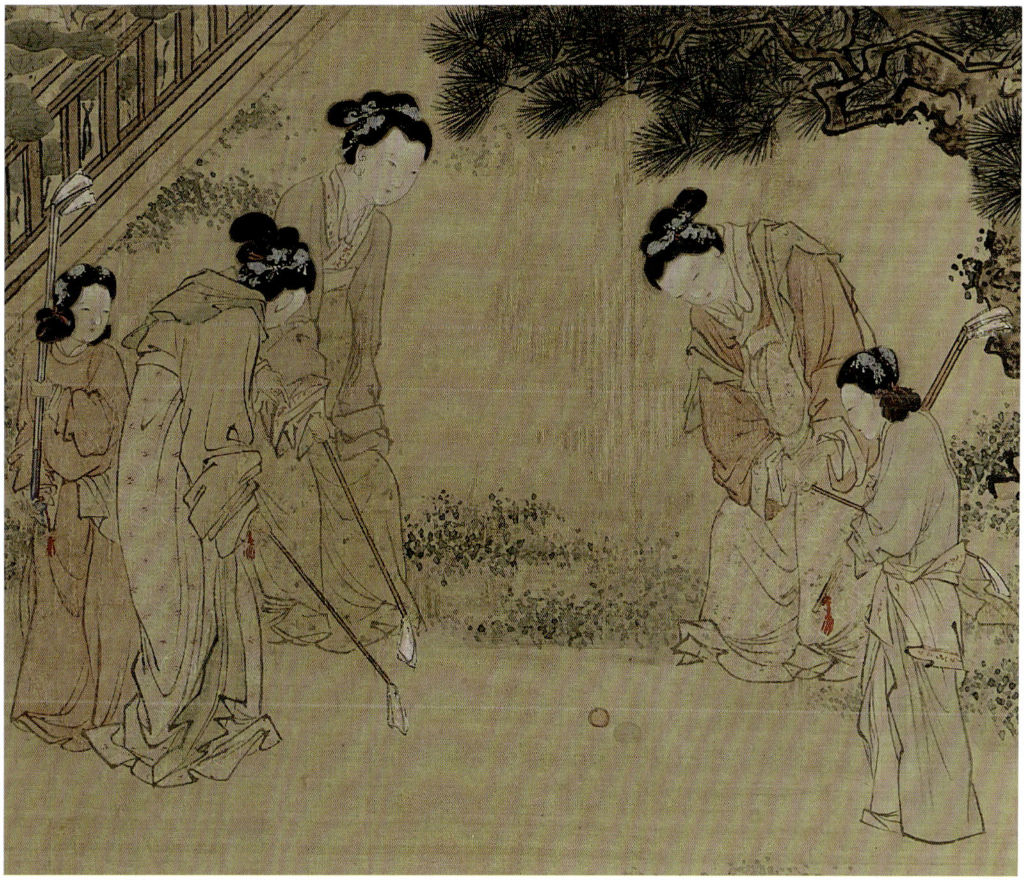

1 For biographical references to Du Jin (act. c.1465–1509), see Little 1987, pp. 7–36.
2 For discussions on defining Du Jin's body of work, see Barnhart et al. 1997b; Little 1999.
3 In the Metropolitan Museum of Art, the Cleveland Museum of Art, the Arthur M. Sackler Museum and Harvard University, and at Villa I Tatti, Florence (see Yashiro 1953, pl. II–V). The 1954 colophon on the Du Jin painting refers to a work by Zhou in the British Museum, now deemed to be a Ming dynasty (1368–1644) copy (1913–0415–0.2).

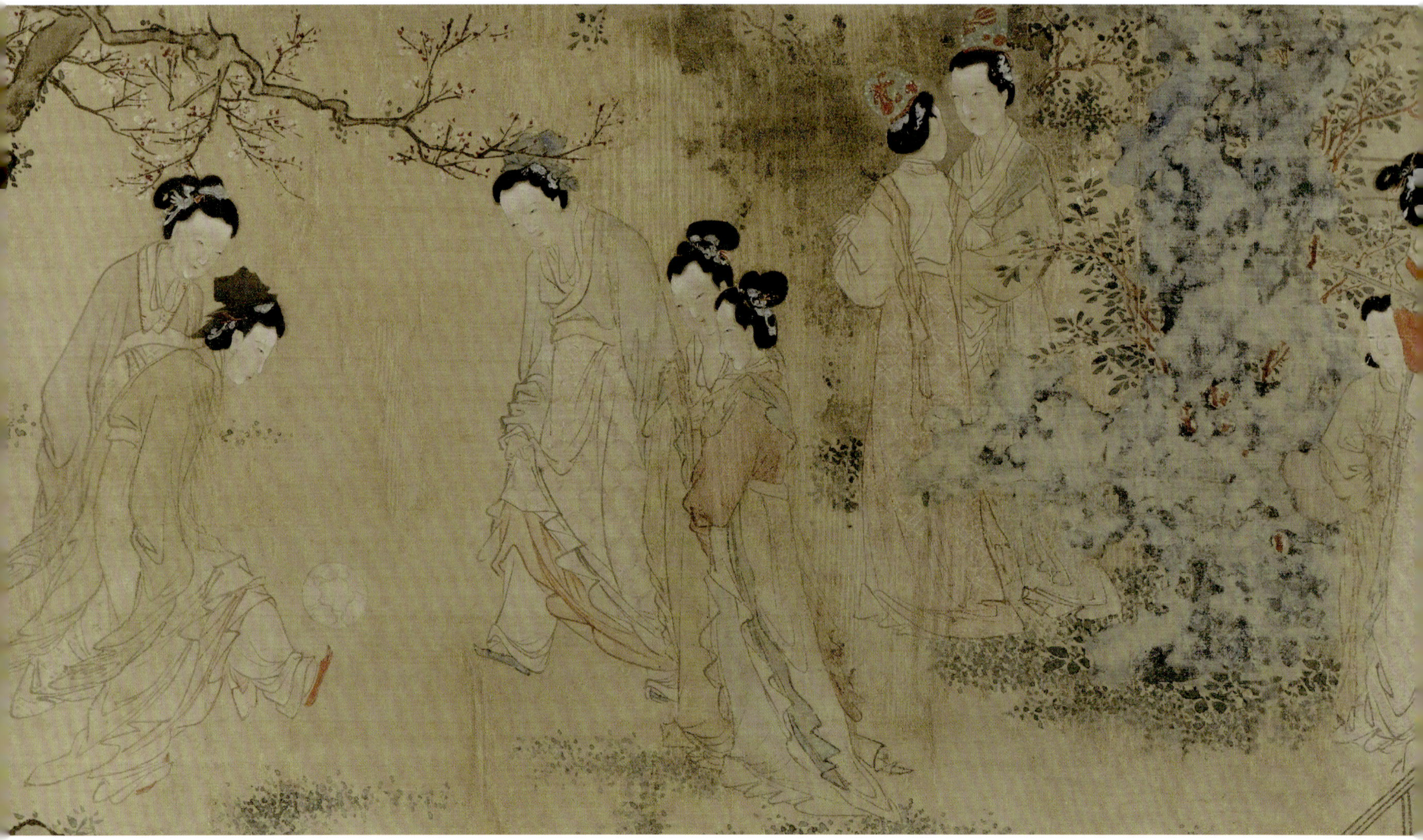

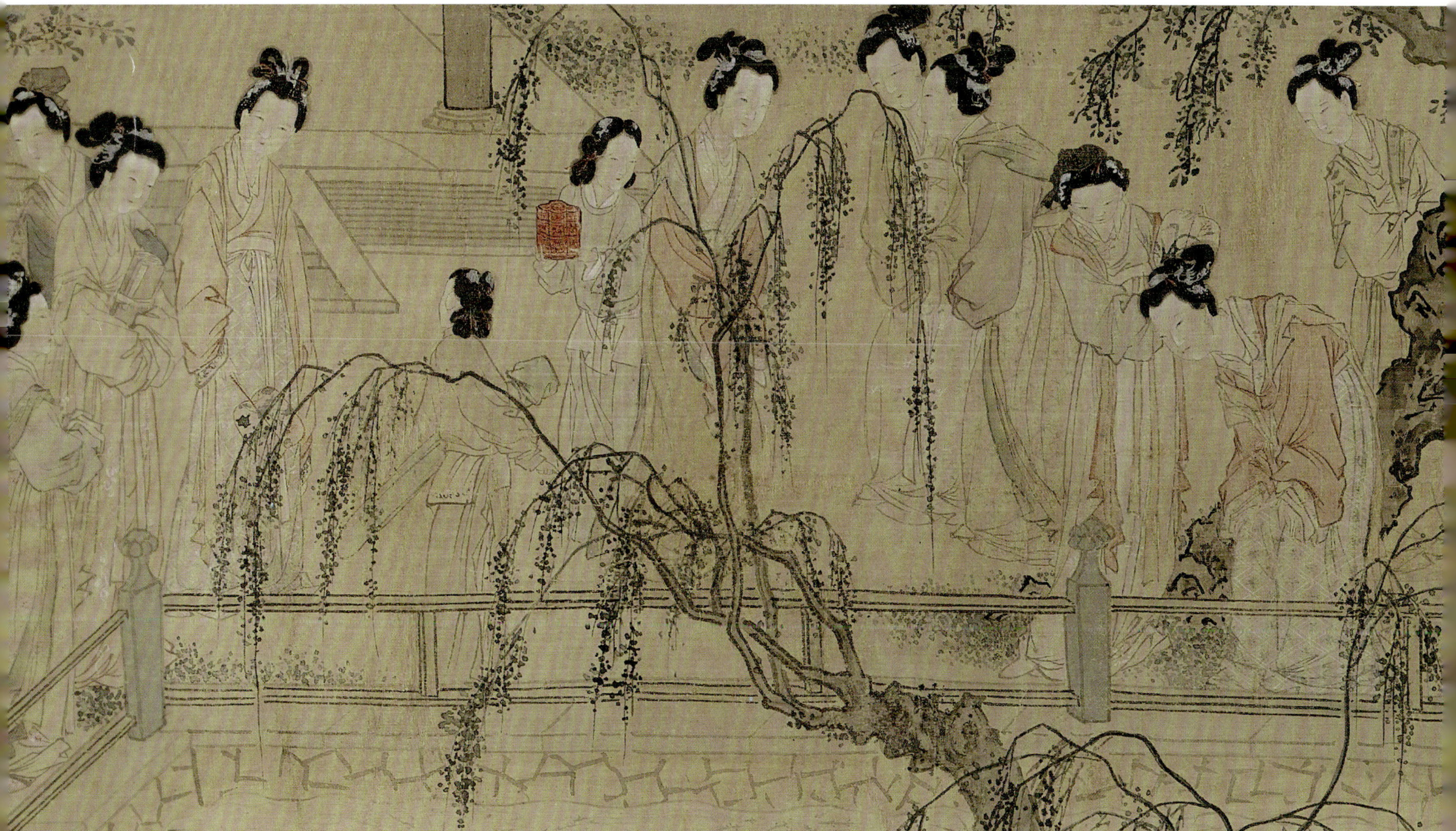

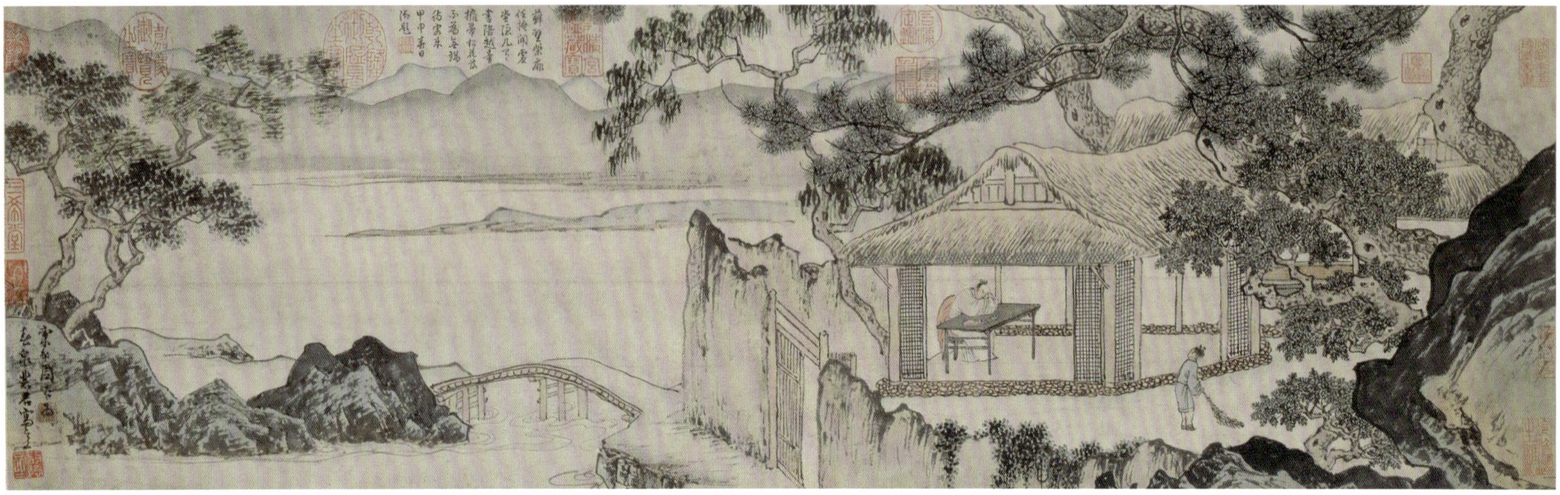

55

ZHOU CHEN (c.1450–1535)

## Dwelling by the Stream in Spring

明 周臣 春泉小隱圖 卷

1475, handscroll, ink and colour on paper,
26 × 85.8 cm
The Palace Museum, Beijing (XIN 47084)

REFERENCE LITERATURE

Cahill 1978; Siggstedt 1982a and 1982b; Fuller 1984; Memphis 1984; Kao 1988; *Complete Collection* 1988, vol.3, p.408; New York and Dallas 1993; Cahill 1994; Yang 1994; Gao 1996; Yang 1997; Zhu (1920) 1997; Wang 1999; Liu in Taipei 2000; Shan 2000; Chen and Lai 2008

On a summer's day, the artist's patron Pei Chunquan has fallen asleep at his desk in his study. Outside the thatched house, in the shade of a group of tall trees extending out behind a rocky outcrop, a servant boy sweeps a yard encircled by crumbling earthen walls. Significantly, the artist has captured the moment when the boy pauses in his activity and turns to look at his dozing master, which gives a light air to the painting and directs the viewer's gaze towards Pei Chunquan as the central focus. The half-open garden gate suggests that Pei might be expecting a visitor, perhaps the artist himself. A wooden bridge links the dwelling to a lakeside path and another group of crisply delineated rocks. The solid surfaces of the rocks in both the first and final sections of the scroll are indicated by dense axe-cut brushstrokes and wet bluish-green washes, which contrast well with the swiftly executed foliage above. The spring issuing from the foreground joins the lake, and is marked by the gentle swells beneath the bridge. Running horizontally across the entire scroll, the distant mountains, subtly defined by a light blue and ink wash, appear in the background and provide illumination for the scholar's reclusive life.

Following the style of a Southern Song dynasty (1127–1279) academy painting, this early work by Zhou Chen conveys a sense of time, the season, the weather and human activity in a landscape setting. The framing of the composition with rocks, tree trunks and branches is a method that was popular with artists of the Zhe school. The painting is without a long inscription or poem to convey the artist's feelings, and bears only a short dedication, a signature and a seal, as was typical of the work of a professional painter.

The flourishing literati culture in the Wu region (centring on Suzhou in Jiangsu Province) around the mid-fifteenth century fostered the rise of the scholar-amateur artist, who personalized his work through poetic inscriptions and used art as a vehicle for individual expression. While Zhou Chen was influenced by the sketchy brushwork of his professional contemporaries in Zhejiang Province, led by Dai Jin (1388–1462), he also combined his style with the literati spirit then prevalent among artists in his hometown such as Du Qiong (1396–1474) and Liu Jue (1410–72), and his work shows a shift from producing paintings for sale to a more integrated and creative approach. Although his name was often overshadowed by his most brilliant students, Tang Yin (1470–1523) and Qiu Ying (1494/5–1552), both of whom were highly regarded (along with Shen Zhou [1427–1509] and Wen Zhengming [1470–1559]) as two of the Four Masters of the Wu School, Zhou Chen's art continued to be influential among his followers in the lower Yangzi Delta. CY

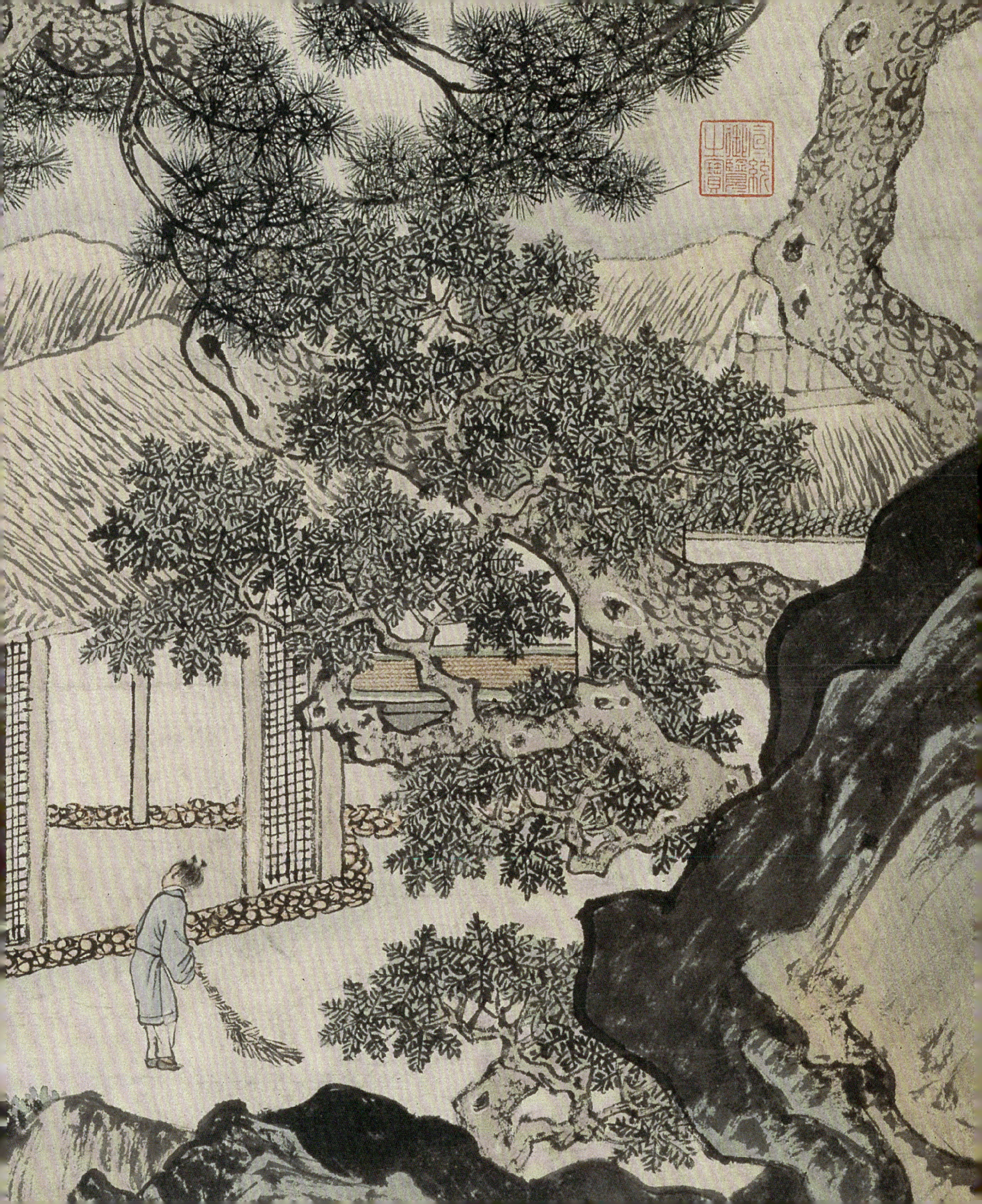

56

LÜ JI (act. 1488–1505)

## Pomegranates, Autumn Mallows, Chrysanthemums, Blue Magpies and Rooster

明 呂紀 榴葵綬雞圖 軸

Last quarter 15th century, hanging scroll, ink and colour on silk, 200.8 × 105.5 cm
The Palace Museum, Beijing

REFERENCE LITERATURE

Taipei 1992b; New York and Dallas 1993; Whitfield 1993; Shan 1996; *A Collection of Paintings by Lin Liang and Lü Ji* 1997; Boston 1997; Shan 1997; Yang 1997; Shan 2000

In vogue since the eighth century, bird-and-flower paintings commonly served to heighten the sophistication of domestic interiors, and became an independent genre. *Pomegranates, Autumn Mallows, Chrysanthemums, Blue Magpies and Rooster* is typical of the bird-and-flower paintings executed for the Ming dynasty (1368–1644) court. Under the leadership of Lü Ji, the most prolific court painter of the Hongzhi emperor's reign (1488–1505), this work was created to serve a practical purpose as an ornate and auspicious piece of art.

The rooster and magpies in the painting have been positioned by the artist in two triangular groups, dividing the image into two halves to form a balanced and rhythmic composition. It is very likely that a second painting would have been matched with this one to form a symmetrical pair, or it may have been one of a set of four representing the four seasons.

Colourful and dramatic, the lower half of the painting depicts a rooster with splendid plumage standing erect as if about to crow, while his dowdy mate is hardly visible behind a rock. Red, white and pale pink chrysanthemums and autumn mallows (*huangshukui; Abelmoschus manihot*) with yellow petals and intense purple centres rise up behind the rocks and the trunk of a pomegranate tree (*Punica granatum*), whose upper branches stretch down towards the left, framing the composition. A pair of blue magpies (*Urocissa erythrorhyncha*) is positioned on the main branch: the male reaches down to extract a pomegranate seed, showing off his long, white-tipped tail feathers, while the female gazes at her mate, exposing the white feathers of her breast. With subtle gradation of colouring and meticulous line drawing, the artist has achieved a punctilious and accurate depiction of their plumage. In contrast, the brushwork used to depict the rocks and tree is in ink monochrome, and is freer, wetter and sparsely coloured, if at all. Although the chrysanthemum leaves are still bright green, the chrysanthemum and mallow flowers, the light touches of brown at the tips of the mallow leaves and the fruit on the pomegranate tree show that the season is autumn.

The choice of plants and birds is auspicious and political as well as seasonal. Typically in season from September, the chrysanthemum is the emblem of a gentleman. The abundant seeds ('zi') of the fruit of the pomegranate are a pun on another meaning of the same Chinese character, 'offspring', and thus symbolize fecundity and numerous progeny. The word for autumn mallow, 'kui', is a pun on 'gui', as in *quangui*, 'influential officials', while the word 'shou' in the title alludes to the silk ribbons (*shoudai*) attached to an official seal, connoting success and promotion in one's political career. Strictly speaking, the Chinese name *shoudainiao* refers to the Asian paradise flycatcher (*Terpsiphone paradisi*), a much smaller tropical bird with an extremely long pair of tail feathers; however, it is clear that the same name, abbreviated to the single character 'shou' (綬), was also applied to the blue magpie, which often appears in Ming bird-and-flower paintings.[1] The rooster (*gongji*) symbolizes high official rank through association with the homophones 'gong' ('duke') and 'ji' ('auspicious'). In grouping chrysanthemums, pomegranates, autumn mallows, magpies and rooster together, this painting was intended to wish the recipient great success in his political career and the continuance of his family fortunes generation after generation. CY

1 Roderick Whitfield, personal communication

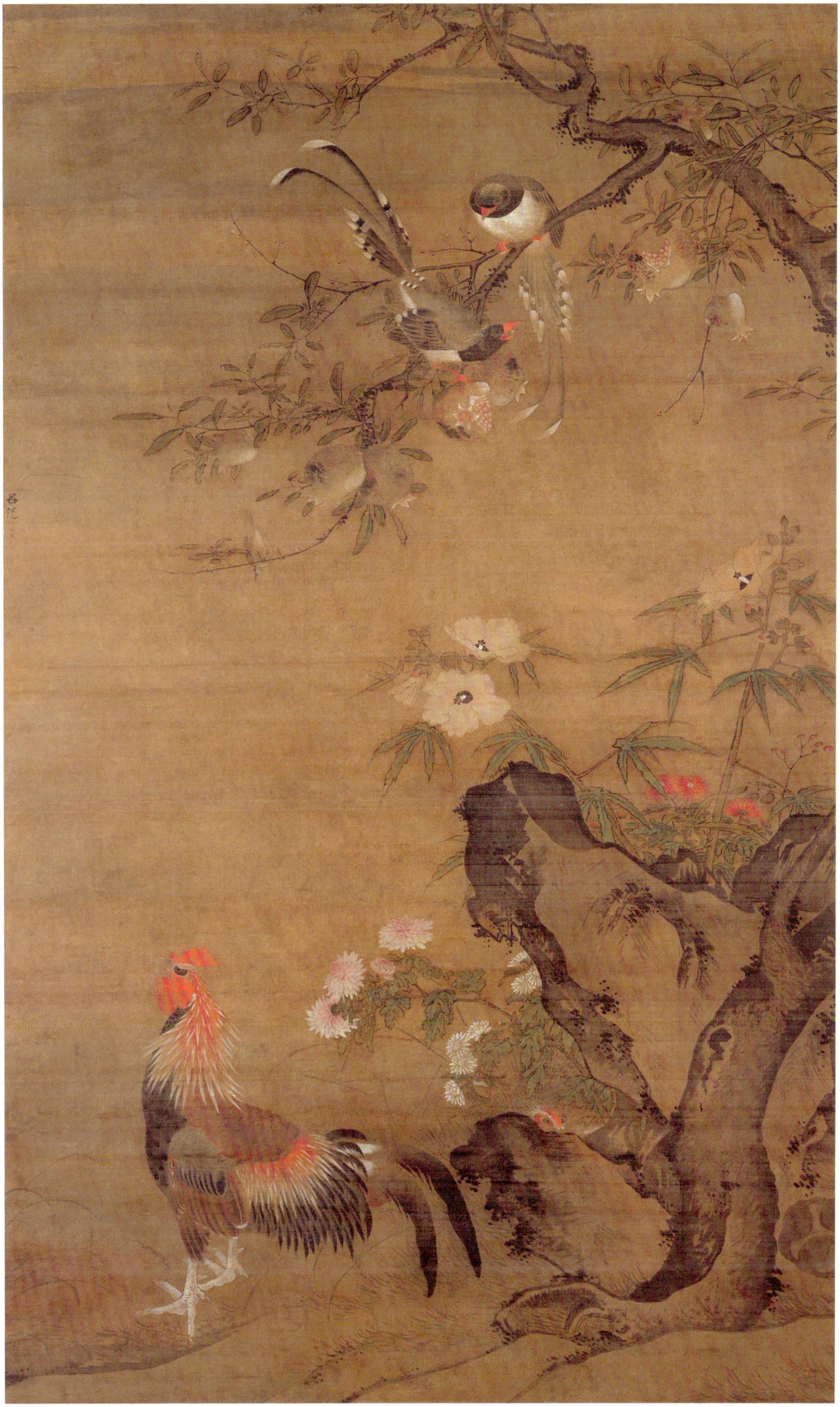

57

SHEN ZHOU (1427–1509)

## Twelve Views of Tiger Hill

明 沈周 虎丘十二景圖 冊

after 1490, album of 12 leaves, ink and light colour on paper, each leaf: 31.1 × 40.2 cm (approx.)
The Cleveland Museum of Art
Leonard C. Hanna, Jr. Fund (1964.371.1–12)

PROVENANCE

Walter Hochstadter; Richard B. Hobart (B, W, F, J)

REFERENCE LITERATURE

Lee 1957, pp. 471–85 and 1966, pp. 2–25, no. 1; Cahill 1978; Kleinhenz 1980, pp. 187–90, no. 155; Ganza 1990; Ma 1990; Wang 1999; Cheng 2009, pp. 127–62

Born into an erudite family in Suzhou in south-eastern China, Shen Zhou was a founding figure of the local Wu school of painting. Although Shen's family members never took the imperial examinations to enter civil service, they were respectable scholars who befriended members of esteemed literary circles as well as cultivating high-ranking officials. Shen eventually inherited the family's extensive cultural network and rich collection of classics and paintings, which helped him to become a celebrated writer, calligrapher, poet and painter. He was acquainted with the different styles of the Song (960–1279) and Yuan (1271–1368) dynasty masters, and succeeded in eloquently melding them together.

Many of Shen Zhou's landscape paintings were based on the extensive travels he made throughout his life within greater Suzhou, including *Twelve Views of Tiger Hill*. Although the album is undated, the thick, rhythmic brushstrokes suggest it was a later work, as those of his earlier style were finer and more densely executed. Some scenes provide a broad overview of the site, while others have a more focused composition.

Tiger Hill is named for a legend in which a white tiger appeared on the hill three days after King Helu (r. 514–496 BCE) was buried there. Already a popular site for excursions and gatherings in the fifteenth century, Tiger Hill appeared frequently in Shen's paintings. Although no particular viewing order is indicated in the album, one possible route is to begin with the welcoming scene of 'Canal Mooring' (Leaf A). Travelling uphill, we pass sites such as 'Pine Retreat' (Leaf C) and 'Enlightened Stone Retreat' (Leaf D), which provided a serene environment for meditation. Apart from the architectural and landscape elements, Shen also carefully observed the various social activities on Tiger Hill. Along the way are people conversing near 'Fool's Spring' (Leaf B) and relaxing at 'Thousand-Man Seat' (Leaf E), and scholars convening at 'Sword Spring' (Leaf F). Arriving at the Thousand-Buddha Hall we have almost reached the summit, and can enjoy a vista of the famous pagoda erected in the tenth century (Leaf G). Many terraces offer breathtaking views from this height (Leaves H and I), and weary visitors can sample the spring water (Leaf J) or rest at a pavilion (Leaf K) as they descend the hill. As we depart, we are afforded a final glimpse of the hill (Leaf L) and are left yearning for more.

The depiction of famous sites rose to popularity as a genre in the Ming dynasty (1368–1644). While references to specific locations were made in the literati landscape painting tradition, many were imaginary tours of places that the painters had never visited. Even if some were based on actual journeys, the paintings were often composite reconstructions of selected memories or a tailored experience for the intended recipient. These 'mind landscapes' were only accessible to a few, and might differ greatly from the site depicted. Shen Zhou painted works in such a manner too, although in the current album he did not sacrifice the site's recognizability for artistic interpretation. Perhaps it was his intention to introduce his beloved Wu region to a greater audience with his objective yet lyrical ink.[1] Rather than presenting a continuous, narrative view of the site as a handscroll, or producing a hanging scroll with a single cropped view, Shen's album offers multiple intimate snippets of Tiger Hill.

Although most of the leaves feature aspects of the lifestyle desirable to scholars, they also integrate people of other professions harmoniously into the landscape – we find boatmen, priests and servants – reflecting the fact that Ming scholars were more socially integrated than their predecessors, whose idealistic life was reclusive. The expressive, accessible quality of the album may explain why Shen's works were well received by a wide audience, from government officials to local artisans. By painting a site beloved by all social classes, the album was the manifestation of a shared cultural experience that fostered regional identity. The artist's revered status as the leading figure of the Wu school further established Tiger Hill as one of the most important cultural landmarks of the region, and it appeared repeatedly in landscapes as late as Xu Yang's (1712–c.1779) depiction of Suzhou in the eighteenth century (cat. no. 76).[2]
JW

1 Ma 1990, p. 130
2 For example, Wen Zhengming (1470–1559), Qian Gu (1508–c.1578) and Xie Shichen (1487–c.1567) also painted Tiger Hill in their works; see Lee 1966? and Cheng 2009.

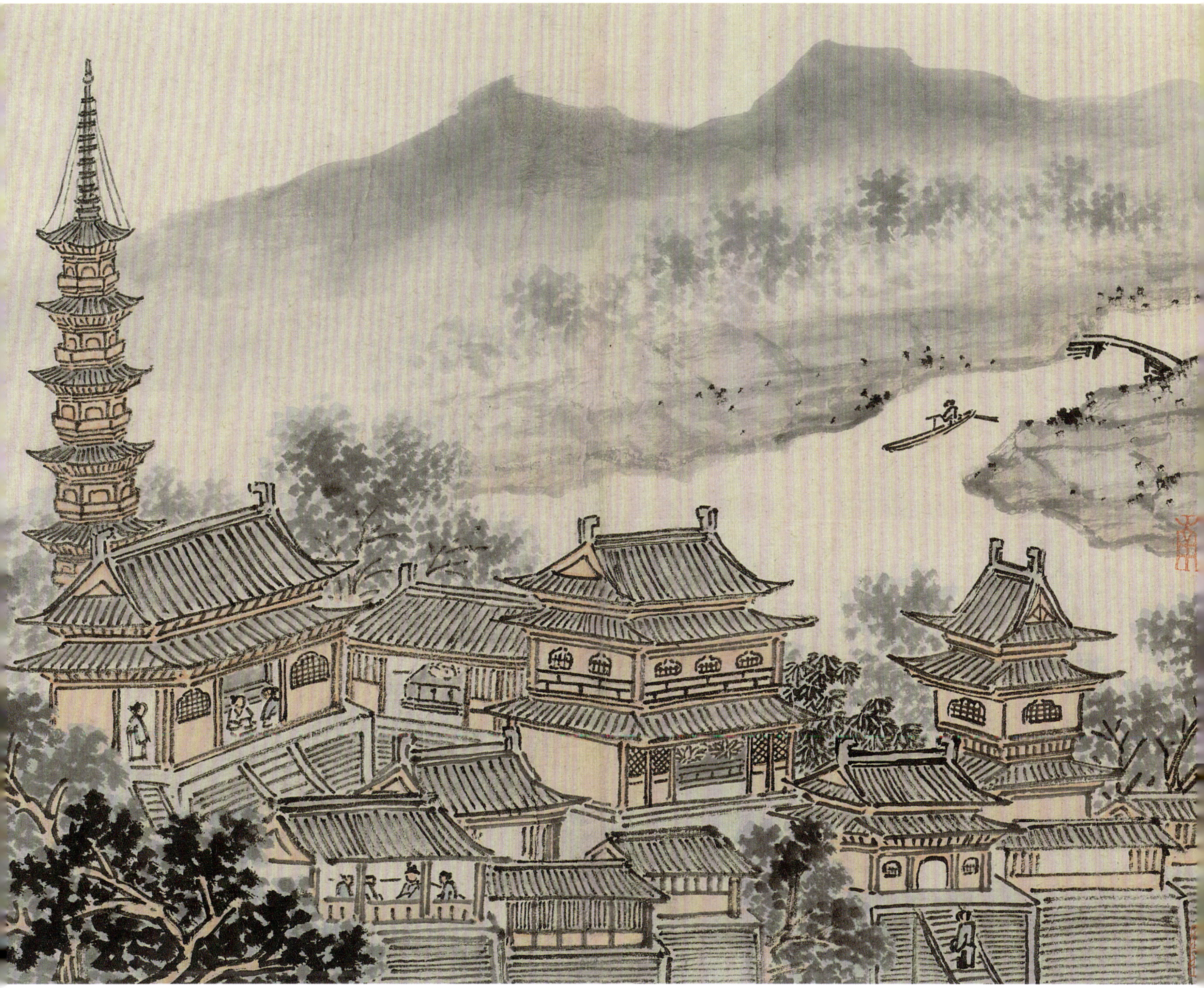

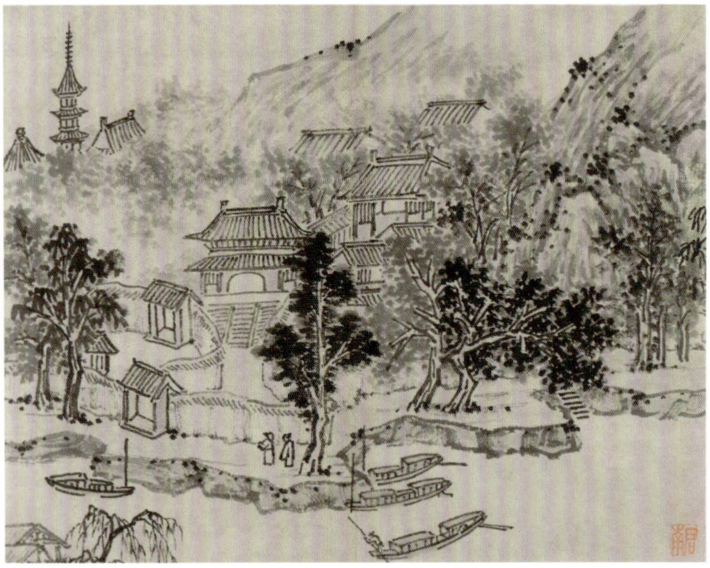
A

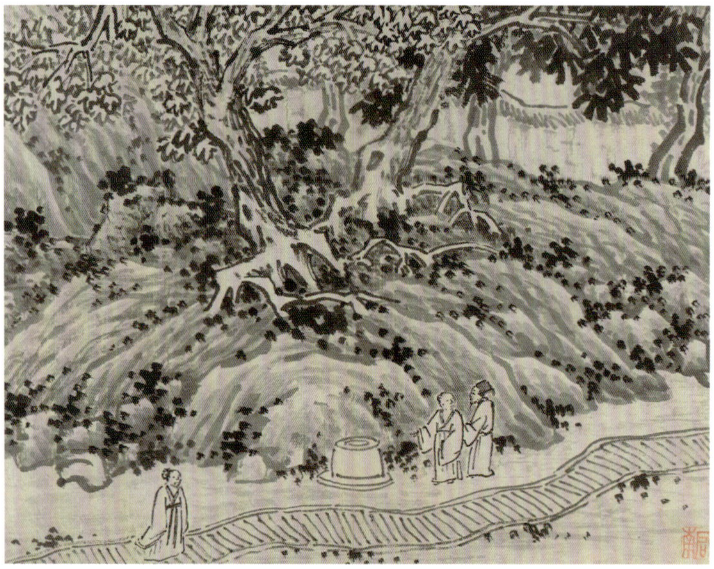
B

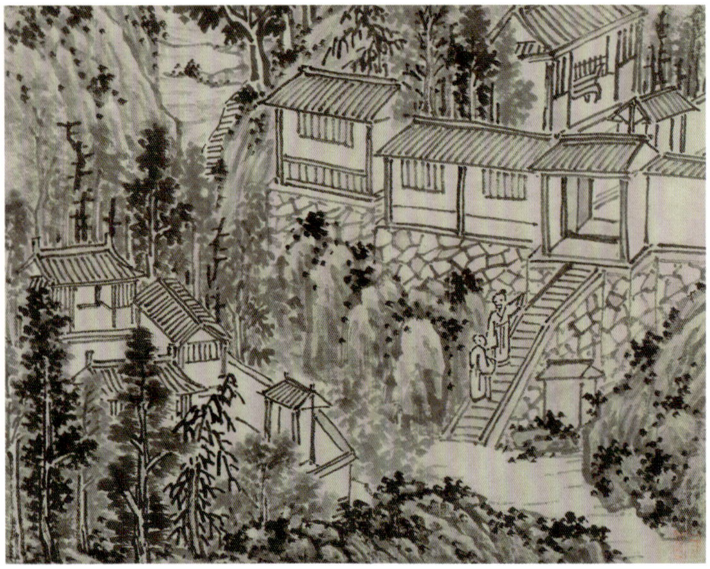
C

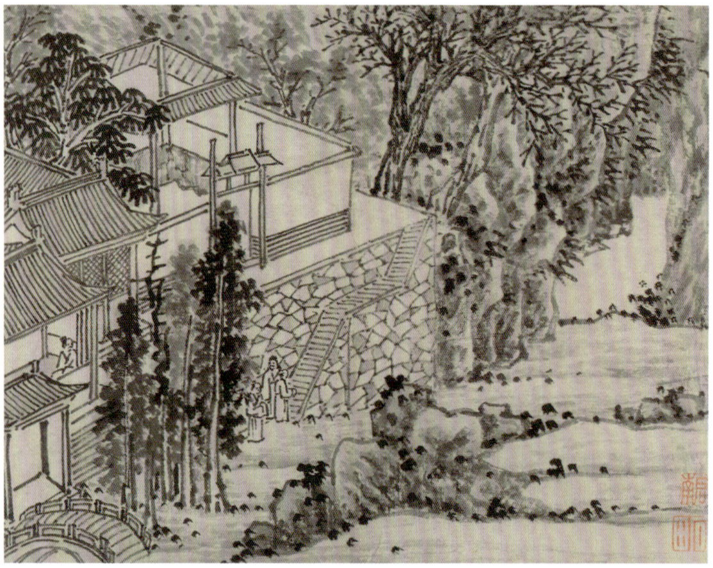
D

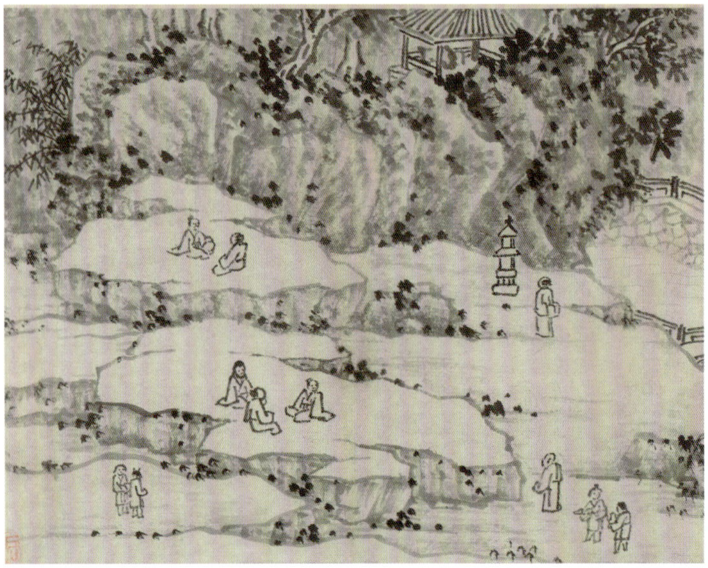
E

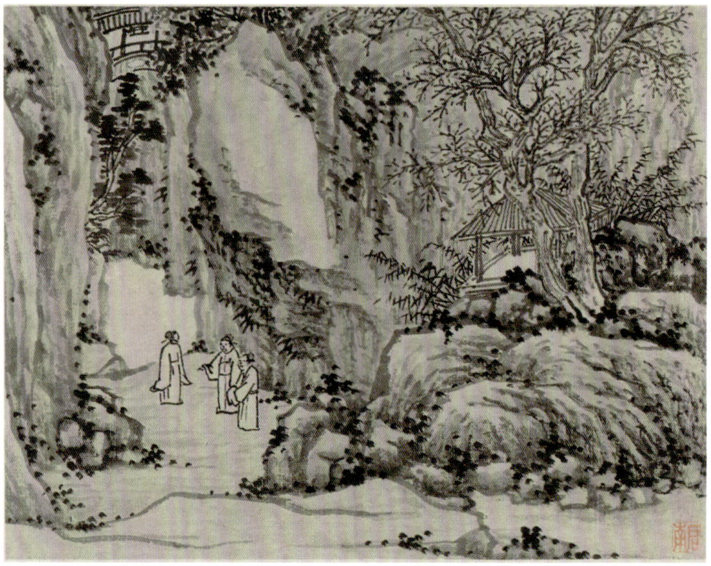
F

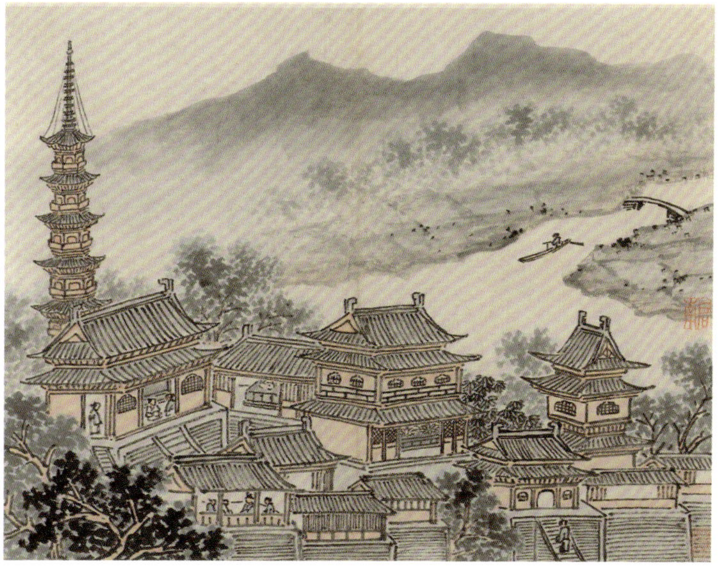
G

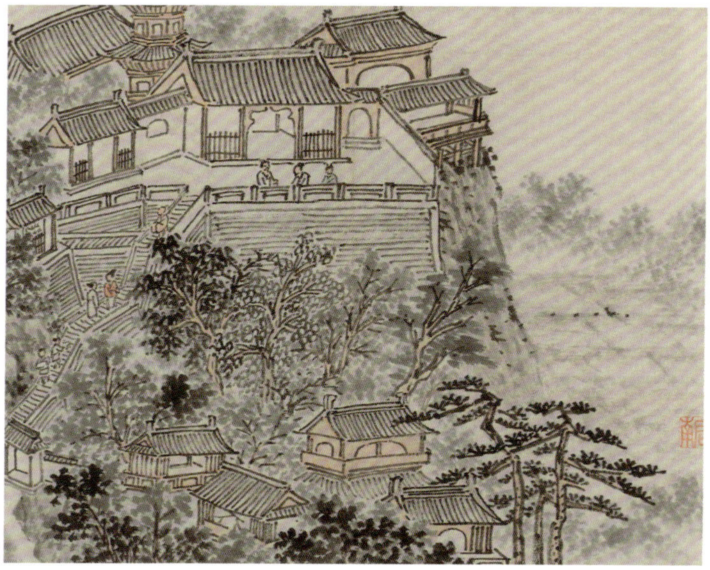
H

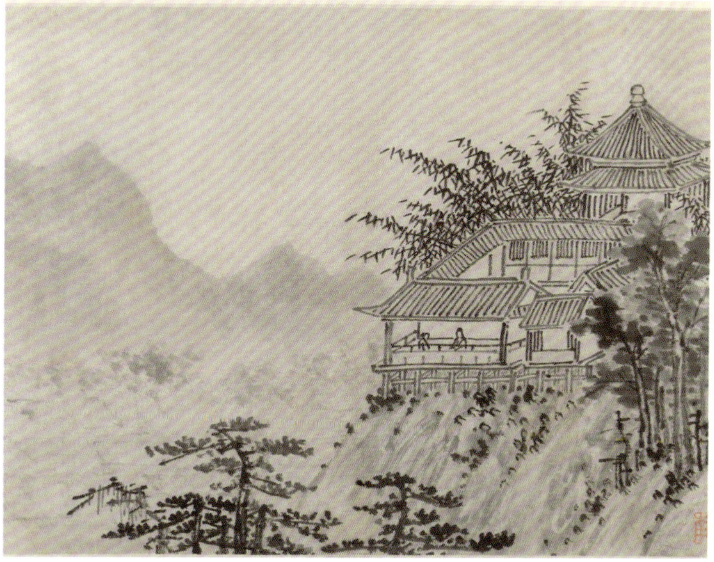
I

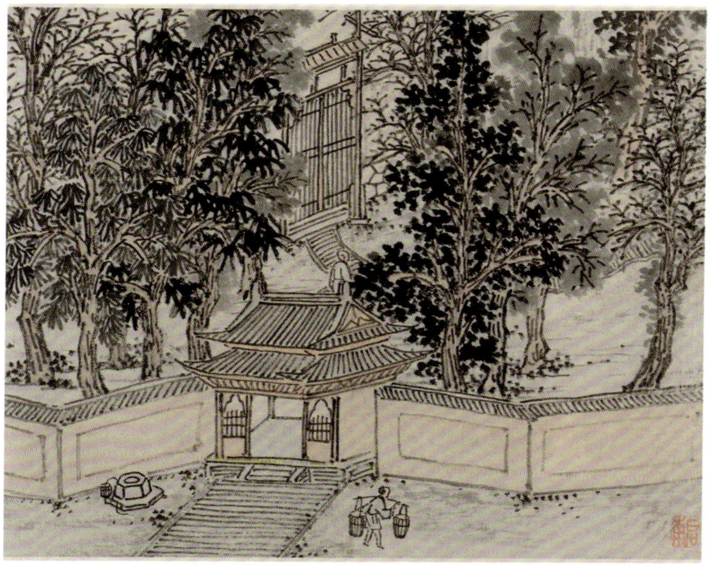
J

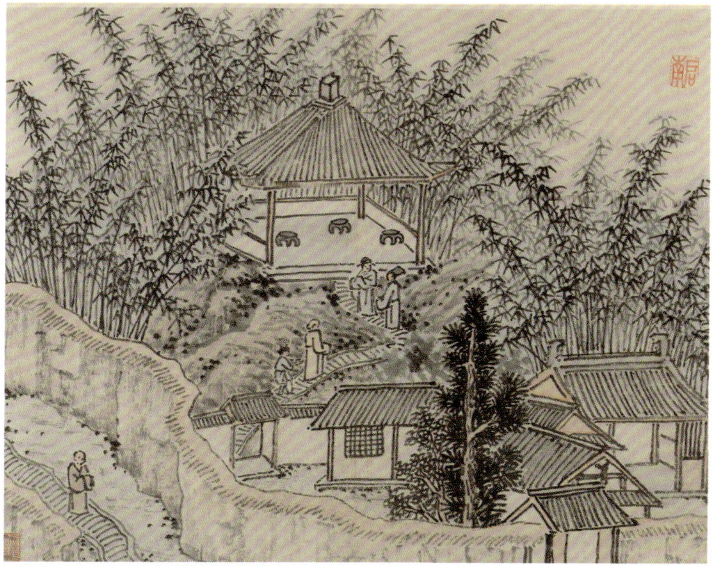
K

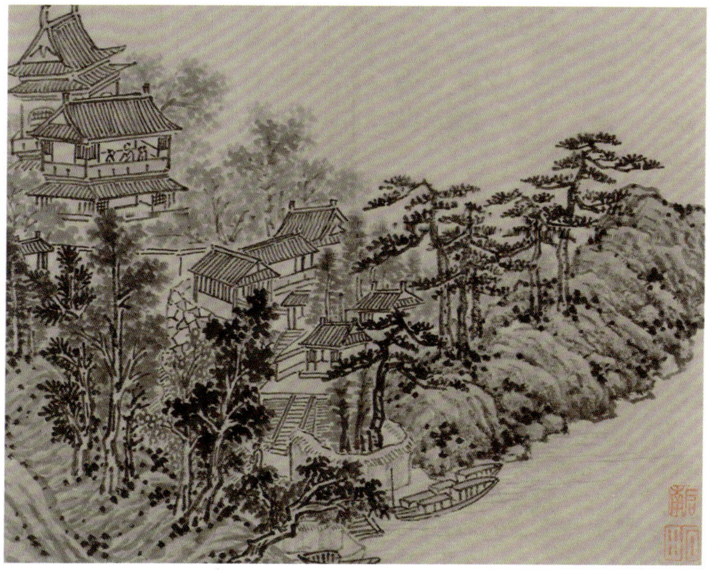
L

58

UNIDENTIFIED ARTIST

## Portrait of Shen Zhou at Age Eighty

明 佚名 沈周像 軸

1506, hanging scroll, ink and colour on silk, 71 × 52.4 cm
The Palace Museum, Beijing (XIN 16641)

REFERENCE LITERATURE

Edwards 1953b, 1962 and 1965; Washington 1973; Yu 1973; Ann Arbor 1976, p. 22; Taipei 1976; Cahill 1978, pp. 57–96 and 157–253; Kohara 1978; Chou 1982; Liscomb 1984; Wang (1782) 1987; *Complete Collection* 1988, vol. 10, pp. 1782–3; Shan 1988; Ma 1990; Vinograd 1992a, pp. 28–9; Chen 1993a; Li 1993; Shen (1469) 1995–9, vol. 1333–402, pp. 311–12 and 382; Wang 1995; Ruan 1996, pp. 35–40; Wang 1999; Clunas 2004; Zi and Geng 2004; Lee 2009; Huang 2010a; Tao 2012

Portraiture has long been an established genre in China, where it is considered different from other categories of figure painting by virtue of realistic representation. A portrait can be understood as a record of certain aspects of a person as seen by another. Whether the physical appearance or social position has been captured by the artist is of little consequence; rather, the underlying conception of portraiture as likeness in Chinese culture requires that a portrait should reveal some sense of the sitter's identity as a particular individual.

Wearing a black hat and a simple cotton robe, the sitter depicted in this portrait is Shen Zhou (1427–1509), who is identified as one of the Four Masters of the Wu School along with Tang Yin (1470–1523), Wen Zhengming (1470–1559) and Qiu Ying (1494/5–1552). Whether to seek participation in court politics like a Confucian official or to pursue individuality and self-cultivation by leading an eremetic life was a difficult choice that preoccupied Chinese scholars over many centuries. Shen settled on the life of a recluse, farmer, scholar and amateur painter; as he commented on the portrait painted of him at age 42, 'for as long as I live, year after year I work on the farm to support my family; day after day I read for my own enjoyment'.[1] The gentle temperament of the farmer-scholar is vividly expressed in this work. Shen's hands are folded across his chest and concealed beneath his capacious robe in a gesture of greeting that signals the sitter's identity as a Confucian scholar and is typical of such portraits. It goes hand in hand with Shen's black silk hat of a man of letters, while his plain light brown robe points to his modest background and humble nature. The facial features and garment are rendered with disciplined linear drawing, each line being steady, even and controlled. The once finely drawn beard and grey hair have now deteriorated.

The wrinkles around Shen's eyes in this work, painted just a few years before his death, are indicated by fine lines with little shading, with a number of brown spots marking his cheeks to show the pigmentation of aged skin. However, the artist was also obliged to follow the guidelines for facial composition in ancestor portraits, such as *santing wuyan*, meaning that the face should be divided into three parts horizontally: from the hairline to the point between the eyebrows, from the eyebrows to the philtrum and from the upper lip to the lower jaw, while the width of the face should be about five times the width of an eye.[2] Even though Shen himself mentions in the colophon that some considered his eyes to be rather small and his jaw too narrow, we can see in this painting that the size and length of the face are proportioned precisely according to the principle of *santing wuyan*.

An extraordinary variety of basic rules, aids and methods came into being in Chinese portraiture, which would be more or less learned by heart so that artists could apply them whenever they wished, spontaneously and without restraint. On the other hand, the visual expression employed in portraits of the literati tended to be distinct from that seen in ancestor portraits from the late Ming (1368–1644) onwards; it could be somewhat more personal and distinctive, and when a work bears no attribution it is often difficult to determine whether it was executed in a workshop or by a single hand, by an artist or a local artisan.

The extant record shows that Shen Zhou commissioned a number of portraits during his lifetime, at the ages of 42, 58, 60, 64, 74, 80 and 83.[3] There is no record of the painter of any of these works. The present portrait is apparently the only one to have survived, making it even more important and offering an insightful rendition of the physiognomy of the great artist, created by a contemporary. Nevertheless, in light of traditional practice in portraiture, is not Shen Zhou's second colophon, 'Like or not like, true or not true? A shadow on paper, a person outside the self', perhaps a telling comment on the likeness? CY

1 Shen (1469?) 1995–9, vol. 1333–02, pp. 311–12
2 Wang 1973
3 Shen (1469?) 1995–9; Ruan 1996, pp. 35–40; *Complete Collection* 1988, vol. 10, pp. 1782–3; Tao 2012

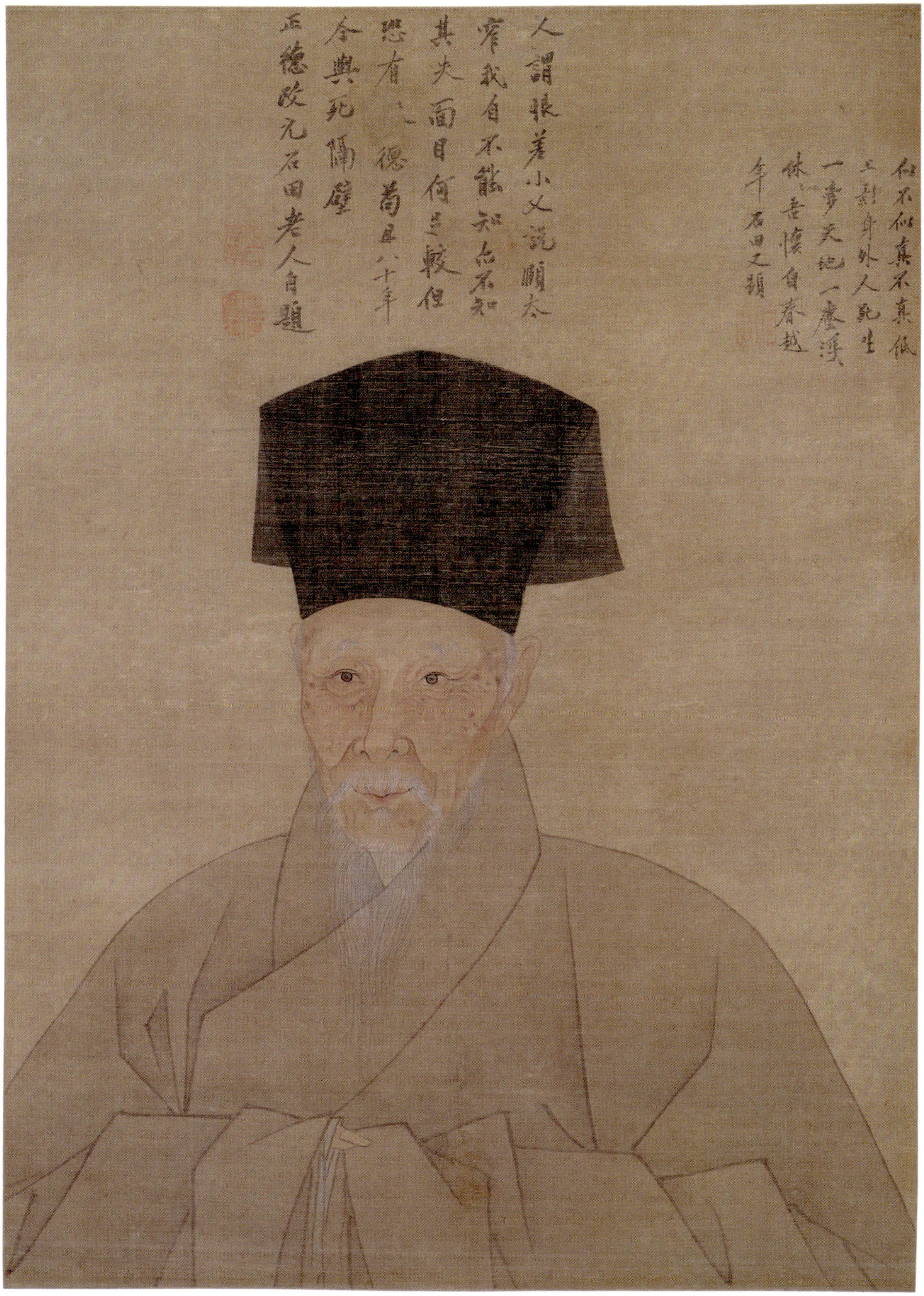
似不似真不真紙
上影身外人死生
一夢天地一塵浮
休〻吾懷自春越
年石田又題
人謂眼差小又說顴太
窄我自不能知亦不知
其失面目何足較但
恐有失德苟且八十年
今與死隔壁
正德改元石田老人自題

59

UNIDENTIFIED ARTIST

## Deity with Phoenix

明 佚名 仙女鳳凰圖 軸

16th century, hanging scroll, ink and light colour on silk, 146.8 × 94.5 cm
The British Museum, London
(1913,0501,0.10)

PROVENANCE

Gift of Sir William Gwynne-Evans, Bt

REFERENCE LITERATURE

Binyon 1927, p. 27; New York and Dallas 1993, fig. 135

The female figure in this painting is of striking beauty, elegance and youth. Depicted in three-quarter profile, the figure turns to our left, or 'westwards', and is accompanied by a phoenix proceeding in the same direction. The graceful bend of her body, the flow of her robes and the floating scarves are all indicative of movement, while her inward look seems to reveal the awareness of her power to seduce.

The motif of the phoenix suggests that the female figure is a depiction of the Daoist deity the Queen Mother of the West (Xiwangmu), also known as Metal Mother (Jin mu). The mythical bird has been a key iconographic symbol of Xiwangmu since at least the Yuan dynasty (1271–1368).[1] However, the phoenix as an attribute of the Queen Mother of the West appears mostly in her crown. Xiwangmu is a patron deity of women and a divine teacher in rulership, and is associated with longevity.[2] Peaches are another attribute of the deity, and refer to the peaches that are said to ripen every 3,000 years in the Queen Mother's paradise on Mount Kunlun. Those upon whom a peach is bestowed gain immortality. Her image here, however, seems to have merged with another Daoist deity, the Mysterious Woman of the Nine Heavens (Jiutian xuannü), who is associated with the arts of war and longevity, and the sexual arts. In her biography, Du Guangting (850–933) describes the Mysterious Woman as a disciple of the Queen Mother of the West, and as a teacher of the Yellow Thearch (Huangdi) who descended through the mists to instruct the Thearch by riding a cinnabar phoenix.[3] Her beauty and youth, as well as the attribute of a scripture as a tool for instruction together with the motif of the phoenix, suggest then that the deity here may be the Mysterious Woman of the Nine Heavens.

The subject matter and style of this scroll imply that the painting was executed by a close follower of the Zhe school artist Wu Wei (c.1459–1508).[4] Wu Wei was a master figure painter, and depicted his subjects with swift, spontaneous brushstrokes. Loose, fluttering scarves are characteristic of his style. Wu is said to have been fond of women, and the female figure features prominently in his oeuvre. He served intermittently at court, and presumably executed his art in the presence of the emperor. Wu's unconventional lifestyle and eccentricity found expression in the spontaneous and bold brushwork of his paintings – a style that continued to be practised by his successors.

A scroll from the former Del Drago collection with a comparable female figure holding a *ruyi* sceptre and a peach (motifs representing the power of rulership and longevity) bears the inscription 'Happiness comes from Heaven' (fig. 61).[5] While the British Museum painting is of exceptional artistic quality and may have been used in various cultural contexts, it is possible that both scrolls were created as gifts to express auspicious wishes to the recipient.

The painting was donated to the British Museum in 1913 by Sir William Gwynne-Evans, who acquired it from the former collection of Arthur Morrison (1863–1945), a London novelist and journalist. After its acquisition by the museum, the scroll was labelled a depiction of 'Lady Lao Yu'. The title was already questioned by Paul Pelliot in 1927, and there seems to be no source that supports Laurence Binyon's title.[6] The scroll came to the museum in a Japanese mount, and has recently been restored and remounted in the Chinese manner. CVS

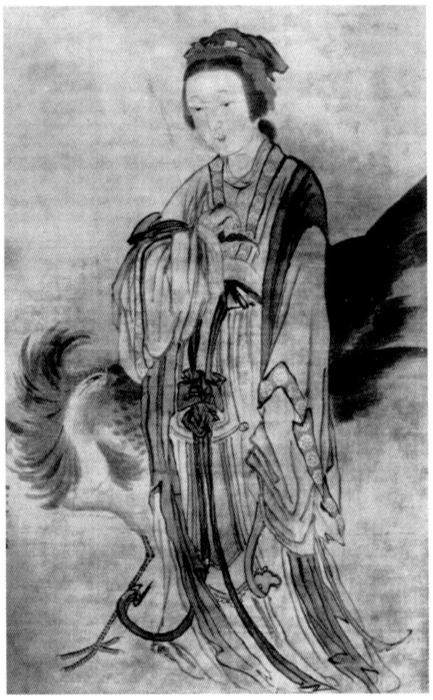

FIG. 61
*Female Figure with Peach and Ruyi Sceptre*
hanging scroll, c.18th century. Ink and colour on silk. Formerly Del Drago Collection (present location unknown)
(After Milan 1931, pl. 28)

The author would like to thank Luk Yu-ping for valuable comments.

1 The Queen Mother of the West is depicted with a phoenix in the murals of the Hall of the Three Purities (Sanqing dian) at the Temple of Eternal Joy (Yongle gong) in Shanxi Province. For a discussion of the iconography and further paintings depicting the Queen Mother of the West, see Stephen Little in Chicago 2000, pp. 276–7, no. 93–4.
2 For the veneration of the Queen Mother of the West during the Tang dynasty (618–907) in particular, see Cahill 1993, esp. pp. 91–102.
3 Ibid., in particular pp. 92, 98
4 For a discussion of Wu Wei (c.1459–1508) and the British Museum painting, see New York and Dallas 1993, pp. 223–47.
5 Milan 1931, pl. 28
6 Pelliot 1927

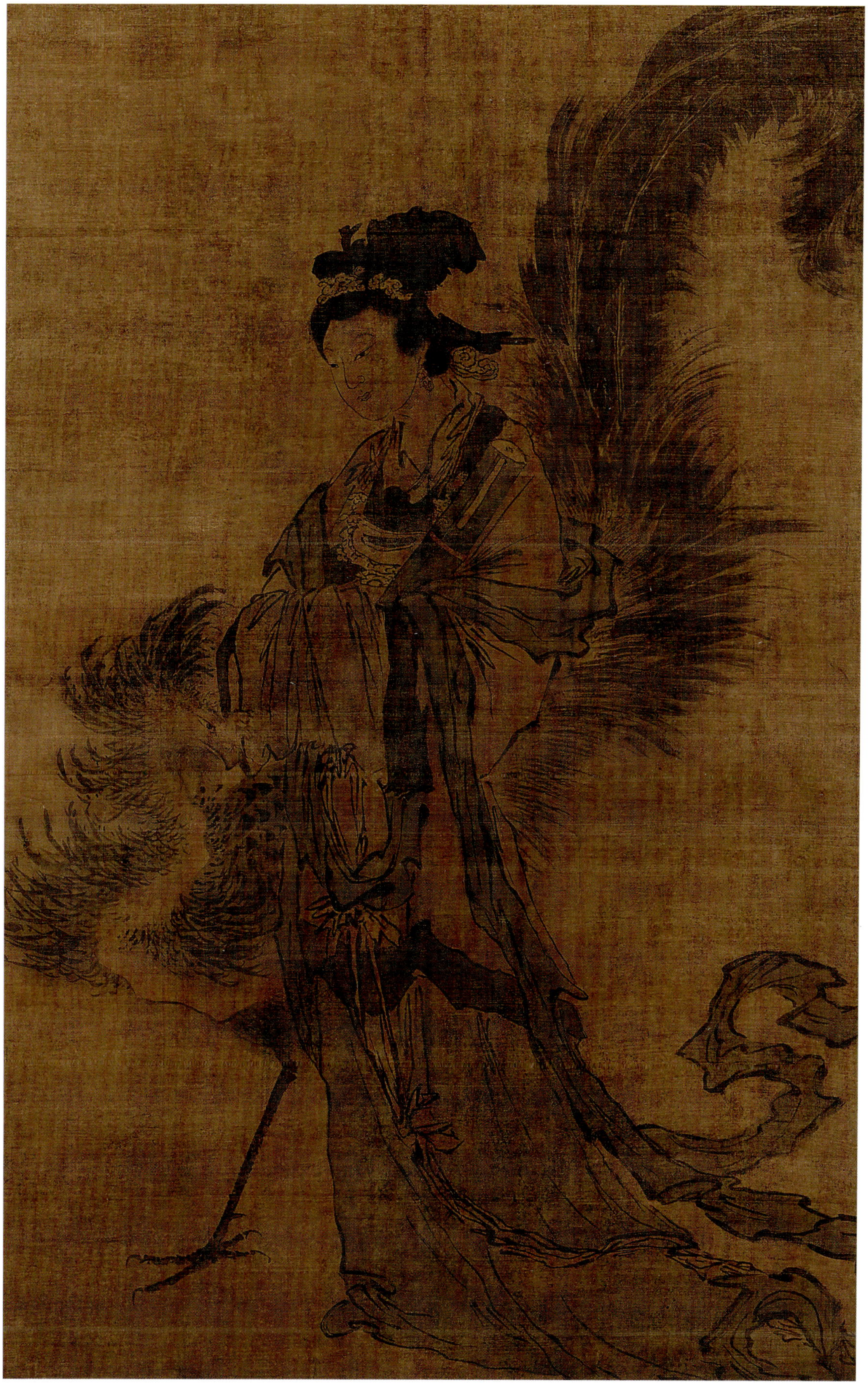

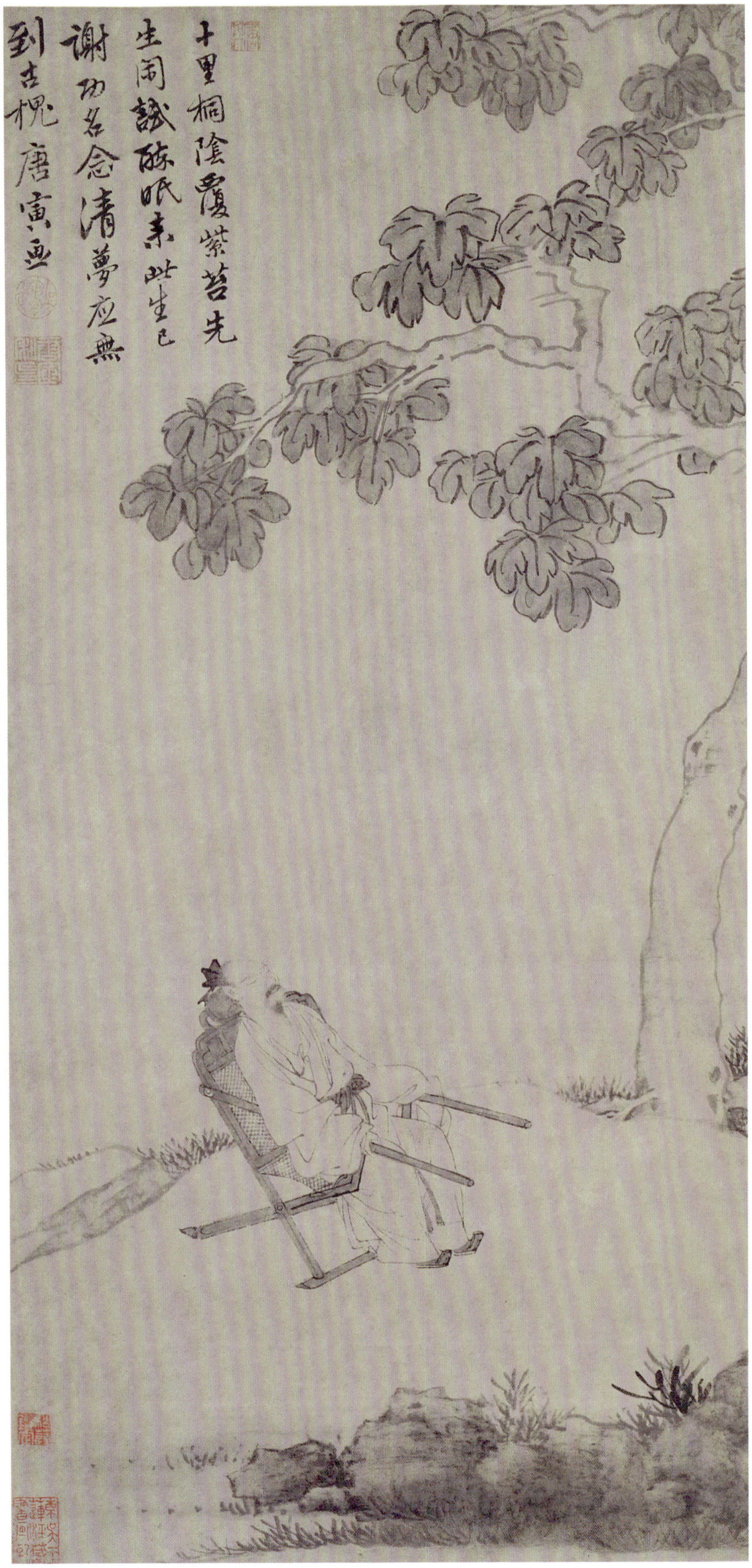
十里桐陰覆紫苔先
生閑試醉眠來此生已
謝功名念清夢應無
到古槐 唐寅畫

60

TANG YIN (1470–1523)

## Pure Dream beneath a Paulownia Tree

明 唐寅 桐蔭清夢圖 軸

first quarter 16th century, hanging scroll, ink and light colour on paper, 62 × 30.8 cm
The Palace Museum, Beijing (XIN 101314)

REFERENCE LITERATURE

Yang 1947; Bian (1682) 1993–8; *Veritable Records of of the Ming Emperor Xiaozong* 1962, vol. 147, p. 9; vol. 148, p. 2; vol. 149, p. 9; vol. 151, p. 1; Yang 1967; Jiang 1976; Siggstedt 1982a and 1982b; Fuller 1984; Memphis 1984; Clapp 1991; Vinograd 1992b; Yang 1994 and 1997; Wang 1999; Liu in Taipei 2000; Shan 2000; Zhou and Zhang 2002; Nemroff 2005

Regarded by his contemporaries as one of the most gifted of the literati, in 1498 Tang Yin received top marks in the provincial examination in Nanjing, and the following year went to Beijing to sit the national examination. However, with a seemingly promising future awaiting him, he was falsely implicated in a charge of bribery involving one of the chief examiners.[1] After being imprisoned, tortured and given a heavy fine, Tang returned to Suzhou in shame, and turned to Chan (J. Zen) Buddhism for solace. In order to earn a living, he was forced to sell paintings and write epitaphs on commission. Living in poverty and afflicted with lung disease, Tang Yin died at the early age of 54.

With all hopes of fame gone, as indicated in the poem accompanying *Pure Dream beneath a Paulownia Tree*, the artist painted this self-portrait after his return from Beijing. Weeds grow vigorously among the scattered rocks in the foreground. In the centre, eyes closed in contemplation, a middle-aged man reclines in a rattan chair in the shade of a paulownia tree. The brushwork used for the figure is elegant and neat. The painting is executed in plain linear style, the natural setting depicted in a soft, free and fluent strokes, with light shading and ink wash on the rocks and leaves. The rather simple and bare backdrop and the clear emphasis on the lone figure's face with its closed eyes convey the contradiction between the artist's outer serenity and indifference to how he might be perceived, and his inner discomfort. Seeing everything as a void, the artist knows his dream will come to nothing. Such underlying sentiments and grievances were shared by many able men of letters who, for various reasons, felt themselves to have been abandoned by society.

Indebted to Zhou Chen (*c.*1450–1535) (cat. no. 55), Shen Zhou (1427–1509) (cat. no. 57) and Du Jin (act. *c.*1465–1509) (cat. no. 54), Tang Yin began to paint seriously only after the age of 30. While his early work is often refined and meticulous, with heavy colouring in the manner of the Southern Song (1127–1279) academy, he gradually turned to monochrome ink in the freehand, eloquent style of the Yuan dynasty (1271–1368) masters. This undated painting represents his later style, showing an affinity to the Yuan brush mode.

Unlike most professional artists, Tang Yin retained his literati spirit, and often personified his subject and expressed his feelings in both paintings and poetry. Depicting the pride and sadness, desolation and consolation of a scholar sitting intentionally in the cool shade of a tree, this painting may have inspired Luo Pin's (1733–99) 1760 portrait *Master Dongxin (Jin Nong)*. It also created a new expression in figure painting, speaking to the hearts of many of those whose talent had gone to waste. CY

1 Tang Yin and Xu Jing (1473–1507) were accused of bribing the servant of the chief examiner, Cheng Minzheng (1445–99), in order to view the examination questions in advance. The accusation was made by Cheng Minzheng's political enemy, Fu Han (1435–1502), and Du Mu (1458-1525), a fellow candidate from Suzhou, who was envious of Tang's talent. Cheng Minzheng was imprisoned and died four days after he was released, whereupon the emperor awarded him a posthumous title, implying his innocence. See Clapp 1991, pp. 5–6; for further details, see Jiang 1976, pp. 37–49.

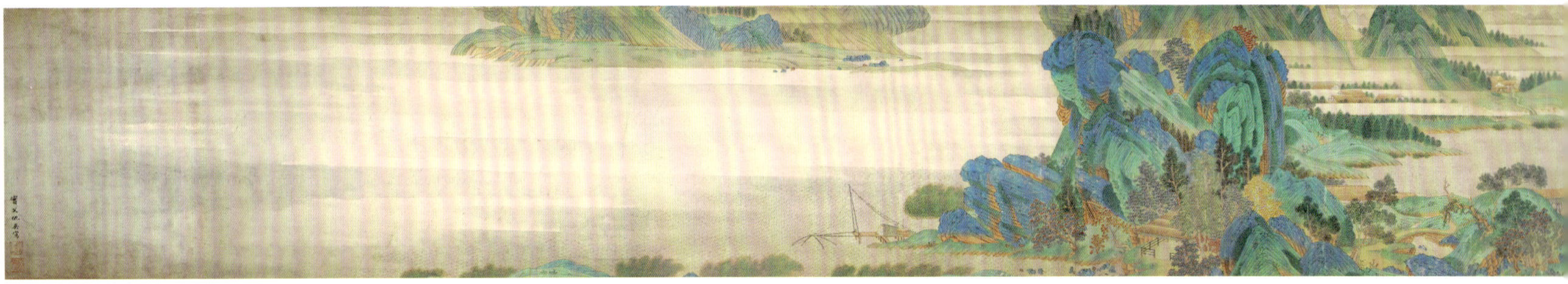

61

QIU YING (1494/5–1552)

## Saying Farewell at Xunyang

明 仇英 潯陽送別圖 卷

first half 16th century, handscroll,
ink and colour on paper, 33.66 × 399.73 cm
The Nelson-Atkins Museum of Art, Kansas City
(46–50)

PROVENANCE

Jean-Pierre Dubosc (1903–88)

REFERENCE LITERATURE

Sickman and Soper 1956, pp. 181–2, pl. 142; Cahill 1978, pp. 209–10, col. pl. 9; Kansas City and Cleveland 1980, pp. 201–3, no. 164; Johnston Laing 2000, figs 5, 8 and 9 (the author argues that the painting in the Nelson is a forgery because it is deviant from Qiu Ying's style, p. 275; the signature of Shifu is also problematic – see p. 277); Blanchard 2007, ill. 17

The painting is based on a famous poem, the 'Song of the Lute', written by Bai Juyi (772–846) in 816. Having been demoted to a rural area, the poet went to bid farewell to his friend, who was hosting a party on a boat at the riverbank of Xunyang. While drinking in the moonlight, the friends heard music being played on a *pipa*, or Chinese lute. The playing was so skilful that they invited the musician to join them on the boat. After playing a song, the musician confessed she had once been a beautiful courtesan in the capital, but had lost her position due to age. Her sorrow quickly aroused Bai's empathy since he felt they shared the same fate.

The melancholic poem is set in a bright blue-and-green landscape, a genre popular during the Tang dynasty (618–907), when Bai Juyi was active. In the Ming dynasty (1368–1644), this archaic style of landscape was often used as a setting to impart an air of antiquity to literary themes. However, in *Saying Farewell at Xunyang*, the landscape is represented beyond a mere setting. Not only is it exquisitely painted with highly detailed elements such as the colourful foliage, flying geese and elegant buildings, but it also becomes fairly manneristic, as evidenced in the geometric slopes of the mountains and the horizontal mists. This style evokes a fantastic wonderland to portray Tang dynasty Xunyang, with key elements of the story, such as the party on the boat and the reflection of the moonlight on the river, pictured literally. At the same time, the wonderland itself offers a visual feast, with additional excitement unessential to the poem: following the boat party, the gorgeous river scene continues for nearly half of the painting, with farmhouses and fishermen adding to the fairy-tale quality.

The painting bears the signature of Qiu Ying and two of his seals. A professional painter of the Wu school (based in Suzhou), Qiu Ying was well known for his paintings of figures and blue-and-green landscapes in a refined style. He was reportedly obliged to hire assistants in his workshop in order to meet the demand for his paintings, and questions have arisen regarding a large number of later figure and landscape paintings that feature possibly spurious signatures. Some scholars have questioned the attribution of *Saying Farewell at Xunyang* as well, on the basis of the style of the signature.[2] Its uniqueness is also challenged by a painting from an album attributed to Qiu Ying in the Palace Museum, Beijing (fig. 62). Both the handscroll in the Nelson-Atkins and the album

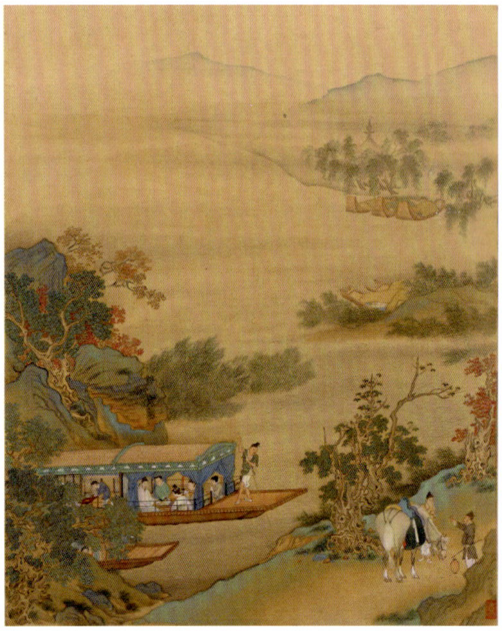

FIG. 62
Qiu Ying (1494/5–1552). *Illustration to the 'Lute Song'*, possibly 1st half 16th century. Leaf from an album of 10 leaves, ink and colour on silk. The Palace Museum, Beijing

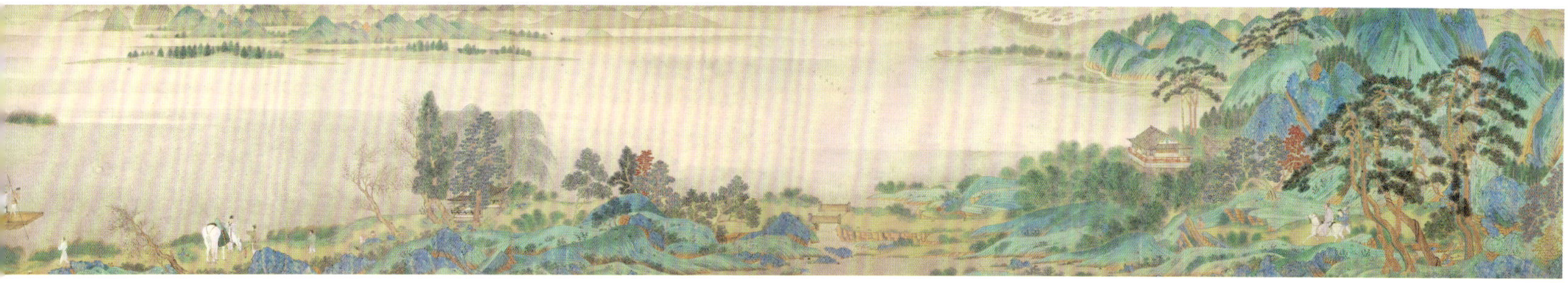

leaf in Beijing show nearly identical images of the poet alighting from a horse and the party scene on the boat. The duplicate versions may have resulted from one painting having been copied from the other, or from both having been based on an earlier model.

Despite the controversy over authorship, the current painting may serve as an example of the visual culture popular in the latter half of the Ming dynasty. It was during the Ming that illustrations for Bai Juyi's 'Song of the Lute' started to appear, and they were especially popular among the Wu school painters. The jewel-toned landscape with its exquisite details and well-known literary theme would have been enjoyed by a wide range of viewers, just as it is today. Perhaps more importantly, this pictorial interpretation of the poem appears to evoke the courtesan culture that prevailed in urban areas, particularly in the circles of scholar-officials. In Ming society, trained courtesans affiliated themselves with the literati culture both through their charms and by honing their skills in music, poetry and painting, and therefore came to be the companions of men of privileged status with a classical education. Read from this perspective, the painting reflects the idea that the courtesan doubles as a mirror image of the poet-official's own failing career. The boat party essential for their rendezvous would have been a common occurrence amid the pleasure boats in a city's licensed quarter, such as those of the famous Qinhuai district in Ming dynasty Jinling (now Nanjing). LL

1 Dates based on Kansas City and Cleveland 1980, p. 201
2 Johnston Laing 2000, pp. 275–8

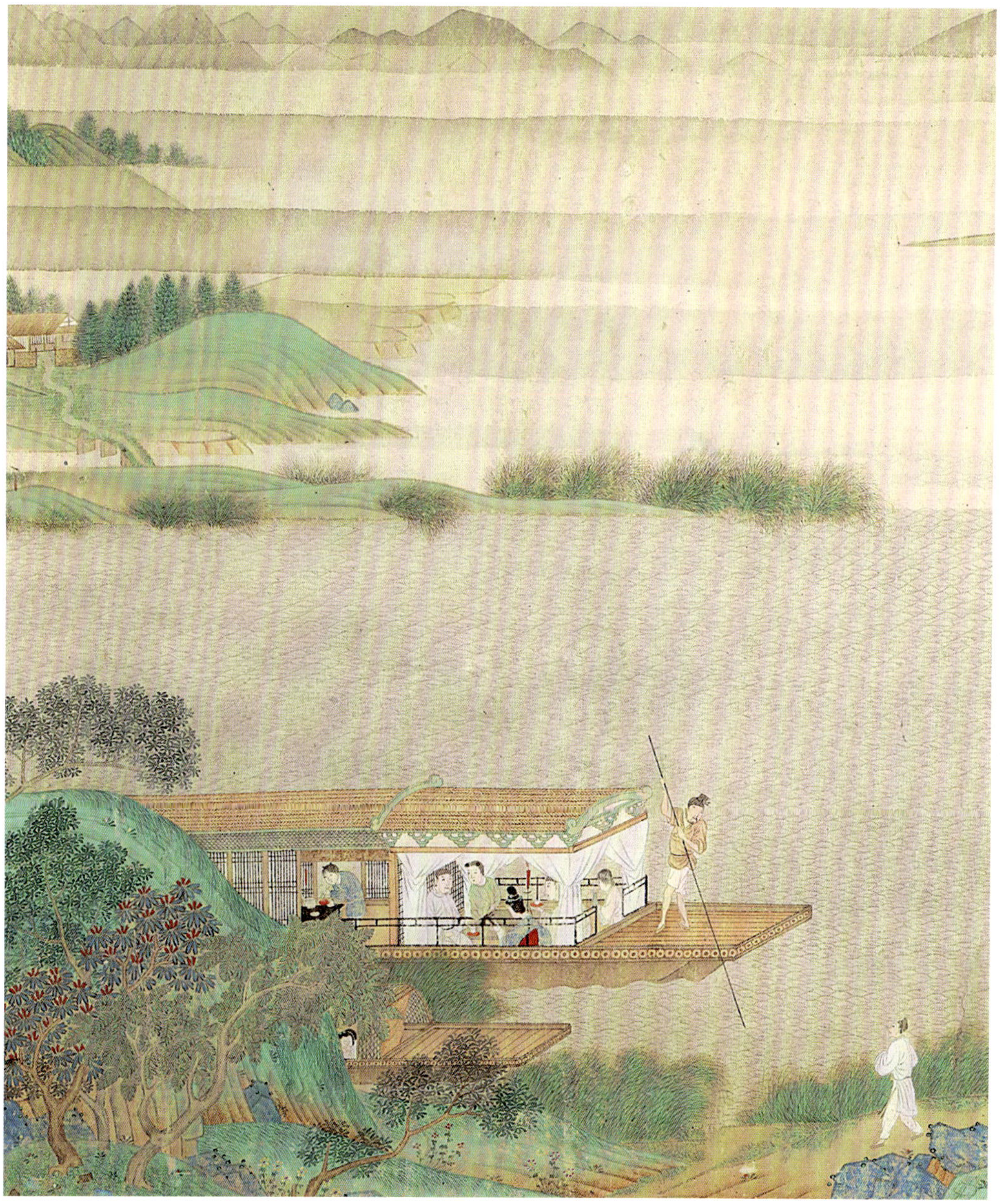

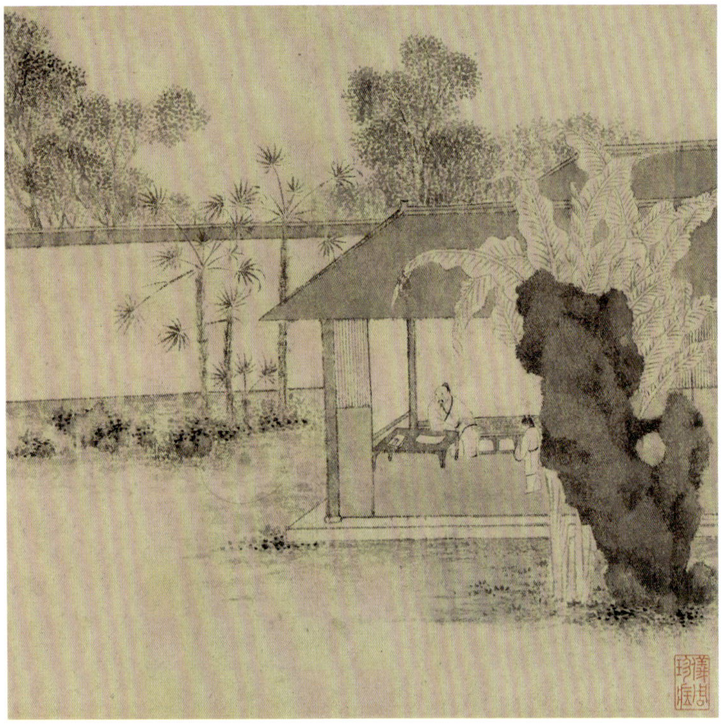

62

WEN ZHENGMING (1470–1559)

## Garden of the Inept Administrator

明 文徵明 拙政園圖詩 冊

1551, album of eight painted leaves with facing leaves inscribed with poems, ink on paper, each leaf 26.4 × 27.3 cm
The Metropolitan Museum of Art, New York
Gift of Douglas Dillon, 1979 (1979.458.1a-ii)

PROVENANCE

Mr and Mrs Earl Morse

REFERENCE LITERATURE

Princeton 1969, pp. 29–31, 66–75, no. 3; Ann Arbor 1976, pp. 175–81, no. LI; Suzhou Museum 1978; Murck and Fong 1980–1, p. 25, fig. 23; New York 1983b, pp. 64–5, 134, no. 22; Clunas 2004, p. 47, fig. 15

Through discipline, talent and sheer longevity, Wen Zhengming became the leading master of the Wu (Suzhou) school of literati painting and the most famous artist in sixteenth-century China. Born into a prosperous scholarly family in the city of Suzhou, the cultural capital of the day, Wen Zhengming was tutored by some of the most illustrious members of that society. In 1478, he was instructed in the classics by family friend Wu Kuan (1435–1504), and by 1489 was studying painting with Shen Zhou (1427–1509). From 1495 to 1522, Wen tried and failed the provincial civil service examination 10 times before being granted an honorary appointment to the Hanlin Academy in today's Beijing. Rapidly disillusioned with official life, he retired from government service after only three years and returned to Suzhou, where he spent his remaining 32 years painting, practising calligraphy and becoming one of the leaders in the cultural life of the city.

In this work, Wen creates idealized images of what has become one of Suzhou's most famous gardens – given the self-effacing title of Garden of the Inept Administrator (Zhuozheng Yuan; also translated as Garden of the Unsuccessful Politician). The garden's owner, Wang Xianchen (1473–c.1543), built it on the site of an old temple during the Jiajing reign (1522–67). In 1535, Wen painted a 31-leaf album of the garden for Wang, accompanying each view with a poem. Sixteen years later he painted this set of eight views, presumably for himself as it bears no dedication, reusing his earlier poems but creating new images. Drawn in a spare, monochrome manner, the paintings exemplify the era's taste for understatement, restraint and modesty. Integrating poetry, calligraphy and painting, the album represents the literati ideal of the 'three perfections'.

Most of the sites Wen depicts are unrecognizable today, but those that are, notably the Hall of Distant Fragrances (Yuanxiang tang), appear far more elegant and substantial than the humble structures illustrated in Wen's album. Evidently, Wen felt free to radically simplify his images, making them appear rustic and quaint rather than attempting to describe the imposing columns and massive tiled roofs that are typical of Suzhou architecture. It was not Wen's intent to depict the garden as it actually appeared, but to evoke the ideal of a humble scholarly retreat in accordance with the garden's self-deprecating name.

It is clear from Wen's commentary that the album leaves do not constitute a tour through the garden's topography. Instead, Wen presents highlights of the garden that give him a chance to explore varied compositional schemas. 'The Bank of Many Fragrances' (Leaf A) is the most balanced and formal view, as suits its position as the opening vista. It offers an elevated frontal view of the elegant hall one encounters upon entering the garden from the residential quarters. Leaf B presents a 'close-up' of 'The Bank of Many Fragrances', where a bridge spans the 'Little Canglang Pond'. 'The Bamboo Bank' (Leaf C) leads the viewer from a gate in the lower left corner of the composition along a zigzag path to a secluded pavilion, where gentlemen gaze out at a quiet grove of bamboo and a pet crane. 'The Banana Balustrade' (Leaf D) reverses the stepped diagonal recession of the previous leaf, framing a study between a banana and massive garden rock at the lower right and a wall lined with windmill palms at the upper left. 'The Fishing Stone' (Leaf E) shows a scholar seated beside the water in the shade of a willow. Seemingly lost in contemplation and with no fishing line in sight, the figure's lack of interest in catching fish may reflect Wen Zhengming's renunciation of an official career. In contrast to this spare composition, 'The Garden of Attracting Birds' (Leaf F) depicts a dense orchard and a vegetable plot tended by a gardener. 'The Jade Spring' (Leaf G) celebrates the owner's discovery of a source of sweet water. It shows a servant drawing water from a well head beneath two paulownia trees. The album's final image, 'The Locust Tree Enclosure' (Leaf H), features a raised terrace encircled by tall trees, where two gentlemen are waited upon by an attendant. Following his accompanying poem, Wen Zhengming gives the precise date when he completed the album: 19 October 1551. MH

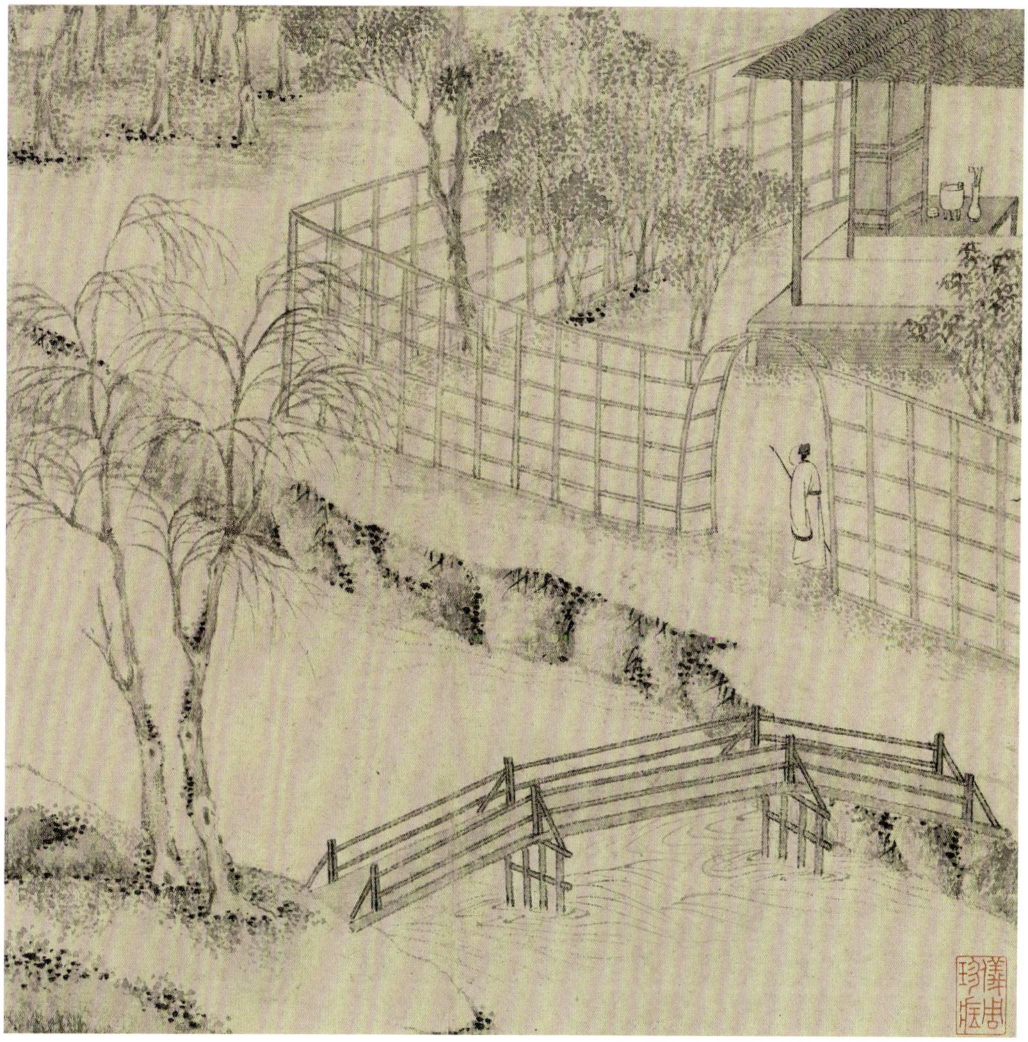

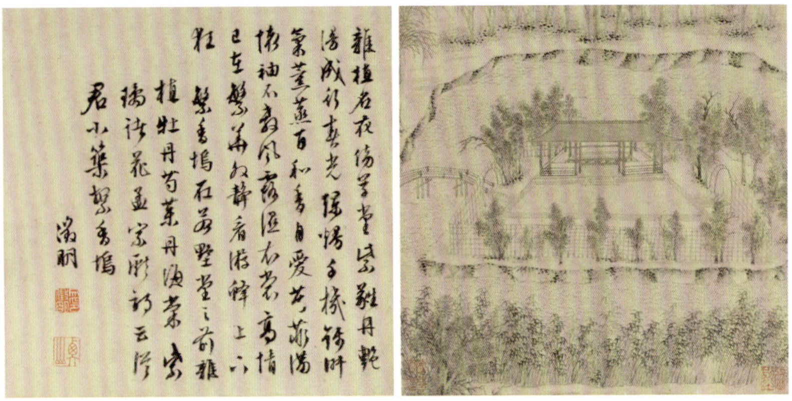

A

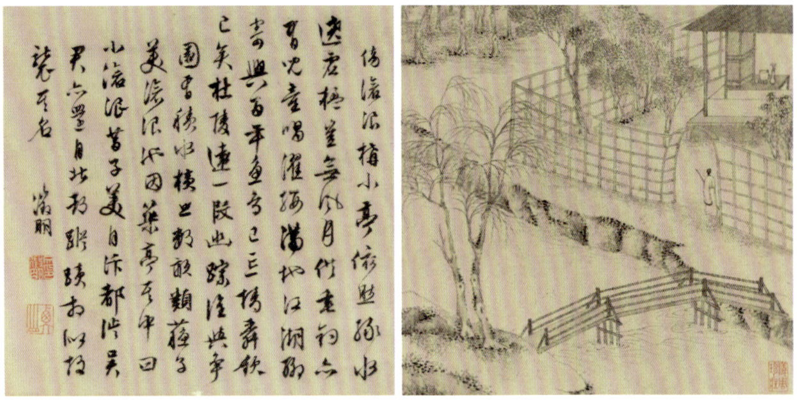

B

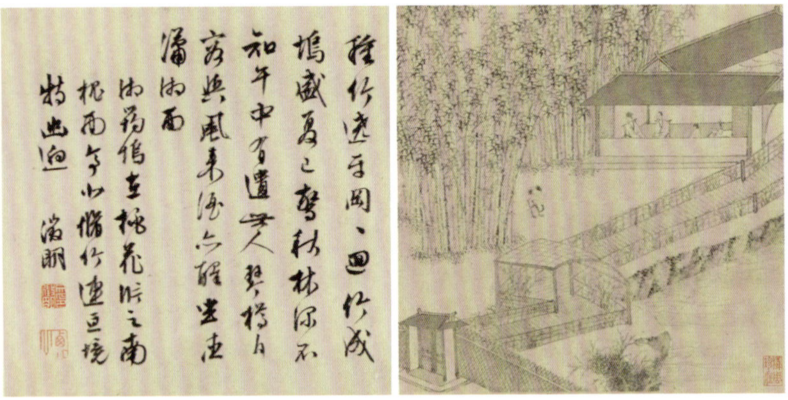

C

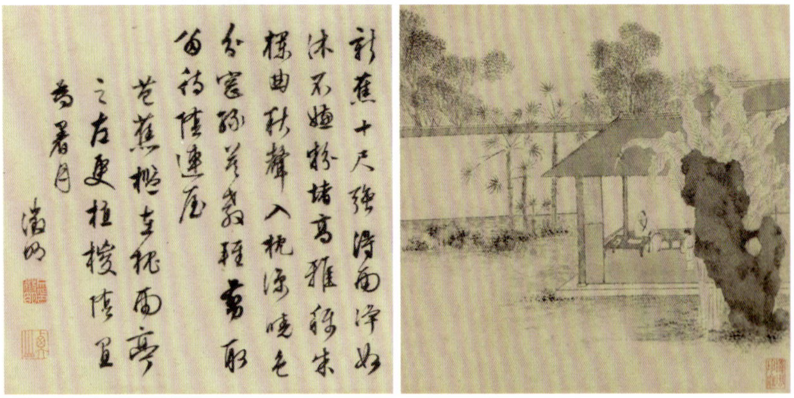

D

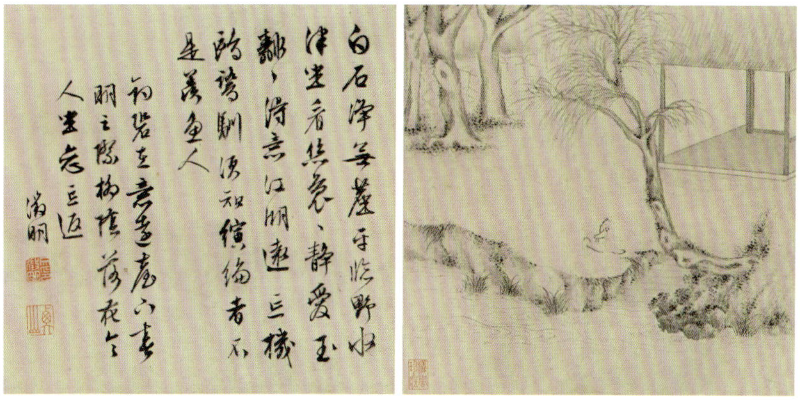

E

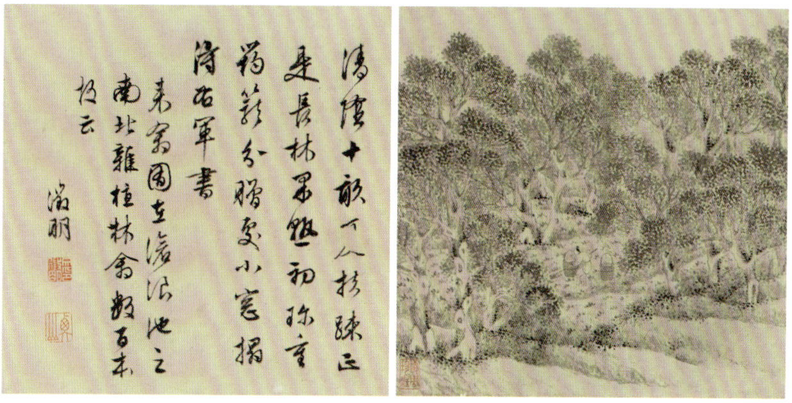

F

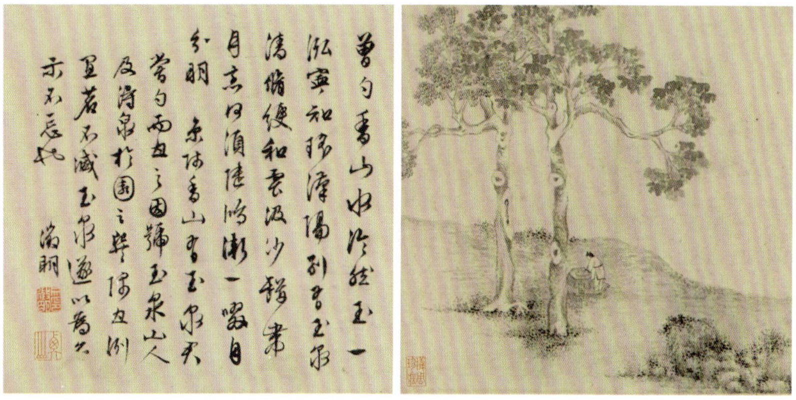

G

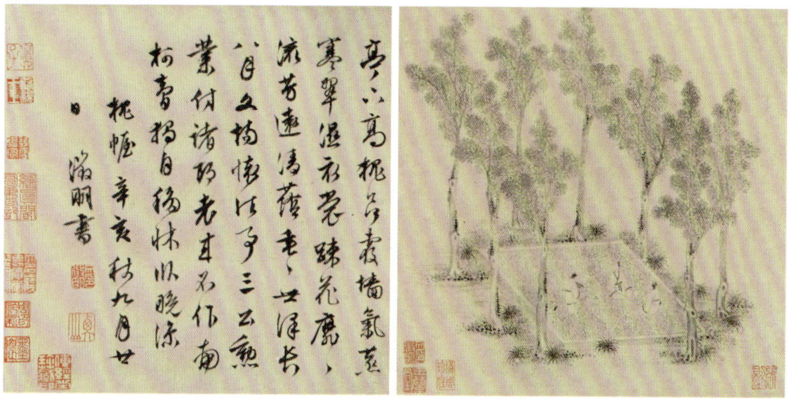

H

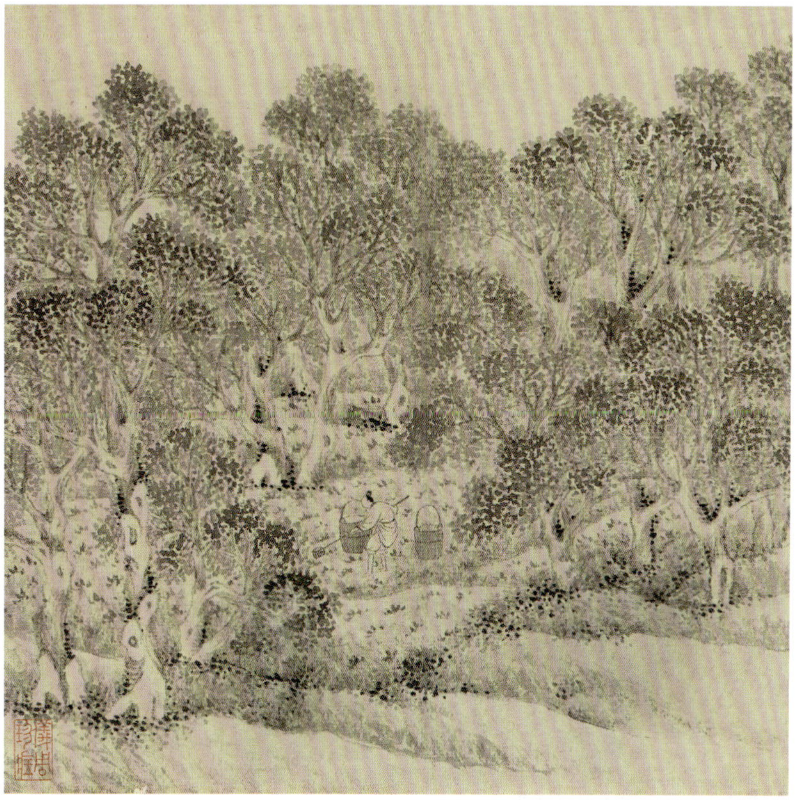

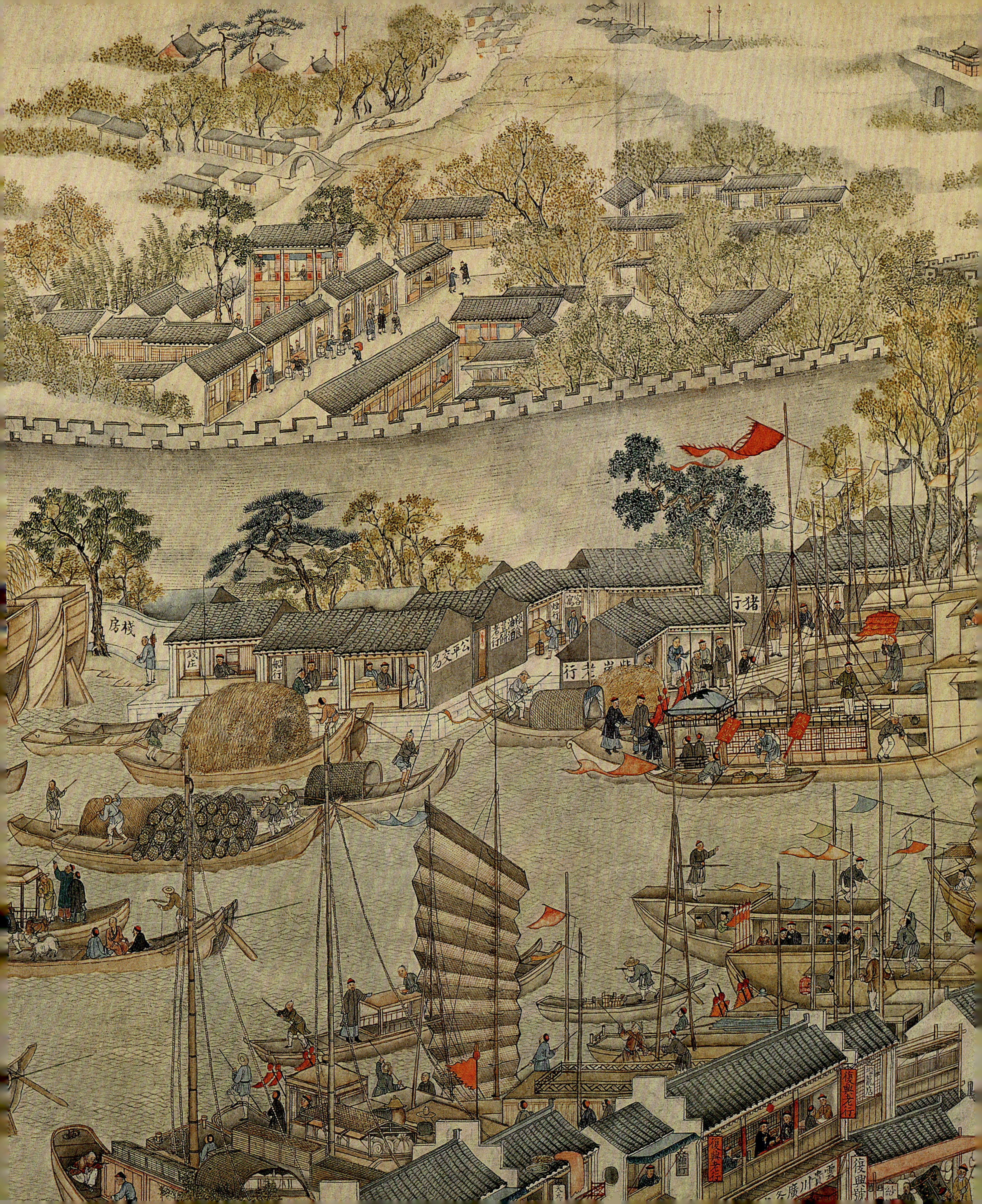
栈房
钱庄
船行
公平交易
烟行
客寓
猪行

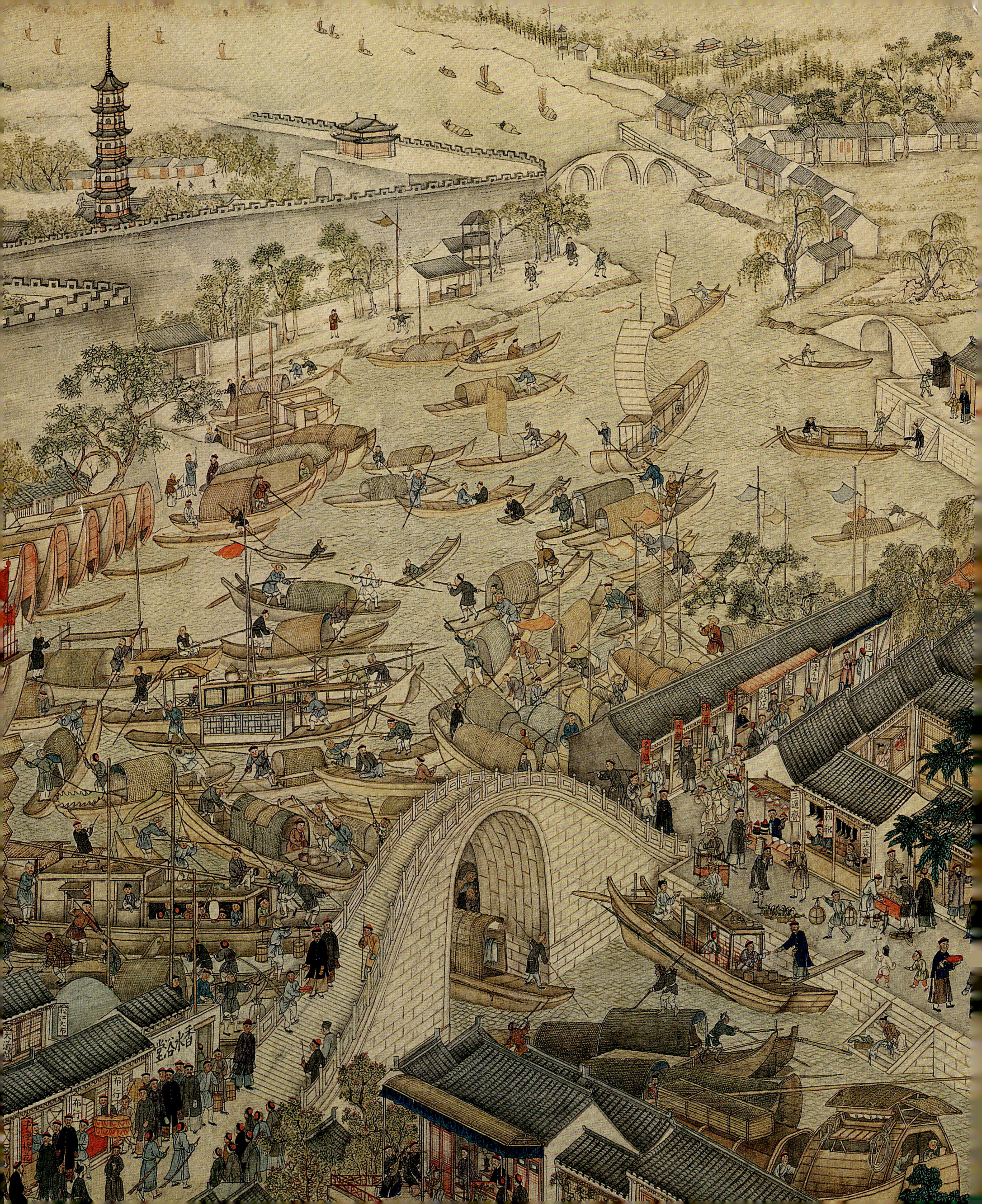

# Paintings 1600–1900

Towards the end of the Ming dynasty (1368–1644), while some painters developed eccentric or mannered styles, one formidable calligrapher and painter came to dominate the scene: Dong Qichang (1555–1636), whose own handscroll *Twin Marvels of Calligraphy and Painting* (cat. no. 63) typifies his somewhat arch rendering of landscape. His self-inscription makes clear that he was inspired by the misty landscapes of the tenth-century master who shared the same family name, Dong Yuan (act. 930s–60s), as transformed by Mi Fu (1051–1107; see cat. no. 18), and claims that he has himself attained the samadhi (state of supreme concentration) of ink play. To complement the painting, Dong also transcribed a poem by Du Fu (712–70), on a visit to the Temple of the Supreme Emperor of Mystery Prime, a title conferred on the philosopher Laozi (act. 6th century BCE) as the divine ancestor of the Tang (618–907) imperial family in 730.[1] His brushwork uses both the 'Mi dots' of the distant mountains, characteristic of Mi Fu, and the 'hemp-fibre' brushstrokes associated with followers of Dong Yuan, such as Huang Gongwang (1269–1354). Thus, despite the apparently sparse nature of the painting itself, with large areas of untouched paper, the messages it conveys are extremely dense, with both Buddhist and Daoist overtones, and explicit references, both textual and visual, to some of the greatest Chinese painters and poets.

In the seventeenth century, the artists of the Orthodox school, that is, the heirs of the literati tradition that Dong Qichang traced back to Wang Wei (699–759), diligently followed Dong's principles to study and transmit the surviving masterpieces of landscape painting from the Song (960–1279) and Yuan (1271–1368) periods through such transformational brushwork. Among them were the Four Wangs: Wang Shimin (1592–1680) and Wang Jian (1598–1677), then their student Wang Hui (1632–1717), and Wang Yuanqi (1642–1715), who all excelled in producing landscapes through developing brush techniques to literally 'write out' compositions in instantly recognizable styles. Wang Shimin was the first to produce an album of reduced-size copies of Song and Yuan landscape paintings in his own and in Dong Qichang's collections: the album, entitled *Revealing the Large through the Small*, as well as several of the originals on which it is based, are in the collection of the National Palace Museum, Taipei. This album set a precedent for other small-scale paintings in a range of Song and Yuan manners, usually concluding with a winter landscape, such as Wang Jian's *Landscapes in the Manner of Old Masters* (cat. no. 68). Wang Hui went even further and produced, not copies, but full-scale paintings inspired by the same masters: his *The Colours of Mount Taihang* of 1669 (cat. no. 67), one of his earliest works, is a handscroll in the grand manner of Fan Kuan (act. c.990–1030), recognizable by the idiom of 'raindrop' touches of the brush used to render the rugged northern landscape. Likewise, Wang Yuanqi's *Early Spring in the Mountains* (cat. no. 75) alludes to a still-extant work (*Early Spring*, 1072; National Palace Museum, Taipei) by Guo Xi (c.1000–c.1090), but the long 'hemp-fibre' brushstrokes are inherited from Huang Gongwang while the composition is radically modern, without the divisions into foreground, middle ground and far distance characteristic of Song landscapes, and fusing Guo Xi's level distance, deep distance and high distance into one unbroken sequence from the foreground to the highest summit. The rhythm of repeated brushstrokes in such paintings gave, for the first time, visible expression to the *longmai* ('dragon veins') and *qiyun* ('breath-resonance') that had ever been the aim of painters since Jing Hao (c.870–c.930) in the tenth century articulated his Six Essentials (*liuyao*, which in turn were a distillation of the Six Methods, *liufa*, of the critic Xie He [act. 6th century]): spirit or breath (*qi*), resonance (*yun*), thought (*si*), scene (*jing*), brush (*bi*) and ink (*mo*).[2]

Dong Qichang's influence is even manifest among the painters, known as the Individualists, who did not follow his prescriptions. Thus Gong Xian (c.1619–89) also makes explicit references in his *Landscape Album* to Dong Yuan and Mi Fu of the Song and Huang Gongwang and Ni Zan (1306–74) of the Yuan. Generally, however, they and their contemporaries followed the spirit, rather than the appearance, of the late Yuan masters: their paintings record their individual experiences and the many places they visited on their travels, and their individual brush styles are totally distinct, reflecting the character of each, as well as recognizable features of place. For instance, Shitao (1642–1707) imbues the album leaves of *Sketches of Calligraphy and Painting by Qingxiang* (cat. no. 71) with his vibrant 'single brushstroke' (*yihua*) and accompanies them with reminiscences in inspired calligraphy, while Bada Shanren (1626–1705), like Shitao a descendant of the Ming imperial house, employs virtuoso ink wash to express his desolation, half a century or more after the Manchu conquest, in *Flowers on the River* (cat. no. 74). In addition, some painters of both schools, orthodox and individualist, exhibit signs of contact with Western culture: thus Wu Li (1632–1718) converted to Christianity and became a Jesuit priest in 1688, and left comments on Western painting,[3] while James Cahill has suggested that European influence, in the form of contemporary European engravings introduced to China by the Jesuits, can be seen in the dramatic contrasts of light and shadow, hitherto unknown in Chinese painting, in the work of Gong Xian and other contemporaries.[4]

Abundant evidence of both continuity and change is visible in the paintings of the eighteenth century as well: in single large hanging scrolls, Yuan Jiang (act. c.1680–1730) often reprises the grand manner of Song landscape painting in combination with imaginary depictions of ancient palaces in the *jiehua* or 'ruled-line' tradition of architectural painters already seen in the painting signed 'Guo Zhongshu' (d.977) (cat. no. 49); his *The Palace of Nine Perfections* (cat. no. 72), however, transposes the subject matter onto a series of narrow borderless hanging scrolls, in which we can see both the antique 'blue-and-green' colouring and clear evidence of an attempt to depict distance by means of an interpretation of Western perspective, with a rising ground plane and a consistent oblique slant to the buildings.

The forces driving changes in the tradition also include a new source of patronage, especially in the lower Yangzi city of Yangzhou, where a newly rich merchant class provided patrons for painters who each cultivated different styles of brushwork and subject matter, some using time-worn themes such as Zheng Xie's (1693–1765) *Bamboo and Rock* (cat. no. 77), others quite extreme, such as Luo Pin's (1733–99) *Ghost Amusement* (cat. no. 78), which displays telling evidence of his having seen Western engravings. In the field of figure painting, the elegant and supremely youthful appearance of Zeng Jing's (1564–1647) *Portrait of Wang Shimin* (cat. no. 64) makes a thought-provoking contrast with the anonymous *Portrait of Shen Zhou at Age Eighty* (cat. no. 58).

The new urban patronage becomes even more manifest in the handscroll *Prosperous Suzhou* (cat. no. 76), a painting of incredible detail, possibly indebted to the splendid handscrolls which the versatile Wang Hui had directed in his later years at the Manchu Qing court to illustrate the southern tours of the Kangxi emperor (r. 1662–1722),[5] while in the final century of the Qing dynasty another development takes hold, as painters migrated from the countryside to the newly prosperous city of Shanghai, where painters such as Ren Yi (1840–95) (cat. no. 79) would come into contact with Western art and customs.

Thus, in this necessarily brief overview of the history of Chinese painting, we see how the tradition was constantly renewed and transformed both by its own practitioners and by the cultural milieux and political events in which they found themselves, including ever more direct contacts with examples of European pictorial art, especially in the form of prints and engravings.

1 Little 2000, p. 182
2 Munakata 1974, p. 11
3 Whitfield 1969, p. 191
4 Cahill 1982, pp. 176–9
5 Hearn 2009



cat. no. 65 (detail)

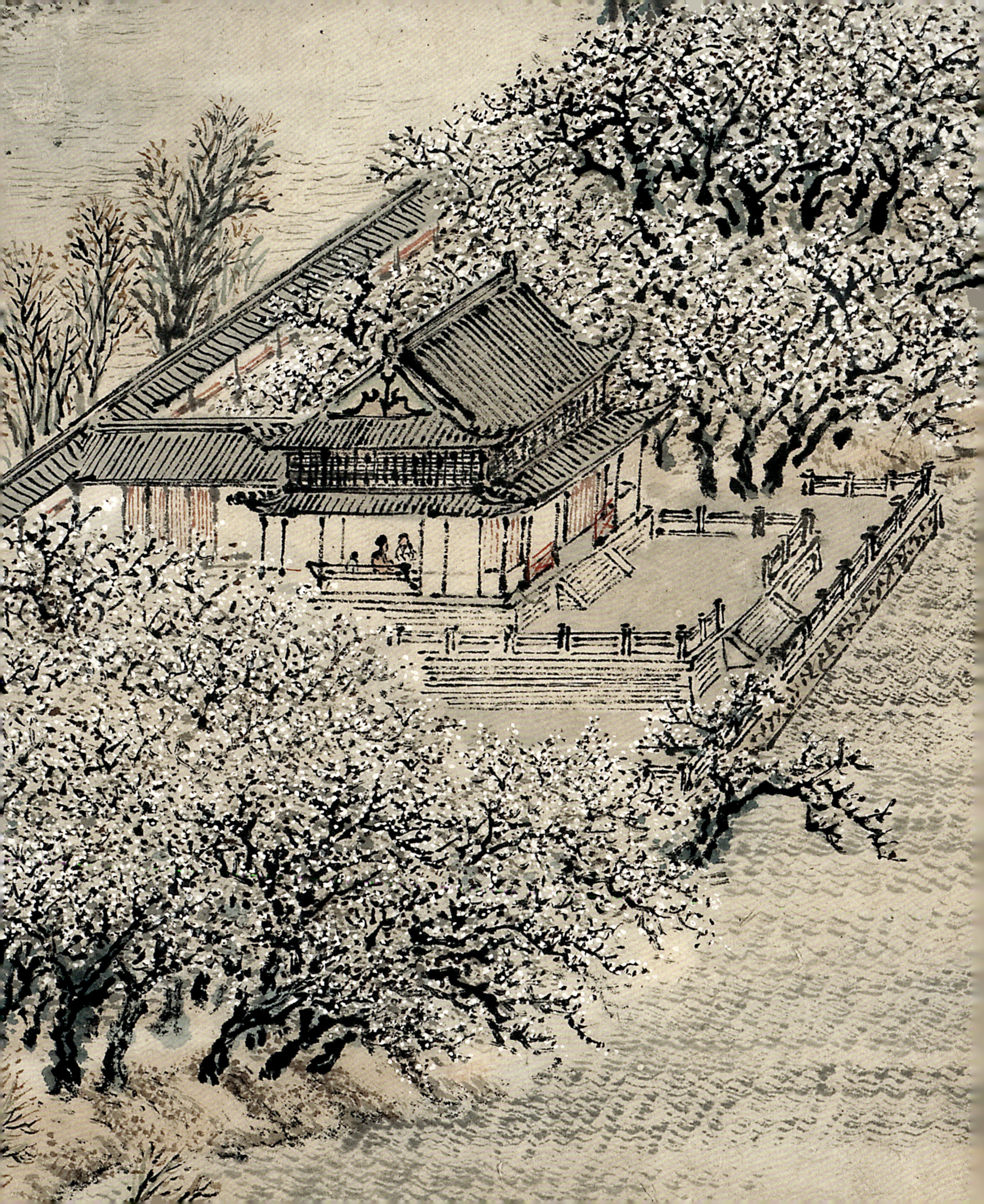

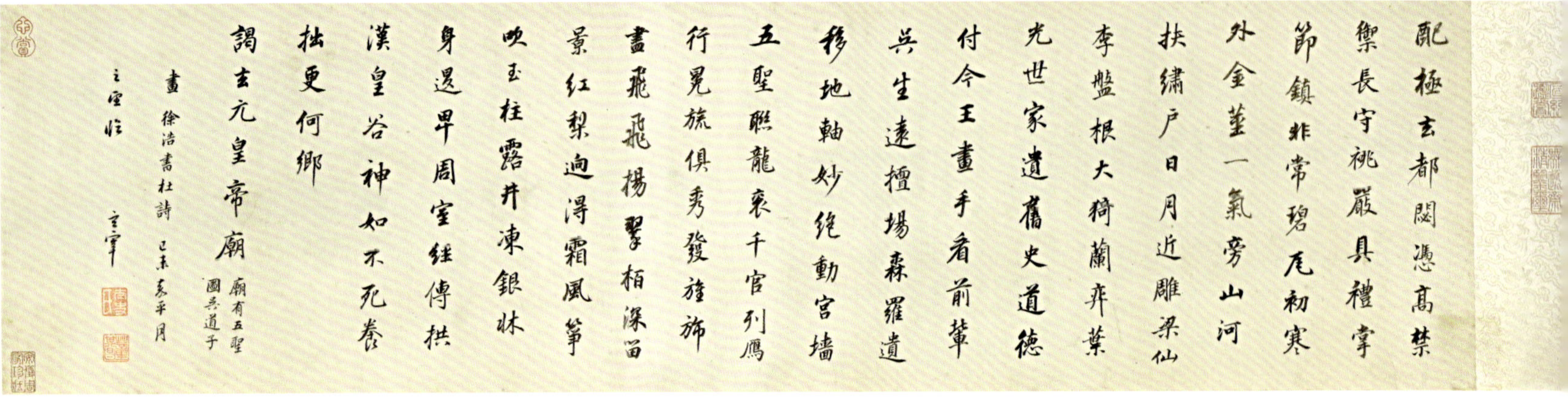

## 63

DONG QICHANG (1555–1636)

### Twin Marvels of Calligraphy and Painting

明 董其昌 書畫合璧 卷

1617 (painting) and 1619 (calligraphy), handscroll, ink on paper, 29.3 × 340.8 cm
Liaoning Provincial Museum (ZONG 4840 SHU 142)

REFERENCE LITERATURE

Dong (1630) 1968; Bush 1971; *Complete Collection* 1988, vol. 3, pp. 441–2; Ren 1988; Hinton 1990; Cahill in Kansas City and Seattle 1992; Liu Fiedler in Kansas City and Seattle 1992; Fong in Kansas City and Seattle 1992; He in Taipei 1992a, p. 89; Hironobu in Kansas City and Seattle 1992; Kansas City and Seattle 1992; Barnhart 1997–8; Dong (mid-17th century) 1999; Chen 2005; Macau 2005; Yang 2005; Chen 2007; Qi 2007

Dong Qichang was born into a modest family in Huating, near Shanghai. After receiving the *jinshi* degree in the civil service examination in 1589, he entered the Hanlin Academy, and later became an imperial tutor (1594) and a minister. The foremost painter, calligrapher and critic of the late Ming period (1368–1644), Dong's theory of the Southern and Northern schools of painting was predominant in the study of Chinese art throughout late imperial China. His high-level government career enabled him to access collections, and his friendship with contemporary eminent collectors also furthered his accomplishment in connoisseurship. Dong's keen interest in collecting ancient paintings is key to understanding his artistic development, stylistic transformations, sources of learning and achievements.[1] This scroll is an example of his realization of *jidacheng*, the 'great synthesis' in painting and calligraphy.

As indicated in the artist's own inscription, the painting in the first half of the scroll was inspired by Dong Yuan's (act. 930s–60s) and Mi Fu's (1051–1107) treatment of the misty landscape of the Xiao and Xiang Rivers in Hunan Province. Dong Qichang owned Dong Yuan's *Xiao and Xiang Rivers* (The Palace Museum, Beijing), Mi Fu's *White Clouds at the Xiao and Xiang Rivers* (now lost) and his son Mi Youren's (1074–1151/1086–1165) *Spectacular Views of the Xiao and Xiang Rivers* (c.1137; The Palace Museum, Beijing),[2] and took these scrolls with him when he paid a second visit to the rivers in 1605. For Dong Qichang, travelling and accessing ancient masterpieces were equally important in enriching one's art. His view was that while the painter who models himself after ancient masters is already among the great, in order to go a step further, one must learn from nature.[3]

Perhaps produced during his journey to Jingkou (now Zhenjiang), Jingxi (now Yixing), Mount Tianping and Lake Tai in Jiangsu Province, this painting shows an affinity with the gentle, damp landscapes of the south.[4] It is evident that Dong had acquired a thorough understanding of the work of Dong Yuan, whose style is closely reflected in this painting, as in the long, dry hemp-fibre brushstrokes that describe the texture of the slopes of the riverbanks. Dong Qichang also borrowed Mi Fu's and Mi Youren's (cat. no. 18) wet ink washes and dots to enhance the depth of the distant mountains and hills, holding the brush sideways on the paper. The contrast between the ink and empty space is striking and purposeful.

Dong's semi-regular script was considered the finest of his day. His brushwork in the second half of the scroll is poised and straightforward, with each stroke exuberant and firm, creating a rhythmic flow between the lines. This piece of writing is a freehand copy of Xu Hao's (703–82) transcription of the poet Du Fu's (712–70) 28-line regulated verse, each line containing five characters. Since Dong collected Xu's calligraphy, he made copies of this piece many times. By repeatedly studying the works of various old masters, Dong captured the spirit of the ancients, and went on to produce powerful work of his own.

This scroll, then, consists of the landscape painting, dated 1617, and the piece of calligraphy, inscribed in 1619. Curiously, the misty landscape does not correspond with the calligraphy of Du Fu's poem, and it is clear that the two works were created individually. The scroll was formerly in the collection of An Qi (1683–1742), and soon after his death, was acquired by the Qianlong emperor (r. 1736–96), who inscribed a poem on it in 1747. As there are no other collectors' seals or colophons prior to An Qi's time, one may conclude that these two pieces by Dong Qichang of similar size and period were for some reason mounted together in a handscroll by An Qi, although they are not thematically related. CY

1 Cahill in Kansas City and Seattle 1992, p. 55
2 Wang (1643) 1994, p. 1023
3 Dong (late 17th century) 1962, p. 27
4 Kansas City and Seattle 1992, p. 510

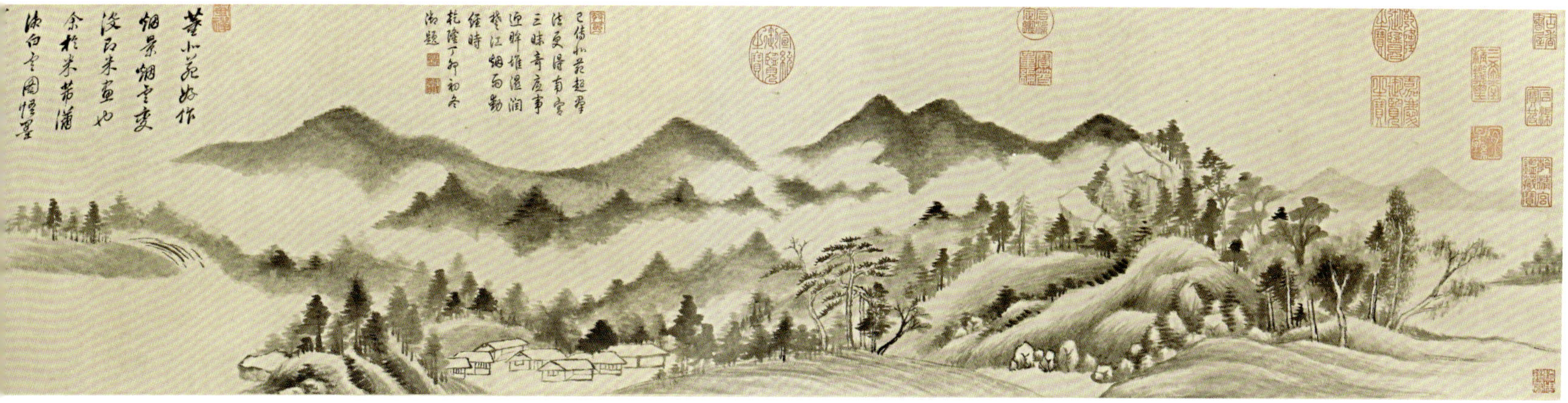

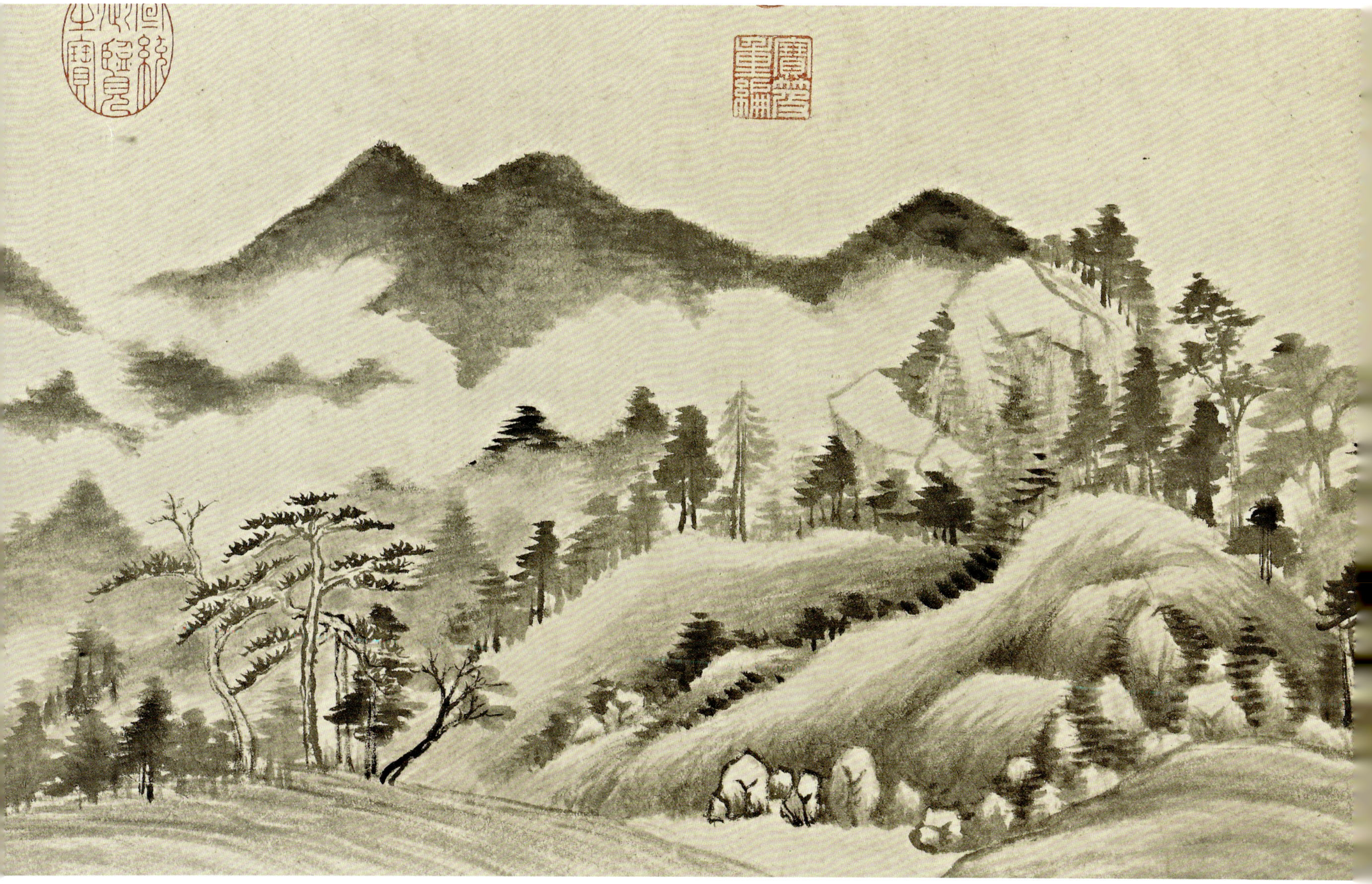

64

ZENG JING (1564–1647)

## Portrait of Wang Shimin (1592–1680)

明 曾鯨 王時敏小像 軸

1616, hanging scroll, ink and colour on silk,
64 × 42.7 cm
Tianjin Museum (65.5.3741)

REFERENCE LITERATURE

Zhou 1981; Cahill 1982a and 1982b; New York 1987; Rogers and Lee 1988; Edwards 1989; Vinograd 1992a; Li and Watt 1993; Liang 1993; Kyoto 1993; Cahill 1994; Kondō 2000 and 2002; Ge 2003; Wang (1916) 2009; Zhang (1739) 2011; Bush and Shih 1985

Wang Shimin (1592–1680) was born into one of the most eminent families in Taicang, Jiangsu Province. Raised by his grandfather, Wang was bought up in a literary environment, and from 1605, was tutored by Dong Qichang (1555–1636), who brought paintings for the boy to study and revealed to him the world of art. Dong also bequeathed his collection to the Wang family when he encountered financial hardship in the late 1610s. He passed his taste in paintings on to Wang Shimin, who himself became a painter, collector and connoisseur.

In 1614, without an examination, Wang Shimin was appointed to the Seal Office through hereditary privilege, in acknowledgement of his grandfather's virtue. The following year, he was called home at the death of his wife: all of their three sons also died, in infancy. This portrait made in 1616 by Zeng Jing was painted during his period of mourning, and depicts a young man with a thoughtful expression wearing a beige-and-white robe and black hat. The sitter's facial features have been carefully rendered in ink, showing Zeng Jing's emphasis on the use of ink rather than a layered colour wash. The painter first outlined his subject and then applied light shading and pale brown to heighten the contrast between light and dark, especially on the eyelids and the skin between the eyes and nose. However, the line under the lip appears quite unnatural, as if added without attention to verisimilitude. The sitter's face is turned very slightly to the right so that the left ear is visible, a deliberately asymmetrical pose that imbues the painting with a sense of motion and makes the sitter appear alert. Although depicted facing front, Wang is not actually looking at the viewer: rather, his expressionless, pensive face gives him an air of wistful contemplation.

Seated cross-legged on a round prayer mat of woven cattail rushes, Wang holds a fly-whisk in his right hand and makes a mudra-like gesture with the left. The delicate hands and polished fingernails indicate his refined background. The outline of the body is merely suggested, being almost entirely covered by a voluminous robe depicted with smooth, elongated, ample and uniform lines. The restrained brushwork reveals the sensitivity, sophistication and orderly nature of the sitter. The combination of the more realistic representation of the face and the invisible body indicated by a limited number of calligraphic lines was fostered principally under the influence of the literati aesthetic, motivated primarily by a wish to portray the sitter's spirit, and to a much lesser extent by an interest in realistic representation. Although the portrait is somewhat true to life in that it captures the lonely sitter's melancholy at a difficult time, the image essentially reveals a level of ideology grounded in the literati tradition. This opposition between lifelikeness and spiritual animation persisted in Chinese portraiture until modern times.[1]

Zeng Jing was one of most prolific and influential portrait painters of late imperial China. Based on traditional portraiture, in later years he placed greater emphasis on a sharp contrast between light and dark in the facial features and added more shading, as seen in *Portrait of Gu Mengyou* (1642; Nanjing Museum). To what extent this reflects Western influence through the activities of Jesuits in China remains debatable. There are more than 20 extant informal portraits made by Zeng Jing of his literati contemporaries, which offer an account of the life, thinking and social network of scholars in the seventeenth century. The portraits of Buddhist monks by Zeng and his student Zhang Qi (act. 1630–53) also made a significant impact on the portraits of the Obaku (Ch. Huangbo) sect of Zen Buddhism in seventeenth-century Japan.[2] CY

1 Gu Kaizhi (c.344–c.406) has long been celebrated as one of the great figure painters known for his insight into character and for his excellence in depicting particular physical details of his sitter. Gu's portrait formula is to emphasize the importance and value of conveying personality and spirit, rather than mere appearance. In the Song dynasty (960–1279), the literati critic Su Shi (1037–1101) wrote: 'If anyone discusses painting in terms of formal likeness, his understanding is close to that of a child' (Bush and Shih [1985] 2012, pp. 224–5). It shows Su's disparagement of representational painting and stiffly formal portraiture, and stresses the value he placed on facial characteristics to convey mental states. Later Chinese painting theory, that of the literati in particular, perpetuated this depreciation of formal portraiture, and consequently excluded portraits from the category of fine art.

2 Zhang Qi (act. 1630–53) painted *Portrait of Feiyin Tongrong* in 1642. This painting was later brought to Japan, and is now in the collection of Manpuku-ji in Kyoto. See Kondō 2000.

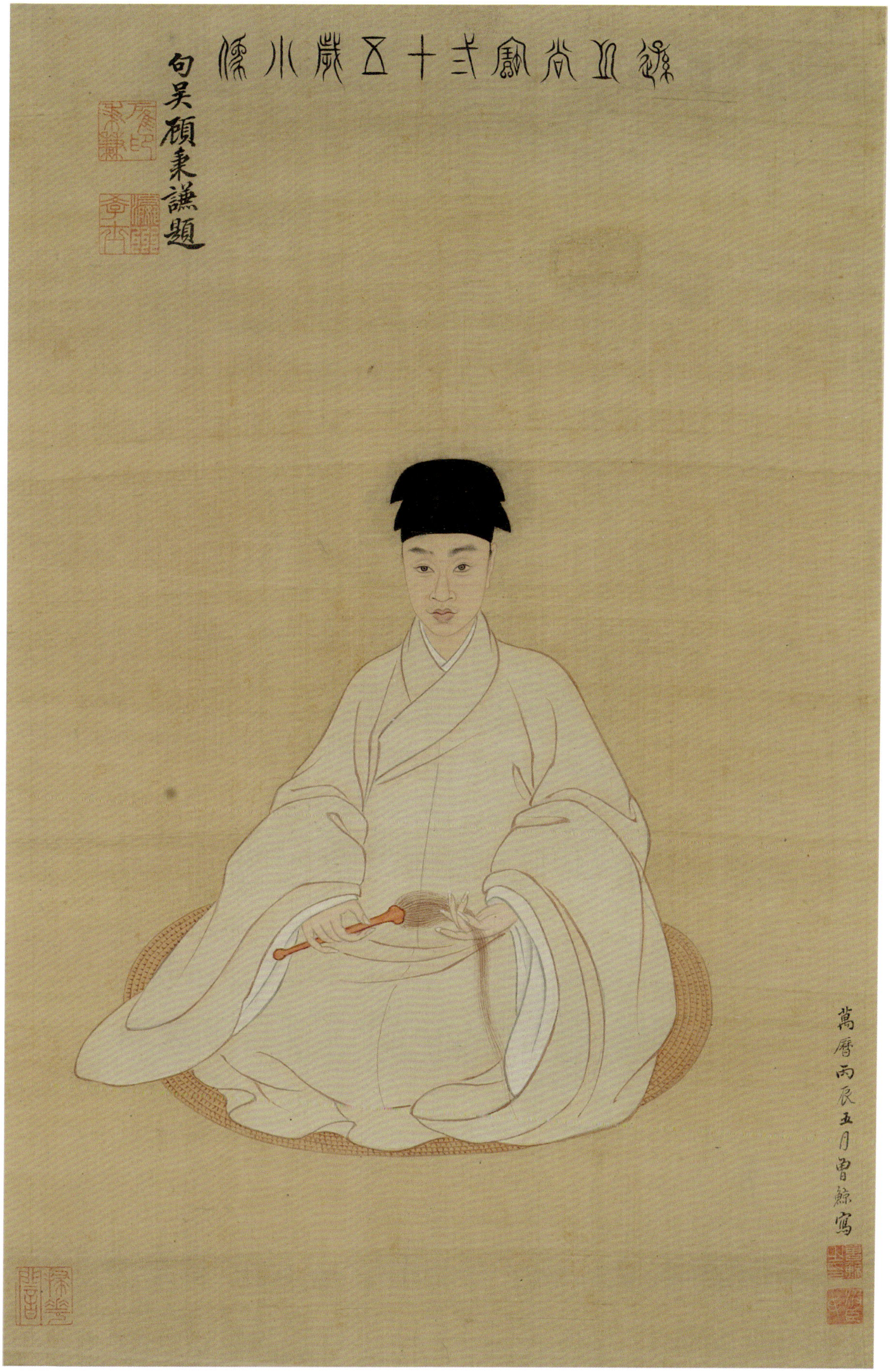
句吳顧秉謙題
萬曆丙辰五月曾鯨寫

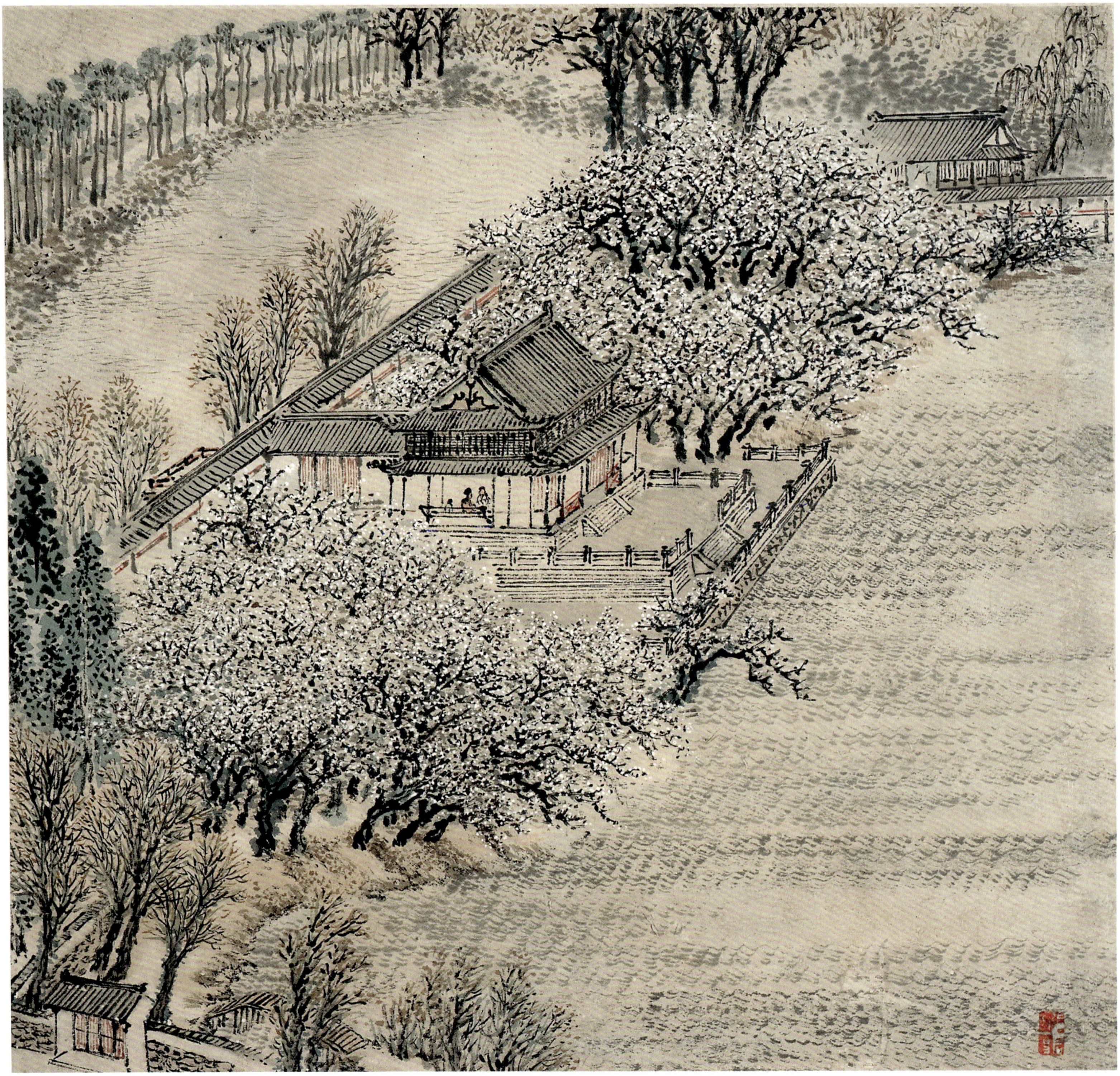

65

ZHANG HONG (1577–after 1652)

## The Zhi Garden

明 張宏 止園圖 冊

1627, two from an album of eight (originally 20) leaves, ink and colour on paper, 32.4 × 34.4 cm
Museum of Asian Art, Berlin (NR 1988–463 a, g)

PROVENANCE
Mochan shanzhuan Collection, purchase 1988

REFERENCE LITERATURE
Cahill 1982a and 1982b, pp. 39–59; *Collection of Ancient Chinese Woodblock Books, Part II* 1994, vol. 8; Gao, Huang and Liu 2012, pp. 15–57

Zhang Hong was born in the town of Hengxi, near Suzhou, in 1577. Very little is known about his life. He initially attempted a scholarly career, but soon switched to painting. He never moved far from Suzhou, where, apart from becoming a well-known painter, he loyally supported his poorer family members with his earnings. His extant works, which are dated between 1613 and 1652, are rooted in the tradition of the great Suzhou painters of the fifteenth and sixteenth centuries, and he is especially known for his monumental landscapes and topographical paintings.[1]

These two leaves from his famous album *The Zhi Garden* (Garden for Resting the Feet) belong to the latter category. The albumn's 20 leaves were split up in the 1950s, and are now held in the Museum of Asian Art, Berlin (eight leaves), and the Los Angeles County Museum of Art (twelve leaves). An inscription on the last leaf, dedicated to a man called 'Master Poet Huishan' (Huishan cizong), dates the album to 1627. Around 1600 – the golden age of the classical Chinese garden – several gardens named 'Zhi Garden' existed in China, and the true identity of the garden painted by Zhang Hong was determined only very recently.[2] This was possible thanks to the discovery of a very rare book published in 1621, the *Zhi Garden Collection*. Compiled by the owner of the garden, the well-known scholar and official Wu Liang (1562–1624), it states that he had the garden made in 1610 just north of the walls of Wujin, a city about halfway between Suzhou and Nanjing, employing the services of the garden architect and painter Zhou Tingce. The book contains poems celebrating the garden's beauty, and names all the buildings within it. Originally written as a record and guide for the owner of and visitors to the real garden, it is now the perfect companion to Zhang Hong's painted record, which, unlike the garden itself, has survived to the present day.

Zhang Hong painted his album three years after the death of its original owner, possibly at the request of a son who had inherited it. The first leaf gives a bird's eye view of the entire garden, and also shows the northern wall and gate of Wujin, as well as a canal with a fortress and bridges. The canal is the Grand Canal, which extends all the way to today's Beijing in the north and Hangzhou in the south. Visitors to the garden would normally have gone there by boat, and indeed, a large pleasure boat is moored at the entrance gate. One may observe that the garden is divided into two parts, separated by a watercourse: the eastern part is dominated by a hexagonal pagoda-shaped structure at the rear, and the western part by a two-storey structure built on a double terrace in a large pond. As in any classical Chinese garden, ponds and watercourses, vegetation, rocks and architecture are ingeniously combined to produce a maximum number of pleasing, usually self-contained views. According to Wu Liang, his garden measured 50 *mu* (about seven acres, or 2.8 hectares) and was thus quite large, with 40 per cent water, 30 per cent earth and rocks, 20 per cent architecture and 10 per cent bamboo and trees.

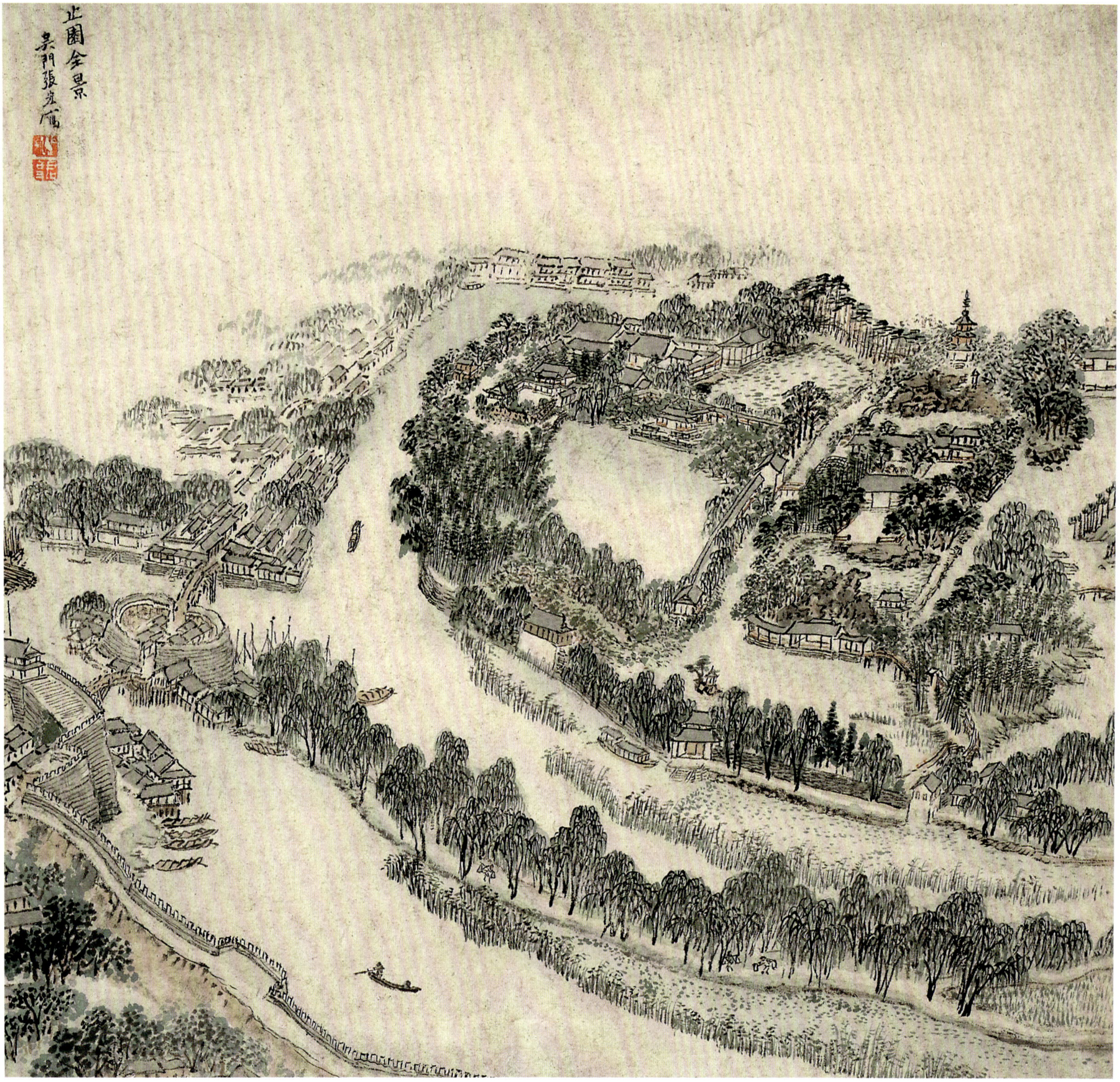

止園全景
吳門張宏寫

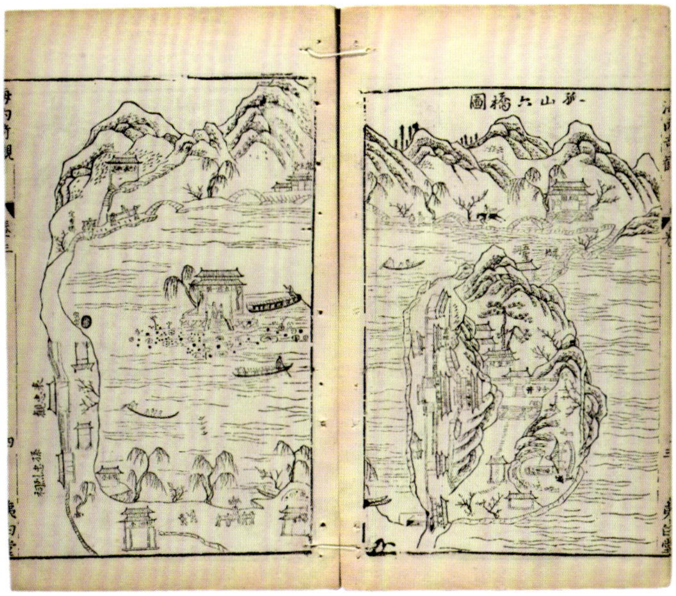

FIG. 63
Yang Erzeng (act. 17th century). *Gushan and the Six Bridges [of West Lake]* from *Amazing Views of the World* (new edition, 1609). Harvard-Yenching Library, Harvard University

The 19 remaining leaves of the album each depict a view in the garden. Leaf 14, exhibited here, shows the Liyun lou (Pear cloud building), the central structure of the western part of the garden. In spite of the building's name, Wu Liang writes clearly that he had planted 700 plum trees here, which we see in full bloom. The large pavilion with its elegant hip-and-gable roof with double eaves, and moon-viewing terrace extending into the pond, has been rendered with great care. Like the overview of the entire garden, this is again a bird's eye view, but seen from the east. This spot, writes Wu Liang, is perfect for viewing plum blossoms and the moon mirrored in the water. It is beautiful always, whether it snows, rains or storms.

Zhang Hong's album, especially the view of the entire garden, has quite a realistic feeling, and the question has been asked whether he was influenced by engravings imported from the West.[3] It is of course entirely possible that both Zhang Hong and Wu Liang had seen Western topographical prints, and Zhang was faced with the challenge of painting a recognizable view of the garden and its situation with respect to the city of Wujin – namely in a flat landscape, which was usually avoided by Chinese painters in favour of mountains, usually imagined or at least embellished. If they did depict flatland, it was typically in commissioned garden paintings. Does the different, 'Western' feeling of Zhang Hong's complete view of the Zhi Garden result from the nature of his commission? It is true that Zhang Hong could have followed older conventions for rendering a park-like landscape with water, buildings and, in this case, hills, like the woodcut of part of the famous West Lake in Hangzhou contained in the work *Amazing Views of the World*, published in Hangzhou in 1609 by Yang Erzeng with illustrations based on paintings by a Chen Yiguan (fig. 63).[4] There, the viewer has to take diametrically different viewpoints within one small landscape print. Although Zhang Hong's painting is very different, it does not in fact use true perspective. The horizon is hidden in haze, as is typical in Chinese painting, while in the Western bird's eye prints that show some similarity with Zhang's leaf, the horizon is clearly demarcated. On the one hand, it seems not impossible that Zhang Hong could have arrived at his bird's eye view on his own, while struggling to find a solution for the problem he faced. On the other hand, he might have remembered the prints recently imported from faraway countries when he was pondering a solution. In either case, the result of his effort was a masterly painting in a novel style. KR

1 Gao, Huang and Liu 2012, p. 19, n. 4; Cahill 1982b, p. 39
2 Gao, Huang and Liu, 2012
3 Cahill 1982a, pp. 17–26
4 *Collection of Ancient Chinese Woodblock Books, Part II* 1994, pp. 214–5

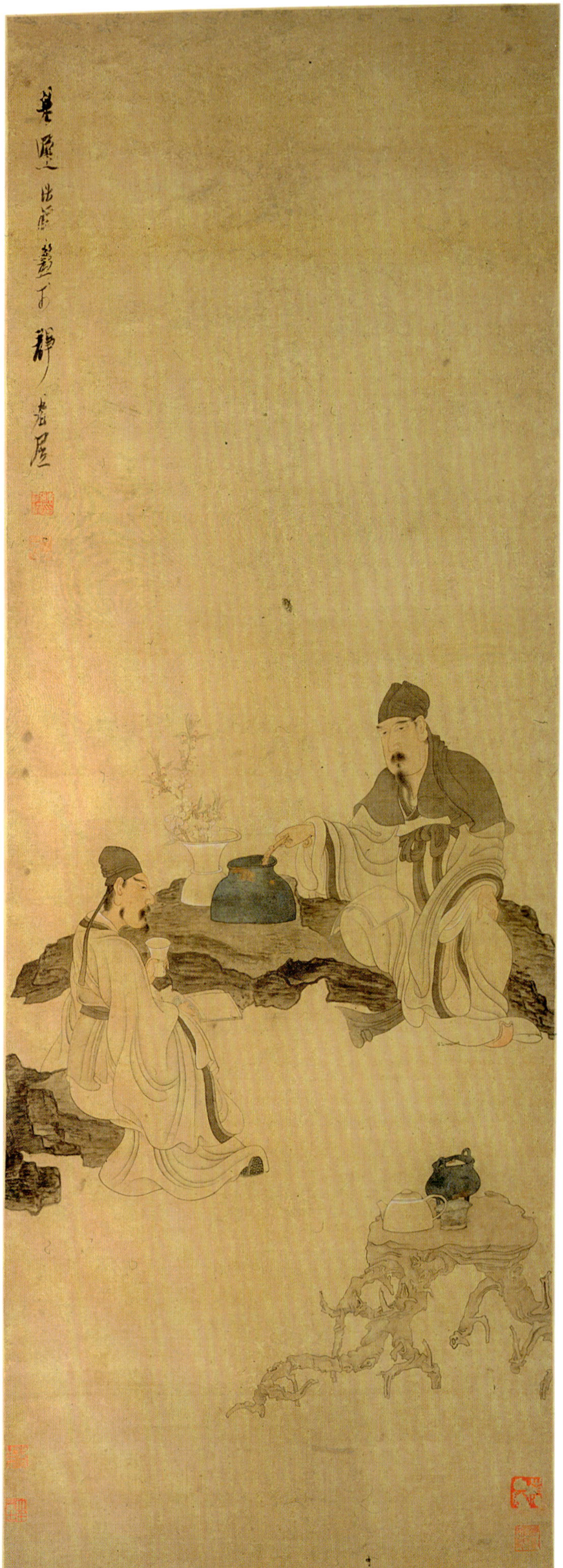

66

CHEN HONGSHOU (1598–1652)

## Versifying under the Influence of Wine

明 陳洪綬 醉吟圖 軸

after 1646, hanging scroll,
ink and colour on silk, 139 × 50.5 cm
Hong Kong Museum of Art
Xubaizhai Collection, 1992 (XL 069)

PROVENANCE

Low Chuck Tiew

REFERENCE LITERATURE

*Chinese Painting and Calligraphy in the Hsü-po Studio* 1983, pl. 7; *Exquisite Gems of Art* 1986, p. 49

Chen Hongshou was a native of Zhuji (present Shaoxing), Zhejiang Province. Born into a scholar-gentry family, Chen was given an early education to prepare him for a career as an official. Exceptionally talented, Chen began to paint at the age of four, copying Li Gonglin's (*c*.1049–1106) works as his model of the *baimiao* ('plain outline') style. Although at 10 he received direct tutelage from the landscape and bird-and-flower master Lan Ying (1585–*c*.1664) in Hangzhou, it was the style of Xu Wei (1521–93) that Chen chose to emulate. Having twice failed the provincial examinations, he began to earn his living as a professional painter and designer for illustrations in woodblock-printed books, and by end of the 1630s, had produced several series of illustrations for the popular historical novel *Water Margin*, the poetry anthology *Nine Songs* and the dramatic work *Romance of the West Chamber*. In 1644, he witnessed the fall of the Ming dynasty (1368–1644) to the Manchus, and in June 1646, retreated briefly to a monastery near Shaoxing. After that Chen became more eccentric, and started using literary names such as 'Laochi' ('Old and Late') and 'Huichi' ('Belated Repentance') to express his remorse for the fall of the Ming and to reflect his identity as a *yimin*, a 'leftover subject' of the previous regime.

Figure painting, which was Chen Hongshou's speciality, brought him fame and status equal to his contemporary, Cui Zizhong (*c*.1595–1644), as manifested in their collective appellation 'Chen of the south and Cui of the north'. *Versifying under the Influence of Wine*, bearing the literary name 'Laochi', shows the typical style of his figure painting, characterized by exaggerated and archaistic forms. Seen in many of his works of this period, wine-drinking is one of the themes Chen fondly used to express his ideal of life in retirement and seclusion. The two scholars here are meticulously defined in brushstrokes resembling iron wire which, together with the smooth and rhythmic drapery folds, are reminiscent of the styles of Li Gonglin and Zhao Mengfu (cat. no. 46), although Chen developed a distinctive method of rendering the folds with subtle shades. Harmoniously integrated with the figures, the wine utensils, stone benches and small table made of eroded root wood are also modelled in minute detail, demonstrating Chen's versatility and competence in painting objects. The linear quality and strong graphic sense in this work are closely related to his woodblock illustrations, at which Chen was also an adept. The archaistic and decorative flavour in his figure painting appealed to popular taste, and demand was such that he produced multiple copies of some of his works with the participation of his studio assistants.

The unusual and decorative characteristics of Chen's paintings profoundly influenced the Eight Eccentrics of Yangzhou in the mid-eighteenth century. His style was imitated by the Shanghai school painters, in particular the Three Rens (Ren Xiong [1823–57], Ren Xun [1835–93] and Ren Yi [1840–95]) in the late Qing dynasty (1644–1911), and more recently even affected the 'New Literati Painting' movement in the late 1980s and early 1990s. SY

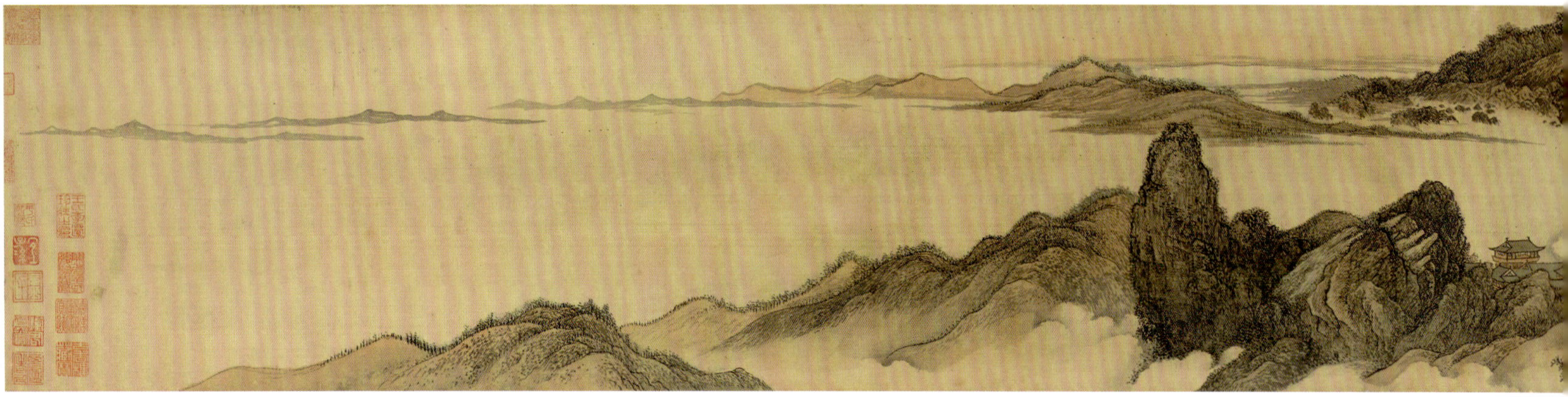

67

WANG HUI (1632–1717)

## The Colours of Mount Taihang

清 王翬 太行山色圖 卷

1669, handscroll, ink and colour on silk,
25.3 × 209.4 cm
The Metropolitan Museum of Art, New York
Gift of Douglas Dillon, 1978 (1978.423)

PROVENANCE

Mr and Mrs Earl Morse

REFERENCE LITERATURE

Zhang (1832) 1932, ch. 4, p. 18; Princeton 1969, pp. 108–13, no. 14; Fong 1970, fig. 5; Princeton 1984, p. 188, fig. 156; Zurich 1996, pp. 162, 226, no. 33; Chen (1915) 2007, pp. 467–70; Chang in New York 2008b; Hearn in New York 2008b; New York 2008b, pls 5, 39a,b

Wang Hui was a child prodigy whose artistic talents were first recognized at the age of 16 by Wang Jian (1598–1677). Later, he spent years as a guest and retainer of the pre-eminent Orthodox master Wang Shimin (1592–1680), who had been a pupil of Dong Qichang (1555–1636). By the late 1660s and early 1670s, Wang Hui had surpassed his mentors, creating extraordinary interpretations of the great masters of antiquity by transforming familiar images into surprising new visions. He summed up his approach to painting as follows: 'I must use the brush and ink of the Yuan [1271–1368] to move the peaks and valleys of the Song [960–1279], and infuse them with the breath-resonance of the Tang [618–907]. I will then have a work of the Great Synthesis.'[1]

*The Colours of Mount Taihang* epitomizes Wang Hui's ability to distil, synthesize and reinterpret his models to create dramatic works inspired by past masterpieces that are, however, distinctly his own. Wang never visited the Taihang mountains in Shanxi Province; rather, he took his inspiration from earlier masterworks, as he makes clear in his inscription: 'Once in the home of a noble family in Guangling [present Yangzhou], I saw a small scroll by Guan Tong [act. *c.*907–23]. With its cloudy peaks racing together in a luxuriant and dense air, it truly pierced my heart and dazzled my eyes. Today, though I remember only a fraction of it, I have followed its method to create this painting, *The Colours of Mount Taihang*. I hope it captures the deep and heroic atmosphere of the north country, rather than merely posturing with pretty details. Three days after the mid-autumn festival in the *jiyou* year [12 September 1669] Wang Hui of Yushan [made] and inscribed [this painting].'[2]

According to Chin-Sung Chang, the source of Wang Hui's inspiration was *Autumn Mountains at Dusk*, a painting attributed to Guan Tong that at the time was owned by Li Zongkong (1618–1701), whose 'noble family' is the one referred to in Wang's inscription.[3] Many of the motifs in *Autumn Mountains* (National Palace Museum, Taipei) reappear in Wang Hui's painting – the imposing foreground promontory looming over a river, and a stream flowing out of a mountain gorge in a series of cascades and spanned by a bridge – but Wang has masterfully rearranged and condensed the monumental hanging scroll composition, transforming it into a handscroll that possesses an entirely new sense of compositional drama. In place of the towering screen of precipitous peaks in *Autumn Mountains*, the first half of Wang's painting cuts off any view into the distance. Instead, Wang confronts the viewer with thrusting near-ground cliffs that nearly collide over the cascading stream. In the second half of the scroll, we emerge from the mountains as the Taihang range descends toward the broad flood plain of the Yellow River. The fulcrum point for this shift in perspective is a temple complex that provides the vantage point from which to view the ensuing panorama. Furthermore, while retaining some of Guan Tong's

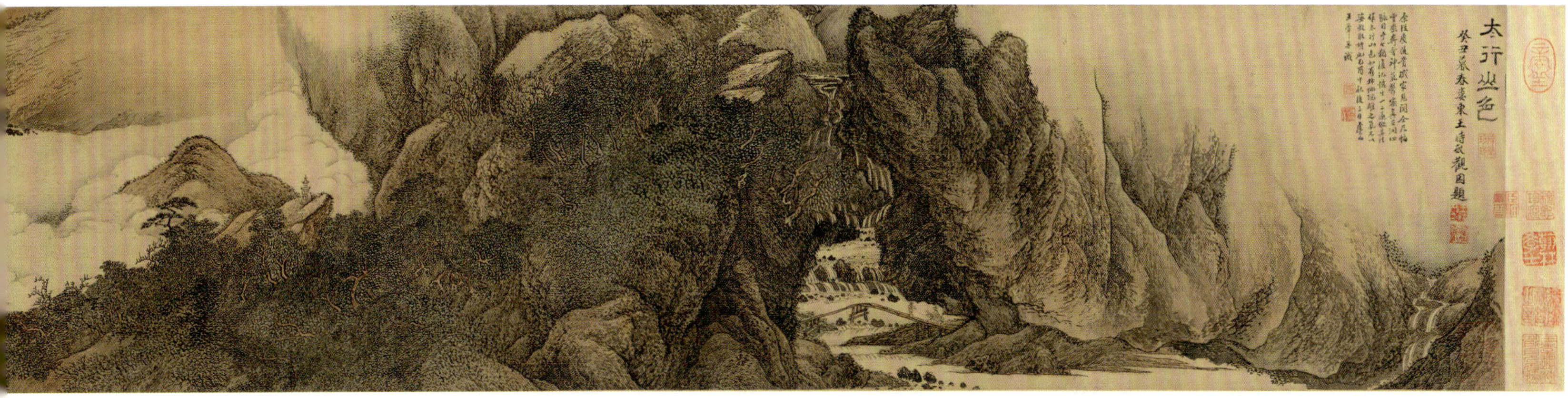

motifs and powerfully animated forms, the texturing and graphic energy of Wang's composition derive from another model, *Travellers amid Streams and Mountains* (National Palace Museum, Taipei) by Fan Kuan (act. *c.*990–1030), a painting owned by Wang Shimin and copied by Wang Hui.[4] Particularly in the opening section, the raindrop stippling of rock surfaces, the peaks topped with dense foliage and the deciduous trees with boldly outlined trunks recall stylistic features of Fan Kuan's masterpiece.

In 1673, Wang Shimin displayed his admiration for *The Colours of Mount Taihang* by inscribing a title in clerical script. Two decades later, Wang Hui's reputation as a master of large-scale compositions was uncontested, and he was selected to direct the pictorial documentation of the Kangxi emperor's (r. 1662–1722) 1689 southern inspection tour, a commission that ensured the apotheosis of the Orthodox school style as the pre-eminent model for the later landscapes of the Qing (1644–1911) academy.[5] MH

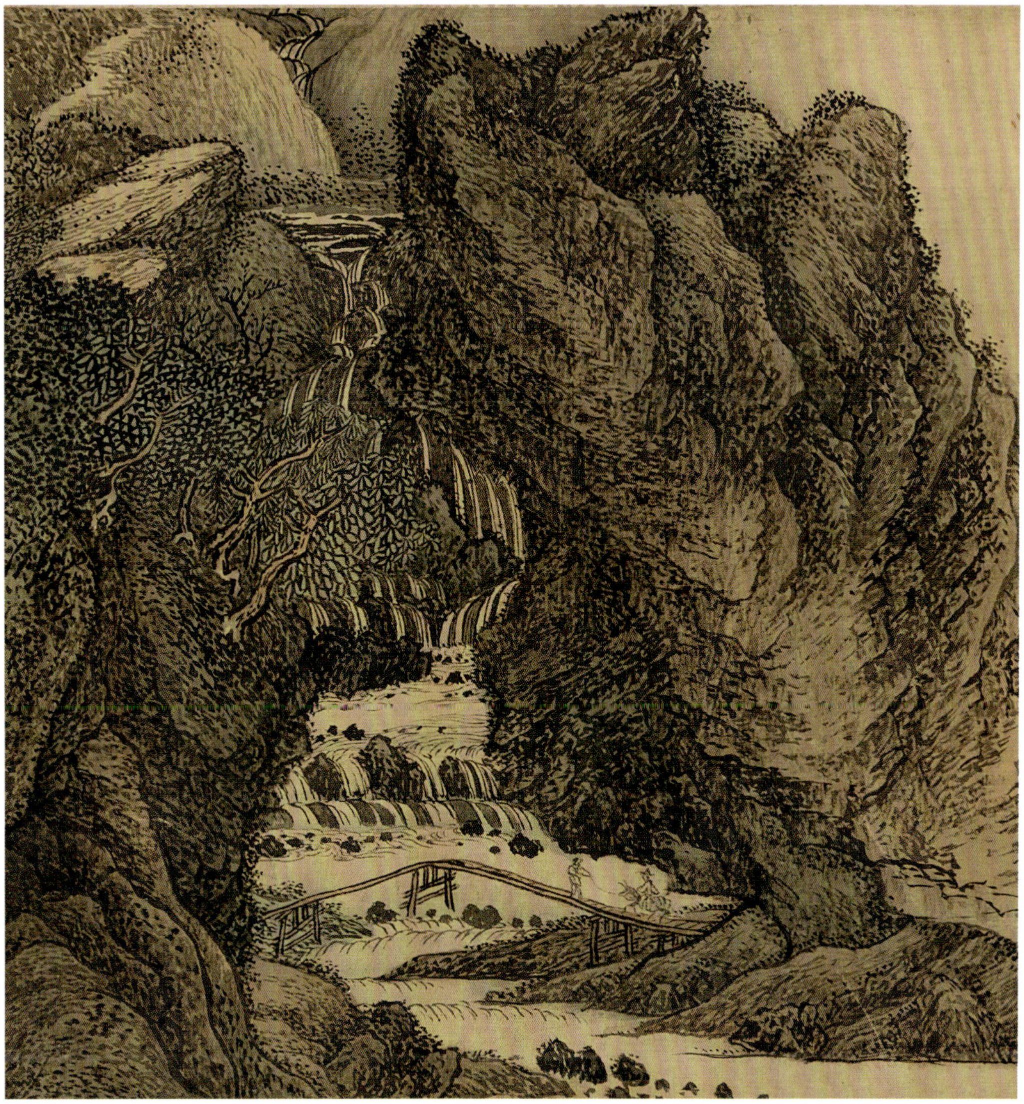

1 Wen Fong in New York 2008b, p. 23, translating a passage from Wang Hui (1632–1717), *Qinghui huaba* (1968 ed.), ch. 4, p. 100
2 Translation adapted from that of Princeton 1969, p. 108
3 For a discussion of Li Zongkong (1618–1701) and his connection to this painting see Chang in New York 2008b, pp. 87–96.
4 For a discussion of Wang Hui's copy of *Travellers amid Streams and Mountains*, see Fong in New York 2008b, pl. 7.
5 See Hearn in New York 2008b.

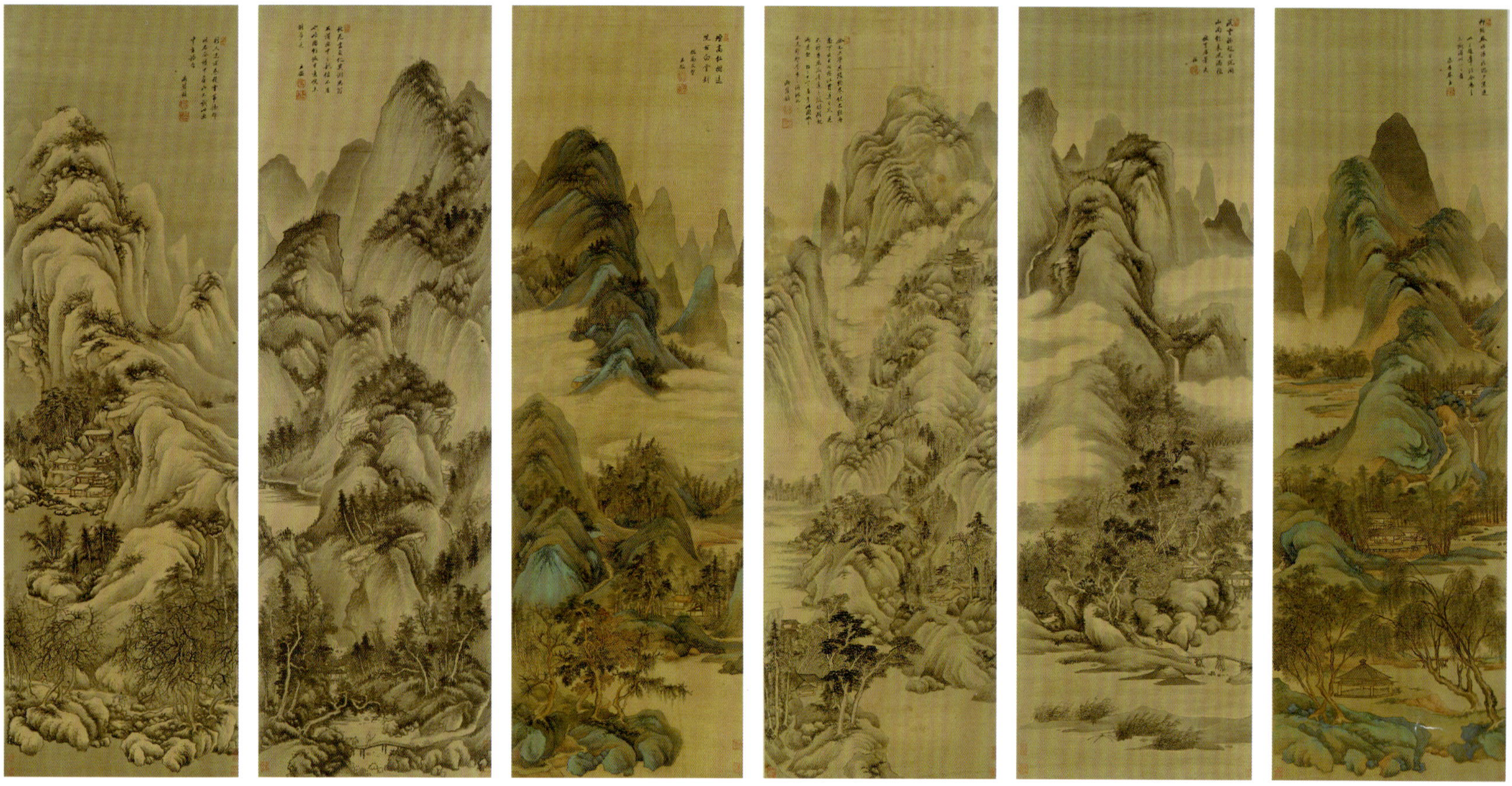

68

WANG JIAN (1598–1677)

## Landscapes in the Manner of Old Masters

清 王鑑 倣古山水圖 屏

1669–73, set of 12 hanging scrolls, ink and colour on silk, each scroll: 162.7 × 51.5 cm
Shanghai Museum (2597)

PROVENANCE

Pang Laichen (1864–1949)

REFERENCE LITERATURE

Pang 1909; Zhongguo gudai shuhua jianding zu 1986–2001, vol. 4, pp. 199–201, Hu 1–2323

The group of artists known as the Four Wangs, comprising Wang Shimin (1592–1680), Wang Jian, Wang Hui (1632–1717) and Wang Yuanqi (1642–1715), are sometimes described as representing the achievements in Chinese landscape painting during the early Qing period (1644–1911). In contrast to the individualist or eccentric tendencies of contemporaneous artists like Bada Shanren (1626–1705), Shitao (1642–1707), Kuncan (1612–after 1674) and Hongren (1610–63), who were sometimes dubbed the Four Monks, the practice of the Four Wangs came to be described as the 'Orthodox school'. These artists saw themselves as inheritors and transmitters of traditional scholar-literati painting. Their aesthetic values were orientated towards the teachings of Dong Qichang (1555–1636), who advocated for the regeneration of scholar-literati painting through the establishment of a 'true' lineage of masters beginning with Wang Wei (699–759), which he called the 'Southern school', and for the systematic study of how landscapes were constructed through old masters.[1]

Wang Jian was born into a prominent family in Taicang, Jiangsu Province. He passed the *juren* or provincial-level civil service exams during the reign of the last Ming emperor, Chongzhen (1628–44), but left service after only eight years, preferring to devote his time to literary and artistic pursuits. His great-grandfather Wang Shizhen (1526–90), a prominent writer and official, had been one of the Later Seven Masters (Houqizi) and a leading light in the *fugu* ('return to antiquity') movement. In fact, Dong Qichang's theories had taken their inspiration from Wang Shizhen. In the 1630s, Wang Jian sought Dong out as his teacher.[2]

Wang Jian was known to have excelled in landscapes, learning techniques from Song (960–1279) and Yuan (1271–1368) painting, and although his compositions were rendered with a wet brush, they still possessed clarity of form. As Wang did not consider painting something simply to be studied, he was not merely a disciple of Dong Qichang but continued to innovate within his practice, incorporating

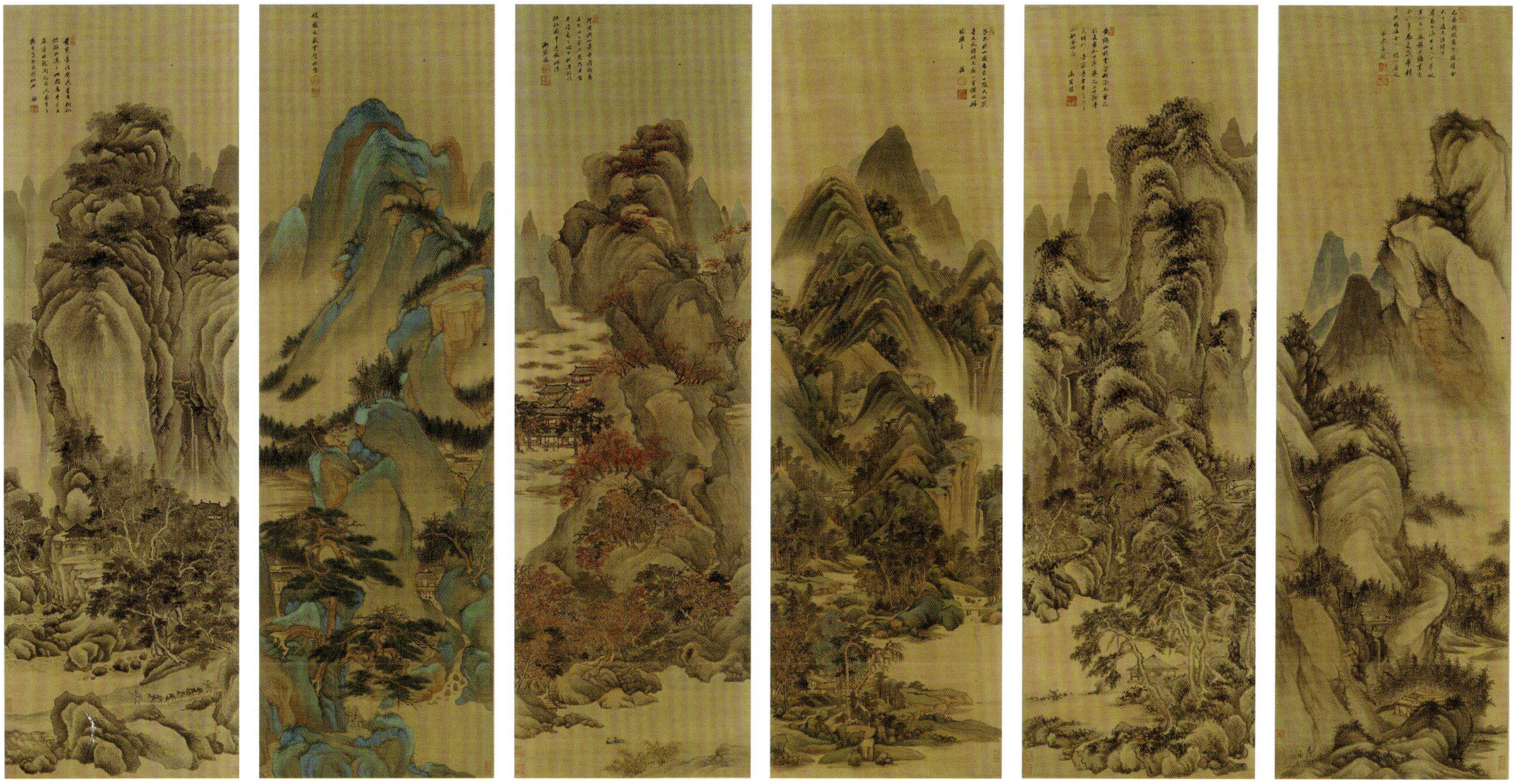

elements from both the Northern and Southern schools into his work. Thus all 12 paintings in this series are evocative of earlier works, with multiple allusions to the brushwork of those artists referenced. However, when viewed together as a set, they are clearly painted by the same hand. This can be seen in the careful layering of landscape forms, from the stones and banks to the soaring peaks near the apex in every painting: a ridge almost like the undulating backbone of a dragon runs through each work. With the exception of one scroll, all the paintings in the set have been rendered in colour, some in the blue-green medium that is an archaistic reference and others with seasonal palettes. In learning from the old masters, Wang Jian was seeking the idea (*yi*) and not the form (*xing*).

While sets of paintings on this scale by artists like Wang Jian were not common, we know from the inscription on the last scroll that this set was intended for the 60th birthday of a friend's father, and would probably have been prominently displayed during the celebrations. It is a late work, begun when the artist was aged 72. As can be read from the other inscriptions, Wang was well acquainted with many leading collectors of his day. While some of the original paintings on which this set was based remain obscure to us today, others are instantly recognizable: *Travellers amid Streams and Mountains* by Fan Kuan (act. *c*.990–1030), for example, is today in the collection of the National Palace Museum, Taipei.[3] The painting was then in the collection of Wang Shimin. Another copy of the work made by Wang Jian for another 12-painting set dated 1670 is also in the collection of the Shanghai Museum. LLZ / YH

1 Fong in New York 2008b
2 For a more detailed biography, see Ho 1992, vol. 2, p. 137. For a new theory of Wang Jian's (1598–1677) date of birth as 1609 instead of 1598, see Bai and Zhang 2009.
3 The configuration of the foreground in the second Fan Kuan (act. *c*.990–1030) copy is different, and it is rendered in a palette suggestive of autumn (see Ho 1992, vol. 1, pp. 362–3 and vol. 2, pp. 140–1; New York 2008b, p. 17, figs 22 and 23).

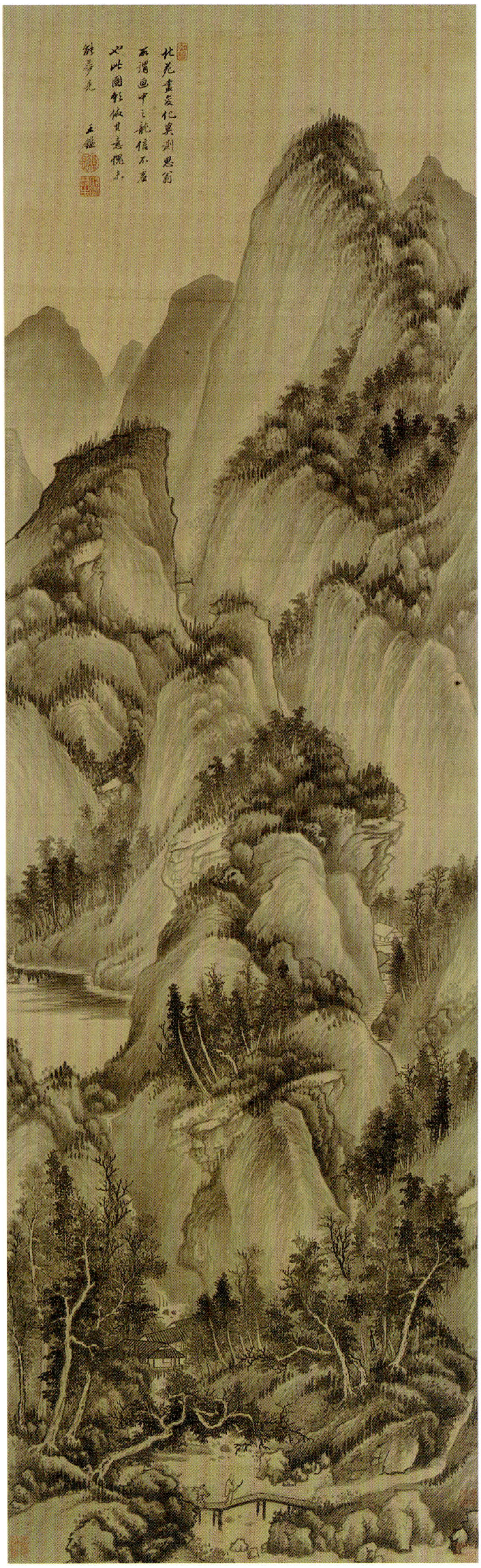

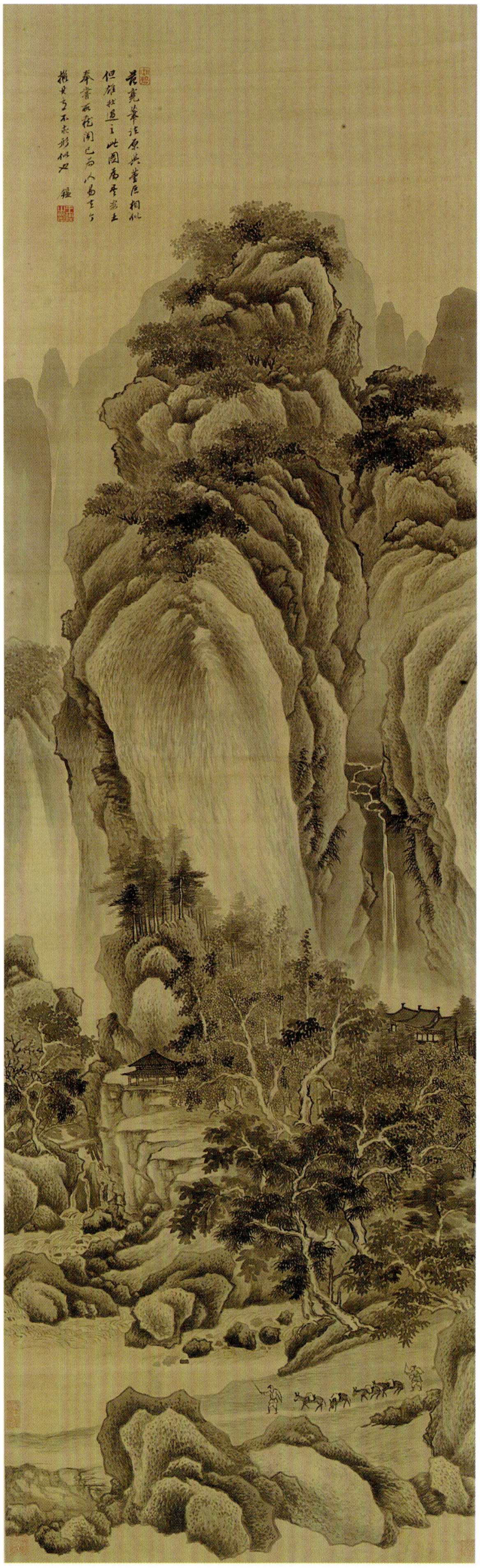

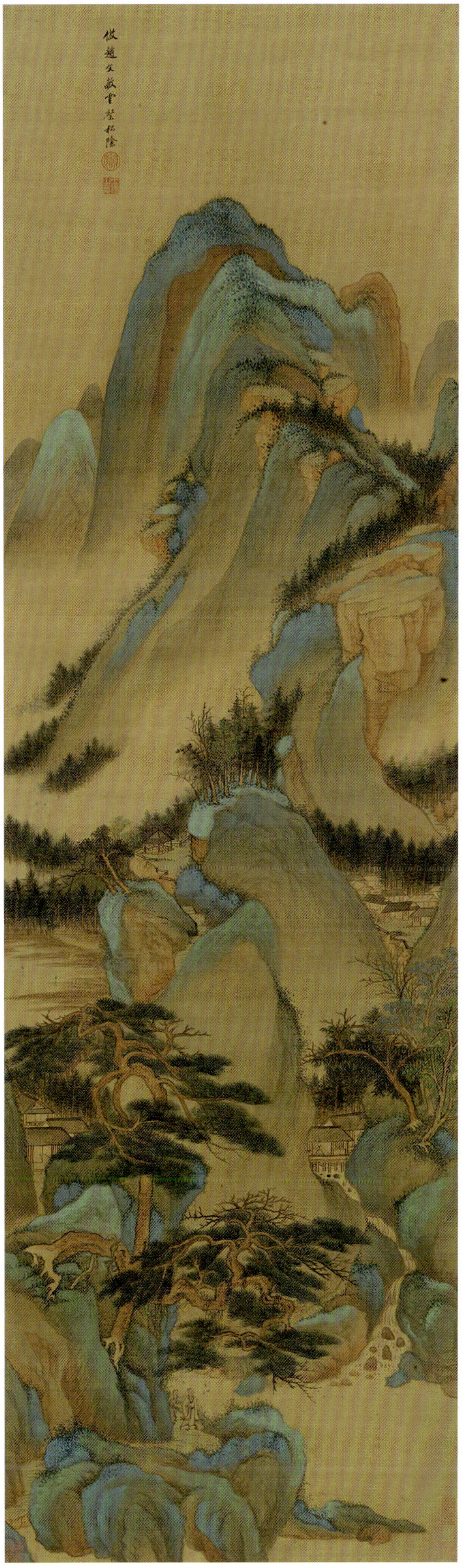
倣趙文敏雪壑松陰

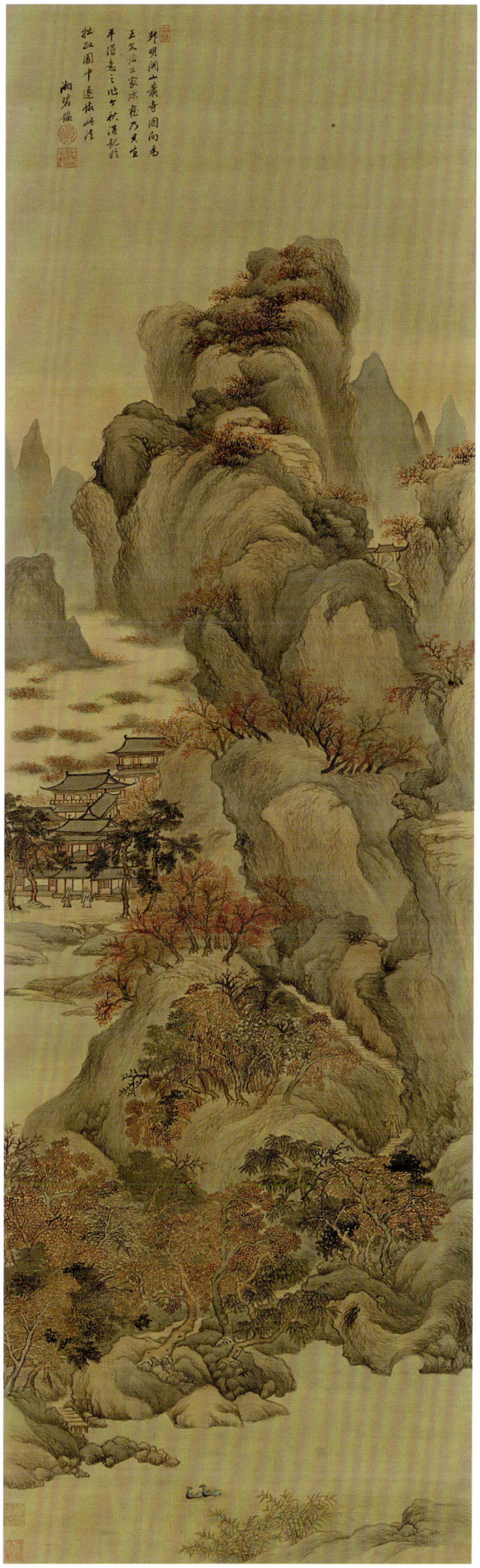

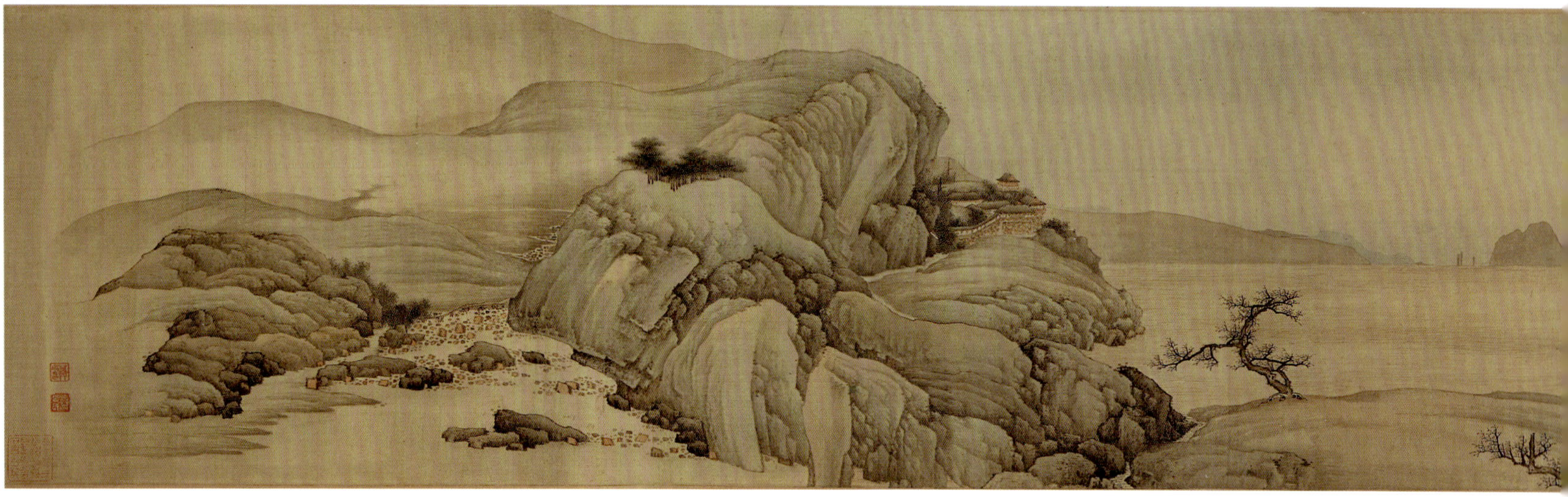

69

FAN QI (1616–after 1694)

## Yangzi Riverscape

清 樊圻 長江圖 卷

1660s, handscroll, ink and colour on silk, 31 × 207 cm
Museum of Asian Art, Berlin (NR 5008)

PROVENANCE

Purchased in 1928 in Beijing through 'General Wang' from Wu Fu

REFERENCE LITERATURE

Ledderose 1998, pp. 183–9

Fan Qi was a professional painter from Nanjing who worked in a variety of styles and covered a broad range of subject matter: flowers, figures, architecture and landscape. Very little is known about his life, but he is customarily considered one of the Eight Masters of Jinling (*Jinling bajia*), a group of painters active in Nanjing in the seventeenth century of whom the most famous was Gong Xian (*c.*1619–89). Among Fan Qi's works, a group of landscapes with a serene, translucent quality stands out, often showing distant views with landscape elements executed in pale, even washes of colour or ink, without or with only very light contour lines. The handscroll *Yangzi Riverscape* is one of the best and most characteristic examples of this group.

Looking at the wide river landscape the painting depicts, one feels immediately that this is an extraordinary work. The mountainous areas at the beginning and end are unlike other Chinese paintings of mountains, and the central part with its wide river vista differs from other panoramic river views. The painting is clearly divided into three sections.

In the opening section, from above and amid a range of tall cliffs, one sees a flat riverscape that gently recedes between low hills to vanish in the far distance. The hills have very few outlines drawn in ink, which is one unusual feature of this work. The sense of depth and distance is created without using the device of clouds and mist – another irregularity. Further, the types of brushstrokes and dots used in more conventional paintings to suggest rocky surfaces are found here only right in the foreground, where they are delicately and sparsely used. A village with finely delineated roof contours looks strangely desolate.

The middle section extends roughly from the square pavilion overlooking the central stretch of water on the right to its fortress-like counterpart dominating the water on the left. Fan Qi was one of the first artists in Chinese art history to paint a true horizon, namely a horizontal line separating heaven and earth. In earlier and most later Chinese painting, including most landscapes by Fan Qi himself, the meeting of earth or water with the sky is ambiguous and blurred by clouds and a misty vagueness. In fact, in the revolutionary horizon line here, which is about 75 centimetres long, there are only two short stretches of about 5 centimetres each where sky and water really touch: at the three boat sails, and to the right of the tip of the tallest tree. Everywhere else, shoals and cliffs in pale grey and brown washes without contour lines appear from behind the

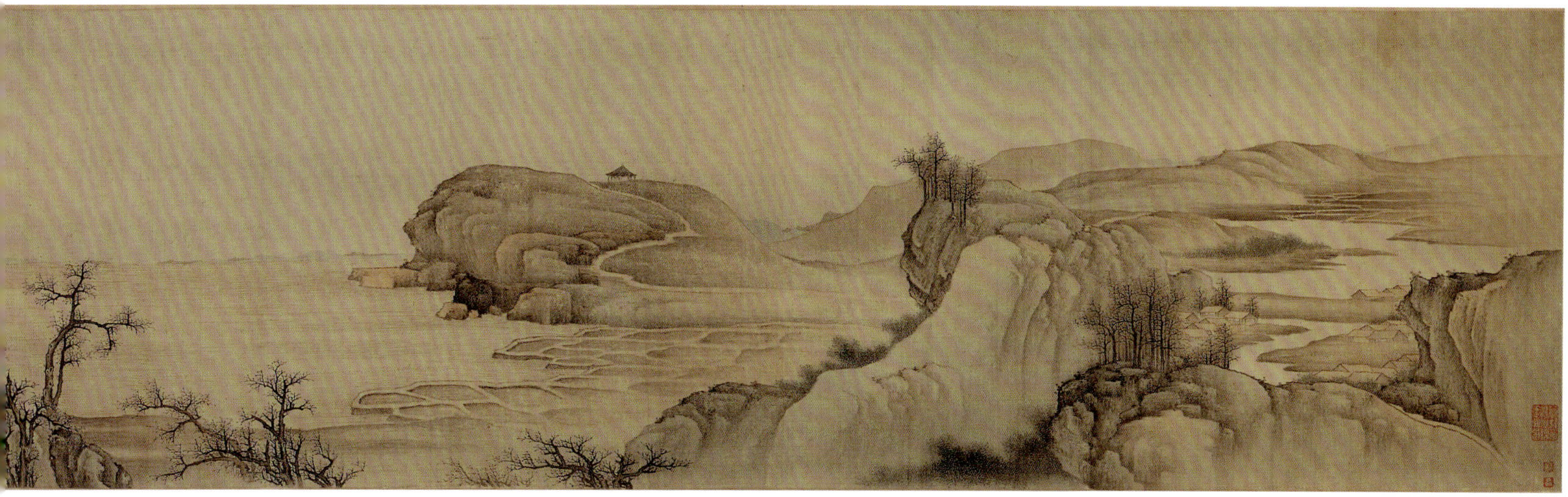

horizon, as if floating on it. It is as if Fan Qi was afraid to show directly the full implications of his line: the earth is round, and even the tallest mountain, if far enough away, sinks beneath the horizon.

The four single trees and tree groups in this section, whose angular branches seem to reach out in communication with each other, are exquisitely positioned. Their verticality contrasts with the flat grid of dammed fields extending into the water at the right.

The left and final section, with its pale mountain slope in the rear continuing beyond the painting's upper edge, seems to fit awkwardly with the horizon in the middle section – but then they were not intended to be viewed together. On its own, the deep vista of a mountain torrent mirrors the river view of the opening section, but with a more desolate, barren atmosphere. The technique of overlaying crags on top of stones set at various angles is seen in a number of Fan Qi's works created in the 1660s, and it is likely that *Yangzi Riverscape* dates from this period.

The horizon line in *Yangzi Riverscape* is a distinctly Western element, but in only a very few of Fan Qi's landscapes is it as clearly marked as it is here. Jesuit missionaries had been active in Nanjing from the end of the sixteenth century, first and foremost among them being Matteo Ricci (1552–1610), who was based in the city from 1595 to 1600. To teach and impress the educated elite, the Jesuits imported illustrated books such as *Civitates Orbis Terrarum*, the famous collection of bird's eye views of European cities published in Cologne by Braun and Hohenberg between 1572 and 1616. This and other illustrated works from Europe were accessible to a fair number of painters in seventeenth-century China, especially in Nanjing. Yet in fact they integrated these Western techniques of rendering the physical world on a flat surface into their own work only to a very limited degree and in subtle ways. Still, those artists – including Fan Qi – were forced to re-evaluate the customary Chinese ways of painting in light of such works, and this could sometimes result in the production of a masterpiece like *Yangzi Riverscape*. KR

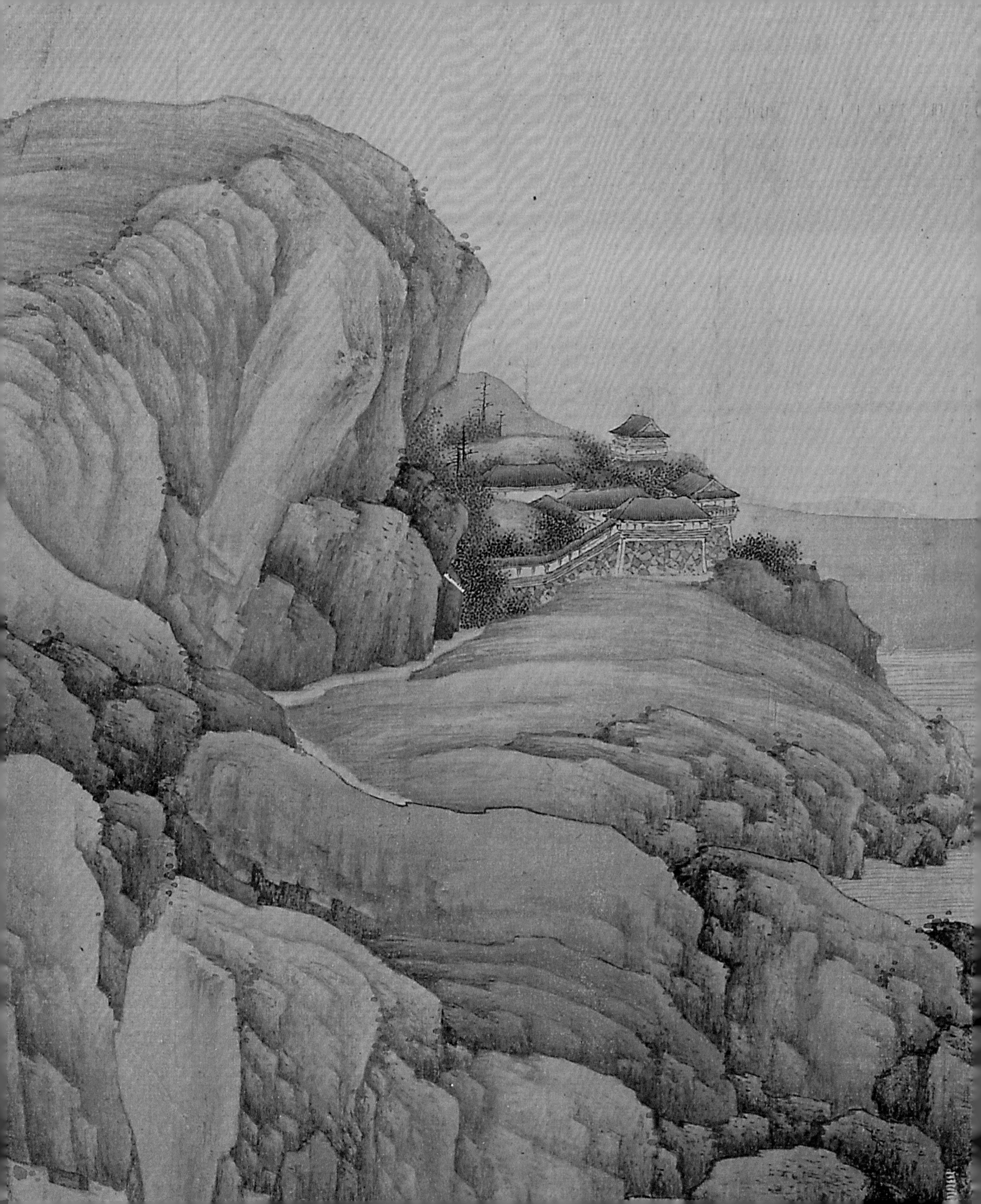

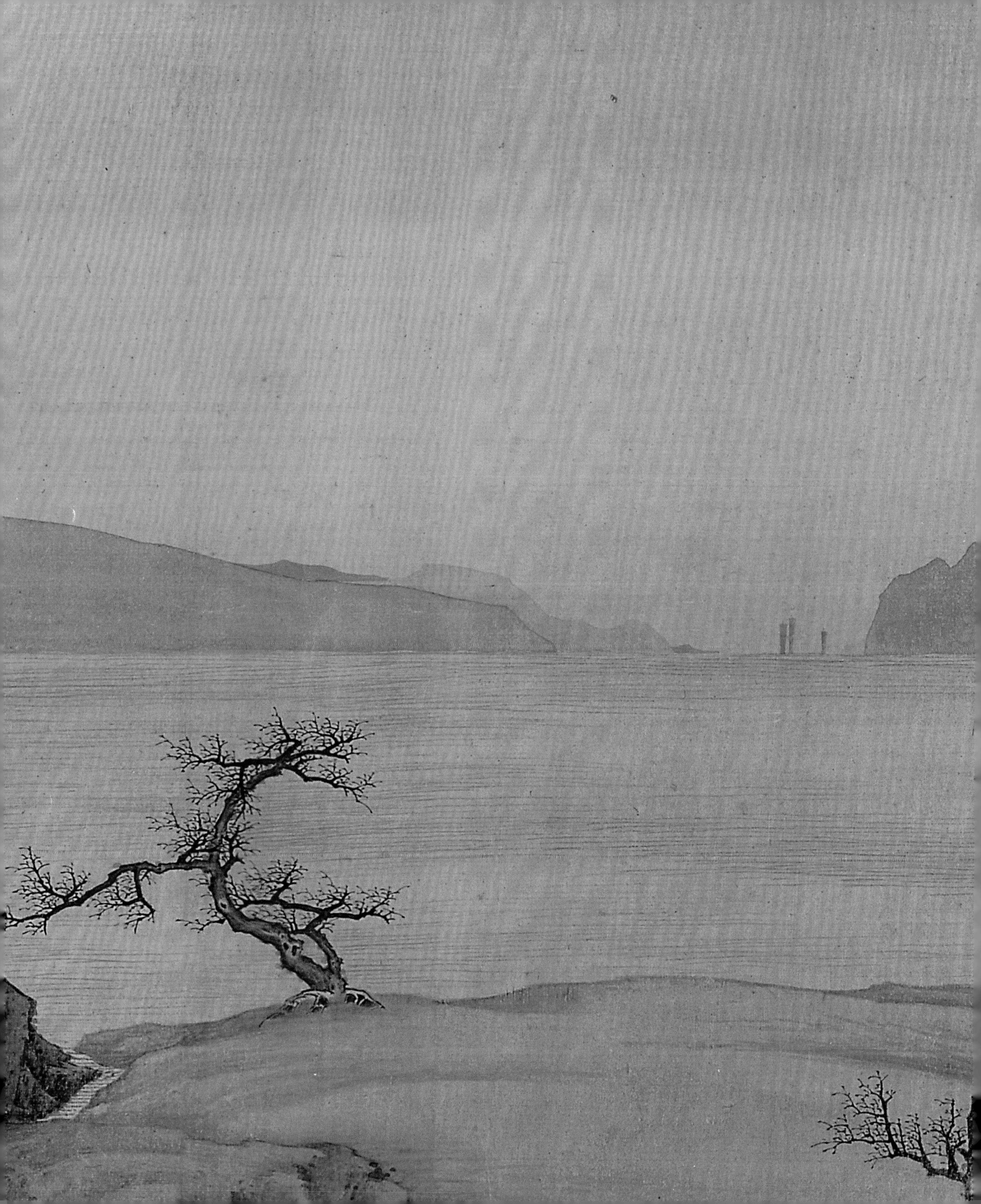

70

## GONG XIAN (c.1619–89)

## Landscape Album

清 龔賢 山水圖 冊

1671, album of 11 leaves, ink and colour on paper, each leaf 24.45 × 45.09 cm
The Nelson-Atkins Museum of Art, Kansas City (60–36/1–11)

PROVENANCE

Kōzō Harada (b.1935)

REFERENCE LITERATURE

New York, Los Angeles and San Francisco 1967; Kansas City 1969, pp. 27–30, no. 8; Wu 1970, figs 15–16; Silbergeld 1976; Kansas City and Cleveland 1980, pp. 279–81, no. 214; Cahill 1982c; Hájek 1991; Hay 1994, pp. 184, 186–7

Gong Xian is perhaps the most important painter of the Nanjing school, so named for a number of artists active in this scenic city located on the lower Yangzi River Delta. This album is one of his best works, and was created during his most productive period, when in his fifties. Gong lived through the period of upheaval that occurred with the dynastic change from the Ming (1368–1644) to the Qing (1644–1911) dynasty in the seventeenth century. Having spent several years as a wanderer due to the political chaos, he came to settle in the scenic Qingliang mountains, in the vicinity of Nanjing. On one of the foothills he built an estate called Half-an-Acre Garden, and here he cultivated a garden and his paintings. How and where he painted is written in the album's colophon (Leaf K) which he signed with his literary name, 'Resident of Half-an-Acre' ('Banmu juren').

The 10 landscape paintings in the album exhibit Gong Xian's genuine vision, demonstrated in the bold approach to composition and brushwork. On most leaves, the tilting terrain elevates the horizon beyond the painting's edge or cuts off the hilltop, creating a grand, panoramic view with a dramatic perspective. His spontaneous and effortless brushwork has crafted many variations of the landscape. Sometimes he translucently sketched, as in Leaf G, whereas at other times he built up dense textures by massing a variety of ink dots over a beige or blue ground, such as Leaf F. The two contrasting modes were termed 'pale Gong' and 'dark Gong' by traditional Chinese connoisseurs. The 'dark Gong' presents a much more dramatic vision, with powerful tonal contrasts that give the effect of light and shadow. His unconventional vision, distinct from any landscape paintings prior to his time, has led some scholars to deem his visual vocabularies greatly enriched by his study of European landscape prints.[1]

The artist's inscriptions on each leaf interestingly voice his creative process. Some tell of startling scenes from his imagination, for example, in Leaf F, where his landscape recalls a friend's longing for home. Most of the inscriptions revere the early painting masters who made up the Orthodox lineage of painting established by Gong's mentor, Dong Qichang (cat. no. 63), one of the most important theorists of Chinese painting. One example, claimed to be inspired by Ni Zan (1306–74, cat. no. 51), is Leaf J, which retains a composition as well as a feeling of desolation typical of Ni's works. However, Gong's version is not only more dramatic, but also emotionally stronger. Dwarfed by the massive hills at the top, a tiny tree resists the strong wind on a sandbar extending into the vast river, surely a symbol of solidarity.

Gong Xian's bleak and sombre landscapes have prompted many scholars to attribute political metaphors to his visual representations, basing their argument on Gong's inter-dynastic career and network.[2] Although he never held an official position, Gong was associated with the scholar-official members of the Fu She, a society involved in political reform that was disbanded at the end of the Ming dynasty. That association contributes to the reason that Gong Xian is often regarded as a *yimin* artist, or a 'left-over subject' nostalgic for the fallen dynasty.

The lack of collectors' seals or records prior to the nineteenth century seems to suggest that Gong Xian's paintings were not widely appreciated until the Shanghai school artists in the early twentieth century revisited the art of the seventeenth-century painters.[3] After the album left China in the early twentieth century, it joined many of Gong's works abroad in Japan, and it was possibly at this time that the leaves were mounted in the hanging scroll format, which would have made them easy to display in Japanese-style rooms. The paintings were reformatted as an album after the scrolls were accessioned by the Nelson-Atkins museum. LL

1 Cahill 1982c, pp. 176–8
2 Silbergeld 1976, p. 570; Hay 1994, pp. 183–4
3 Hájek 1991, p. 43

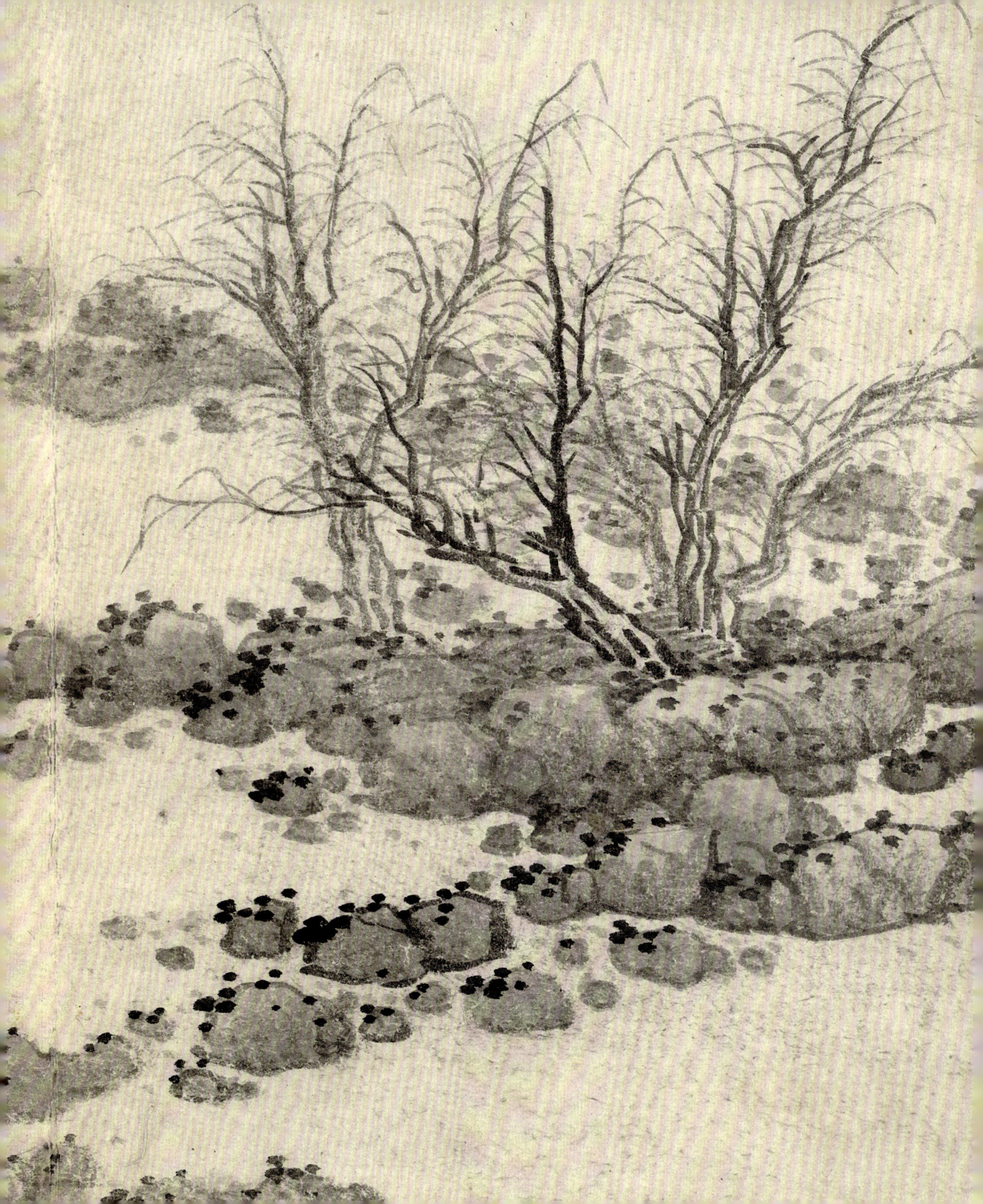

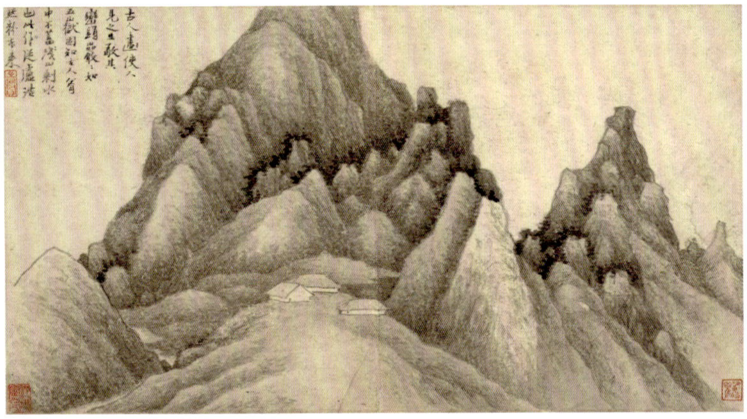
A

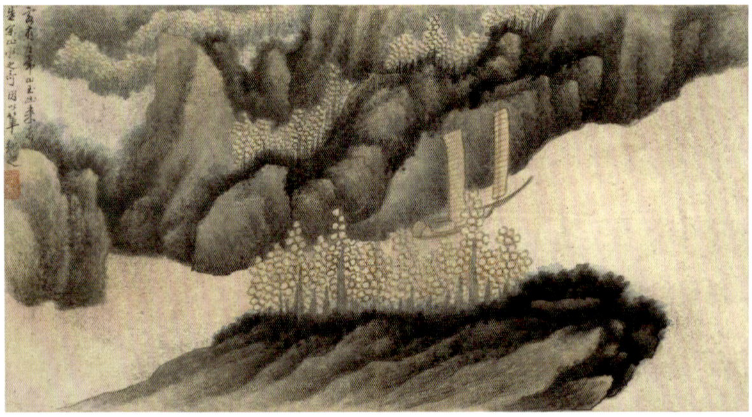
B

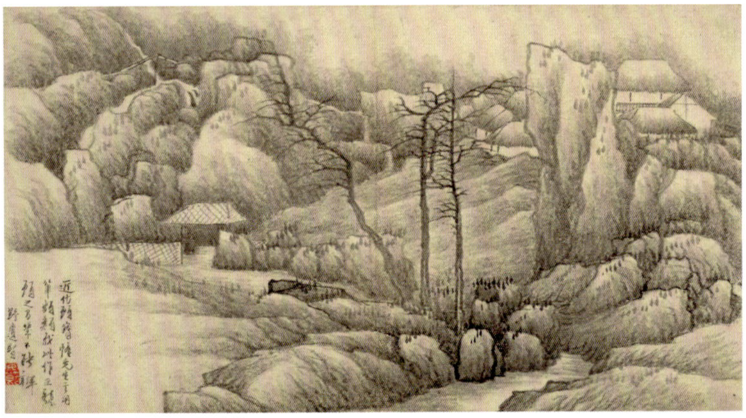
C

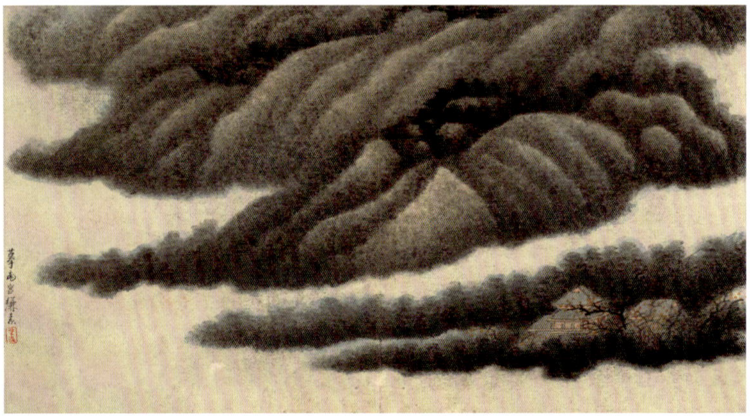
D

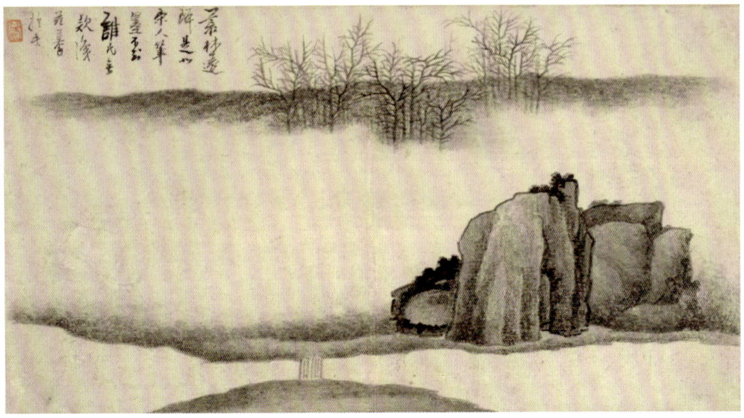
E

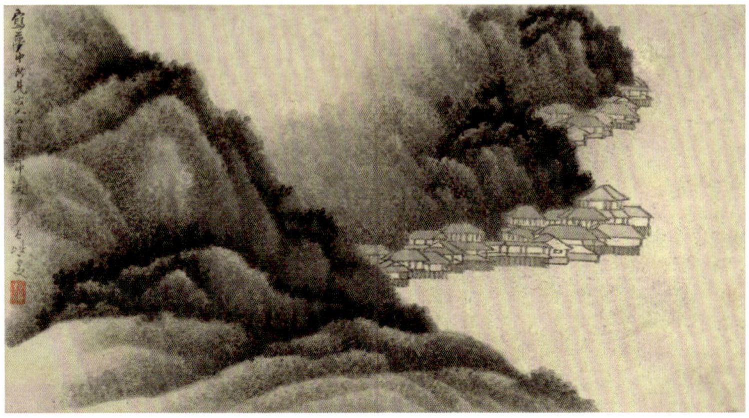
F

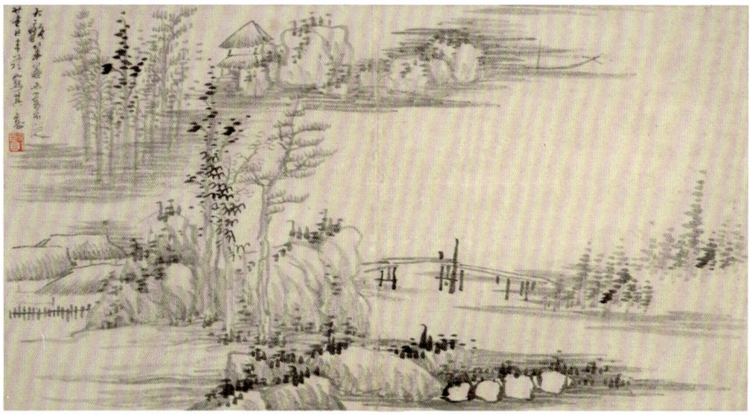

G

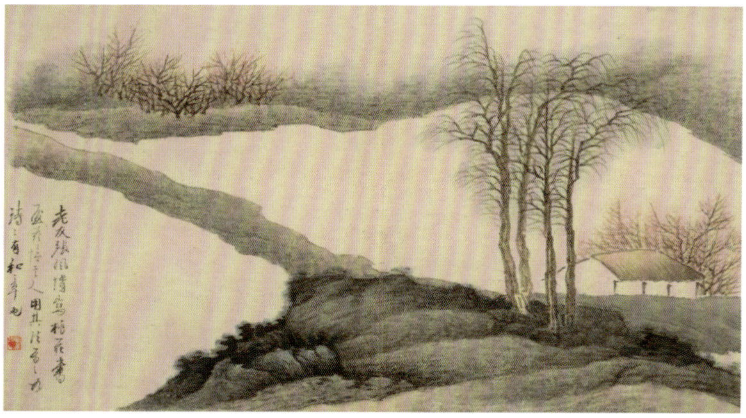

H

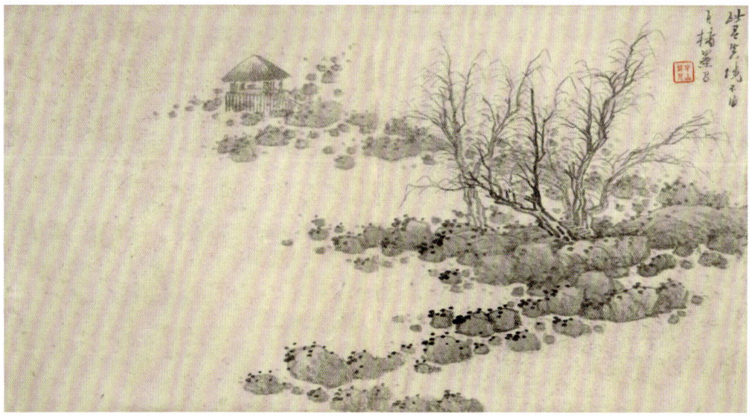

I

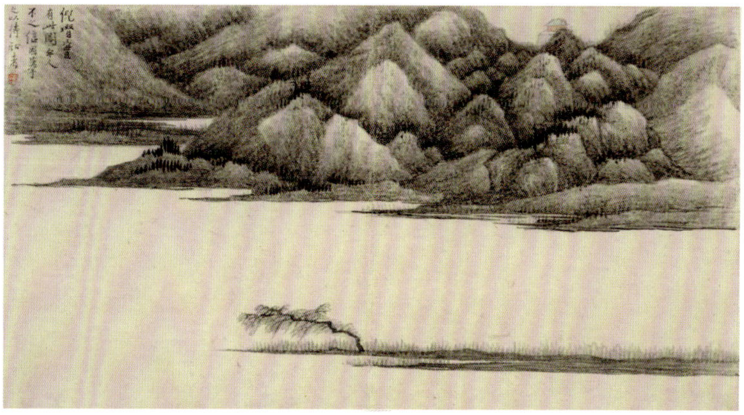

J

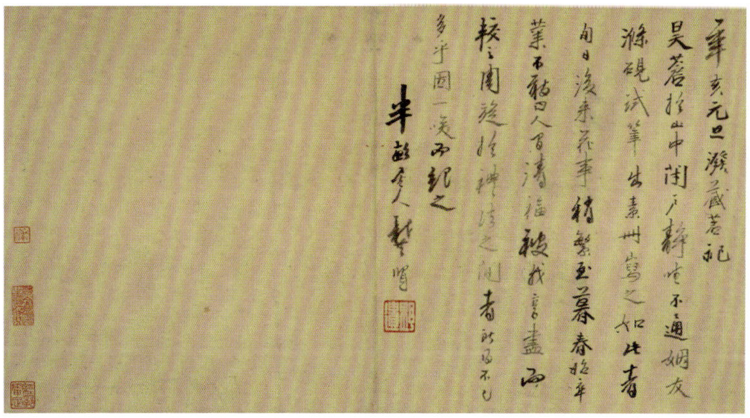

K

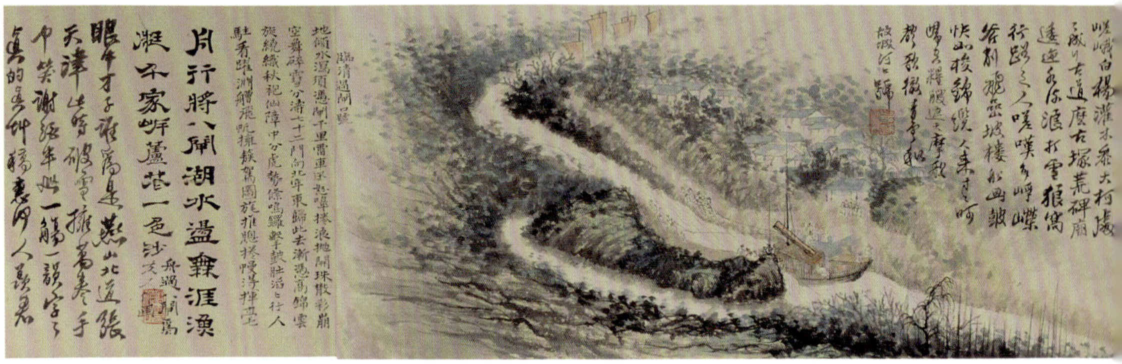

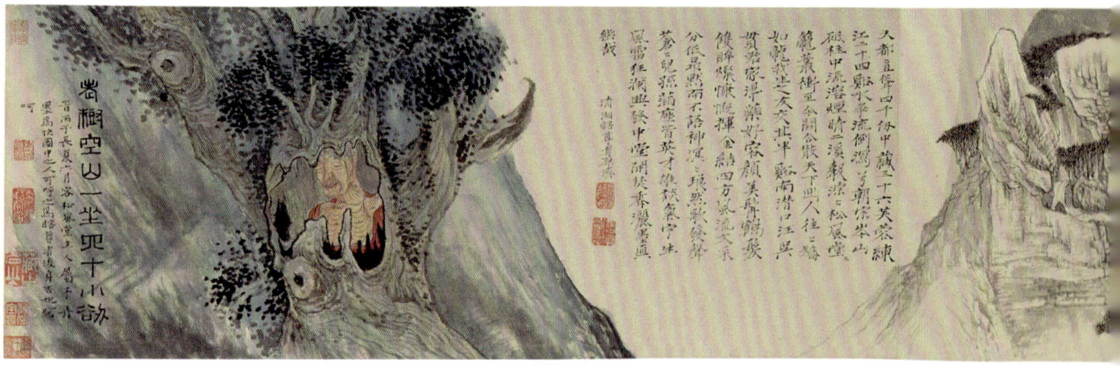

71

SHITAO (1642–1707)

## Sketches of Calligraphy and Painting by Qingxiang

清 石濤 清湘書畫稿 卷

1696, handscroll, ink and colour on paper, 25.6 × 421.5 cm
The Palace Museum, Beijing (XIN 147048)

REFERENCE LITERATURE

Ann Arbor 1967, p. 40; Wu 1967; Fraser 1989; Vinograd 1992a, p. 62 and 1995; Liu Fiedler 1998; Hay 2001; *A Compendium of Chinese Paintings* 1997–2001, vol. 26, pp. 8 and 32–3; Wang 2002; Macca 2004, pp. 530–1; Wang 2005; Zhu 2005; Park 2007; Zhang and Gao 2008

Shitao, originally named Zhu Ruoji, was a scion of the Ming (1368–1644) imperial family. After the Manchu conquest of 1644, the orphaned Shitao was smuggled to the safety of Buddhist temples, and took ordination at Baoen Guangxiao Temple in Quanzhou, Guangxi Province. Leaving Quanzhou at the age of 16, he wandered alone from place to place in the south and practised meditation in the mountains, beside rivers and in temples. After a brief and faltering conversation with the Kangxi emperor (r. 1662–1722) in 1684, he spent nearly three years (1689 to 1692) in Beijing, but failed to gain imperial sponsorship for his art and returned. As a professionalized amateur painter, Shitao often recalled his personal memories in his paintings, and this handscroll of sketches, bearing disparate dates of 1691 and 1696, is one of the most vivid examples: it portrays events both from his time in Beijing and his journey south via the Grand Canal, albeit in no particular order.

In the summer of 1696, Shitao was invited to stay at Pine Wind Hall in She County, Anhui Province. He was requested to create this scroll by his host, Cheng Jun (1638–1704), who was a wealthy merchant and well-regarded art patron. 'Qingxiang' in the title is one of Shitao's many literary names, referring to the Qingxiang estate in Quanzhou where he first found refuge as monk. The handscroll includes six paintings and 13 poems, mostly written before he arrived in the south. The first four poems are without accompanying paintings, and describe Shitao's activities and situation in Beijing. The opening poem reveals the artist's heavy heart when bidding farewell to his friends upon his departure; the second and third are dedicated to his patrons of high official rank, Wang Renyue and Tu Na; and the fourth is a nostalgic letter to his teacher Mei Qing (1623–97) in the south, relating his wish to return to Yangzhou. The calligraphy, in the style of Ni Zan (1306–74), is meticulous and careful, with sharp-edged and angular strokes.

The following five poems and three sketches describe Shitao's boat journey on the Grand Canal in the autumn of 1692. The gathering scene of literati in Botou, Shandong Province is represented in diagonal composition, with two distinct types of brushwork: the fine lines encircling the leaves and structuring the boat, and detailing the interactions between the figures half hidden beneath the slope, provide

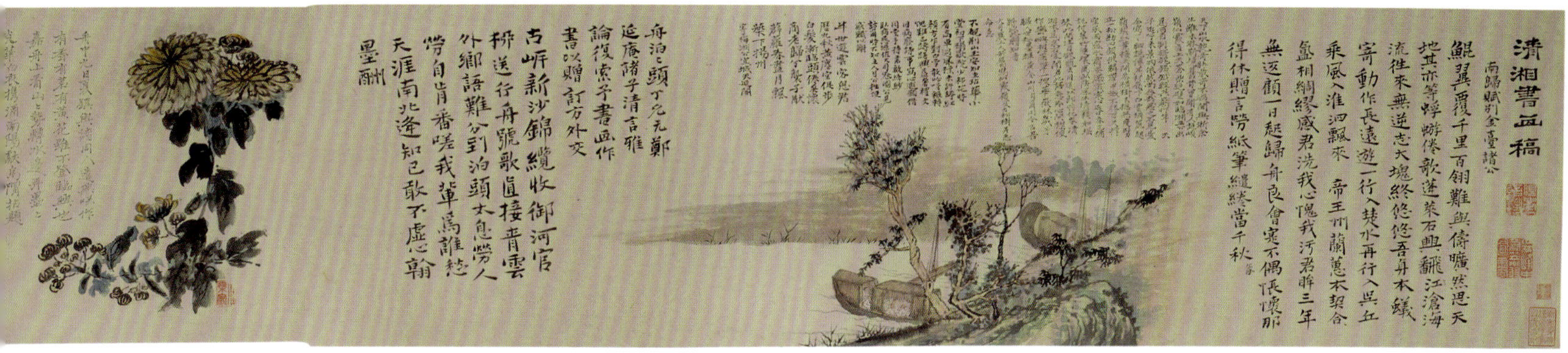


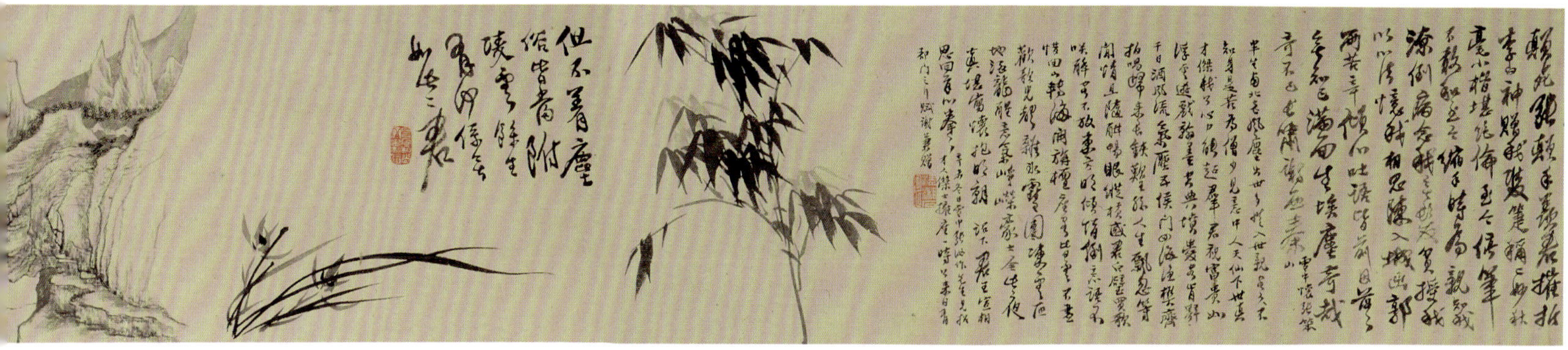

an elegant, intimate atmosphere; and the trembling thick lines, bold ink wash and wet coloured dots texturing the rocks, trees and riverbanks suggest the corresponding effects of gentle wind, movement and unconfined air, as also implied by the ripples on the water. In the next scene, the yellow chrysanthemum not only stands for their enjoyable gathering in Xiazhen at the Chongyang Festival on the ninth day of the ninth month, it also recalls the foremost hermit-poet Tao Qian's (365–427) homecoming. The third sketch describes a rather unusual subject: instead of drawing a famous scenic spot in the beautiful landscape along the canal, the artist has depicted groups of labourers towing boats at the lock – teams of 10 workers each have climbed the slope beside the canal to pull the boats against the current. The long brush-strokes represent the rapid flow of the water, while sails in the distance signify the busy canal traffic. The thick ink and blue dots of the brush-strokes added on top of the extensive lines on the riverbanks impart an extra intensity and restlessness to the scene of toil at the sluice gate.

The tenth to the twelfth poems and the fourth sketch are dedicated to Zhang Lin and Zhang Shu, two salt merchants living in Tianjin. The combination of orchid and bamboo symbolizes the nature of a gentleman, in praise of the Zhang brothers. Depicted without outlines and using ink wash, the two plants have a clean, pure appearance. The paler ink of the orchid, occasionally accented with darker ink on the elongated leaves, creates a sense of physicality and vividness. As if to intensify the sentiments of the still life, the calligraphy inserted in the middle evokes the exaggerated and boldly written running script of Huang Tingjian (1045–1105).

The thirteenth poem and accompanying landscape painting are dedicated to Cheng Jun. For Shitao, the ultimate tribute to his host, a native of Anhui, could be none other than the incomparable peaks of Anhui's famous mountain, Huangshan. Painted in the style of the Anhui school using the plain-drawing technique and dry linear brushwork, the jagged cliffs, outstretched pine and ponderous peaks encircle the lone traveller to create a private, enclosed space. Such a life of solitude suggests a focus on the inner self, perhaps reflecting Shitao's host residing in the mountains in his latter years as well as Shitao's own quietude after his years of longing for recognition in Beijing. The last sketch, which continues to look inward, is a sentimental depiction of a Buddhist monk in a red robe meditating in a hollow tree. The swirling lines representing the wrinkled, loose skin of the monk's exposed upper body and face harmonize with the swirling brush-strokes depicting the rough texture of the tree. The sharp outlines of the foreground against the blurred background formed of relentless, layered strokes and washes would seem to suggest a contradiction: in his state of stillness, the monk is unaffected by the flow of time and all activity beyond his small world, which is powerless to disturb his meditation.

The fact that the events depicted in this scroll do not follow a strict geographical or chronological sequence makes it very different from a conventional travel painting. Although dedicated to Cheng Jun, the scroll is in fact a highly personal account, culminating in an enduring moment of self-revelation. CY

72

YUAN JIANG (act. c.1680–1730)

## The Palace of Nine Perfections

清 袁江 九成宮圖 屏

1691, set of 12 hanging scrolls,
ink and colour on silk, 207 × 563.2 cm
The Metropolitan Museum of Art, New York,
Purchase, The Dillon Fund Gift, 1982 (1982.125a–l)

PROVENANCE

Jeoung-kyu Lee

REFERENCE LITERATURE

New York 1983b, pp. 105–11, 138, no. 40; Murck 1988; Zurich 1996, pp. 146–7, 152–3, 226, no. 31

During the early Qing dynasty (1644–1911), the city of Yangzhou, situated on the Grand Canal about 65 kilometres north of the Yangzi River, was the distribution centre for salt gathered from the Huai'an salterns and a hub for shipments of tax grain to the capital.[1] Recovering rapidly from its near destruction in 1645 when Manchu forces brutally suppressed Ming loyalist resistance, burning the city and decimating the population, Yangzhou by the end of the seventeenth century had become the wealthiest commercial entrepôt in the empire and a major centre of artistic activity.[2]

The professional painter and Yangzhou native Yuan Jiang thrived in this milieu. Yuan specialized in intricately described visions of palatial complexes set within sumptuous blue-and-green landscapes. Reviving the monumental landscape style of the Tang (618–907) and Song (960–1279) dynasties, Yuan catered to the current vogue of large-scale hanging scrolls and multi-panelled screen paintings as decoration in the ostentatious mansions of Yangzhou's mercantile elite. He was assisted in this work by several other artists, including his son or nephew Yuan Yao (act. 1730–after 1778), who continued to practise the family style into the late eighteenth century.[3]

*The Palace of Nine Perfections*, one of Yuan Jiang's earliest extant works, is a screen-like set of 12 scrolls that takes as its subject an eighth-century imperial retreat located in the hills north of the Tang capital, Chang'an (present Xi'an). Destroyed by the end of the ninth century, the Palace of Nine Perfections was a splendid residence with grounds so vast it was necessary to travel on horseback between halls – as suggested here by the two mounted figures riding through the covered corridor that zigzags through the mountains to the left of the central hall. Yuan envisions the ancient royal complex as a utopia, inserting Qing-style buildings into a fantastic landscape that suggests the enchanted realm of the immortals. Set on a broad marble terrace and overlooking a pond filled with lotus, the central hall, for example, was inspired by Buddhist depictions of Amitābha's Pure Land (cat. no. 9), in which the halls of that paradise are approached across a lotus pond.

In his inscription, Yuan states that he is 'imitating antiquity', but for other paintings he links this style to that of Guo Zhongshu (d.977), the tenth-century master of 'ruled-line' (*jiehua*) architectural renderings (cat. no. 49). The sumptuous palette and narrative detail relate the work far more directly, however, to the sixteenth-century revival of the Southern Song (1127–1279) academy manner popularized by Qiu Ying (1494/5–1552).[4] What distinguishes Yuan's interpretation of the Song style are a greatly enlarged scale, an expansive treatment of space and landscape elements that contradict nature. On the looming rock cliff, for example, a pine tree grows upside down.

Yuan Jiang executed *The Palace of Nine Perfections* just two years after the Kangxi emperor (r. 1662–1722) visited Yangzhou on his second southern inspection tour, and it seems likely that the inclusion of a regal entourage – with the Emperor and his parasol bearer prominently featured in the foreground – was inspired by the ceremonial processions of that imperial visit.[5] The painting is one of only a handful of works by Yuan in which he records the date, using not only the usual cyclical characters but also the Kangxi reign title, a formal device which suggests that the commission may have come from an official or a patron with imperial connections, for whom Kangxi's visit may have had special significance. Combining legend and architectural fantasy with thinly veiled references to contemporary events, Yuan's painting is a celebration of the grandiose materialistic lifestyle to which the high society of Yangzhou aspired. MH

1 The discussion of this painting is excerpted from my essay in Zurich 1996, pp. 146–7, 152–3.
2 For an eyewitness account of the Manchu destruction of Yangzhou in 1645, see Wang (1645) 1937. For an account of Yangzhou's prosperity during the Qing, see Ho 1954.
3 For Yuan Jiang (act. c.1680–1730), Yuan Yao (act. 1730–after 1778) and other members in this circle, see Cahill 1963 and 1966; Nie 1982; Murck 1988.
4 For examples of Qiu Ying's (1494/5–1552) architectural paintings in a coloured landscape, see Taipei 1989, nos 5, 6.
5 The connection between the imperial procession depicted in this painting and the Kangxi emperor's 1689 southern tour was first suggested by Alfreda Murck in Murck 1988, p. 236.

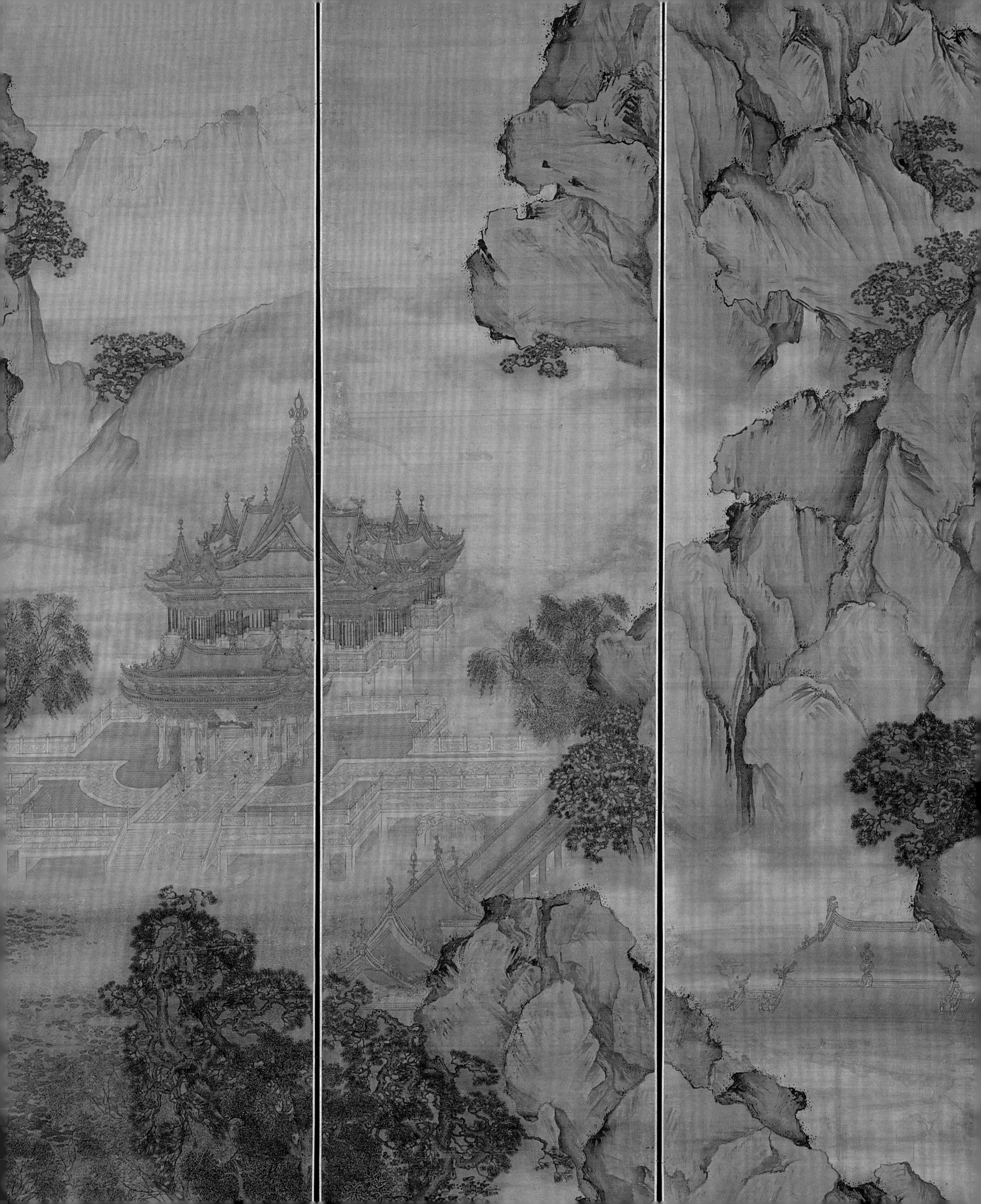

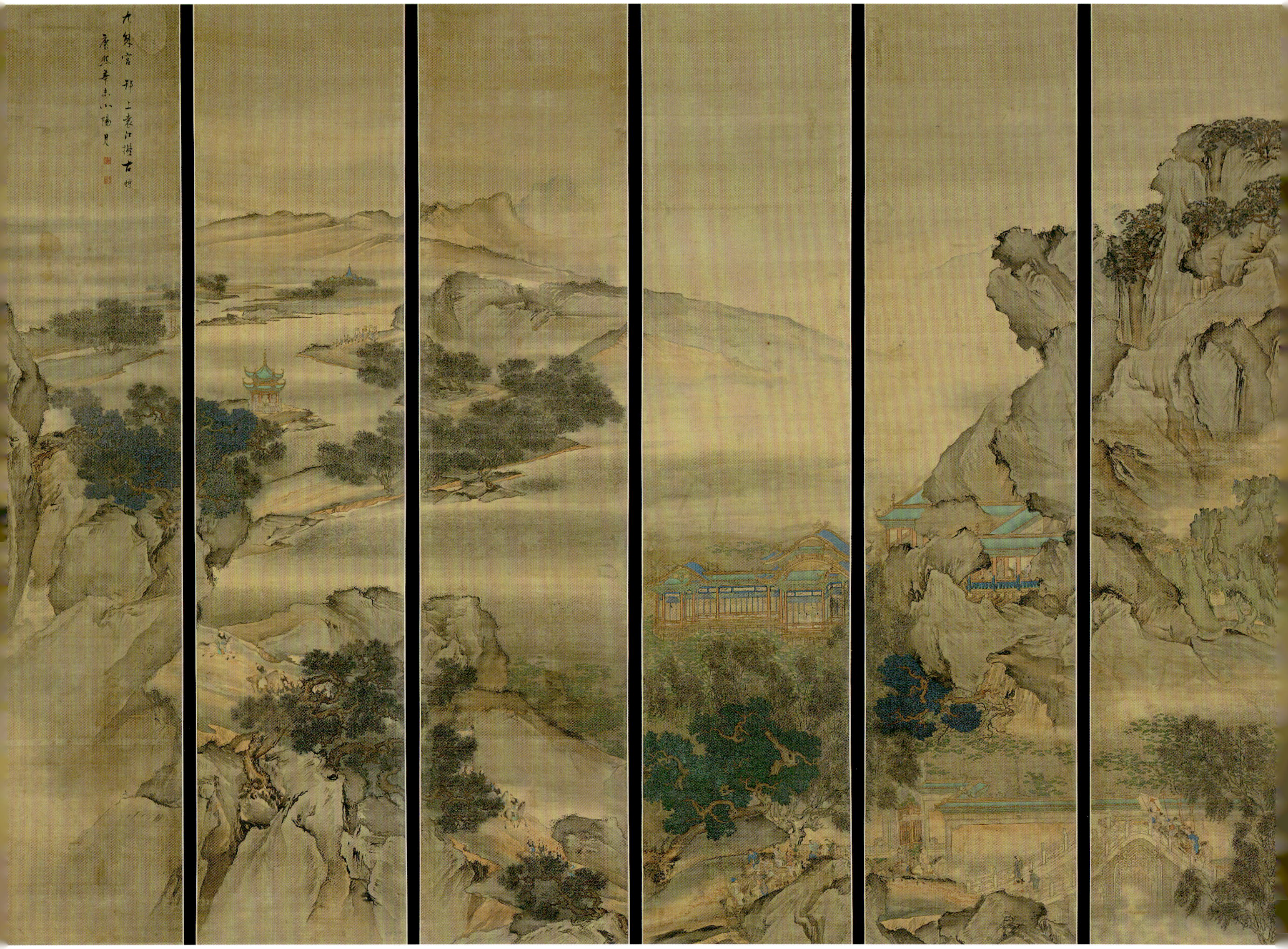
九成宮 邗上袁江擬古
康熙辛未小陽月

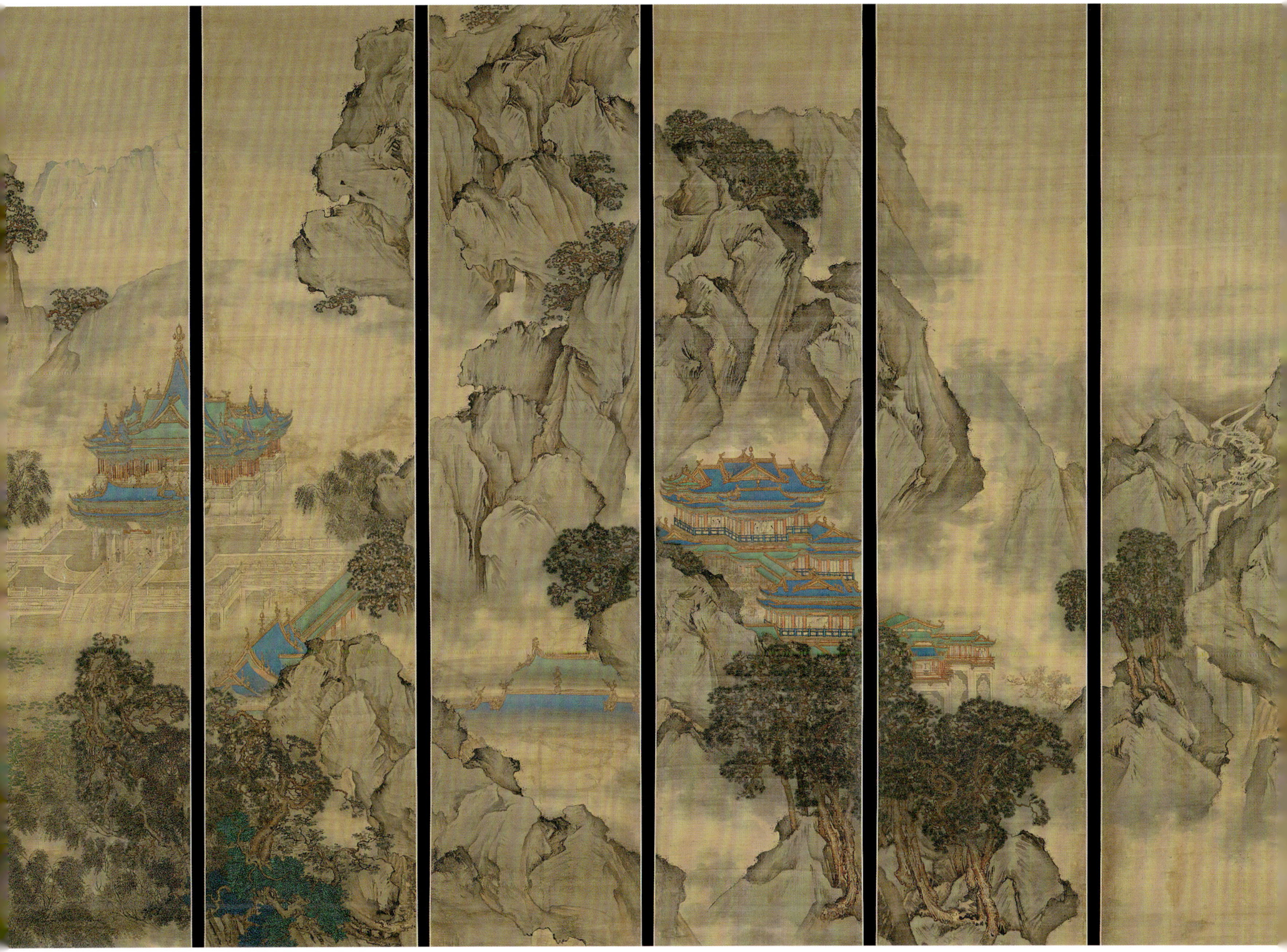

73

FA RUOZHEN (1613–96)

## Clouds and Mist in the Mountains

清 法若真 雲煙疊嶂圖 軸

c.1690, hanging scroll, ink on paper, 206.3 × 75.5 cm
Museum of Far Eastern Antiquities, Stockholm (NMOK-050)

PROVENANCE

Purchased in Beijing in 1929–30

REFERENCE LITERATURE

Sirén 1938, vol. 2, pl. 184, 1945, pp. 102–4 and 1956–8, vol. 6, pl. 357a; New York, Los Angeles and San Francisco 1967, no. 22; Leijon 1981, p. 144; Suzuki et al. 1982–3, vol. 2, no. E020-054; Chin 1984, pp. 100–3; *Chinese Art in Overseas Collections* 1990, pl. 78; Kansas City and Seattle 1992, no. 148

Fa Ruozhen was a native of Jiaozhou in Shandong Province, and came from a family of scholars and officials. He obtained his *jinshi* degree in 1646, and had a long career as an official until he was removed from office in 1670 after being implicated in the impeachment against the collector and official Zhou Lianggong (1612–72). At the end of his career he served as a provincial administrative commissioner of Anhui Province, where the famous Mount Huang (Huangshan) is situated. After his retirement from office he lived in reclusion in the Huangshan area for more than 20 years before returning to his hometown, some two years before his demise. He was well known for his poetry, calligraphy and landscape paintings, as well as for his broad knowledge of the *Five Classics*. Most of his dated paintings are from his period of retirement.

This landscape scroll is executed in a monumental style, with billowing clouds floating among towering cliffs and mist-filled trees. The imposing view is reminiscent of the large mountainous landscapes of the Northern Song period (960–1279), and it is possibly this classical quality which makes nineteenth-century collector Wu Cizhi in his inscription on the mounting associate it with the Tang dynasty (618–907) poet Wang Wei's (699–759) famous lines: 'Cold mountains grow ever more azure-grey, Autumn's floods churn more loudly each passing day.'

As often seen in seventeenth-century landscape paintings, mass and space are ambiguously rendered. The energetic contours outlining the outcrops and at places sometimes even the clouds are combined with rather heavy shading and texture strokes, resulting in blurred spatial relationships – it is sometimes difficult to decide whether cliffs and rocks are protruding or receding. The space is relatively constricted, the clouds and mist failing to create any sense of depth. The crags reaching almost to the top of the painting contribute to an almost claustrophobic atmosphere.

The painting is undated, but the style corresponds to Fa Ruozhen's landscapes from around 1690, namely from a period very late in his life.[1]

Considering the artist's renown as a poet and calligrapher, the lack of signature and date is somewhat surprising. It is possible that the painting was originally part of a tripartite work consisting of multiple hanging scrolls, with Fa Ruozhen's signature and date on one of the other paintings. The towering peak here suggests that this scroll may have been the central piece. MS

1 Kansas City and Seattle 1992, vol. 2, p. 166

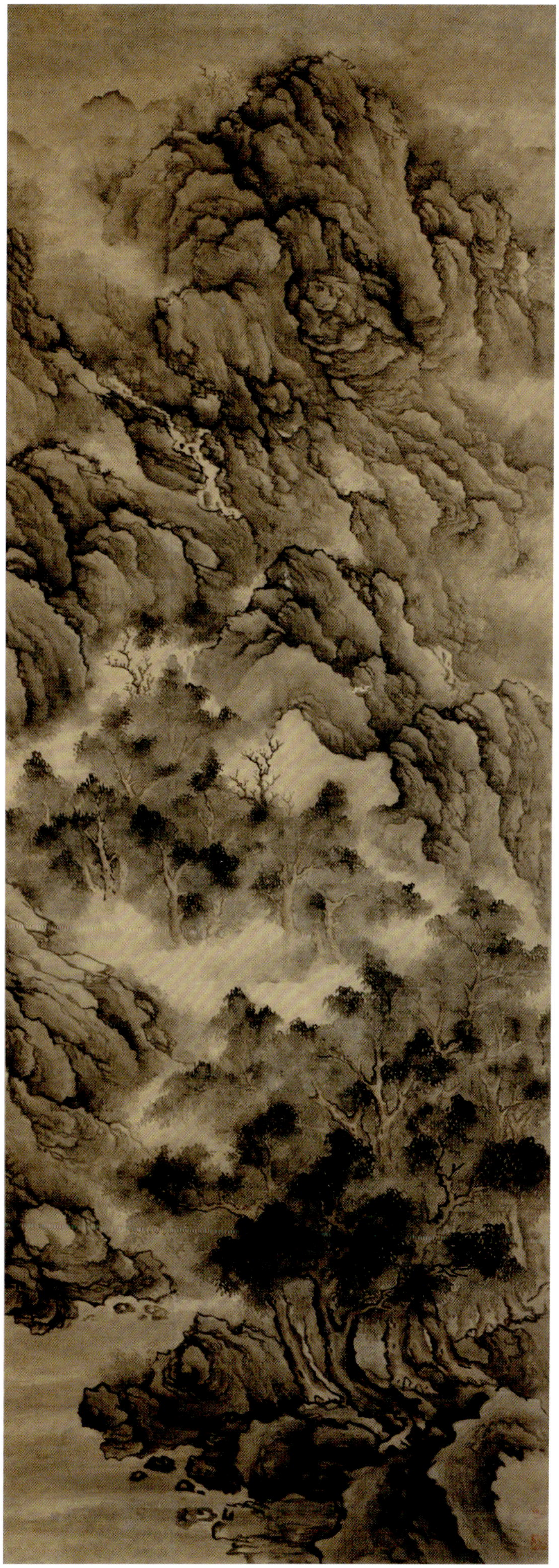

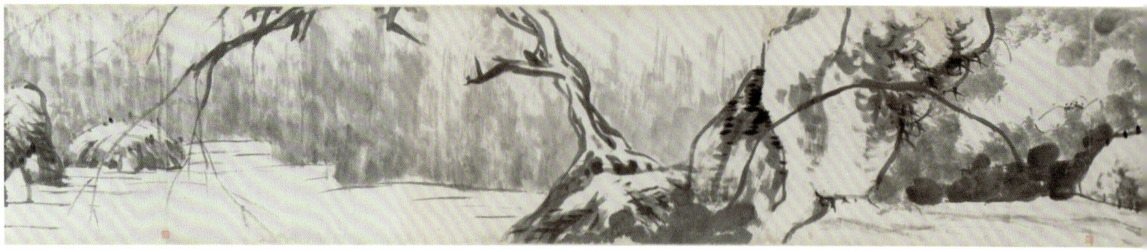

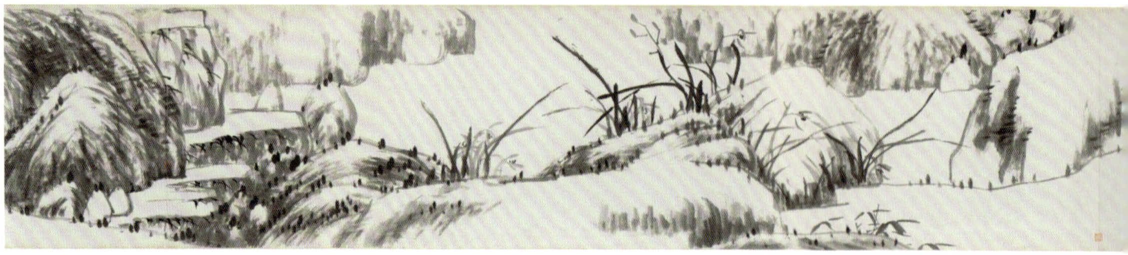

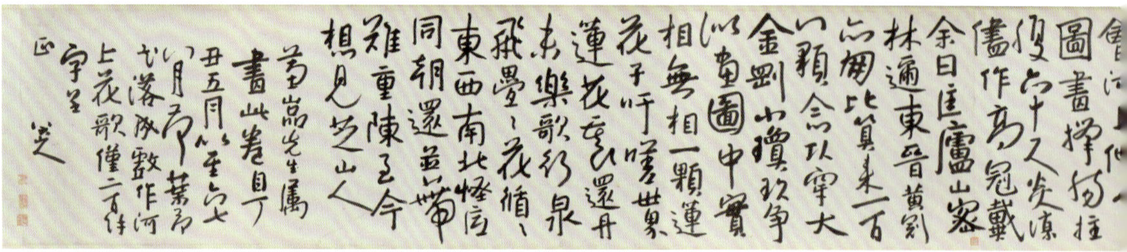

74

BADA SHANREN (1626–1705)

## Flowers on the River

清 八大山人 河上花圖 卷

1697, handscroll, ink on paper, 47 × 1292.5 cm
Tianjin Museum (58.5.372)

REFERENCE LITERATURE

New Haven 1990; *A Compendium of Chinese Paintings* 1997–2001, vol. 5, pp. 10, 56–65; Shan 2002; Washington 2003; Zhu 2010

Ours is the first era in which Bada Shanren has been given due recognition. Since the early twentieth century, Chinese scholars and artists have hailed him as one of the greatest painters of all time and credited him with revitalizing Chinese painting. Yet in his own time, Bada was regarded as an enigma, and his art considered strange and incomprehensible. Few of his contemporaries knew him, and many thought him mad. Indeed, this was probably just the image he sought to maintain in order to protect himself – even the name 'Bada Shanren' is a pseudonym. Bada was born into a branch of the Ming imperial family in 1626, in Nanchang, Jiangxi Province. He grew up in an artistic environment – both his father and grandfather were artists. When he was 18, however, Manchu forces captured Beijing, where they ousted the last emperor of the Han-Chinese Ming dynasty (1368–1644) and established a new dynasty, the Qing (1644–1911). The following year, they occupied Nanchang. Subsequently, Bada's immediate family perished, and for personal safety he became a Chan Buddhist monk, living for the next 30 years as an abbot in the hinterland of Jiangxi. In the late 1670s, however, conflicted by a yearning to return to secular life, he decided to return to normal society, but suffered a severe nervous breakdown that lasted several years. Eventually he recovered, and for the rest of his life lived quietly in his hometown as a professional painter, calligrapher and poet.

In a way, Bada was an artist of his time. Like many of his contemporaries, he practised the arts of the Chinese scholar. At a young age, he had rigorously studied the style of the early master Ouyang Xun (557–641), and later that of the Ming calligrapher and painter Dong Qichang (1555–1636), among many others. He also emulated the exaggerated style of the Song (960–1279) calligrapher Huang Tingjian (1045–1105). As well, Bada was a serious student of poetry. His fascination with obscure metaphors, riddles and humour was due partly to his broad interest in classical poetry and partly to his training in Chan poetry and *gong'an* (J. *koan*) during his time as a Buddhist monk. This tendency to incorporate a wide range of influences is also present in his art, where he explored the long tradition of Chinese painting, studying the work of old masters such as Muxi

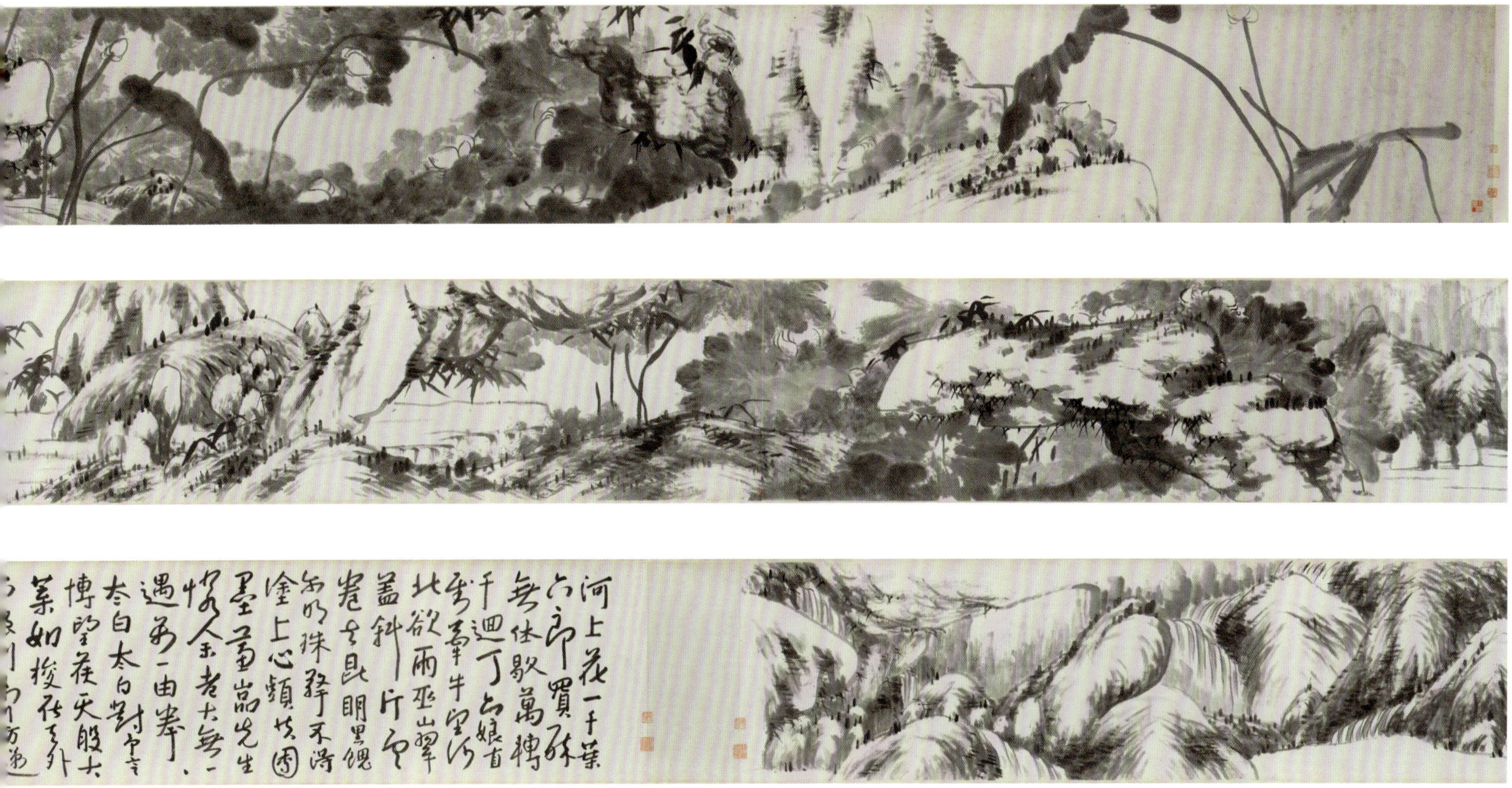

(d.c.1281), Ni Zan (1306–74), Shen Zhou (1427–1509) and Xu Wei (1521–93). Dong Qichang especially had a powerful impact on his style. Among all his contemporaries, in fact it was Bada who most brilliantly showed an ability to synthesize the tradition and elevate the art of painting into the highest mode of personal expression. His art is emotionally intense and completely original, as testified by *Flowers on the River*. Painted for one of his young friends, Huiyan (probably a descendent of a merchant living in Yangzhou),[1] the work took him four months (June–September 1697) to complete. The scroll consists of nine sheets of paper (47 × 183 cm each) joined together, and including the poem at the end, reaches 14 metres, making it the longest scroll he ever created.

The lotus was Bada's most frequently painted subject. In his later period, he used seals and alternative literary names that referred to the flower, such as 'Zaifu' ('In the Lotus'), 'Zaifu shanfang' ('Mountain Studio in the Lotus') and 'Heyuan' ('Lotus Garden'). For someone who had spent 30 years as a monk, the lotus no doubt served as a reminder of the Buddha. In Daoism the flower represents longevity, the lotus seeds being used as an elixir ingredient in alchemy. The lotus was also an enduring symbol of a high-minded gentleman in Confucian thought: rising up from the mud and murky water, it emerges in the pure air, as the Song philosopher Zhou Dunyi (1017–73) expressed it in his influential essay *Adoration of the Lotus*. However, as Bada's art is always extremely autobiographical, the lotuses in this work must have had a particularly personal meaning in connection with this moment in his life. He was already 72 years old in 1697, which was eight years before his death. Some scholars have interpreted the flowers as the artist's melancholic reflection on his own life cycle, from budding youth, to maturity and death.[2] Yet, reading the lengthy poem at the end, one finds a jubilant man completely free from all anxieties and desires, enjoying every moment of creating his work:

> The 108 rosary beads
> Can be made of great diamonds,
> Or little jade stones,
> But how can they compare with,
> in my picture,
> A single lotus seed that is visible but does
> not exist?
> Alas! The entire world is within my lotus.
> Have I transmuted the ingredients of
> the Elixir?
> Happily singing my way,
> I immerse myself in the splashes of spring
> water and the sprays of flowers.
> East and west, south and north after
> all are the same.

While searching for Bada's personal intentions in the image is important in understanding his art, it should not eclipse the appreciation of the artist's breathtaking handling of form, tonality, texture and gesture. Contemplating this masterpiece, viewers cannot help but feel they are re-enacting the process of painting. ZH

1 Zhu 2010, pp. 282–3
2 Shan 2002, p. 297

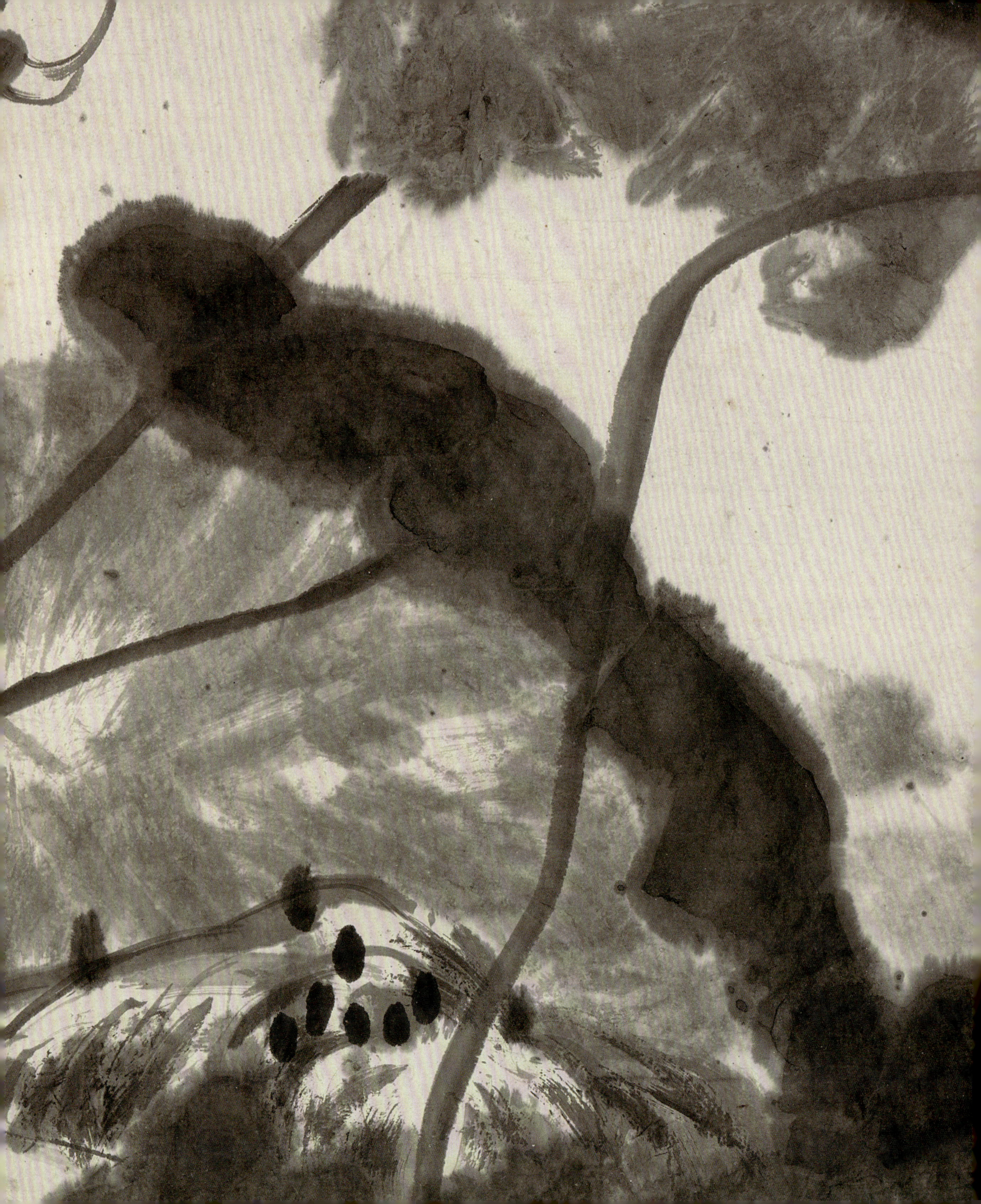

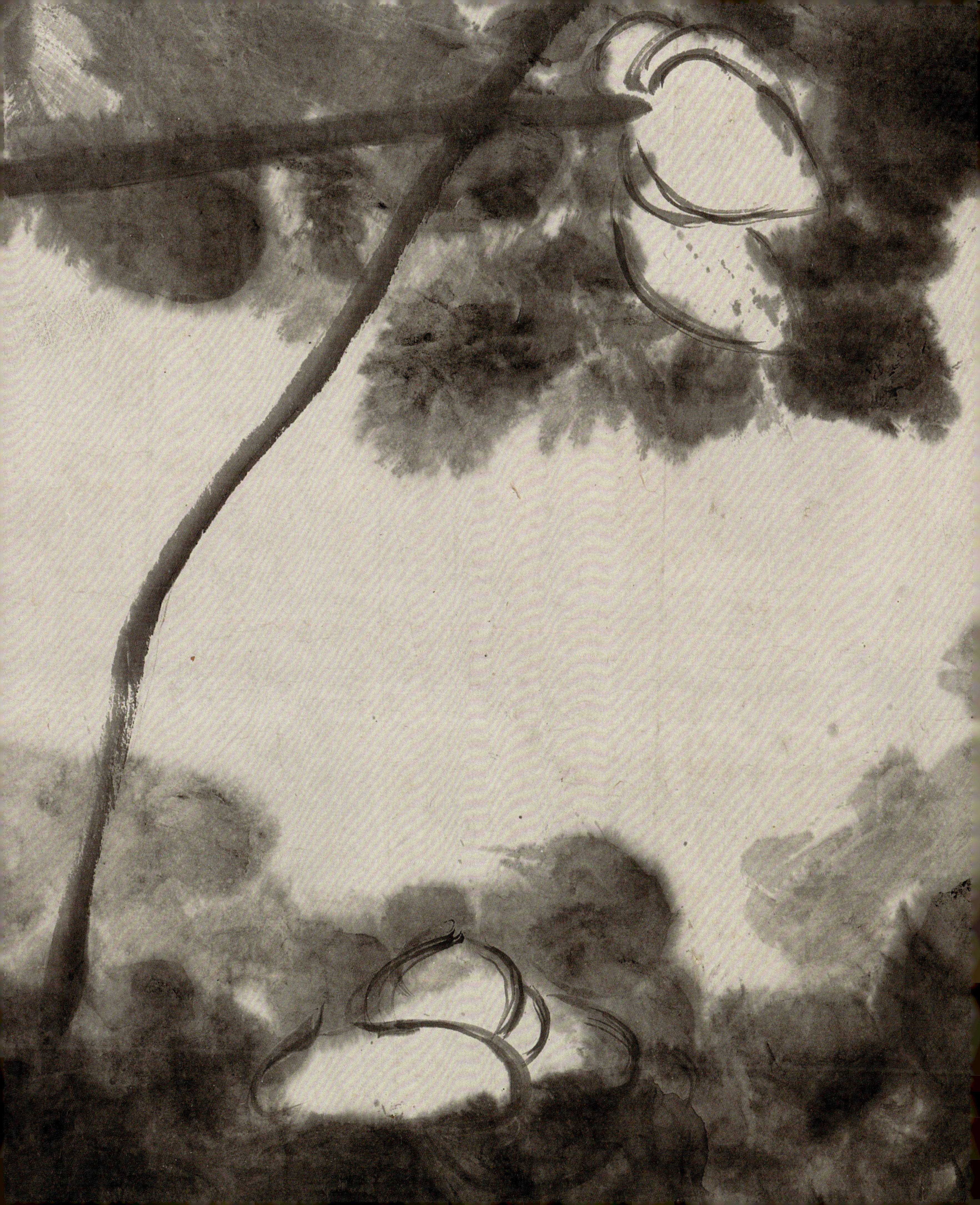

75

WANG YUANQI (1642–1715)

## Early Spring in the Mountains

清 王原祁 山中早春圖 軸

1705, hanging scroll, ink and colour on paper, 100.1 × 44.7 cm
Liaoning Provincial Museum
(ZONG 26188 SHU 2632)

REFERENCE LITERATURE

Wang 1973; Wen 1980; Cahill 1982a; Rogers and Lee 1988; Wu 1991; Zheng 1992; Duoyun bianji bu 1993; Taipei 1997; Wang (c.1680) 2000; Wan 2010; Wang 2010b

The leading literati painter in the late seventeenth century and the Kangxi emperor's (r. 1662–1722) favourite artist, Wang Yuanqi inherited the orthodox style and his taste in painting from Dong Qichang (1555–1636) through his grandfather Wang Shimin (1592–1680). Wang Yuanqi was raised in a scholarly environment in Taicang, Jiangsu Province, and from an early age received an education in art both from his grandfather and from the famous painters visiting their home. In 1670, he was awarded the *jinshi* degree in the civil service examination, and then appointed an assistant inspector for the provincial examinations. He was made magistrate of Renxian, in the former northern province of Zhili, in 1681, and by 1712 had been appointed senior vice president of the Ministry of Revenue, a position he held until his death in 1715.

More than once, Wang complained in writing that his heavy responsibilities prevented him from painting. As his inscription on this painting, dated 1705, relates, Wang 'had no time to paint for anyone' unless he was occasionally freed from official duties, and it took him almost half a year to finish this spring landscape. In another account dated 1707, Wang wrote: 'When I play with the pliant brush and enter into and leave the styles of various masters of the Song and Yuan, it is like being face-to-face with the ancients themselves. Although I cannot imitate exactly their forms and spirit, to some extent a single encounter is still model enough for lodging conceptions and broadening the heart.'[1] His passion for the old masters is thus apparent. His style derives from the Four Masters of the Yuan (1271–1368), and his art theory is especially related to Huang Gongwang (1269–1354).

In the book *Desultory Jottings at a Rainy Window*, Wang discusses the art of landscape painting and the key concepts of *longmai* ('dragon vein'), *kaihe* ('opening and closing') and *qifu* ('rising and falling') in representing the physiognomy and geomancy of actual scenery.[2] Such ideas and knowledge, for which he was indebted to his grandfather Wang Shimin, were transmitted into the composition of this painting. On the left is the land, with rolling hills stretching up and down into the middle plane; on the right, the open space signifying water dominates the foreground, and the mountains only begin to appear in the middle plane with a bridge linking the two foothills; they are joined by a towering mountain range in the centre, depicted in an 'S' shape like a dragon vein extending into the distance.

The painting is executed in a highly articulate and alluring manner. The artist has used his brush sideways to create the dots on the mountain peaks and tree leaves, while the many-toned pale browns and greens produced with vibrant and moist brushwork give a sense of early spring. Not only does this work display the physical characteristics of a landscape, but its intricate conception draws viewers into the painted world, to experience what the artist experienced and to explore a poetic space created from nature. CY

1 Rogers and Lee 1988, p. 176
2 Wang 1973, p. 170

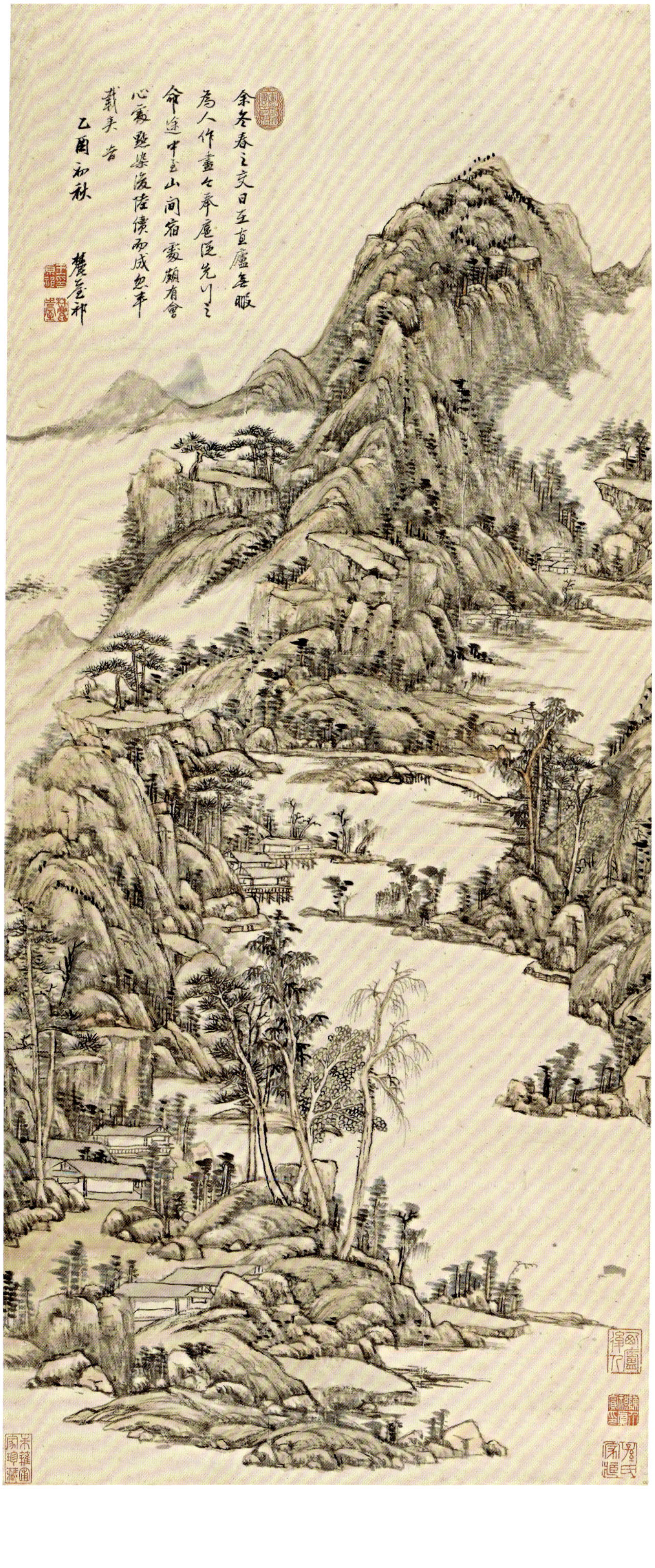
余冬春之交日至直廬無暇
為人作畫今奉廬陵先生之
命途中至山間宿處頗有會
心處題詠後陸續而成忽半
載矣昔
乙酉初秋
麓臺祁

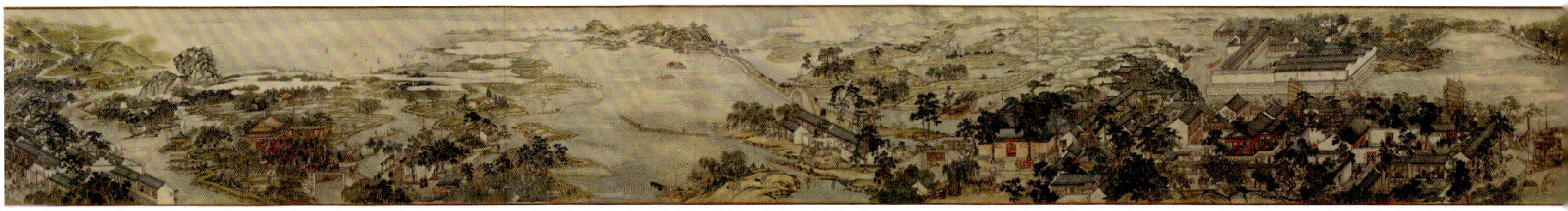

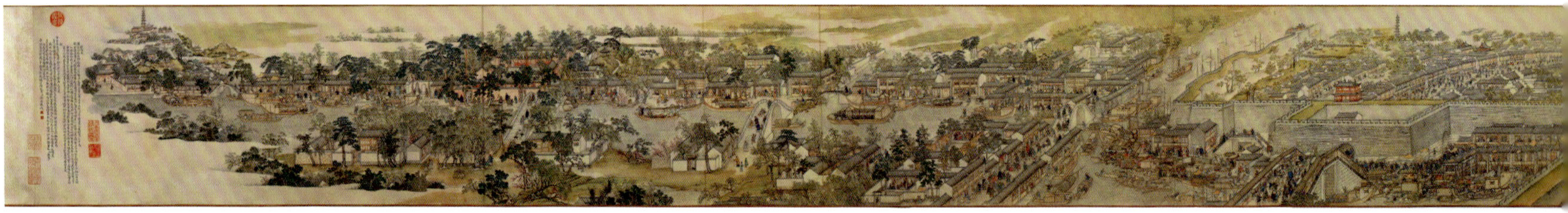

76

XU YANG (1712–c.1779)

## Prosperous Suzhou

清 徐揚 姑蘇繁華圖 卷

1759, handscroll, ink and colour on silk, 39 × 1241 cm
Liaoning Provincial Museum (ZONG 2938 SHU 240)

REFERENCE LITERATURE

*Prosperous Suzhou* 1986; Hockney 1993; Fan 2003; Ma 2008; Nie 2008

This exceptionally long scroll, known in its time as *The Affluent Life in the Prosperous Age*, was painted in the imperial workshop within the Forbidden City in Beijing on commission of the Qianlong emperor (r. 1736–96). The production process began in 1756 and was completed in 1759,[1] and must have been exacting. According to the general practice of the imperial workshop during this period, for major commissions like this one, the master artist would first have produced a draft scroll in ink on paper and then submitted it for the Emperor's approval; only after the draft had been approved would the workshop have been issued with the requisite silk and expensive mineral pigments to execute the final work. At this stage, a team of painters who had been trained to work in the master artist's style – some specializing in human figures and others in architectural elements or landscape – would have been assigned to paint specific areas in accordance with their expertise, while the master artist closely supervised them to ensure stylistic consistency and monitor overall progress.

In spite of its enormous scale and lavish colours, as well as the immense effort involved in its execution, this scroll was not intended for public display. Apart from the Emperor himself, probably very few members of the court had access to it. In other words, it was not an ordinary propaganda piece. Kept locked away in a storeroom of the Forbidden City, it was created as a historical document for posterity as evidence of the Qing (1644–1911) rulers' governance of a prosperous empire. The Emperor's extraordinary ambition is made explicit in the opening sentences of the colophon written by the master artist, Xu Yang: 'Only my dynasty has such a thriving government and culture, surpassing the achievements of the Three Dynasties [Xia (c.22nd/21st–c.17th century BCE), Shang (c.17th–c.11th century BCE) and Zhou (c.1100–256 BCE)]. Its geographical area and the size of its population are unprecedented. Your Subject is so fortunate to have met with this flourishing age.'

Xu Yang was a native of Suzhou, economically and artistically the richest city in China. Before being recruited to the imperial workshop, he lived in the commercial district of the city and enjoyed a reputation as a respected professional painter; his contribution to a local gazetteer project was highly regarded among local officials. When the Qianlong emperor made his first southern inspection tour in 1751, he visited Suzhou, and was greatly enamoured of the city. Xu, then aged 40, had the opportunity to present an album of his paintings to the Emperor, and was subsequently summoned to the capital to serve as a court artist. At court Xu's talent was recognized right away, and he was immediately paid the salary of an artist of the first rank. Within two years he was also given the honorary title *juren*, a designation usually reserved for scholars who had passed provincial-level civil examination.[2] Given the important status of Suzhou in the empire, Xu's connection with the city and the favourable

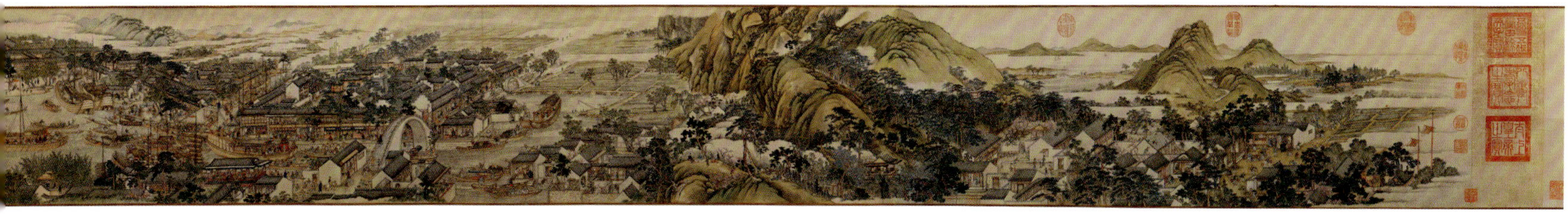

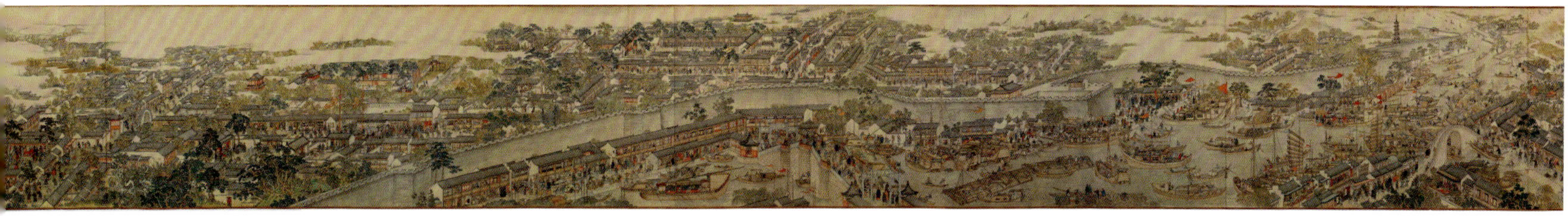

impression he had made on Qianlong during the southern inspection tour, it is perhaps unsurprising that the Emperor selected Suzhou to represent his reign. As for Xu Yang, while he appears simply to have been carrying out the Emperor's wishes, his intimate knowledge of his hometown makes the painting an invaluable record of daily life in eighteenth-century China.

Set in late spring, this depiction of urban life in Suzhou begins with a morning landscape of Lingyan Hill, on the western outskirts of the city. It then travels east through a town called Mudu, where the spectacle of a local wedding slowly unfolds; next comes a bucolic scene of Lake Shi, followed by the metropolis itself. The artist leads us to approach the city from its south-west corner, with its cluster of wharves and workshops of different trades. From this point, we are directed northward via the Grand Canal along the city wall, where we witness urban life in ever greater intensity. In this section, the wall gradually moves downwards to allow a better view inside the city walls; here, we see commercial streets and shops with people selling goods as well as the prefectural government offices, in which the prefectural examination is taking place. Moving further north, we reach the climax of the urban episode at the gate called Changmen, the busiest place in the city, where commerce and trade are most concentrated. Xu creates the ambience of the locale through his depiction of the dense congregation of people and businesses at the foot of the massive city gate, on the waterfront and Hongqiao Bridge, and on the boats and rafts. The scroll unfolds further to show the commercial activity extending beyond the city and gradually fading away as people prepare for their nocturnal visit to Tiger Hill in the evening mist.

The use of the European approach to perspective is noticeable, especially in sections where streets and houses inside the city wall are depicted receding into the far distance. Nevertheless, the basic method of spatial construction is derived from that used in *Along the River during the Qingming Festival* (fig. 46) the seminal urban landscape masterpiece created by Zhang Zeduan (act. early 12th century) in the twelfth century. This method, whose principle is similar to modern axonometric projection, allows the viewer simultaneously to look over the buildings at one moment, wander along a street and observe the details of the goods in the shops at another, and turn into a back lane and peek into a private garden at yet another. Above all, it frees one from observing from a fixed point. To paraphrase David Hockney's words, this is what the viewer finds exciting.[3] ZH

1 See Ma 2008, p. 261
2 Nie 2008, pp. 151, 160
3 Hockney 1993, p. 128

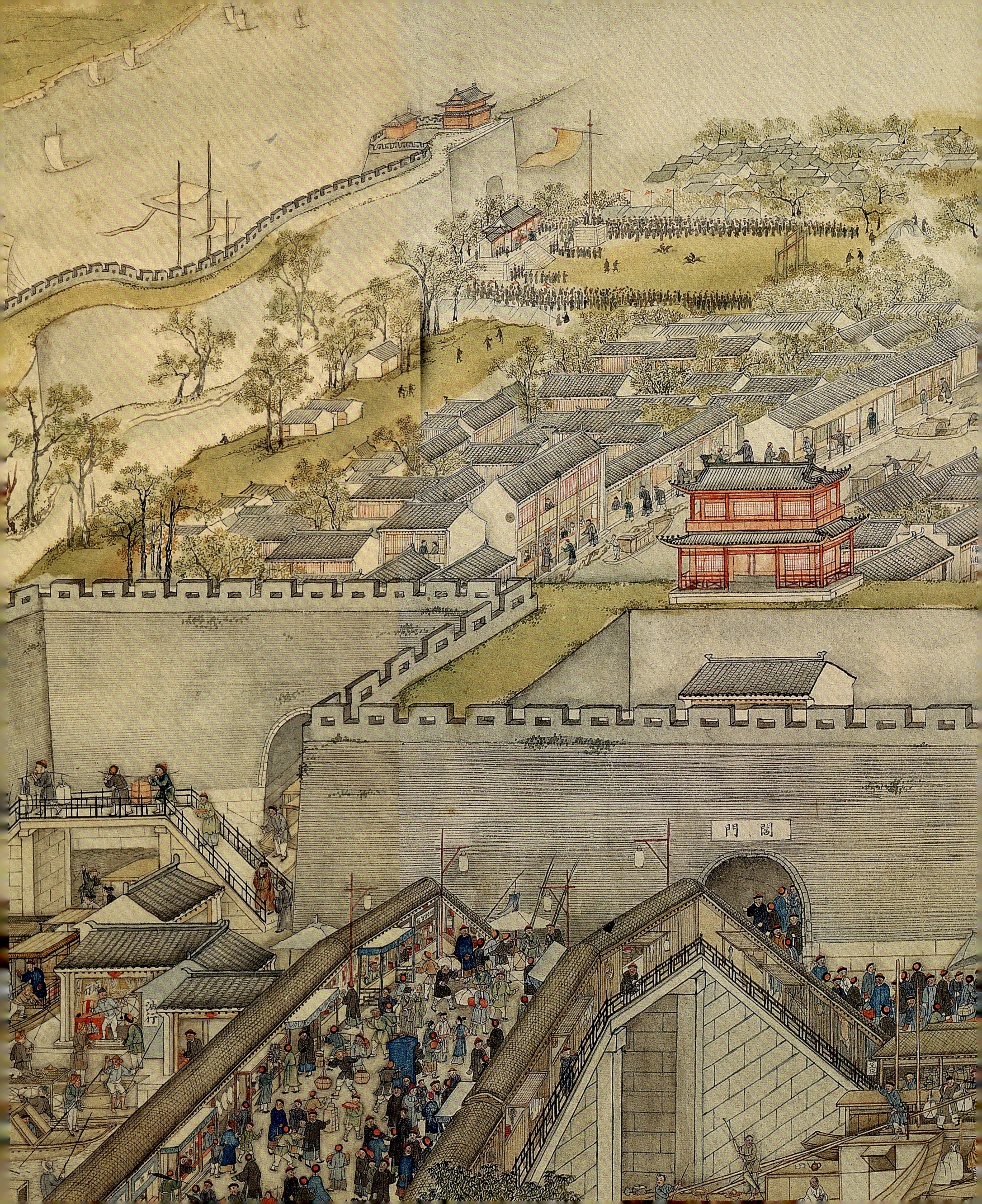
閶門
油行

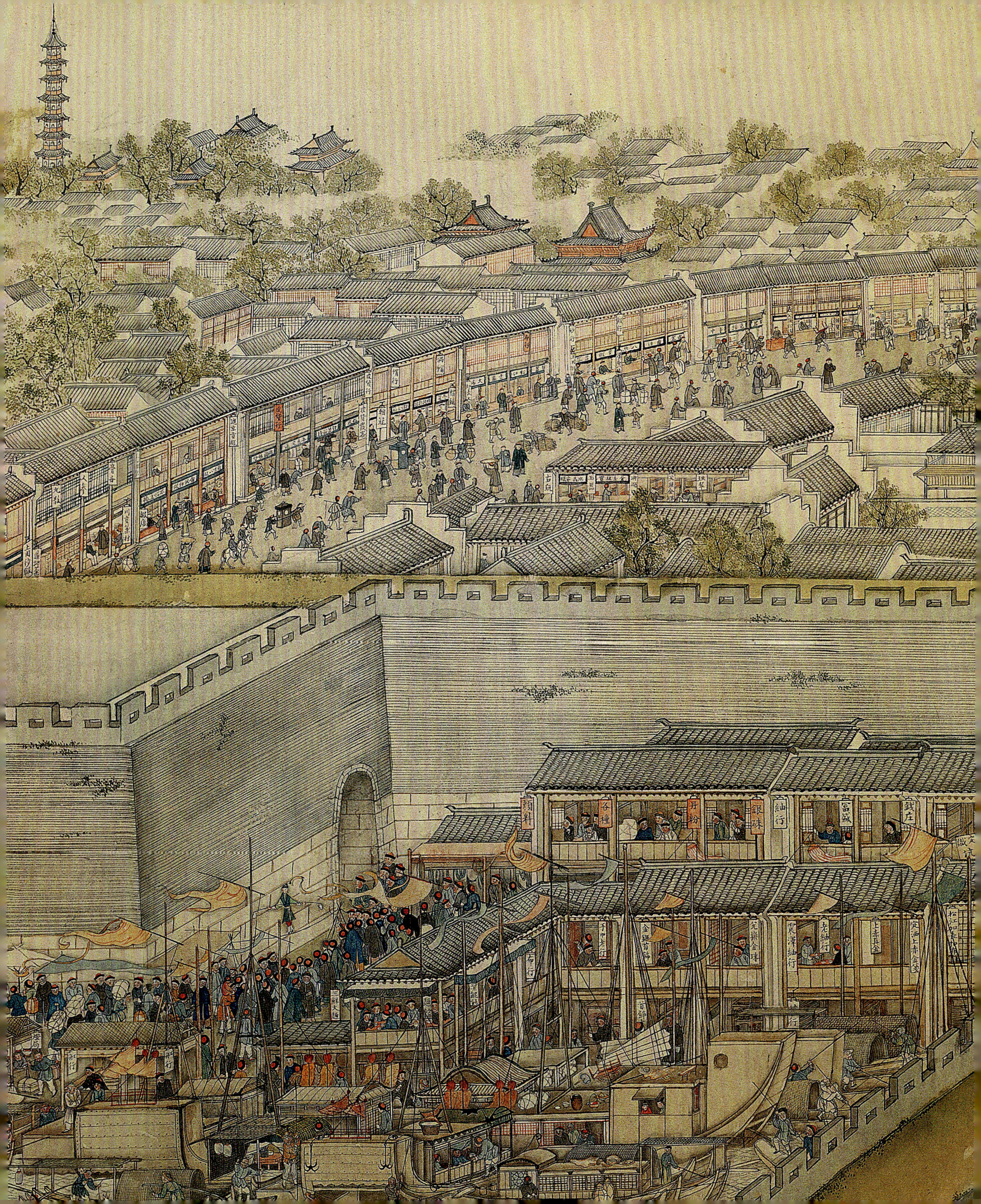

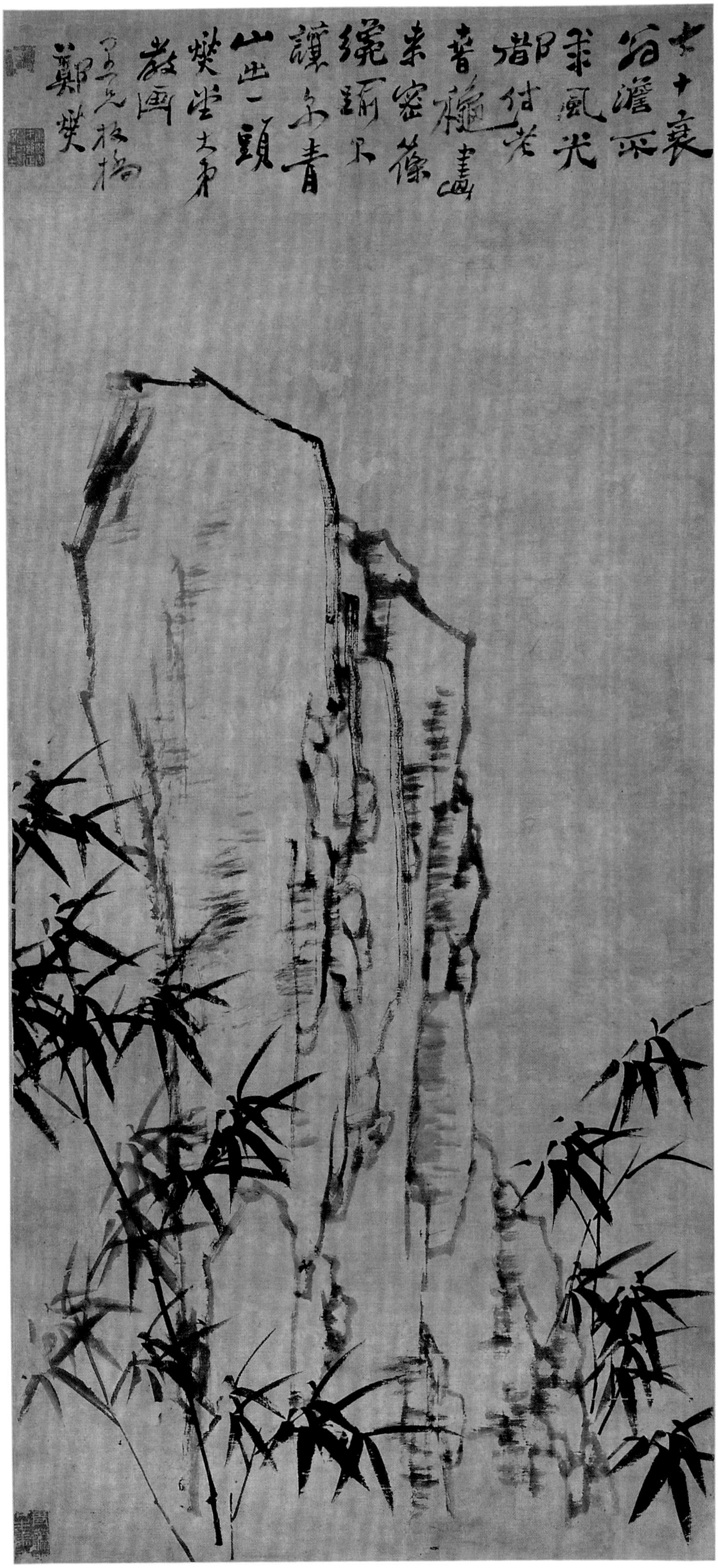

77

ZHENG XIE (1693–1765)

## Bamboo and Rock

清 鄭燮 竹石圖 軸

c.1762, hanging scroll, ink on paper, 170 × 79 cm
Museum of Asian Art, Berlin (NR 5335)

PROVENANCE

Purchased in 1927 in Tianjin from Zhang Zhitan (1883–1946)

REFERENCE LITERATURE

Ledderose 1998, pp. 233–7, no. 31; Pohl 1990; Zhou 1996

Zheng Xie, better known by his literary name Banqiao, came from a scholarly family in Xinghua, Jiangsu Province. In 1711, he passed the lowest of the three imperial examinations, and around the same time befriended the painter Li Shan (1686–1762), who became one of his artistic mentors. In 1714 he moved to Yangzhou, one of the commercial and artistic centres of eighteenth-century China. He lived a bohemian life and frequented the entertainment quarters of the city, but at the same time made a name as a poet, calligrapher and painter. He greatly admired, and was influenced by, Xu Wei (1521–93) and Shitao (1642–1707), two of the most famous individualist masters of the past. However, hardly any of Zheng's works from this early period have survived. In his late 30s, Zheng returned to Confucian studies, passing the provincial examination in 1732 and the metropolitan examination in 1736. From 1742, he worked as a district magistrate in Shandong Province. In 1746–7, during his tenure, he had to cope with a great famine, which made him feel ill prepared and powerless, as he expressed in his writings more than once. In 1753, at the age of 60, he retired as an official and returned to Yangzhou, resuming his life as a famous and eccentric painter – perhaps the most famous of a group of loosely related artists with close ties to this city that since the late nineteenth century have been labelled the 'Eight Eccentrics of Yangzhou'. He rarely painted anything other than depictions of bamboo, rocks and orchids in monochrome ink.

Painting bamboo has a long tradition in China. Since it bends but does not break it was regarded as a symbol for the Confucian scholar-official, and as in this painting, was often combined and contrasted with rock, signifying a solid pillar stone or minister. Zheng Xie knew the great masters of bamboo painting personally, and frequently commented on them in the inscriptions he wrote to his bamboo paintings, although he developed his own unique style. He consistently painted the leaves and stems in solid black and grey ink strokes, and never in the other prevalent style of bamboo painting, by tracing contour lines. He grew bamboo in his garden and made a lifelong study of the plant, observing that the bamboo's shadow fluttering on paper creates a natural painting, and that he received plenty of inspiration from its silhouette projected by the sun and moon on window paper and white-washed walls, without following any master.[1]

The calligraphic inscription added to this painting is in Zheng Xie's characteristic style, and combines characters in running, standard and archaic clerical scripts. It evidences Zheng's study of and admiration for early inscriptions as found on engraved stones from the second to the sixth century, and gives his writing a kind of ruggedness, quite different from mainstream calligraphy in the tradition of the fluent writing style of Wang Xizhi (303–65).

The 'big younger cousin' to whom the painting is dedicated in the inscription is very likely Zheng Mo, a son of a paternal uncle of Zheng Xie, 24 years his junior. Zheng Xie treated him like a son, and in the 1730s–40s wrote a series of 16 family letters to him that have since become famous.

The three seals impressed by Zheng on his work all refer to his life and painting:

> I passed the first Imperial Examination in the Kangxi reign [1662–1722], the second in the Yongzheng reign [1722–36] and the third in the Qianlong reign [1736–96].
>
> Humble servant studying with the Wisteria Master, expressing his admiration for the painter Xu Wei, whose literary name was Qingteng
>
> How could I have achieved this through effort?

The last seal, expressing the Daoist view that a true work of art is created naturally and without effort, is supposed to have been carved by Zheng Xie himself.[2]

*Bamboo and Rock*, painted in or around 1762, is a highly representative work by Zheng Xie that combines his painting, calligraphy and seal carving. Zheng produced some of his works commercially; in fact, he is one of the literati painters to admit without embarrassment that he lived from selling his paintings. Over 20 similar paintings of bamboo with rock from the 12 years between 1754 and 1765 have been transmitted, and it is likely that he created many more. With its large format and fine inscription dedicated to a favourite cousin, however, this painting is certainly not the least significant of the group. KR

1 Pohl 1990, p. 140
2 Zhou 1996, p. 215

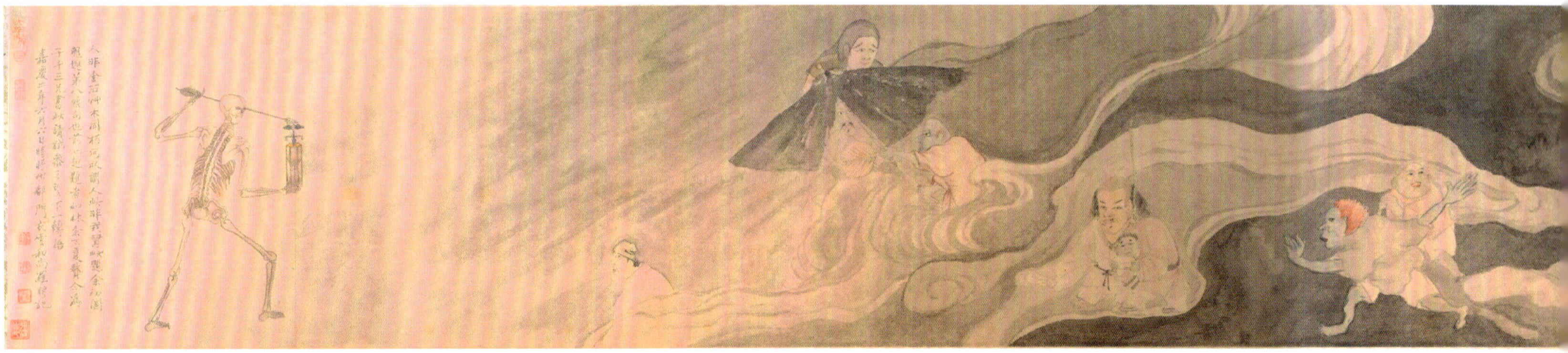

78

LUO PIN (1733–99)

## Ghost Amusement

清 羅聘 鬼趣圖 卷

1797, handscroll, ink and light colour on paper,
26.7 × 257.2 cm
Hong Kong Museum of Art
Xubaizhai Collection (XL 158)

REFERENCE LITERATURE

Hondius 1610; Hong Kong 1992; Wang and Zhou 1992; Chen 1993b; Zhang 1999; Hay 1999; Koon in New York 2009; Woodall 2012

The youngest representative of a group of leading scholar-painters loosely defined as the 'Eight Eccentrics of Yangzhou', Luo Pin specialized in a wide range of subjects, from figures to flowers, plants and scenery. He received numerous commissions for his work from wealthy merchants and officials, both in Yangzhou and in other places such as Beijing, where he spent many years. However, he also produced religious and other paintings with a moralizing theme. The present work belongs in the latter category.

*Ghost Amusement* was painted for an as yet unidentified patron in 1797 and derives its subject matter from an earlier and better-known scroll completed around 1766, which now belongs to the Reseel Fok Family Collection in Hong Kong. The Fok painting consists of eight pictures in varying sizes mounted as a handscroll. In order to imbue the forms of the ghosts with a sense of immateriality, Luo soaked the paper with water and painted while it was damp, causing the otherwise defined lines to bleed into ink washes. With the 1797 scroll, Luo integrated the individual pictures into a unified composition and employed swirls of dark mists and clouds to connect and at the same time divide them into different scenes. Other changes here include the more lineal approach, the extensive application of dark-toned ink washes for the background and above all, the reduction of the pair of skeletons facing one another in the final scene to a single animated skeleton, which thrusts an arrow across a taut cord connected to an hourglass held in its other hand.

Apart from the skeletons, almost all the ghosts were possibly drawn from earlier Chinese paintings, notably those depicting the Demon Queller Zhong Kui, a popular guardian figure since the Tang dynasty (618–907). Perhaps as a result of visits to local temples, Luo Pin came into contact with the images of ghosts in paintings used in the 'Water and Land' ritual, a Buddhist rite for the dead – his mentor Jin Nong (1687–1763) had also been interested in the subject. However, although Jin drew some supernatural beings in at least one of his albums, he never incorporated them into an entire composition. At any rate, Luo's works fascinated contemporary viewers, and indeed, together with Pu Songling's (1640–1715) literary masterpiece *Strange Stories from a Chinese Studio*, published also in 1766, triggered a 'ghost craze' in elite circles in the second half of the eighteenth century. Over the years, Luo's friends and later admirers wrote more than 160 colophons on the sheets following the paintings in the Fok scroll and continuing onto the borders of the mount surrounding the individual pictures. The 1797 scroll indicates that the infatuation persisted for more than three decades.

Yet, the later scroll was not intended to be a replica of the Fok version, as Luo's own inscription makes clear. The latter invites his patron (and the viewer today) to focus on and contemplate the morality of the final skeleton scene. Instead of the pair of skeletons,[1] Luo's new imagery is borrowed from *Pictorum aliquot celebrium, praecipué Germaniae inferioris, Effigies*, a pictorial history of eminent Netherlandish painters published by Hendrik Hondius the elder in 1610. Uncannily, Hondius's skeleton print is also the final image in the *Effigies*, where it is entitled 'Post Funera Vita' and bears an inscription stating:

> Pale Death attacks all. We have to obey it. No colour or honour is of any help here. For those who have lived well, there is LIFE AFTER BURIAL. [As for] those who have painted well, consider that they live in Death. A new life is set out in lifelike paintings: let each set out to be able to live after death.[2]

How did Luo Pin access Hondius's print? Did he see it as a single leaf or as part of an album? Was he aware of the art-historical nature of the book or the meaning of the print? The answer to these intriguing questions remains to be found. ZH

1 Jonathan Hay has traced its source to Andrea Vesalius's (1514–64) *De humani corporis fabrica* (1613). See Hay 1999, pp. 219–21.

2 The inscription is translated by Daniel Hadas. See www.courtauld.org.uk/netherlandishcanon/image-tombstone/72.html (accessed 12 November 2012).

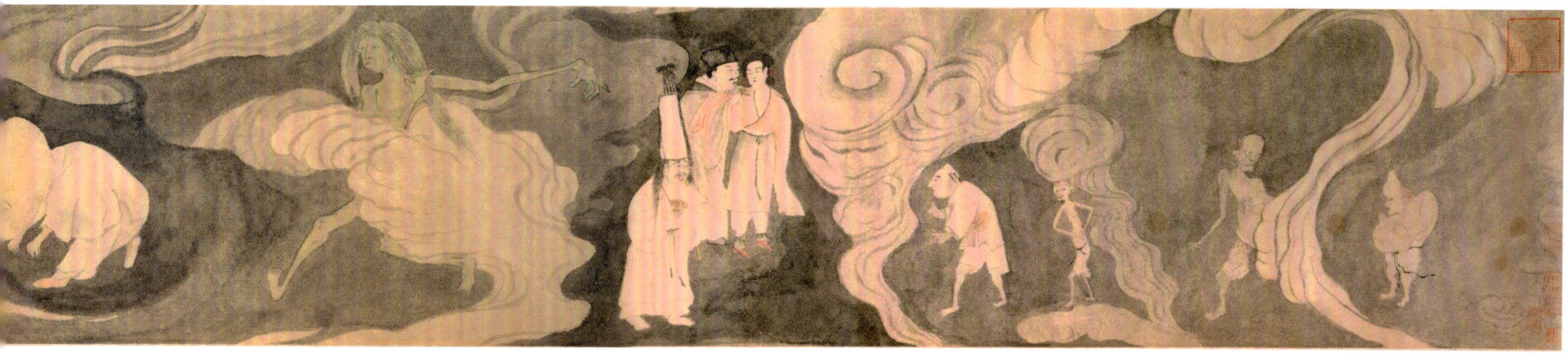

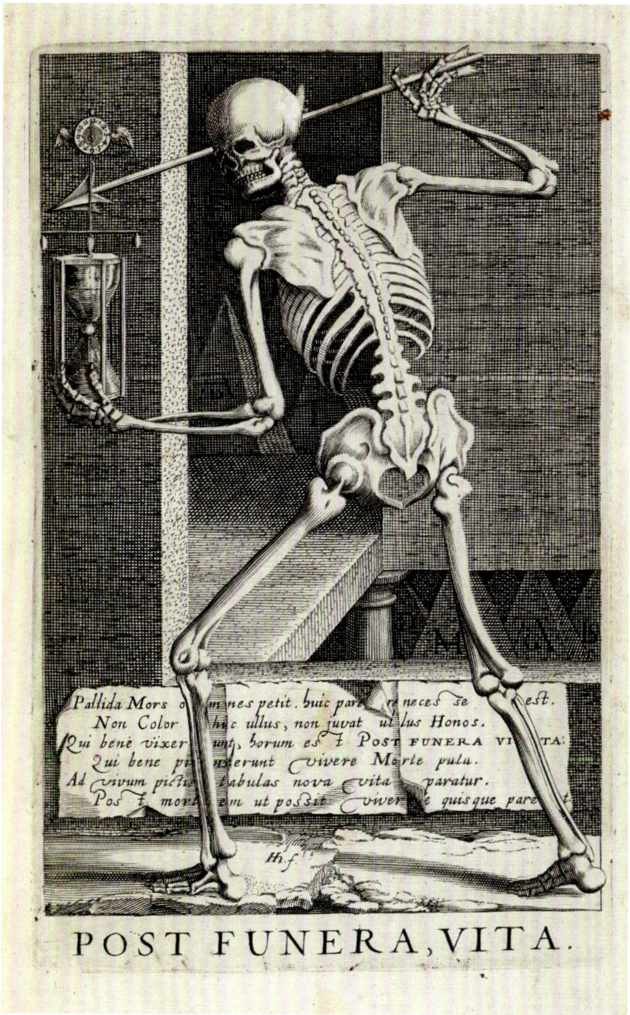


FIG. 64
Hendrik Hondius the elder (1573–1650).
*Post Funera Vita: After Burial, Life* engraving from *Pictorum aliquot celebrium praecipué Germaniae inferioris* (The Hague, 1610)

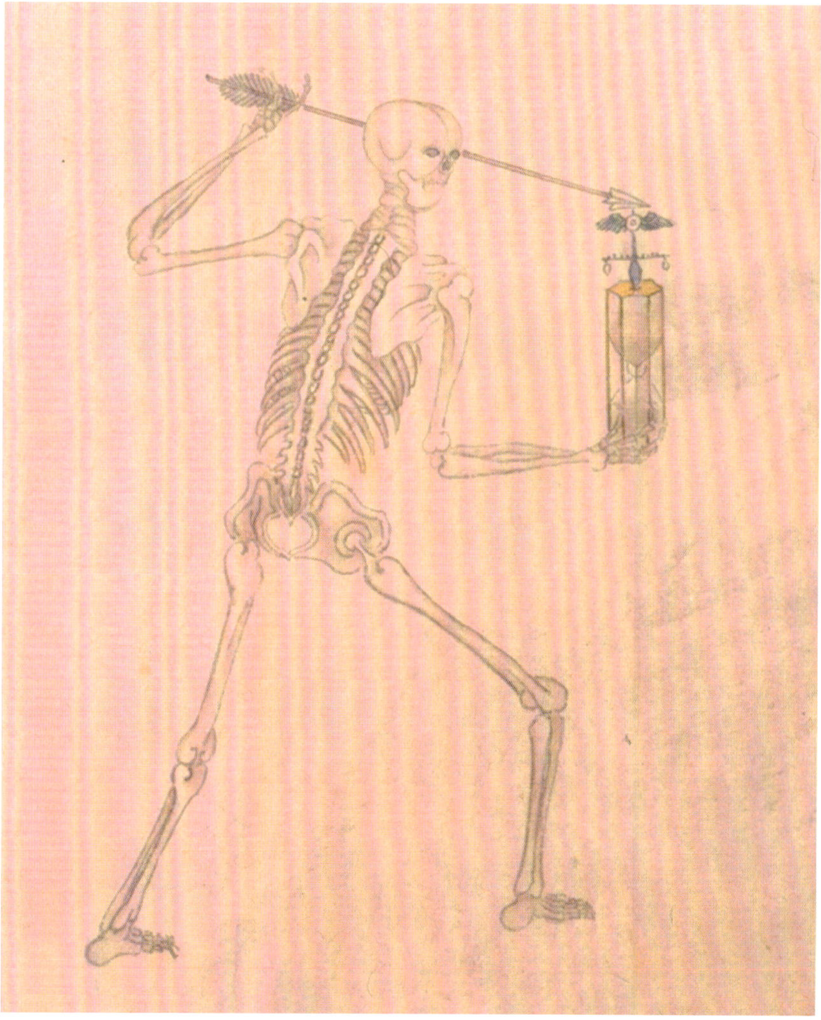

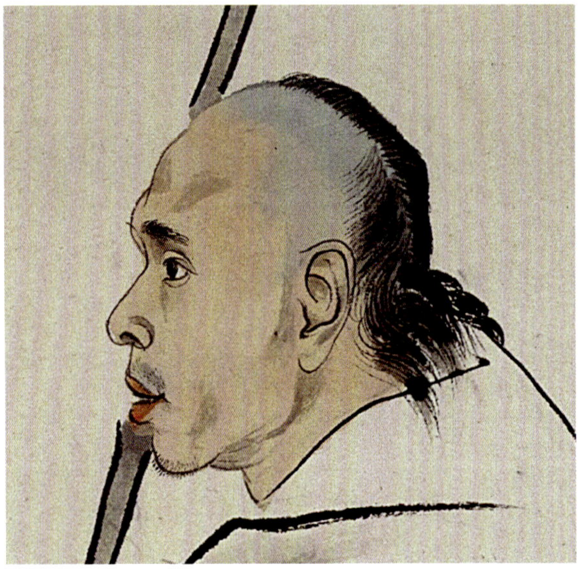

79

REN YI (1840–95)

## Portrait of Gao Yongzhi as Calligrapher-Beggar

清 任頤 高邕之像 軸

1887, hanging scroll, ink and light colour on paper, 129.4 × 48 cm
The Palace Museum, Beijing

REFERENCE LITERATURE

Wang (1875) 1969, pp. 136–7; Li 1978; Lee 1981; Gong 1982; Fu and Cai 1984; Xue 1987; Yang (1919) 1988; Ding 1989; Huang (1883) 1989; Vinograd 1992a, pp. 147–9; Xue 1994; Zhang 1994; Cahill 1995; Pan 1997, p. 173, no. 90; Chou 1998; Wue 2001; Lai 2005; Kuo 2007; Yang 2007; Yeh 2007; Yang 2009 and 2011

Ren Yi, more usually known as Ren Bonian, was born in Xiaoshan, Zhejiang Province. As a leading and successful professional painter in nineteenth-century Shanghai, Ren was a pioneer of the artistic direction of the Shanghai school, which was to cater for the new class of merchant patrons and international customers.

Portraits occupy a special place in Ren Bonian's oeuvre, and over time their number and range of expression increased, as did the emphasis on individualism, self-expression and attention to anatomy. In Huang Shiquan's (1852–1925) *Record of Dream Images from Songnan* of 1883, he speaks specifically of Ren Bonian's skill in portraiture: 'He uses a boneless technique to differentiate and highlight the face and countenance. From a distance, his portraits radiate health and vitality, as if alive. However, he keeps his skill secret; for those he does not know, he will not easily take up his brush.'[1] Ren is known to have made 41 portraits of his artist friends, whose names are found in the book *Ink Forest of Shanghai* and other contemporary records on art. His portraits of well-known artists not only give us a catalogue of those who were active in the Shanghai and Suzhou areas, but are also indicative of Ren's own prominent role in the art world of his time.

The sitter in this portrait, Gao Yongzhi, was born into a literary family in Hangzhou with a fine art collection, and was a well-regarded calligrapher and painter in Shanghai. In 1909, he founded the Yu Garden Charitable Association of Calligraphy and Painting there, with the aim of restoring the Chinese art tradition through the collective effort of the artists. Although Gao was ten years younger than Ren Bonian, his passion for Bada Shanren (1626–1705) was shared with Ren, and had a significant impact on the latter's art after they met in the late 1870s.

Gao Yongzhi was skilled at and fond of calligraphy, and called himself 'the calligrapher-beggar'. Thus when Ren portrayed Gao here, the painter boldly laughed at his best friend, casting him as a rather subdued beggar with unkempt hair, torn clothes and an open basket filled with brushes and ink stones. However, the emphasis on light and shading in Gao Yongzhi's face combines with the stark profile to create an effect of vivid presence and something of the representational power of a photographic likeness. Apart from works by missionary-painters in the imperial court in the eighteenth century, previously a full-face eye was used in informal portraits where the face was shown in profile; Ren Yi was the first to depict the eye from a side view.[2] The artist's naturalistic representation of Gao's features here thus indicates his awareness of Western-style painting.

As the biggest treaty port in late Qing dynasty (1644–1911) China, Shanghai was a commercial centre teeming with rich merchants, compradors and other foreign influences. The prosperous economy provided good employment opportunities, and appealed to those seeking fame and fortune. In this portrait of the artist as beggar, however, Ren presents a somewhat dark view of the position of the city's artists. CY

1 Huang (1883) 1989, pp. 102–3
2 Zhang 1994

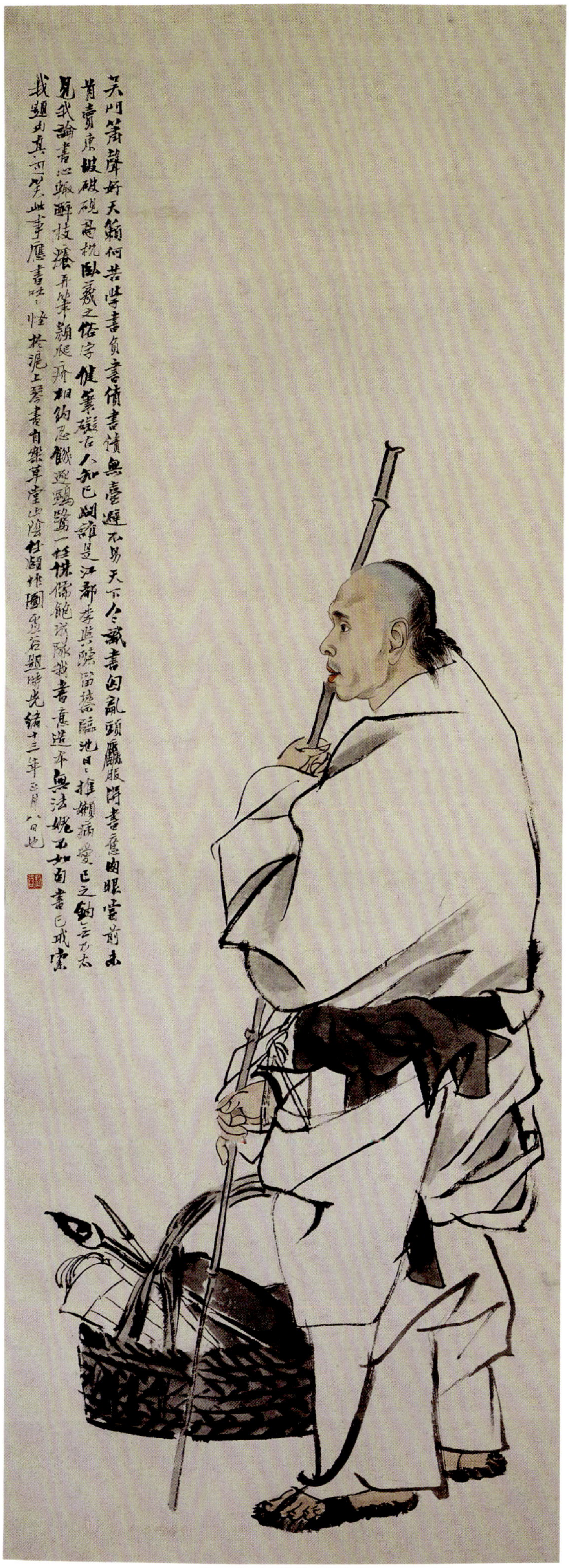

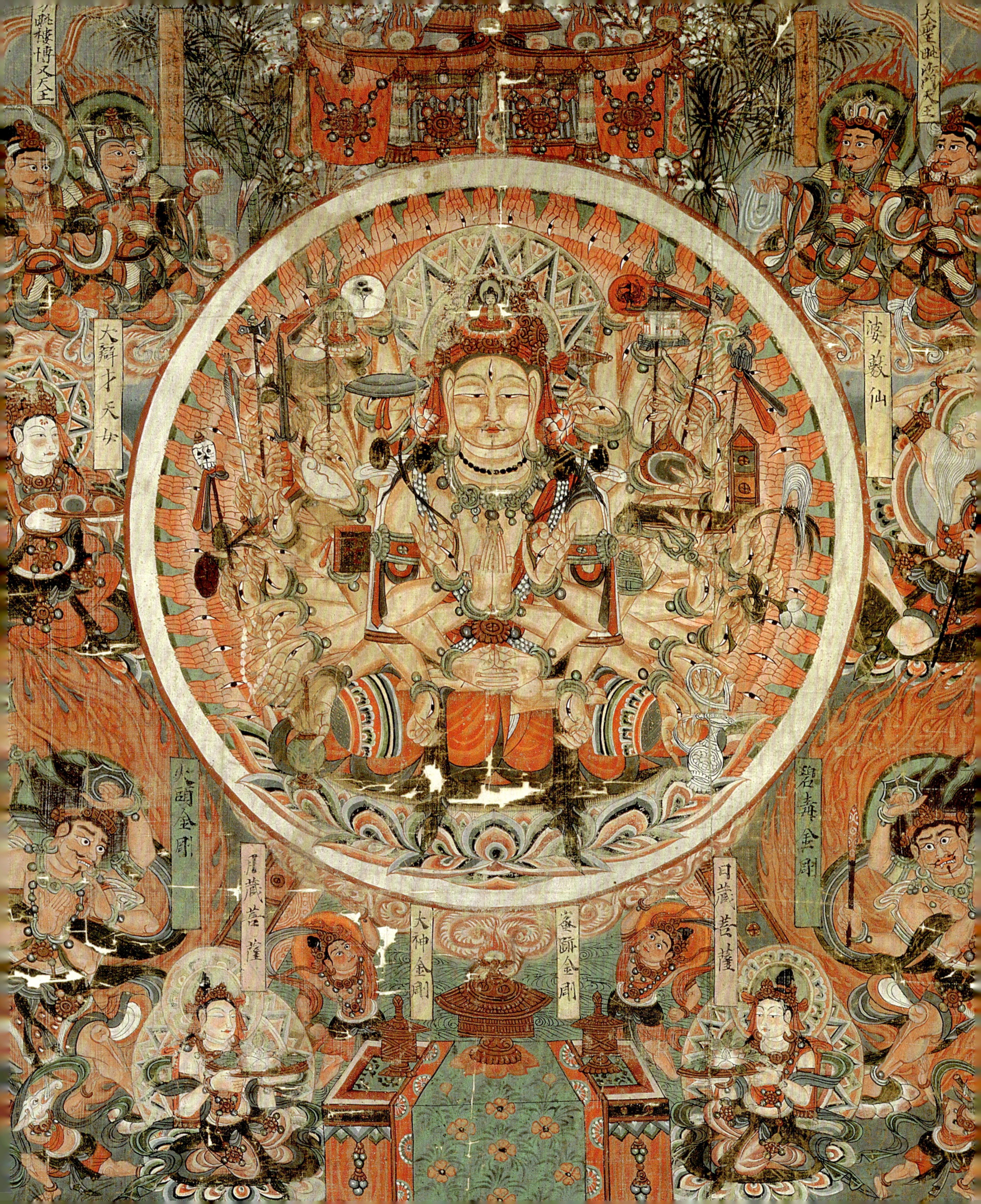
毗樓博叉天王
婆藪仙
火頭金剛
碧毒金剛
大神金剛
日藏菩薩

# APPENDIX

## INSCRIPTIONS, MARKS AND SEALS

Transcriptions by Lin Yi-hsin and Jennifer Wong, and edited by Zhang Hongxing, who also translated the texts unless noted otherwise. Information on collectors' colophons and seals provided by lending institutions.

### 4

UNIDENTIFIED ARTIST

**The Bodhisattva Dizang (Kṣitigarbha)**

Bodhisattva
菩薩

Given with all her heart by Zhang, wife, in the seventeenth year of the Kaiyuan reign [729]

妻張一心供養開元十七年

(Translation adapted from the work of Valérie Zaleski)

### 8

UNIDENTIFIED ARTIST

**Itinerant Monk Accompanied by a Tiger**

An image of the *tathāgata* Baosheng (Prabhūtaratna), painted on behalf of [my] deceased younger brother Zhiqiu on the occasion of the fast of the third period of seven days [after his death], and offered in his praise.

寶勝如來一軀。意為亡弟知球三七齋畫造慶讚供養

(Translation by Hero Friesen in collaboration with Roderick Whitfield, Giés 1996, vol. 3, p.152)

### 9

UNIDENTIFIED ARTIST

**Bodhisattva as Guide of Souls**

Bodhi[sattva] who leads the way

引路菩[薩]

(Translation by Roderick Whitfield)

### 12

UNIDENTIFIED ARTIST

**Guanyin of the Thousand Hands and Thousand Eyes**

(Order: right to left, top to bottom)

Vaiśravaṇa, the great saint, guardian king of the north
北方大聖毗沙門天王

Virūdhaka, guardian king of the west
西方毗樓勒叉天王

Dhṛtarāṣṭra, guardian king of the east
東方提頭賴叉天王

Virūpākṣa, guardian king of the south
南方毗樓博叉天王

The ascetic Vasu
婆藪仙

The goddess of eloquence (Sarasvatī)
大辯才天女

Blue Poison Vajra
碧毒金剛

Sun Receptacle (Sūryagarbha)
日藏菩薩

Secret Traces Vajra (Guhyapada)
密跡金剛

Great Deva Vajra
大神金剛

Moon Receptacle (Candragarbha)
月藏菩薩

Fire-Head Vajra
火頭金剛

*vināyaka*
毗那也歌

*vināyaka*
毗那耶歌

Water-Moon Avalokiteśvara
水月觀音

Those who would like to hunt treasures must go to the ocean; those who would like to excel precious goodness in their future life must sow seeds in the field of blessing. This is your devout disciple, steward of the Military Commissioner, Vice-Director for Transport, Grand Master for Glorious Happiness with Silver Seal and Blue Ribbon, and the Acting Adviser to the Heir Apparent, Ma Qianjin. I am dressed in scholar's robes, exposed to the influence of the ancient sages Yao and Shun, and fully prepared for creating this piece of writing. I have reviewed my past acts, and made new plans for my future, vowing to detest evil matters and refrain from other beliefs; work for the good causes and keep my own beliefs. In the first month of autumn, at the full moon [i.e. the fifteenth day of the seventh month, day of the *avalambana* the Buddhist festival of the dead], thinking with affection of my dear parents whose traces are become hard to see, I summoned a skilful artist. At the same time as he executed a funerary portrait [of my mother], I, with great respect, had him make a painting of the great compassionate bodhisattva Guanshiyin with his attendants, and also a painting of Guanyin of moon and water, in two panels. Guanyin saves people, protects the country, supports the fallen, and blesses those who have even committed crimes or lost their faith. Therefore, all those who come to pay respect adore him; they are able to recognize their wrong paths, and receive further protection. As the ceremony draws to its end, we all have accumulated his blessing for the three generations and avoided falling into the hell – together we are on the path towards the enlightenment. Written in the eighth year of Tianfu reign, *guimao* [943 AD], the thirteenth day of the seventh moon.

竊以求珎寶者，須投滄海，要來世之勝因者，須種福田。
厥有清信弟子、節度押 衙、知副後槽使、銀青(光)祿大夫、
撿校太子賓客馬千進，儒襟舜海，煦影堯曦，睹垂露以馳心，
想懸針而驛慮。是以修諸故事，創此新圖。憎惡業，遠誡他門，愛善
緣，近逼自戶。時遇初秋，白月團圓，憶戀慈親，難睹靈跡，遂召良工，
乃邈真影之間，敬畫大悲觀世音菩薩一驅并侍從，又畫水月觀音一軀
二鋪。觀音救民護國，濟拔沉淪，願罪棄倦之流，亦福祉之覆體。
遂使往來瞻禮，莫不傾心，顯悟迷途，暗增殊佑。慶讚將畢，
福資三世，不值泥黎，緣及有情，同超覺路。于時天福八年歲次癸卯
七月十三日題記。

Offered with a sincere heart [for my] deceased mother, *née* Zhang, *upāsikā* of the Sudden Awakening of the Mahayana from Sanjie Temple

亡妣三界寺大乘頓悟優[婆]姨阿張一心供養

(Part of the translation comes from work of Hero Friesen in collaboration with Roderick Whitfield, Giès 1996, vol. 3, pp. 93–4)

### 13

UNIDENTIFIED ARTIST; traditionally attributed to ZHANG SENGYOU (ACT. 490–540)

**The Five Planets and Twenty-eight Constellations**

Painting of the Divine Appearances of the Five Planets and Twenty-Eight Constellations

五星及廿八宿神形圖

Submitted by Court Gentleman Consultant, Administrative Aide of Longzhou, Expectant Official of the Academy of Scholarly Worthies and also Grand Astrologer Liang Lingzhan

奉義郎、龍州別駕、集賢院待制、仍太史梁令瓚上

Jupiter is heroic and righteous, and controls ruling authorities and benefits. His temple can be built near the imperial gates. Worship with white joss papers and silver utensils and offer white plants as food. Avoid polychromy and weeping. This planet represents righteous sovereignty.

歲星神，豪俠勢利。立廟可於君門，祭用白幣，器用銀，
食上 [尚] 白鮮。諱彩色，忌哭泣。歲星為君王。

cat. no. 12 (detail)

Mars ingests fire. Worship with raw meat and strong liquor. Use copper utensils and red joss papers, and kill animals to release blood [for offering]. The ceremonial implements are weapons, but use only after the drum dance. Avoid weeping and be benevolent [towards him]. Yinghuo is like a wilful and violent lordly prince. The temple of Mars can be built near military gates.

熒惑星神，食火。祭用血肉酒，器用赤銅，幣用赤，殺牲釁血，祭具戰器鼓舞，然後祭之。忌哭泣，善事。熒惑，嬌暴公子。熒惑廟可致[置]軍門。

Saturn resides in the palace of black fog and cloud. Offer [him] black sesame oil, vegetables and drinking water. Worship with black joss papers and iron utensils. Abstain from luxury and lechery. Saturn is like an imperial censor, and appropriate for [consulting] matters concerning water and earth. Erect his shrine next to an agricultural field or a small river islet.

鎮星神，以黑煙霧為宮。祭用烏麻油，蔬食，飲水，幣用故黑，器用鐵，戒在奢婬。鎮星是御史。宜水土事，立祠農疇水渚傍。

Venus should be worshipped with an assembly of female musicians. Use golden utensils and yellow joss papers [for offering]. Meat dishes may be presented, but avoid killing animals and weeping. The temple of Venus is like a women's palace in yellow. The temple is decorated in yellow, but also embellished with the five colours. Venus is like an imperial consort.

太白星神，祭用女樂，器用金，幣用黃，食用血肉，不殺牲，亦忌哭泣。太白廟女宮中黃，屋飾皆黃，仍被[披]五彩。太白，后妃也。

Mercury represents an official. She is knowledgeable of the conditions of the entire country, and is also adept at managing official papers, reading the almanac, performing administrative duties and delivering [documents], as well as enforcing law and order in society. Mercury serves [the office] in the daytime and is always in the vicinity of the Sun. Worship with bluish-green [materials]. Use jade utensils and bluish-green joss papers, and offer vegetables and fish. Her temple can be erected near the minister's residence, such as the Secretariat.

辰星神，功曹也。知天下，理文墨、曆術、典吏、傳送，執天下綱紀。辰星，白御也，常不離日。祭用碧，器用碧玉，幣用碧色，祭用蔬水類、〔魚屬〕。廟可致[置]於相府也，中書省是。

Painting of the Divine Appearances of the Twenty-Eight Constellations

二十八宿神形圖

Horn is wise and brave. He is optimistic and proficient in music and the almanac. His first name is Yunfang or Xianshuai, and surname is Chizhen.

角星神，聰睿勇智，受快樂，通律歷。名芸芳，弌[一]名先率，姓熾振。

Neck is honest and sincere. He is skilled in battle arrays. His name is Xianzhan.

亢星神，性淳，質清平，通於戰陣，名賢戰。

Root. His temple is ninety thousand miles [wide], which takes a long time to reach. His first name is Fenping and surname is Zhaiwei.

氐星神，廟有九萬里，通於數紀之會。名枌評，姓為翟衛。

Chamber is malevolent and tyrannical. He is lecherous and begot many children. He spreads demonic rumours and utters maledictions. Both human and non-human, as well as a man and woman, he is truly a hermaphrodite. His temple is more than one hundred thousand miles wide and has an eery and sinister atmosphere. His first name is Hansun and surname is Guanjijian.

房星神，性毒雄，多淫多子，妖訛咒咀，淫祀兩形，與丈夫婦人，更為雄雌。廟一十萬餘里，廟欹邪廣。名含孫，姓為管紀踐。

Heart has an extremely malevolent character. He is lecherous and begot many children. He spreads demonic rumours and utters maledictions. Both human and non-human, as well as a man and woman, he is truly a hermaphrodite. His temple is one hundred thousand miles wide and has an eery and sinister atmosphere. His first name is Zhaogui and surname is Fangguan.

心星神，性多毒，多淫多子，妖訛咒咀，淫祀兩形，與丈夫婦人，更為雄雌。廟十萬里，廟欹邪廣。名招貴，姓房館。

Tail can impeach all gods without being impeached by them. His first name is Kaidang and surname is Zhangsi.

尾星神，能刻[劾]眾神，而不受眾神刻[劾]。名闓當，姓為張兕。

Winnowing-basket howls like a female tiger. He never submits to human beings and uses his power only to hurt all beings [on earth]. He is skilled in warfare. His first name is Shichang and surname is Tan. Note: Tu could be Tu.

箕星神，吼如母大蟲，不受人制，獨用能害物，通於兵。名士常，姓為談，注云：土或為吐。

Dipper can control yin and yang. The size of his temple is uncertain. His first name is Zhuang □ and surname is Judu.

斗星神，能起伏陰陽，其廟無定準里數。名狀□，姓拒堵。

Ox is skilled in curing many diseases. He offers divinations with malicious flattery. He often performs fortune-telling irresponsibly, and uses blandishment to persuade people. His first name is Lüexuchi and surname is Juanxu.

牛星神，善醫多病，受占候陰陽諂邪，妄說禍福，能以諂辭扇動人。名略緒熾，姓蠲徐。

Woman is lascivious, covetous and calumnious, but skilled in curing many diseases. She offers divinations with malicious flattery. She often performs fortune-telling irresponsibly, and uses blandishment to persuade people. Her temple is 56 thousand miles wide. Her first name is Seshu.

女星神，淫亂貪讒，善醫多病。受占候陰陽諂邪，妄說禍福，能以諂辭扇動人。廟廣五萬六千里。名為色舒。

Emptiness understands the calendrical systems and mathematics. His first name is Kaiyang and surname is Mingpijiang.

虛星神，明歷術。名闓陽，姓明辟疆。

Rooftop is fond of weeping. Opinionated and righteous, he likes chaos and carnage. His temple is 56 thousand miles wide. His first name is Tuichang and surname is Lüjiasheng.

危星神，好哭泣，剛腹嫉惡，好亂好殺，廟廣五萬六千里，名推長，姓呂賈生。

Inscription by an unidentified author (after 1744); seals by Emperor Huizong 徽宗 (r. 1101–25); colophon (dated 1636) and seals by Dong Qichang 董其昌 (1555–1636); colophon and seals by Chen Jiru 陳繼儒 (1558–1639); seals by Liang Qingbiao 梁清標 (1620–91); colophon and seal by An Qi 安岐 (1683–1742); seal by Prince Zheng, Wuergonga 烏爾恭阿 (d.1846); seals by Wanyan Jingxian 完顏景賢 (1875–1931); unidentified seals; illegible seals

## 14

UNIDENTIFIED ARTIST; traditionally attributed to LI CHENG (919–67) and WANG XIAO (act. 1st half 10th century)

### Reading the Memorial Stele

Figures [by] Wang Xiao; trees and rocks [by] Li Cheng

王曉人物，李成樹石

Inscription by the artists; seal by Sun Chengze 孫承澤 (1592–1676); seals by Liang Qingbiao 梁清標 (1620–91); seals by An Qi 安岐 (1683–1742); seals by the Qianlong emperor 乾隆 (r. 1736–96); seals by Yun Li 允禮 (1697–1738); seal by Li Zuoxian 李佐賢 (1807–76); unidentified seals

## 15

POSSIBLY YAN WENGUI (967–1030)

### Landscape with Pavilions

Secretary of □ Prefecture [and] Treasurer of □ Yun County Yan Wengui □

待詔□州□筠縣主簿燕文貴□

Frontispiece, colophon and seal by Fu Shan 傅山 (1607–84); title and seal by Nagao Kō 長尾甲 (1864–1942); seals by Zhao Zizhou 趙子晝 (1089–1142); colophon and seals by Yang Sisheng 楊思聖 (1617–61); colophon (dated 1663) and seal by Yin Yue 殷岳 (1603–70); colophons (dated 1893 and 1901) and seals by Li Zaixian 李在銑 (act. late 19th–early 20th century); colophon (dated 1893) and seal by Weng Tonghe 翁同龢 (1830–1904); colophon (dated 1897) and seals by Sun Yuwen 孫毓汶 (1833–99); colophons (dated 1910 and 1911) and seals by Wanyan Jingxian 完顏景賢 (1875–1931); seals by Guo Weimin 郭衛民 (dates unknown); unidentified seals; illegible seals

## 16

POSSIBLY EMPEROR HUIZONG (1082–1135; r. 1101–25)

### Court Ladies Preparing Newly Woven silk

Label strip, colophon (dated 1898) and seals by Luo Wenbin 羅文彬 (1845–1903); title and seals by Emperor Zhangzong 章宗 (r. 1190–1208); colophon and seal by Zhang Shen 張紳 (act. 14th century); title, colophons (dated 1697 and 1699) and seals by Gao Shiqi 高士奇 (1645–1703); seal by Jin Futing 金黼廷 (act. 1st half 19th century); unidentified seals

## 17

POSSIBLY EMPEROR HUIZONG (1082–1135; r. 1101–25)

### Auspicious Cranes

On the evening of the day after *shangyuan*, in the *renchen* year of the Zhenghe reign [1112], suddenly auspicious clouds coalesced and descended over the Duanmen [palace gate], illuminating it. Every one of those assembled raised his head to gaze at them. Suddenly, a flock of cranes appeared, flying and calling in the sky. There were two cranes that came to rest, face-to-face, at the tips of the owl-tails [roof ridge-end ornaments], entirely at ease and composed. The others all wheeled in the sky, as if according to a set rhythm. Among the residents of the capital city moving to and fro, there was none who did not bow down and gaze up in reverence and sigh in wonder over this marvel at length. For a time the cranes did not disperse, but then they zigzagged back to the north-west and scattered. Moved by this auspicious sign, I therefore made this poem to record its particulars:

政和壬辰上元之次夕，忽有祥雲拂鬱，低映端門，眾皆仰而視之。
倏有群鶴飛鳴於空中，仍有二鶴，對止於鴟尾之端，頗甚閑適，
餘皆翺翔，如應奏節。往來都民，無不稽首瞻望，嘆異久之。
經時不散，迤邐歸飛西北隅散。感茲祥瑞故作詩以紀其實：

Just as the sky grows light, rainbow-hued clouds brush the [palace watchtower's] roof ridge.
Immortal birds, proclaiming good auspices, suddenly come with their measured gambolling [into the court].
Soaring windborne, truly companions of the Three Mountains (Isles of Immortality),
Two by two, they present in review their venerable, noble forms.
They seem to be imitating the blue *luan* [phoenix-like mythical birds with five-coloured feathers] that roosted atop the jewelled halls,
Could they be the like of the (auspicious) red geese that gathered at Heaven's Pond?
Lingering, they sound their pure and limpid calls and face the cinnabar watchtower [of the Emperor's palace residence],
Therefore [having witnessed all of this], the ignorant and unsure are brought to certainty.

Imperially composed, imperially painted and written. [Cipher:] First Man Under Heaven.

清曉觚稜拂彩霓，仙禽告瑞忽來儀。
飄飄元是三山侶，兩兩還呈千歲姿。
似擬碧鸞棲寶閣，豈同赤雁集天池。
徘徊嘹唳當丹闕，故使憧憧庶俗知。

御製御畫並書"天下一人"簽押

Inscription and seal by the artist; colophon and seals by monk Laifu 釋來復 (1319–91); seal by Hu Xingjian 胡行簡 (*jinshi* 1342); seal by Xiang Yuanbian 項元汴 (1525–90); seals by the Qianlong emperor 乾隆 (r. 1736–96); seal by the Jiaqing emperor 嘉慶 (r. 1796–1820); seal by the Xuantong emperor 宣統 (r. 1908–11); seal by the Dongbei Museum 東北博物館 (1949–59) [now the Liaoning Provincial Museum]; unidentified seal

(Translation adapted from the work of Maggie Bickford, Ebrey and Bickford 2006, pp. 461–2, with reference to Sturman 1990, p. 33)

## 18

MI YOUREN (1074–1151/1086–1165)

### Cloudy Mountains

Label strip and seal by Wu Hufan 吳湖帆 (1894–1968); colophon (dated 1200) by Wang Yisun 王沂孫 (*c.*1230–*c.*1291); colophon (dated 1290) and seals by Xianyu Shu 鮮于樞 (1246–1302); colophon and seal by Guo Tianxi 郭天錫 (1244–1302); colophon (dated 1437) and seals by Fang Mian 方勉 (act. mid-15th century); colophon (dated 1438) and seal by Song Zheng 宋拯 (act. mid-15th century); seal by Lu You 陸友 (act. *c.*1280–1340); seals by Liang Qingbiao 梁清標 (1620–91); seals by the Qianlong emperor 乾隆 (r. 1736–96); seals by the Jiaqing emperor 嘉慶 (r. 1796–1820); seals by the Xuantong emperor 宣統 (r. 1908–11); seals by Wang Jiqian 王季遷 [C.C. Wang] (1906–2002); seal by Xu Bangda 徐邦達 (1911–2012); unidentified seals; illegible seals

## 19

QIAO ZHONGCHANG (act. late 11th – early 12th century)

### Illustration to the Second Prose Poem on the Red Cliff

On the fifteenth of the tenth lunar month of the same year [1082] I set out on foot from Snow Hall, intending to return to Lin'gao. Two guests accompanied me as we passed Yellow Dirt Hill. Dew had fallen, and the trees had shed all their leaves. Our shadows lay on the ground, and we gazed up at the bright moon. Delighted by our surroundings, we sang back and forth to teach each other as we walked. After some time, however, I heaved a sigh: 'I have guests but no wine; and even if I had wine, I have no food to go with it. The moon is bright and the wind fresh. Are we going to waste such a fine evening as this?' One of my guests said: 'Today at sunset I caught a fish in my net. It has a large mouth and tiny scales, and looks just like a Song River bass. But where can we get wine to go with it?'

是歲十月之望，步自雪堂，將歸於臨皋。二客從予，過黃泥之坂。
霜露既降，木葉盡脫，人影在地，仰見明月，顧而樂之，行歌相答。
已而嘆曰：「有客無酒，有酒無肴，月白風清，
如此良夜何！」客曰：「今者薄暮，舉網得魚，巨口細鱗，
狀如松江之鱸。顧安所得酒乎？」

We returned to my house and consulted my wife. She said: 'We do have one jug of wine I hid away, keeping it for just such an emergency.' Taking the wine and the fish . . .

歸而謀諸婦。婦曰：「我有斗酒，藏之久矣，以待子不
時之須。」於是攜酒與魚，

. . . we went boating again below the Red Cliff. The river made a noise as it flowed, and the sheer cliff rose a thousand feet. The peak was towering and the moon tiny. The water level had fallen, and the rocks on the bottom were exposed. How many months had it been since my last visit? And yet the landscape seemed completely unfamiliar to me.

復遊於赤壁之下。江流有声，斷岸千尺；山高月小，水落石出。
曾日月之幾何，而江山不可復識矣。

So thinking, I picked up my robe and began to climb. I stepped over jutting rocks, pushed back undergrowth . . .

予乃攝衣而上，履巉岩，披蒙茸，

. . . squatted on tigers and leopards . . .

踞虎豹，

. . . and climbed along scaly dragons until I could pull myself up to the perilous nests of the hawks and look down into the River Lord's palace in the depths. My two guests were quite unable to follow me. All at once I let out a long, low whistle. The trees and grasses shook; the mountains sang out and the valleys answered; a wind arose and the water surged. I grew apprehensive and melancholy, humbled and fearful, and felt so cold that I knew I could not remain there long.

登虬龍，攀栖鶻之危巢，俯馮夷之幽宮。蓋二客不能從焉。
劃然長嘯，草木震動，山鳴谷應，風起水湧。予亦悄然而悲，
肅然而恐，凜乎其不可留也。

I climbed down and got back into the boat. We rowed out into the middle of river, then let the boat drift freely about and come to rest wherever it would. By that time it was nearly midnight and there was no sign of life anywhere around us. Just then a lone crane appeared, cutting across the river from the east. Its wings were as big as cartwheels, and it wore a black skirt and white robe. It let out a long, grating cry and swooped down over our boat before continuing westward.

反而登舟，放乎中流，聽其所止而休焉。時夜將半，四顧寂寥。適有
孤鶴，橫江東來。翅如車輪，玄裳縞衣，戛然長鳴，掠予舟而西也。

A short while later the guests departed, and I, too, went home to sleep. I dreamed of a Daoist dressed in a fluttering feather robe who passed before Lin'gao. He bowed to me and said: 'Did you enjoy your outing to the Red Cliff?' I asked his name, but he lowered his gaze and made no reply. 'So! Aha!' I said. 'Now I understand. Last night it was you who flew screeching over my boat, wasn't it?' The Daoist turned away with a smile . . .

須臾客去，予亦就睡。夢二道士，羽衣翩僊，過臨皋之下，揖予而
言曰：「赤壁之遊樂乎？」問其姓名，俛而不答。「嗚呼！噫嘻！
我知之矣。疇昔之夜，飛鳴而過我者，非子也耶？」道士顧笑，

. . . and just at that moment I woke up. I opened the door to look, but he was nowhere in sight.
予亦驚寤。開戶視之，不見其處。

Inscription by the artist; colophon (dated 1123) by Zhao Lingzhi 趙令畤 [Zhao Delin 趙德麟] (1061–1134); colophon by Wu Andao 武安道 (dates unknown); seals by Liang Shicheng 梁師成 (*c.*1063–1126); seals by Liang Qingbiao 梁清標 (1620–91); seal by the Jiaqing emperor 嘉慶 (r. 1796–1820); seals by the Xuantong emperor 宣統 (r. 1908–11); seals by John M. Crawford, Jr. 顧洛阜 (1913–88)

(Translation adapted from the work of Ronald Egan, Egan 1994, pp. 245–6)

## 20

HU SHUNCHEN (act. early 12th century)

### Farewell to Hao Xuanming, Envoy to Qin

Groves of cassia are 'Summoning the Recluse',
You could compose [a song of] 'Roaming Far'.
Green maples begin to show crimson,
The white dew is just right for autumn.
Floating clouds above jade peaks become twilit,
While majestic mists retreat at the Qin frontier pass.
Moved by separation, I give you this painting –
And in my desolation, I climb the heights.

On the second day of the ninth month in the fourth year [1122] of the *Xuanhe reign-period* [1119–26], [He] Xuanming *Dacan* has received the assignment of envoy to Qin [Shaanxi]; and I have made this to commemorate his departure – [signed] Hu Shunchen.

叢桂方招隱，君猶賦遠遊。
青楓初試絳，白露正宜秋。
玉疊浮雲暮，秦關正氣收。
離情付圖畫，悵我一登樓。

宣和四年九月二日，玄明大參有使秦之命，作此紀別，胡舜臣

Inscription by the artist; colophon by Cai Jing 蔡京 (1047–1126); colophon (dated 1344) by Wu Rui 吳睿 (1298–1355); colophon (dated by 1484) and seals by Shen Zhou 沈周 (1427–1509); seals by Tao Cheng 陶成 (act. Ming dynasty [1368–1644]); 6 seals by Xiang Yuanbian 項元汴 (1525–90); colophon and seal by Liu Yong 劉墉 (1719–1814); colophon and seals by Weng Fanggang 翁方綱 (1733–1818); colophon (dated 1804) and seals by Qian Yue 錢樾 (1743–1815); colophon (dated 1805) and seal by Zhang Wentao 張問陶 (1764–1814); colophon (dated 1805) and seal by Zhou Houyuan 周厚轅 (act. Qing dynasty [1644–1911]); colophons (dated 1809 and 1834) and seals by Wu Rongguang 吳榮光 (1773–1843); seal by Cai Zhiding 蔡之定 (1748–1834); seal by Yi Bingshou 伊秉綬 (1754–1815); unidentified seals

(Translation by Elizabeth Brotherton, Brotherton 2000/2001)

21
LI GONGNIAN (act. early 12th century)
**Winter Evening Landscape**

Gongnian

公年

Inscription and traces of seal by the artist; seals by Lu Xingzhi 陸行直 (1275–after 1349); seal by Wang Xianchen 王献臣 (1473–c.1543); seal by DuBois Schanck Morris (1873–1956); damaged seal

22
UNIDENTIFIED ARTIST; traditionally attributed to ZHU RUI (act. 1st half 12th century) or a follower
**Bullock Carts Travelling over Rivers and Mountains**

Painted respectfully by Your Subject Zhu Rui

臣朱銳恭畫

Apocryphal inscription by Zhu Rui 朱銳 (act. 1st half 12th century); seal by Prince Yi, Hongxiao 弘曉 (1722–78); seal by Ye Menglong 葉夢龍 (1775–1832); seal by Liang Qingbiao 梁清標 (1620–91); colophon (dated 1825) and seal (on reverse) by Lu Kun 盧坤 (1772–1835); unidentified seal

(Translation by Nancy Berliner)

23
ZHOU JICHANG (act. 2nd half 12th century)
**Luohans Bestowing Alms on Suffering Human Beings**

[Previously from] Jinghai County in Tongzhou and now living at Tingchuan Bridge in Fenghuang Village, Wu County in Pingjiang Prefecture, the Buddhist Gao Zhiwen donated his wealth to commission this sacred image for the Hui'an Temple of Ming Prefecture. [He wishes] to accumulate merit and virtues for his deceased grandfather Digong, grandmother Xu and father Site ... [so that] they can become saints and achieve Buddhahood. On the fifteenth day of the twelfth lunar month, in the *jiachen* year of the Chunxi reign [1184], [written by] the Buddhist monk Yishao and painted by Zhou Jichang

通州靜海縣寄居平江府吳縣鳳凰鄉艇舡橋居住弟子高之問, 捨財置此聖幀, 入明州惠安院常住, 供養功德, 伏用追薦, 亡祖迪功、亡祖母許氏、亡考四特, 奏□□□□□□□□後心, 願成聖□, 同登佛果, 淳熙甲辰季冬望日題, 幹僧義紹周季常筆

24
ZHOU JICHANG (act. 2nd half 12th century)
**Luohans in a Bamboo Grove Receiving Offerings**

Living in Lushan at Yangtang Village, the female Buddhist Ye Nianqiniang and the male [Buddhist] Bao Anli donated their wealth to commission this [painting] for the Hui'an Temple, in order to help accumulate merit and virtues so as to complete acts of faith until satisfaction. In the *gengzi* year, also the seventh year of the Chunxi reign [1180], written by the Buddhist monk Yishao and painted by Zhou Jichang

陽堂鄉鹿山保住女弟子葉氏廿七娘、□□□男包安禮等施財此入惠安院, 常住供養功德, 隨心圓滿, 庚子淳熙七年, 幹僧義紹書, 周季常筆

25
UNIDENTIFIED ARTIST; traditionally attributed to HU GUI (act. c.907–c.960)
**Qidan (Khitan) Falconer with Horse**

Seal by Mu Ang 沐昂 (1379–1445); seal by Wanyan Jingxian 完顏景賢 (1875–1931)

26
UNIDENTIFIED ARTIST
**Travelling Caravan in Snow**

□ Dong

□東

Inscription by the artist

27
MA YUAN (act. late 12th–early 13th century)
**Bare Willows and Distant Mountains**

Ma Yuan
馬遠

Inscription by the artist (partly damaged); seals by Xiang Yuanbian 項元汴 (1525–90)

28, 29
XIA GUI (act. 1180–1230)
**Sailboat in Rainstorm**

Xia Gui

夏圭

Inscription by the artist; seal by Mu Ang 沐昂 (1379–1445); seal by Wanyan Jingxian 完顏景賢 (1875–1931)

EMPEROR XIAOZONG (1127–94; r. 1163–89)
**Calligraphy of Poem by Su Shi in Semi-cursive and Regular Scripts**

The ceaseless river rain always lulls me to sleep,
Winds beat the cliffs all day to move my boat along.

平生睡足連江雨, 盡日舟行擘岸風。

Inscription and seal by the artist; inscription possibly by Ruan Yuan 阮元 (1764–1849); seal by Mu Ang 沐昂 (1379–1445); seal by Wanyan Jingxian 完顏景賢 (1875–1931)

(Translation by Wu Tung, Boston 1997, p. 178)

31
EMPEROR LIZONG (1205–64; r. 1225–64)
**Poem by Huangfu Ran in Regular Script**

Still I yearn to see my parents in every crowd.
Here, white clouds always touch the eastern mountains.
Sitting alone, I burn incense and recite sutras.
The mountain is deep; the temple, ancient; and snow, everywhere.

戀親時見在人羣, 多在東山就白雲。
獨坐焚香誦經處, 深山古寺雪紛紛。

Inscription and seals by the artist; seal by Ruan Yuan 阮元 (1764–1849); seal by Wanyan Jingxian 完顏景賢 (1875–1931)

(Translation by Wu Tung, Boston 1997, p. 182)

32
UNIDENTIFIED ARTIST; traditionally attributed to FAN KUAN (act. c.990–1030)
**Temple among Snowy Hills**

Label strip by an unidentified author; seal by Emperor Wenzong 文宗 (r. 1328–29 and 1329–32); seals by Xiang Yuanbian 項元汴 (1525–90); seal by Zhang Xiaosi 張孝思 (act. early 17th century); seal by Wanyan Jingxian 完顏景賢 (1875–1931); damaged seal

33
POSSIBLY WU BING (act. late 12th–early 13th century)
**Bamboo Twig with Grasshopper**

Painted by Wu Bing

吳炳畫

Seal by Xiang Yuanbian 項元汴 (1525–90); seal by Wu Mouhe 吳懋和 (dates unknown); seal by Yu Teng 于騰 (1832–90); unidentified seals

34
UNIDENTIFIED ARTIST; traditionally attributed to ZHOU WENJU (act. 961–75)
**Child with His Pets in a Flower Garden**

Seal by Wanyan Jingxian 完顏景賢 (1875–1931)

37
LIU YUAN (act. 13th century)
**Sima Yu's Dream of the Courtesan Su Xiaoxiao**

Made by Liu Yuan of Pingshui [in] the Crafts Office, a disciple of Santang Wang

三堂王門人祗應司平水劉元製

Inscription and seal by the artist; colophon and seals by Yang Zhongying 楊重英 (d.1788); seal by Liu Ding (dates unknown); colophon and seals by Zhang Heng 張珩 (1915–63); unidentified seals; illegible seal

(Translation adapted from the work of Ellen Avril, Avril 1997, p. 60)

38
CHEN RONG (c.1189–c.1268)
**Nine Dragons**

The *Picture of Nine Dragons* was painted in the spring of the *jiachen* year [1244]. This scroll has come back into the possession of my son-in-law Xian Li. Does not a divinely inspired thing surely find its allotted place?

九龍圖作於甲辰之春, 此畫復歸於甥館仙李之家, 神物固有所屬耶

A real dragon stole a glance at the engraving at Chu;
In Jinling, two dragons flew away when the pupil of the eye was added.
When Zhuliang had already become an immoral, Zhang followed him;
How ashamed was Liu Dongwei when laughed at by the dragon couple!

The eight scrolls of Wu's dragon were not worth hanging.
When drunk I spit the painting from within.
And the waves of Longmen [the Dragon Gate] or of Sanxia [the Three Gorges] are like mountains,
Sending great roars from the depths into heaven.
The flying dragon appears from the gorge and flies toward the river of spring;
The force of Jiuhe [the Nine Rivers] does not subdue him.
A dragon is like a *ce mu* [Red-leaf] on the Tianchi [Pond of Heaven];
The fungus aroused the land of mist and cloud.
Again, the goddess Qi Nü has been punished by *juntian* [the Lord of Heaven];
Lei Gong [the God of Thunder] struck mountains, and heaven and earth were black.
The glistening jade dragon rubbed scales against inaccessible cliffs;
[Dragon-like] big newt, he seems to avoid the visitor from Yangling.
The golden snake [lightning] flashed when the dragon awoke from his snoring;
His sharp-rising horns became Haimen [the Gate of the Sea].
His grinding tenth and sharp talons grasped the bright moon;
The dance of Tianwu [the God of Sea] shook the base of heaven;
Over the thunderheads, the dragon taught his sons to make lightning;
The oldest dragon was in the fifth picture.
Two dragons relieved the people during the year of drought;
In the night the horse's mane turned over the *tian piao* [Ladle of Heaven].
The warm waves of peach blossom time had reached the third level [of Mount Kunlun];
Who dares to climb Yumen, the most hazardous place?
Blue whiskers and deep red beards grew when fire was burning off their tails;
Thunder of the tenth lunar month followed them as they fled upwards.
The Marquis of Shu slept peacefully in Nanyang's Wu(xiang);
All the figures were painted as strange and old.
They saved their superhuman strength waiting for the future;
In the world the people prayed for heavy rain.
Suoweng [Chen Rong] painted the picture of nine dragons.
His wonderful brushwork was unequalled in this world.
Looking from afar, cloud and water were like flying movement;
So that one feels it was done by the hand of a god.
Longgong [Dragon King] from Xuancheng had nine sons.
All of them entered the old man's picture.
Who will paint two cows for me?
Do not put the golden bridle on one of them.

The colophon of the picture *Nine Deer* was written by Fuweng [Huang Tingjian; 1045–1105], and the picture *Nine Horses* was praised by Polao [Su Shi; 1037–1101]. Suoweng's dragons are like neither deer nor horses. How could I dare to follow in the footsteps of Master Su and Master Huang? I simply put this down to record the year and the month.

楚中寫鑿真龍窺，金陵點眼雙龍飛。
諸梁羽化張亦去，雌雄笑殺劉洞微。
八軸吳龍不堪掛，醉余吐出胸中畫。
龍門三峽浪如山，從臾漲天聲大價。
飛龍出峽駕春江，九河之勢不敢降。
一龍天池戴赤木，菌蠢猛省雲霧邦。
鈞天奇女又遭謫，雷公擘山天地黑。
玉龍皎皎摩蒼崖，蟠玩似避陽陵客。
鼾鼻睡起金蛇奔，嶄然頭角當海門。
摩牙厲爪攫明月，天吳起舞搖天根。
雲頭教子掣金鑠，第五圖中龍最老。
兩龍遍活黎與蒸，馬鬃夜半天瓢倒。
桃花浪暖透三層，禹門岌嶪誰敢登。
蒼髯絳鬣火燒尾，十月霹靂隨飛騰。
蜀侯高臥南陽武，貌出全形奇且古。
神功收斂待時來，天下蒼生望霖雨。
所翁寫出九龍圖，筆端妙處世所無。
遠觀雲水似飛動，即之疑是神所摹。
宣城龍公生九子，盡入老翁圖畫裡。
阿誰為我屠雙牛，一牛莫著金籠頭。

九鹿之圖跋於涪翁，九馬之圖贊於坡老，所翁之龍雖非鹿馬並，然欲效蘇、黃二先生贊跡，則余豈敢姑述，以志歲月。

Inscriptions and seal by the artist; colophon (dated 1306) by Dong Sixue 董思學 (late 13th–early 14th century); colophon (dated 1331) and seals by Zhang Sicheng 張嗣成 (d.1344); colophon and seals by Wu Quanjie 吳全節 (1269–1346); colophon and seal by Ouyang Xuan 歐陽玄 (1283–1357); colophon and seals by Zhang Zhu 張翥 (1287–1368); colophon (dated 1380) and seals by Wang Boyi 王伯易 (act. 14th century); seals by Geng Zhaozhong 耿昭忠 (1640–86); colophon and seals by Yin Jishan 尹繼善 (1695–1771); colophon and seal by Liu Tongxun 劉統勳 (1700–73); colophon and seals by Yu Minzhong 于敏中 (1714–79); colophon and seals by Dong Bangda 董邦達 (1699–1769/74); colophon and seals by Qiu Yuexiu 裘日修 (1712–73); colophon and seals by Wang Jihua 王際華 (1717–76); colophon and seals by Qian Weicheng 錢維城 (1720–72); colophon and seals by Chen Xiaoyong 陳孝泳 (1715–79); colophon (dated 1767) and seals by the Qianlong emperor 乾隆 (r. 1736–96); seal by the Jiaqing emperor (r. 1796–1820), seal by Prince Gong, Yixin 弈訢 (1833–98)

(Translation adapted from the work of Tseng 1957, pp. 17 and 19)

## 39, 40

UNIDENTIFIED ARTIST; traditionally attributed to SHI KE (act. 10th century)

### Two Chan Patriarchs Harmonizing Their Minds

Scroll 1

Apocryphal seal by Li Yu 李煜 (937–78); apocryphal seals by Emperor Huizong 徽宗 (r. 1101–25); unidentified seal

Scroll 2

1st year of Qiande [919], 8th month, 8th day; west Shu; painted by Shi Ke; second Chan patriarch in contemplation

乾德改元八月八日，西蜀石恪寫二祖調心圖

Apocryphal inscription by the artist; apocryphal seals by Emperor Gaozong 高宗 (r. 1127–62); unidentified seals

## 41

UNIDENTIFIED ARTIST (mid-13th century); traditionally attributed to ZHIWENG (act. early 13th century)

### Meeting between Yaoshan and Li Ao

All moments of enlightenment come in a flash,
Why distrust your eye and value your ear?
Just as between the water and the clouds,
Don't say there is nothing there.
[signed] Lengquan Guangwen

全機劈面來，賤目而貴耳。
便是水雲間，莫道無餘事。

住泠泉 廣聞

Inscription and seals by Yanxi Guangwen 偃溪廣聞 (1189–1263)

(Poem translated by Maxwell Hearn)

## 42

UNIDENTIFIED ARTIST; traditionally attributed to MUXI (d. c.1281)

### Slumbering Budai

Seal by Zen'ami 善阿弥 (act. 2nd half 14th century)

## 43

UNIDENTIFIED ARTIST; traditionally attributed to MUXI (d. c.1281)

### Monk Mending Clothes in the Morning Sun

One thread passing through the eye of a needle,
Patches the holes in a tattered garment.
Biting down firmly with one's jaws,
Immediately it is broken.

Dongsou Yuankai at Yuji [Jade Desk Pavilion] respectfully eulogizes

針孔一絲，破衣補漏。
咬定牙關，當下便斷。

玉几東叟元愷敬贊

Inscription (dated between 1314 and 1320) and seal by Dongsou Yuankai 東叟元愷 (act. 1314–40); unidentified seal

(Translation by Michelle C. Wang, Levine and Lippit 2007, p. 126)

## 44

GONG KAI (1222–1307)

### Emaciated Horse

Ever since the clouds and mist fell upon the Heavenly Pass,
Empty have been the twelve stables of the previous dynasty.
Who is there today to lament over the bones of this noble steed?
In the setting sun, along the sandy shore, he casts a shadow like a mountain.

One of the classics [*Classic of Judging Horses*, attributed to Po Lo] says that a horse's ribs should be slender and numerous. An ordinary horse has only ten ribs. One with more than this is a noble steed. But only a thousand-league horse has as many as fifteen ribs. If you want to paint the bones beneath the flesh, especially if you intend to make fifteen ribs visible, they will only be visible if the horse if emaciated. Therefore I have made this image in order to show that the extraordinary deterioration of this thousand-league horse is not something to be avoided.

[Written by] Gong Kai of Huaiyin, [who is like] lone wood and lofty water.

一從雲霧降天關，空盡先朝十二閑。
今日有誰憐駿骨，夕陽沙岸影如山。

經言馬肋貴細而多，凡馬僅十許肋，過此即駿足。惟千里馬多至十有五肋。假令肉中畫骨，渠能使十五肋現于外？現於外非瘦不可。因成此相 以表千里之異，尪劣非所諱也。 淮陰龔開水木孤清書

Inscription and seals by the artist; title, colophons (one dated 1748) and seals by the Qianlong emperor 乾隆 (r. 1736–96); apocryphal colophon and seals by Yang Weizhen 楊維禎 (1296–1370); apocryphal colophon by Ni Zan 倪瓚 (1306–74);

colophon and seal by Gong Su 龔璛 (1266–1331); colophon and seals by Chen Shen 陳深 (1260–1344); colophon and seals by Yu Zhuo 俞焯 (dates); colophon and seals by Yang Zhu 楊翥 (1369–1453); colophon and seals by Xie Jin 謝晉 (d.c.1427); colophon and seals by Liu Yi 劉益 (dates); colophon (dated 1436) and seals by Xu Cheng 徐理 (1407–72); colophons (one dated 1578) and seals by Xiang Yuanbian 項元汴 (1525–90); colophon (dated 1698) and seals by Gao Shiqi 高士奇 (1654–1703); colophon by Liang Shizheng 梁詩正 (1697–1763); colophon and seals by Wang Youdun 汪由敦 (1692–1758); colophon and seal by Shen Deqin 沈德潛 (1673–1769); seal by Li Rihua 李日華 (1565–1635); seal by Li Zhaoheng 李肇亨 (1592–1664); seal by An Qi (1683–1742); seal by Lu Shusheng 陸樹聲 (d.1933); seal by Wanyan Jingxian 完顏景賢 (1875–1931)

(Includes translation by Jerome Silbergeld, Silbergeld 1985, p. 169)

## 45

QIAN XUAN (c.1235–before 1307)

### Doves and Pear Blossoms after Rain

The old man of Zha River, Qian Xuan Shunju

霅谿翁錢選舜舉

Inscription and seals by the artist; colophon and seals by Mou Yan 牟巘 (1227–1311); colophon and seals by Ke Jiusi 柯九思 (1290–1343); colophon and seals by Bao Xun 鮑恂 (c.1300–after 1382); colophon and seals by Qian Liangyou 錢良右 (1278–1344); colophon and seals by Zhang Wenzai 張文在 (act. Yuan dynasty [1271–1368]); colophon and seals by Sun Hua 孫華 (1338–58); colophons and seal by Sun Xin 孫莘; colophon and seal by Shen Cun 沈存 (act. Yuan dynasty); colophon and seals by Zhang Tianying 張天英 (act. 1335); colophon and seal by Lin Fufeng 林附鳳 (dates unknown); colophon and seals by Zou Liang 鄒亮 (act. 1436); colophon and seals by Qiu Dayu 丘大祐 (dates unknown); seals by Xiang Yuanbian 項元汴 (1525–90); seal by Zhang Hao 張浩 (c.1700); seal by Bi Yuan 畢沅 (1730–97); seal by Bi Long 畢瀧 (1733–97); seal by Zhang Heng 張珩 (1915–63); unidentified seals

(Translation by Nora Ling-yün Shih, Avril 1997, p. 62)

## 46

ZHAO MENGFU (1254–1322); ZHAO YONG (1289–after 1360); ZHAO LIN (act. 2nd half 14th century)

### Grooms and Horses

On the tenth day of the first lunar month in the second year of the Yuanzhen reign [11 February 1296], I painted this *Groom and Horse* for Surveillance Commissioner Feiqing's pure enjoyment. Zhao Mengfu of Wuxing inscribed this.

元貞二年正月十日作人馬圖以奉飛卿廉訪清玩。吳興趙孟頫題

During autumn in the eighth lunar month of the nineteenth year (*jihai*) of the Zhizheng reign [1359], I was staying in Wulin. One day, Han Jieshi visited me and informed me of the kind offer of the Songjiang magistrate, Xie Boli. Jieshi was asked to show me my father's painting, *Groom and Horse*, in [Xie's] collection. [He then] requested me to also paint a *Groom and Horse* at the end of this scroll to extend [the work]. As I respectfully viewed [my father's] painting, feelings of joy and sorrow intermingled and I could not put it down. Although I am not acquainted with Boli, I am deeply appreciative of his noble intention. Therefore, I happily agreed to do the painting, so that it can be given to Jieshi to pass on to Boli. Written by Zhao Yong

至正十九年己亥秋八月，余寓武林。一日韓介石過余，道松江同知謝伯理雅意，俾介石持所藏先平章所畫人馬見示，求余於卷尾亦作人馬以繼之。拜觀之餘，悲喜交集，不能去手。余雖未識伯理，嘉其高致，故慨然為作，以授介石，歸之伯理云。趙雍書

Xie Boli from Yunjian has long had the *Man and Horse* painting by my grandfather, Weiguogong [Zhao Mengfu], in his collection. Having had it mounted as a scroll, he asked my father to paint [the same subject] at the end, and requested me [to do so as well]. I do not know why Boli wishes to have [a work by] all three generations of my family, but if he did not have such refined taste, he would not concern himself with such a thing. Therefore, I could not refuse his request, and agreed [to paint]. The time now is the fifteenth day of the tenth lunar month, winter of the *jihai* year in the Zhizheng reign [1359]. Written by 'the gentleman for managing affairs' of the Jiangzhe region and proofreader of the Secretariat, Zhao Lin

雲間謝伯理氏，舊藏先大父魏國公所畫人馬圖。裝潢成卷，復口家君作于後，而亦以命余。竊惟伯理之口豈欲侈吾家三世之所傳歟。自非篤於文[?]雅不能用心若此也，遂不辭而承命。 時至正己亥冬十月望日也。承事郎江浙等處行中書省檢校官趙麟識

Inscription and seal by Zhao Mengfu; inscription by Zhao Yong; inscription and seal by Zhao Lin; label strip by an unidentified author; colophon (dated 1405) and seals by Hu Cheng 胡誠 (act. early 15th century); colophon (dated 1403) and seals by Shen Danian 沈大年 (act. early 15th century); colophon and seals by Chen An 陳安 (act. early 15th century); colophon and seals by Zou Hui 鄒誨 (act. early 15th century); colophon and seals by Shanzhu 善住 (act. early 15th century); colophon by Liu Yue 劉嶽 (*jinshi* 1414); colophon and seals by Jugong 李居恭 (act. early 15th century); colophon (dated 1425) and seals by Yuan Heng 袁衡 (act. early 15th century); colophon and seals by Chen Hongshou 陳洪綬 (1598–1652); seals by An Qi 安岐 (1683–1742); seals by the Qianlong emperor 乾隆 (r. 1736–96); seal by the Jiaqing emperor 嘉慶 (r. 1796–1820); seals by the Xuantong emperor 宣統 (r. 1908–11); seals by Zhu Xingzhai 朱省齋 (1900–?); seals by Zhang Daqian 張大千 (1899–1983); seals by Xu Wenbo 徐雯波 (c.1927–?); seals by John M. Crawford, Jr. 顧洛阜 (1913–88)

(Translation of Zhang Mengfu's inscription adapted from the work of Maxwell Hearn, Hearn in New York 2010, p. 238)

## 47

ZHENG SIXIAO (1239–1316)

### Ink Orchid

I have been asking Xihuang [an ancient hermit] with my head bowed:
Who were you – and why did you come to this land?
I opened my nostrils before making the painting,
And there, floating everywhere in the sky, is the antique fragrance undying.
Suonan Weng [Zheng Sixiao].

向來俯首問羲皇，汝是何人到此鄉。
未有畫前開鼻孔，滿天浮動古馨香。

所南翁

On the fifteenth day of the first lunar month in the *bingwu* year [1306], [I] made this one scroll.

丙午正月十五日作此壹卷。

Inscriptions and seals by the artist; colophon and seal by Chen Shen 陳深 (1260–1344); colophon and seals by Wang Yu 王育 (act. Yuan dynasty [1271–1368]); colophon and seals by Lie Zhe 列哲 (act. Yuan dynasty [1271–1368]); colophon and seal by monk Yuze 釋餘澤 (1277–?); colophon and seal by Wei Junmin 魏俊民 (act. Yuan dynasty [1271–1368]); colophon and seal by Chen Yu 陳昱 (act. Yuan dynasty [1271–1368]); colophon and seal by Zheng Yuanyou 鄭元祐 (1292–1364); colophon and seal by monk Deqin 釋德欽 (act. Yuan dynasty [1271–1368]); colophon and seals by Wang Mian 王冕 (1287–1359); colophon and seal by Hu Xi 胡熙 (act. Yuan dynasty [1271–1368]); colophon by Duan Tianyou 段天祐 (*jinshi* 1324); colophon by Han Yi 韓奕 (1334–1406); colophon (dated 1511) by Zhu Yunming 祝允明 (1460–1526); seals by Zhang Xiaosi 張孝思 (act. c.mid-17th century); seal by Da Zhongguang 笪重光 (1623–92); seals by Song Luo 宋犖 (1634–1713); seals by the Qianlong emperor 乾隆 (r. 1736–96); seal by the Jiaqing emperor 嘉慶 (r. 1796–1820); seals by the Xuantong emperor 宣統 (r. 1908–11); unidentified seals

(Includes translation by Wai-kam Ho, Cahill 1976, p. 16)

## 48

WANG MIAN (1287–1359)

### Fragrant Snow at Broken Bridge

Chilly plum blossoms fill branches of white jade;
Scattered by a warm breeze, [petals] flutter like snowflakes.
The 'Recluse of Solitary Hill' [Lin Bu] remains true to himself,
But who carries the song of reed pipes across Broken Bridge?

Yuanzhang

一樹寒梅白玉條，暖風吹亂雪飄飄。
孤山處士情如故，誰載笙歌過斷橋。

元章

Inscription and seals by the artist; label strip by Shen Jin'an 沈覲安 (1901–75); colophon (dated 1568) and seals by Gu Dadian 顧大典 (*jinshi* 1568); colophon and seal by Zhang Fengshi 張逢時 (1917–90); seal by the Qianlong emperor 乾隆 (r. 1736–96); seal by Wang Jiqian 王季遷 [C.C. Wang] (1906–2002); unidentified seals

(Translation by Maxwell Hearn)

## 49

UNIDENTIFIED ARTIST; traditionally attributed to GUO ZHONGSHU (d.977)

### The Summer Palace of Emperor Minghuang

Zhongshu

忠恕

Apocryphal inscription by the artist; seal by Gu Wenbin 顧文彬 (1811–89)

## 50

UNIDENTIFIED ARTIST (act. 14th century)

**Bodhidharma Crossing the Yangzi on a Reed**

The reeds bloom, the wind rises, and the crests of waves are high,
The Shaoshi cliff lies ahead, a far road to travel,
Beyond the world of kalpas [an aeon in the Buddhist cycle of cosmic time], a single flower blossoms into five petals,
My heels are now readied for the whipping of a rattan cane.

Respectfully eulogized by Monk Qingyu

蘆花風起浪頭高，少室岩前去路遙。
刼外一花開五葉，腳跟正好喫藤條。

比丘清欲拜贊

Inscription and seals by Liaoan Qingyu 了庵清欲 (1288–1363)

(Translation adapted by Malcolm McNeill from the work of Wai-kam Ho, Kansas City and Cleveland 1980, pp. 124–5)

## 51

NI ZAN (1306–74)

**Woods and Valleys of Mount Yu**

Chen Fan (? – 168) once prepared a bed,
When Xu Ru (97–168) came to visit.
How sweet is the water from Yan You's [Yan Yan] (506–443 BCE) well.
Yet Yu Zhong's [Zhongyong, second son of the legendary Supreme King of Zhou during the Shang dynasty (16th–11th century BCE)] shrine is neglected and desolate.
We watch the clouds and daub with our brushes;
We drink wine and write poems.
The joyful feelings of this day
Will linger long after we have parted.

On the thirteenth day of the twelfth [lunar] month in the *xinhai* year [1372], I visited Master Bowan, observed and wrote the woods and valleys of Mount Yu and inscribed a five-word poem to record this travel. Ni Zan

陳蕃懸榻處，徐孺過門時。
甘洌言游井，荒涼虞仲祠。
看雲聊弄翰，把酒更題詩。
此日交歡意，依依去後思。

辛亥十二月十三日，訪伯琬高士，目寫虞山林壑并題五言以記來游。倪瓚

Inscription by the artist; colophon (dated 1759) and seals by Emperor Qianlong 乾隆 (r. 1736–96); inventory character and seals by Xiang Yuanbian 項元汴 (1525–90); seal by Geng Zhaozhong 耿昭忠 (1640–86); seal by An Qi 安岐 (1683–c.1746); seal by Chen Kuilin 陳夔麟 (1855–1928); seal by Xu An 徐安 (act. 20th century); seal by Tan Jing 譚敬 (1911–91); seal by Wang Jiqian 王季遷 [C.C. Wang] (1907–2003); seal by Zhang Heng 張珩 (1915–61); unidentified seal

(Poem translated by Wen Fong, Fong 1992, p. 490, with expanded notation.)

## 52

DAI JIN (1388–1462)

**Spring Clouds in the Linggu Mountains**

Qiantang [Hangzhou] Dai Jin

錢唐 戴進

Inscription and seals by the artist; colophon and seal by Nie Danian 聶大年 (1402–55); colophon and seal by Dong Qichang 董其昌 (1555–1636); seal by Xu Zhigu 許志古 (act. Ming dynasty [1368–1644]); colophon and seals by Sun Chengze 孫承澤 (1592–1676); seals by Liang Qingbiao 梁清標 (1620–91); seals by Fang Guancheng 方觀承 (1698–1768); colophon and seals by Li Zuoxian 李佐賢 (1807–76); seals by Shao Songnian 邵松年 (1848–1923/4)

## 53

UNIDENTIFIED ARTIST; traditionally attributed to REN RENFA (1255–1327)

**The Four Pleasures: Music, Chess, Calligraphy and Painting**

On each one of the four paintings:

Ziming

子明

Apocryphal inscription and seal by the artist

## 54

DU JIN (act. c.1465–1509)

**Court Ladies in the Inner Palace**

Seals by the artist; seal by Yang Shining 楊士凝 (*juren* 1717); colophons (dated 1845 and 1861) and seals by Zhang Xianghe 張祥河 (1785–1862); colophon (dated 1954) and seal by Liu Cha 柳垞 (act. 20th century); seals by Lin Xiongguang 林熊光 (1897–1971); seal by Liu Qian 劉遷 (1903–90)

## 55

ZHOU CHEN (c.1450–1535)

**Dwelling by the Stream in Spring**

Dongcun, Zhou Chen, painted the 'idea' of Pei Chunquan's dwelling

東村周臣為春泉裴居寫意

Inscription and seal by the artist; seals by Gu Kexue 顧可學 (1482–1560); seals by Zhu Zhichi 朱之赤 (act. late 16th–early 17th century);[1] seal by Prince Guoyi, Aisin Gioro Yinli 胤禮 (1697–1738); inscription and seals by the Qianlong emperor 乾隆 (r. 1736–96); seal by the Jiaqing emperor 嘉慶 (r. 1796–1820); seal by the Xuantong emperor 宣統 (r. 1908–11); unidentified seal

1 Although this painting bears the seals of Zhu Zhichi, the title was not included in Zhu's catalogue, see Zhu (1920) 1997.

## 56

LÜ JI (act. 1488–1505)

**Pomegranates, Autumn Mallows, Chrysanthemums, Blue Magpies and Rooster**

Lü Ji

呂紀

Inscription and seal by the artist

## 57

SHEN ZHOU (1427–1509)

**Twelve Views of Tiger Hill**

LEAF A
Distant View of Tiger Hill from the Canal Mooring

LEAF B
The Fool's Spring

LEAF C
The Pine Retreat

LEAF D
The Enlightened Stone Retreat

LEAF E
The Nodding Stone Terrace, Tiger Hill, and the Thousand-Man Seat

LEAF F
The Sword Spring, Tiger Hill

LEAF G
The Thousand Buddha Hall and the Pagoda of the 'Cloudy Cliff' Monastery

LEAF H
The Five Sages Terrace

LEAF I
The Thousand Acres of Clouds

LEAF J
Tiger-Flight Spring at the Back Gate

LEAF K
Bamboo Pavilion, Tiger Hill

LEAF L
Cloud-Climbing Pavilion

Seals by the artist; colophon and seal by Yao Yuanzhi 姚元之 (1776–1852); seals by Hou Shigong 侯世恭 (possibly 19th century)

(All titles from Kansas City and Cleveland 1980, pp. 187–190.)

## 58

UNIDENTIFIED ARTIST

**Portrait of Shen Zhou at Age Eighty**

There are those who think the eyes are slightly small,
Or the jaw too narrow;
Since I wouldn't know how I look,
I cannot tell what is missing (in the portrait).
Of what importance are my face and eyes?
My only fear is lack of virtue.
Drifting through these 80 years,
Now death is only a wall away.

First year of the Zhengde reign [1506], old man Shitian, inscribed by himself.

人謂眼差小，又說頤太窄，
我自不能知，亦不知其失。
面目何足較，但恐有失德，[1]
苟且八十年，余與死隔壁。

正德改元石田老人自題

Like or not like,
True or not true?
A shadow on paper,
A person outside the self.
Death and life, a single dream,
Heaven and earth, a dusty stream
Floating or resting,
Happily I live the rest of my life.

Passing the year [1507], inscribed by Shitian

似不似，真不真。
紙上影，身外人。
死生一夢，天地一塵。
浮浮休休，吾懷自春。

越年石田又題

Inscriptions (dated 1506 and 1507) and seals by Shen Zhou 沈周 (1427–1509); seals by Tan Jing 譚敬 (1911–91)

(Translation by Chia-ling Yang with reference to Edwards 1976, p. 22 and Vinograd 1992, pp. 28–9)

1 Part of the character 失 (*shi*; 'lack') is missing owing to damage on the painting.

## 60

TANG YIN (1470–1523)

### Pure Dream beneath a Paulownia Tree

For ten *li* the paulownia shadows cover the purple moss.
The gentleman is at leisure, feeling an intoxicated sleep.
For this lifetime, he has already renounced thoughts of rank and fame.
The pure sleep should not have the dreams of grandeur.

Painted by Tang Yin

十里桐陰覆紫苔，先生閑試醉眠來。
此生已謝功名念，清夢應無到古槐。

唐寅畫

Inscription and seals by the artist; unidentified seals

(Poem translation adapted from the work of Richard Vinograd, Vinograd 1992a, pp. 94–5)

## 61

QIU YING (1494/5–1552)

### Saying Farewell at Xunyang

Painted by Shifu Qiu Ying

仇英實父繪

Inscription and seals by the artist; frontispiece andseals by Zhu Zhifan 朱之蕃 (1558–1624); colophon (dated 1614?) and seals by Xie Guanbiao 謝官表 (act. early 17th century); seals by Sun Kuotu 孫擴圖 (act. 1736–55); seals by Jean-Pierre Dubosc (1903–88)

## 62

WEN ZHENGMING (1470–1559)

### Garden of the Inept Administrator

LEAF A

Fanxiang Wu 繁香塢 ('The Bank of Many Fragrances')

Various kinds of flowers are planted next to the thatched house:
Purple luxuriance and red beauty in random array.
The spring radiance and brilliance embroider them with a thousand artifices.
In the good air and scented mist a hundred fragrances mix.
I love the scents that fill my bosom and sleeves,
I do not heed the wind or the dew that wets my clothes.
My lofty thoughts are already beyond the noisy world.
Aloof, I watch the bees flying up and down.

The Bank of Many Fragrances is in front of Ruoshutang. It is planted with a mixture of various kinds of peonies, begonias, wisteria and other flowers. Meng Zongxian (act. *c.*1161–90) said in a poem: 'Beside your small house is a bank of many fragrances' [i.e. the name is taken from this poem]. Zhengming

雜植名花傍草堂，紫蕤丹豔漫成行。
春光爛熳千機錦，淑氣薰蒸百和香。
自愛芳菲滿懷袖，不教風露濕衣裳。
高情已在繁華外，靜看遊蜂上下狂。

繁香塢在若墅堂之前，雜植牡丹、芍藥、丹(桂)、海棠、紫璃諸花。
孟宗獻詩云：“從君小築繁香塢。”徵明

LEAF B

Xiao Canglang 小滄浪 ('Little Canglang Pond')

Once a small pavilion was built by the Canglang [pond];
The green water still surrounds its empty railings.
Here there are always the wind and moon to offer to the fisherman,
And boys, too, singing 'Wash your hat tassels!'
Rivers and lakes fill the whole land, enough for my enjoyment,
For a hundred years the fish and birds have forgotten walls.

Shunqing [see below] is dead, Du Ling [Du Fu] (712–70) far away –
As a paragon of hermits who will compete with me?

The garden has several *mu* of water reservoirs, like Su Zimei's [Su Shunqing (1008–48) of the Song dynasty, who had a Canglang pavilion at Suzhou] Canglang ponds. So a pavilion was built amongst them, and called the little Canglang. Formerly Zimei returned from the capital, Bian. Our lord from Wu [i.e. the owner of the garden, Wang Xianchen (1473–*c.*1543)], also came back from the northern capital. The name is taken from this coincidence of their travels. Zhengming

(偶)傍滄浪構小亭，依然綠水繞虛楹。
豈無風月供垂釣，亦有兒童唱濯纓。
滿地江湖聊寄興，百年魚鳥已忘情。
舜欽已矣杜陵遠，一段幽蹤誰與爭。

園有積水，橫亘數畝，類蘇子美滄浪池，因築亭其中，曰小滄浪。
昔子美自汴都徙吳，君亦還自北都，蹤跡相似，故襲其名。徵明

LEAF C

Xiangyun Wu 湘筠塢 ('The Bamboo Bank')

Bamboos are planted around the low mound
Forming a bank of bamboo around the edge.
In full summer it already seems to be autumn,
So deep is the wood, one cannot tell when it is noon.
In its midst is one who has abandoned the world,
Enjoying himself with a *qin* and a goblet.
When a wind stirs he wakes too from drunkenness
To sit and listen to the rain on the bamboo leaves.

The Bamboo Bank is south of the Peach-blossom rill and north of the Huaiyuting. It is planted all around with bamboos, and is especially quiet and secluded. Zhengming

種竹繞平岡，岡回竹成塢。盛夏已驚秋，林深不知午。
中有遺世人，琴樽自容與。風來酒亦醒，坐聽瀟湘雨。

湘筠塢在桃花沜之南，槐雨亭北，修竹連亙，境特幽迴。徵明

LEAF D

Bajiao Jian芭蕉檻 ('The Banana Balustrade')

The new banana is more than ten feet tall;
After rain it is clean as though washed.
It does not dislike the high whitened wall,
It elegantly matches the curved balustrade.
Autumn sounds come into the cool pillow,
Morning colours divide the green window
Let no one tell the heedless shears to take it,
Leave it until the shade reaches the house.

The Banana Balustrade is to the left of the Huaiyuting. Later, palms were planted, to make a suitable shade for the summer months. Zhengming

新蕉十尺強，得雨淨如沐。不嫌粉堵高，雅称朱欄曲。
秋聲入枕涼，曉色分窗綠。莫教輕剪取，留待陰連屋。

芭蕉檻在槐雨亭之左，更植椶陰，宜為暑月。徵明

LEAF E

Diao Gong 釣䂬 ('The Fishing Stone')

The white stone is clean and dustless;
Flat, it overhangs the stream of wild water.
I sit and watch the line rolling,
I take quiet pleasure in the jade-like turning [of the water].
I enjoy rivers and lakes, far off,
I forget cares, and terns and egrets become tame.
You must know that he who stretches his line,
Is not one who desires [to catch] fish.

The Fishing Stone is below the Yiyuan Tai [Pavilion of Distant Thoughts]. At the time of spring brightness, the shade of the willows and the falling flowers make one sit so absorbed as to forget to return. Zhengming

白石淨無塵，平臨野水津。
坐看絲裊裊，靜愛玉粼粼。
得意江湖遠，忘機鷗鷺馴。
須知纜綸者，不是羨魚人。

釣䂬在意遠臺下，春明之際，柳陰落花，令人坐恋忘返。徵明

LEAF F

Laiqin Yu 來禽囿 ('The Garden of Attracting Birds')

Here in summer a cool shade spreads over ten *mu*.
That is when the fruits begin to ripen in the long orchard.
At the place where the precious heavy baskets are divided and given away.
In a small window, I have got a rubbing of Youjun's [Wang Xizhi] (303–65) calligraphy.

The Garden of Attracting Birds consists of several hundred apple trees [*linqin*, literally 'wood-birds'] planted on both sides of the Canglang Pond.

清陰十畝夏扶踈，正是長林果熟初。珎重筠籠分贈處，
小窗搨得右軍書。

來禽囿在滄浪池之南，北雜植林禽數百本，故云。徵明

**LEAF G**

Yu Quan 玉泉 ('The Jade Spring')

Once I ladled water from Xiangshan
Cool as a stream of jade.
Would you know that as far as Yao [the 7th star of the Dipper]
is from the Milky Way
There is another clear jade spring?
Preparing a rope, I draw water with the clouds,
In an earthen jar, I boil it with moonlight.
What need of Lu Hongjian [Lu Yu (733–c.804), a tea master
in the Tang]?
At the first sip you will yourself decide.

At Xiangshan in the capital there is a jade spring where the Master often ladled the water and made tea, and called himself 'Yuquan Shanren' ['Hermit of the Jade Spring'] after it. When he struck a spring in the south-east corner of the garden, and the jar kept [its water] cold and suitable for tea, no less than that of the jade spring, he gave it this name, to show that he would not forget. Zhengming

曾勺香山水，冷然玉一泓。
寧知瑤漢隔，別有玉泉清。
修綆和雲汲，沙瓶帶月烹。
何須陸鴻漸，一啜自分明。

京師香山有玉泉，君嘗勺而甘之，因號玉泉山人。及得泉於園之巽隅，甘冽宜茗，不減玉泉，遂以為名，示不忘也。徵明

**LEAF H**

Huai Wo 槐幄 ('The Locust Tree Enclosure')

Below the pavilion a tall locust tree falls over the wall,
Mist on the cold leaves wets my clothes.
The scattered flowers are sparse but their scent travels far,
The cool shade falls all around, of lasting benefit to the world.
The literary contests of the eighth moon recall past doings,
When the honours of the three ministers were entrusted
to the candidates.
Since I became old I have not dreamt of Nanke,
Alone I move my bed to lie in the cool of the evening.

The Locust Tree Enclosure, on the twentieth day of the ninth lunar month during autumn of the *xinhai* year [1551]. Wen Zhengming wrote.

亭下高槐欲覆牆，氣蒸寒翠濕衣裳。
踈花靡靡流芳遠，清陰垂垂世澤長。
八月文場懷往事，三公勳業付諸郎。
老來不作南柯夢，猶自移床卧晚涼。

槐幄。辛亥秋九月廿日，徵明書

Inscriptions and seals by the artist; colophon (dated 1822) and seal by Yongxing, Prince Cheng 永瑆 (1752–1823); colophon (dated 1930) and seal by Naitō Torajirō 内籐虎次郎 (1866–1934); seals by Zhang Xiaosi 張孝思 (act. 17th century); seals by An Qi 安岐 (1683–1742); seals by Zhou Zuoxin 周祚新 (act. 1st half 17th century); seal by Yongrong 永瑢 (1743–90); seal by Yixin, Prince Gong 奕訢 (1833–98); seals by Baoxi 寶熙 (1871–1930); unidentified seals

(All translations are adapted from the work of Roderick Whitfield, Princeton 1969, pp. 66–9)

## 63

DONG QICHANG (1555–1636)

### Twin Marvels of Calligraphy and Painting

**1**

Dong Beiyuan [Dong Yuan] (act. 930s–60s) liked to depict misty landscapes, yet the transformations of mist and clouds were best represented by Mi [Fu] (1051–1107). Pondering on Mi Fu's *White Clouds at the Xiao and Xiang Rivers*, I begin to understand the deep delight in ink play. The third lunar month in the *dingmao* year [1617], inscribed by Siweng

董北苑好作烟景，烟雲變沒即米画也。余於米芾瀟湘白雲圖悟墨戲三昧。 丁卯三月思翁識

**2**

Beside the Pole Star is the Dark Capital,[1]
Enclosing it, the barricades soar skywards.
The ancestral temple is kept in all propriety,
Following strict rules with integrity.
Its glazed tiles shine in the frost,
Its bronze pillars link together.
Landscapes decorate its embroidered doors,
Sun and moon are carved on its beams.
The coiling roots of the divine Li are great,
Flourishing like orchids, with shining leaves.[2]
[Laozi's (act. 6th century BCE)] family has been handed
down in ancient history,
The *Daode [jing]* has been transmitted to the rulers of today.
Talented painters follow ancient masters,
Master Wu Daozi (c.685–758) is by far the best.
In sheer numbers, his works shake the world's axis,
Marvels of perfection, his murals move the palace walls.[3]
The Five Sages in their dragon robes,
A thousand officials, lined up like swallows.[4]
The emperor's crown with its elegant tassels,
Banners and flags flapping in the wind.
When the cypress stays green in the scene,
Russet pears glow bright in the frost.
The wind chimes blow by the jade pillars,
Frozen silver bejewels the dewy well.
[Laozi] bowed out when the Zhou fell low,
His enduring writing was passed to the Han emperors.
As his valley spirit never dies,
What other place is better than this retreat?

'Paying respect to the Supreme Xuanyuan Emperor's [Laozi] Temple'.
The temple has a painting of the Five Emperors, painted by Wu [Dao]zi.
Xu Hao (703–82) wrote out Du [Fu]'s verse. Xuanzai [Dong Qichang] made this tracing copy on the fifteenth day of the twelfth lunar month in the *jiwei* year [1619].

配極玄都閟，憑高禁禦長。
守祧嚴具禮，掌節鎮非常。
碧瓦初寒外，金莖一氣旁。
山河扶繡戶，日月近雕梁。
仙李盤根大，猗蘭奕葉光。
世家遺舊史，道德付今王。
畫手看前輩，吳生遠擅場。
森羅移地軸，妙絕動宮牆。
五聖聯龍袞，千官列雁行。
冕旒俱秀發，旌旆盡飛揚。
翠柏深留景，紅梨迥得霜。
風箏吹玉柱，露井凍銀牀。
身退卑周室，經傳拱漢皇。
谷神如不死，養拙更何鄉。

謁玄元皇帝廟，廟有五聖圖，吳道子畫，徐浩書杜詩。
己未嘉平月之望臨。玄宰

Inscriptions (dated 1617 and 1619) and seals by the artist; inscription (dated 1747) and seals by the Qianlong emperor 乾隆 (r. 1736–96); seal by the Jiaqing emperor 嘉慶 (r. 1796–1820); seal by the Xuantong emperor 宣統 (r. 1908–11); seals by An Qi 安岐 (1683–1742)

(Translation by Roderick Whitfield and Chia-Ling Yang)

1 The Temple of the Supreme Emperor of Mystery Prime [Li Er, known as Laozi], situated on Mt Beimang north of Luoyang, and renamed Taiwei Miao in 743; see Little 2000, p. 62.
2 Li: 'plum tree', but also the family name of both Laozi and the Tang imperial family, who claimed Laozi as their ancestor
3 William Acker translates this couplet: 'Its checkered throng of varied forms turns the earth on its axle; Its subtleties past hope of imitation make the palace walls tremble'; Acker 1954, p. 362.
4 Five Sages: the five mythical rulers of ancient China (Shennong, Yao, Shun, Yu and Tang). Wu Daozi's murals of the Five Sages with their Thousand Officials are mentioned by Zhu Jingxuan (c.785–c.848) in his *Celebrated Painters of the Tang Dynasty* of circa 840.

## 64

ZENG JING (1564–1647)

### Portrait of Wang Shimin

**1**

In the fifth lunar month of the *bingchen* year of the Wanli reign [1616], painted by Zeng Jing

萬歷丙辰五月曾鯨寫

**2**

Portrait of Xunzhi [Wang Shimin's courtesy name], minister of the imperial seals office, at the age of 25. Inscribed by Gu Binqian from Juwu [the ancient Wu Kingdom]

遜之尚寶弍十五歲小像。句吳顧秉謙題

Inscription and seals by the artist; inscription and seals by Gu Bingqian 顧秉謙 (c.1550–after 1628); seal by Wang Yuanqi 王原祁 (1642–1715)

(Translation by Chia-ling Yang)

## 65

ZHANG HONG (1577– after 1652)

### The Zhi Garden

Overall View of the Zhi Garden. Written by Zhang Hong from Wumen [Suzhou]

止園全景。吳門張宏寫

Inscription and seals by the artist

(Translation adapted from the work of Wai-Kam Ho, Kansas City and Seattle 1992, vol. II, p. 116)

## 66

CHEN HONGSHOU (1598–1652)

**Versifying under the Influence of Wine**

Painted by Laochi Hongshou in the Jingzhe Ju (The Hermit's Studio)

老遲洪綬畫於靜者居

Inscription and seals by the artist; seals by Mo Meixi 莫梅谿 (dates unknown); seals by Zhang Daqian 張大千 (1899–1983)

(Translation by Szeto Yuen-kit)

## 67

WANG HUI (1632–1717)

**The Colours of Mount Taihang**

Once in the home of a noble family in Guangling [present Yangzhou], I saw a small scroll by Guan Tong [act. *c*.907–23]. With its cloudy peaks running together in a luxuriant and dense air, it truly pierced my heart and dazzled my eyes. Today, though I remember only a fraction of it, I have followed its method to create this painting, *The Colours of Mount Taihang*. I hope it captures the deep and heroic atmosphere of the north country, rather than merely posturing with pretty details. Three days after the mid-autumn festival in the *jiyou* year [1669], Wang Hui of Yushan [made] and inscribed [this painting]

余從廣陵貴戚家見關仝尺幅，雲巒奔會神氣鬱密，真足洞心駭目。予今猶復記憶其一二，遂倣其法作太行山色，似有北地沉雄之氣，不以姿致取妍也。己酉中秋後三日。虞山王翬並識

Inscription and seals by the artist; label strip by Ziweng 自翁 (possibly act. 19th century); frontispiece (dated 1816) and seals by Pan Yijun 潘奕雋 (1740–1830); inscription (dated 1673) and seals by Wang Shimin 王時敏 (1592–1680); colophons (one dated 1815) and seals by Chen Chongben 陳崇本 (act. *c*.1775–after 1815); seals by Wang Wenbo 王文伯 (act. *c*.1662–1722); seals by Xu Naipu 許乃普 (1787–1866); seal by Chen Kuilin 陳夔麟 (1855–1928); seals by Zhang Daqian 張大千 (1899–1983); seals by Earl Morse (1908–88); seals by Wang Jiqian 王季遷 [C.C. Wang] (1906–2002)

(Translation adapted by Maxwell Hearn from the work of Roderick Whitfield, Princeton 1969, p. 108)

## 68

WANG JIAN (1598–1677)

**Landscapes in the Manner of Old Masters**

**1**

The travellers return from remote lanes, bringing with them the lingering glow of accumulated snow. There is a picture in these poetic lines by Youcheng [Wang Wei] (701–61), is there poetry in my picture? Xiangbi [Wang Jian's literary name], Jian.

行人返深巷，積雪帶余暉。此右丞詩中畫也，不識此畫中有詩否？湘碧鑒

**2**

Beiyuan's [Dong Yuan] (act. 945–60) paintings are unpredictable. Siweng [Dong Qichang] (1555–1636) call them dragons among paintings. Truthful Siweng's word is. My desire is only to emulate [Dong Yuan's] spirit, but I'm embarrassed to say that [dragons] cannot even be seen in my dreams. Wang Jian.

北苑畫變化莫測，思翁所謂畫中龍，信不虛也。此圖欲仿其意，愧未能夢見。王鑒

**3**

Encircled by mounds of mangrove, the ancient hall is obscured by white clouds. In the manner of Ma Wenbi [Ma Wan] (act. late 14th century). Wang Jian.

壇高紅樹繞，院古白雲封。仿馬文璧。王鑒

**4**

In the *yiwei* year [1655], I travelled with Zhang Yue'an shijun [Zhang Xuezeng] (act. *c*.1634–57) by boat in the south. We made the journey to view a handscroll by Jiang Guandao [Jiang Shen] (*c*.1090–1138). [Upon seeing the painting,] the subtley of the painting had a profound affect on us. We took two months to examine it from beginning to end. [Since then] almost twenty years have passed! This painting is done in the manner of Jiang. Despite the criticism I might attract, why should I not attempt to 'learn to walk in Handan'. Don't you think? Xiangbi, Jian.[1]

予乙未年與張約庵使君聯舟南下，出其所藏江貫道長卷見示。妙有幽微淡遠之致，得縱觀兩月，忽忽將二十寒暑矣。此圖仿之，不免邯鄲學步之誚。何如？何如？湘碧鑒

**5**

Dark clouds emerge as the sun sets over the creek;
As the heavy rains arrive, a frenzied wind whips through the tower.[2]
After the brush idea (*biyi*) of Li Tang (*c*.1049–*c*.1130). Jian.

溪雲初起日沉閣，山雨欲來風滿樓。仿李唐筆意。鑒

**6**

The willow pond overflows with spring rain;
At the flowering bank, the sun slowly sets.[3]
[I] have used a combination of brushwork from the Three Zhaos [Zhao Lingran (Northern Song dynasty [960–1127]), Zhao Boju (*c*.1120–70) and Zhao Mengfu], but does this work resemble them slightly? Master of Ranxiang'an.

柳塘春水漫，花塢夕陽遲。以三趙筆法合為之，未識得似一二否？染香庵主

**7**

[Although] the brushwork of Fan Kuan (d. after 1023) is not unlike that of Dong [Yuan and] Ju[ran] (act. 960–86), it is more majestic. The original [by Fan Kuan] on which this painting is based was once in the collection of Wang Fengcheng [Wang Shimin] (1592–1680), but I am told it has been acquired by some else.[4] This work only evokes the spirit of Fan Kuan and not its form-likeness. Jian.

范寬筆法原與董巨相似，但雄壯過之。此圖為吾婁王奉常所藏，聞已為人易去。今擬其意，不求形似也。鑒

**8**

After Zhao Wenmin's [Zhao Mengfu] (1254–1322) *Cloudy Valley Shady Pines*.

仿趙文敏《雲壑松陰》

**9**

Shuming's [Wang Meng] (1308–85) *Solitary Temple in the Mountains*, which has always been a treasure in the family collection of Wang Wenke gong [Wang Ao] (1450–1524), is one of the works the artist himself well pleased. This autumn I was able to view the painting at the Zhuozheng yuan [Garden of the Inept Administrator],[5] and so I copied its brush method. Xiangbi, Jian.

叔明《關山蕭寺圖》，向為王文恪公家珍藏，乃其生平得意之作。今秋得觀於拙政園中，遂仿此法。湘碧鑒

**10**

Zijiu's [Huang Gongwang] (1269–1354) *Autumn Mountains* is in the collection of Jingkou Zhang family [Zhang Kunchen] (Ming dynasty [1368–1644]). Dong Wenmin [Dong Qichang] considers it a masterpiece by Dachi [Huang] and this painting is a copy of the original. Jian.

子久《秋山圖》為京口張氏收藏。董文敏謂此大痴一生傑作，此圖擬之。鑒

**11**

I saw *Cloudy Valleys Shady Pines* by the Woodcutter of Yellow Crane Mountain [Wang Meng] in Sun Shaozai's [Sun Chengze] (1592–1676) studio in Chang'an some twenty years ago. It used to appear in my dreams, now I recall it and emulate its idea. I wonder if it corresponds? Xiangbi, Jian.

黃鶴山樵《雲壑松陰》，余曾見於長安孫少宰齋，已二十余年矣。時形之夢寐，返思其意為之，不知合作否？湘碧鑒

**12**

At the beginning of autumn in the *jiyou* year [1669], Brother Daqian came to visit me at my home in Bantang [Jiangsu province]. He brought white silk for my humble brush, intending my works to be a gift for his father Mister Gongji during his 60th birthday celebrations in spring of the *guichou* year [1673]. For him, I especially painted 12 works in the manner of old masters. Wang Jian from Loudong.

己酉新秋寓半塘精舍，大千道兄過訪，以尊翁公濟先生六十華誕在癸醜小春，預出絹素索余拙筆，為是歲華封之祝，特仿古十二幀以應之。婁東王鑒

Inscriptions and seals by the artist.

(Translation by Yin Hwang.)

1 Zhang Xueceng was one of the Nine Friends of Painting. He took up the post as Prefect of Suzhou in 1654. Reference to an ancient story that warns against the dangers of imitation. It tells of a young man who tried so hard to learn how to walk elegantly like the people in Handan [Hebei province] that he eventually forgot how to walk and could only crawl.

2 The first two lines are taken from the well-known poem 'The Eastern Tower in Xianyang' by Xu Hun (*jinshi* 832).

3 The first two lines are taken from a poem by Yan Wei (act. 766–79).

4 He was referring to *Travellers Among Streams and Mountains* (now in the National Palace Museum, Taipei).

5 The Garden of the Inept Administrator still survives in Suzhou today. It was the subject of two albums by Wen Zhengming and one, dated 1551, is in the collection of The Metropolitan Museum of Art (cat. no. 62).

## 69

FAN QI (1616–after 1694)

**Yangzi Riverscape**

Seals by the artist; label strip and seals by Zhu Zhixi 祝之錫 (dates unknown); seal by Wu Qingbo 吳晴波 (act. Republican period [1912–49]); unidentified seals

## 70
GONG XIAN (c.1619–89)
### Landscape Album

**LEAF A**
'High Peaks with Buildings in the Manner of Lu Hong'
Painting of the ancients compels respect and admiration from the viewer,
Their peaks as steep and majestic as the Five Sacred Mountains,
From this one knows that they harboured no remnants of little hills or rivers in their breasts.
This work derives from a study sketch by Lu Haoran [Lu Hong 盧鴻 (active 8th century)].

古人畫使人見之生敬，其巒頭巖嚴如五嶽，固知古人胸中不蓄殘山剩水也。此作從盧浩然粉本來。

**LEAF B**
'River Scene with Boats'
A guest who came here from Changshan and Yushan tells me of the marvels of the landscape there. Taking up my brush, I tried it here.

客有自常山、玉山來者，告余山水之奇，因以筆試之。

**LEAF C**
'Mountain Valley with Cottages'
The brushwork of Mr. Gu Baozhuang, a man of the recent time, quite resembles my own. The present work falls in between Gong and Gu; one can scarcely tell who did it. Yeyi Xian.

近代顧寶幢先生，其用筆頗類我。此作在龔顧之間，幾不能辨。
野遺賢

**LEAF D**
'Mountains and Mist-Filled Valleys'

Imitating Nangong's [Mi Fu 米芾 (1051–1107)] [painting] on silk.

摹南宮縑素。

**LEAF E**
'Desolate Grove on the Far Bank'

'Desolate Grove on the Far Bank' is the brush and ink of a man of the Northern Song. Yet we do not know who he is, there being neither inscription nor signature. It is now imitated here.

荒林遠岸是北宋人筆墨，不知誰氏，無款識，茲摹於此。

**LEAF F**
'Village on a Mountainous Lakeshore'

Having painted what I saw in a dream, a friend says: 'the shores of the lakes in our Zhejiang often have spots like this.'

寫夢中所見，友人云吾浙中湖干多有此處。

**LEAF G**
'Lakeshore with Cottages'

Dachi's [Huang Gongwang 黃公望 (1269–1354)] brush and ink also come from Dong [Dong Yuan 董源 (?–around 962)] and Ju [Juran 巨然 (active second half of 10th century)]. The painting conveys this thought.

大癡筆墨未嘗不從董巨來，茲寫其意。

**LEAF H**
'The Peach Blossom Studio'

My old friend Chang Feng [d. 1662] often paints the Peach-Blossom Studio. This picture uses his idiom to remember him. It is like adapting stanzas to harmony in poetry.

老友張風慣寫桃花書屋。茲憶其人，用其法為之，如詩之有和章也。

**LEAF I**
'Pavilion on a Lake'

The scenery depicted here exists in the reality and does not come from the paper and brush.

此有其境，不得自楮墨間。

**LEAF J**
'Lone Tree in a Mountainous Lake'

Ni Tsan (1301–1374) really did paint such a view, but people nowadays don't believe it. I imitate it here, to wait for those who would understand.

倪瓚實有此圖，今人不之信。因摹之，以待知者。

**LEAF K**
Colophon

On New Year's Day of the *xinhai* year [1671], sprinkling some tea about that I had specially set aside, I made sacrifice to the vast heavens. In the mountains I sealed my door and sat quietly, communicating with neither relatives nor friends. Having washed my ink-stone and tried out my brush, I brought out this blank album. I painted away like this for some ten days, but then my "flower activities" became somewhat burdensome, and it was already the end of spring before I finished it. I dare not say that I have enjoyed in full measure the unalloyed happiness in this world, and yet, compared with those who always act according to rules and etiquette, is not what I have attained a little more? I record this here with a smile. Resident of Half-an-Acre, Gong Xian.

辛亥元旦，潑藏茗祀昊蒼。於山中閉戶靜坐，不通姻友，滌硯試筆出素冊寫之，如此者旬日。後來花事稍繁,至暮春始卒業。不敢日人間清福被我享盡，而較之周旋於禮法之間者，所得不已多乎。因一笑而記之。半畝居人龔賢

Inscriptions, colophon and seals by the artist; seals by Baoxi 寶熙 (1871–30); seal by Jin Cheng 金城 (1878–1926); colophon (dated 1918) and seals by Luo Zhenyu 羅振玉 (1866–1940)

(Translation adapted from the work of Mark F. Wilson, Kansas City and Cleveland 1980, pp.279–81)

## 71
SHITAO (1642–1707)
### Sketches of Calligraphy and Painting by Qingxiang

Sketches of calligraphy and painting by Qingxiang [Shitao]

清湘書畫稿

**POEM 1**
'Going South, Bidding Farewell to the Lords of the Golden Terrace'[1]

The wings of the *kun* cover a thousand *li*;
The Hundred Birds are no match for it.
But in the vastness of Heaven and Earth,
Even it is like an insect.
Tiring, he leans on Penglai's rock,
Reviving, he soars over streams and oceans.
He comes and goes without hindrance;
Nature always moves at a measured pace.

My life began like that of an ant,
My movements have led me to travel far.
At first entering the waters of Chu;
Then journeying to the hills of Wu.
Riding the wind I came to the Huai and Si,
On a breeze I reached the imperial fief.
*Lan* and *hui* orchids originally formed a close covenant;[2]
The generative forces of nature were bound together.
I was touched that my Lord purified my heart;
I am ashamed that I sullied my Lord's gaze.
For three years I did not look back [to the south];
But suddenly, I rushed for my boat.

True accord is not accidental;
My regret will never end.
The [farewell] poems you gave, labouring with brush and paper,
I shall treasure for a thousand years.

南歸賦別金臺諸公

鯤翼覆千里，百翎難與儔。
曠然思天地，其亦等蜉蝣。
倦欹蓬萊石，興飜滄海流。
往來無逆志，大塊終悠悠。
吾身本蟻寄，動作長遠遊。
一行入楚水，再行入吳丘。
乘風入淮泗，飄來帝王州。
蘭蕙本契合，氤氳相綢繆。
感君洗我心，愧我污君眸。
三年無反顧，一日起歸舟。
良會寔不偶，悵懷那得休。
贈言勞紙筆，繾綣當千秋。

**POEM 2**
Of all the wonderful landscapes in the world,
Even the most singular cannot surpass Min and Zhe.[3]
Although in my life I still haven't visited these places;
In the past I have always heard that people said so.
Precipitous mountain ranges, and rosy clouds ascending straight to heaven;
Dark green peaks, broken-off cliff, as if an abyss.
Mr Wang goes out to govern these two provinces;[4]
Streaming banners and iron axes thread through the mountains.
Last year he was summoned by the Son of Heaven [and left for Beijing];
Wanting to know if the scenery he parted from was still the same.
Pondering but unable to see it, passionately [he asked] me to paint it;
Each and every view he explained, with its special qualities:
Below the mountains white clouds rise across the foothills,
At the tops of the mountains red leaves stretch to the heavens.
Reaching over the trees, on an entirely different scale
Separately there stands a pine, spreading in every direction.
Its scales and armour of tender needles seek no victories,
At a hundred feet it grasps the sky, receiving rain and dew.
First to stand the ice and frost in the heart of winter;
Now with the spring warmth, it is still advancing.
Jade-green bamboo gives shade for ten thousand *mu* around;[5]
The wind generates sounds as pure as music from a jade zither.
Gazing on this scenery, one wants to fly away;
My eyes transform Gentleman Jiang into immortal peaks.[6]

I, Qingxiang, was originally a guest of springs and rocks;
When I heard these words from my lord, my heart grew cooler still.
Opening my collar I then imagine being in the mountain and isles;
Lowering the brush in a single sweep, mountains and forests bloom.
The years and months rush by in the world of men,
But pigments and ink glitter more than gold.

Mountains and streams have been the same from past
to present;

I dedicate this painting to the one who knows my tune.

Dasinong (minister of home affairs and finance), Wang Renyue [Wang Zhi], entrusted me to execute *The Mountain Range of Rosy Clouds* and *The Old Pine Tree* to explain fully their meaning.

天下山水孰奇壯，最奇不過閩與浙。
余生雖未游斯境，舊昔曾聞有人說。
峻嶺仙霞直上天，蒼岳絕壁如臨淵。
王公出為兩省制，旂旄鐵鉞經其巔。
昨年天子近呼來，景物依然尚念哉。
思之不見愛余寫，一一細說傳其材。
嶺下白雲橫麓起，嶺頭紅葉接天開。
參橫樹木總無度，劈立一松勘四顧。
披鱗帶甲嫩不勝，百尺撐空承雨露。
冰霜蚤勵歲寒心，近日春光猶託付。
翠竹連環萬畝陰，風生清籟如瑤琴。
此間注目欲飛去，目送江郎羽化岑。
清湘本為泉石客，聞君此語愈冷心。
開襟便作巒嶼想，落筆一搜華嶽林。
歲月驅人世，粉墨輝黃金。
山川自爾同今古，吾將以此贈知音。
大司農王人嶽屬寫仙霞嶺及古松樹並悉命意

**POEM 3**

Not recognizing the jade from Jing Mountain [in Hubei],
How would one know that the tablet would be flawed
or brilliant?'[7]
In my small studio, I had just settled in,
In the lonely courtyard, a few transplanted flowers.
It happened that a tall carriage came by,
The praises of his reputation had not yet been sung.
When the young man sat then before me,
How should this old fellow dare respond in poetry?
Tossing and turning, it is hard to be sincere,
Ambivalence flourishes more extravagantly.
Manners and writing were put aside owing to my illness,
The business of poetry describes the heart's depth.
Wishing to lend a hand to my friend,
I open the red silk curtains and begin to write.

As I lay ill in the Ciyuan Temple in Beijing, it happened that the Dasikou (minister of justice) Mr Tu (d.1697) came to pay a visit. At that time I didn't know that the master's son [Tu] Yue had already left, so I composed this by way of apology.

不覩荊山玉，安知圭玷華。
小堂初下榻，獨院少移花。
時有高車過，風標未許誇。
紅顏方乍對，白雪敢吟呀。
輾轉忱難已，躊躇興益奢。
禮文因病廢，詩事寫心遐。
願借同堂手，持書起絳紗。

臥病慈源，值大司寇圖公見訪。
爾時不知主人月公往便，感賦以謝。

**POEM 4**

Half my life a monk, wandering like a cloud
For nine years I have longed for you.
Through the yellow dust, in vain I tread,
White hairs slowly appear on my head.
Now being tired, I think of the four recluses in Shang Mountain;
Let me return, following in Ziyou's footsteps.[8]
In hermit's costume, in the last month of spring,
On a floating leaf, I shall sail down to Yangzhou.

Sent to Mei Yuangong [Mei Qing 梅清] (1623–97) in Tianyange Studio of Xuancheng [in Anhui Province].

半世遊雲客，思君歷九秋。
黃塵空促步，白髮漸臨頭。
倦矣懷商老，歸兮襲子猷。
薜蘿春盡月，飄葉下揚州。

寄梅淵公宣城天延閣

**POEM 5**

The boat is moored at Botou.[9] As for [my companions] Ding Yunyuan, Zheng Yan'an and the rest, their speech is pure and their discussions are elegant. [They have]repeatedly asked me for calligraphy and painting. I have written this to present to them and to commemorate my friendship with people of the ordinary world.

Like new sand on the ancient shore, the 'silken cords' gather;[10]
Imperial river and 'official willows' greet the traveller's boat.[11]
Loud songs resound to the blue beyond the clouds;
Speaking our native dialect all the way to Botou, it's hard to part.
With deep sighs the labourers, labouring of their own accord;
Alas for our generation, for whom are we so sad?
To Heaven's limits south and north, I encounter those who
know me;
How could I not with purest heart present this brush and
ink to you?

舟泊泊頭。丁允元、鄭延庵諸子清言雅論，復索予書畫，作書以贈，訂方外交

古岸新沙錦纜收，御河官柳送行舟。
號歌直接青雲外，鄉語難分到泊頭。
太息勞人勞自肯，番嗟我輩為誰愁。
天涯南北逢知己，敢不虛心翰墨酬。

**POEM 6**

After nine days on the boat, I and my colleagues dispelled sad thoughts with laughter, writing and merry-making in Xiazhen.[12]

We had incense, we had tea and we had chrysanthemums,
Although we didn't climb up, our spirits were high.
From the boat we viewed the winding mountain features,
At the water's edge we played with ink, ink that was lustrous
and fine.

Men in white robes brought wine, a gift from Nanyang,
We in our black hats set 'Xiazhen' as our theme.[13]
Generally those who travel feel very lonely and desolate,
Level sands and shallow waters stretch to the edge of the sky.

舟中九日。 夏鎮與諸同人遣興笑作

有香有茗有黃花，雖不登臨興也嘉。
舟上看山山勢轉，水邊弄墨墨光華。
白衣攜酒南陽獻，烏帽拈題夏鎮呀。
總是客途寥寂甚，平沙淺水接天涯。

**POEM 7**

'Work Chants on the Gucheng River'[14]

A thousand turns, a hundred bends on the Gucheng River,[15]
Slanting east, stretching west, dividing the craggy peaks.
White poplars, clustered trees, branches touching the heavens,
Here and there lining up along ancient trodden tracks.
Old tombs, desolate stelae, ancestral temples along its
winding course;
Water flowing, waves crashing, against the snow wolf's lair.
Passengers who come this way heave many a sigh,
Soaring and axe-cut sheer, those overhanging cliffs.
On larger boats the painted drums beat fast like a
weaver's shuttle,

The haulers drag them inch by inch, oh!
Returning empty, the grain barges scrape past the sky;
The sound of their singing penetrates the very clouds
in heaven.

故城河口號

千迴百折故城河，東傾西長分嵯峨。
白楊灌木參天柯，處處成行古道麼。
古塚荒碑廟逶迤，水流浪打雪狼窩。
行路之人嗟嘆多，崢嶸斧削飛嵒坡。
樓船畫鼓快如梭，錦纜人來寸寸呵。
歸空糧艘遮天摩，歌聲歌徹青雲和。

**POEM 8**

'Work Chants at the Linqing Locks'[16]

The land slants, the water drains, one must rely upon the locks,
Like thousand-*li* thunder chariots, a swift and angry roar.
Curling waves cast back, with pearls of tinted spray,
Tumbling in space, dancing shards, snow-splitting waves.
Seventy-two gates stand firm against the north;
Going east from here, the water level gradually rises.
The bright clouds twist and turn, weaving an autumn coat,
The immortal banks divide the land in stripes.
Strike the gongs, beat the drums, in strong unceasing din,
Travellers stop to watch the barges leap the water.
Flying sails clustered together, riding with decorated flags;
Push open the window, roll up the blinds, let me wield
the brush!

臨清過閘口號

地傾水瀉須憑閘，千里雷車迅怒嘷。
捲浪拋開珠散彩，崩空舞碎雪分濤。
七十二門向北牢，東歸此去漸憑高。
錦雲旋繞織秋袍，仙障中分虎勢條。
鳴鑼擊鼓壯滔滔，行人駐看躍淵艚。
飛帆擁簇駕圖旄，推窗卷幔得揮毫。

**POEM 9**

Our boat is about to pass the eighth lock,[17]
The lake waters stretch endlessly away.
Fishing boats of a thousand families along the banks;
The reed plumes are of one colour with the sand.

The boat is passing the eighth lock; I paint [this] for my friends.

舟行將八閘，湖水盪無涯。
漁艇千家岸，蘆花一色沙。

舟過八閘為友人作畫

**POEM 10**

'In the Snow, Thinking of Zhang Benshan (Zhang Shu)'

Who is the gentleman my eyes behold?
On the road north of Yan Mountain [in Hebei],
Mr Zhang Tianjin.[18]
He comes crunching through the snow with his ten
thousand books;
[Cups] in hand, we laugh and toast; the wine's half gone.
One cup, one rhyme, each word perfect;
Whether writing regular or cursive, to whom to give it?
I admire you, crazier than 'Crazy Zhang'[19]

I admire you, twisting and breaking the spirit of Li Bo (701–62).
That you bestow upon me a fan is simply splendid;
Write with fine brush, your small standard script is outstanding.[20]
Now I shall halt my brush, for I dare not match;
Now I shall stay my hand, give time for my friend.
You know I am down on my luck;
You worry about this penniless monk.
You guide me with Buddhist teaching;
You inspire me with our shared thoughts.
It is a hardship for both, me to enter the city and you to come
to the village,
This inclination of our minds, this pouring out of feeling,
must be our past affinity.
How lonely to be without close friends,
With a face full of life's dust.
How odd, and yet not odd;
With this long lament, I take my leave of [Mt] Xitai.[21]

眼中才子誰為是，燕山北道張天津。
此時破雪擁萬卷，手中笑謝酒半巡。
一觴一韻字字真，的真草稿惠何人。
羨君顛死張顛手，羨君摧折李白神。
贈我雙箑稱上妙，秋毫小楷堪稱倫。
至今停筆不敢和，至今縮手時為親。
知我潦倒病，念我無髮貧。
授我以心法，憶我相思陳。
入城出郭兩苦辛，傾心吐語皆前因。
落落無知己，滿面生埃塵。
奇哉奇不已，長嘯謝西秦。

雪中懷張笨山

**POEM 11**

Through half a lifetime of dust blown from south to north,
Though I have left the world, my friends of the world are
dearer to me.
Being a stranger for so long, not even aware of my own suffering,
As a monk I hardly meet anyone with whom to share my ideas.
Like a celestial immortal come to this world, with talent
outstanding,
My friend's force of mind is able to leap beyond the crowd.
You see that fortune and fame are but floating clouds,
You take your ease with brush and ink and ancient books.
To keep a beloved guest, you refuse the 'Thousand-day' wine,[22]
Your free-spirited character surpasses the portals of the
'Five Nobles'.[23]
In the four seas the fishermen [recluses] follow your rhythm
and song,
Chanting 'Long Sword, come home!' sighing for the emperor's
descendants.
Man's life flits by so one might as well relax,
Drink without restraint, till one cannot see straight.
I am moved that you used white jade to buy songs and laughter,[24]
This tipsy guest carries on until the east is bright.
Pour out emotions, tip over thoughts, words are not begrudged,
Turn the mountains, roll the seas, reach enlightenment.[25]
Sitting, the guests all say let joy be unconfined,
Their songs a mix of sound, with ice and snow around.
Frozen clouds envelop the earth, the wine dragon awakens;
Their resolve is lofty and noble, every one a hero.
This night with true resolve, set free our cherished wish,
Tomorrow for a decree, published by our imperial lord.

Thinking of you, these memories are engraved on my mind. On a snowy winter's day of the *xinwei* year [1691], Mr Zhang Ruzuo received me.[26] Many talented men and outstanding scholars are gathered at his seat. Tomorrow, Mr Zhang journeys to the capital Beijing. In thanks I present this poem as a gift.

半生南北老風塵，出世多從入世親。
客久不知身是苦，為僧少見意中人。
天仙下世真才傑，我公心力能超群。
君視富貴如浮雲，遊戲翰墨空典墳。
愛客肯辭千日酒，風流氣壓五侯門。
四海漁樊齊拍唱，歸來長鋏歎王孫。
人生飄忽等閒情，且隨酣暢眼縱橫。
感君白璧買歌笑，醉客不放東方明。
傾情倒意語不惜，回山轉海開旃檀。
座客皆言不盡歡，歌兒聲雜冰雪團。
凍雲匝地酒龍醒，意氣崢嶸豪士全。
此夜真堪寫懷抱，明朝詔下君王宣。

相思回首心拳拳，辛未冬日雪中，張汝作先生見招才人傑士擁座一時，公來日有都門之行。賦謝兼贈

**POEM 12**

Only to be free of the dusty world,
Ever to be with the chaste clouds.
No other concerns in the rest of my life
Can compare with these two gentlemen.

但不著塵俗，皆當附凌雲。
餘生有何係，無如此二君。

**POEM 13**

Tiandu Peak rises four thousand spans,[27]
Hidden within it are 36 ethereal worlds.
Lan River has 24 streams[28]
Rushing and tumbling under the majestic mountain.
Mt Cen's immovable pillar standing midstream,[29]
Yan and Qing, twin rivers, sounding cascades.
Pine Wind Hall faces Longcong Mountain,[30]
Those born here are now spread out in the world,
So many outstanding, as strong as dragons.
Of the friends of my life, half I met here;
Wang, Wu and Guan from south of the river,[31]
Jun is talented in medicine and handsome.[32]
With fine beard, white hair, a bright pair of eyes,
Generous with his money, helping on all sides.
Charming and knowledgeable, and discriminating,
He can be silent, unspeaking, but of deepest spirit,
Clear and musical, his voice is bold and strong,
Children and grandchildren fill his house, all talented,
When he talks aloud, his breath is wind and thunder,
When he gets excited, the whole hall opens.
Burning incense, splashing ink, in true reclusive fashion,
Qingxiang, the blind arhat, Yuanji.

天都直聳四千仞，中藏三十六芙蓉。
練江二十四谿水，爭流倒瀉兮朝宗。
岑山砥柱中流溶，煙晴二溪聲淙淙。
松風堂在籠叢衝，至今開合散天下。
出入往往矯如龍，我生之友交其半。
谿南潛口汪吳貫，君家得藥好容顏。
美髯鶴髮雙眸燦，慷慨揮金結四方。
風流文采分低昂，默而不語神溟溟。
琅然歌發聲蒼蒼，兒孫滿座皆英才。
雄談氣宇生風雷，狂瀾興發中堂開。
焚香灑墨真幽哉，清湘瞎尊者原濟。

Inscription and dedication at the end of the scroll:
Old tree, deserted mountain, I once sat for 40 small kalpas.
In the long summer, the sixth lunar month of the *bingzi* year [1696], at my guest stay at Pine Wind Hall. The Master [Cheng Jun] entrusted me to play with ink for delight. Oughtn't we to call the man in the picture the next incarnation of the blind arhat? Ha ha!

老樹空山一坐四十小劫。時丙子長夏六月客松風堂。
主人屬予弄墨為快。 圖中之人可呼之為瞎尊者後身否也? 呵呵

Inscriptions and seals by the artist; seal by Xiang Yuan 項源 (1736–1850); inscription (dated 1927) and seal by Zeng Xi 曾熙 (1861–1930); seals by Pang Yuanji 龐元濟 (1864–1949); unidentified seals

(Translation by Roderick Whitfield and Chia-Ling Yang, with reference to Fraser 1989, pp.47–65)

1 Jintai, the Golden Terrace, was one of the eight famous scenes to the south-east of Beijing. It refers to Beijing in this context.
2 *Lan* and *hui* (*Lysimachia foenum-graecum Hance*) are both fragrant orchids.
3 Min and Zhe, i.e. Fujian and Zhejiang Provinces
4 Wang Zhi (1614–95), also known as Renyue, received the highest marks in the national examinations in 1655, and was the administrator in Guangdong (1666) and Jiangxi (1687) Provinces and viceroy of Min-Zhe (Fujian and Zhejiang Provinces) (1688). When Emperor Kangxi (r. 1662–1722) journeyed to Zhejiang in 1689, he praised Wang Zhi for being incorruptible and righteous. Soon after this meeting Wang was summoned by the Emperor to Beijing, and in the fifth lunar month of 1689 became Hubu shangshu or Dasinong, minister of home affairs and finance. This poem was written a year after Wang's arrival in Beijing, so perhaps between 1690 and 1691. It indicates that Shitao made two paintings, *The Mountain Range of Rosy Clouds* and *The Old Pine Tree*, to illustrate the scenery in Zhejiang and Fujian at Wang Zhi's request: it may have been written on one of these two paintings as a dedication. See Wu 1967, p. 58; Fraser 1989, p. 9.
5 10,000 *mu* are equivalent to approximately 667 hectares.
6 A mountain in Zhejiang Province
7 The allusion is to King Wen, the Zhou dynasty (c.11th century BCE–256 BCE) founder, who hired a skilled jade craftsman to cut a stone that had been presented as jade and rejected by two earlier rulers. The couplet relates how Shitao did not realize that his youthful visitor had been Tu Yuepo, who inherited his wonderful qualities from his father, Tu Na (known as Tu Jintang, minister of justice from 1688 to 1697), to whom this poem is dedicated. At that time, Shitao was unwell and was staying for a while at Ciyuan Temple in the Jinyu Chi ('Goldfish pond') district in south Beijing.
8 Ziyou: Wang Huizhi (d.388), the fifth son of the famous calligrapher Wang Xizhi (303–65)
9 Botou (literally, 'Quayside'): an important staging post on the Grand Canal, just south of Cangzhou in Hebei Province
10 Silken cords: that is, gaily decorated pleasure boats
11 In the eleventh century, willows were planted along the banks of the Grand Canal.
12 Xiazhen: an old town in Weishan County, Shandong Province, on the Grand Canal

13 Worn by hermits
14 The title is actually written at the end of the poem.
15 Gucheng: on the Grand Canal at the border between Hebei and Shandong Provinces, 100 kilometres south of Botou
16 Linqing: in Shandong Province, on the Grand Canal, just south of the border with Hebei Province
17 There were eight new locks built along the Grand Canal in Yi County in Shandong by 1651, at the end of the Ming dynasty (1368–1644) and the beginning of the Qing (1644–1911): Taizhuang, Houqian, Dunzhuang, Dingmiao, Wannian, Zhangzhuang, Desheng and Hanzhuang.
18 Zhang Tianjin: Zhang Shu (1659–1704), also known as Benshan and Nianyi, was a native of Funing, yet residing in Tianjin in Hebei Province. Hence, Shitao gave him the nickname Zhang 'Tianjin' in the poem. He was talented at composing poetry and calligraphy after Zhang Xu's (act. c.700–50) style.
19 Zhang Xu, famous for his 'wild cursive' calligraphy
20 Literally, 'with autumn hair' – for the highest-quality brushes, the hairs of the wolf or other animals are taken in the autumn, when they are in top condition.
21 There is a Mt Xitai near Luoyang. Perhaps a play on Zhang Shu's name Benshan ('original mountain').
22 According to Zhang Hua (act. 3rd century), a wine that would make one happily drunk for a thousand days.
23 Renowned for hospitality in the Han dynasty (206 BCE–220 CE).
24 The phrase 'with gold and white jade, buy songs and laughter' is the first line of a poem written in 753 by Li Bo (701–62) to see off his friend Yuan Canjun. They had journeyed through the Taihang Mountains to Taiyuan, where Li was royally entertained by his friend and his father.
25 Literally, 'open the sandalwood [throne and obtain samadhi]', a phrase from the *Avatamsaka Sūtra*; T 1739.36.981a11
26 Zhang Lin, also known as Ruzuo and Lu'an, was the older brother of Zhang Shu. On Zhang Lin, see Zhang and Gao 2008.
27 Tiandu, Celestial Capital Peak, 1,829 metres high, is one of the three main peaks of Huangshan (Mount Huang) in Anhui Province.
28 Lan River runs through Anhui Province; twenty-four of its tributaries flow from Huangshan.
29 Mt Cen lies north of Shexian, the capital of Anhui Province, and south-east of Huangshan.
30 Songfeng Tang (Pine Wind Hall) was the studio of Cheng Jun (see below), to whom Shitao dedicated this work. His family counted many brilliant personages.
31 Fengnan River in She County, Anhui Province
32 Cheng Jun (1638–1704), also known as Geren and Su'an, was a wealthy merchant in Anhui residing between Hangzhou and Yangzhou for business. His studio, Pine Wind Hall, was located south of She County in Anhui. He was a patron to Shitao and Bada Shanren; several paintings by Shitao were dedicated to him, including *Listening to the Stream* (Shanghai Museum; 1701) and *Bird's-eye View of the Mountain* (Sichuan Provincial Museum; 1703). See Zhu 2005, pp. 364–8.

## 72

YUAN JIANG (act. c.1680–1730)

**The Palace of Nine Perfections**

'The Palace of Nine Perfections'. An imitation of the ancient style by Yuan Jiang from Hanshang [Yangzhou] in the *xiaoyang* [Indian summer], or tenth, lunar month of the *xinwei* year of the Kangxi reign [1691]

九成宮。邗上袁江擬古，時康熙辛未小陽月

Inscription and seals by the artist; label strips by an unknown artist

(Translation by Shi-yee Liu)

## 73

FA RUOZHEN (1613–96)

**Clouds and Mist in the Mountains**

Seals by the artist; colophon (dated 1855) and seals by Wu Cizhi 吳慈治 (act. mid-19th century)

## 74

BADA SHANREN (1626–1705)

**Flowers on the River**

The flowers on the river,
Have a thousand leaves.
When the wind blows, they sway ceaselessly like the gorgeous drunken young man Liulang [Zhang Zongchang, a 7th-century courtier].
Twisting and turning thousands of times, with postures as captivating as Madam Ding Liuniang's [a courtesan in the Sui dynasty (581–618)],
They dance and move far away until reaching the Cowherd (Altair) who overlooks the northern side of the galaxy.
As the rain is about to descend on Mount Wu, the verdant leaves began to lean to the side;
When the wind blows over, the sea of clouds drives away the darkness on the pond.
Droplets on lotus leaves are as plump as pearls and untouchable;
I painted them over with blots of dark ink in my mind.
Mr Huiyan pitied my old age and loneliness, summoning Li Bo [701–62] for a meeting.
Li Bo said to me:
The lotus leaves are as vast as
The land conquered by Marquis Bowang [Zhang Qian (164–114 BCE)].
The leaves move in the wind back and forth like a shuttle,
As if to be carried beyond the sky.
They dance elegantly and swiftly, like Madam Liuniang wielding her sword.
They are as exuberant as those in Wu and Yue in the eighth month,
And they are the pictures created by the Immortal on the River.
The lotus stems are as tall as sixty feet,
Far away from the warmth and coldness of the world, the flowers wear a tall hat.
I replied:
I live on Mount Kuanglu,
Where there are dense forests,
The Eastern Jin dynasty [317–420] Daoist monk [Lu Xiujing (406–77)] is also my neighbour.
The 108 rosary beads
Can be made of great diamonds,
Or little jade stones,
But how can they compare with, in my picture,
A single lotus seed that is visible but does not exist?
Alas! The entire world is within my lotus.
Have I transmuted the ingredients of the Elixir?
Happily singing my way,
I immerse myself in the splashes of spring water and the sprays of flowers.
East and west, south and north after all are the same.
Day and night different things are too complicated to expound,
Now I only want to meet the hermit of Mount Zhi.

Mr Huiyan asked me to make this painting. Beginning in the fifth lunar month of the *dingchou* year [1697] through the sixth, seventh and eight lunar months, the lotus leaves and flowers gradually came into being. Playfully I composed this 'Song of Flowers on the River', which is only slightly over 200 words. Hereby I submit them for correction. Bada Shanren

河上花，一千葉。六郎買醉無休歇。萬轉千迴丁六娘，直到牽牛望河北。欲雨巫山翠盖斜，片雲卷去昆明黑。饋爾明珠擎不得，涂上心頭共團墨。蕙嵒先生憐余老大無一遇，萬一由拳拳太白。太白對予言：博望侯，天般大。葉如梭，在天外。六娘劍術行方邁。團圞八月吳兼會，河上仙人正圖畫。撐腸拄腹六十尺，炎涼盡作高冠戴。余曰：匡廬山，密林邇，東晉黃冠亦朋比。算來一百八顆念頭穿，大金剛，小瓊玖，爭似圖畫中，實相無相，一顆蓮花子。吁嗟世界蓮花裏。還丹未？樂歌行，泉飛疊疊花循循。東西南北怪底同。朝還並蒂難重陳，至今想見芝山人。

蕙嵒先生屬畫此卷，自丁丑五月以至六七八月，荷葉、荷花落成，戲作〈河上花歌〉，僅二百餘字，呈正。八大山人

Inscription by the artist; colophon and seal by Prince Cheng, Yongxing 成親王永瑆 (1752–1823); seals by Xu Naipu 許乃普 (1787–1866); colophon and seals by Xu Shichang 徐世昌 (1855–1939)

## 75

WANG YUANQI (1642–1715)

**Early Spring in the Mountains**

Between winter and spring, I was on duty at the Zhilu [Imperial Study] during the day and had no time to paint for anyone. Under the current imperial orders, I have been appointed to the advance party.[1] On the way to the lodging in the mountains, I had quite an inspiration [to paint]. After painting the initial dots and washes, I completed this work gradually – suddenly it has been half a year!
Early autumn of the *yiyou* year [1705], Lutai Qi [Wang Yuanqi]

余冬春之交，日在直廬，無暇為人作畫。今奉扈從先行之命，途中至山間宿處，頗有會心處，點染後陸續而成，忽半載矣。
時乙酉初秋麓臺祁

Inscription and seals by the artist; seal by Zhu Zhipu 朱稚圃 (act. 18th century); seal by Chen Jieqi 陳介祺 (1813–84); unidentified seal

(Translation by Chia-Ling Yang)

1 Emperor Kangxi (r. 1662–1722) undertook six tour inspections to the south between 1684 and 1707. Wang was appointed to prepare for the fifth tour inspection in 1705.

## 76

XU YANG (1712–c.1779)

### Prosperous Suzhou

Only my dynasty has such a thriving government and culture, surpassing the achievements of the Three Dynasties [Xia (c.22nd/21st–c.17th century BCE), Shang (c.17th–c.11th century BCE) and Zhou (c.1100–256 BCE)]. Its geographical area and the size of its population are unprecedented. Your Subject is so fortunate to have met with this flourishing age. He has depicted its peacefulness in this *Prosperous Suzhou* scroll, so his painting skills are of some use. The painting begins with Lingyan Hill, travels east through Mudu, passes Heng Hill, crosses Lake Shi and proceeds to Shangfang Hill. From the northern bank of Lake Tai and between Shi and He Hills, it enters the city of Gusu [Suzhou]. After exiting the gate Changmen through the three gates Feng, Pan and Xu, it turns toward Shantang Bridge and ends at Tiger Hill. Along the way, [one can admire the] steepness of the city walls and moats, the multiplicity of the official structures and the beauty of the landscapes. Then [in the suburbs], there are fishermen and woodcutters, peasants and weavers here and there; [in the city,] merchants gather like clouds to form markets, and shops line up tidily like fish scales – these all make the city the great metropolis of the south-east. [As for the social customs,] wine is offered to the elderly in the springtime to wish them longevity and honour them with respect. Marriages are arranged at a suitable time, following the appropriate rituals. [Regarding education,] huge candles with multiple flames are burned to recruit talent in the examination halls [at night]; the fragrance of ten thousand books diffuses from the teachers' seats in private schools. Farmers sing joyfully in the fields, while travellers chant on their journeys. This harmonious and prosperous atmosphere is beyond the capacity of painting to represent. Generation after generation, the rulers of our dynasty have bestowed their profound benevolence and benefaction [upon the people] for over a hundred years. [Two years ago,] His Majesty's grace returned [to this region] again, and beneficent acts were performed more than ever. The people of this land rejoice in gratitude as they are so joyous and fortuitous, and encourage one another to become moral citizens of this prosperous age – how could all of this be coincidental? When Confucius left for the State of Wei, he constantly planned cultural and educational reforms, yet [his efforts] were to no avail. Today, [his vision] has finally blossomed to the fullest extent. Despite His Majesty working diligently day and night, He treats his people as one would a wounded patient, and never diminishes in His care for them. Hence, [this country] retains its stability and increasing prosperity, and will forever be peaceful and auspicious. As a courtier serving the inner court, I am obliged to depict the thriving governance of the Emperor although being incapable of capturing its full brilliance. The painting was completed in the ninth lunar month of the *jimao* year of the Qianlong reign [1759], and is inscribed respectfully by Your Subject Xu Yang.

欽 惟我國家, 治化昌明, 超軼三代。幅員之廣, 生齒之繁, 亙古未有。臣幸遭逢之盛, 圖寫太平, 為《盛世滋生圖》一卷, 臣執藝所有事也。其圖自靈巖山起, 由木瀆鎮東行, 過橫山, 渡石湖, 歷上方山。從太湖北岸, 介獅、和兩山間, 入姑蘇郡城。自葑、盤、胥三門出閶門外, 轉山塘橋, 至虎邱山止。其間城池之峻險, 廨署之森羅, 山川之秀麗 ; 以及漁樵上下, 耕織紛紜;商賈雲屯, 市廛鱗列, 為東南一都會。至若春樽獻壽, 尚齒為先, 嫁娶朱陳, 及時成禮。三條燭燄, 或掄才於童子之場 ; 萬卷書香, 或受業於先生之席。耕者歌於野, 行者咏於塗。熙皞之風, 丹青不能盡寫。要皆自我朝聖聖相承, 深仁厚澤, 淪浹於百有餘年之久。我皇上鑾輿再幸, 行慶施惠, 有加無已。斯地斯民, 故能感激鼓舞, 樂樂利利, 交相勸勉, 共為盛世之良民, 豈偶然哉。昔孔子適衛, 惓惓於富教之謨, 而未之行焉。至今日而全盛矣, 大備矣。皇上宵旰憂勞, 猶且視民如傷, 無時少釋。所以保泰持盈, 永太平福澤於無疆者也。臣執事內庭, 能不益加觀感以摹寫帝治光昌於萬一乎? 圖成於乾隆己卯九月 臣徐揚敬跋

Inscription and seal by the artist; seals by the Qianlong emperor 乾隆 (r. 1736–96); seal by the Jiaqing emperor 嘉慶 (r. 1796–1820); seals by the Xuantong emperor 宣統 (r. 1908–11); seal by the Dongbei Museum 東北博物館 (1949–59) [now the Liaoning Provincial Museum]

## 77

ZHENG XIE (1693–1765)

### Bamboo and Rock

An elderly gentleman of seventy am I, calm, without ambition.
My age of adventure belongs to years long past.
I painted dense, short bamboo stalks, hardly over one foot tall,
And let you, green mountain, surpass them by a head's length.

Painted for my big younger cousin to comment on – your humble older brother Zheng Xie, also named Banqiao

七十衰翁澹不求, 風光都付老春秋。
畫來密篠澹踰尺, 讓爾青山出一頭。

燮堂大弟教畫, 墨兄板橋鄭燮。

Inscription and seals by the artist; label strip and seal by Yang Zhaojun 楊昭儁 (act. Republican period [1912–49])

(Translation by Klaas Ruitenbeek)

## 78

LUO PIN (1733–99)

### Ghost Amusement

'The human body is unlike metal and stone, it decays like grass and wood; but what is a human being? It is not in my possession.' These are sentences in the inscription for the eighth picture of my first *Ghost Amusement* painting. The inscriptions for the seven pictures before it are as abundant as trees in a forest, so I will not note them here. Today I inscribe this for Ziqian, my third brother, and invite him to try to contemplate its meaning in the hope it will prompt a turning word. On the sixth day of the six month in the second year of Jiaqing [1797], as I am about to depart the capital, written by Monk Yiyun, Luo Pin.

「人非金石, 草木同朽 ; 何以謂人, 此非我有」。此題余初圖鬼趣第八幀句也。前七趣題者如林, 余不复贅, 今為子千三兄書此, 請試參之, 望下一轉語。嘉慶二年六月六日, 時將出都門, 衣雲和尚羅聘

Inscription and seals by the artist; colophon (dated 1932) and seals by Wu Hufan 吳湖帆 (1894–1968); colophon (dated 1933) and seal by Xu Chengyao 許承堯 (1874–1946); colophon (dated 1934) and seals by Shou Nie 壽鑈 (1885–1949); colophon (dated 1941) and seals by Lin Sijin 林思進 (1873–1953); seal by Zhan Shanzi 張善孖 (1882–1940); seals by Zhang Daqian 張大千 (1899–1983); seals by Liu Zuochou 劉作籌 (1911–1993); unidentified seal.

## 79

REN YI (1840–95)

### Portrait of Gao Yongzhi as Calligrapher-Beggar

In Wu City [Suzhou] the sound of the flute is music for Heaven,
Why take so much trouble to study and be indebted to calligraphy?
Calligraphy debts respect no one, and evading them is not easy,
All the world is quite clear about calligraphy.
Untidy hair and dirty clothes: you get the idea,
Clear-eyed [buyers] before me, and still unwilling to sell.
Dongpo dozed off when his ink stone broke,[1]
Xizhi's strong brush was halted by aberrant characters.[2]
If you ask me which ancient calligrapher knew my tune,
It would be Li from Jiangdu and Cai from Chenliu.[3]
All day by the ink pond,[4] just an excuse for laziness,
Passionate about one's own writing, isn't that too much?
I love to discuss calligraphy, it blows my mind,
Itching to ply my brush, like a scab on my face.
Agreeing to endure a fast, to pursue the gulls,[5]
Or let a troop of dwarves eat till they are full.
The ideas in my calligraphy have no method in them,
Shame, unknowing, to beg for writing, just be warned,
Asking for my poor writing, I have to laugh,
This request for calligraphy is just too, too odd.

In Thatched Hall of Self Indulgence in Music and Books [Studio of Ren Yi], painted by Ren Yi of Shanyin and inscribed by Xugu on the eighth day of the first month, the thirteenth year of the Guangxu reign [1887]

吳門簫聲好天籟, 何苦學書負書債。
書債無台避不易, 天下人人識書丐。
亂頭麤服得書意, 肉眼當前未肯賣。
東坡皴俔高枕臥, 羲之俗字健筆礙。
古人知己問誰是, 江都李與陳留蔡。
臨池日日推懶病, 愛己之鉤無乃太。
見我論書心輒醉, 技癢弄筆類爬疥。
相約忍飢逐鷗鷺, 一任侏儒飽成隊。
我書意造本無法, 愧不如自書己戒。
索我題句真可笑, 此事應書咄咄怪。

於滬上琴書自樂草堂, 山陰任頤作圖, 虛谷題。
時光緒十三年正月八日也

Inscription (dated 1887) and seal by Xugu 虛谷 (1821–96)

(Translation by Chia-Ling Yang, with reference to Richard Vinograd, Vinograd 1992a, p .147)

1 Su Shi (1037–1101)
2 Wang Xizhi (303 65), universally recognized as the father of Chinese calligraphy
3 Li Yong (678–747), Tang dynasty (618–907) master of *xingshu* or 'running script'; and Cai Yong (132–92), Han dynasty (206 BCE–220 CE) master of *lishu* or 'clerical script'. This is a pun on 'Yong': Li Yong and Cai Yong, both famous calligraphers, shared the same given name as Gao Yong[zhi].
4 Practising calligraphy so diligently that the pond water becomes black
5 The image is from a poem by Su Shi, 'On the Ninth Day, Seeking Zhou and Li on the Lake and Not Finding Them'.

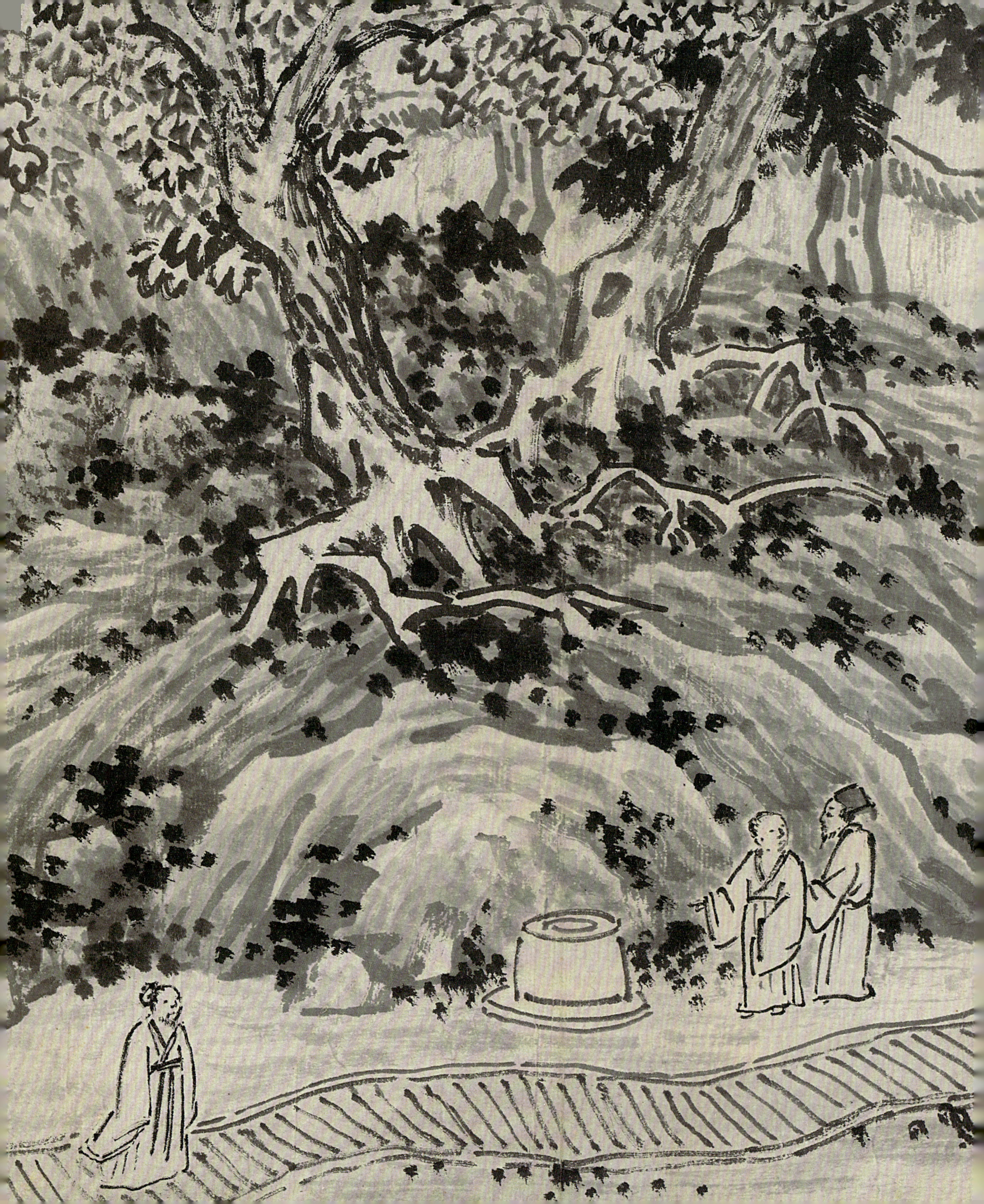

# BIBLIOGRAPHY


*A Collection of Paintings by Lin Liang and Lü Ji* 1997
*A Collection of Paintings by Lin Liang and Lü Ji* (Lin Liang, Lü Ji huaji 林良呂紀畫集), Liu Zheng (刘正) and Liu Jianping (刘建平) (eds), Tianjin 1997

*A Collection of Paintings by Zhao Mengfu* 1995
*A Collection of Paintings by Zhao Mengfu* (Zhao Mengfu huaji 趙孟頫畫集), Shanghai 1995

*A Compendium of Chinese Paintings* 1997–2001
*A Compendium of Chinese Paintings* (Zhongguo huihua quanji 中國繪畫全集), 30 vols, Beijing 1999

*A Compendium of Song Paintings* 2008
*A Compendium of Song Paintings* (Song hua quanji 宋畫全集), Zhejiang daxue Zhongguo gudai shuhua yanjiu zhongxin (浙江大學中國古代書畫研究中心) (ed.), 28 vols, Hangzhou 2008

ACKER 1954
William R.B. Acker (trans. & annot.), *Some T'ang and Pre-T'ang Texts on Chinese Painting*, Leiden 1954

AKIYAMA 1965
Akiyama Terukazu (秋山光和), 'A Study of Two Silk Paintings from Dunhuang Representing a Monk Carrying Sutras and Accompanied by a (Tonkō-ga tora wo tsureta angya sō wo meguru kōsatsu – perio shōrai kinue ni irei no shōkai wo chūshin ni 敦煌画「虎をつれた行脚僧」をめぐる考察ペリオ将来絹絵二遺例の紹介を中心に), *The Journal of Art Studies* (Bijutsu kenkyū 美術研究), vol. 238 (February 1965), pp. 1–21

ALTIERI 1983
Daniel Altieri, 'The Painted Visions of the Red Cliffs', *Oriental Art*, vol. XXIX, no. 3 (1983), pp. 252–64

AMSTERDAM 1992
*Discarding the Brush. Gao Qipei (1672–1734) and the Art of Chinese Finger Painting*, Klaas Ruitenbeek (ed.), exh. cat., Rijksmuseum Amsterdam, Amsterdam 1992

AN (1742) 1993–8
An Qi (安岐), *A Catalogue of Paintings and Calligraphy I Have Observed* (Moyuan huiguan 墨緣彙觀), painting section, vol. 10, reprinted in *A Compendium of Writings on Calligraphy and Painting in China* (Zhongguo shuhua quanshu 中國書畫全書), Lu Fusheng (盧輔聖) (ed.), 14 vols, Shanghai 1993–8; preface to original edition 1742

ANDERSON 1886
William Anderson, F.R.C.S., *Descriptive and Historical Catalogue of a Collection of Japanese and Chinese Paintings in the British Museum*, London 1886

ANN ARBOR 1967
Richard Edwards, *The Painting of Tao-chi*, exh. cat., Ann Arbor 1967

ANN ARBOR 1976
Richard Edwards, *The Art of Wen Cheng-ming (1470–1559)*, exh. cat., The University of Michigan Museum of Art, Ann Arbor 1976

AVRIL 1997
Ellen Avril, *Chinese Art in the Cincinnati Art Museum*, Cincinnati Art Museum, Cincinnati 1997

AWAKAWA 1971
Yasuichi Awakawa, *Zen Painting*, John Bester (trans.), Tokyo 1971

BAI AND ZHANG 2009
Bai Qianshen (白謙慎) and Zhang Hui (章暉), 'An Investigation of Wang Jian's Birthdate' (Wang Jian shengnian kao 王鑑生年考), *Chinese Painting and Calligraphy* (Zhongguo shuhua 中國書畫), no. 11 (2009), pp. 60–4

BAKER 1993
Richard Stanley Baker, 'Cultural Hegemony and the Decoration of the Zashiki in the Muromachi Period' (Muromachi jidai no zashiki kazari to bunkateki shudōken 室町時代の座敷飾りと文化的主導権), in *Japanese Art: the Complete Works* (Nihon bijutsu zenshū 日本美術全集), vol. 11, Toda Teisuke (戸田禎佑) (ed.), Tokyo 1993, pp. 68–73

BARNHART 1997–8
Richard M. Barnhart, 'Dong Qichang and Western Learning: A Hypothesis in Honor of James Cahill', *Archives of Asian Art*, vol. 50 (1997–8), pp. 7–16

BARNHART ET AL. 1997A
Richard M. Barnhart, James Cahill, Lang Shaojun, Nie Chongzheng, Wu Hung, Yang Xin, *Three Thousand Years of Chinese Painting*, New Haven and London, 1997

BARNHART ET AL. 1997B
Richard M. Barnhart, James Cahill, Maxwell K. Hearn and Stephen Little, 'The Tu Chin [Du Jin] Correspondence, 1994–95', *Kaikodo Journal* 5 (Autumn 1997), pp. 8–45

BARNHART, IRIYA AND NAKATA 1977
Richard M. Barnhart, Iriya Yoshitaka (入矢義高) and Nakata Yujiro (中田勇次郎), 'Dong Yuan, Juran' (Tō Gen, Kyonen 董源, 巨然), in *Essence of Chinese and Japanese Literati Paintings* (Bunjinga suihen 文人畫粹編), vol. 2, Tokyo 1977

BÉGUIN 2000
Gilles Béguin, 'Le musée Cernuschi, un siècle d'histoire', in *Musée Cernuschi. Arts de l'Asie*, Paris 2000, pp. 7–11

BELL 1917
Hamilton Bell, *Early Chinese Paintings in the Museum of Fine Arts, Boston*, New York 1917

BIAN (1682) 1993–8
Bian Yongyu (卞永譽), *Analyses of Calligraphy and Painting in the Hall of Testing Antiquity* (Shigu Tang shuhua huigao 式古堂書畫彙考), painting section, vol. 16, reprinted in *A Compendium of Writings on Calligraphy and Painting in China* (Zhongguo shuhua quanshu 中國書畫全書), Lu Fusheng (盧輔聖) (ed.), 14 vols, Shanghai 1993–8; preface to original edition 1682

BICKFORD 1996
Maggie Bickford, *Ink Plum: The Making of a Chinese Scholar-Painting Genre*, Cambridge 1996

BICKFORD 2002–3
Maggie Bickford, 'Huizong and the Aesthetic of Agency', *Archives of Asian Art*, vol. 53 (2002–3), pp. 71–104

BICKFORD 2006
Maggie Bickford, 'Huizong's Paintings: Art and the Art of Emperorship', in *Huizong and Late Northern Song China: The Politics of Culture and the Culture of Politics*, Patricia Ebrey and Maggie Bickford (eds), Cambridge, MA 2006, pp. 131–70

BINYON 1927
Laurence Binyon, *Chinese Paintings in English Collections* (*Ars Asiatica*, vol. IX), Paris and Brussels 1927

BIRMINGHAM, AL 1987
Alice R.M. Hyland, *Deities, Emperors, Ladies and Literati: Figure Painting of the Ming and Qing Dynasties*, exh. cat., Birmingham Museum of Art, Birmingham, AL 1987

BLANCHARD 2006
Lara C.W. Blanchard, 'Huizong's New Clothes: Desire and Allegory in Court Ladies Preparing Newly Woven Silk', *Ars Orientalis*, vol. 36 (2006), pp. 111–35

BLANCHARD 2007
Lara C.W. Blanchard, 'A Scholar in the Company of Female Entertainers: Changing Notions of Integrity in Song to Ming Dynasty Painting', *Nan nü: Men, Women and Gender in Early and Imperial China*, vol. 9 (2007), pp. 189–246

BOSTON 1973
Jan Fontein and Wu Tung, *Unearthing China's Past*, exh. cat., Museum of Fine Arts, Boston 1973

BOSTON 1997
Wu Tung, *Tales from the Land of Dragons: 1,000 Years of Chinese Painting*, exh. cat., Boston Museum of Fine Arts, Boston 1997

BOSTON 2010
Sheng Hao, *Fresh Ink: Ten Takes on Chinese tradition*, exh. cat., Boston Museum of Fine Arts, Boston 2010

BRACK 2010
Matthew Brack, 'A Technical Study of Portable Tenth-century Paintings from Dunhuang in US Collections', Conservation and the Eastern Mediterranean: Contributions to the 2010 IIC Congress (2010)

BRINKER 1973–4
Helmut Brinker, 'Ch'an Portraits in a Landscape', *Archives of Asian Art*, vol. 27 (1973–4), pp. 8–29

BROTHERTON 2000–1
Elizabeth Brotherton, 'Two Farewell Handscrolls of the Late Northern Song', *Archives of Asian Art*, vol. 52 (2000–1), pp. 44–62

BÜGENER 2013 (forthcoming)
Annette Bügener, 'Die Heldengalerie des Qianlong-Kaisers: Ein Beitrag zur chinesischen Porträtmalerei im 18. Jahrhundert', PhD dissertation, University of Heidelberg 2013 (forthcoming)

*Bulletin of the Museum of Fine Arts, Boston* 1912
*Bulletin of the Museum of Fine Arts, Boston* (December 1912)

*Bulletin of the Museum of Fine Arts, Boston* 1917
*Bulletin of the Museum of Fine Arts, Boston* (December 1917), pp. 67–73

BURKUS-CHASSON 2005
Anne Burkus-Chasson, 'Visual Hermeneutics and the Act of Turning the Leaf: A Genealogy of Liu Yuan's Lingyan Ge', in Cynthia J. Brokaw and Kai-Wing Chow (eds), *Printing and Book Culture in Late Imperial China*, Berkeley 2005, pp. 371–416

BUSH 1969
Susan Bush, 'Literati Culture under the Chin (1122–1234)', *Oriental Art*, vol. XV, no. 2 (1969), pp. 103–12

BUSH 1971
Susan Bush, *The Chinese Literati on Painting: Su Shih (1037–1101) to Tung Ch'i-ch'ang (1555–1636)*, Cambridge, MA 1971

BUSH AND SHIH 1985
Susan Bush and Hsio-yen Shih, *Early Chinese Texts on Painting*, Cambridge, MA 1985

CAHILL 1958
James Cahill, 'Ch'ien Hsuan and His Figure Painting', *Archives of the Chinese Art Society of America*, vol. 12 (1958), pp. 11–29

CAHILL 1960
James Cahill, *Chinese Painting*, Lausanne 1960

CAHILL IN NEW YORK 1962D
James Cahill, 'Ode on the Red Cliff (Part II)', in *Chinese Calligraphy and Painting in the Collection of John Crawford, Jr.*, Laurence Sickman (ed.), exh. cat., The Pierpont Morgan Library, New York 1962, pp. 72–5

CAHILL 1963
James Cahill, 'Yüan Chiang and His School', *Ars Orientalis*, vol. 5 (1963), pp. 259–72

CAHILL 1966
James Cahill, 'Yüan Chiang and His School', *Ars Orientalis*, vol. 6 (1966), pp. 191–212

CAHILL 1978
James Cahill, *Parting at the Shore: Chinese Painting of the Early and Middle Ming Dynasty*, New York and Tokyo 1978


cat. no. 57, leaf B (detail)

CAHILL 1982A
James Cahill, *The Compelling Image: Nature and Style in Seventeenth-Century Chinese Painting*, Cambridge, MA and London 1982

CAHILL 1982B
James Cahill, *The Distant Mountains: Chinese Painting of the Late Ming Dynasty*, 1570–1644, New York and Tokyo 1982

CAHILL 1982C
James Cahill, 'Hung-jen and Kung Hsien: Nature Transfigured', in *The Compelling Image: Nature and Style in Seventeenth-Century Chinese Painting*, Cambridge, MA and London 1982, pp. 146–83

CAHILL IN KANSAS CITY AND SEATTLE 1992
James Cahill, 'Tung Ch'i-ch'ang's Painting Style: Its Sources and Transformations', in *The Century of Tung Ch'i-ch'ang*, Wai-kam Ho and Judith G. Smith (eds), exh. cat., vol. 1, The Nelson-Atkins Museum of Art, Kansas City and Seattle 1992, pp. 55–79

CAHILL 1994
James Cahill, *The Painter's Practice: How Artists Lived and Worked in Traditional China*, New York 1994

CAHILL 1995
James Cahill, 'Ren Xiong and His Self-Portrait', *Ars Orientalis*, vol. 25 (1995), pp. 119–32

CAHILL 1998
James Cahill, 'Some Alternative Sources for Archaistic Elements in the Paintings of Qian Xuan and Zhao Mengfu', *Ars Orientalis*, vol. 28 (1998), pp. 64–75

CAHILL 1992
Suzanne E. Cahill, 'Sublimation in Medieval China: The Case of the Mysterious Woman of the Nine Heavens', *Journal of Chinese Religions*, vol. 20 (1992), pp. 91–102

CAHILL 1993
Suzanne E. Cahill, *Transcendence and Divine Passion. The Queen Mother of the West in Medieval China*, Stanford 1993

CAO 1975
Cao Xun (曹汛), 'The Wooden House Containing the Coffin in The Liao Tomb at Yemaotai' (Yemaotai Liao mu zhong de guanchuang xiaozhang 葉茂台遼墓中的棺床小帳), *Wenwu* 文物, no. 12 (1975), pp. 49–63

CHANG 1991
Chang Feng-Ch'i (張豐吉), *Brushes* (Bi 筆), Zhanghua 1991

CHANG IN NEW YORK 2008B
Chin-Sung Chang, 'Wang Hui: The Evolution of a Master Landscapist', in *Landscapes Clear and Radiant: the Art of Wang Hui* (1632–1717), Maxwell K. Hearn (ed.), exh. cat., The Metropolitan Museum of Art, New York 2008, pp. 87–96

*Changes, Images and Fashion* 2008
*Changes, Images and Fashion: Modern Chinese Painting*, 1796–1949, *Conference Proceedings* (Shibian xingxiang, liufeng: zhongguo jindai huihua 1796–1949, xueshua yantaohui lunwenji 世変· 形象· 流風：中国近代絵画 1796–1949 学術研討会論文集), Hung-hsi mei-shu wen-chiao Foundation (財団法人鴻禧藝術文教基金会), Taipei 2008

CHAVANNES 1904
Edouard Chavannes, 'La peinture chinoise au musée du Louvre', *T'oung pao*, vol. 5, no. 3 (1904), pp. 310–31

CHAVANNES AND PETRUCCI 1914
Edouard Chavannes and Raphaël Petrucci, *La peinture chinoise au Musée Cernuschitu*, Brussels and Paris 1914

CHEN (1915) 2007
Chen Kuilin (陳夔麟), *Catalogue of Calligraphy and Painting of the Baoyu Ge Studio* (Baoyu Ge shuhua lu 寶迂閣書畫錄), vol. 1, reprinted in A Collection of *Selected Historical Catalogues of Calligraphy and Paintings Catalogue* (Lidai shuhualu jikan 歷代書畫錄輯刊), Guojia tushuguan (comp.), vol. 13, Beijing 2007; preface to original edition 1915

CHEN 1956
Chen Rentao (陳仁濤), *Annotated Catalogue of Lost Calligraphies and Paintings from the Qing Palace Collection* (Gugong yiyi shuhua mu jiaozhu 故宮已佚書畫目校註), Hong Kong 1956

CHEN 1984
Chen Gaohua (陳高華), *Documentary Sources of Painters in Song, Liao and Jin Dynasties* (Song, Liao, Jin huajia shiliao 宋遼金 畫家史料), Beijing 1984

CHEN 1993A
Chen Zhenghong (陳正宏), *A Chronology of Shen Zhou* (Shen Zhou nianpu 沈周年譜), Shanghai 1993

CHEN 1993B
Chen Jinling (陳金陵), 'A Chronology of Luo Pin' (Luo Pin nianpu 羅聘年譜), in *A Chronology of the Eight Eccentrics of Yangzhou* (Yangzhou 'Baguai' nianpu 揚州八怪年譜), Bian Xiaoxuan (卞孝萱) (ed.), Nanjing 1993, pp. 375–424

CHEN 2003
Chen Dexin (陳德馨), 'Zhao Yong's Noble Steeds and the Social Roles of Horse Paintings in the Yuan Dynasty' (Cong Zhao Yong *Junma tu* kan hua ma tu zai Yuandai shehui wangluo zhong de yunzuo 從趙雍《駿馬圖》看畫馬圖在元代社會網絡中的運作), *Journal of Art History* (Meishu shi yanjiu jikan 美術史研究集刊), vol. 15 (2003), pp. 133–67

CHEN 2004
Chen Zhenghong 陳正宏, 'The perfect combination of poetry and painting in the context of the social system of the upper-class in early modern' (China Shiga gappeki to kinseichūgokushishin no shakōhōshiki 詩畫合璧と近世中國士紳の社交方式), *Journal of Kansai University Society for the Study of Chinese Literature* (Kansai daigakuchūgokubungakukaikiyō 關西大學中國文學會紀要), no. 25 (2004)

CHEN 2005
Chen Haoxing (陳浩星), *The Light of the Southern School: The Calligraphy and Painting of Dong Qichang* (Nanzong beidou: Dong Qichang de shuhua yishu 南宗北斗: 董其昌的書畫藝術), Macau 2005

CHEN 2007
Chen Ci (陳辭), *A Compendium of Dong Qichang* (Dong Qichang quanji 董其昌全集), Shijiazhuang 2007

CHEN AND LAI 2008
Chen Jiejin (陳階晉) and Lai Yu-chih (賴毓芝), *Tracing the Che [Zhe] School in Chinese Painting* (Zhuisuo Zhepai 追索浙派), Taipei 2008

CHENG 2009
Cheng Wen-huei 鄭文惠, 'Cultural Writing of Huqiu Landscape in Middle Ming Dynasty' (Gonggong yuanlin yu renwen jiangou: Mingdai zhongqi Huqiu dijing de wenhua shuxie 公共園林與人文建構：明代中期虎丘地景的文化書寫', *National ChengChi University Chinese Journal* (Zhengda zhongwen xuebao 政大中文學報), no. 11 (2009), pp. l27–62

CHI 1984A, 1984B AND 1985
Chi Jo-hsin (嵇若昕), 'Wang Mian and the Development of Ink Plum Painting, Part 1, 2, 3' (Wang Mian yu momei hua de fazhan 王冕與墨梅畫的發展 [上] [中] [下]), *National Palace Museum Research Quarterly* (Gugong xueshu jikan 故宮學術季刊), vol. 2, no. 1 (1984), pp. 37–58; vol. 2, no. 2 (1984), pp. 41–66; and vol. 2, no. 3 (1985), pp. 69–82

CHICAGO 2000
Stephen Little, *Taoism and the Arts of China*, exh. cat., Art Institute of Chicago, Chicago 2000

CHIN 1984
Chin Shunshin (Chen Shunchen 陳舜臣), *Biographies of Chinese Painters* (Chūgoku gajin den 中国画人伝), Tokyo 1984

*Chinese Art in Overseas Collections* 1985
*Chinese Art in Overseas Collections: Painting* (Haiwai yizhen: huihua 海外遺珍: 繪畫), National Palace Museum, Taipei 1985

*Chinese Art in Overseas Collections* 1990
*Chinese Art in Overseas Collections: Painting Part III* (Haiwai yizhen: huihua 海外遺珍: 繪畫[再續]), vol. III, National Palace Museum, Taipei 1990

*Chinese Cave Temples: the Mogao Caves at Dunhuang* (1983) 1987
*Chinese Cave Temples: the Mogao Caves at Dunhuang* (Chūgoku sekkutsu: Tonkō bakkokutsu 中國石窟:敦煌莫高窟), Dunhuang Institute (敦煌文物研究所) (ed.), reprinted Beijing 1987; original edition Tokyo 1983

*Chinese Painting and Calligraphy in the Hsü-po Studio* 1983
*Chinese Painting and Calligraphy in the Hsü-po Studio* (Kyo Hakusai-zö shogasen 虚白齋藏書畫選), Tokyo 1983

CHISHOLM 1963
Lawrence W. Chisholm, *Fenollosa: The Far East and American Culture*, New Haven and London 1963

CHOU 1982
Chou Ju-hsi (ed.), 'The Methodology of Reversal in the Study of Wen Cheng-ming', in *Essays in Commemoration of the Golden Jubilee of the Fung Ping Shan Library* (1932–1982), Chan Ping-leung et al. (eds), Hong Kong 1982, pp. 428–37

CHOU 1998
Chou Ju-hsi, *Art at the Close of China's Empire*, Tempe, AZ 1998

CLAPP 1991
Anne de Coursey Clapp, *The Painting of T'ang Yin*, Chicago 1991

CLAYPOOL 2005
Lisa Claypool, 'Zhang Jian and China's First Museum', *The Journal of Asian Studies*, vol. 64, no. 3 (August 2005), pp. 567–604

CLEVELAND 1964
'Year in Review for 1964', *The Bulletin of The Cleveland Museum of Art*, vol. 51, no. 10 (1964), pp. 236–66

CLEVELAND 1968
Sherman E. Lee and Wai-kam Ho, *Chinese Art Under the Mongols: The Yüan Dynasty* (1279–1368), exh. cat., The Cleveland Museum of Art, Cleveland 1968

CLEVELAND 1986
'1985 Annual Report', *The Bulletin of The Cleveland Museum of Art*, vol. 73, no. 6 (1986), pp. 219–75

CLUNAS 2004
Craig Clunas, *Elegant Debts: The Social Art of Wen Zhengming*, Honolulu and London 2004

COHEN 1992
Warren I. Cohen, *East Asian Art and American Culture: A Study in International Relations*, New York 1992

*Collection of Ancient Chinese Woodblock Books, Part II* 1994
*Collection of Ancient Chinese Woodblock Books, Part II* (Zhongguo gudai banhua congkan erbian 中国古代版画丛刊二编), 10 vols, Shanghai 1994

COLOGNE 2010
Clarissa von Spee, *The Perfect Brush. Chinese Painting 1300–1900/Der Perfekte Pinsel. Chinesische Malerei 1300–1900*, exh. cat., Museum of East Asian Art, Cologne 2010

*Complete Collection* 1988
*Complete Collection of Imperial Treasures of the Stone Canal* (Bidian zhulin, Shiqu baoji hebian 祕殿珠林石渠寶笈合編), 12 vols, Shanghai 1988

*Complete Collection of Chinese Architecture* 1996–2003
*Complete Collection of Chinese Architecture: Domestic Architecture* (Zhongguo jianzhu yishu quanji, zhaidi jianzhu 中國建築藝術全集, 宅第建築), 24 vols, Beijing 1996–2003

CUI 2000
Cui Lequan (崔樂泉), *Ancient Sports in Chinese Cultural Relics* (Zhongguo gudai tiyu wenwu tulu 中国古代体育文物图录), Beijing 2000

DENG (1168–73) 1993–8
Deng Chun (鄧椿), *Painting Continued* (Huaji 畫繼), reprinted in *A Compendium of Writings on Calligraphy and Painting in China* (Zhongguo shuhua quanshu 中國書畫全書), 14 vols, Lu Fusheng (盧輔聖) et al., (eds), vol. 2, Shanghai 1993–8, pp. 703–24

*Dictionary of Chinese Artists* (1924) 1980
*Dictionary of Chinese Artists* (Zhonggguo meishujia renming cidian 中國美術家人名辭典), Yu Jianhua (俞劍華) (comp.), Shanghai 1980; original edition 1924

DING 1989
Ding Xiyuan (丁羲元), *Ren Bonian – Chronology, Essays, Miscellanies and Works* (Ren Bonian – nianpu, lunwen, zhencun, zuopin 任伯年 – 年譜, 論文, 珍存, 作品), Shanghai 1989

DING 1991
Ding Xiyuan (丁羲元), 'Disputing Qiao Zhongchang's *Illustration to the Second Prose Poem on the Red Cliff* scroll' (Qiao Zhongchang *Hou Chibi fu tujuan* bianyi 喬仲常《後赤壁賦圖卷》辯疑), *Duoyun* 朵雲, no. 31 (1991), pp. 29–37

DONG (1630) 1968
Dong Qichang (董其昌), *Writings of Dong Qichang* (Rongtai ji 容臺集), Taipei 1968

DONG (late 17th century) 1962
Dong Qichang (董其昌), *The Eye of Painting* (Huayan 畫眼), in *Compilation of Writings on Art* (Yishu congbian 藝術叢編), Taipei 1962

DONG (mid-17th century) 1999
Dong Qichang (董其昌), *Miscellaneous Notes from the Huachan Studio* (Huachanshi suibi 畫禪室隨筆), Shanghai 1999

DŌTANI 1951
Dōtani Ken'yū (堂谷憲勇), (explanation of the plates), *World collection of art* (Sekai bijutsu zenshū 世界美術全集), vol. 14, Heibonsha 1951

DRÈGE 1981
Jean-Pierre Drège, 'Papiers de Dunhuang, essai d'analyse morphologique des manuscrits chinois datés', *T'oung pao*, vol. 67, no. 3 (1981), pp. 305–17

DUNKERTON ET AL. 1991
Jill Dunkerton, Susan Foister, Dillian Gordon and Nicholas Penny, *Giotto to Dürer: Early Renaissnace Painting in The National Gallery*, New Haven 1991, pp. 187–8

DUOYUN BIANJI BU 1993
Duoyun bianji bu (朵雲編輯部), *A Study of the Four Wangs of the Early Qing* (Qingchu si Wang huapai yanjiu 清初四王畫派研究), Shanghai 1993

EBINE 1971
Ebine Toshio (海老根聰郎), plate commentary, in *Japanese Art in Colour* (Genshoku nihon no bijutsu 原色日本の美術), Yonezawa Yoshiho (米沢嘉圃) and Tanaka Jirō (中田勇次郎) (eds), vol. 29, *Paintings Brought into Japan* (Shōrai kaiga 請来絵画), Tokyo 1971, p. 99

EBINE 1978A
Ebine Toshio (海老根聰郎), plate commentary, in *Compendium of Ink Painting* (Suiboku bijutsu taikei 水墨美術体系), Toda Teisuke (戸田禎佑) (ed.), vol. 3, *Muxi, Yujian* (Mokkei, Gyokkan 牧谿, 玉澗), Tokyo 1978, p. 166

EBINE 1978B
Ebine Toshio (海老根聰郎), plate commentary, in *Compendium of Ink Painting* (Suiboku bijutsu taikei 水墨美術体系), Toda Teisuke (戸田禎佑) (ed.), vol. 3, *Muxi, Yujian* (Mokkei, Gyokkan 牧谿, 玉澗), Tokyo 1978, p. 164

EBINE 1976
Ebine Toshio (海老根聰郎), plate commentary, *The Higashiyama Treasures – Focusing on New Historical Material Concerning the Zakkashitsu-in Seal* (Higashiyama gyomotsu – zakkashitsu-in ni kansuru shin shiryō o chūshin ni 東山御物 –『雑華室印』に関する新史料を中心に), Tokyo and Nagoya 1976

EBINE 1977
Ebine Toshio (海老根聰郎), *Chinese Paintings of the Yuan dynasty on Buddhist and Daoist Figural Subjects* (Gen jidai dōshaku jinbutsu-ga 元時代道釈人物画), Tokyo 1977

EBINE 2000
Ebine Toshio (海老根聰郎), 'Ink Figure Painting – A Look at Neglected Works' (Suiboku jinbutsuga – kuchiru o megutte 水墨人物画 – 朽をめぐって), in *A New History of World Art – Japan* (Sekai bijutsu daizenshū – tōyō hen 世界美術大全集 – 東洋編), vol. 6, Shimada Hidemasa (嶋田英誠) Nakazawa Fujio (中澤富士雄) (eds), *Southern Song, Jin* (Nansō, kin 南宋, 金) Tokyo 2000

EBREY 2008
Patricia B. Ebrey, *Accumulating Culture: The Collection of Emperor Huizong*, Seattle 2008

EBREY AND BICKFORD 2006
Patricia B. Ebrey and Maggie Bickford (eds), *Emperor Huizong and Late Northern Song China: The Politics of Culture and the Culture of Politics* (*Harvard East Asian Monographs* 266), Cambridge, MA and London 2006

ECKE 1972
Tseng Yu-ho Ecke, 'Emperor Hui-tsung the Artist', PhD dissertation, New York University, 1972

EDWARDS 1953a
Richard Edwards, 'Ch'ien Hsuan and Early Autumn', *Archives of the Chinese Art Society of America*, vol. 7 (1953), pp. 71–83

EDWARDS 1953b
Richard Edwards, 'The Field of Stones: A Preliminary Study of the Art of Shen Chou (1427–1509)', PhD dissertation, Harvard University 1953

EDWARDS 1962b
Richard Edwards, *The Field of Stones: A Study of the Art of Shen Chou* (1427–1509), Baltimore 1962

EDWARDS 1965
Richard Edwards, 'Shen Chou and the Scholarly Tradition', *The Journal of Aesthetics and Art Criticism*, vol. 24 (1965), pp. 45–52

EDWARDS 1989
Richard Edwards, *The World Around the Chinese Artist: Aspects of Realism in Chinese Art*, Ann Arbor 1989

EGAN 1994
Ronald C. Egan, *Word, Image, and Deed in the Life of Su Shi*, Cambridge 1994

ESKENAZI 2012
Giuseppe Eskenazi, in collaboration with Hajni Elias, *A Dealer's Hand: The Chinese Art World through the Eyes of Giuseppe Eskenazi*, London 2012

*Essence of Chinese and Japanese Literati Paintings* 1974–9
*Essence of Chinese and Japanese Literati Paintings* (Bunjinga suihen 文人畫粹編), 20 vols, Tokyo 1974–9

*Etymological Dictionary of Chinese Language* 1988
*Etymological Dictionary of Chinese Language* (Ciyuan 辭源), Beijing 1988

*Exquisite Gems of Art* 1986
*Exquisite Gems of Art* (Yiyuan duoying 藝苑掇英), no. 31 (1986)

FAIRBROTHER 1991
Trevor Fairbrother, *Brice Marden: Boston: A 'Connection' Project at the Museum of Fine Arts Boston*, Boston 1991

FAN 2003
Fan Jinmin 范金民, 'A Portrait of the Commercial Prosperity in Qing Dynasty Suzhou: *Prosperous Suzhou*' (Qingdai Suzhou chengshi gongshang fanrong de xiezhao: *Gu Su fanhua tu* 清代蘇州城市工商繁榮的寫照: 姑蘇繁華圖), *Forests of History* (Shilin 史林), no. 5 (2003), pp. 104–15

FENOLLOSA 1912
Ernest Francisco Fenollosa, *Epochs of Chinese and Japanese Art: An Outline History of East Asiatic Design*, 1853–1908, 4 vols, London 1912

FONG 1960
Wen C. Fong, 'The Problem of Ch'ien Hsuan', *Art Bulletin*, vol. 42, no. 3 (September 1960), pp. 173–89

FONG 1963
Wen C. Fong, 'A Statement of Method', *Oriental Art*, vol. IX, no. 2 (1963), pp. 3–8

FONG 1970
Wen C. Fong, 'Orthodoxy and Change in Early Qing Landscape Painting', *Oriental Art*, vol. XVI, no. 1 (1970), pp. 38–44

FONG 1992
Wen C. Fong, *Beyond Representation: Chinese Painting and Calligraphy, 8th–14th Century*, Princeton Monographs in Art and Archaeology, no. 48, New York 1992

FONG AND HEARN 1982
Wen C. Fong and Maxwell K. Hearn, 'Silent Poetry: Chinese Paintings in the Douglas Dillon Galleries', *The Metropolitan Museum of Art Bulletin*, vol. 39, no. 3 (1982), pp. 1, 4–80

FONG IN KANSAS CITY AND SEATTLE 1992
Wen C. Fong, 'Tung Ch'i-ch'ang and Artistic Renewal', in *The Century of Tung Ch'i-ch'ang*, Wai-kam Ho and Judith G. Smith (eds), exh. cat., vol. 1, The Nelson-Atkins Museum of Art, Kansas City and Seattle 1992, pp. 43–54

FONG IN NEW YORK 2008B
Wen C. Fong, 'Wang Hui and Repossessing the Past', in *Landscapes Clear and Radiant: The Art of Wang Hui* (1632–1717), Maxwell K. Hearn (ed.), exh. cat., The Metropolitan Museum of Art, New York 2008, pp. 27–32

FRASER 1989
Sarah E. Fraser, 'Journey without a Destination: Shi Tao's 1696 *Qingxiang Sketches of Calligraphy and Painting*', MA thesis, University of California 1989

FU 1988
*Complete Collection of Chinese Art* (Zhongguo meishu quanji 中國美術全集), *Paintings* (Huihua bian 繪畫編), vol. 3, *Song Dynasty Paintings, Part I* (Liang Song huihua, shang 兩宋繪畫, 上), Fu Xinian (傅熹年) (ed.), Beijing 1988

FU 2005
Fu Dongguang 傅東光, 'A preliminary Study of Mounting Style at the court of Emperor Qianlong' (Qianlong neifu shuhua zhuanghuang chutao 乾隆內府書畫裝潢初探), Palace Museum Journal (Gugong bowuyuan yuankan 故宮博物院院刊), no. 2 (2005) p. 111–21

FU AND CAI 1984
Fu Hua (富华) and Cai Geng (蔡耕), *Collected Album of Paintings by Xugu* (Xugu huace 虛谷畫冊), Beijing 1984

FUJITA 1989
Fujita Shinya (藤田伸也), plate commentary, in *Painting of the Song Period* (Sōdai no kaiga 宋代の絵画), Nara 1989

FULLER 1984
Germaine F. Fuller, 'Spring in Chiang-nan: Pictorial Imagery and Other Aspects of Expression in Eight Wu School Paintings of a Traditional Literary Subject', PhD dissertation, The University of Chicago 1984

GANZA 1990
Kenneth Stanley Ganza, 'The Artist as Traveler: The Origin and Development of Travel as a Theme in Chinese Landscape Painting of the Fourteenth to Seventeenth Centuries', PhD dissertation, Indiana University, 1990

GAO 1996
Gao Musen (高木森), 'A Study of Two Professional Painters in the Wu Region – Zhou Chen and Qiu Ying' (Lun Wuzhong liangwei zhiye huajia – Zhou Chen yu Qiu Ying' 論吳中二位職業畫家 – 周臣與仇英), *National Palace Museum Monthly* (Gugong wenwu yuekan 故宮文物月刊), vol. 162, no. 9 (1996), pp. 4–27

GAO, HUANG AND LIU 2012
Gao Juhan (James Cahill 高居翰), Huang Xiao (黃曉) and Liu Shanshan (劉珊珊), *Garden Paintings in Old China* (Buxiude linquan: Zhongguo gudai yuanlin huihua 不朽的林泉: 中國古代園林繪畫), Beijing 2012

GE 2003
Ge Xiaolin (葛曉琳), *Wang Shimin*, 1592–1680 (王時敏, 1592–1680), Beijing 2003

GIÈS ET AL. 1994
*Les arts de l'Asie centrale: La collection Paul Pelliot du Musée national des arts asiatiques Guimet*, Jacques Giès, Michel Soymié and Jean-Pierre Drège et al. (eds), 2 vols, Tokyo 1994 [translated in *The Arts of Central Asia: the Pelliot Collection in the Musée Guimet*, Hero Friesen with Roderick Whitfield (trans.), London 1996]

GIÈS 1996
*The Arts of Central Asia: the Pelliot Collection in the Musée Guimet*, Jacques Giès (ed.), Hero Friesen with Roderick Whitfield (trans.), 3 vols, Chicago 1996

GOLDMAN 2006
Paul Goldman, *Looking at Prints, Drawings and Watercolours: A Guide to Techincal Terms*, London 2006

GOMI 1971
Gomi Mitsuko (五味充子), 'Genetic Problems: Court Ladies Preparing Newly Woven Silk Scroll, Copy of Zhang Xuan's Original by Huizong' (Den Kisō mo Chō Ken tōrenzu no seiritsuni kansuru kōsatsu 伝徽宗摹張萱搗練圖の成立に関する考察), *Journal of the Japan Art History Society* (Bijutsushi 美術史), vol. 21, no. 1 (July 1971), pp. 1–16

GONG 1982
Gong Chanxing (龔產興), *Research on Ren Bonian* (Ren Bonian yanjiu 任伯年研究), Tianjin 1982

GRIFFITHS 1996
*Landmarks in Print Collecting: Connoisseurs and Donors at the British Museum since* 1753, Antony Griffiths (ed.), London 1996

VAN GULIK 1958
R.H. van Gulik, *Chinese Pictorial Art as Viewed by the Connoisseur: Notes on the Means and Methods of Traditional Chinese Connoisseurship of Pictorial Art, Based upon a Study of the Art of Mounting Scrolls in China and Japan*, Istituto Italiano per il Medio ed Estremo Oriente, Rome 1958

GUO 2010
Guo Wenlin (郭文林), *Premiere Techniques of Copying Calligraphy and Paintings* (Shuhua linmo jichu jifa 書畫臨摹基础技法), Beijing 2010

HACKIN 1923
Joseph Hackin, *Guide-catalogue du Musée Guimet*, Paris 1923

HÁJEK 1991
Lubor Hájek, 'A Landscape album by Gong Xian dated 1637', *Orientations*, vol. 22, no. 8 (August 1991), pp. 43–9

HANDLER 1993
Sarah Handler, 'The Chinese Screen: Movable Walls to Divide, Enhance and Beautify', *Journal of the Classical Chinese Furniture Society* (Summer 1993), pp. 4–31

HARADA 1939
Harada Bizan (原田尾山) et al., *Works of Art in the Sōraikan Collection* (Sōraikan kinsho 爽籟館欣賞) second edition, Osaka 1939

HARADA 1940
Harada Bizan (原田尾山), 'Hu Shunchen and Cai Jing's handscroll presented to Hao Xuanming on the occasion of his being dispatched to Qin' (Ko Shunshin Sai Kei okuka Ku Genmei shihata zu-maki 胡舜臣蔡京送郝玄明使秦圖卷), *The Journal of Art Studies* (Bijutsu kenkyū 美術研究), vol. 104 (1940)

HARADA 2012
*Special Issue: China and East Asia – Modern Collection Formation and a Context for Research* (Tokushū: chūgoku to higashiajia – kindai no korekushon keisei to kenkyū no haikai 特集中国と東アジア – 近代のコレクション形成と研究の背景), Harada Heisaku (ed.), *Art Forum 21* (Bijutsu forum 21 美術フォーラム 21), vol. 26 (2012)

HARRIST 1997
Robert E. Harrist Jr., 'The Legacy of Bole: Physiognomy and Horses in Chinese Painting', *Artibus Asiae*, vol. 57, no. 1/2 (1997), pp. 135–56

HASHIMOTO 1997
Hashimoto Yoshihiko (橋本義彥), *The History of the Shōsō-in* (Shōsō-in no rekishi 正倉院の歴史), Tokyo 1997

HATA 1997
Hata Kōhei (秦恒平), *A Distant View of the Monkey – Painting and Discussions on Culture* (Saru no enkei — etosetora bunkaron 猿の遠景 – 絵とせとら文化論), Tokyo 1997

HATA 2004
Hata Yasunori (畑靖紀), 'Knowledge of Southern Song Dynasty Imperial Academy Painting in Muromachi Period Japan: Focusing on the Xia Gui and Liang Kai Handscrolls in the Collection of the

Ashikaga Shoguns' (Muromachi jidai no nansō intaiga ni taisuru ninshiki o megutte – Ashikaga shōgunke no Ka Kei to Ryō Kai no gakan o chūshin ni 室町時代の南宋院体画に対する認識をめぐって – 足利将軍家の夏珪と梁楷の画巻を中心に), *Art History* (*Bijutsu-shi* 美術史), vol. 156 (2004); pp. 427–43

HAY 1983
John Hay, 'Values and History in Chinese Painting, I: Hsieh Ho Revisited', *RES: Anthropology and Aesthetics*, no. 6 (Autumn 1983), pp. 72–111

HAY 1985
John Hay, 'Surface and the Chinese Painter: The Discovery of Surface', *Archives of Asian Art*, vol. 38 (1985), pp. 95–123

HAY 1989
Jonathan Hay, 'Khubilai's Groom', *RES: Anthropology and Aesthetics*, no. 17/18 (Spring/Autumn 1989), pp. 117–39

HAY 1994
Jonathan Hay, 'The Suspension of Dynastic Time', in *Boundaries in China*, John Hay (ed.), London 1994, pp. 171–97

HAY 1999
Jonathan Hay, 'Culture, Ethnicity, and Empire in the Work of two Eighteenth-Century "Eccentric" Artists', *RES: Anthropology and Aesthetics*, no. 35 (Spring 1999), pp. 201–23

HAY 2001
Jonathan Hay, *Shitao: Painting and Modernity in Early Qing China*, Cambridge 2001

HE 1998
He Shizhe (賀世哲), 'Donors' Name Labels' (Gongyangren tiji 供養人題記), in *Dictionary of Dunhuang Studies* (Dunhuang xue da cidian 敦煌學大辭典), Ji Xianlin (季羨林) (ed.), Shanghai 1998, pp. 181

HEARN IN NEW YORK 2008B
Maxwell K. Hearn, 'Art Creates History: Wang Hui and *The Kangxi Emperor's Southern Inspection Tour*', in *Landscapes Clear and Radiant: the Art of Wang Hui (1632–1717)*, Maxwell K. Hearn (ed.), exh. cat., The Metropolitan Museum of Art, New York 2008, pp. 128–83

HINTON 1990
David Hinton, *The Selected Poems of Tu Fu*, London 1990

HIRONOBU IN KANSAS CITY AND SEATTLE 1992
Kohara Hironobu, 'Tung Ch'i-ch'ang's Connoiseurship in T'ang and Sung Painting', in *The Century of Tung Ch'i-ch'ang*, Wai-kam Ho and Judith G. Smith (eds), exh. cat., vol. 1., The Nelson-Atkins Museum of Art, Kansas City and Seattle 1992, pp. 81–103

HO 1954
Ho Ping-ti, 'The Salt Merchants of Yang-chou: A Study of Commercial Capitalism in Eighteenth Century China', *Harvard Journal of Asian Studies*, vol. 17 (1954), pp. 130–68

HO 1992
Ho Chuan-hsing (何傳馨), 'Calligraphy on Du Fu's verse "Paying Homage to the Supreme Xuanyuan Emperor's [Laozi] Temple"' (Ming Dong Qichang Du Fu "Ye Xuanyuan Huangdi miao shi" 明董其昌杜甫謁玄元皇帝廟詩), in *Special Exhibition Catalogue of Beauty in Calligraphy* (Shufa zhimei tezhan tulu 書法之美特展圖錄), exh. cat., Ho Chuan-hsing (ed.), National Palace Museum, Taipei 1992

HOCKNEY 1993
David Hockney, *That's the way I see it*, London 1993

HONDIUS 1610
Hendrik Hondius the elder, *Pictorum aliquot celebrium, praecipué Germaniae inferioris, Effigies*, The Hague 1610

HONG KONG 1992
*A Gift of Heritage: Selection from the Xubaizhai Collection of Chinese Painting and Calligraphy* (Gu cui jin cheng: Xubaizhai cang Zhongguo shuhua xuan 古萃今承 : 虛白齋藏中國 書畫選), exh. cat., Hong Kong Museum of Art, Hong Kong 1992

HONG KONG 1997
*From Beijing to Versailles: Artistic Relations between China and France*, exh. cat., Hong Kong Museum of Art, Hong Kong 1997

HU (1816) 1972
Hu Jing (胡敬), *Miscellaneous Notes from the Xiqing Studio* (Xiqing zhaji 西清劄記), vol. 4, pp. 7b–8b, reprinted in *Mr Hu's Three Publications on Painting and Calligraphy* (Hu shi shuhua kao san zhong 胡氏書畫考三種), Taipei 1972, pp. 208–10; original edition 1816

HUANG (1883) 1989
Huang Shiquan (黃協勛), *Record of Dream Images from Songnan* (Songnan mengying lu 淞南夢影錄), reprinted Shanghai 1989; original edition 1883

HUANG 1985
*Complete Collection of Chinese Art* (Zhongguo meishu quanji 中國美術全集), *The Great Tradition of Textile Printing, Dyeing, Weaving and Embroidery* (Yinran zhixiu gongyi meishu de guanghui chuantong 中國美術全集, 編 6, 印染織繡, 上), Huang Nengfu (黃能馥) (ed.), Beijing 1995

HUANG 2010A
Huang Chao-cheng (黃朝政), 'A Discussion of the Thought and Character of Literati Portraits in the Ming and Qing Dynasties' (Shilun Ming Qing wenren xiaoxianghua zhong de sikao yishi yu biaoxian tezheng 試論明清文人肖像畫中的思考意識與表現特徵), *Journal of Calligraphy and Painting* (Shuhua yishu xuekan 書畫藝術學刊), vol. 8 (2010), pp. 125–56

HUANG 2010B
Michelle Ying-Ling Huang, 'British Interest in Chinese painting, 1881–1910. The Anderson and Wegener collections of Chinese painting in the British Museum', *Journal of the History of Collections* (2010), pp. 1–14

HUNG 2007
Hung Sun-Hsin (洪順興), 'The Role of Brass Ring in Hanging Scroll Mounting' (Kan bu jian de yingxiong, guaizhou muhou de luosiding – tonghua' 看不見的的英雄，掛軸幕後的螺絲釘—銅環), *National Palace Museum Monthly* (Gugong wenwu yuekan 故宮文物月刊), no. 7 (2007), pp. 92–7

HUNG 2009
Hung Sun-Hsin (洪順興), 'Treatise on the Mounting of Zhou Jiazhou and Wang Chong "Qianzi"' (Cong Wang Chong "Qianzi" tan Zhou Jiazhou "Zhuanghuang zhi" yu benfu shoujuan zhuangbiao 從王寵千字文談周嘉胄《裝潢志》與本幅手卷裝裱), *National Palace Museum Monthly* (Gugong wenwu yuekan 故宮文物月刊,) no. 12 (2009), pp. 100–7

IETSUKA 1997
Ietsuka Tomoko (家塚智子), 'The Institution and Transformation of the Dōbōshū' (Dōbōshū no sonzai keitai to hensen 同朋衆の存在形態と変遷), *Studies in the Performing Arts* (Geinoshi kenkyū 芸能史研究), vol. 136 (1997), pp. 35–57

IETSUKA 1998
Ietsuka Tomoko (家塚智子), 'Duties and Kinship Ties of the Dōbōshū' (*Dōbōshū no shokushō to ketsuen* 同朋衆の職掌と血縁), *Studies in the Performing Arts* (Geinoshi kenkyū 芸能史研究), vol. 141 (1998), pp. 84–95

IETSUKA 2001
Ietsuka Tomoko (家塚智子), 'Evaluating the Dōbōshū from the Viewpoint of Cultural History' (*Dōbōshū no bunkashi ni okeru hyōka o megutte* 同朋衆の文化史上における評価をめぐって), *Studies in the Performing Arts* (Geinoshi kenkyū 芸能史研究), vol. 155 (2001), pp. 38–49

IETSUKA 2009
Ietsuka Tomoko (家塚智子), 'On the Dōbōshū' (Dōbōshū ni tsuite 同朋衆について), *Studies in History and Geography* (Rekishi to chiri 歴史と地理), vol. 627 (2009)

IETSUKA 2010
Ietsuka Tomoko (家塚智子), 'The Reception of Karamono in the Muromachi Period – the Dōbōshū and Objects from China' (Muromachi jidai ni okeru karamono no juyō – Dōbōshū to karamono 室町時代における唐物の受容 – 同朋衆と唐物), in *Intriguing Asia* (Ajia yūgaku アジア遊学), vol. 134, *Metalworking in East Asia* (Higashi ajia o meguru kinzoku kōgei 東アジアをめぐる金属工芸), Tokyo 2010, pp. 208–23

IHARA 2004
*Special Issue: Huizong and His Times* (Tokushū: kisō to sono jidai 特集:　徽宗とその時代), *Intriguing Asia* (Ajia yūgaku アジア遊学), Ihara Hiroshi (ed.), vol. 64, Tokyo 2004

ISE 1930
Ise Senichirō (伊勢専一郎), *Works of Art in Sōraikan Collection* (Sōraikan kinsho 爽籟館欣賞), Osaka 1930

ITAKURA 1998
Itakura Masaaki (板倉聖哲), *The handscroll Noble Horse by Gong Kai; On the collection of the Osaka Municipal Museum of Art* (Kyō Kai hitsu Shun-kotsu zumaki (Ōsaka shiritsu bijutsukan zō ni tsuite 龔開筆『駿骨圖巻』; 大阪市立美術館藏について), *Gekkan shinika* 月刊しにか, (October 1998)

ITAKURA 2001
Itakura Masaaki (板倉聖哲), 'The Significance of Qiao Zhongchang's *Illustration to the Second Prose Poem on the Red Cliff* from The Nelson-Atkins Museum of Art' (Kyō Chūjō Kōsekihekifu no shiteki ichi 喬仲常「後赤壁賦圖巻」[ネルソン· アトキンア美術館]の史的位置), *Kokka* 國華, no. 1270 (2001), pp. 9–22

ITAKURA 2002
Itakura Masaaki (板倉聖哲), 'Pictures of Screen Paintings on the Wall of a Tang Tomb' (*Tō bohekiga ni egakareta byōbuga* 唐墓壁画に描かれた屏風画), *Studies in Art History* (Bijutsushi ronsō 美術史論), vol. 18 (2002), pp. 61–86

ITAKURA 2004
Itakura Masaaki (板倉聖哲), 'The Emperor's Gaze – Huizong's Auspicious Cranes (Liaoning Provincial Museum)' (Kōtei no manazashi – kisō zuikaku zumaki [ryōneishō hakubutsukan] 皇帝の眼差し – 徽宗「瑞鶴図巻」遼寧省博物館), *Intriguing Asia* (Ajia yūgaku アジア遊学), vol. 64 (2004), pp. 128–39

ITAKURA 2006
Itakura Masaaki (板倉聖哲), 'Poetry and Landscape Handscroll Presented to Hao Xuanming on the occasion of his being dispatched to Qin, by Hu Shunchen' (Ko Shunshin-hitsu okuka Ku Genmei shihata zu-maki' 胡舜臣筆送郝玄明使秦圖巻), *Kokka* (國華), vol. 110, no. 1329 (July 2006), pp. 48–50

ITAKURA 2008
Itakura Masaaki, 'Text and Images: The Interrelationship of Su Shi's *Odes on the Red Cliff* and Illustration of the *Later Ode on the Red Cliff* by Qiao Zhongchang', in *The History of Painting in East Asia: Essays on Scholarly Method*, Naomi Noble Richard and Donald E. Brix (eds), Taipei 2008, pp. 421–42

ITAKURA 2011
Itakura Masaaki (板倉聖哲), 'A Re-examination of Tang Dynasty Paintings – Looking at Murals Depicting Folding Screens' (Tō jidai kaiga ni kansuru fukugenteki kōsatsu – byōbuhekiga ni chūmoku shite 唐時代絵画に関する復元的考察 – 屏風壁画に注目して), in *Rokuon Zasshū: Bulletin of Nara National Museum* (Rokuon zasshū Nara kokuritsu hakubutsukan kiyō 鹿苑雑集 奈良国立博物館紀要), no. 13 (2011)

ITAKURA 2012A
Itakura Masaaki (板倉聖哲), 'East Asian Painting Collections of the Bakumatsu Period in Historical Context – A Look at Tani Bunchō' (*Bakumatsuki ni okeru higashiajia kaiga korekushon no shiteki ichi – tani bunchō no shiten kara* 幕末期における東アジア絵画コレクションの史的位置谷文晁の視点から), *Studies in Art History* (Bijutsushi ronsō 美術史論叢), vol. 28 (2012), pp. 27–44

ITAKURA 2012B
Itakura Masaaki (板倉聖哲), 'Painting Appreciation in Early Modern and Modern Japan and the Transformation of the Image of the Chinese Artist – the Case of Wang Jianzhang' (Kinsei, kindai nihon ni okeru chūgoku kaiga kanshō to gakazō no henyō – Ō Kenshō no baai 近世·　近代日本における中国絵画鑑賞と画家像の変容 – 王建章の場合), *Art Forum 21* (*Bijutsu forum 21* 美術フォーラム 21), vol. 26 (2012), pp. 126–32

ITAKURA 2013
Itakura Masaaki (板倉聖哲), 'The Development of Iconography in the Depiction of the Orchid Pavilion Gathering in East Asia' (Higashi ajia ni okeru rantei kyokusui zuzō no enkai 東アジアにおける蘭亭曲水宴図像の展開), *Studies in Art History* (Bijutsushi ronsō 美術史論叢), vol. 29 (2013)

JAMES ET AL. 1997
Carlo James, Caroline Corrigan, Marie Christine Enshaian, Marie Rose Greca, *Old Master Prints and Drawings: A Guide to Preservation and Conservation*, Amsterdam 1997

JERA-BEZARD AND MAILLARD 1985
Robert Jera-Bezard and Monique Maillard, 'Origine et montage des bannières peintes de Dunhuang', *Arts Asiatiques*, vol. 40, no. 1 (1985) pp. 83–91

JERA-BEZARD AND MAILLARD 1989
Robert Jera-Bezard and Monique Maillard, 'Le rôle des bannières et des peintures mobiles dans les rituals du bouddhisme d'Asie centrale', *Arts Asiatiques*, vol. 44 (1989), pp. 57–67

JIA (6th century) 1998
Jia Sixie (賈思勰), *Principal Techniques for the Welfare of the People* (Qimin yaoshu 齊民要術), Yangzhou, reprinted Beijing 1998; facsimile of a Ming dynasty edition

JIANG 1976
Jiang Zhaoshen (江兆申), *A Study of Tang Yin* (Guanyu Tang Yin de yanjiu 關於唐寅的研究), Taipei 1976

JIANG 1985
Jiang Boqin (姜伯勤), 'The painting guilds and painting academy in Dunhuang' (Dunhuang de huahang yu huayuan 敦煌的畫行與畫院), in *The proceedings of national symposium on Dunhuang 1983* (1983 quanguo Dunhuang xueshu taolunhui wenji 1983 年全國敦煌學術討論會文集), Lanzhou 1985, pp. 171–91

JIANG 2009
Jiang Feide (姜斐德 Alfreda Murck), *Poetry and Painting in Song China: The Subtle Art of Dissent* (Songdai shihua zhong de zhengzhi yinqing 宋代詩畫中的政治隱情), Beijing 2009

JIANGSU PROVINCIAL MUSEUM 1959
*Selected Epigraphic Sources of the Ming and Qing Dynasties in Jiangsu Province* (Jiangsu sheng Ming Qing yilai beike ziliao xuanji 江苏省明清以来碑刻资料选集), Jiangsu Provincial Museum (江苏省博物馆) (ed.), Beijing 1959

JIN 1982
Jin Weinuo (金維諾), 'Visit to Boston' (Fangwen Boshidun 訪問波士頓), *Art Research* (Meishu yanjiu 美術研究), no. 1 (1982), pp. 78–84

JIN 2004
Jin Weinuo (金維諾), 'The Court Painting in the Tang Dynasty and its Influences' (Tangdai gongting huihua jiqi yingxiang 唐代宮廷繪畫及其影響), *Calligraphy and Painting in China* (Zhongguo shuhua 中國書畫), no. 1 (January 2004), pp. 24–43

JOHNSTON LAING 2000
Ellen Johnston Laing, '*Suzhou Pian* and Other Dubious Paintings in the Received "Oeuvre" of Qiu Ying', *Artibus Asiae*, vol. 59, no. 3/4 (2000), pp. 265–95

KAKUI 1984
Kakui Hiroshi (角井博), 'The Issue of Yu Ji's Colophon Originally Attached to the 'Two Chan Patriarchs' scroll' (Niso chōshin-zu den Seki Kaku ga jūyō bunkazai ni fuzoku suru Gushū batsu no mondai「二祖調心図<伝石恪画· 重要文化財>に付属する虞集跋の問題」), *Museum*, 400 (1984), pp. 22–34

KANSAS CITY 1969
Marc F. Wilson, *Kung Hsien: Theorist and Technician in Painting. A Loan Exhibition … May 1, 1969 – July 15, 1969*, exh. cat., *The Nelson Gallery and Atkins Museum Bulletin*, vol. IV, no. 9, Kansas City 1969

KANSAS CITY AND CLEVELAND 1980
Wai-kam Ho, Sherman E. Lee, Laurence Sickman and Marc F. Wilson, *Eight Dynasties of Chinese Painting: The Collections of the Nelson Gallery-Atkins Museum, Kansas City, and The Cleveland Museum of Art*, exh. cat., The Nelson-Atkins Museum of Art, Kansas City and The Cleveland Museum of Art, Cleveland 1980

KANSAS CITY AND SEATTLE 1992
*The Century of Tung Ch'i-ch'ang*, Wai-kam Ho and Judith G. Smith (eds), exh. cat., 2 vols, The Nelson-Atkins Museum of Art, Kansas City and Seattle 1992

KAO 1988
Kao Mayching (高美慶), *Ming Dynasty Paintings in the Palace Museum* (Gugong bowuyuan cang Mingdai huihua 故宮博物院藏明代繪畫), Hong Kong 1988

KAWAI 2002
Kawai Masatomo, 'Reception Room Display in Medieval Japan', in *Kazari: Decoration and Display in Japan: 15th–19th Centuries*, Tsuji Nobuo and Nicole Rousmaniere (eds), London 2002, pp. 32–41

KAWAZOE AND MINAGAWA 2011
'Karamono and East Asia – a History of Cultural Exchange Focusing on Imported Items' (Karamono to higashiajia – hakusaihin o meguru bunkakōryū shi 唐物と東アジア – 舶載品をめぐる文化交流史, *Intriguing Asia* (Ajia yūgaku アジア遊学), Kawazoe Fusai (河添房江) and Minagawa Masaki (皆川雅樹) (eds), vol. 147 (2011)

KENT 2001
Richard K. Kent, 'Ch'iao Chung-ch'ang's Illustration of Su Shih's "Latter Prose Poem on the Red Cliff": Pai-miao (Plain Line Drawing) as Heuristic Device', *Taida Journal of Art History* (Guoli Taiwan daxue meishushi yanjiu jikan 國立臺灣大學美術史研究集刊), no. 11 (September 2001), pp. 95–132

KIHARA 2007
Kihara Toshie (鬼原俊枝), 'Concerning the Triptych *Shaka Descending the Mountain* and *Snowy Landscapes* [National Treasure], and the Collection Seal Reading "Dōyū"' (Kokuhō *Shussanshaka-zu, Sekkei sansui-zu* sanbukutsui to 'dōyū' no kanzō-in ni tsuite 国宝出山釈迦図· 雪景山水図三幅対と「道有」の鑑蔵印について), *Cultural Properties Monthly* (Gekkan bunkazai 月刊文化財), vol. 525 (June 2007), pp. 37–43

KINBARA 1938
Kinbara Seigo (金原省吾), *Muxi* (Mokkei 牧溪), *A Series of Oriental Art Literature* (Tōyō bijutsu bunkō dai 3-kan, Atorie-sha 東洋美術文庫), Tokyo 1938

KLOSE 2009
Wolfgang Klose (Hg.), *Wilhelm von Bode – Otto Kümmel. Briefwechsel aus 20 Jahren 1905–1925*, Karlsruhe 2009

KOHARA 1967
Kohara Hironobu (古原宏伸), plate commentary, in *Asiatic Art in Japanese Collections* (Tōyō bijutsu 東洋美術), Tanaka Ichimatsu (田中一松), Yonezawa Yoshiho (米澤嘉圃) and Kei Kawakami (川上涇) (eds), vol. 1, *Painting I* (Kaiga I 絵画 I), Tokyo 1967

KOHARA 1978
Kohara Hironobu (古原宏伸), *Shen Zhou, Wen Zhengming* (Shin Shū, Bun Chōmei 沈周，文徵明), Tokyo 1978

*Kokka* 1912
'Sung Picture of a Boy Playing' (宋畫端午戲嬰圖), *Kokka* 國華, vol. 22, no. 262 (March 1912)

*Kokka* 1918
'Monkey, attributed to Mao Song' (Den Mō Shō hitsu saru zu 伝毛松筆猿図), *Kokka* 國華, vol. 29, no. 340, (September 1918), pp. 91

*Kokka* 1923
'Boston Museum's *Luohan* Paintings from Daitoku-ji Temple' (Bosuton Bijutsukan ni tsutawareru kyū Daitokuji no Rakanzu ボストン美術館に傳はれる舊大德寺の羅漢図), *Kokka* (國華), vol. 33, no. 393 (1923), pp. 251–53

KONDŌ 2000
Kondō Hidemi (近藤秀實), 'Zeng Jing, a Portrait Painter of the Ming Dynasty and Japanese Obaku-shu Portraits' (Zeng Jing yu Huang Bo huaxiang – Zhong Ri huihua jiaoliu zhi yiduan 曾鯨與黄檗画像 – 中日繪畫交流之一端), *Palace Museum Journal* (Gugong bowuyuan yuankan 故宮博物院院刊) (May 2000), pp. 78–86

KONDŌ 2002
Kondō Hidemi (近藤秀實), *Painting School of Pochen [Zeng Jing]* (Pochen huapai 波臣畫派), Jilin 2002

KŌNO 2001
Kōno Motoaki (河野元昭), 'Bunchō and the Study of Chinese Painting – Koshi Gafu and Hyōkaku Kishō-zu' (*Bunchō no chugokuga gakushū – koshi gafu to hyōkaku kishō-zu* 文晁の中国画学習 – 『顧氏画譜』と『漂客奇賞図』), *Kokka* 國華, vol. 107, no. 1273 (November 2001), pp. 13–25

KŌNO 2002
Kōno Motoaki (河野元昭), 'Bunchō and the Study of Chinese Painting – Shoga Kōkan and Shūko Jisshu' (*Bunchō no chugokuga gakushū – shoga kōkan to shūko jisshu* 文晁の中国画学習 – 『書画甲観』と『集古十種』), *Studies in Art History* (Bijutsushi ronsō 美術史論叢), vol. 18 (2002), pp. 35–60

KOON IN NEW YORK 2009
Yeewan Koon, 'Ghost Amusement', in *Eccentric Visions: the Worlds of Luo Ping*, Kim Karlsson, Alfreda Murck and Michele Matteini (eds), exh. cat., The Metropolitan Museum of Art, New York, 2009, pp. 182–99

KUO 2007
*Visual Culture in Shanghai, 1850s–1930s*, Jason Kuo (ed.), Washington, DC 2007

KYOTO 1982
Nishigami Minoru (西上実), *The beauty of birds and flowers – painting and design* (Kachō no bi – kaiga to ishō 花鳥の美 – 繪畫と意匠), exh. cat., Kyoto National Museum, Kyoto 1982

KYOTO 1983
Nishigami Minoru (西上実), *Landscape* – idea and art (Sansui – shisō to bijutsu 山水 – 思想と美術), Kyoto National Museum, Kyoto 1983

KYOTO 1993
Nishigami Minoru (西上実), *The Art of Obaku: Formation of the Culture of the Edo Period* (Obaku no bijutsu: Edo jidai no bunka o kaeta mono 黄檗の美術：江戸時代の文化を変えたもの), Kyoto National Museum, Kyoto 1993

KYOTO 2006
Kobayashi Yūko (小林優子), 'Aspirations of the Literati Artist – Appreciating Wang Jianzhang' (Akogare no bunjin gaka – Ō Kenshō o meguru shōgan no itonami 憧れの文人画家王建章をめぐる賞玩のいとなみ), *Literati of the Modern Era* (Kindai bunjin no itonami 近代文人のいとなみ), Naritasan Calligraphy Art Museum, Kyoto 2006

LACHMAN 1989
Charles H. Lachman (trans. & annot.), *Evaluations of Sung Dynasty Painters of Renown: Liu Tao-ch'un's Sung-cha'ao Ming-hua P'ing*, Leiden and New York 1989

LAI 2005
Yu-Chih Lai, 'Surreptitious Appropriation: Ren Bonian (1840–1895) and Japanese Culture in Shanghai, 1842–1895', PhD dissertation, Yale University 2005

LAWTON AND MERRILL 1993
Thomas Lawton and Linda Merrill, *Freer a Legacy of Art*, Washington DC 1993

LEDDEROSE 1973
Lothar Ledderose, 'Subject Matter in Early Chinese Painting Criticism', *Oriental Art*, vol. XIX, no. 1 (1973), pp. 1–15

LEDDEROSE 1995
Lothar Ledderose, 'Collecting Chinese Painting in Berlin', *Europe Studies China, Papers from an International Conference on the History of European Sinology*, London 1995, pp. 175–201

LEDDEROSE 1998
Lothar Ledderose, *Orchideen und Felsen. Chinesische Bilder im Museum für Ostasiatische Kunst Berlin*, Staatliche Museen zu Berlin – Preussischer Kulturbesitz, Berlin 1998

LEE 1957
Sherman E. Lee, 'Some Problems in Ming and Ch'ing Landscape Painting', *Ars Orientalis*, vol. 2 (1957), pp. 471–85

LEE 1966
Sherman E. Lee, 'Literati and Professionals: Four Ming Painters', *The Bulletin of the Cleveland Museum of Art*, vol. 53, no. 1 (January 1966), pp. 2–25.

LEE 1972
Sherman E. Lee, 'Zen in Art: Art in Zen', *The Bulletin of The Cleveland Museum of Art*, vol. 59, no. 9 (1972), pp. 239–60

LEE 1981
Stella Yu Lee, 'The Figure Painting of Jen Po-nien (1840–1896), the Emergence of a Popular Style in Late Chinese Painting', PhD dissertation, University of California 1981

LEE 2001
Lee Hui-shu, *Exquisite Moments: West Lake & Southern Song Art*, New York 2001

LEE 2009
Lee Chun-yi, 'Daoism and the art of Shen Zhou (1427–1509)', PhD dissertation, Arizona State University 2009

LEE AND HO 1980
Sherman E. Lee and Wai-kam Ho, 'The Nature and Significance of the Collection of Liang Ch'ing-Piao', in *Proceedings of the International Conference on Sinology, Section of History of Arts*, vol. 10, Taipei 1980, pp. 101–57

LEIJON 1981
Per-Olow Leijon, 'Chinese Paintings', *Arts of Asia*, vol. 11, no. 6 (November–December 1981), pp. 135–46

LI (1318–9) 1993–8
Li Kan (李衎), *Manual of Bamboo Painting* (Zhu pu 竹譜), first edition 1318–9, reprinted in *A Compendium of Writings on Calligraphy and Painting in China* (Zhongguo shuhua quanshu 中國書畫全書), 14 vols., Lu Fusheng (盧輔聖) et al (eds), vol. 2, pp. 733–4, Shanghai 1993–8

LI 1978
Li Yu (李渝), *Ren Bonian: The People's Painter of the Late Qing* (Ren Bonian: Qingmo di shimin huajia 任伯年: 清末的市民畫家), Taipei 1978

LI 1990
Li Wai-yee, 'Dream Visions of Transcendence in Chinese Literature and Painting', *Asian Art*, vol. III, no. 4 (Autumn 1990), pp. 53–78

LI 1991
Li Chu-tsing, '*Grooms and Horses* by Three Members of the Chao Family', in *Words and Images*, Alfreda Murck and Wen C. Fong (eds), New York 1991, pp. 199–220

LI 1993
Li Chu-tsing (李鑄晉), 'The Early Development of Shen Zhou' (Shen Zhou zaonian de fazhan 沈周早年的發展), in Palace Museum (故宮博物院), *A Study of the Wu School of Painting* (Wumen huapai yanjiu 吳門畫派研究), Beijing 1993

LI 1996
Li Zhizhong (李致忠), *A Story of Ancient Chinese Books* (Zhongguo gudai shuji shihua 中國古代書籍史話), Beijing 1996

LI 2003
Li Chu-tsing (李鑄晉), '*Grooms and Horses* by the Three Generations of the Zhao Family of Wuxing' (Wuxing Zhao shi sanshi *Ren ma tu* juan 吳興趙氏三世人馬圖卷), in *Autumn Colours on the Que and Hua Mountains: Zhao Mengfu's Life and Painting* (Que Hua qiuse: Zhao Mengfu de shengping yu huayi 鵲華秋色；趙孟頫的生平與書藝), Taipei 2003, pp. 99–132

LI 2012
Li Song (李淞), 'One Chen Rong and Two Suo Wengs' (Yige Chen Rong, Liangge Suo Weng 一個陳容兩個所翁), in *Masterpieces of Early Chinese Painting and Calligraphy in American Collections* (Han mo hui cui: Meiguo shoucang Zhongguo Wudai Song Yuan shuhua zhenpin zhan 翰墨薈萃: 美國收藏中國五代宋元書畫珍品展), Shanghai Museum, Shanghai 2012, pp. 378–9

LI AND WATT 1993
Li Chu-tsing (李鑄晉) and James Watt (屈志仁), 'Wang Shimin and Dong Qichang' (Wang Shimin yu Dong Qichang' 王時敏與董其昌), in Duoyun bianji bu (朵雲編輯部), *A Study of the Four Wangs of the Early Qing* (Qingchu si Wang huapai yanjiu 清初四王畫派研究), Shanghai 1993, pp. 449–62

LIANG 1993
*Selected Works of Chinese Portraiture* (Zhongguo xiaoxianghua xuanji 中國肖像畫選集), Liang Baiquan (梁白泉) (ed.), Nanjing 1993

LIANG 1996
*The Art of the Dunhuang Caves: The Mogao Caves, Caves 321, 329 and 335 (Early Tang)* (Dunhuang shiku yishu: Mogaoku di 321, 329, 335 ku [chu Tang] 敦煌石窟藝術: 莫高窟第 321, 329, 335 窟), Liang Weiying (梁尉英) (ed.), Jiangsu 1996

LIAONING SHENG BOWUGUAN 1975
Liaoning sheng bowuguan, 'The Liao tomb discovered at Yemaotai, Faku' (Faku Yemaotai liaomu jilue 法庫葉茂臺遼墓記略) *Wenwu* (文物) no. 12 (1975), pp. 26–36

LIN 1985
Lin Jiazhi (林家治), 'The Difficult Life of Qiu Ying' (Qiu Ying qiongku de yisheng 仇英窮苦的一生), *Duoyun* 朵雲, no. 1 (May 1985), pp. 201–5

LIPPIT 2009
Yukio Lippit, 'Apparition painting', RES: *Anthropology and Aesthetics*, no. 55/56 (Spring/Autumn 2009), pp. 61–86

LISCOMB 1984
Kathlyn Lannon Liscomb, 'Early Ming Painters: Predecessors and Elders of Shen Zhou (1427–1509)', PhD dissertation, University of Chicago 1984

LITTLE 1987
Stephen Little, 'Du Jin, Tao Cheng, and Shi Zhong: Three Scholar-Professional Painters of the Early Ming Dynasty', PhD dissertation, Yale University 1987

LITTLE 1999
Stephen Little, 'Du Jin's *Enjoying Antiquities*: A Problem in Connoisseurship', in *Issues of Authenticity in Chinese Painting*, Judith G. Smith and Wen C. Fong (eds), New York 1999, pp. 189–220

LITTLE 2000
Stephen Little, *Taoism and the Arts of China*, Berkeley 2000

LIU 1972
Liu Jiu'an (劉九庵), 'Some Questions on the Paintings Discovered in the Tomb of Zhu Tan' (Zhu Tan mu chutu huajuan de jige wenti 朱檀墓出土畫卷的幾個問題), *Wenwu* 文物, no. 8 (1972), pp. 64–6

LIU 1990
Liu Jiu'an (劉九庵), 'Alias Paintings by Suzhou Artists and Some Distinctive Examples' (Wumen huajia zhi biehao tu ji jianbie julie 吳門畫家之別號圖及鑑別舉例), *Palace Museum Journal* (Gugong bowuyuan yuankan 故宮博物院院刊), no. 3 (1990), pp. 54–61

LIU 1993
Liu Shangheng (劉尚恒), 'Price List of Several Loyalist Artists in the Early Qing' (Qing chu yimin yuyi zhi jiage 清初遺民鬻藝之價格), *Wenxian* (文獻), no. 2 (1993), p. 168

LIU 2002
Heping Liu, '*The Water Mill* and Northern Song Imperial Patronage of Art, Commerce and Science', *The Art Bulletin*, vol. 84, no. 4 (December 2002), pp. 566–95

LIU 2005
Cary Y. Liu, 'Chinese Architectural Aesthetics: Patterns of Living and Being between Past and Present', in *House, Home, Family: Living and Being Chinese*, Ronald G. Knapp and Kai-yin Lo (eds), Honolulu 2005, pp. 139–59

LIU FIEDLER 1998
Shi-yee Liu Fiedler, 'From Buddhism to Daoism: A Study of Shitao's *Sketches of Calligraphy and Painting*', unpublished paper, 1998

LIU FIEDLER IN KANSAS CITY AND SEATTLE 1992
Shi-yee Liu Fiedler, 'Chronology of T'ung Ch'i-ch'ang's Works and Inscriptions', in *The Century of Tung Ch'i-ch'ang*, Wai-kam Ho and Judith G. Smith (eds), exh. cat., vol. 2, The Nelson-Atkins Museum of Art, Kansas City and Seattle 1992, pp. 485–575

LIU IN TAIPEI 2000
Liu Fangru (劉芳如), 'Introduction' (Qianyan 前言), in *Four Masters of Figure Painting in the mid-Ming Dynasty: Du Jin, Zhou Chen, Tang Yin and Qiu Ying* (Ming zhongye renwuhua sijia tezhan: Du Jin, Zhou Chen, Tang Yin, Qiu Ying 明中葉人物畫四家特展：杜堇, 周臣, 唐寅, 仇英), exh. cat., National Palace Museum, Taipei 2000, pp. 10–47

LOEWE 1993
*Early Chinese Texts: A Bibliographic Guide, Society for the Early China, Institute of East Asian Studies*, Michael Loewe (ed.), Berkeley 1993

LONDON 1910
British Museum, *Guide to an Exhibition of Chinese and Japanese Paintings (fourth to nineteenth century, A.D.)*, exh. cat., London 1910

LONDON 1914A
The British Museum, *Guide to an Exhibition of Paintings, Manuscripts and other Archaeological Objects Collected by Sir Aurel Stein, KCIE, in Chinese Turkestan*, exh. cat., London 1914

LONDON 1914B
The British Museum, *Guide to an Exhibition of Chinese and Japanese Paintings Principally from the Arthur Morrison Collection*, exh. cat., London 1914

LONDON 1936
*The Chinese Exhibition: A Commemorative Catalogue of the International Exhibition of Chinese Art, Royal Academy of the Arts, November 1935–March 1936*, exh. cat., Royal Academy of Arts, London 1936

LOS ANGELES 1957
*The Arts of the T'ang Dynasty*, exh. cat., Los Angeles County Museum of Art, Los Angeles 1957

LU 1993–8
*A Compendium of Writings on Calligraphy and Painting in China* (Zhongguo shuhua quanshu 中國書畫全書), 14 vols, Lu Fusheng (盧輔聖) et al. (eds), Shanghai 1993–8

LU 1997
Lu Zongrun, 'A Summary of the Development of the Art of Mounting Calligraphy and Painting in the Qing Dynasty' (Qingdai shuhua zhuangbiao gongyi fazhan gaishu 清代書畫裝裱工藝發展概述), *Historical Artefacts: Bulletin of the National Taiwan Museum of History* (Lishi wenwu yuekan 歷史文物月刊), April 1997, pp. 93–103

LU 2004
*A Study of Dai Jin and the Zhe School – Special issue* (Dai Jin yu Zhepai yanjiu 戴進與浙派研究), Lu Fusheng (ed.), *Duoyun* 朵雲, vol. 61 (2004)

LUOYANG SHI DI'ER WENWU GONGZUO DUI 1992
Luoyang shi di'er wenwu gongzuo dui (洛陽市第二文物工作隊), 'A Song Tomb Discovered at Mangshan, Luoyang' (Luoyang Mangshan Songdai bihua mu 洛陽邙山宋代壁畫墓), *Wenwu* 文物, no. 12 (1992), pp. 37–51

LYONS AND PARIS 1991
Alan Kennedy with Vira Linhartova, *Manteau de nuages: kesa japonais : XVIIe-XIXe siècles*, exh. cat., Musée Historique des Tissus, Lyons, Paris Musée National des Arts Asiatiques Guimet, Paris 1991

MA 1990
Ma Jen-mei, 'Shen Chou's Topographical Landscape', PhD dissertation, University of Kansas 1990

MA 1997
Ma De (馬德), *Documentary sources of Dunhuang artisans* (Dunhuang gongjiang shiliao 敦煌工匠史料), Gansu renmin chuban she, Lanzhou 1997

MA 2008
Ma Ya-chen (馬雅貞), 'Mediating between Local Society and the Centre: the Dual Character of *The Affluent Life in the Prosperous Age*' (Zhongjie yu difang yu zhongyang zhijian: *Shengshi zisheng tu* de shuangchong xingge 中介於地方與中央之間：《盛世滋生圖》的雙重性格), *Taida Journal of Art History* (Guoli Taiwan daxue meishushi yanjiu jikan 國立台灣大學美術史研究集刊), no. 24 (2008), pp. 259–322

MACAU 2004
Chen Haoxing (陳浩星), *Rules by the Masters: Paintings and Calligraphies by Bada and Shitao in the Collections of the Palace Museum and Shanghai Museum* (Zhiren wufa: Gugong, Shangbo zhencang Bada Shitao shuhua jingpin 至人無法: 故宮, 上博珍藏八大石濤書畫精品), exh. cat., Macau Museum of Art, Macau 2004

MACAU 2005
Chen Haoxing (陳浩星), *The Light of the Southern School: Special Catalogue on the 450th Anniversary of the Birth of Dong Qichang* (Nanzong beidou: Dong Qichang dansheng sibai wushi zhounian shuhua teji 南宗北斗: 董其昌誕生四百五十週年書畫特集), exh. cat., Macau Museum of Art, Macau 2005

MACGREGOR 1994
*Sir Hans Sloane, Collector Scientist, Antiquary: Founding Father of the British Museum*, Arthur MacGregor (ed.), London 1994

MACOUIN 2009
Francis Macouin, 'Émile Guimet', in *Dictionnaire critique des historiens de l'art*, Philippe Sénéchal (ed.), Paris 2009 (www.inha.fr/IMG/article_PDF/article_a2357.pdf) (accessed December 2012)

MAEDA 1975
Robert J. Maeda, 'Chieh-Hua: Ruled-line painting in China', *Ars Orientalis*, vol. 10 (1975), pp. 123–41

MARX 2007–8
Barbara Marx, 'Medici Gifts to the Court of Dresden', *Studies in Decorative Arts. The Bard Graduate Center for Studies in Decorative Arts, Design, and Culture*, vol. XV, no. 1 (Fall–Winter 2007–8), pp. 46–83

MASAKI 1933
Masaki Tokuzo, 'Monkey, attributed to Mao Song' (Den Mō Shō hitsu saru zu 伝毛松筆猿図), in *The Journal of Art Studies* (Bijutsu kenkyū 美術研究), vol. 17 (1933), pp.37–8

MATSUMOTO 1932
Matsumoto Eiichi (松本栄一), 'On a T'ang Buddhist Painting from Tun-huang Dated 729' (Tonkō shutsu kaigen nendai ga ni tsuite 燉煌出開元年代畫に就て), *Kokka* 國華, vol. 43, no. 511 (June 1932), 153–8

MATSUSHIMA 1976
Matsushima Junsei (松島順正), 'On Folding Screens in the Shōsō-in' (Shōsō-in no byōbu ni tsuite 正倉院の屏風について), *Journal of the Archives and Mausolea of the Department of the Imperial Household Agency* (Kunaichō shoryobu kiyō 宮内庁書陵部紀要), no. 28 (1976), pp. 1–15

MAUCUER 2011
Michel Maucuer, 'In the House of a Greek Mandarin', *Arts of Asia*, vol. 41, no. 4 (2011), pp. 42–53

McCAUSLAND 2000
Shane McCausland, 'Zhao Mengfu (1254–1322) and the Revolution of Elite Culture in Mongol China', PhD dissertation, Princeton University 2000

McCAUSLAND 2003A
Shane McCausland, *First Masterpiece of Chinese Painting: The Admonitions Scroll*, London 2003

McCAUSLAND 2003B
*Gu Kaizhi and the Admonitions Scroll*, Shane McCausland (ed.), London 2003

McCAUSLAND 2011
Shane McCausland, *Zhao Mengfu: Calligraphy and Painting for Khubilai's China*, Hong Kong 2011

MENG 2000
Meng Sihui (孟嗣徽), 'An Iconographic Study of the 'Five Planets and Twenty Eight Constellations' Scroll' (Wuxing ershibaxiu shenxing tu tuxiang kaobian 孟嗣徽《五星廿八宿神形圖》圖像考辨), Study of History of Art (Yishushi yanjiu 藝術史研究), no. 2 (2000), pp. 517–56

MILAN 1931
*Le Pitturi Chinesi Della Raccolta Del Drago esposte nel castello Sforzesca di Milano (Novembre 1931–Febraio 1932)*, exh. cat., Milan 1931

MIYAZAKI 2011
Noriko Miyazaki, 'The Current State of Japanese Research on Chinese Art History and Related Issues: With a Focus on the History of Ming and Ch'ing Painting', *Acta Asiatica. Bulletin of The Institute of Eastern Culture*, no. 100 (Tokyo 2011), pp. 67–84

MONOD-BRUHL 1939
Odette Monod-Bruhl, *Guide du Musée Guimet: avec introductions concernant l'histoire, les religions et les arts des différents pays*, Paris 1939

MURCK 1988
Alfreda Murck, 'Yuan Jiang: Image Maker', in *Chinese Painting under the Qianlong Emperor: The Symposium Papers in Two Volumes*, Ju-hsi Chou and Claudia Brown (eds), *Phoebus*, vol. 6, no. 2 (1988), pp. 228–59

MURCK AND FONG 1980–1
Alfreda Murck and Wen C. Fong, 'A Chinese Garden Court: The Astor Court at The Metropolitan Museum of Art', *The Metropolitan Museum of Art Bulletin*, vol. 38, no. 3 (1980–1), pp. 2–64

MURCK AND FONG 1991
*Words and Images: Chinese Poetry, Calligraphy and Painting*, Alfreda Murck and Wen C. Fong (eds), Princeton University Press, Princeton 1991

MURRAY 1995
Julia K. Murray, 'Buddhism and early narrative illustration in China', *Archives of Asian Art*, vol. 48 (1995), pp. 17–31

MUSEUM OF FINE ARTS, BOSTON 1944
Museum of Fine Arts, *Fifteen Hundred Years of Chinese Painting*, Museum of Fine Arts, Boston 1944

MUSEUM OF FINE ARTS, BOSTON 1975
Museum of Fine Arts, *Illustrated Handbook*, Museum of Fine Arts, Boston 1975

MUSEUM OF FINE ARTS, BOSTON 1982
Museum of Fine Arts, *Asiatic Art in the Museum of Fine Arts, Boston*, Museum of Fine Arts, Boston 1982

MUSEUM OF FINE ARTS, BOSTON 1991
Museum of Fine Arts, *Selected Masterpieces of Asian Art, 1890–1990: Museum of Fine Arts, Boston*, Tokyo 1991

MUSEUM OF FINE ARTS, BOSTON 1992
Museum of Fine Arts, *Selected Masterpieces of Asian Art*, Museum of Fine Arts, Boston 1992

NAGOYA 2008
*Exploring the Treasures of the Muromachi Shoguns* (Muromachi shōgunke no shihō o saguru 室町将軍家の至宝を探る), exh. cat., Tokugawa Art Museum, Nagoya 2008

NAGOYA AND BOSTON 1999
Museum of Fine Arts, *Okakura Tenshin to Bosuton Bijutsukan – Okakura Tenshin and the Museum of Fine Arts, Boston*, exh. cat., Nagoya and Boston Museum of Fine Arts, Boston 1999

NAKAGAWA 1983
Nakagawa Kenji, 'Gong Kai's painting *Noble Horse*' (Kyōkai hitsu Shun-kotsu 龔開筆「駿骨圖」), in Osaka Municipal Museum of Art Bulletin (Ōsaka shiritsu bijutsukan kiyō), 1983

NAKATA AND FU 1981–3
Nakata Yujiro (中田勇次郎) and Fu Shen (傅申), *Masterpieces of Chinese Calligraphy in American and European Collections* (Ōbei shūzō chūgoku hoshō meisuki zenshū 歐米收藏: 中國法書名蹟集,明清篇), 2 vols, Tokyo 1981–3

NARA 1997
*Yuan dynasty painting – A century of the Mongol world empire* (Gen jidai no kaiga—Mongoru sekai teikuni no isseiki 元時代の繪畫 – モンゴル世界帝國の一世紀), exh. cat., Museum Yamato Bunkakan, Nara 1997

NARA 2008
Tsukamoto Maromitsu (塚本麿充), *Lofty landscapes – the Li-Guo tradition in China and Korea* (Sūkō naru sansui –chūgoku, chōsen rikakukei sansuiga no keifu 崇高なる山水 – 中國· 朝鮮、李郭系山水の系譜), exh. cat., Yamato Bunkakan, Nara 2008

NARA 2009
*Sacred Ningbo, Gateway to 1300 Years of Japanese Buddhism* (Seichi Ninpo [Ninpo]: Nihon Bukkyo 1300-nen no genryu: subete wa koko kara yatte kita 聖地寧波 (ニンポー): 日本仏教1300年の源流 : すべてはここからやって来た), exh. cat., Nara National Museum, Nara 2009

NATIONAL MUSEUMS OF BERLIN 2009
National Museums of Berlin, *Deutsch-Russischer Museumsdialog. Verlust und Rückgabe*, Berlin 2009

NATIONAL MUSEUMS OF BERLIN 2012
National Museums of Berlin, *Auf Grünwedels Spuren. Restaurierung und Forschung an Zentralasiatischen Wandmalereien*, Leipzig 2012

NEEDHAM 1959
Joseph Needham, with the research assistance of Wang Ling, *Science and Civilisation in China*, vol. 3, *Mathematics and the Sciences of the Heavens and the Earth*, Cambridge 1959

NEMROFF 2005
Lauren S. Nemroff, 'The Figure Paintings of Tang Yin (1470–1524)', PhD dissertation, New York University 2005

NEW HAVEN 1977
Shen C.Y. Fu, in collaboration with Marilyn W. Fu, Mary G. Neill and Mary Jane Clark, *Traces of the Brush: Studies in Chinese Calligraphy*, exh. cat., Yale University Art Gallery, New Haven 1977

NEW HAVEN 1985
Maggie Bickford and Mary Gardner Neill, *Bones of Jade – Soul of Ice: The Flowering Plum in Chinese Art*, exh. cat., Yale University Art Gallery, New Haven 1985

NEW HAVEN 1990
Wang Fang-yu and Richard Barnhart, *Master of the Lotus Garden: The Life and Art of Bada Shanren (1626–1705)*, Yale University Art Gallery, New Haven 1990

*New History of World Art 1997–2001*
*A New History of World Art – Oriental* (Sekai bijutsu daizenshū – tōyō hen 世界美術大全集 – 東洋編), Tokyo 1997–2001

*New Trends in Art 1992*
*New Trends in Art* (Geijutsu shinchō 芸術新潮), no. 1 (1992)

NEW YORK 1962A
James Cahill, *The Art of Southern Song China*, exh. cat., Asia House Gallery, New York 1962

NEW YORK 1962B
Laurence Sickman, *Chinese Calligraphy and Painting in the Collection of John M. Crawford, Jr.*, exh. cat., Pierpont Morgan Library, New York 1962

NEW YORK 1972
Richard Barnhart, *Wintry Trees, Old Forests: Some Landscape Themes in Chinese Painting*, exh. cat., New York 1972

NEW YORK 1973
Wen C. Fong, with catalogue by Marilyn Fu, *Sung and Yuan Paintings*, exh. cat., The Metropolitan Museum of Art, New York 1973

NEW YORK 1983a
Richard M. Barnhart, *Along the Border of Heaven: Sung and Yuan Paintings from the C.C. Wang Family Collection*, exh. cat., New York 1983

NEW YORK 1983b
Richard M. Barnhart, *Peach Blossom Spring: Gardens and Flowers in Chinese Painting*, exh. cat., The Metropolitan Museum of Art, New York 1983

NEW YORK 1987
Chu-tsing Li and James Watt, *The Chinese Scholar's Studio: Artistic Life in the Late Ming Period*, exh. cat., New York 1987

NEW YORK 1997
Robert E. Harrist Jr. and Virginia Bower, *Power and Virtue: The Horse in Chinese Art*, exh. cat., China Institute Gallery, New York 1997

NEW YORK 2000
Jonathan Chaves, *The Chinese Painter as Poet*, exh. cat., China Institute Gallery, New York 2000

NEW YORK 2001
Hui-shu Lee, *Exquisite Moments: West Lake & Southern Song Art*, exh. cat., China Institute Gallery, New York 2001

NEW YORK 2007
*Awakenings: Zen Figure Painting in Medieval Japan*, Gregory P.A. Levine and Yukio Lippit (eds), exh. cat., Japan Society Gallery, New York 2007

NEW YORK 2008A
Maxwell K. Hearn, *How to Read Chinese Paintings*, exh. cat., The Metropolitan Museum of Art, New York 2008

NEW YORK 2008B
*Landscapes Clear and Radiant: the Art of Wang Hui* (1632–1717), Maxwell K. Hearn (ed.), exh. cat., The Metropolitan Museum of Art, New York 2008

NEW YORK 2008C
Willow Hai Chang, *The Last Emperor's Collection: Masterpieces of Painting and Calligraphy from the Liaoning Provincial Museum*, exh. cat., China Institute Gallery, New York 2008

NEW YORK 2009
*Eccentric Visions: the Worlds of Luo Ping*, Kim Karlsson, Alfreda Murck and Michele Matteini (eds), The Metropolitan Museum of Art, New York, 2009

NEW YORK 2010
*The World of Khubilai Khan: Chinese Art in the Yuan Dynasty*, James C.Y. Watt (ed.), exh. cat., The Metropolitan Museum of Art, New York 2010

NEW YORK AND DALLAS 1993
Richard M. Barnhart with Mary Ann Rogers and Richard Stanley-Baker, *Painters of the Great Ming: The Imperial Court and the Zhe School*, Richard M. Barnhart (ed.), exh. cat., The Metropolitan Museum of Art, New York and Dallas Museum of Art, Dallas 1993

NEW YORK, LOS ANGELES AND SAN FRANCISCO 1967
James Cahill, *Fantastics and Eccentrics in Chinese Painting*, exh. cat., Asia House Gallery, New York, LACMA, Los Angeles and M.H. de Young Memorial Museum, San Francisco 1967

NIE 1982
Nie Chongzheng (聶崇正), *Yuan Jiang and Yuan Yao* (Yuan Jiang yu Yuan Yao 袁江與袁耀), Shanghai 1982

NIE 2008
Nie Chongzheng (聶崇正), *Qing Court Painting and the Influence of the West* (Qinggong huihua yu xihua dongjian 清宮繪畫興西畫東漸), Beijing 2008

NISHIDA 2000
Hiroko Nishida, 'The Collection and Appreciation of Chinese Art Objects in 15th and 16th Century Japan, and their Legacy', in *Collecting Chinese Art. Interpretation and Display* (Colloquies on Art and Archeology in Asia no. 20), Stacey Pierson (ed.), London 2000, pp. 9–18

NISHIYAMA 2011
Nishiyama Mika (西山美香), 'Ashikaga Yoshimitsu's Internalization of the Song Dynasty Emperor Huizong – Kyoto's Shōkoku-ji and Kaifeng's Daxiangguo Temple' (*Ashikaga yoshimitsu no uchinaru sōchō kōtei – kyoto shōkokuji to kaifū daishōkokuji* 足利義満の内なる宋朝皇帝 – 京都相国寺と開封大相国寺), *Intriguing Asia* (Ajia yūgaku アジア遊学), vol. 142 (2011), pp. 145–61

OGAWA 1980
Ogawa Yūsuke (小川裕充), 'Imagination in Tang and Song landscape painting—from the po'mo style to Early Spring and Dream Journey through the Xiao and Xiang Rivers' (Tō-sō sansui gashi ni okeru imajineshon – hatsuboku kara sōshunzu, shōshōgayū-zu made (jō) (chū) (shita) 唐宋山水畫史におけるイマジネーション – 潑墨から「早春圖」「瀟湘臥游圖巻」まで（上）（中）（下）( parts 1, 2, and 3), *Kokka* 國華, vol. 87 (1980), no. 1034, pp. 5–17; 1035, pp. 35–45; and 1036, pp. 25–36

OGAWA 1981
Ogawa Hiromitsu (小川裕充), 'Famous Paintings in the Academy' (Inchf no meiga 院中の名画), *Essays on Chinese painting in Honour of Prof. Suzuki Kei's Sixtieth Birthday* (Chugoku kaigashi ronshu: Suzuki Kei sensei kanreiki-kinen 鈴木敬先生還暦記念中国絵画史論集), Tokyo 1981, pp. 23–85

OGAWA 1990
Ogawa Hiromitsu (小川裕充), 'One hundred landscape paintings (13): Yan Wengui, Landscape with Pavilions' (Chūgoku sansuiga hyakusen 13: En Bunki Kōzanrōzu 中國山水畫百選 13: 燕文貴江山樓觀圖), *Eastern Book Review* (Tōhō 東方), no. 117 (1990)

OGAWA 1994
Ogawa Hiromitsu (小川裕充), 'One Hundred Landscape Paintings (50): Li Rongjin, Han Palace' (Chūgoku sansuiga hyakusen 50: Ri Yōkin kan'enzu 中國山水畫百選 50: 李容瑾漢苑圖), *Eastern Book Review* (Tōhō 東方), no. 154 (1994)

OGAWA 1996
Ogawa Hiromitsu (小川裕充), 'Auspicious Cranes, by Huizong' (Kisō hitsu zuikaku zumaki 徽宗筆瑞鶴図巻), *Studies in Art History* (Bijutsushi ronsō 美術史論叢), vol. 12 (1996), pp. 129–37

OGAWA 1997
Ogawa Hiromitsu (小川裕充), 'Continuity of Spatial Composition in Song and Yuan Landscape Painting' (Sōgen sansuiga niokeru kōsei no denshō 宋元山水画における構成の伝承), *Studies in Art History* (Bijutsushi ronsō 美術史論叢), vol. 13 (1997), pp. 111–23

OGAWA 2008
Ogawa Hiromitsu (小川裕充), 'Transition of Treatment of Silk During the Song Dynasty: Sitting Portraits of Successive Emperors of the Northern and Southern Song Dynasties on a Silk Support' (Sōdai no yōkenhō ni tsuite – ryōsō rekidai kōtei zazō wo chūshinni 宋代の用絹法について–両宋歴代皇帝坐像を中心に), *Studies in Art History* (Bijutsushi ronsō 美術史論叢), vol. 24 (2008), pp. 73–80

OSAKA 1980
*Song and Yuan Art* (Sō-gen no bijutsu 宋元の美術), exh. cat., Osaka Municipal Museum of Art, Osaka 1980

OSAKA AND SHANGHAI 1994
Nakagawa Kenji (中川憲一), *Famous Chinese Paintings and Calligraphy from the Osaka Municipal Museum of Art and the Shanghai Museum* (Ōsaka shiritsu bijutsukan Shanhai hakubutsukan kuranaka kokushoga meihin zuroku 大阪市立美術館· 上海博物館藏中國書畫名品圖), exh. cat., Osaka Municipal Museum of Fine Arts and Shanghai Museum 1994

OUYANG 2008
Ouyang Moyi (歐陽摩一), 'Name Labels and Long Inscriptions in the Han Stone Carvings' (Lun Han huaxiangshi wenzi bangti he tiji 論漢畫像石文字榜題和題記", *Southeast Culture* (Dongnan wenhua 東南文化), no. 1 (2008), pp. 61–5

PAINE 1964
Robert Treat Paine, *Figure Compositions of China and Japan, from the Collection of the Museum of Fine Arts, Boston*, Museum of Fine Arts, Boston 1964

*Paintings of the Musée national des arts asiatiques-Guimet, Paris 1968*
*Paintings of the Musée national des arts asiatiques Guimet, Paris* (Gime tōyō bijutsukan ギメ東洋美術館), Tokyo 1968

PAN 1979
Pan Jixing (潘吉星), *A History of Papermaking Techonology in China* (Zhongguo zaozhi jishu shigao 中國造紙技術史稿), Beijing 1979

PAN 1997
Pan Shenliang (潘深亮), *Masterpieces of the Shanghai School* (Haishang mingjia huihua 海上名家繪畫), Hong Kong 1997

PAN AND MA 1985
Pan Yushan (潘玉閃) and Ma Shichang (馬世長), *The Former Building Sites in Front of the Mogao Caves* (Mogaoku kuqian diantang yizhi 莫高窟窟前殿堂遺址), Beijing 1985

PANG 1909
Pang Yuanji (龐元濟), *Record of Famous Paintings in the Studio of Emptiness* (Xuzhai minghua lu 虛齋名畫錄), Shanghai 1909

PARIS 1947
*Manuscrits et peintures de Touen-Houang: Mission Pelliot 1906–1909: collections de la Bibliothèque nationale et du Musée Guimet*, exh. cat., Bibliothèque nationale, Paris 1947

PARIS 1976
*La Route de la soie: les arts de l'Asie centrale ancienne dans les collections publiques françaises*, exh. cat., Grand Palais, Paris 1976

PARIS 1995–6
*Sérinde, Terre de Bouddha*, Jacques Giès and Monique Cohen (eds), exh. cat., Grand Palais, Paris 1995–6

PARIS 2002
*Afghanistan, une histoire millénaire*, exh. cat., Paris Musée National des Arts Asiatiques Guimet, Paris 2002

PARIS 2004
*Montagnes celestes: Trésors des musées de Chine*, Jacques Giès (ed.), exh. cat., Grand Palais, Paris 2004

PARIS 2006
Mael Bellec, 'La collection Jean-Pierre Dubosc (1904–1988)', in *Les Très Riches Heures de la Cour de Chine. Chefs-d'oeuvre de la peinture impériale des Qing 1662–1796*, Marie-Catherine Rey (ed.), exh. cat., Musée Guimet, Paris 2006

PARIS 2009
Eric Lefebvre, *Six siècles de peintures chinoises. Oeuvres restaurées du Musée Cernuschi*, exh. cat., Musée Cernuschi, Paris 2009

PARK 2007
Park Hyoeun (박효은 〔저자〕), 'Boundaries of Poetry and Painting Embodied in Shitao's *Qingxiang Sketches of Calligraphy and Painting* of 1696' (Seogdo-eui ch'eonyugbaeggusib-nyeon jag Ch'eongsang seohwa go-e guhyeon-doen sihwa-eui keonggye 石濤의 1696年作《清湘書畫稿》에구현된詩畵의境界), *Studies in Art History* (Misul sahag 美術史學), vol. 21, no. 8 (2007), pp. 7–40

PELLIOT 1927
Paul Pelliot, 'Revue – Laurence Binyon, *Les peintures chinoises dans les collections d'Angleterre* (1927)', *T'oung pao*, vol. XXV (1927), pp. 415–17

PENG 1988
Peng Xinwei (彭信威), *A History of Money in China* (Zhongguo huobi shi 中國貨幣史), Shanghai 1988

PHILADELPHIA 1984
Jean Gordon Lee, *Philadelphians and the China Trade, 1784–1844*, exh. cat., Philadelphia Museum of Art, Philadelphia 1984

PIERSON 2011
Stacey Pierson, 'From Market and Exhibition to University: Sir Percival David and The Institutionalization of Chinese Art History in England', in *Collecting China. The World, China and A History of Collecting*, Vimalin Rujivacharakul (ed.), Newark 2011, pp. 130–7

PITMAN 2002–3
Jennifer Pitman, 'China's Presence at the Centennial Exhibition, Philadelphia, 1876', *Studies in the Decorative Arts*, vol. 10, no. 1 (2002–3), pp. 35–73

PLESTERS 1993
Joyce Plesters, 'Ultramarine Blue, Natural and Artificial', in *Artist's Pigments: A Handbook of Their History and Characteristics*, vol. 2, Ashok Roy (ed.), National Gallery of Art, Washington, DC pp. 37–65

POHL 1990
Karl-Heinz Pohl, *Cheng Pan-ch'iao: Poet, Painter and Calligrapher*, Monumenta Serica Monograph Series XXI, Nettetal 1990

PRINCETON 1969
Roderick Whitfield and Wen C. Fong, *In Pursuit of Antiquity: Chinese Paintings of the Ming and Qing Dynasties from the Collection of Mr. and Mrs. Earl Morse*, exh. cat., Princeton University Art Museum, Princeton 1969

PRINCETON 1976
*Japanese Ink Paintings from American Collections: The Muromachi Period, an Exhibition in Honor of Shouiro Shimada*, exh. cat., Yoshiaki Shimizu and Carolyn Wheelwright (eds), Princeton University Art Museum, Princeton 1976

PRINCETON 1984
Wen C. Fong, Alfreda Murck, Shou-Chien Shih, Pao-chen Ch'en and Jan Stuart, *Images of the Mind: Selections from the Edward L. Elliott Family and John B. Elliott Collections of Chinese Calligraphy and Painting at the Art Museum, Princeton University*, exh. cat., Princeton University Art Museum, Princeton 1984

*Princeton University Art Museum* 2007
*Princeton University Art Museum Handbook of the Collections*, Princeton University Art Museum, Princeton 2007

*Prosperous Suzhou* 1986
*Prosperous Suzhou* (Gu Su fanhua tu 姑蘇繁華圖), Hong Kong 1986

QI 2007
*Chronological List of Calligraphy and Painting by Dong Qichang* (Dong Qichang shuhua biannian tumu 董其昌書畫編年圖目), Qi Yuan (齊淵) (ed.), Beijing 2007

QIAN 2004
Qian Gonglin, *Chinese Fans: Artistry and Aesthetics*, San Francisco 2004

REN 1988
Ren Daobin (任道斌), *Chronology of Dong Qichang* (Dong Qichang xinian 董其昌繫年), Beijing 1988

RENKAI 1991
Yang Renkai (杨仁恺), *The Appearance and Disappearance of National Treasures – A Brief Look at Paintings and Calligraphies Lost from the Imperial Palace* (Guobao chenfu lu – Gugong sanyi shuhua jianwen kaolüe 國寶沉浮錄 – 故宮散佚書畫見聞考略), Shanghai 1991

RIBOUD 1970
Krishna Riboud, *Tissus de Touen-Houang conservés au Musée Guimet et à la Bibliothèque nationale*, Mission Paul Pelliot, vol. XIII, Paris 1970

ROBINSON 1984
James Jay Robinson, 'The Vitality of Style: Aspects of Flower and Bird Painting During the Yuan Dynasty (1279–1368)', PhD dissertation, University of Michigan 1984

ROGERS AND LEE 1988
Howard Rogers and Sherman E. Lee, *Masterworks of Ming and Qing Painting from the Forbidden City*, Lansdale, PA 1988

ROGERS AND WOHLAUER 1996
Malcolm Rogers and Gilian Wohlauer, *Treasures of the Museum of Fine Arts, Boston*, Boston 1996

ROGERS IN NEW YORK AND DALLAS 1993
Mary Ann Rogers, 'Visions of Grandeur: The Life and Art of Dai Jin', in Richard M. Barnhardt, Mary Ann Rogers and Richard Stanley-Baker, *Painters of the Great Ming: The Imperial Court and the Zhe School*, exh. cat., The Metropolitan Museum of Art, New York and Dallas Museum of Art, Dallas 1993, pp. 127–94

ROWLEY 1947
George Rowley, *Principles of Chinese Painting*, Princeton 1947

RUAN (1791) 1854
Ruan Yüan (阮元), *Random Notes of the Stony Moat* (Shiqu suibi 石渠隨筆), Beijing 1854; original edition 1791

RUAN 1996
Ruan Rongchun (阮榮春), *Shen Zhou* (沈周), Jilin 1996

SAN FRANCISCO 2008
He Li and Michael Knight, *Power and Glory: Court Arts of China's Ming dynasty*, exh. cat., Asian Art Museum – Chong-Moon Lee Center for Asian Art and Culture, San Francisco 2008

SAWAMURA 1916
Sawamura Sentarō (帰鞍子), 'Ancient Paintings on the Theme of "in the Morning Sun"' (Koga chōyō-zu 古画朝陽図), *Kokka* 國華, vol. 27, no. 314 (July 1916), pp. 17

SCHMITT 2006
Camille Schmitt, 'Montures impériales: les rouleaux horizontaux' and 'Technique picturale à la Cour de Qianlong', in Marie-Catherine Rey, *Les Très Riches Heures de la Cour de Chine*, Paris 2006, p. 115 and 117

SCHMITT 2011
Camille Schmitt, *La médecine de l'art, conservation-restauration traditionnelle des peintures chinoises montées en rouleaux, à partir de textes de la dynastie* Ming, Arles 2011

SEKI 2002
Seki Shūichi (関周一), 'The Distribution and Consumption of Karamono' (Karamono no ryūtsū to shōhi 唐物の流通と消費), *Bulletin of the National Museum of Japanese History* (Kokuritsu rekishiminzoku kenkyūhōkoku 国立歴史民俗博物館研究報告), vol. 92 (2002), pp. 87–111

SHA 1987
Sha Menghai (沙孟海), 'An investigation of brush-holding method in ancient times' (Gudai shufa zhibi chutan 古代書法執筆初談), in *Collected Essays on Calligraphy* (Sha Menghai lunshu conggao 沙孟海論書叢稿), Sha Menghai (沙孟海) (ed.), Shanghai 1987, pp. 204–6

SHA 2006
Sha Wutian (沙武田), 'Research on Realist and Descriptive Sketches from Dunhuang – with Discussion of the Realist Portrait Art in Dunhuang Painting' (Dunhuang xiezhen miaozhen huagao yanjiu – jian lun Dunhuang hua zhi xiezhen xiaoxiang yishu 敦煌寫真邈真畫稿研究 – 兼論敦煌畫之寫真肖像藝術), *Journal of Dunhuang Studies* (Dunhuang xue jikan 敦煌學輯刊), no. 51 (2006), pp. 43–62

SHAN 1988
Shan Guoqiang (單國強), 'The Nature of Portraiture in Ancient Times' (Shilun gudai xiaoxianghua xingzhi 試論古代肖像畫性質), *Palace Museum Journal* (Gugong bowuyuan yuankan 故宮博物院院刊), no. 4 (1988), pp. 50–60

SHAN 1996
Shan Guoqiang (單國強), *Lü Ji* (呂紀), Taipei 1996

SHAN 1997
Shan Guoqiang (單國強), 'Reflections on the Biographies of Lin Liang and Lü Ji' (Lin Liang, Lü Ji shengping kaolüe' 林良, 呂紀生平考略) *Palace Museum Journal* (Gugong bowuyuan yuankan 故宮博物院院刊) (January 1997), pp. 1–6

SHAN 2000
Shan Guoqiang (單國強), *A History of Ming Painting* (Mingdai huihua shi 明代繪畫史), Beijing 2000

SHAN 2002
Shan Guoqiang (單國強), *Studies in Ancient Calligraphy and Paintings* (Gushuhua lunji 古書畫論集), Beijing 2002

SHAN 2004
Shan Guoqiang (單國強), 'An Investigation of Dai Jin's Life' (Dai Jin shengping shiji kao 戴進生平事跡考), *Duoyun* 朵雲, no. 61 (2004), pp. 116–31

SHANDONG PROVINCIAL MUSEUM 1972
Shandong Provincial Museum (山東省博物館), 'Report on the Discovery of the Ming Tomb of Zhu Tan' (Fajue Ming Zhu Tan mu jishi 發掘明朱檀墓紀實), *Wenwu* 文物, no. 5 (1972), pp. 25–36

SHANGHAI 2010
*A Thousand Years of Colour – Treasures of Painting from the Tang, Song and Yuan in Japanese and Chinese Collections* (Qiannian danqing – Riben Zhongguo cang Tang Song Yuan huihua zhenpin 千年丹青 – 日本中国藏唐宋元绘画珍品), exh. cat., Shanghai Museum, Shanghai 2010

SHANGHAI 2012
*Masterpieces of Early Chinese Painting and Calligraphy in American Collections* (Han mo hui cui: Meiguo shoucang Zhongguo Wudai Song Yuan shuhua zhenpin zhan 翰墨薈萃: 美國收藏中國五代宋元書畫珍品展), exh. cat., Shanghai Museum, Shanghai 2012

SHANGHAI MUSEUM 2005
*Classics of Painting and Calligraphy – Ancient Paintings and Calligraphies in the Collections of the Palace Museum and the Shanghai Museum* (Shuhua jingdian – Gugong bowuyuan, Shanghai bowuguan Zhongguo gudai shuhua cangpin ji 书画经典–故宫博物院、上海博物馆中国古代书画藏品集), Shanghai Museum (上海博物馆) (ed.), Beijing 2005

SHAO (1254) 1975–89
Shao Tan (邵曇), *A True Record of the Five Schools* (Wujia zhengzong zan 五家真宗讚), reprinted in *Supplement to the Manji Edition of the Buddhist Canon* (Manji shinsan dai Nihon zokuzōkyō 卍新纂大日本續藏經), vol. 78, no. 1554, Tokyo 1975–89; original edition 1254

SHE 1988
She Cheng (佘城), *A New Investigation of the Imperial Painting Academy in the Northern Song* (Bei Song tuhuayuan xintan 北宋圖畫院之新探), Taipei 1988

SHEN (1469) 1995–9
Shen Zhou (沈周), 'Verse for Portrait at the Age of Forty-Two' (Sishier sui xiangzan 四十二歲象贊), reprinted in *Poems of Shitian (Shen Zhou)* (Shitian gao 石田稿), in *Complete Collections of the Four Treasuries, Continued Belles Lettres Section* (Xuxiu siku quanshu – jibu 續修四庫全書 – 集部), Shanghai 1995–9, vol. 1333–02, pp. 311–12, 382; originally written in 1469

SHIH 1984
Shou-ch'ien Shih, 'Eremitism in Landscape Paintings by Ch'ien Hsuan (*c.*1235–before 1307)', PhD dissertation, Princeton University 1984

SHIMADA 1976
Shimada Hidemasa (嶋田英誠),'A Preliminary Study of Yan Wengui's Work and its Importance in Northern Song Lansacape Painting' (En Bunki no denshō sakuhin to sono hokusō sansuiga shijō ni shimeru ichi ni tsuite no ichishiron 燕文貴の傳承作品と、その北宋山水畫史上に占める位置についての一試論), *Journal of the Japan Art History Society* (Bijutsushi 美術史), vol. 26, no. 1 (November 1976), pp.39–58

SHIMAO 1989
Shimao Arata (島尾新), 'The Taste for Chinese Painting in the Fifteenth Century' (Jūgo seikinii okeru chūgoku kaiga shumi 十五世紀における中国絵画趣味), *Museum*, vol. 463, no. 10 (1989)

SHIMAO 1994
Shimao Arata (島尾新), 'Ink Painting from Noami to the Kano School' (Suibokuga – Nōami kara kano-ha e 水墨画 – 能阿弥から狩野派へ), *Japanese Art* (Nihon no bijutsu gō 日本の美術), no. 338 (1994), pp. 1–98

SHIMAO 2006
Shimao Arata (島尾新), 'Meeting Places and Karamono – The Mechanism and Function of Symbols of Power in the Early Muromachi Period' (Kaisho to karamono – Muromachi jidai zenki no kenryoku hyōshō sōchi to sono kinō 会所と唐物 – 室町時代前期の権力表象装置とその機能), in *Spatial History: Architecture-City-Territory* (Shirizu toshi kenchiku rekishi シリーズ都市· 建築· 歴史), vol. 4, *Culture and Site in the Medieval Period* (Chūsei no bunka to ba 中世の文化と場), Tokyo 2006

SHIMAO IN TOKYO 2004
Shimao Arata (島尾新), 'Fantasy Images – Chinese Painters in the Higashiyama Gyomotsu' (Higashiyama gyomotsu gensō – imeji no naka no chūgoku gajintachi 東山御物幻想イメージのなかの中国画人たち), in *Elegant and Noble in Soul: Southern Song Painting at the Nezu Institute of Fine Arts* (Nansō kaiga: saijō gachi no sekai 南宋絵画 – 才情雅致の世界), exh. cat., Nezu Museum, Tokyo 2004, pp. 25–36

SHIMIZU 1980
Yoshiaki Shimizu, 'Six Narrative Paintings by Yin Tuoluo', *Archives of Asian Art*, vol. 32 (1980), pp. 6–37

SHIMOSAKA 2003
Shimosaka Mamoru (下坂守), 'Iconography and Structure in Pilgrimage of the Ashikaga Shogun to the Wakamiya Hachimangū Shrine' (Wakamiya hachimangū-zō ashikaga shōgun wakamiya hachimangū sankei emaki no zuzō to gamen kōsei 若宮八幡宮蔵『足利将軍若宮八幡宮参詣絵巻の図像と画面構成), in *Painting the Medieval Age in Japan – An Analysis of Narrative Illustration* (Egakareta nihon no chūsei – ezu bunseki-ron 描かれた日本の中世 – 絵図分析論), Kyoto 2003

*Shinbi taikan* 1899
*Selected Relics of Japanese Art* (Shinbi taikan 真美大観), series 3, Kyoto 1899

SICKMAN AND SOPER 1956
Laurence Sickman and Alexander Soper, *The Pelican History of Art: The Art and Architecture of China*, Nikolaus Pevsner (ed.), Harmondsworth 1956

SIGGSTEDT 1982A
Mette Siggstedt, 'Zhou Chen: The Life and Paintings of a Ming Professional Artist', *The Museum of Far Eastern Antiquities, Bulletin*, vol. 54 (1982), pp. 1–239

SIGGSTEDT 1982B
Mette Siggstedt, 'Zhou Chen: The Life and Paintings of a Ming Professional Artist', PhD dissertation, Institutionen för Orientaliska Språk, Stockholm 1982

SILBERGELD 1976
Jerome Silbergeld, 'Political Landscapes of Kung Hsien in Painting and Poetry', *Journal of the Institute of Chinese Studies of the Chinese University of Hong Kong*, vol. 8, no. 2 (December 1976), pp. 561–74

SILBERGELD 1985
Jerome Silbergeld, 'In Praise of Government: Chao Yung's Painting, "Noble Steeds" and Late Yuan Politics', *Artibus Asiae*, vol. 46 (1985), pp. 159–202

SILBERGELD 1995
Jerome Silbergeld, 'Back to the Red Cliff: Reflections on the Narrative Mode in Early Literati Landscape Painting', *Ars Orientalis*, vol. 25 (1995), pp. 19–38

SIRÉN 1927
Osvald Sirén, *Chinese Paintings in American Collections*, Paris and Brussels 1927

SIRÉN 1933
Osvald Sirén, *A History of Early Chinese Painting*, London 1933

SIRÉN 1938
Osvald Sirén, *Later Chinese Painting*, 2 vols, New York 1938

SIRÉN 1945
Osvald Sirén, *Kinesiska och japanska målningar och skulpturer i Nationalmuseum*, Stockholm 1945

SIRÉN 1956–8
Osvald Sirén, *Chinese Painting: Leading Masters and Principles*, 7 vols, New York 1956–1958

SOCIETY FOR THE RESEARCH OF COLLECTIONS 2012
Society for the Research of Collections of Chinese Painting in the Kansai Region, *Past and Future in the Collections of Chinese Painting of the Kansai Region* (Kansai chūgoku shoga korekushon no kako to mirai 関西中国書画コレクションの過去と未来), Nishinomiya 2012

SOFUKAWA 2006
*Iconography of Chinese art* (Chu-goku bijutsu no zuzo-gaku 中國美術の圖像學), Sofukawa Hiroshi (曾布川寛) (ed.), Kyoto 2006

SONG 1957
Song Lian (宋濂), 'The Origins of Painting' (Hua yuan' 畫原), in *Chinese Painting Theories Edited by Category* (Zhongguo hualun leibian 中國畫論類編), Yu Jianhua (俞劍華) (ed.), Beijing 1957

SOPER 1951
Alexander C. Soper, *Kuo Jo-Hsu's Experience in Painting (T'u-hua chien-wen chih): An Eleventh Century History of Chinese Painting*, Washington, DC 1951

SOPER 1958
Alexander C. Soper, 'T'ang Ch'ao Ming Hua Lu. Celebrated Painters of the T'ang Dynasty by Chu Ching-hsüan of T'ang', *Artibus Asiae*, vol. 21, no. 3/4 (1958), pp. 204–30

VON SPEE 2008
Clarissa von Spee, *Wu Hufan. A Twentieth Century Connoisseur in Shanghai*, Berlin 2008

VON SPEE 2010
Clarissa von Spee, *The Printed Image in China: From 8th to 21st Centuries*, London 2010

VON SPEE 2012
Clarissa von Spee, 'Victoria Contag. Revisiting her collection, career and scholarship' (unpublished paper), London 2012

STRÖBER 2004
Eva Ströber, 'Earliest Documented Ming-Porcelain', *The International Ceramic Fair and Seminar* (London 2004), pp. 26–35

STURMAN 1989
Peter Sturman, 'Mi Youren and the inherited literati tradition: dimensions of ink-play', PhD dissertation, Yale University 1989

STURMAN 1990
Peter Sturman, 'Cranes Above Kaifeng: The Auspicious Image at the Court of Huizong', *Ars Orientalis*, vol. 20 (1990), pp. 33–68

STURMAN 1995
Peter Sturman, 'The Donkey Rider as Icon: Li Cheng and Early Chinese Landscape Painting', *Artibus Asiae*, vol. 55, 1/2 (1995), pp. 43–97

SU (1082) 1986
Su Shi (蘇軾), *A Collection of Writings by Su Shi* (Su Shi wenji 蘇軾文集), 6 vols, Beijing 1986

SUFUKAWA 1977
Sofukawa Hiroshi (曾布川寛), 'A study of the landscape painting of the Five Dynasties and the early Northern Song period – Jing Hao, Guan Tong, Guo Zhongshu, and Yan Wengui' (Godai kita sō shoki sansuiga no ichikōsatsu – Kei Kō, Seki Dō, Kaku Chūjo, En Bunki 五代北宋初期山水畫の一考察 – 荊浩· 關仝· 郭忠恕· 燕文貴), *Journal of Oriental Studies* (The Toho Gakuho 東方學報), vol. 47 (1977), pp. 123–214

SUGIMOTO 2008
Sugimoto Ichibun (杉本一樹), *Shosoin: Its History and Treasures* (Shōsōin: rekishi to hōmotsu 正倉院 : 歴史と宝物), reprinted Tokyo 2008; first edition 1967

SULLIVAN 1965
Michael Sullivan, 'Notes on early Chinese screen painting', *Artibus Asiae*, vol. 27, no. 3 (1965), pp. 239–64

SULLIVAN 1967
Michael Sullivan, 'They speak of eternal things', *Stanford Today* (Summer 1967), pp. 2–6

SUN (1660) 1970
Sun Chengze (孫承澤), *Whiling Away the Summer in the Gengzi Year* (Gengzi xiaoxia ji 庚子消夏集), Yishu shangjian xuanzhen 藝術賞鑑選珍) (ed.), reprinted in *Selected Historical Painting Catalogues*, Taipei 1970; preface to original edition 1660

SUN 1962
Sun Zubai (孫祖白), *Mi Fu, Mi Youren* (米芾, 米友仁), in *Compendium of Chinese Painters* (Zhongguo huajia congshu 中國畫家叢書), Shanghai 1962

SUN AND SUN 2001
Sun Ruxian (孫儒僩) and Sun Yihua (孫毅華), *A Compendium of the Dunhuang Caves* (Dunhuang shiku quanji 敦煌石窟全集), vol. 21, *Paintings of Architecture* (Jianzhu hua 建築畫), Hong Kong 2001

SUNG 2009
Hou-mei Sung, *Decoded Messages: The Symbolic Language of Chinese Animal Painting*, New Haven 2009

*Supplement to the Manji Edition of the Buddhist Canon* 1975–89
*Supplement to the Manji Edition of the Buddhist Canon* (Manji shinsan Dai Nihon zokuzōkyō 卍新纂大日本續藏經), 88 vols, Tokyo 1975–89

SUZHOU MUSEUM 1978
Suzhou Museum (蘇州市博物館), 'Garden of the Inept Administrator' (Zhuozheng Yuan 拙政園), *Wenwu* 文物, no. 6 (1978), pp. 85–7

SUZUKI 1978
Suzuki Kei (鈴木敬), *A Compendium of Ink Painting: Li Tang, Ma Yuan, Xia Gui* (Suiboku bijutsu taikei: Ri Tō, Ba En, Ka Kei 水墨美術大系: 李唐· 馬遠· 夏珪), vol. 2, Tokyo 1978

SUZUKI 1981
Suzuki Kei (鈴木敬), *A History of Chinese Painting* (Chūgoku kaigashi 中國繪畫史), vol. 1, Tokyo 1981

SUZUKI 1985
Suzuki Kei, *A History of Chinese painting* (Chūgoku kaigashi 中國繪畫史), vol. 2, Tokyo 1985

SUZUKI AND AKIYAMA 1973
*Chinese Art* (Chūgoku bijutsu 中國美術), Suzuki Kei (鈴木敬) and Akiyama Terukazu (秋山光和) (eds), 5 vols, Tokyo 1973

SUZUKI ET AL. 1982–3
*A Comprehensive Illustrated Catalogue of Chinese Paintings: American and Canadian Collections* (Chūgoku kaiga sōgō zuroku: Daiikkan, Amerika-Kanada hen 中國繪畫總合圖錄: 第1巻 アメリカ· カナダ篇), Suzuki Kei (鈴木敬) et al. (eds), 5 vols, Tokyo 1982–3

SZE 1978
Mai-mai Sze (trans. & ed.), *The Mustard Seed Garden Manual of Painting: A Facsimile of the 1887–8 Shanghai Edition*, Princeton University Press, Princeton 1978

TAIPEI 1976
*Ninety Years of the Wu School* (Wupaihua jiushinian 吳派畫九十年), exh. cat., National Palace Museum, Taipei 1976

TAIPEI 1989
*Exhibition Catalogue of Works by Qiu Ying* (Qiu Ying zuopin zhan tulu 仇英作品展圖錄), exh. cat., National Palace Museum, Taipei 1989

TAIPEI 1992A
*Special Exhibition Catalogue of Beauty in Calligraphy* (Shufa zhimei tezhan tulu 書法之美特展圖錄), exh. cat., Ho Chuan-hsing (何傳馨) (ed.), National Palace Museum, Taipei 1992

TAIPEI 1992B
*Special Exhibition of Flower and Bird Paintings by Lü Ji* (Lü Ji huaniao tezhan 呂紀花鳥特展), exh. cat., National Palace Museum, Taipei 1992

TAIPEI 1997
*Landscape Paintings by Wang Yuanqi of the Qing: Special Exhibition of Hanging Scrolls* (Qing Wang Yuanqi hua shanshui: huazhou tezhan 清王原祁畫山水：畫軸特展), Itakura Masaaki (板倉聖哲) (ed.), exh. cat., National Palace Museum, Taipei 1997

TAIPEI 2000
*Four Masters of Figure Painting in the mid-Ming Dynasty: Du Jin, Zhou Chen, Tang Yin and Qiu Ying* (Ming zhongye renwuhua sijia tezhan: Du Jin, Zhou Chen, Tang Yin, Qiu Ying 明中葉人物畫四家特展：杜堇, 周臣, 唐寅, 仇英), exh. cat., National Palace Museum, Taipei 2000

TAIPEI 2006
*Grand View: Special Exhibition of Northern Song Painting and Calligraphy* (Daguan: Bei Song shuhua tezhan 大觀: 北宋書畫特展), exh. cat., National Palace Museum, Taipei 2006

TAIPEI 2010
*Dynastic Renaissance: Art and Culture of the Southern Song* (Wenyi shaoxing: Nansong yishu yu wenhua tezhan 文藝紹興: 南宋藝術與文化特展), Ho Chuan-Hsing (ed.), exh. cat., The National Palace Museum, Taipei 2010

*Taishō Shinshū Daizōkyō* (SAT 2012)
*The Taishō Revised Edition of the Tripitaka* (Taishō Shinshū Daizōkyō 大正新脩大藏經), SAT Taishō Shinshū Daizōkyō Text Database ver. 2012 (SAT 2012)

TAJIMA 2004
Tajima Isao (田島公), 'Book Collections and the Transmission of Writings – Imperial Libraries and Storehouses In Ancient and Medieval Times' (Tenseki no denrai to bunko – kodai, chūsei no tennōke yukari no bunko, hōzō o chūshin ni 典籍の伝来と文庫 – 古代 · 中世の天皇家ゆかりの文庫 · 宝蔵を中心に), in *A History of Japan through the Ages* (Nihon no jidaishi 日本の時代史), vol. 30, *History and Source Materials* (Rekishi to sozai 歴史と素材), Tokyo 2004

TAJIMA 2006A
Tajima Isao (田島公), 'Themes and Conclusions Concerning Imperial Libraries and Storehouses in Bibliographic Research' (Tennōke yukari no bunko, hōzō no mokurokugakuteki kenkyū no seika to kadai 天皇家ゆかりの文庫 · 宝蔵の『目録学的研究』の成果と課題), *Studies in Narrative Literature* (Setsuwa bungaku kenkyū 説話文学研究), no. 41 (2006)

TAJIMA 2006B
Tajima Isao (田島公), 'Changes in Imperial Libraries and Storehouses during the Mediaeval Age' (Chūsei tennōke no bunko hōzo no hensen 中世天皇家の文庫・宝蔵の変遷), in *Research on Libraries of the Imperial Palace and the Court Nobility* (Kinri kuge bunko kenkyū 禁裏・公家文庫研究), vol. 2, Kyoto 2006

TAKAGI 1935
Takagi Bun (高木文), *On the Transmission of Muxi and Yujian's Famous Paintings, Eight Views of the Xiao and Xiang* (Mokkei gyokkan meibutsu shōshōhakkei e no denrai to kōsatsu 牧谿玉澗名物瀟湘八景絵の伝来と考察), Tokyo 1935

TAKAGISHI 2004
Takagishi Akira (高岸輝), 'Tosa Yukihiro and the Development of the Tosa School' (Tosa yukihiro to tosa-ha no tenkai 土佐行弘と土佐派の展開), in *Painting and the Muromachi Nobility – a Study of the Early Tosa School* (Muromachi ōken to kaiga – shoki tosa-ha kenkyū 室町王権と絵画 – 初期土佐派研究), Kyoto 2004

TAKAGISHI 2011
Takagishi Akira (高岸輝), 'Longing for the Emperor – the Muromachi-dono Collection and Paintings of the Emperor' (Kōtei e no akogare – muromachidono korekushon to kōtei no kaiga 皇帝へのあこがれ – 室町殿コレクションと『皇帝の絵画』), in *Dreams of China – Karamono and Diplomacy in the Muromachi Period* (Chūka gensō – karamono to gaikō no muromachijidai shi 中華幻想 – 唐物と外交の室町時代史), Tokyo 2011

TAKEI 1998
Takei Akio (竹居明男), 'Temple Storehouses [Sutra Repositories] and the Culture of the Insei Era' (Ji'in no hōzō [kyōzō] to inseiki no bunka 寺院の宝蔵 [経蔵] と院政期の文化), in *Cultural History of Ancient Buddhism in Japan* (Nihon kodai bukkyō no bunkashi 日本古代仏教の文化史), Tokyo 1998

TAKENAMI 1998
Takenami Haruka (竹浪遠), plate commentary, *New History of World Art: Oriental* (Sekai bijutsu daizenshū, tōyō hen 世界美術大全集: 東洋編), vol. 5, *Five Dynasties, Northern Song, Liao and Xixia* (Godai hokusō ryō seika 五代・北宋・遼・西夏), Ogawa Yūsuke (小川裕充), Yuba Tadanori (弓場紀知) (eds), Tokyo 1998

TAKENAMI 2010
Takenami Haruka (竹浪遠), 'An Evaluation of Li Cheng and the Formation of his Literary Painter Image in the Northern Song Dynasty' (Hokusō niokeru Ri Sei no hyōka to sono bunjin gakazō keisei nitsuite: shison, kanshōsha, Rikakukei gaka tono kakawari kara 北宋における李成の評価とその文人画家像形成について: 子孫・鑑賞者・李郭系画家との関わりから), *Bulletin of Kurokawa Institute of Ancient Cultures* (Kobunka kenkyū 古文化研究), vol. 9 (2010), pp. 45–76

TAKENAMI 2011
Takenami Haruka (竹浪遠), plate commentary, *Exploring Chinese painting and calligraphy* (Chūgoku shoga tanbō 中國書畫探訪), Tokyo 2011, p. 73

TANAKA 1941
Tanaka Toyozo (田中豊蔵), plate commentary, *Gwasetu: journal of Far Eastern Art* (画説), no. 54 (June 1941)

TANAKA 1944
Tanaka Toyozo (田中豊蔵), plate commentary, *The Journal of Art Studies* (Bijutsu kenkyū 美術研究), no. 135 (March 1944), pp. 35–8

TANAKA, AKIYAMA AND TANAKA 1938
*Masterpieces of Painting of the Song and Yuan* (Sō-gen meiga shū 宋元名画集), Tanaka Kisaku (田中喜作), Akiyama Teruo (秋山光夫) and Tanaka Ichimatsu (田中一松) (eds), Tokyo 1938

TANG 1967
*Collected Criticism of Ci Poetry* (Cihua congbian 詞話叢編), Tang Guizhang (唐圭璋) (ed.), 12 vols, Taipei 1967

TAO (1360–68) 1963
Tao Zongyi (陶宗儀), *A Collection of Writings at Spare Time* (Chuogeng lu 輟耕錄), Taipei 1963

TAO 2012
Tao Yuzhi (陶喻之), 'Comments on Extant Portraits of Shen Zhou and Inscriptions' (Shen Zhou chuanshi xiaoxianghua ji tishu shiyi 沈周傳世肖像畫題書拾遺), paper presented at the symposium on the Wu school at the Suzhou Museum, 2012

*The Art of China* 1977–82
*The Art of China* (*Chūgoku no bijutsu* 中國の美術), 6 vols, Kyoto 1977–82

THOTE 1997
Alain Thote, 'At the Source of Modern French Sinology: Édouard Chavannes', *Orientations*, vol. 28, no. 6 (1997), pp. 42–7

TODA 1967
Toda Teisuke (戸田禎佑), plate commentary, *Asiatic Art in Japanese Collections* (Tōyō bijutsu 東洋美術), Tanaka Ichimatsu (田中一松), Yonezawa Yoshiho (米澤嘉圃) and Kei Kawakami (川上涇) (eds), vol. 1, Painting I (Kaiga I 絵画 I), Asahishinbunsha, Tokyo 1967

TODA 1973
*Compendium of Ink Painting* (Suiboku bijutsu taikei 水墨美術大系), vol. 3, *Muxi, Yujian* (Mokkei, Gyokkan 牧谿玉澗) Toda Teisuke (戸田禎佑) (ed.), Tokyo 1973

TODA 1988
Toda Teisuke (戸田禎佑), 'The Use of 'Gold' in Painting of the Southern Song Academy' (Nansōin taiga ni okeru 'kin' no shiyō ni tsuite 南宋院体画における「金」の使用について), in *Kokka* 國華, no. 1116 (1988)

TOKAGAWA 1984
Tokagawa Yoshinobu, 'The Japanese Monkey that Travelled to Song China' (Sō ni wattata nihonzaru 宋に渡った日本猿), *Tankō* 淡交 (April 1984)

TOKYO 1929
*Masterpieces of Chinese Paintings of the Tang, Song, Yuan and Ming Dynasties* (Tō-Sō-Gen-Min meiga taikan 唐宋元明名画大観), 2 vols, exh. cat., Tokyo Metropolitan Art Gallery, Tokyo 1929

TOKYO 1962
Nakamura Tanio (中村渓男), *Song and Yuan Painting* (Sō gen no kaiga 宋元の絵画), exh. cat., Tokyo National Museum, Tokyo 1962

TOKYO 1995
*Yamanoue Sōji – On the Proper Use of Fine Tea Utensils* (Yamanoue Sōji – Tenshō jūyon nen no *me* 山上宗二 – 天正十四年の眼), exh. cat., The Gotoh Museum, Tokyo 1995

TOKYO 1996A
*Ink Mists: Zen Paintings by Muxi* (Mokkei: dōkei no suibokuga 牧谿 – 憧憬の水墨画), exh. cat., The Gotoh Museum, Toyko 1996

TOKYO 1996B
*Shirukurōdo daibijutsuten – Grand Exhibition of Silkroad Buddhist Art* (シルクロード大美術展), exh. cat., Tokyo Metropolitan Art Museum, Tokyo 1996

TOKYO 2000
*Gold Brocade and Satin Damask – Textiles that Enhance the Famous Utensils of the Tea Ceremony* (Kinran donsu – chaseki no meihin o hikitateru orimono 金襴・緞子 – 茶席の名品を引き立てる織物), Yoshioka Akemi (吉岡明美) (ed.), exh. cat., Nezu Museum, Tokyo 2000

TOKYO 2004
*Elegant and Noble in Soul: Southern Song Painting at the Nezu Institute of Fine Arts* (Nansō kaiga: saijō gachi no sekai 南宋絵画 – 才情雅致の世界), exh. cat., Nezu Museum, Tokyo 2004

TOKYO 2013
*Wangxi Zhi: Master Calligrapher* (Tokubetsuten – shosei Ōgishi 特別展 – 書聖王羲之), exh. cat., Tokyo National Museum, Tokyo 2013

TOKYO AND NAGOYA 1976
*Higashiyama Gyomotsu – New Materials on the 'Zakkeshitsu-in' Seal* (Higashiyama gyomotsu – Zakkeshitsu-in ni kansuru shin shiryō o chūshin ni 東山御物 – 『雑華室印』に関する新資料を中心に), exh. cat., Nezu Museum and Tokugawa Art Museum, Tokyo and Nagoya 1976

TOKYO NATIONAL MUSEUM 1979
*Illustrated Catalogue of Tokyo National Museum* (Tokyo Kokuritsu Hakubutsukan zuhan mokuroku, Chugoku kaiga hen 東京国立博物館図版目録〈中国絵画篇〉), Tokyo National Museum, Tokyo 1979

TOMINAGA 1974
Tominaga Soichi, *National Gallery of Art, Washington, Museum of Fine Arts, Boston, Art Institute of Chicago and the Museum of Modern Art, New York*, Tokyo 1974

TOMITA 1933
Tomita Kojiro, *Portfolio of Chinese Paintings in the Museum (Han to Sung periods)*, Boston 1933

TOMITA 1990
Tomita Kojiro, *A History of the Asiatic Department: A Series of Illustrated Lectures Given in 1957 by Kojiro Tomita (1890–1976)*, Museum of Fine Arts, Boston 1990

TÖRMÄ 2002
Minna Törmä, *Landscape Experience as Visual Narrative: Northern Song Dynasty Landscape Handscrolls in the Li Cheng-Yan Wengui Tradition*, Helsinki 2002

TÖRMÄ 2006–7
Minna Törmä, 'Osvald Sirén: Tracing his Path in Art History', *Zürich Studies in the History of Art, Georg Bloch Annual, University of Zürich, Institute of Art History*, vol. 13/14 (2006–7), pp. 333–9

TÖRMÄ 2007
Minna Törmä, 'The 1920s: A Decade of Change in the Life of Osvald Sirén', in *The Shaping of Art History in Finland*, Renja Suominen-Kokkonen (ed.), Helsinki 2007, pp. 157–68

TÖRMÄ (forthcoming)
Minna Törmä, *Enchanted by Lohans: Osvald Sirén's Journey into Chinese Art*, Hong Kong (forthcoming)

TORONTO 2002
Ka Bo Tsang, *More Than Keeping Cool: Chinese Fans and Fan Paintings*, exh. cat., Royal Ontario Museum, Toronto 2002

TSENG 1957
Tseng Hsien-Chi, 'A Study of the Nine Dragon Scroll', *Archives of the Chinese Society of America*, vol. 11 (1957), pp. 16–39

TSUKAHARA 1991
Tsukahara Akira (塚原晃), 'Mapping the Transmission of Eight Views of the Xiao and Xiang by Muxi and Yujian' (Mokkei Gyokkan shōshōhakkeizu – sono denrai no keifu 牧谿・玉澗瀟湘八景図 – その伝来の系譜), *Bulletin of the Graduate Division of Literature of Waseda University, supplement* (Waseda daigaku daigakuin bungaku kenkyūka kiyō bessatsu 早稲田大学大学院文学研究科紀要別冊), vol. 17, Waseda University 1991

TSUKAMOTO 2011A
Tsukamoto Maromitsu (塚本麿充), *Exploring Chinese painting and calligraphy* (Chūgoku shoga tanbō 中國書畫探訪), Nigensha 2011

TSUKAMOTO 2011B
Tsukamoto Maromitsu (塚本麿充), 'Imperial Cultural Properties and Kaifeng in the Early Northern Song – the Culture of the Imperial Court and the Buddhist temples Qisheng Chanyuan and Daxiangguo Temple' (Kōtei no bunbutsu to hokusō shoki no kaibutsu – keiseizen'in, shōkokuji, kyūtei o meguru bunbutsu to sono imi ni tsuite, ue / shita 皇帝の文物と北宋初期の開封 – 啓聖禅院、大相国寺、宮廷をめぐる文物とその意味について[上・下]), *The Journal of Art Studies* (Bijutsu kenkyū 美術研究), vol. 1, vol. 404 (2011) pp. 1–36

TSUKAMOTO 2011C
Tsukamoto Maromitsu (塚本麿充), 'Imperial Cultural Properties and the Society of the Northern Song Dynasty – From the Perspective of Cultural Exchange' (Kōtei no bunbutsu to hokusō no shakai – nihon bunbutsu no kōryū kara no shiten 皇帝の文物と北宋の社会 – 日本文物の交流からの視点), BI, no. 5 (2011)

TSUKAMOTO 2012
Tsukamoto Maromitsu (塚本麿充), 'Imperial Cultural Properties and Kaifeng in the Early Northern Song – the Culture of the Imperial Court and the Buddhist Temples Qisheng Chanyuan and Daxiangguo Temple' (Kōtei no bunbutsu to hokusō shoki no kaibutsu – keiseizen'in, shōkokuji, kyūtei o meguru bunbutsu to sono imi ni tsuite, ue / shita 皇帝の文物と北宋初期の開封 – 啓聖禅院、大相国寺、宮廷をめぐる文物とその意味について[上・下]), *The Journal of Art Studies* (Bijutsu kenkyū 美術研究), vols 1 and 2, vol. 406 (2012), pp. 1–26

TSURUTA 1971
Tsuruta Takeyoshi (鶴田武良), plate commentary, *Encyclopedia of Japanese Art in Colour* (Genshoku nihon no bijutsu 29 原色日本の美術・29, 請来美術 (繪画・書)), 小學館, 1971, p. 42

VANDIER-NICOLAS 1974–6
Nicole Vandier-Nicolas, *Bannières et peintures de Touen-houang conservées au Musée Guimet*, Mission Paul Pelliot, vols XIV and XV, Paris 1974–6

VEIT 2001
Willibald Veit, 'Ein Erster Besuch. Die Sammlung des Museums für Ostasiatische Kunst Berlin in der Eremitage in St. Petersburg', *Ostasiatische Zeitschrift, Neue Serie*, vol. 2 (Autumn 2001), pp. 35–40

VEIT IN LEDDEROSE 1998
Willibald Veit, 'Frühlingswolken in den Linggu-Bergen', in Lothar Ledderose, *Orchideen und Felsen. Chinesische Bilder im Museum für Ostasiatische Kunst Berlin*, National Museums of Berlin - Preussischer Kulturbesitz, Berlin 1998, pp. 101–6

VENICE 1954
*Mostra d'arte cinese: Catalogo/Exhibition of Chinese Art Catalogue*, Jean-Pierre Dubosc (ed.), exh. cat., Palazzo Ducale, Venice 1954

*Veritable Records of the Ming emperor Xiaozong* 1962
*Veritable Records of the Ming emperor Xiaozong* (Ming Xiaozong shilu 明孝宗實錄), Taipei 1962

VINOGRAD 1992A
Richard Vinograd, *Boundaries of the Self: Chinese Portraits, 1600–1900*, Cambridge 1992

VINOGRAD 1992B
Richard Vinograd, 'Image of the Artist in Seventeenth-Century Chinese Portraiture', in *Boundaries of the Self: Chinese Portraits, 1600–1900*, New York 1992, pp. 94–5

WAKIMOTO 1934
Wakimoto Jūkurō (脇本十九郎), 'Concerning the Gardener Zen'ami and the "Zen'a" Seal on Song and Yuan Paintings' (Teishi zen'ami to sō gen gajiku ni nosesuru 'Zen'a' kanshiki-in ki ni tsuite 庭師善阿弥と宋元画軸に載する「善阿」鑑蔵印記に就いて), *The Journal of Art Studies* (Bijutsu kenkyū 美術研究), vol. 26 (February 1934), pp. 18–31

WAN 2010
Wan Xinhua (萬新華), 'Portrait, Family, Identity – A Discussion of Yu Zhiding's *Portrait of Wang Yuanqi* in Plain Outline' (Xiaoxiang, jiazu, rentong – cong Yu Zhiding baimiao *Wang Yuanqi xiang* zhou tanqi 肖像家族認同 – 從禹之鼎白描<王原祁像>軸談起), *Chung Cheng Journal of Chinese Studies* (Zhongzheng daxue zhongwen xueshu niankan 中正大學中文學術年刊), vol. 6 (2010), pp. 211–45

WANG (1643) 1993–8
Wang Keyu (汪砢玉), *The Coral Net: A Record of Painting by Wang* (Wang shi shanhu wang minghua tiba 汪氏珊瑚網名畫題跋), painting section, vol. 8, reprinted in *A Compendium of Writings on Calligraphy and Painting in China* (Zhongguo shuhua quanshu 中國書畫全書), Lu Fusheng (盧輔聖) (ed.), vol. 5, Shanghai 1994; preface to original edition 1643

WANG (1645) 1937
Wang Xiuchu (王秀楚), *A Record of Ten Days in Yangzhou* (Yangzhou shiri ji 揚州十日記), reprinted in 'A Memoir of Ten Days' Massacre at Yangchow', Lucien Mao (trans.), *Under Heaven* (Tianxia 天下), vol. 4, no. 5 (May 1937), pp. 515–37; original edition 1645

WANG (1782) 1987
Wang Ao (王鏊), 'Tomb Inscription of Shitian [Shen Zhou]' (Shitian muzhiming 石田墓誌銘), reprinted in *Collected Essays of Thunder and Marsh* (Zhenze ji 震澤集), vol. 29, 17b–20a, in *Complete Collections of the Four Treasuries, Belles Lettres Section* (Siku quanshu – jibu 四庫全書 – 集部), Shanghai 1987, vols 171–24

WANG (1875) 1969
Wang Tao (王韜), 'A Comment on the Seven Best Painters and Calligraphers of the Tongzhi Period' (Tongzhi nianjian lun Hujiang shuhua qijue' 同治年間論滬江書畫七絕), reprinted in *A Collection of Jottings on Shanghai* (Yingruan zazhi 瀛壖雜志), Taipei 1969; original edition 1875

WANG (1916) 2009
Wang Shimin (王時敏), *Collected Writings of Mr Wang Yanke (Wang Shimin)* (Wang Yanke xiansheng ji 王煙客先生集), reprinted Shanghai 2009; original edition 1916

WANG 1967
Wang Jiqian (王季遷; C.C. Wang), 'Ni Zan's Paintings' (Ni Yunlin zhi hua 倪雲林之畫), *National Palace Museum Quarterly* (Gugong jikan 故宮季刊), vol. 1 (April 1967), pp. 15–46

WANG 1973
Wang Yuanqi (王原祁), 'Desultory Jottings at a Rainy Window' (Yuchuang manbi 雨窗漫筆), completed in c.1683; reprinted in *Extended Collection of Chinese Painting Theories* (Zhongguo hualun xubian 中國畫論續編), Yu Jianhua (俞劍華) (ed.), Hong Kong 1973, pp. 169–73

WANG 1991
Wang Yikun (王以坤), *A Study of the Evolution of Mounting Paintings and Calligraphy* (Shuhua zhuanghuang yange kao 書畫裝潢沿革考), Beijing 1991

WANG 1995
Chi-ying Alice Wang, 'Revisiting Shen Zhou (1427–1509)', PhD dissertation, Indiana University 1995

WANG 1996
Wang Jinyu (王進玉), 'A Study of Ultramarine Blue in the Cave Temples of Dunhuang, Maijishan and Binlingsi' (Dunhuang, Maijishan, Binlingsi shiku qingjinshi yanliao de yanjiu 敦煌麥積山炳靈寺石窟青金石顏料的研究), Kaogu (考古), no. 10 (1996), pp. 77–99

WANG 1999
Wang Jiacheng (王嘉誠), *Biographies of the Four Masters of the Ming: Shen Zhou, Wen Zhengming, Tang Yin and Qiu Ying* (Ming sijia zhuan: Shen Zhou, Wen Zhengming, Tang Yin, Qiu Ying 明四家傳：沈周, 文徵明, 唐寅, 仇英), Taipei 1999

WANG (C.1680) 2000
Wang Yuanqi (王原祁), *Inscriptions on Paintings by Lutai* (Lutai tihua gao 麓臺題畫稿), reprinted Shanghai 2000; completed c.1680

WANG 2002
Wang Shiqing (汪世清), 'A Case Study of Shitao' (Shitao sankao 石濤散考), *Duoyun* 朵雲, vol. 56 (2002), pp. 18–66

WANG 2003
Wang Cheng-hua, 'Imperial Treasures, Art Exhibitions, and National Legacy: The Institute for Exhibiting Antiquities in the 1910s', paper presented at *Memory Links: To Self, Country, and Culture in Chinese History*, East Asian Studies Center, Indiana University, 30 October–2 November 2003

WANG 2005
*The Poems of Shitao* (Shitao shilu 石濤詩錄), Wang Shiqing (汪世清) (ed.), Shijiazhuang 2005

WANG 2006
Wang Guo (王果), 'History of Screens in Ancient China' (Zhongguo Gudai Pingfeng Sheji Yuanliu 中國古代屏風設計源流), MA thesis, Suzhou University, Suzhou 2006

WANG 2007
Eugene Y. Wang, '"Picturing Idea" and Its Cultural Dynamics in Northern Song China', *The Art Bulletin*, vol. 89, no. 3 (September 2007), pp. 463–81

WANG 2010A
Wang Huimin (王惠民), 'A Study of the Depictions of Guanyin Bestowing Treasure and Guanyin Bestowing Sweet Dew in Mogao Cave 205' (Mogao ku di 205 ku Shi bao Guanyin yu Shi ganlu Guanyin tuxiang kaoshi 莫高窟第205窟施宝观音与施甘露观音图像考释), *Dunhuang Studies Quarterly* (Dunhuangxue jikan 敦煌學季刊), no. 1 (2010), pp. 58–65

WANG 2010B
Selena Shen Wang, 'Wang Yuanqi and Orthodox Self-Reflection in Early Qing China', PhD dissertation, University of Pennsylvania 2010

WANG AND ZHOU 1992
Wang Fengzhu (王鳳珠) and Zhou Jiyin (周積寅), *A Chronological List of the Calligraphy and Paintings of the Eight Eccentrics of Yangzhou* (Yangzhou Baguai shuhua nianbiao 揚州八怪書畫年表), Nanjing 1992

WANG ET AL. (1708) 1969
Wang Yuanqi (王原祁) et al., *Record of Painting and Calligraphy commissioned by Kangxi Emperor* (Pei wen zhai shu hua pu 佩文齋書畫譜) reprinted Beijing 1969; completed 1708

WANG IN NEW HAVEN 1990
Wang Fangyu, 'The life and art of Bada Shanren', in *Master of the Lotus Garden: The Life and Art of Bada Shanren (1626–1705)*, Richard M. Barnhart and Judith G. Smith (eds), Yale University Press, New Haven 1990

WANG, LI AND P'AN 1979
Wang Te-yi (王德毅), Li Rung-tsun (李榮村) and P'an Po-cheng (潘柏澄), *A Dictionary of Yuan Biographies* (Yuan ren chuanji ziliao suoyin 元人傳記資料索引), Taipei 1979

WANG, SUN AND SONG ET AL. (1708) 1991
Wang Yuanqi (王原祁), Sun Yueban (孫岳頒), Song Junye (宋駿業) Wu Jing (吳暻) and Wang Quan (王銓), *A Record of Painting and Calligraphy Commissioned by the Kangxi Emperor* (Peiwen Zhai shuhua pu 佩文齋書畫譜), 5 vols, reprinted Shanghai 1991; original edition 1708

WAPPENSCHMIDT 2007
Friderike Wappenschmidt, '"Was Man Chostlichs, Fremds und Seltzames sieht." Ostasiatische Exponate im Inventar der Münchner Kunstkammer von 1598', *Ostasiatische Zeitschrift, Neue Serie*, vol. 14 (Autumn 2007), pp. 9–20

WARD WITH ROWLANDS 1987
*A Bountiful Decade: Selected Acquisitions 1977–1987*, Roger Ward with Eliot W. Rowlands (eds), The Nelson-Atkins Museum of Art, Kansas City 1987

WASHINGTON 1973
Thomas Lawton, *Chinese Figure Painting, Fiftieth Anniversary Exhibition II – Freer Gallery of Art*, exh. cat., Freer Gallery of Art, Washington DC 1973

WASHINGTON 1984
Margaret C.S. Christman, *Adventurous Pursuits: Americans and the China Trade, 1784–1844*, exh. cat., National Portrait Gallery, Washington DC 1984

WASHINGTON 2003
*In Pursuit of Heavenly Harmony: Paintings and Calligraphy by Bada Shanren from the Estate of Wang Fangyu and Sum Wai*, Joseph Chang and Qianshen Bai (eds), exh. cat., Freer Gallery of Art, Washington DC 2003

WASHINGTON 2003
Joseph Chang, Qianshen Bai and Stephen Allee, *In Pursuit of Heavenly Harmony: Paintings and Calligraphy from the Estate of Wang Fangyu and Sum Wai*, exh. cat., Freer Gallery of Art, Washington DC 2003

WATSON 1968
Burton Watson, *The Complete Works of Chuang Tzu*, New York 1968

WEIDNER 1994
*Latter Days of the Law: Images of Chinese Buddhism, 850–1850*, Marsha Weidner (ed.), Lawrence, KS 1994

WEIDNER 2001
*Cultural Intersections in Later Chinese Buddhism*, Marsha Weidner (ed.), Honolulu 2001

WEITZ 2002
Ankeney Weitz, *Zhou Mi's Record of Clouds and Mist Passing Before One's Eyes: An Annotated Translation*, Leiden, Boston and Cologne 2002

WEN 1980
Wen Zhaotong (溫肇桐), *Wang Yuanqi* (王原祁), Shanghai 1980

WEN (1637) 1987
Wen Zhenheng (文震亨), *Superfluous Things* (Zhangwu zhi 長物 志), in *Complete Collections of the Four Treasuries* (Siku quanshu – jibu 四庫全書), Shanghai 1987, vol. 872

WEN 2008
Wen Renjun (聞人軍), *Annotation of the Artificers' Record* (Kaogong ji yizhu 考工記譯注), Shanghai 2008

WEN 2013
Wen Renjun (trans. & annot.) [published as Jun Wenren], *Ancient Chinese Encyclopedia of Technology*, Routledge, New York 2013

WEN, PU AND YANG 2008
Wen Tai-Shiang (溫台祥), Pu Yen-Kuan (浦彥光) and Yang Shih-Jung (楊時榮), *A Discussion of the Making and Conservation of Books* (Shi shuji zhuanghuang yu baocun guanxi yanjiu 釋書籍裝潢與保存關係研究), *Interdisciplinary Journal of Taiwan Library Administration* (Taiwan tushuguan guanli jikan 臺灣圖書館管理季刊), vol. 3, pt 3 (July 2008), pp. 96–117

WHITEHILL 1970
Walter Muir Whitehill, *Museum of Fine Arts, Boston; A Centennial History*, Cambridge, MA 1970

WHITFIELD 1976
Roderick Whitfield, 'Chinese Paintings from the collection of Archduke Ferdinand II', *Oriental Art*, vol. XXII, no. 4 (1976), pp. 406–16

WHITFIELD 1982–5
Roderick Whitfield, *The Art of Central Asia. The Stein Collection in the British Museum*, 3 vols, Tokyo 1982–5

WHITFIELD 1993
Roderick Whitfield, *Fascination with Nature. Plants and Insects in Chinese Painting and Ceramics of the Yuan Dynasty (1279–1368)*, Seoul 1993

WHITFIELD 2003
Roderick Whitfield, 'On Some Fragments of a Dunhuang Painting in the Collection of the British Museum' (Dai Ei hakubutsukan shōzō no Tonkō kaiga dampen ni tsuite 大英博物館所蔵の敦煌繪畫斷片について), *Ars Buddhica* (Bukkyō geijutsu 佛教藝術), *Special issue: One Hundred Years of Dunhuang Studies* (Tokushū: Tonkōgaku no hyakunen 特集 敦煌學の百年), no. 271 (2003), pp. 48–56

WHITFIELD 2004
Susan Whitfield, *Aurel Stein and the Silk Road*, London 2004

WHITFIELD AND FARRER 1990
Roderick Whitfield and Anne Farrer, *Caves of the Thousand Buddhas. Chinese Art from the Silk Road*, New York 1990

WILKINSON 1981
Stephen Wilkinson, 'Paintings of "The Red Cliff Prose Poems" in Song Times', *Oriental Art*, vol. XXVII, no. 1 (1981), pp. 76–89

WINTER 2008
John Winter, *East Asian Paintings: Materials, Structures and Deterioration Mechanisms*, London 2008

WIRGIN 1989
*The Ernest Erickson Collection in Swedish Museums*, Jan Wirgin (ed.), Stockholm 1989

WOODALL 2012
Joanna Woodall, *Picturing the Netherlandish Canon*, online exhibition catalogue, www.courtauld.org.uk/netherlandishcanon (accessed 12 November 2012)

WU (late 13th–early 14th century) 1984
Wu Zimu (吳自牧), *Record of the Millet Dream* (Mengliang lu 夢粱錄), reprinted Hangzhou 1984; original edition late 13th–early 14th century

WU (1713) 1993–8
Wu Sheng (吳升), *Record of Great Art* (Daguan lu 大觀錄), painting section, vol. 17, reprinted in *Collection of Writings on Chinese Calligraphy and Painting* (Zhongguo shuhua quanshu 中國書畫全書), Lu Fusheng (盧輔聖) et al. (eds), vol. 8, Shanghai 1994; preface to original edition 1713

WU (17th century) 1993–8
Wu Qizhen (吳其貞), *Records of Painting and Calligraphy* (Shuhua ji 書畫記), painting section, vol. 5, reprinted in *Collection of Writings on Chinese Calligraphy and Painting* (Zhongguo shuhua quanshu 中國書畫全書), Lu Fusheng (盧輔聖) (ed.), vol. 8, Shanghai 1994; original edition 17th century

WU 1967
Wu Tung, 'Tao-chi: A Chronology', in *The Painting of Tao Chi 1641–ca. 1720*, Richard Edwards (ed.), Michigan 1967, pp. 53–62

WU 1996A
Wu Tung, *Masterpieces of Chinese Painting from the Museum of Fine Arts, Boston: Tang through Yuan Dynasties*, 2 vols, Museum of Fine Arts, Boston 1996

WU 1970
William Wu, 'Kung Hsien's Style and His Sketchbooks', *Oriental Art*, vol. XVI, no. 1 (1970), pp. 72–80

WU 1991
Wu Yuming (吳聿明), *A Study of the Loudong School of Painting* (Loudong huapai yanjiu 婁東畫派研究), Nanjing 1991

WU 1996B
Wu Hung, *The Double Screen: Medium and Representation in Chinese Painting*, London 1996

WU 2009
Wu Shixin (吳世新), *A Story of Xuan Paper* (Zhongguo xuanzhi shihua 中國宣紙史話), Beijing 2009

WUE 2001
Roberta Wue, 'Picturing the Artist: Ren Bonian (1840–1896) and Portraits of the Shanghai Art World', PhD dissertation, New York University, New York 2001

XIE 1957
Xie Zhiliu (謝稚柳), *Famous Paintings of the Tang, Five Dynasties, Song and Yuan Periods* (Tang, Wudai, Song, Yuan mingji 唐五代宋元名跡), Shanghai 1957

XIE 1989
Xie Zhiliu (謝稚柳), *A Complete Collection of Song Huizong* (Song Huizong Zhao Ji quanji 徽宗趙佶全集), Shanghai 1989

XU 1974
Xu Bangda (徐邦達), *A Chronological List of Paintings and Calligraphies* (Lidai liuchuan shuhua zuopin bian nianbiao 歷代流傳書畫作品編年表), Hong Kong 1974

XU 1979
Xu Bangda (徐邦達), 'Paintings from the Hand of Huizong and the Issue of his Substitute Painters' (Song Huizong Zhao Ji qinbi hua yu daibi de kaobian 宋徽宗趙佶親筆畫與代筆的考辨), *Palace Museum Journal* (Gugong bowuyuan yuankan 故宮博物院院刊) (January 1979), pp. 62–8

XU 1981
Xu Bangda (徐邦達), *An Introduction to the Connoisseurship of Ancient Calligraphy and Painting* (Gu shuhua jianding gailun 古書畫鑑定概論), Beijing 1981

XU 1984
Xu Bangda (徐邦達), *Issues of Forgery and Misattribution in Ancient Calligraphy and Paintings* (Gu shuhua wei'e kaobian 古書畫僞訛考辨), Nanjing 1984, pp. 228–9

XU 1994
Xu Bangda (徐邦達), *Revised Chronological List of Surviving Paintings of All the Dynasties* (Gaiding lidai liuchuan huihua nianbiao 改訂歷代流傳繪畫年表), Beijing 1994

XU 1997
Xu Bangda (徐邦達), *Revised Inventroy of the Calligraphy and Paintings in the Former Qing Palace Collection* (Chongding Qing gugong jiucang shuhua lu 重訂清宮舊藏書畫錄), Beijing 1997

XU 2000
Xu Jianrong (徐建融), *Inscriptions and Seal Marks on Calligraphy and Painting* (Shuhua tikuan tiba qianyin 書畫題款題跋鈐印), Shanghai 2000

*Xuanhe Painting Catalogue* (1120) 1964
*Xuanhe Painting Catalogue* (Xuanhe huapu 宣和畫譜), Yu Jianhua (俞劍華) (annot.), reprinted Beijing 1964; original edition 1120

XUE 1987
Xue Yongnian (薛永年), 'Reflections on Ren Bonian' (Ren Bonian de qishi 任伯年的啟示), *Chinese Paintings* (Zhongguo hua 中國畫), no. 4 (1987), pp. 31–8

XUE 1994
Xue Yongnian (薛永年), *Masters of Modern Chinese Painting – Ren Bonian* (Zhongguo jinxiandai mingjia huaji – Ren Bonian 中國近現代名家畫集 – 任伯年), Taipei 1994

YAMABE 2012
Nobuyoshi Yamabe, 'A Comparison of the Transformation Tableaux of the *Amitāyus Visualization Sūtra* and of the *Favour Repayment Sūtra*, in Buddhist Meditation: Texts, Tradition and Practice', *paper presented at the 6th Biennial International Conference*, K.J. Somaiya Centre for Buddhist Studies, vol. 19 (2012)

YAMAGUCHI 1993
Yamaguchi Seiichi, 'Der Kunstmarkt in der frühen Meiji-Zeit', in *Japan und Europa, 1543–1929, Essays*, Berlin 1993, pp. 66–73

YAMAMOTO IN NAGOYA 2008
Yamamoto Taiichi (山本泰一), *Zen'ami in the Age of Ashikaga Yoshimitsu and Collection Seals Associated with Him* (Ashikaga Yoshimitsu jidai no zen'ami to kanzōin ni tsuite 足利義満時代の善阿弥と鑑蔵印について), in *Exploring the Treasures of the Muromachi Shoguns* (Muromachi shōgunke no shihō o saguru 室町将軍家の至宝を探る), exh. cat., Tokugawa Art Museum, Nagoya 2008

YAMASHITA 2000
Yamashita Yūji (山下裕二), 'Approaching a Masterpiece: the Painting "Monkey" attributed to Mao Song' [14–16] (Meiga ni chikazuku den Mō Shō hitsu saru-zu (14–16) 名画に近づく 伝毛松筆 猿図 (14～16)), in *Studies in the Tea Ceremony* (Chadō no kenkyū 茶道の研究), vol. 45 (2000); no. 2, pp. 36–9; no. 3, pp. 36–9; no. 4, pp. 32–5

YANG (1919) 1988
Yang Yi (楊逸), *The Ink Forest of Shanghai* (Haishang molin 海上墨林), reprinted Taipei 1988; preface to original edition 1919

YANG 1980
Yang Boda (楊柏達), 'Supplementary Report on the Lacquer Objects Found in the Ming Tomb of Zhu Tan' (Ming Zhu Tan mu chutu qiqi buji 明朱檀墓出土漆器補記), *Wenwu* 文物, no. 6 (1980), pp. 70–4

YANG 1947
Yang Jing'an (楊靜盦), *A Chronology of Tang Yin* (Tang Yin nianpu 唐寅年譜), Shanghai 1947

YANG 1967
*A Treatise on Ming Painting Studies* (Mingren huaxue lunzhu 明人畫學論著), Yang Jialuo (楊家駱) (ed.), Taipei 1967

YANG 1975
Yang Renkai (杨仁凯), 'On Dating and Other Issues of the Paintings Excavated from the Liao Tomb at Yemaotai' (Yemaotai Liao mu chutu guhua de shidai ji qita 葉茂台遼墓出土古畫的時代及其他), *Wenwu* 文物, no. 12 (1975), pp. 37–9

YANG 1977
Yang Li-Kui (楊麗圭), 'A Study of Zheng Sixiao, with an Annotation of His Poetry' (Zheng Sixiao yanjiu jiqi shi qianzhu 鄭思肖研究及其詩箋注), M.A. thesis, Chinese Culture University, Taipei 1977

YANG 1994
Yang Xin (楊新), *Ming and Qing Paintings in the Palace Museum* (Gugong bowuyuan cang Ming Qing huihua 故宮博物院藏明清繪畫), Beijing 1994

YANG 1997
Yang Xin (楊新), 'The Ming Dynasty (1368–1644)', in Richard M. Barnhart, *Three Thousand Years of Chinese Painting*, New Haven and London 1997, pp. 197–249

YANG 2005
Yang Dunyao (楊敦堯), 'A Preliminary Study of Dong Qichang's Reconstruction of Dong Yuan's *Summer Mountains*' (Dong Qichang jiangou Dong Yuan *Xiashan tu* zhi chutan 董其昌建構董源《夏山圖卷》之初探), in *Collected Essays on Calligraphy and Painting in Honour of Professor Su Fengnan on his Retirement* (Su Fengnan jiaoshou fuwu gongshi sishinian tuixiu jinian shuhua yishu lunwen ji 蘇峰男教授服務公職四十年退休紀念書畫藝術論文集), Taipei 2005, pp. 459–66

YANG 2007
Chia-Ling Yang, *New Wine in Old Bottles – The Art of Ren Bonian in Nineteenth-Century Shanghai*, London 2007

YANG 2009
Chia-Ling Yang, 'The Crisis of the Real – Photography and Portraiture in Late Nineteenth-Century Shanghai', in *Looking Modern: East Asian Visual Culture from Treaty Ports to World War II*, Jennifer Purtle and Hans B. Thomsen (eds), Chicago 2009, pp. 20–37

YANG 2011
Yang Chia-Ling (楊嘉玲), *A Painted Dream of Shanghai: Ren Bonian's World of Ink and Brush* (Huameng Shanghai: Ren Bonian de bimo shijie 畫夢上海：任伯年的筆墨世界), Taipei 2011

YASHIRO 1944
Yashiro Yukio (矢代幸雄), 'The Five Planets and the Twenty-eight Lunar Mansions handscroll' (Gosei nijūhachi shukushin-kei zumaki 五星二十八宿神形圖卷), *The Journal of Art Studies* (Bijutsu kenkyū 美術研究), vol. 139 (1944)

YASHIRO 1953
Yashiro Yukio (矢代幸雄), 'Again on the Song Copy of the Scroll "Ladies of the Court" by Zhou Wenju' (saisetsu sōmo Shū Bunku kanchūzu 再説宋摹周文矩宮中圖), *The Journal of Art Studies* (Bijutsu kenkyū 美術研究), vol. IV, no. 169 (1953), pp. 157–62

YE (1128) 1984
Ye Mengde (葉夢得), *Miscellaneous Notes by Stone Grove* (Shilin yanyu 石林燕語), reprinted in *Documentary Sources of Painters in Song, Liao and Jin Dynasties* (Song, Liao, Jin huajia shiliao 宋遼金 畫家史料), Chen Gaohua (陳高華) (ed.), Beijing 1984; completed 1128

YEH 2007
Wen-hsin Yeh, *Shanghai Splendor: Economic Sentiments and the Making of Modern China, 1843–1949*, Berkeley, Los Angeles and London 2007

YI 2001
Yi Ruofen (衣若芬), 'Battles and Journeys: Illustrating Eulogies of the Red Cliff' (Zhanhuo yu qingyou: Chibitu tiyong lunxi 戰火與清遊: 赤壁圖題詠論析), *National Palace Museum Research Quarterly* (Gugong xueshu jikan 故宮學術季刊), vol. 18, no. 4 (2001), pp. 63–102

YIN 1988
Yin Jinan (尹吉男), 'An Initial Acquaintance with the Calligraphy and Paintings from the Tomb of Wang Zhen' (Guanyu Huai'an Wang Zhen mu chutu shuhua de chubu renshi 關於淮安王鎮墓出土書畫的初步認識), *Wenwu* 文物, no. 1 (1988), pp. 65–72

YOKOHAMA 1996
Wu Tung, *Masterpieces of Song and Yuan Paintings from the Museum of Fine Arts, Boston* (Bosuton bijutsukan no shihō chūgoku sō genga meihinten zuroku ボストン美術館の至宝：中國宋・元畫名品展), exh. cat., Sogo Museum of Art, Yokohama 1996

YONEDA 1998A
Yoneda Yūsuke (米田雄介), *The History and Preservation of the Shōsō-in Treasures* (Shōsō-in hōmotsu no rekishi to hozon 正倉院宝物の歴史と保存), Tokyo 1998

YONEDA 1998B
Yoneda Yūsuke (米田雄介), *The Shōsō-in and Japanese Culture* (Shōsō-in to nihon bunka 正倉院と日本文化), Tokyo 1998

YONEDA 2000
Yoneda Yūsuke (米田雄介), *The Shōsō-in and the Heian Period – the Path to Japanization* (Shōsō-in hōmotsu to heian jidai – wafuka e no michi 正倉院宝物と平安時代 – 和風化への道), Tokyo and Kyoto 2000

YONEZAWA 1954
Yonezawa Yoshiho (米澤嘉圃), 'Paintings with the Zen'a Seal [Society for Research on Muromachi Period Ink Painting]' (Zen'a-in no aru gafuku [Muromachi jidai suibokuga kenkyūkai kiji] 善阿印のある画幅 [室町時代水墨画研究会記事]), *Journal of the Japan Art History Society* (Bijutsushi 美術史), no. 11 (January 1954)

YONEZAWA 1963
Yonezawa Yoshiho (米澤嘉圃), 'Yanxi Guangwen's Eulogy on *Meeting Between Yaoshan and Li Ao*' (Enkei Kōken san *Gakusan Li Kō Zenkai zu* 偃溪廣聞贊藥山李翺禪會圖), *Kokka* 國華, no. 859 (October 1963), pp. 20–6

YU 1973
*Extended Collection of Chinese Painting Theories* (Zhongguo hualun xubian 中國畫論續編), Yu Jianhua (俞劍華) (ed.), Hong Kong 1973

YU 1988
Yu Fei'an, *Chinese Painting Colors: Studies of their Preparation and Application in Traditional and Modern Times*, Jeremy Silbergeld and Amy McNair (trans.), Hong Kong, Seattle and London 1988

YU 1992
Yu Zhonghang (于中航), 'A Short Biography of the Northern Song Landscapist Li Gongnian (Bei Song shanshui huajia Li Gongnian xiao kao 北宋山水畫家李公年小考), *Wenwu* (文物), no. 7 (1992), pp. 94, 74

YÜ 1994
Yü Chün-fang, 'Guanyin: The Chinese Transformation of Avalokiteshvara', in *Latter Days of the Law: Images of Chinese Buddhism, 850–1850*, Marsha Weidner (ed.), Lawrence, KS 1994, pp. 151–81

YU 2010
Yu Hui (余輝), 'A Study of Landscapes by Li Tang and by Post- Li Tang Artists' (Li Tang yu hou Li Tang shanshui yanjiu 李唐與後李唐山水研究), in Symposium Proceedings of Dynastic Renaissance: Art and Culture of the Southern Song (Shaoxing wenyi: nan Song yishu yu wenhua xueshu yantao hui 紹興文藝: 南宋藝術與文化學術研討會), National Palace Museum, Taipei 2010, pp. 475–506

ZAINIE 1978
Carla M. Zainie, 'Sources for Some Early Japanese Ink Paintings', *The Bulletin of The Cleveland Museum of Art*, vol. 65, no. 7 (1978), pp. 232–46

ZHANG (1739) 2011
Zhang Geng (張庚), 'Zeng Jing' (曾鯨), reprinted in *A Record of Qing Painting* (Guochao huazheng lu 國朝畫徵錄), Hangzhou 2011; original edition 1739

ZHANG (1832) 1932
Zhang Dayong (張大鏞), *Records of Painting and Calligraphy of the Ziyiyue Studio* (Ziyiyue Zhai shuhua lu 自怡悅齋書畫錄), reprinted 1932; original edition 1832

ZHANG 1994
Zhang Hongxing, 'From Slender Eyes to Round: A Study of Ren Yi's Portraits in the Context of Contemporary Photography,' manuscript, 1994

ZHANG 2003
Zhang Hongxing, 'The Nineteenth-Century Provenance of the Admonitions Scroll: A Hypothesis', in Shane McCausland, *Gu Kaizhi and the Admonitions Scroll*, London 2003, pp. 277–94

ZHANG 2005
Zhang Hongxing, 'Rereading Inscriptions in Chinese Scroll Painting: The Eleventh to the Fourteenth Centuries,' *Art History*, vol. 28, no. 5 (2005), pp. 606–25

ZHANG 1995
Zhang Zining (張子寧; Joseph Chang), 'A Further Study of the Handscroll *Grooms and Horses by the Three Generations of the Zhao Family*' (*Yetan Zhao shi sanshi renma tu* juan 也談《趙氏三世人馬圖》卷), in *Collected Essays on Zhao Mengfu* (Zhao Mengfu yanjiu lunwen ji 趙孟頫研究論文集), Shanghai 1995, pp. 767–76

ZHANG 1999
Zhang Yuming (張郁明), 'Luo Pin and his Artistic Development' (Luo Pin yu tade yishu daolu 羅聘和他的藝術道路), in *Collected Essays on the Yangzhou School of Painting* (Yangzhou huapai yanjiu wenji 揚州畫派研究文集), Tianjin 1999, pp. 234–68

ZHANG 2007
Zhang Peijun (張培君), 'A Study of the donors' image in the painted banners from the Library Cave' (Dunhuang cangjingdong chutu yihua zhong gongyangren tuxiang chutan 敦煌藏經洞出土遺畫中供養人圖像初探), *Dunhuang Research* (Dunhuang yanjiu 敦煌研究), vol. 104, no. 4 (2007), pp. 91–7

ZHANG 2012
Zhang Ming (張鳴), 'A Discussion of Su Shi's Poem Visualized in Qiao Zhongchang's *Illustration to the Second Prose Poem on the Red Cliff*' (Tantan Qiao Zhongchang *Hou Chibi fu tu* dui Su Shi *Hou Chibi fu* yishu yiyun de shijue zaixian 談談喬仲常《後赤壁賦圖》對蘇軾《後赤壁賦》藝術意蘊的視覺再現), in *A Close Look at the Five Dynasties, Song, and Yuan Paintings and Calligraphies in American Collections* (Han mo hui cui: xidu Meiguo cang Zhongguo Wudai Song Yuan shuhua zhenpin 翰墨薈萃: 細讀美國藏中國五代宋元書畫珍品), Beijing 2012, pp. 284–95

ZHANG AND GAO 2008
Zhang Jindong (張金棟) and Gao Chaoying (高朝英), 'A Study of *Poem of Suixian Hall*, a Calligraphy in Running Script by an Old Man Sleeping on a Tiger – with Additional Comments on the Eminent Scholars from the Beijing Area, Zhang Lin and Zhang Shu, Part II' (Huwo laoren xingshu *Suixian Tang shi lüshi* kao – jiantan jifu xianzhe Zhang Lin, Zhang Shu [xia] 虎臥老人行書《遂閑堂時律詩》考 – 兼談畿輔先哲張霖, 張霔 [下]), *Stories of Cultural Relics* (Wenwu chunqiu 文物春秋), no. 2 (2008), pp. 59–68

ZHAO 1995
Zhao Xiaohua (趙曉華), 'Discovering Zhou Fang through a painted screen: *Ladies Adorning their Hair with Flowers* in the Liaoning Provincial Museum' (Heyou jian Zhou Fang, Yiru huaping zhong: Liaoning sheng bowuguan cang Zanhua shinu tu 何繇见周昉,移入画屏中: 遼寧省博物館藏簪花仕女圖), *Chinese Art Newspaper* (Zhongguo wenwu bao 中國文物報), no. 420, 2 February 1995

ZHAO 2011
Zhao Feng (趙豐) (ed.), *Textiles from Dunhuang in French Collections*, Shanghai 2011

ZHENG 1948
Zheng Zhenduo (鄭振鐸), *Paintings of the Tang, Song and Later Periods in the Collection of Yunhui Zhai* (Yunhui Zhai cang Tang Song yilai minghua ji 韞輝齋藏唐宋以來名畫集), Shanghai 1948

ZHENG 1982
Zheng Zhuolu (鄭拙廬), *Ni Zan* (倪瓚), Shanghai 1982

ZHENG 1992
Zheng Wei (鄭威), 'A Chronology of Wang Yuanqi' (Wang Yuanqi nianpu 王原祁年譜), *Duoyun* 朵雲, vol. 39 (1992), pp. 88–119

ZHENG 1997
Zheng Binglin (鄭炳林), 'Prices of Commodities in Dunhuang in late Tang and Five Dynasties Period' (Wan Tang Wudai Dunhuang maoyi shichang de wujia 晚唐五代敦煌貿易市場的物價), *Dunhuang Research* (Dunhuang yanjiu 敦煌研究), no. 3 (1997), pp. 14–32

ZHENG 2004
Zheng Binglin (鄭炳林), 'A Study in Commodities in Dunhuang in late Tang and Five Dynasties Period' (Wan Tang Wudai Dunhuang shangye maoyi shichang yanjiu 晚唐五代敦煌商業貿易市場研究), *Journal of Dunhuang Studies* (Dunhuang xue jikan 敦煌學輯刊), vol. 45, no. 1 (2004), pp. 103–18

ZHONGGUO GUDAI SHUHUA JIANDING ZU 1986–2001
*Illustrated Catalogue of Selected Works of Chinese Painting and Calligraphy* (Zhongguo gudai shuhua tumu 中國古代書畫圖目), Zhongguo gudai shuhua jianding zu (中國古代書畫鑑定組) (ed.), 24 vols, Beijing 1986–2001

ZHOU (1280–90) 1993
Zhou Mi (周密), *Wild Talks of the Eastern Qi* (Qidong yeyu 齊東野語), reprinted in *Collected Historical Writings on Mounting Techniques of Calligraphy and Painting, with Annotation and Translation into Modern Chinese* (Shuhua zhuangbiao jiyi jishi 書畫裝裱技藝輯釋), Du Bingzhuang (杜秉庄) and Du Zixiong (杜子熊) (eds), Shanghai 1993, pp. 208–21; completed in 1280–90

ZHOU (c.1290) 1882
Zhou Mi (周密), *Former Events in Wulin [Hangzhou]* (Wulin jiushi 武林舊事), reprinted in *Collected Historial Writings on Wulin [Hangzhou]* (Wulin zhanggu congbian 武林掌故叢編), 12 vols, Ding Bing (丁丙) (ed.), Hangzhou 1882; completed c.1290

ZHOU (1650–1) 1993
Zhou Jiazhou (周嘉胄), *Treatise on Mounting* (Zhuanghuang zhi 裝潢志), reprinted in *Collected Historical Writings on Mounting Techniques of Calligraphy and Painting, with Annotation and Translation into Modern Chinese* (Shuhua zhuangbiao jiyi jishi 書畫裝裱技藝輯釋), Du Bingzhuang (杜秉庄) and Du Zixiong (杜子熊) (eds), Shanghai shuhua chuban she, Shanghai 1993, pp. 1–140; completed in 1650–1

ZHOU 1981
Zhou Jiyan (周積寅), *The Portraiture of Zeng Jing* (Zeng Jing de xiaoxianghua 曾鯨的肖像畫), Beijing 1981

ZHOU 1996
Zhou Jiyin (周積寅), *Research Compendia for the Great Masters of Chinese Painting of the Ming and Qing Dynasties* (Ming-Qing Zhongguo hua dashi yanjiu congshu 明清中國畫大師研究叢書), *Zheng Banqiao* (鄭板橋), Changchun 1996

ZHOU 2003
*Chinese Paitnings from Wei, Jin to Five Dynasties* (Zhongguo minghua shang xi: Wei, Jin zhi Wu Dai huihua 魏晉至五代繪畫), Zhou Linsheng (周林生) (ed.), Shijiazhuang 2003

ZHOU AND ZHANG 2002
*A Compendium of Tang Bohu* (Tang Bohu quanji 唐伯虎全集), Zhou Daozhen (周道振) and Zhang Yuezun (張月尊) (eds), Hangzhou 2002

ZHU (1920) 1997
Zhu Zhichi (朱之赤), *A List of Calligraphies and Paintings in the Collection of Zhu Wo'an (Zhu Zhichi)* (Zhu Wo'an cang shuhua mu 朱臥庵藏書畫目), reprinted in *Fine Art Series* (Meishu congshu 美術叢書), Huang Binhong (黃賓虹) and Deng Shi (鄧實) (eds), Nanjing 1997, pp. 1023–38; original edition Shanghai 1920

ZHU 1952
Zhu Xingzhai (朱省齋), *Xingzhai's Notes on Paintings* (Xingzhai duhua ji 省齋讀畫記), Hong Kong 1952

ZHU 2005
Zhu Liangzhi (朱良志), *A Study of Shitao* (Shitao yanjiu 石濤研究), Beijing 2005

ZHU 2010
Zhu Liangzhi (朱良志), *A Study of Bada Shanren* (Bada Shanren yanjiu 八大山人研究), Hefei 2010

ZI AND GENG 2004
*The Wu School of Painting – Shen Zhou, 1427–1509* (Wumen huapai – Shen Zhou, 1427–1509 吳門畫派 – 沈周), Zi Du (紫都) and Geng Jing (耿靜) (eds), Beijing 2004

ZOU (1758) 1993
Zou Yigui (鄒一桂), *Painting Manual of Xiaoshan* (Xiaoshan huapu 小山畫譜), reprinted in *Collected Historical Writings on Mounting Techniques of Calligraphy and Painting, with Annotation and Translation into Modern Chinese* (Shuhua zhuangbiao jiyi jishi 書畫裝裱技藝輯釋), Du Bingzhuang (杜秉庄) and Du Zixiong (杜子熊) (eds), Shanghai 1993, pp. 354–62; completed in 1758

ZURICH 1996
Richard M. Barnhart, Wen C. Fong and Maxwell K. Hearn, *Mandate of Heaven: Emperors and Artists in China: Chinese Painting and Calligraphy from The Metropolitan Museum of Art, New York*, exh. cat., Museum Rietberg, Zurich 1996

# ACKNOWLEDGEMENTS

THE VICTORIA AND ALBERT MUSEUM'S previous and current directors, Sir Mark Jones and Martin Roth are the true begetters of the ambitious exhibition that this book accompanies. Without their inspirational initiative and guidance, and subsequent firm commitment, there could be no exhibition.

The organisation of such a display can only be possible through the expertise and hard work of a vast number of people. I owe huge thanks to my closest collaborators, Jennifer Wong (Assistant Curator) and Sarah Gage (Exhibition Co-ordinator) who have worked with enthusiasm and dedication. Sarah, with the assistance of Natalia Ferreiro and former colleague Isabel Escudero, and with the support of Linda Lloyd-Jones, Stephanie Cripps, Rebecca Lim, Lizzie Hines, Diana McAndrews, and other colleagues in Exhibitions and Loans, has tirelessly managed the loans and all aspects of design, transport and installation. Thanks also go to Susanna Haddon for her sterling work on the exhibition labels, and to Peter Kelleher for producing a film for the exhibition.

Stanton Williams conceived a beautifully minimalistic design that fits the nature of the exhibition. We thank Paul Williams, Anna Hesketh, and Tom Harvey for bringing their expertise into the project. Our thanks also go to their collaborators on graphic design, Ian Cartlidge and Ben Tibbs of Cartlidge Levene.

The publication of this exhibition catalogue has created enormous demands. My thanks go to Tom Windross and to other colleagues in V&A Publishing, especially Mark Eastment, Clare Davis, Davina Cheung and Zara Anvari, and Liz Edmunds and Vicky Haverson for their picture research. I am also particularly grateful to Philip Lewis for the book's design and to Frances McDonald for her editorial skills – as well as to Trista Selous and Carol Morland for their translations. I would like to thank all the contributors to the exhibition catalogue for their expertise and commitment, and Lin Yi-Hsin for his great work on the transcriptions and translations of inscriptions in the appendix.

Among the V&A colleagues who have contributed to this project, I am particularly grateful to Beth McKillop, an East Asia specialist and Deputy Director of the Museum, for her warm encouragement, inspiring spirit and thoughtful guidance; to Damien Whitmore, Olivia Colling, Jane Rosier, and especially Zoë Franklin, Lucy Hawes and Charlotte Wood in Public Affairs; to Jane Lawson, Jo Ani, Laura Sears and Sophie Hargroves in Development; to Jo Prosser, Annabelle Dodd, Matt Thomas, Malcolm Sutherland and Steve Lewis in VAE; to Annabel Judd and colleagues in Design; to Susan Catcher, Richard Ashbridge and colleagues in Conservation; to Thomas Phongsathorn at the V&A Magazine; to James Beardsworth in Members; Elizabeth Bullock in the Web Team; to colleagues in Learning, especially Matilda Pye and Rebecca English; to colleagues at Events, Gallery Services, Estate, Safety and Security and Technical Services; and to colleagues in the Research Department where much work for this project has been conducted, including Glenn Adamson, Christine Guth, Marta Ajmar, Ghislaine Wood, and Helen Woodfield. My special thanks go to colleagues of Asian Department, my home department, for their patience and aid when needed, including Anna Jackson, Ming Wilson, Luisa Mengoni, Helen Persson, Xiaoxin Li, former colleague Pauline Le Moigne, and especially our senior specialist of Japanese art and design Rupert Faulkner who kindly undertook a fruitful research journey with me to Japan.

Around a third of objects in the exhibition come from five museums in China. The loans are made possible with the support of the State Administration for Cultural Heritage (SACH) and the Embassy of the People's Republic of China in the United Kingdom of Great Britain and Northern Ireland. For their support, we thank ambassador Liu Xiaoming and minister-councillor Xiang Xiaowei. For SACH we thank the director, Li Xiaojie, and the vice-directors Song Xinchao and Gu Yucai. We are particularly grateful to Duan Yong, Zhang Jianxin and Xin Lujiang for their advice on practical matters. Art Exhibitions China (AEC) was instrumental in liaising with all lending institutions and in bringing together the entire group of loan objects to Beijing for packing and shipment. We would like to thank their director Wang Jun, the vice-directors Yao An and Zhou Ming, and the former vice-director Yin Jia. Our special thanks go to Qian Wei, Feng Xue, Li Wei, and Dai Penglun for their work on all fronts. The generosity and collegiality of the five lending institutions has been extraordinary. We are especially thankful to the following individuals: at the Palace Museum, director Shan Jixiang, vice-director Li Ji, Wang Lei of the Foreign Affairs Office, and curator Wang Hu of the Calligraphy and Painting Department; at Shanghai Museum, director Chen Xiejun, executive vice-directors Li Zhongmou and Chen Kelun, and Zhou Yanqun, head of the Foreign Affairs Office, and curator Ling Lizhong; at Liaoning Provincial Museum, director Ma Baojie, vice-director Liu Ning, and Liu Yun; at Tianjin Museum, director Bai Wenyuan, his predecessor Chen Zuo, and Yu Ying; and at Dunhuang Academy director Fan Jingshi and executive vice-director Luo Huaqing. For the loan of two paintings from the Xubaizhai Collection at Hong Kong Museum of Art, we are thankful to chief curator Eve Tam and curator Szeto Yuen-kit. Sebastian Wood the British Ambassador to China has kindly offered his support during the negotiation of China loans.

For loans from Japan, we are grateful to all the lending institutions and their staff involved, especially the following individuals: at Tokyo National Museum, director Zeniya Masami, curator Tsukamoto Maromitsu; at Kyoto National Museum, director Sasaki Johei, curator Kure Motoyuki and his predecessor Nishigami Minoru; and at Osaka Municipal Museum of Art, director Masahiro Shino and curator Yumino Takyuki. Additional thanks to Mr Kure of Kyoto National Museum for facilitating the loan of a painting deposited in his museum by a private collector. We also wish to thank Asaka Hiroshi and Tanaka Kentaro at Agency for Cultural Affairs, Fine Art Division, Cultural Properties Department, for providing general guidance to loans from Japanese collections.

In the United States, we are very grateful to all our lending institutions and their staff, especially director Malcolm Rogers, Jane Portal, chair of Department of Asia, Oceania and Africa, and curator Nancy Berliner at the Museum of Fine Art in Boston; director Tomas P. Campbell, and Maxwell K. Hearn, chair of Department of Asian Art at The Metropolitan Museum of Art in New York; director Julián Zugazagoitia, senior curator Colin Mackenzie and curator Lu Ling-En at the Nelson-Atkins Museum of Art in Kansas City; director David Franklin and curator Anita Chung at the Cleveland Museum of Art; director Aaron Betsky and curator Sung Hou-Mei at Cincinnati Art Museum; and director James Christen Steward and curator Cary Liu at Princeton University Art Museum.

In continental Europe and Britain, we wish to thank the following individuals and their affiliated institutions for lending their objects: at Musée Guimet in Paris, president Olivier de Bernon and his predecessor Jacques Giès, and curator Valérie Zaleski; at Asian Art Museum in Berlin, director Klaas Ruitenbeek; at National Museums of World Culture in Stockholm, director Sanne Houby-Nielsen, former curator Mette Siggstedt and curator Si Han; at the British Museum, director Neil MacGregor, Jan Stuart, keeper of Asian Department, and curator Clarissa von Spee; and at the British Library, chief executive officer Roly Keating and Kristian Jensen.

The research for this exhibition and publication has benefited from the help of many people, but I would like to express my utmost gratitude to Jane Portal and Maxwell Hearn for their collegiality and generosity. My thanks also go to the following individuals: Jane Weeks of the British Council, Rose Kerr of Sir Percival David Foundation Trust, Carmen Yau of the Bei Shan Tang Foundation in Hong Kong, Sun Shuyun in London, Ann Paludan in Carlisle, Lucas Nickel and Yin Hwang of the School of Oriental and African Studies, Frances Wood of the British Library, Nixi Cura and Minna Törmä of Christie's Education London, Gigi Chang in Shanghai/Hong Kong, Nanny Kim in Cologne, Fan Jingzhong of the China Academy of Art in Hangzhou, Yu Hui and Zu E of the Palace Museum in Beijing, Zhao Feng of China National Silk Museum in Hangzhou, Jerome Silbergeld of Princeton University, Wu Hung of the University of Chicago, Eugene Wang of Harvard University, Craig Clunas of University of Oxford, Itakura Massaki and Yamazaki Noriko of the University of Tokyo, Feng Mingzhu, Ho Chuan-Hsing, Lai Yi-Man, Cheng Shu-Fang and Chen Yun-Ru of the National Palace Museum in Taipei, Lai Yu-Chih, Shih Shou-Chien and Wang Cheng-Hua of Academia Sinica in Taipei, Hou Shixin of Xinjiang Autonomous Region Museum in Urumqi, Zhao Shengliang and Wang Jinyu of Dunhuang Academy in Dunhuang, and Xu Bing, Xu Ping and Zheng Yan of the Central Academy of Fine Art in Beijing.

Finally, I owe immeasurable debts to my family and teachers, to Ruihua and Zhichun for their enthusiasm and support, to my parents and siblings in Nanjing for their understanding, and to Roderick Whitfield and Youngsook Pak for their acts of great kindness over many years.

ZHANG HONGXING
October 2013

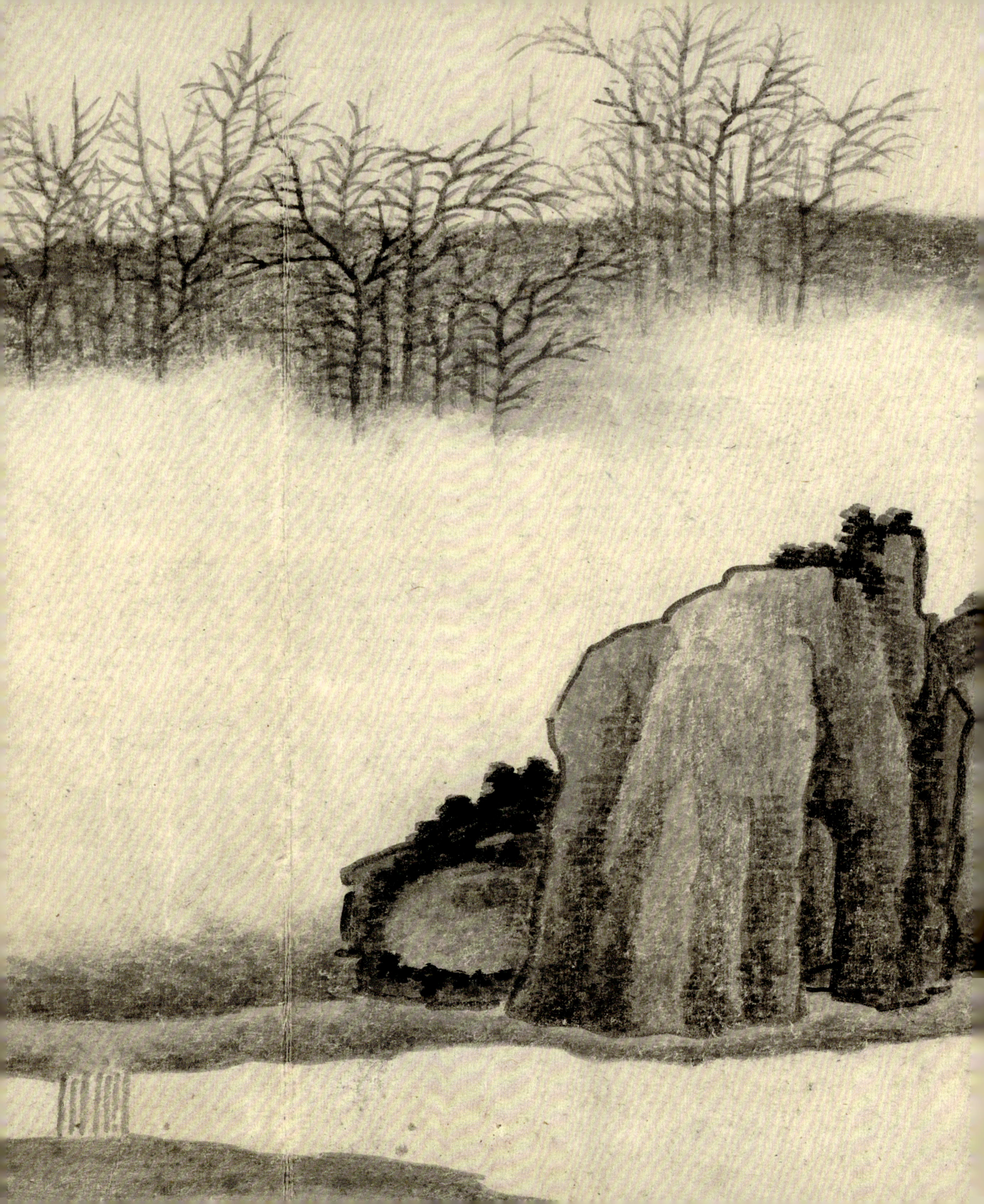

# INDEX

NOTE

Page references in *italics* refer to illustrations.

cat. no. 13 (detail)

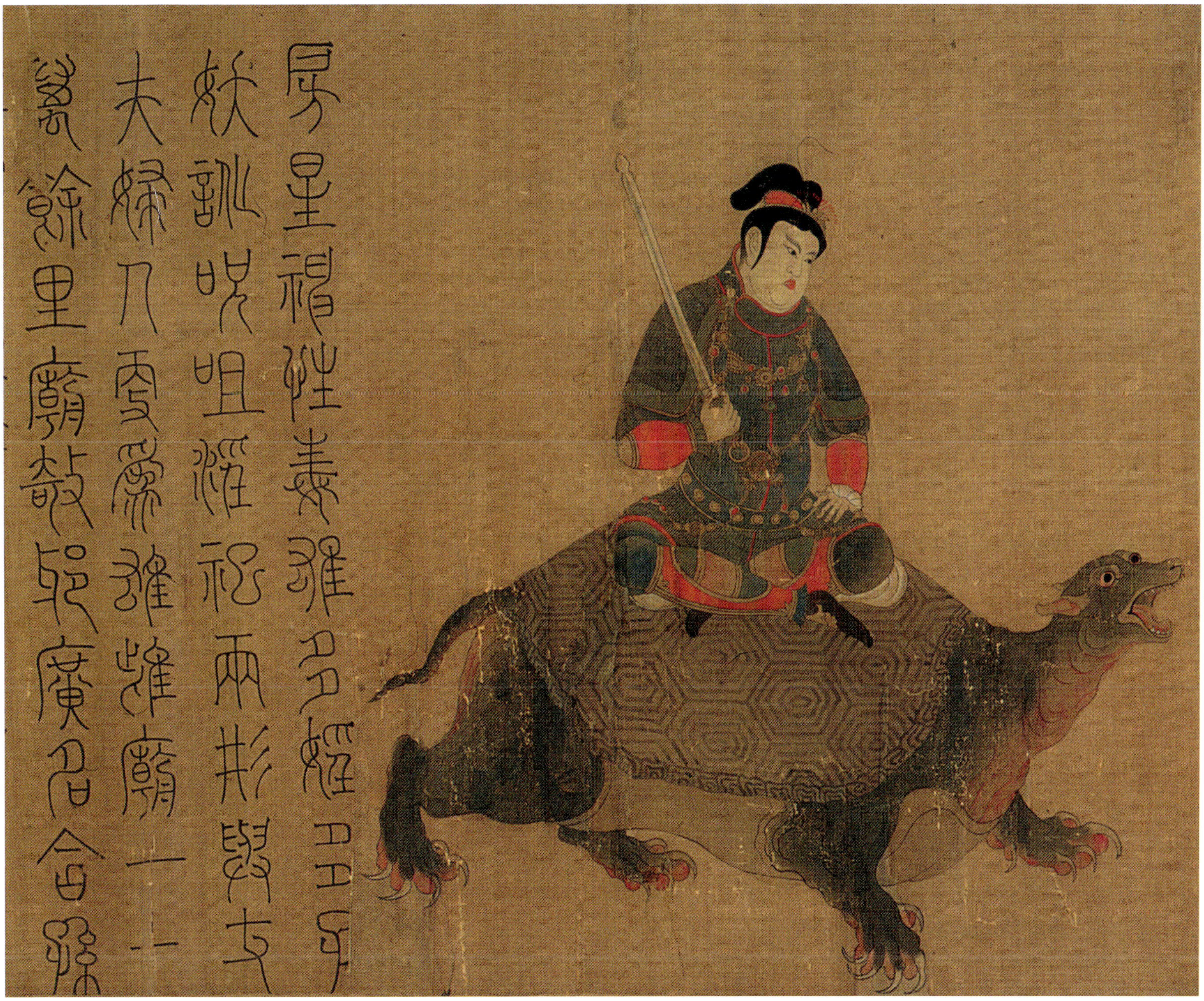

# PICTURE CREDITS

© Baoji Museum Baoji Museum Collection: fig. 13; © The Trustees of the British Museum: cat. nos 1 (p. 10, detail), 9 (p. 64, detail), 59; figs 8–9, 23, 26, 36, 38; © The British Library Board: fig. 64; © Musée Cernuschi / Roger-Viollet: fig. 37; Cincinnati Art Museum, Ohio, USA / John J. Emery Endowment / The Bridgeman Art Library: cat. nos 37, 45; © The Cleveland Museum of Art: cat. nos 48, 50, 57; © Courtesy of Datong Museum: fig. 28; © Courtesy of Dunhuang Academy: figs 14, 16, 29, 30; © Musée Guimet, Paris, Dist. RMN-Grand Palais/image musée Guimet: cat. nos 6, 10, 11 (pp. 118–19, detail); © Harvard College Library, Harvard-Yenching Library, Harvard University: fig. 63; Courtesy Hunan Provincial Museum: fig. 1; Kunsthistorisches Museum, Vienna: fig. 35; © Courtesy of Kyoto National Museum: cat. nos 42, 43; © The Liaoning Provincial Museum Collection: cat. nos 17 (fig. 47), 63, 75, 76 (fig. 21, pp. 266–7, detail); figs 5–7, 11, 32, 52–3; © 2013. Image copyright The Metropolitan Museum of Art / Art Resource NY / Scala, Florence: cat. nos 18, 41, 46, 48 (pp. 202–3, detail), 51, 62, 67, 72; The Museum of Far Eastern Antiquities, Stockholm / Östasiatiska Museet: cat. nos 33, 73; Photograph © 2013 Museum of Fine Arts, Boston: cat. no. 16 (fig. 34, p. 78 and jacket, details), 22–5, 27–32, 34, 36, 38 (pp. 148–9, detail); figs 2, 22; © Collection of the National Palace Museum, Taipei: figs 15, 17, 19, 20, 31, 59; The Nelson-Atkins Museum of Art, Kansas City: cat. nos 19 (Photo: John Lamberton), 61 (pp. 113–14, 235, details) (Photo: John Lamberton) 70 (Photo: Jamison Miller); © Osaka City Museum of Fine Arts: cat. nos 13 (fig. 60), 14, 15, 20, 44, 47, 49 (p. 4, detail); © The Palace Museum Collection: cat. nos 49, 55 (pp. 230–1, detail), 56, 60, 71, 79; figs 4, 10, 24–5, 33, 46, 62; © 2013. Princeton University Art Museum / Art Resource NY / Scala, Florence: cat. no. 21; fig. 27; © Private collection, Kyoto: cat. no. 26; Foto: © Rheinisches Bildarchiv Köln: fig. 39; © RMN-Grand Palais (Musée Guimet, Paris): cat. nos 2 (P. Pleynet), 3 (Mathéus), 4 (Daniel Arnaudet), 5 (Mathieu Ravaux), 7 (Daniel Arnaudet), 8 (Thierry Ollivier), 12 (Thierry Ollivier); figs 40 (Richard Lambert), 49 (René-Gabriel Ojéda), 58 (Michel Urtado); © The Shanghai Museum Collection: cat. nos 54, 68; © The Shōsō-in Repository, The Imperial Household Agency: fig. 41; Image courtesy of Clarissa von Spee: fig. 61; Staatliche Museen zu Berlin, Museum für Asiatische Kunst / Jürgen Liepe: cat. nos 52, 65 (p. 271, detail), 69, 77; © Tenryū-ji, Kyoto / Courtesy of Nara National Museum: figs 42–3; © The Tianjin Museum Collection: cat. nos 64, 74 (pp. 2–3, 306–7, details); Image: TNM Image Archives: cat. nos 35, 39–40, 53; figs 35, 44–5; © V&A Images: figs 18, 50-1; © Image courtesy of Roderick Whitfield: figs 54–7; Photograph © Xinjiang Uyghur Autonomous Region Museum: fig. 3; Xubaizhai Collection, Hong Kong Museum of Art: cat. no. 79